Object-Oriented Programming for the Macintosh™

Kurt J. Schmucker

Hayden Book Company
A DIVISION OF HAYDEN PUBLISHING COMPANY, INC.
HASBROUCK HEIGHTS, NEW JERSEY

To Karen

Acquisitions Editor: BILL GROUT
Production Editor: RONNIE GROFF
Composition and production: TECHART, SAN FRANCISCO
Cover photo-illustration: RON MORECRAFT
Cover design: JIM BERNARD
Printed and bound by: COMMAND WEB OFFSET, INC.

Library of Congress Cataloging-in-Publication Data

Schmucker, Kurt J.
Object-oriented programming for the Macintosh.

Includes index.
1. Macintosh (Computer)—Programming. I. Title.
QA76.8.M3S35 1986 005.265 86-7668
ISBN 0-8104-6565-5

Printed in the United States of America

1	2	3	4	5	6	7	8	9	Printing
86	87	88	89	90	91	92	93	94	Year

Foreword

Macintosh applications are easy to use, but until recently they were difficult to program. Their nontraditional user interface refused to yield to traditional software engineering techniques. Now, a new technique has emerged to make Macintosh application development easier. It is called object-oriented programming.

In the 1960s, Kristen Nygaard and Ole-Johan Dahl of the Norwegian Computing Center needed a language to cope with complex simulation problems. Many simulations involve the interplay of objects such as gas molecules and walls, or customers, tellers, and bank accounts. Nygaard and Dahl decided to make the object concept an explicit feature in their programming language, Simula. Simula makes it easy to model a portion of the world as an interacting set of objects.

Simula never attained the popularity of competitors like Fortran, Pascal, and C, but its ideas have been adopted by many language designers. The expanding roster of object-oriented languages includes Planner, Smalltalk, Objective-C, LOOPS, Object Pascal, and C++. A few of these languages are becoming available on the Macintosh. For example, my group at Apple has developed versions of Smalltalk-80 and Object Pascal. Kriya Systems has developed Neon, and other companies have indicated that they plan to introduce object-oriented language compilers and interpreters in the near future.

Object-oriented programming is still an evolving discipline. Professor Nygaard himself is currently participating in the design of a new object-oriented language, Beta. Researchers around the world, including several at Apple, are investigating new variations of the technique, including visual programming languages that allow certain simple programs to be implemented in hours instead of days.

The subject of the book you are holding is not research but practical application development. Larry Rosenstein, Scott Wallace, Ken Doyle, and other Macintosh experts at Apple have devised a model of the "typical" Macintosh application structured in terms of objects such as windows, documents, and commands. They have embodied their model in a software library called MacApp. If you choose to use MacApp to develop a Macintosh application, it will probably save you months of effort as compared with the traditional approach. With MacApp, you need only code the differences between your specific application and the "typical" one MacApp models. In addition, the use of MacApp will make your application more consistent with Apple's user interface standards and will make it easier for you to meet customer expectations of reliability and error recovery. MacApp programs can be written in various high-level languages as well as in Assembler. This book includes a thorough introduction to MacApp and some of its languages.

MacApp is not the first object-oriented software library to model a window-oriented user interface. During the 1970s, Alan Kay's Learning Research Group (LRG) at Xerox Palo Alto Research Center developed a system and language called Smalltalk that used a window-oriented user interface and included an object-oriented library. LRG scientists led by Dan Ingalls developed several versions of Smalltalk, starting with a children's language called Smalltalk-72 and culminating in a professional programmer's version known as Smalltalk-80. The user interface library of Smalltalk-80 is called Model-View-Controller or MVC. To my knowledge, this book is the first to explain the concepts of MVC as they are expressed in the standard Smalltalk-80 release. It also describes the Lisa ToolKit, a predecessor of MacApp that ran on the Lisa, and provides excellent summaries of Neon, ExperCommonLisp, Object Logo, and Objective-C.

MacApp has been available as a Lisa-to-Macintosh cross-development system since February 1985. At the time of this writing, Apple is testing a Macintosh standalone version in preparation for release to a wider user community. The company will provide a manual, sample programs, and reference material with the MacApp release, but is counting on independent authors to provide tutorials. The book in your hands is unique in that the author took an early interest in MacApp and worked closely with Apple for over a year to gather information for his text. His book is written for experienced programmers, and assumes some knowledge of Pascal and an acquaintance with the user interface of the Macintosh. The author has actually implemented an interesting Macintosh application, QuadWorld, and uses it to illustrate the concepts he teaches.

Object-oriented programming is not a subject to be absorbed in one Sunday afternoon. The author has undertaken to guide the reader through the thickets barring access to this strange but powerful concept. In the first part of the book, he examines the foundations of the subject from many sides and explores it to many depths. Then the author introduces MacApp itself through the QuadWorld example. The reader who lacks immediate interest in the details of Macintosh programming can skim these sections and move on to the advanced topics, including an excellent survey of object-oriented languages. The insightful appendix on user interface design is independent of the rest of the book and will be of interest to a wide audience. It has been included here because of its obvious importance to anyone designing a Macintosh application.

If you have access to a Macintosh while you are reading this material, you can put your learning to the test and reinforce it with practice. If you have written an application for another machine and want to port it to the Macintosh, this guide can help you in restructuring it for the new user interface. If you have been harboring an exciting idea for an interactive application, then after you have mastered the lessons herein, you will be in a better position than ever to try it out. Whatever your plans, let me welcome you to object-oriented programming, and show you to the entrance that is this book.

Larry Tesler
Cupertino, California

About This Book

The Macintosh is more than simply the subject of this book—it is the means by which all of the book's text, figures, and sample programs were created. The thirteen chapters and the two appendices were written and edited with Microsoft Word, each chapter a separate Word document. The original manuscript was prepared on a Macintosh XL and transmitted to the various editors either via the AppleTalk network or on diskette for editing and revision on their Macintoshes. The original keystrokes on my XL's keyboard were "captured" electronically by the typesetter, producing the type you are now reading. Early versions of the manuscript were printed on the Apple ImageWriter and the Apple LaserWriter for review during MacApp's development stage.

The programs in this book were developed either in the Lisa Workshop (Object Pascal and Clascal) or on the Macintosh itself (Smalltalk, Neon, Object Logo, and ExperCommonLISP). The eight listings included in the book were either generated in the Lisa Workshop and then "Maccom"ed over to the Macintosh to become Microsoft Word documents, or were text files generated directly on the Macintosh itself and then formatted with Microsoft Word.

Nearly all of the more than 200 hundred illustrations in this book were produced on the Macintosh using either MacDraw or MacPaint. These, too, were given to the production editors at Hayden in electronic form. These original MacDraw figures were then edited at Hayden to produce the final figures on these pages.

Were it not for the Macintosh's excellent manuscript- and figure-preparation capabilities, this book would have taken considerably longer to prepare. Moreover, a task of this magnitude gave many of these application programs, compilers, and interpreters a real workout, enabling me to discover several bugs that were then communicated to the respective developers. Because of this effort, these may be bugs that you will never see.

Preface

This is a book intended for Macintosh application programmers, not for Macintosh end users. Accordingly, the second-person "you" refers to such a programmer and we reserve the term "user" for the ultimate end users of your software. To most effectively profit from reading this book, you should be comfortable at least reading Pascal or C, and have some familiarity with the basic concepts of computer graphics, especially with the QuickDraw graphics library on the Macintosh. A general introduction to programming for Macintosh would also be useful. To this end, Chernicoff's *Macintosh Revealed—Unlocking the Toolbox* (Hayden, 1985) provides an excellent introduction to both QuickDraw (in Chapter 5) and Macintosh programming (in Chapters 6 and 7). It is highly recommended as a companion volume to this one, though many of the details explained in *Macintosh Revealed* are handled for you automatically when you adopt the object-oriented approach to developing Macintosh software. In addition, you should have a user's working knowledge of several application programs on the Macintosh, as many of these are used as examples throughout the book.

This book is organized in two major sections. Section I is an introduction to object-oriented programming with all examples taken from Object Pascal, an object-oriented extension of Pascal. Individuals who wish to learn only the basics of this technology will find that this section is self-contained and will enable them to produce sophisticated Pascal applications on the Macintosh. Section II covers the other object-oriented languages on the Macintosh as well as some advanced topics in object-oriented programming. Those who need a more in-depth understanding of object-oriented programming, or who wish to use the object-oriented approach from languages other than Pascal, will need to read both Section I and II.

Of course, the term "Macintosh" refers to the entire Macintosh family of computers, including the Lisa, the predecessor of the first Macintosh. The Lisa is the host of several operating systems and environments. One operating system, MacWorks, turns the Lisa into a "Macintosh XL"—a system that can run almost all Macintosh software, including object-oriented software, without modification. Another operating system runs the "Lisa 7/7 Office System," a multi-tasking, window environment that also can run programs written in one object-oriented language, Clascal. Yet another environment is the Lisa Workshop, a program development environment that can be used to develop programs in several of the object-oriented languages discussed in this book.

There are few details in this book about the Lisa Workshop or the other programming environments in which object-oriented programs are prepared. There are several reasons for this. First, the mechanics of compiling and linking programs and of dealing with various text editors are completely independent of using an object-oriented language to produce Macintosh applications. Second, some object-oriented languages described here have their own peculiar environments which are supplied with the language's compilers and linkers. Little insight into object-oriented programming would be gained by examining these. Third, the Macintosh Programmer's Workshop which may become the most popular programming environment, will not be available until several months after this book is published.

A couple of formatting conventions are used throughout this book. Code fragments as well as procedure and variable names are set off by a special font like this:

```
FUNCTION TQuadApplication.DoMakeDocument (itsDocKind:INTEGER):
   TDocument;
VAR quadDocument: TQuadDocument;
BEGIN
   NEW (quadDocument);
   quadDocument.IQuadDocument;
   DoMakeDocument := quadDocument;
END;
```

and information that, while important, is auxiliary or advanced is set off from the rest of the text with a colored background like this:

Definitions

Shaded boxes like this contain "by-the-way" information that provides side comments, advanced discussions, helpful hints, or a discussion of cases that are exceptions to the general rule being discussed. You may choose to skip over, or merely browse such boxes the first time you read a section.

Acknowledgments

A book like this is never the result of just one person's labor. Many people advised and assisted me during the eighteen months in which this book was written.

Larry Tesler of Apple Computer was my main technical contact at Apple. Larry, the leader of the Object Oriented Systems team in the Apple Advanced Development group, read every one of the many drafts of this book, suggested so many improvements that I lost count, and spent countless hours talking with me about object-oriented programming. Without his assistance, this book would probably never have been started or finished. I am also grateful to Larry for allowing me to participate in the α and β-test of MacApp and to participate in the MacApp development meetings whenever I was in Cupertino.

The entire Object Oriented Systems team at Apple assisted me by reading various drafts and advising me on the implementation of the programs used as examples throughout the book. Among those who went to extraordinary efforts to assist me were Larry Rosenstein, Scott Wallace, Ken Doyle, Dan Ingalls, Barry Haines, Jonathan Simonoff, Harvey Alcabes, and Mark Lentczner. Eileen Mayes assisted me by making sure that I had the latest software and all the necessary technical notes and documentation. Each of these individuals endured numerous phone calls from me and were always willing to discuss the latest changes in MacApp, help me solve a minor crisis, or provide any background I needed. It was indeed a pleasure to have been associated with this group of professionals during the design and implementation of the Toolkit and MacApp.

Bryan Lockwood, Sally Breckenridge, and Chet Wisinski, all colleagues of mine at Productivity Products International, read the final manuscript and suggested many changes under the short deadlines that always seem to occur during the final days of finishing a book. Special thanks to Tom Love, President of PPI, for giving me sufficient time to finish this project when there were equally pressing tasks elsewhere.

Many other individuals assisted in dealing with the languages their companies market: Guru Jees of Kriya, and Chuck Duff, Mark Achler, and Reese Warner formerly of Kriya (NEON); Denison Bolay of Expertelligence (ExperCommonLISP); Jeremy Jones and Glenn Forrestor of Coral Software (Object Logo); Brad Cox of Productivity Products International (Objective-C); and Evelyn van Orden of Xerox Corporation (Smalltalk).

Gene Velazques of Flacon Microsystems and John Sauer of The Comm Center were the Apple Authorized Dealers who helped me obtain the sometimes scarce hardware and software for my Lisa and Macintosh. On many occasions these individuals loaned me equipment or found supplies that were just not available anywhere.

Joen Makower of Tilden Press edited the final manuscript, producing consistency and clarity in a draft that lacked both in many places.

Bill Grout of Hayden, Martha Steffen of Apple, and literary agent Raphael Sagalyn worked together on the publication details and, in general, brought this book to market.

Finally, my wife Karen was an understanding computer widow during this book's preparation, for which I am forever appreciative. Equally important, she was my most frequent "typical Macintosh user," upon whose experiences many of my conclusions about the Macintosh user interface were drawn. She also ran the entire manuscript through a spell checker to correct my typing—a task that took many hours just before the Christmas holidays.

My heartfelt thanks to all for their assistance, without which this book could not have come to fruition. Any errors or inaccuracies that remain are, of course, mine.

—Kurt J. Schmucker
Crofton, Maryland

Contents

CHAPTER

1

Why Object-Oriented Programming?

BEFORE MacApp

"Developing software for the Macintosh is a bitch."
Dash Chang, President
Chang Labs—Developers of Macintosh Ledger and Rags to Riches

AFTER MacApp

"I was able to build a working prototype of my entire application in less than five months. I never would have completed this without MacApp."
Carl Nelson, President
Carl Nelson and Associates—Developers of NaVision, a chart drawing and navigation application for yachts

Programming a sophisticated Macintosh-style application using traditional software engineering techniques can be difficult. Your program must respond to a variety of different types of events, from simple text entry to mouse clicking in scroll bars and alert boxes. All this must be done extremely efficiently and, more importantly, it must be done essentially the same as in other Macintosh applications. An application program on Macintosh that doesn't highlight selected text by inverting it on the screen, doesn't pull down menus from the top of the screen but rather pulls them up from the bottom, or reverses the way scroll arrows worked would be "hard to use." It simply wouldn't find a high degree of acceptance among Macintosh users. As you know, a major advantage of the Macintosh over other personal computers is that all applications have similar user interfaces. Unfortunately, what is good for the user usually means extra work on the part of the developer, and indeed, applications for the Macintosh tend to require a tremendous amount of complex code.

This complex code is usually developed by individually crafting a program that manages the various types of interactive "events" that can occur while the application is running—window events, menu events, keyboard events, insertion of microdiskettes, and mouse movements, for example. Interactions unique to an individual application (such as creating a new task in MacProject, moving polygons in MacDraw, or designing a new iconic symbol in Filevision) are handled by this software, as are interactions that are the same across all Macintosh applications (such as resizing a window, opening one of an application's documents, or activating a desk accessory). The fact that application-unique and application-independent events are all handled by the same program means that the task of producing even a simple Macintosh application requires a tremendous amount of development "overhead," compared to the development of the code that really defines the application. This overhead consists primarily of implementing major portions of the Macintosh User Interface Standard.

The User Interface Standard is the total of all the things about an application and about the Macintosh that the user sees and does—the exact shape and style of windows, the ways in which text editing takes place, the use of dialog boxes, and much more. (You can find details about the Macintosh User Interface Standard in Appendix A.) The standard, while a tremendous boon for Macintosh users, is a tremendous technical barrier for Macintosh software developers, especially first-time developers. Consider, for example, the main event loop in the small application program, Sample, used in *Inside Macintosh* as a tiny example of the basic structure of a Macintosh application (Figure 1-1). Note that only the underlined portion of this main event loop deals with the features specific to this application; the majority of the code deals with the standard user interactions of pulling down menus, moving and activating windows, and dealing with desk accessories.

```
REPEAT                                 {call Desk Manager to perform any periodic }
  SystemTask;                          { actions defined for desk accessories}
  TEIdle(textH);                       {call TextEdit to make vertical bar blink}

  IF GetNextEvent(everyEvent, myEvent) {call Toolbox Event Manager to get the next }
    THEN                               { event that the application should handle}
      CASE myEvent.what OF             {case on event type}

      mouseDown:            {mouse button down: call Window Manager to learn where}
        CASE FindWindow(myEvent.where, whichWindow) OF

        inSysWindow:        {desk accessory window: call Desk Manager to handle it}
          SystemClick(myEvent.whichWindow);
```

```
      inMenuBar:          {menu bar: call Menu Manager to learn which command, }
        DoCommand(MenuSelect(myEvent.where));    { then execute it}

      inDrag:             {title bar: call Window Manager to drag}
        DragWindow(whichWindow,myEvent.where, dragRect);

      inContent:                          {body of application window: }
        BEGIN                             { call Window Manager to check whether }
          IF whichWindow <> FrontWindow   { it's the active window and make it }
            THEN SelectWindow(whichWindow { active if not}
            ELSE
              BEGIN                       {it's already active: call QuickDraw to }
              GlobalToLocal(myEvent.where); { convert to window coordinates for }
                                          { TEClick, use Toolbox Utility BitAnd to }
              extended := BitAnd(myEvent.modifiers,shiftKey) <> 0;  { test for Shift }
              TEClick(myEvent.where, extended, txtH);  { key down and call TextEdit }
              END;                                     { to process the event}
        END;        {of inContent}

      END;      {of mouseDown}

    keyDown, autoKey:                     {key pressed once or held down to repeat}
      BEGIN
      theChar := CHR(BitAnd(myEvent.message, charCodeMask));  {get the character}
      IF BitAnd(myEvent.modifiers, cmdKey) <> 0 {if Command key down, call Menu }
        THEN DoCommand(MenuKey(theChar))   { Manager to learn which command, }
        ELSE TEKey(theChar, textH);        { then execute it; else pass }
      END;                                 { character to TextEdit}

    activateEvt:
      BEGIN
      IF BitAnd(myEvent.modifiers,activeFlag) <> 0
        THEN                        {application window is becoming active: }
          BEGIN                     { call TextEdit to highlight selection }
          TEActivate(textH);        { or display blinking vertical bar, and call }
          DisableItem(myMenus[editM], undoCommand);     { MenuManager to disable }
          END                       { Undo (since application doesn't support Undo)}
        ELSE
          BEGIN                     {application window is becoming inactive: }
          TEDeactivate(textH);      { unhighlight selection or remove blinking }
          EnableItem(myMenus(editM], undoCommand);    { vertical bar, and enable }
          END;                      { Undo (since desk accessories may support it)}
      END;     {of activateEvt}

    updateEvt:
      BEGIN                                          {window appearance needs updating}
      BeginUpdate(WindowPtr(myEvent.message)); {call Window Manager to begin update}
      EraseRect(thePort↑.portRect);            {call QuickDraw to erase text area}
      TEUpdate(thePort↑.portRect,textH);       {call TextEdit to update the text}
      EndUpdate(WindowPtr(myEvent.message));   {call WindowManager to end update}
      END;    {of updateEvt}

    END;     {of event case}

UNTIL doneFlag;
```

Figure 1-1 The main event loop portion of a small Macintosh application program that does not use object-oriented techniques. The only portion of this program unique to the application being developed is underlined—the majority is code that must be present in most Macintosh applications. Although this code is common to most applications, it is individually crafted by each developer. The programming languages discussed in this book provide a solution to this productivity inefficiency.

Notes

Inside Macintosh, written by Apple and published by Addison-Wesley, is the authoritative reference manual for programming the Macintosh. It is required reading for any serious Macintosh developer. The sample program, Sample (a portion of which is reproduced in this chapter), is contained in full in the first chapter (A Road Map) of *Inside Macintosh* and is reproduced here with the permission of Apple and Addison-Wesley.

This sample program, and indeed almost all Macintosh applications, fits the basic model shown in Figure 1-2, in which the application programmer designs a set of custom subroutines and a custom main program that coordinates the execution of these custom routines as well as an assortment of supplied routines. In this approach, the supplied subroutine library (the Macintosh Toolbox) acts as a set of immutable building blocks that the programmer assembles, with his or her own glue, into the desired application program.

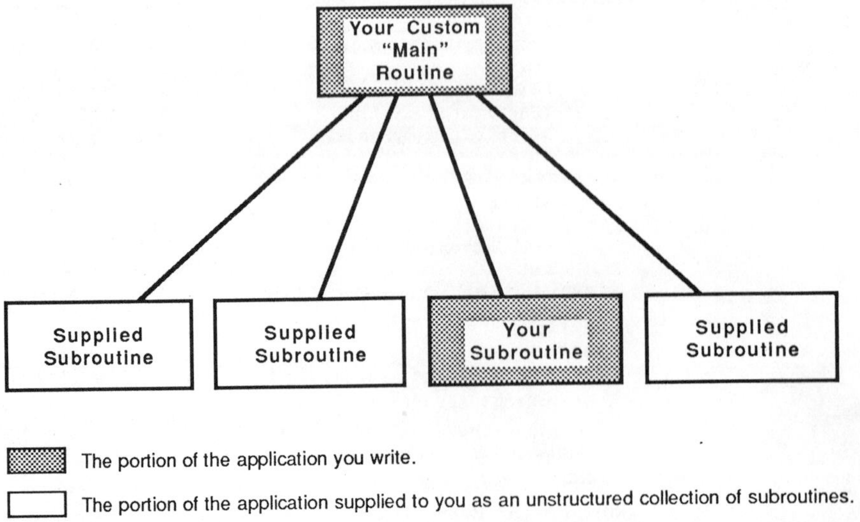

Figure 1-2 The basic organization for a Macintosh application. Here, the developer has hand-crafted a main routine, implementing on his or her own many features of the Macintosh User Interface Standard. Such applications are usually designed from scratch by the developer.

This approach, while taking advantage of the Toolbox to assist in developing applications that conform to the Macintosh User Interface Standard, still has a significant amount of development inefficiency—the code that implements much of the Macintosh User Interface Standard must be reengineered by each developer. This code, which can be complex and difficult to develop, is represented in Figure 1-2 by much of the custom main routine—a routine totally crafted by the developer.

There ought to be a better way.

For example, there ought to be a way in which the code common to most Macintosh applications could be shared, or at least reused. Clearly, the Toolbox accomplishes this to some extent, but couldn't this packaging of reusable components go further, extending into the area of this main routine and into the rudimentary control of the portions of the interface standard common to most applications? Let's suppose there was a way to do this—that is, there was a way to package much of the custom main routine so it could be reused easily. Let's call this reusable main program an *expandable application* and explore what types of properties it must have to be truly useful to Macintosh developers.

The Expandable Application

An expandable application, if one existed, would provide a way of overcoming much of the development inefficiency that now exists by providing a reusable, blank application that implements much of the Macintosh User Interface Standard. Applications developed by customizing this framework would fit the basic model shown in Figure 1-3. Here, a basic skeleton consisting of a main routine and most of its subroutines are supplied to you, the application programmer. You then, must have the ability to:

- Append code to some subroutines of the expandable application.
- Modify other subroutines.
- Add new subroutines at various points in the flow of control.

With such capabilities, you would not be unduly restricted in either designing or implementing an application. In addition, this expandable application would have to handle many user interactions by itself, without "bothering" you. Interactions of this "automatic" type include window resizing, menu handling, window movements, basic text editing, and printing an application's documents from the Finder—in short, the features common to all Macintosh applications. This framework architecture, as shown in Figure 1-3, is slightly more complex that that of the traditional architecture, shown in Figure 1-2.

This slight increase in complexity, however, results in a considerable decrease in the amount of code that you have to design, implement, and test. (While this may sound like science fiction, keep reading—today's science fiction has a habit of becoming tomorrow's science fact.)

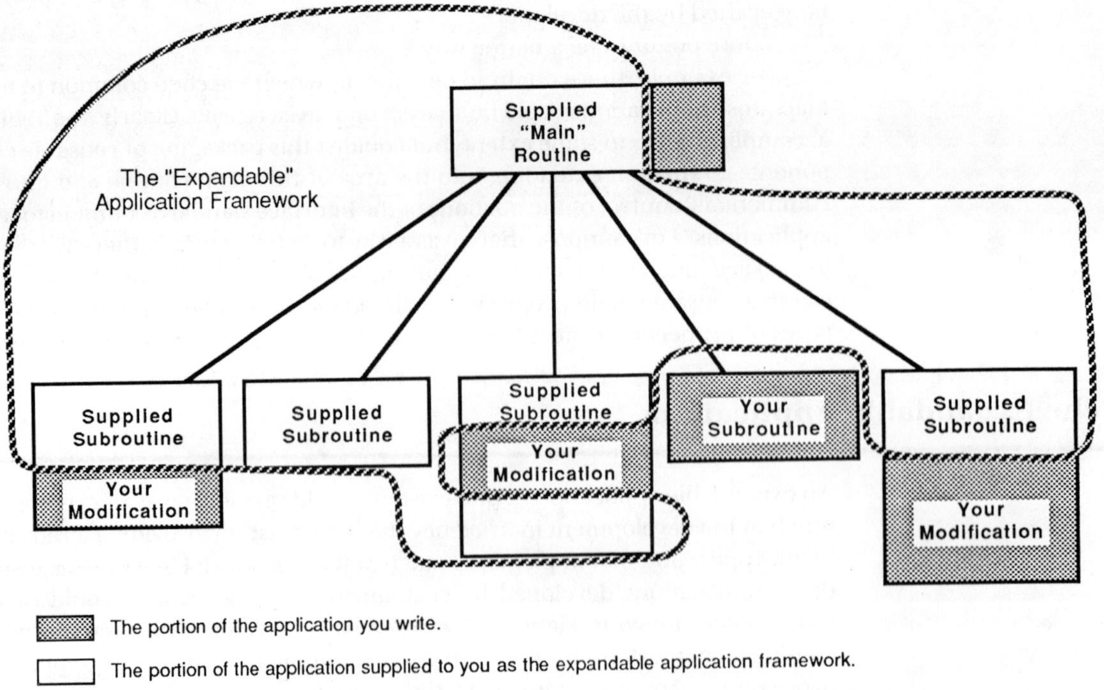

Figure 1-3 The basic organization for a Macintosh application designed with the expandable application framework. The developer implements only those portions of the application that are different from other Macintosh applications. Applications designed in this way can be very easily built incrementally, starting with a working but minimal base application that is easily expandable.

Let's examine one possible way in which this expandable application might be implemented. Suppose you took a more complete version of the central event loop from Sample and, instead of the underlined portion (the application-unique portion), you inserted a subroutine call to MyApplicationEvent(relativeMouseDownPosition). As an application developer you could then write your own MyApplicationEvent routine, link it with this generic event loop, and get an application that properly handled all events, the major difference being that in this hypothetical development path you need only write the code that handled the kinds of events unique to his application. You could follow essentially the same approach to provide other known subroutines that performed certain application-specific tasks, yet whose control was standard, like:

- a HighlightSelection routine that would invoke an application-specific routine for highlighting whatever screen objects the program used. After all, different applications highlight in different ways. Some even highlight the same thing in different ways: consider the ways in which MacPaint, MacDraw, and MacProject highlight rectangles, for example (Figure 1-4). This HighlightSelection routine would be called by the expandable application when a window was reactivated.
- a ReadDocumentFromDisk routine that would be invoked when the user selected a particular document in the Open Which Document? dialog box. (The Open Which Document? dialog box is a standard component and thus is part of the expandable application).

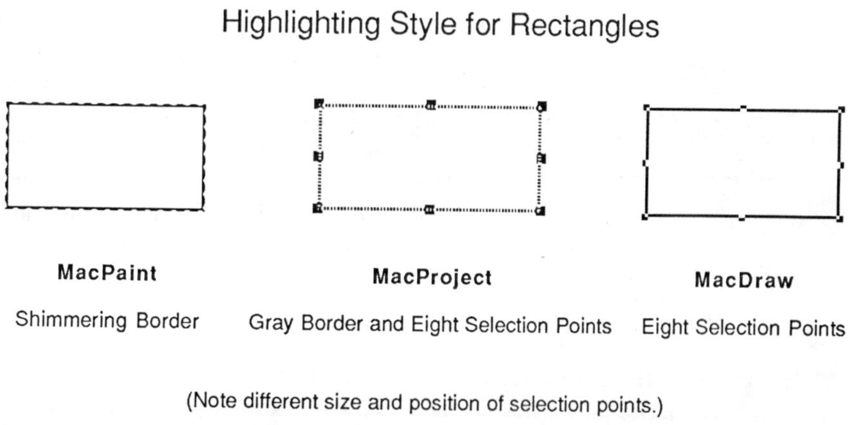

Figure 1-4 Highlighting of the current selection can vary among in different applications, even when the object being highlighted is the same. Here we see a rectangle as highlighted in MacProject, MacDraw, and MacPaint. This need to support application-dependent highlighting methods limits the design choices for the manner of implementing a Macintosh expandable application. What is needed to provide this flexibility in the expandable application is a manner of encapsulating the programs that work on a particular type of data with that data. Object-oriented programming provides that encapsulation feature, along with many others.

While such an architecture might sound attractive at first, it won't give you the properties you want for an expandable application. It simply isn't flexible enough. In the HighlightSelection example, how will the expandable application know about several different types of selections or, equivalently, how will you make use of only one HighlightSelection routine, when your application has five different types of selections? How will one ReadDocumentFromDisk routine suffice when the application naturally has two types of documents (like Microsoft Word, which has both manuscripts and glossaries)? What you need is a way for the expandable application to invoke a HighlightSelection routine that is appropriate to the current selection, or a ReadDocumentFromDisk routine that is specific to the type of document to be read. However, how can a generic, expandable application be written to both "know" about the application's data types and yet still be generic?

The basic problem here (but not the only one) is that there is no way in a standard programming language such as Pascal or C to encapsulate specific procedures that act upon only a certain type of data together with that data. This is exactly the approach of *object-oriented programming.* With object-oriented programming there is a way for the expandable application to contain a statement to the effect of: "Invoke the highlight procedure that is appropriate to the current selection, whatever that selection type is." Such a statement works even when the data type of the current selection is something far beyond what the original expandable-application designers had in mind. This feature of object-oriented programming has been termed, somewhat whimsically, "call-by-desire" to differentiate it from the more standard call-by-reference and call-by-value ways of invoking a routine. This name, while slightly in jest, does convey the fact that the "what" has been divorced from the "how" in this mechanism; the calling program merely indicates that highlighting, for example, is needed at a certain point, without indicating how that highlighting is to be done. The current selection itself will decide the "how" by calling the appropriate procedure directly (See Lamar Ledbetter and Brad Cox, "Software-ICs," *BYTE,* Volume 10, Number 6 (June 1985), pp. 307-316).

MacApp—The Expandable Macintosh Application

Such an expandable appliction has been designed using the encapsulation techniques of object-oriented programming. "MacApp" (the Expandable Macintosh Application) is the collective name for this reusable main program plus a set of special subroutines that implement most features of the Macintosh User Interface Standard. MacApp "sits on top of" the Macintosh Toolbox to provide a framework for building new Macintosh applications. MacApp is written in a variant of Pascal that supports the encapsulation of data and programs necessary to build an expandable application. (This Pascal variant is called "Object Pascal" and is discussed in Chapter 3.) You can build new applications using MacApp as the application framework if you write your application in Object Pascal, or in other object-oriented programing languages, such as Objective-C or ExperCommonLisp (Chapter 13). You can even write in macro assembler and still make use of the MacApp framework.

The Object-Oriented Approach

The existence of the Macintosh User Interface Standard makes MacApp, and object-oriented programming in general, a very powerful software development tool for several reasons. The most basic of these, as you will see in the next chapter, is that object-oriented programming enables developers to design "intelligent" combinations of data and software in prepackaged software components called *objects*. These components can then be used repeatedly without change. As one example of this, MacApp defines such a software object that mimics the behavior of a Macintosh window. This window object "knows" how to respond to mouse presses in its title bar by moving about the screen as well as how to respond to resizing, how to open and close on the screen, and so on. When you use such an object in an application, this behavior "comes for free." Moreover, there is a mechanism whereby you can add to the behavior of these objects, in effect saying "Give me a standard Macintosh window object, but one that is split with panes in a certain way and can respond to panel resizing requests correctly."

Objects are not limited to entities you can see on the screen like icon objects and window objects. This object-oriented encapsulation in MacApp also makes it possible to provide an framework for undoable commands, for example. This is done with another kind of MacApp object, a command object. These objects "know" what actions should be performed when a particular command is done or undone. To add a new undoable command to an application built on the MacApp framework, you design one of these command objects. In designing it, you program what actions this object should take when doing and when undoing the command. Then you merely "drop" this comand object into the MacApp framework. MacApp will have this command object execute the appropriate action at the appropriate time.

With object-oriented programming, you construct independent little "computers" that can perform their own computations and which interact with each other by passing messages back and forth. This model can break the static binding of data and programs present in conventional languages.

Conventional languages such as Pascal, Ada, and C provide a rich set of data types plus the ability to extend the number of data types. In some sense, this extensibility allows you to mold the computer into a form more appropriate to the problem at hand, thus simplifying the task of designing a program to solve that problem. By designing your own data types, you are building new units of data, that can later be operated upon by your procedures. Unfortunately, the correspondence governing which procedures operate upon which types of data is something you must keep in mind during program design. This correspondence is not difficult to manage when the system is small, but becomes more and more difficult as the system grows. Even for those cases in which the correspondence can be managed, it still is a barrier to code reusability. This is because this correspondence forces your design to limit the types of data it can process, both now and in the future. Later, trying to reuse a procedure or other piece of code from this system almost invariably means a new type of data must be processed, necessitating a change to the code. So much for reusability. Consider, for example, an electronic mail system designed to handle only text messages. Trying to use that same system to build a new electronic mail system that handles text, graphics, and voice messages is harder than starting from scratch. Indeed, software is usually considered so unreusable that many professionals would never consider trying this conversion of a text-only electronic mail system. Despite the fact that the basic algorithms for dealing with the entities being mailed through the system are identical in both cases, there is little reusability because these basic algorithms are usually "cluttered" with information about the types of data with which they deal.

This cluttering of procedures with the data type information (which may later need to change) also increases program maintenance costs. Consider a program that makes extensive use of case statements to differentiate between the actions required with different data types. Such a program would have many occurrences of statements like the following one, taken from a program that manipulates various types of quadrilaterals, each with a routine optimized for the particular geometric constraints present in each type of polygon:

```
CASE quad.tag OF
    quadrilateral:  DrawQuadrilateral(quad);
    trapezoid:      DrawTrapezoid(quad);
    parallelogram:  DrawParallelogram(quad);
    rhombus:        DrawRhombus(quad);
    square:         DrawSquare(quad)

END;
```

Suppose you subsequently want to add rectangles to this program. This means that throughout your code, you must differentiate the treatment of rectangles from that of other quadrilaterals. To do so, you must go through the entire program, find every instance of a use of the "tag" field used to distinguish the various type of quadrilaterals, change these instances, then recompile the program. Multiply this effort by that needed to find some less obvious portions of a program you didn't write and you can quickly see that the modification of programs with these types of constructs is difficult and costly.

Even this type of modification, bad as it is, is possible only when you have the source code available to you. When the system you need to modify is in a compiled library or in ROM, this type of change, difficult as it might be to accomplish with the source code, is impossible.

The basic problem here is that you have had to clutter your basic algorithms for the operation of the entire system with information about the types of data being dealt with now, rather than being able to express the basic algorithms themselves in a manner independent of the kinds of data they will manipulate. This cluttering is often referred to as the *static binding of procedures and data* because the program cannot dynamically accommodate new types of data. The strong static link between procedures and data types makes the job of modifying a program more difficult.

Object-oriented programming provides you with a solution to the types of problems exemplified by the quadrilateral-drawing problem outlined above. In this approach, the quadrilateral-drawing case statement becomes:

Send the message DrawYourself to each quadrilateral.

(Unfortunately, we presently must express this message sending in English. Soon we will see exactly how this is written in several different object-oriented programming languages.) Note how this message-sending statement in an object-oriented approach is independent of any changes you might wish to make to improve the efficiency of rectangle drawing—you simply have to reprogram the rectangle object to execute the more efficient code; you needn't go back and change the way that the system "hangs together."

The Effect of Using the Object-Oriented Approach

Case studies have shown that the object-oriented approach to programming can result in significant reductions in both development time and the size of the source code required to perform a given set of functions. In some instances, the development time using object-oriented programming has been one-quarter of that for conventional procedure-oriented programming for the same application program and the resulting size of the source code has been one-tenth as large.(See the two articles by Brad J. Cox for more details: "Message/Object Programming: An Evolutionary Change in Programming Technology," *IEEE Software* Volume 1, Number 1 (January 1984), pp. 50-61, and "Object-Oriented Programming in C," *UNIX Review*, October/November 1983, pp. 67-70.) You may have heard that these gains are at the price of significant performance penalties. This is simply not the case and, in fact, some of the applications we develop in later chapters run faster because they are object-oriented. Combined, these factors make the object-oriented approach attractive for many new application programs.

You will see that object-oriented programming is particularly well-suited to the types of highly interactive, user-friendly applications that are the very basis of the Lisa and Macintosh revolution. This is because the level of interaction between the user and the Macintosh application program can be mirrored directly in the interaction between the objects that form the basis of an object-oriented system. Form follows function when the observable behavior of the application reflects the structure of the application itself. The great complexity of a program like MacDraw, Filevision, or MacProject can be made manageable with such an approach to the architecture of the underlying system.

Object-Oriented Languages

This object-oriented approach can be exploited in conventional languages, but it often requires that you manage intricate software with complex data structures. A better solution is to use languages that inherently support this approach to software design, languages known as *object-oriented languages.* A number of these languages now exist and several are available on the Macintosh. Those who like to learn completely new languages may want to explore this new approach to software design in Smalltalk—a language whose very essence is the object-oriented approach to software design. Those who feel more comfortable using already familar languages may want to explore the object-oriented extensions to these languages. In this book, we discuss object-oriented extensions to Pascal, C, Forth, LISP, and assembly language. Using these extensions won't require you to learn a new language, but rather only to adopt a new approach in the use of a familiar language—an approach with the benefits of object-oriented programming mentioned above.

Notes

Languages for object-oriented programming did not begin with Macintosh, but have their beginnings in the much older language, SIMULA. SIMULA, however, used the object-oriented metaphor only for a small portion of the language; objects were not the centerpiece around which the design and use of the language revolved. The basic notions of object-oriented programming and the terminology now uniformly used by all examples of object-oriented programming languages are derived from the programming language and programming environment of Smalltalk, the result of a ten-year research project conceived by Alan Kay and conducted at the Xerox Palo Alto Research Center (PARC). In fact, the term "object-oriented language" itself came from the PARC Smalltalk research. One of the primary goals of this project was to design a programming language and environment that would facilitate the production of highly interactive programs that executed on powerful personal computers.

Such computers, like the Macintosh, now commonplace, were merely visions of what might be possible in the foreseeable future when the Smalltalk research efforts began. Placing mainframe-size computational power and memory into a personal computer made reasonable and cost-effective new approaches to programming that were previously considered to be "wasteful" of machine resources. One innovation is the raster approach to computer graphics. High-resolution raster systems require a large amount of memory for the screen bitmap and character fonts. In the case of Macintosh, the screen bitmap requires 22K while the fixed set of font files on my Macintosh occupies over 500K on disk.(In this regard, my Macintosh may be somewhat unusual—authors tend to go a little "font crazy" with a system like Macintosh. This may be a reaction to so many years of dealing with systems that give you one poorly designed font.) Another new approach made possible by the increase in both processing power and memory was object-oriented programming.

The individuals at PARC in those days foresaw (and in some cases, created) the hardware advances that would lead soon to inexpensive powerful personal computers and they began to think about the problem of using that computer power in a way to deliver the best total system to an individual. In doing so, they did not follow the less risky, but also less rewarding, path of designing tomorrow's software for today's machines. Rather, they tried to develop tomorrow's software for tomorrow's machines—a much more difficult task and one in which they succeeded. Their work led to the revolutionary notions of multiple, overlapping windows on the face of a high-resolution display that was an integral component of the powerful personal workstation, the extensive use of a flexible pointing device called a mouse, and the concepts of object-oriented programming—concepts that have now spread to several languages besides Smalltalk.

In this book, we discuss several object-oriented programming languages currently available on Macintosh—Object Pascal, Smalltalk-80, Neon (a Forth derivative), ExperCommonLisp (a LISP derivative), Object Logo, Object Assembler, Objective-C, and Lisa Clascal—and provide you with a basis for using other object-oriented programming languages that become available. To simplify the presentation, Object Pascal is used exclusively in the discussion and examples in the introductory chapters of this book (Section I). All other languages are presented in Section II.

Object-Oriented Programming and the Macintosh User Interface

While this object-oriented approach is useful for the development of any software, it is particularly attractive if a standard user interface has been defined, because in that case one group of programmers can define the software objects that implement this standard and provide these reusable components to other developers as building blocks. This is exactly what MacApp is—a collection of software objects that mimic the behavior required by the Macintosh User Interface Standard. Before you can understand how to use these MacApp objects as a base for new applications you must first understand the basic concepts of object-oriented programming (Chapter 2) and the syntax for the variant of Pascal that supports these concepts (Chapter 3).

Thus, the motivation for an expandable application is firmly rooted in the Macintosh User Interface Standard and a strong foundation in this standard is needed before further discussing the ways in which this expandable application is designed and used. As developers, you'll need a more thorough understanding and a more explicit vocabulary for this user interface than that needed by most other Macintosh users. There are several ways in which this understanding and vocabulary can be acquired:

1. using and studying a wide variety of Macintosh software,
2. reading the general treatment of the Macintosh User Interface Standard presented in *Inside Macintosh*, or
3. reading the more specific treatment especially designed for MacApp programmers in Appendix A of this book.

The best approach for you depends on a number of factors, but the bottom line is this: as a Macintosh software developer, you must have a thorough understanding of the Macintosh User Interface Standard—without this knowledge, your software will not meet the expectations of its users. Accordingly, the remainder of this book assumes this knowledge.

CHAPTER

2

The Basics of Object-Oriented Programming

This chapter provides a framework for the rest of the book. It defines the basic terminology of object-oriented programming and presents a high-level conceptual model for structuring your data and programs. Once you have an understanding of the jargon and structure, the chapter introduces a simple application that is used throughout the book to illustrate the concepts and usage of object-oriented programming, the QuadWorld Application.

The Basic Concepts of Object-Oriented Programming

There are several basic concepts in the use of object-oriented programming languages that have no counterparts in traditional programming languages or approaches to programming. Because these concepts are shared by all of the languages we discuss in this book, they are introduced in a general setting here. The minor variations present in each language, as well as each language's syntax, are described in later chapters.

There are four notions central to object-oriented programming: object, class, method, and inheritance. Because they are interdependent, it is not possible to explain just one of these concepts in any detail without also discussing the others. Because they interlock to provide a new framework for programming, you must understand all of them together or none at all. We explain these notions in ever-expanding detail until the total explanation encompasses all of them and shows their interrelationships.

Objects

Objects are a combination of the conventional programming notions of data and procedures. However, unlike conventional programming systems, which represent these two components independently and require the programmer to manage their interaction, object-oriented programming systems combine data and the specific procedures that operate on that data. This joint entity is called an *object*. To invoke an object's procedure, you send the object a *message*. The object will interpret that message and will execute one of its procedures—a procedure that operates on its private data.

This concept simplifies your program considerably. Consider, for example, a simple object representing an upright rectangle. It could be defined as follows:

Object: myUprightRect1
Internal Data: topLeft: Point,
bottomRight: Point
Messages: center

where the message center instructs the rectangle object to calculate its center and return that information. To determine the object's center, you simply send it the message center. It takes care of the rest.

Notes

Bear in mind that this hypothetical example object is not representative of the objects you will be using to program Macintosh applications. It is unrealistically simple so that you can first study the concepts of object-oriented programming without letting the details get in the way.

This approach hides the internal details of how an object functions from the program that uses the object. You could change the definition of the object myUprightRect1 to:

Object: myUprightRect2
Internal Data: top, right, bottom, left: **INTEGER**
Messages: center

without making any changes to the application program that uses it. The only difference between these two objects is the kind of data they store internally. The object myUprightRect1 has two pieces of data, each of which is a point, while the object myUprightRect2 has four pieces of data, each of which is an integer. Either object can be used interchangeably in an application. The internal details of how these objects actually calculate their centers different, but these differences will not affect the use of these objects. This is a crucial point.

In some sense then, messages tell objects what is to be done but not how it is to be accomplished. In fact, the "how" is specifically hidden inside the object. Objects act like modularized units that can be combined to provide the desired total system—little autonomous computers that pass messages back and forth as part of a larger system.

Classes

Object-oriented programming could get tedious if you had to describe the message behavior of every object separately. Groups of objects that respond in the same way to the same messages can be described at once by describing their *class.* This grouping notion in object-oriented programming is in many ways analogous to the standard Pascal notion of describing a user-defined data type that can be used for many different variables. Objects are referred to as *instances* of their classes, just as standard Pascal variables are instances of their data types. In Object Pascal, in fact, a class is referred to as an *object type* because it is declared similarly to standard Pascal's RECORD type.

Notes

While all object-oriented languages use the same basic set of concepts, they do not all use the same terminology to describe these concepts. We emphasize Object Pascal terminology in the first section of this book and introduce the terminology of other languages in Section II. Chapter 10 contains a table comparing the terminologies used in all the languages surveyed in this book.

A class is specified by describing the names and types of variable data contained in an instance of one of its objects as well as listing all the messages to which these instances, or objects, will respond. This variable data is called the class's *instance variables* and the set of messages is called the class's *protocol.*

(There also are some other components of a class, but let's tackle one new concept at a time.) Thus, if you had many objects like myUprightRect1 and myUprightRect2, you could specify a class called UprightRect:

Class: UprightRect
Instance Variables: topLeft: Point,
bottomRight: Point
Messages: center (returns Point)

and three instances, or objects, of class UprightRect would be defined as:

Object Name: myRect **Class Name:** UprightRect
Instance Variables: topLeft = (100, 200),
bottomRight = (300, 400)

Object Name: yourRect **Class Name:** UprightRect
Instance Variables: topLeft = (400, 200),
bottomRight = (500, 450)

Object Name: foo **Class Name:** UprightRect
Instance Variables: topLeft = (127, 311),
bottomRight = (327, 456)

Definitions

In practice, objects do not have names, just addresses like other dynamically allocated data structures. An object's address is called a *reference.* A reference can be assigned to a variable, which then serves as a temporary, non-unique name for the object.

The basic idea is that the class describes the structure of its instances and the objects themselves contain the variable data, similar to the relationship of standard Pascal data types to their variables. Another analogy is to see classes as templates for creating new objects. As you will see in Chapter 10, the Objective-C language uses this analogy by describing one of the many roles of a class as a *factory.* You can think of a factory as a cookie cutter that stamps out new instances of its class, new objects, whenever necessary. All instances of a given class have the same structure although the actual data stored in any one object may be different from the data stored in another object of the same type, just as all cookies stamped out with the same cookie cutter have the same shape even if they are made of different types of dough and decorated differently.

Most classes are not as simple as UprightRect. Consider, for example, the object that represents a quadrilateral (a four-side geometric figure) in a real application, QuadWorld, that we will be developing in this book. (QuadWorld is explained more thoroughly in the final section of this chapter.) A quadrilateral object responds to the following messages, as well as some other ones:

QuadWorld Quadrilateral Object Messages	Response when received
AsText	Creates and returns a textual description of the quadrilateral.
Center	Computes and returns the quadrilateral's center.
EnclosingRectangle	Creates and returns the smallest upright rectangle that completely encloses the quadrilateral.
RotateBy	Rotates the quadrilateral by given angle.

The objects myUprightRect1 and myUprightRect2 used above, are interchangeable even though they have different ways of structuring their instance variables. So, too, the way in which the internal computations are performed when any of these messages are sent to a Quadrilateral object could be changed without affecting your use of this quadrilateral object in an application program. In effect, the rest of your program can be structured around the notion of a quadrilateral as an independent computer that responds in certain ways to certain commands. This would permit you to easily "lift" a new type of quadrilateral object from another program that extends the standard quadrilateral behaviors, then "drop" it into your application. You also could "drop" a newly improved quadrilateral implementation into your application (an implementation in which the same messages are recognized, but which, say, operates much faster because of the more optimal design of the code executed when a particular message is received). Modularity and portability are thus enhanced.

This may not seem too important for a quadrilateral object, but consider how these same notions would apply to the concept of a Window object, and Icon object, or a SpreadsheetCell object. With these notions modularized in this way, you can construct a new application or modify an existing one easily and quickly by replacing an implementation of a Window class with another that has more functionality, or one implementation of an Icon object by another which has a more efficient implementation of some of its standard behavior, or one implementation of a SpreadsheetCell by another that uses a more compact way of storing its instance variables. These changes could be made to the classes used in the application without affecting the remainder of the application because the object-oriented approach hides the details of the implementation from the rest of the software.

With this type of programming approach, the viewpoint for applications development switches from inside to outside. You interconnect various objects—one that "knows" how to behave as a window, another that knows how to behave as an icon, and still another that knows how to behave as a spreadsheet cell—all without knowing how these entities actually work. This switch of viewpoints is subtle and is usually accompanied by the "aha!" of insight when you realize its potential for the first time.

When there is a large library of these classes, this object-oriented approach to system design allows you to design your own Macintosh-style system, tailored to any particular application domain with a minimum of time and effort. If the requirements for a particular system called for pop-up menus, scroll arrows that worked in a certain unusual way, an application-specific spreadsheet, and access to the AppleTalk network, for example, you can assemble the independent parts from the class library, then "glue" them together into an electronic desktop environment. You needn't redesign the inner workings of any objects or even worry about their interaction to any appreciable degree. This is exactly what MacApp offers you—a library of classes that provide all the pieces you need for developing a Macintosh application.

Methods

So far we have focussed on the data described by an object's class. But classes also define procedures that "know" how to operate on the object's data. These procedures are called *methods,* and they govern the behavior and functionality intrinsic to an object. (In some of the languages we will be discussing, these methods turn out to be the only way to operate on these data.) To invoke one of these methods, you send a message to an instance of the class. A message acts as a selector that specifies which of its methods an object should activate. The object itself then selects the appropriate method. In effect, what happens is that the object receives a message describing what is to be accomplished (For example, "Respond by telling me your center" or "Draw yourself on the screen"), not how to do it (For example, "Run procedure XYZ on yourself") Because objects are highly sophisticated, the message sender just indicates what it desires the object to do without having to worry about anything else. This trust has been termed the "call-by-desire" invocation technique and it is central to object-oriented programming and the idea of an expandable application. With this, you don't need to know how a method works, you only need to know which message will obtain the behavior you desire. Once a class of objects has been fully defined, with instance variables and a set of messages and methods, you can "drop" it into your program with little or no modification.

Inheritance

The fourth basic concept in object-oriented programming is inheritance. As children inherits their parents' characteristics, so too, descendent classes can inherit the instance variables and methods of their ancestor classes. In this way, you do not have to explicitly describe the message behavior of each class. Classes can be described as exhibiting all the message behavior and variable data of some other class, plus some additional message behavior and data. A side effect of designing classes this way is the overall structure that is imposed on clases in your application, a feature not appreciably present in the user-defined data types of standard Pascal and thus one that distinguishes between type definition in Pascal and object definition in Object Pascal.

Typically, in object-oriented programming this class structure can be accomplished in two ways: *simple hierarchical inheritance* or *multiple inheritance,* but because Object Pascal does not have multiple inheritance and because it is a more advanced concept in object-oriented programming, we will delay its discussion until Chapter 10 and focus here on the simpler form of inheritance. Simple hierarchical inheritance occurs when a class is described in terms of one other class immediately above it in a single line of parentage. This parent class is called its *superclass* generically, and its *immediate ancestor* in Object Pascal. This results in a tree-structured hierarchy, such as the one shown in Figure 2-1 with each new class being identical to its immediate ancestor class except for any additional characteristics that you specifically identify. The newly defined class is called a *subclass* of the original parent class generically, and an *immediate descendant* in Object Pascal. An immediate descendant is a further specialization of the class of objects, in much the same way that a robin or a wren, for example, is a special type of bird. Robins and wrens possess characteristics common to all birds, but also possess other distinguishing characteristics. So, too, an immediate descendant possesses all the instance variables of its immediate ancestor and access to all of the ancestor's methods as well as some additional instance variables and methods.

Overriding Inherited Methods

There are two ways to alter what a new class inherits from its superclass. You can simply add instance variables and methods, or you can *override* an inherited method. When a descendant redeclares an already defined method, it is declaring that its own, more specialized version of the method is to be performed instead of its parent's. What this means is that even though the same message is sent, different methods are invoked; the class of an object determines which methods are used to respond to messages sent to that object.

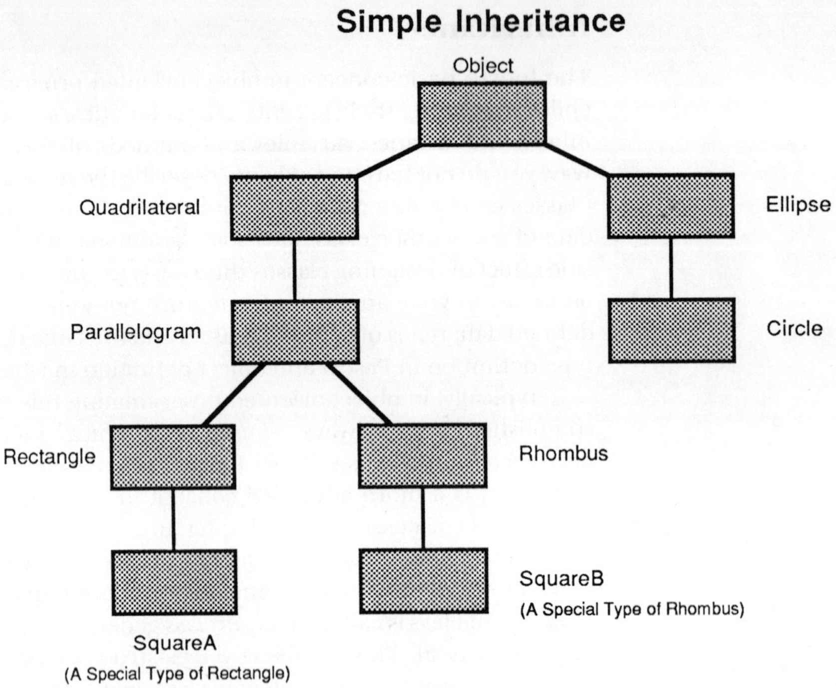

Figure 2-1 Simple hierarchical inheritance. As shown here, this can be represented graphically as a tree. All the languages in this book provide this type of inheritance.

Let us look at a very small example. In Figure 2-2, classes are represented by rectangles and methods by circles, a convention we use throughout this book. Class GAMMA in this figure is a subclass of class BETA which in turn is a subclass of class ALPHA. Class ALPHA defines three methods with selectors *a*, *b*, and *c*. Class BETA defines one method with selector *d* and overrides the *a* method inherited from class ALPHA (for a total of four methods – the method *d*, which is defined in class BETA, the methods *b* and *c*, which are defined in ALPHA but inherited by BETA, and the method *a*, which is overridden in BETA). Class GAMMA defines one method with selector *e*, overrides the *a* method inherited from class BETA, and overrides the *c* method inherited from class ALPHA (for a total of five methods). Thus, class BETA overrides the *a* method of class ALPHA, and class GAMMA overrides the *a* method of class BETA and the *c* method of class ALPHA. Note that any method not specifically overridden in a descendant is inherited unchanged from the ancestor. For example, both BETA and GAMMA inherit ALPHA's *b* method automatically.

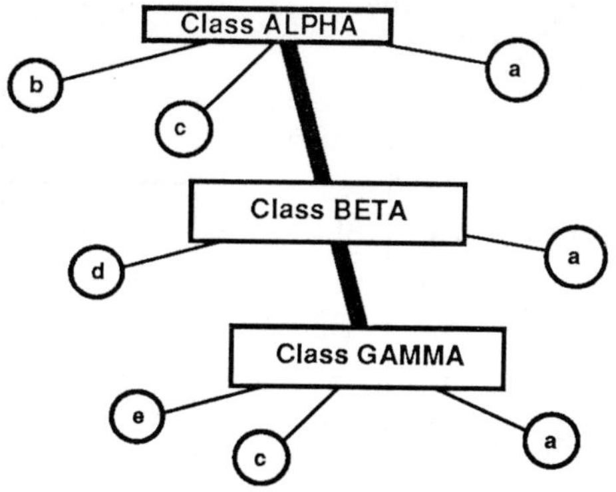

Figure 2-2 A small example of overridden methods and simple inheritance.

In effect, when a message is sent to an object, the system looks to see if the class of that object has a method corresponding to that method. If so, that method is executed. If not, the system looks for a method with that message in the class's ancestor. Let us look at the table in Figure 2-3 to see what this means in practice. Let myAlpha be an instance of class ALPHA, myBeta of class BETA, and myGamma of class GAMMA. Then Figure 2-3 shows what methods are executed when certain messages are sent to these objects. As you can see, sending the message *a* to the object myBeta invokes the method *a* in class BETA – this is the simplest case because the message can be resolved in the class of the object that received the message. Sending the message *b* to the object myGamma invokes the method *b* of class ALPHA. This is the next most complicated case because the message has to be resolved in one of the ancestor classes of the class of the object that received the message. In this example, the system first tried to find a method in class GAMMA with the selector *b.* Finding none, it then tried to find a method with selector *b* in GAMMA's superclass, class BETA. Finding none there, it tried and found a method with selector *b* in BETA's superclass, class ALPHA. This method was executed. Sending the message *d* to the object myAlpha represents the most complicated case: an error detected a run-time. In this last example, the system first tried to find a method in class ALPHA with the selector *d.* Finding none, it tried to find a method with selector *d* in ALPHA's superclass, presumably the class Object, the eventual ancestor of all classes. Finding none, it tried further by searching the superclass of Object, but found no superclsas. At that point a standard error handling procedure was invoked. This error occurred because, in the context of this small example, instances of class ALPHA cannot respond to the message *d.*

to the object \ Send the message:	a	b	c	d	e
`myAlpha`	ALPHA.a	ALPHA.b	ALPHA.c	—	—
`myBeta`	BETA.a	ALPHA.b	ALPHA.c	BETA.d	—
`myGamma`	GAMMA.a	ALPHA.b	GAMMA.a	BETA.d	GAMMA.e

Figure 2-3 The message resolution table for the set of classes in figure 2-2.

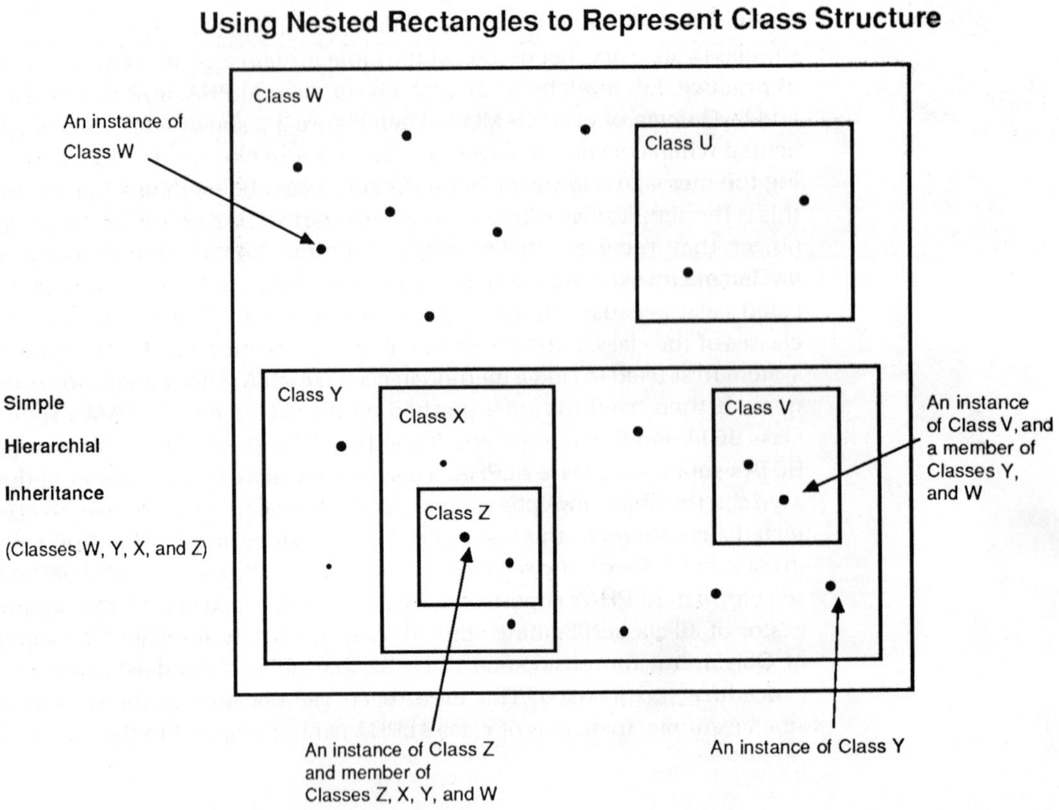

Figure 2-4 The nested rectangle representation for class structure. This is the class representation style common in the Smalltalk literature.

Notes

A more detailed model of the implementation of an object-oriented programming language is given in the next section, but for now it is sufficient to realize that this method-selection scheme allows you to override any method, whether it is a method you wrote yourself, one stored in a system library, or even one stored in ROM. You override a method by defining a new descendant class and by reimplementing the method for a particular message in the original ancestor class's protocol. When that message is received by objects that are instances of your new class, your overriding method will be executed automatically instead of the method in the original ancestor class.

Definitions

An alternate notational convention is sometimes adopted that depicts classes and instances using nested rectangles for the classes and dots for the instances. In this diagramming method, class A is a subclass (an immediate descendant) of class B if A's rectangle is immediately enclosed by B's rectangle and it is a superclass (an immediate ancestor) of class C if C's rectangle is immediately enclosed by A's rectangle. Several examples of this graphic convention are shown in Figure 2-4. In particular, you can see in Figure 2-4 that class Z is a subclass of class X, that class U is a subclass of class W, that class X is a superclass of class Z, and that class W is a superclass of class Y. In addition to the immediate ancestor-immediate descendant relationship, class A is said to be an *ancestor* of class B if there is a sequence of classes from A to B such that each class in this sequence is the immediate descendant of the class preceding it. When this is true, you can also say that class B is a *descendant* of class A. Instances of classes are represented as dots within the rectangles of Figure 2-4. An object is an *instance* of the class represented by its immediately enclosing rectangle and a *member* of any class represented by an enclosing rectangle. In particular, you can see in Figure 2-4 that class W is an ancestor of class Z because classes W, Y, X, and Z form an ancestor-descendant chain. For the same reason, class Z is a descendant of class W and all instances of class Z are members of class W.

Any hierarchy must have a starting point, and this ancestor-descendant strategy and inheritance structure works only if you have at least one *root class* from which to derive all other classes. All object-oriented programming languages we discuss in this book call this root class Object (or something very similar). All other classes are derived from Object or one of its descendant classes.

Class Libraries

As you can imagine, choosing the set of messages for a new class is an important step in its design. The messages of a new descendent class should specify exactly the desired behavior structure for all instances of the class. The most efficient way to design a new application is to start with those classes in the class library that are "closest" to your needs, then derive your own new descendent classes from these, making as few modifications as are necessary to provide the specific type of behavior for your application. One of the most difficult tasks you'll face is to be sufficiently familiar with the class libraries (the classes and their message protocols) for any language you are usng so as to minimize "reinventing the wheel." Since most Macintosh developers use two or more languages in developing a single application, minimizing the learning time is an important goal. To help you learn them, the designers of Macintosh object-oriented languages have made a concerted effort to make all their basic expandable application class libraries as similar to each other as is practical. Language differences make complete equivalence impossible, so there are differences, but due to their efforts you can get double or triple benefit from learning the class libraries because you will be learning them for all languages at once. Moreover, because of this similarity in class libraries, several companies are working on automated aids for converting, say, a Smalltalk-80 program into an Objective-C or an Object Pascal program. These aids do not provide fully automatic conversion between languages, but they take much of the drudgery out of the conversion process and assist in the inevitable syntax confusion that results when any programmer is working simultaneously in two languages.

A Conceptual Model for Object-Oriented Languages

The manner in which objects, messages, classes, instances, and methods are implemented vary from language to language, even for languages present on Macintosh. While some implementation details are discussed in the chapters concentrating on individual languages, a language-independent implementation model is probably more useful to most application developers. In this section, we establish a model that we can use throughout this book, regardless of which language we are discussing. By necessity, such a model must provide only the crudest picture of the manner in which object-oriented systems are actually implemented. Nonetheless, it can help you structure your new application design.

Graphic Notation Conventions

In describing this model, we use some special graphic notation conventions for representing objects and classes. Figure 2-5 gives the conventional format for an object's structure and Figure 2-6 shows how a typical object uses this notation, with the "is_an_instance_of" link pointing to the class of the object so that you can know of which class this object is an instance, and with the instance-variables area holding the actual values of the object's instance variables.

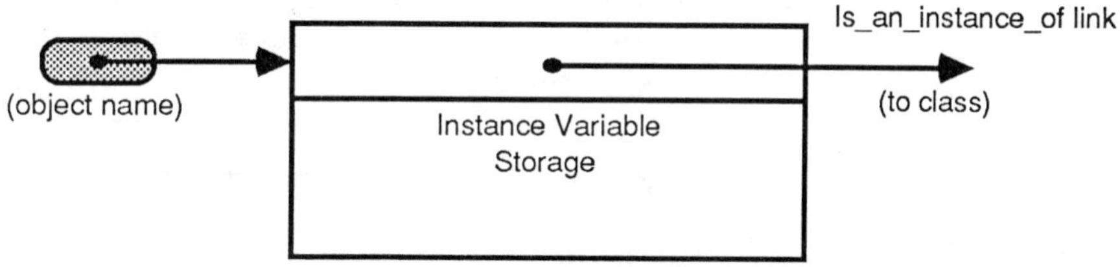

Figure 2-5 A graphical notation for objects. Note that the instance variables of the object can themselves be other objects. The "name" of the object is a pointer variable that points to the object's record.

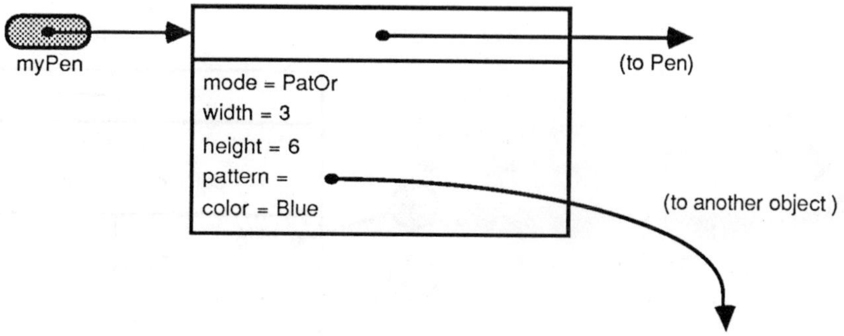

Figure 2-6 A typical object in the graphical notation of figure 2-5. The class of this object is shown in Figure 2-8.

Figure 2-7 shows what the conventional format for the structure of a class looks like. As you can see, there is a link pointing upward to the class's immediate ancestor (its superclass), and the instance-variables area holds a template for the instance variables needed when an instance is created. Finally, there is a message and method dispatch table that indicates which messages in the class's protocol call which methods for a given class. Figure 2-8 shows how an actual class, Pen, would use this notation convention.

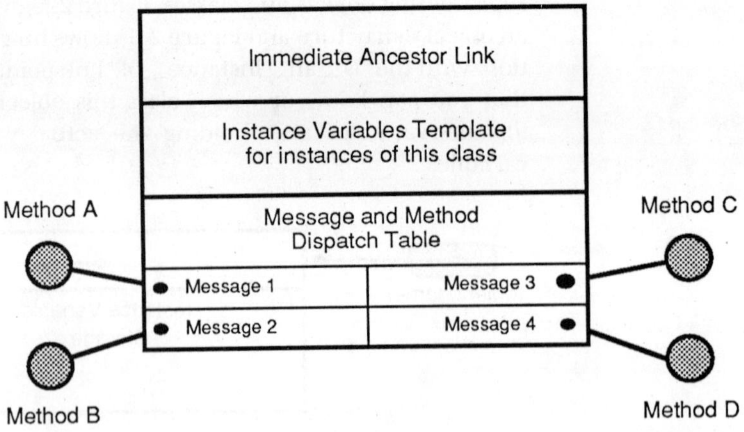

Figure 2-7 A graphical notation for classes. In this notation, the procedures and functions that are the methods for a class are shown as small gray circles.

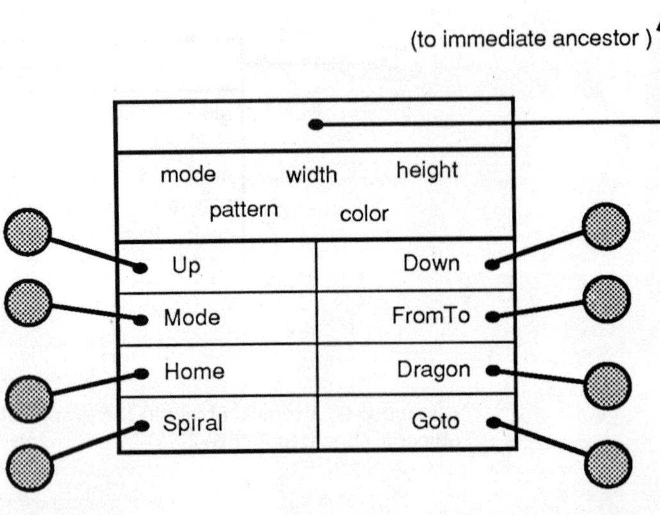

Figure 2-8 A typical class in the graphical notation of figure 2-7. Note that the template for generating objects of this class ("Mode, Width, Height, Pattern, Color") is stored in the class.

As you can see, in our model, both classes and objects are represented by complex record structures à la Pascal, with each object "record" having a field linking it to its class and each class "record" pointing to its immediate ancestor, or superclass. Within each object record there are fields for each of that object's instance variables and within each class record there are pointers to each of the procedures and functions that implement that specific class's methods. In order to minimize the memory requirements for the class hierarchy, the only messages in the class record are the additional messages to which the class responds—that is, the new or overriding messages. A fuller example of these relationships, for the classes ALPHA, BETA, and GAMMA (first shown in Figure 2-2), appears in Figure 2-9. (Note the root class of Object *included above the* ALPHA class.) The message protocols for these classes are:

Object (Immediate Ancestor is NIL)
Instance Variables: (*none*)
Methods: WhatClass, IsNil, Copy, Release, Display

ALPHA (Immediate Ancestor is Object)
Instance Variables: x1: **INTEGER;**
x2: **BOOLEAN;**
Methods: a, b, c

BETA (Immediate Ancestor is ALPHA)
Instance Variables: y1: **STRING;**
y2: **BOOLEAN;**
y3: **REAL;**
Methods: a, d

GAMMA (Immediate Ancestor is BETA)
Instance Variables: z1: **POINTER;**
Methods: a, c, e

In our model, when a message is sent to a particular instance of a class (an object), first the "is_an_instance_of" link is traversed to find the appropriate class, then the method table in that class is searched to see if a method corresponding to that message is found. If it is, that method is executed for that object. (This is what would happen when the message ***a*** is sent to the object myAlpha in Figure 2-9, for example.) If that method table does not contain a method corresponding to that message, the class's ancestor link is traversed to find the immediate ancestor of that class. The method table of that immediate ancestor is searched for a method corresponding to the message. If one is found, that method is executed for the object that originally received the message. (This is what would happen when the message ***d*** is sent to the object myGamma in Figure 2-9, for example, or when the object myAlpha is sent the message IsNil.) If that method table (in the ancestor class) does not contain an appropriate method, its ancestor link is traversed in turn—and so on until either a method for the message is found or the search fails in the method table of the class Object and an error routine is called.

Notes

In actual practice, real implementations of object-oriented languages use caching and a variety of other techniques to make this method lookup very fast. In addition, some languages permit you to assist in this task by indicating the plausibility that a method actually will be invoked.

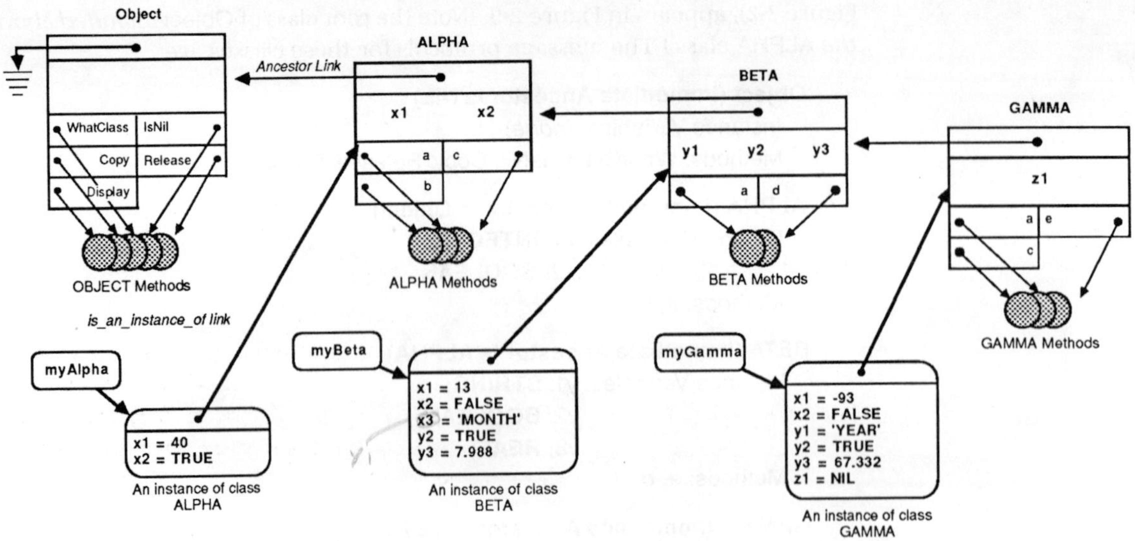

Figure 2-9 A simple implementation model for object-oriented languages. This model demonstrates how the notions of objects, messages, classes, instances, and methods can be implemented using standard programming language techniques. While this model accurately reflects the behavior of the object-oriented languages described in this book, it is not necessarily the manner in which they are actually implemented on Macintosh.

The SELF Pseudo-Variable

As this ancestor chain is traversed during the search for the message received, the system must remember to which object the message was being sent and it must have a way of referring to that object. This is done with a special pseudo-variable SELF. When you want one method to invoke another, analogous to one procedure calling another, you need to use this pseudo-variable. This can be seen by considering how the definition of the a method in class Beta (in Figure 2-9), would be implemented if you wanted the same object that received the *a* message to be sent the *d* message. This is how it would be coded in Object Pascal, although all other object-oriented languages use this pseudo-variable similarly:

```
PROCEDURE BETA.a
BEGIN
  .
  .
  .
  SELF.d;
  .
  .
  .
END;
```

Accessing Overridden Methods

There are times when you don't want to invoke the method of the current receiving class, but rather want to invoke the overridden method of its ancestor, or superclass. A common example of this is when you want to free objects that you no longer need. In languages without automatic garbage collection, which includes most languages we discuss in this book, you have to manage the space these objects occupy by yourself. In most cases, you can simply send the object the message Free to return the memory it occupies to the heap of available memory and, because the root class Object implements this message, all objects will respond to it. Sometimes, however, they may not do so correctly because some instance variables of the object may themselves be references to objects that need to be deallocated at the same time. Consider a class OMEGA whose object instances have two instance variables, a and b, each of which refers to an object. To free an instance of class OMEGA, you must first free the objects referred to by its instance variables. This would be done in Object Pascal in the following way:

```
PROCEDURE OMEGA.Free;
BEGIN
  a.Free;         { Send the message "Free" to the "a" component }
  b.Free;         { Send the message "Free" to the "b" component }
  INHERITED Free; { Invoke the free method of OMEGA's superclass }
END;
```

The last line of this procedure cannot be **SELF.Free** because this would result in an endless recursion of **OMEGA**'s free method, to say nothing of attempting to free already deallocated objects—a no-no. Rather, you should free all of the instance variable objects unique to the **OMEGA** class, then invoke the "higher-level" free method to properly deal with the rest. Syntactically, this is done in Object Pascal with the **INHERITED** qualifier. Use of this qualifier does, in fact, send a message to SELF, but it starts the method search in the super class of **OMEGA** and not the class **OMEGA** itself. Thus you avoid the problems noted above. Here, too, all object-oriented languages we will discuss have this concept of accessing overridden methods, although some use slightly different terminology.

Warning

There is a problem with our conceptual model in that the model predicts that the time to resolve a message will be related to the length of the ancestor-descendent chain from the class of the object that receives the message to the class that is found to contain the corresponding method in those cases in which several different methods are present in the system with the same message names. This is simply not true of real implementations. Indeed, one empirical study by Brad Cox has demonstrated that a cleverly implemented method call results in a constant time to resolve a message and that this time is only twice as long as a procedure call. (See his article for more details: "Message/Object Programming: An Evolutionary Change in Programming Technology," *IEEE Software*, Volume 1, Number 1 (January 1984), pp. 50-61.) Other less scientific studies indicate similar subjective response time for users. This is the only important inaccuracy in our model. We will have to be content, however, with our conceptual model as it stands, keeping in mind its one minor flaw, because presenting the actual algorithms used for message resolution in real systems is beyond the scope of this book.

A Brief Introduction to QuadWorld

Throughout this book we work with a single basic application in several languages to better compare the relative strengths and weaknesses of the object-oriented languages available on the Macintosh and to provide for the needs of programmers with different language preferences. To keep our discussion (and this book) of reasonable length, this application must be fairly small yet representative of all Macintosh applications. We call our application QuadWorld, and in this section, we give you a brief introduction to the concepts and functions QuadWorld includes so that you have a contextual framework for the references and discussions that begin in Chapter 3. In later chapters, we provide complete implementations of QuadWorld in three different languages and partial implementations in each of the other languages we discuss in the book.

QuadWorld enables you to draw and manipulate various types of quadrilaterals: squares, rectangles, parallelograms, rhombi, and other quadrilateral objects. In QuadWorld you can enter or delete any of these objects and rotate them about their centers. When you draw them, you needn't worry about the specific geometric constraints uniquely associated with any of them, such as rhombi, for example—these are taken care of automatically. In many Macintosh applications, users need more than one way to view the same information. To show you how this can be programmed, QuadWorld includes two distinct representations of the quadrilaterals—a graphical one that draws a picture of each quadrilateral and a tabular one that lists a textual representation of the same quadrilaterals. You may select either representation of a quadrilateral object and both the graphical and the tabular representations will be highlighted. Figure 2-10 shows the desired window layout for QuadWorld.

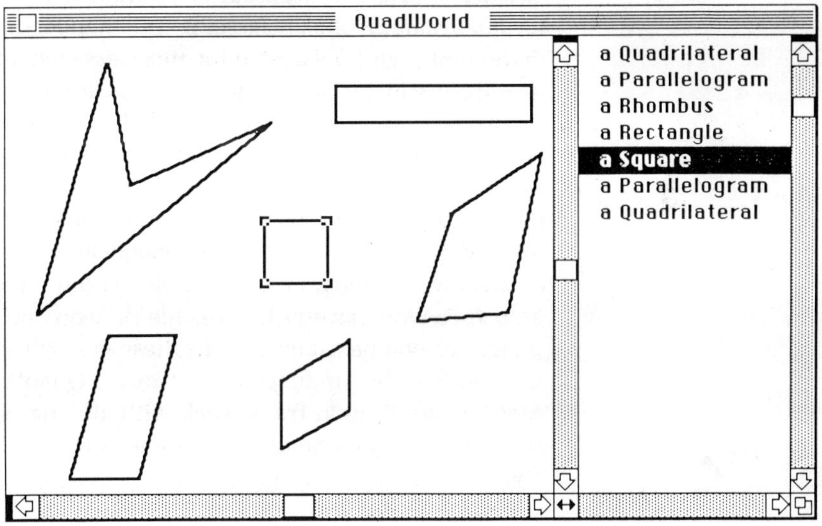

Figure 2-10 The QuadWorld screen design. This application program will be used as the major example for all object-oriented languages described in this book.

The QuadWorld user interface is heavily dependent upon the high-resolution Macintosh graphics screen and on the mouse-and-menu command schemes it popularized as you can see by the following list of features that will be provided in each QuadWorld implementation:

- A large, scrollable drawing area for the quadrilaterals.
- The ability to enter a quadrilateral interactively with graphically displayed feedback and without concern for the unique geometric constraints associated with the more specialized types of quarilaterals.
- The ability to select a quadrilateral by selecting either of its displayed representations and to have both representations automatically highlight for you.
- The ability to delete any or all quadrilaterals.
- The ability to rotate a quadrilateral about its center by any desired angle;
- The ability to adjust the relative sizes of the graphical and tabular areas.
- The ability to undo any action (add, delete, delete all, rotate).

These features are achievable in all object-oriented languages, with varying degrees of difficulty depending on the language and the application framework it provides.

QuadWorld naturally lends itself to the inheritance style that characterizes object-oriented programming, and the desired class hierarchy structure for quadrilateral object classes is shown in Figure 2-11. The methods included in the first high-level design for this class structure are also shown in this figure. Here you can see that Square is descended from Rectangle (because a square is a special type of rectangle—one with equal sides), Rhombus is descended from Parallelogram (a rhombus is a special type of parallelogram—one with equal sides), and so forth. In addition, note that most messages, with their associated methods, for the entire hierarchy of Quadrilateral classes are defined at the highest level, the Quadrilateral class.

As with almost everything else about QuadWorld, this particular class structure won't always be possible or won't be the best choice for each language we will be examining. In these cases, it will be modified slightly to accommodate the language's constraints. QuadWorld is constructed from the MacApp application framework with all languages that support it, and from other application frameworks, such as Lisa Toolkit and Smalltalk MVC, with those languages that do not.

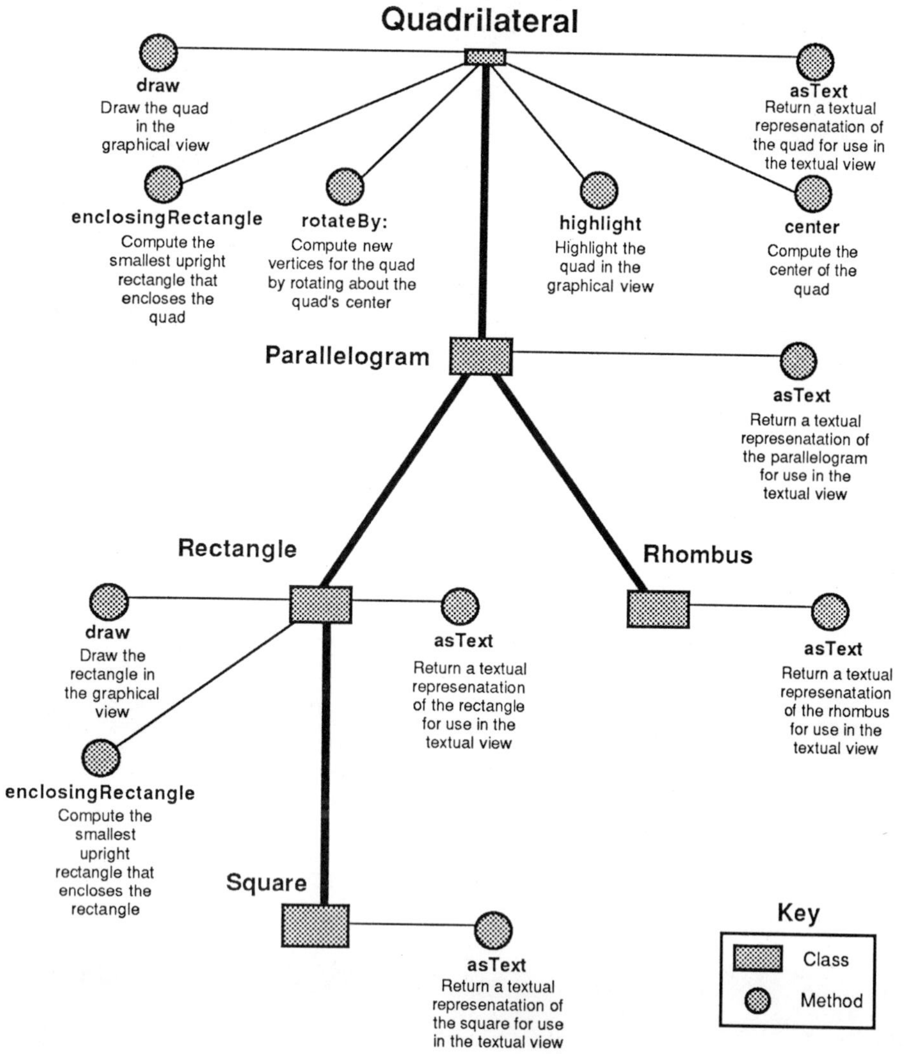

Figure 2-11 The desired QuadWorld class structure. This is the most natural class structure for the Quad World application.

CHAPTER

3

Object Pascal

Object Pascal is Apple's second object-oriented extension to the Pascal language. (The first extension, Clascal, was intended only for the Lisa Office System and is discussed in Chapter 12.) Object Pascal has all the benefits of being the second Pascal extension—its design contains all of the good features and none of the bad ones of its predecessor. In addition, because it was known to be possible to design such an extension (having already done Clascal), the emphasis on this attempt was simplicity and elegance. The result is that you have to learn very few new concepts to use Object Pascal. The syntax for Object Pascal was jointly designed by the Apple Clascal team and Niklaus Wirth, the designer of Pascal, who was invited to Apple's Cupertino headquarters specifically for this project. Apple's team also solicited the opinions of many Clascal application programmers (including those of the author) to guide the design of this new language.

Providing support for the concepts of object-oriented programming in a real programming language can be accomplished in two general manners: designing a totally new programming language around these basic concepts (the *pure* object-oriented language approach) or grafting these concepts onto an existing language (the *hybrid* approach). The only example of a pure object-oriented language in this book is the Smalltalk language discussed in Chapter 11. All other languages, including Object Pascal, are hybrids. The full capabilities of Pascal are available to the Object Pascal programmer for developing application programs, along with new capabilities of classes, methods, and messages; in short, all the features of object-oriented languages are added to those of Pascal. Each approach, pure and hybrid, has its particular strengths, but many people consider the hybrid approach to be superior for the following reasons:

- Hybrid languages enable you to choose between an object-oriented approach and a conventional procedural one on a case-by-case basis in developing a single system. Often, certain parts of a system are more naturally designed using the object-oriented approach while other parts are more naturally implemented with a procedural approach. With a hybrid language, you can use the best tool for each task rather than being forced to use one approach throughout whether or not it is appropriate.
- Hybrid languages enable you to make use of existing libraries or to reuse significant portions of older systems written in the more common version of that language. For both Pascal and C, this is a significant body of software. In addition to these older, procedurally-based subroutine libraries, you can use the class libraries provided with the language—the MacApp library, for example, in the case of Object Pascal.
- Hybrid languages create less of a "culture shock" for both programmers and their managers. The languages on which these are based are already well-known, so the use of an object-oriented extension is not seen as such a radical move.
- Hybrid languages often can be learned in less time, again because they are based on languages most programmers know. Rather than trying to learn an entirely new language from scratch, you need only learn how the object-oriented extensions are added to the language.
- Hybrid languages allow you to choose between the method call and the procedure call. While the method call—accomplished by sending a message to an object and having the object decide which method to invoke to accomplish the task—is an extremely powerful way of encapsulating data and programs, it is more "expensive" (in terms of execution time) than a straight procedure call. In many cases this expense is well worth it. However, there are cases, such as heavy numerical computations, where it is not. Hybrid languages allow you the flexibility of choosing the method call approach when that power is needed and falling back to the procedure call when it is not.

Notes

When implemented in a sufficiently clever manner, one study reported an overhead of a method call as small as 1.75 times as that of the standard procedure call and other implementers claim even more impressive results. (Cox, B., "Message/Object Programming: An Evolutionary Change in Programming Technology," IEEE Software, Volume 1, Number 1, January 1984, pp. 50-61.) Note that this does not mean an application designed using object-oriented principles and implemented using an object-oriented language will run 1.75 times slower than one designed and implemented using standard techniques. This overhead applies only to the method call statements, not to the application as a whole. The run-time penalty for using object-oriented techniques is usually less than 10 percent and many applications actually run faster when implemented using an object-oriented programming language used in conjunction with an application framework like MacApp. (See further discussions of efficiency in Chapter 6 .)

These characteristics of hybrid object-oriented languages do not mean that any Pascal program can easily be changed to make extensive use of Object Pascal's extensions nor that a Pascal programmer can write an object-oriented program in Object Pascal without some training or, more important, without adopting a new way of organizing software. An object-oriented language requires a considerably different approach to program design—an approach reflected in the structure of the source code itself and in the thought processes used in designing that code. While a full discussion of the characteristics of object-oriented design that distinguish it from standard procedural design is outside the scope of this book, we can point out that object-oriented design is concerned with a different type of modularity than procedural design. In an object-oriented design, the unit of modularity is the class; in procedural design the unit of modularity is the procedure. In object-oriented design you have building blocks that have different characteristics, such as inheritance, that, greatly influence the overall design of the application. (For a more detailed discussion of object-oriented design, see *An Object-Oriented Design Handbook for Ada™ Software,* 1985, published by the EVB Corporation, Rockville, MD.)

Objects and Classes in Object Pascal

Standard Pascal has four structured types: array types, set types, file types, and record types. In Object Pascal, new classes are defined as additional kinds of structured types in an extension to the syntax and semantics of standard Pascal-type statements. One new structured type, called the *object type,* most closely resembles the record type in that it can be composed of a number of fields of differing data types. Basically, the fields of the Object Pascal object type are one of two varieties: data fields that contain the instance variable data associated with the objects of this class or pointers to that data; and method fields that point to the procedures and functions that implement the methods of the class.

Definitions

Strictly speaking, from this point on we will be describing Apple's implementation of Object Pascal for the Macintosh: Macintosh Workshop Pascal. The term "Object Pascal" really describes a generically defined extension to the Pascal standard. Any company can implement and market Object Pascal for any machine. As of this writing, no other Object Pascal implementations were available but several were planned.

Before we can see exactly how this syntax is extended to provide for the definition of Object Pascal classes, we must digress briefly to explain one of the most useful extensions of Macintosh Workshop Pascal over that of standard Pascal—the compilation unit.

Notes

There are many other very useful extensions to standard Pascal in Macintosh Workshop Pascal, including arbitrarily typed functions, the ability to directly call C and assembly language routines, and short-circuited boolean expression evaluation. See the Macintosh Workshop Pascal Reference Manual for details.

Unlike standard Pascal, Macintosh Workshop Pascal enables you to define separately compiled libraries. These libraries, called *units,* are defined in two parts: the interface part, which defines the externally known constants, variables, types, and the calling sequences for the externally known procedures and functions in the unit; and the implementation part, which provides the bodies of those procedures and functions defined in the interface part as well as private constants, variables, data types, procedures, and functions. Units provide a means for new data types, and their associated functions and procedures, to be packaged for use by Pascal programmers without having to release the source code for the programs or reveal parts of the package not intended for public use. To be used in an application program, only the unit's interface portion must be made available in source form; the implementation portion can be released as an object file only. Figure 3-1 diagrams this relationship between a unit and a program that uses the unit. An excellent example of a use of this unit facility in Macintosh Workshop Pascal is the Quickdraw graphics library, which provides Macintosh with the drawing speed needed for windows, icons, rulers, and other items.

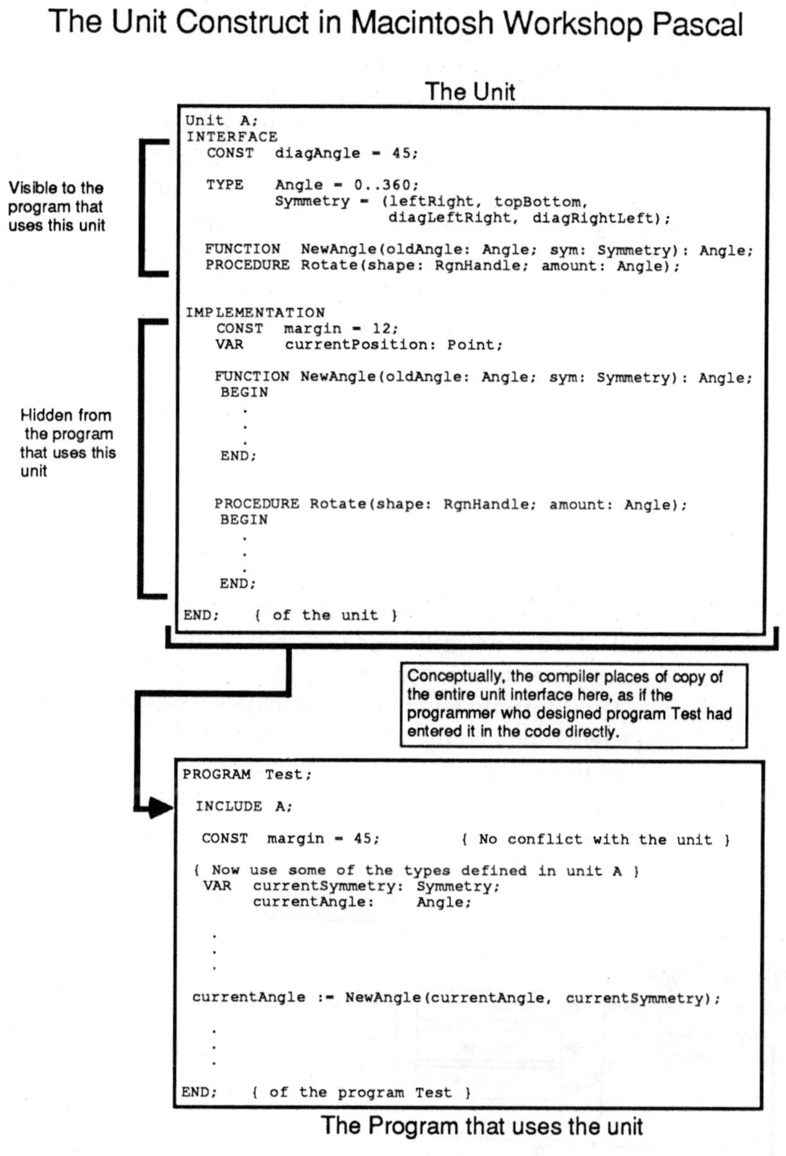

Figure 3-1 The unit construct in Macintosh Workshop Pascal. This construct is usually used to design a set of classes for an Object Pascal application.

When defining Object Pascal classes, this two-part unit is used frequently. The interface part describes the data template of the new classes you want to define and lists their additional or redefined messages. The implementation part defines the method bodies, which are executed when those messages are sent to instances of the classes. This unit structure reinforces the idea that the groups of classes they define are like building blocks to be used to construct your programs. In fact, having to use this unit structure makes most people code their classes so that they are even more portable and generic.

The implementation part of a unit can be used for more than just the methods of classes defined in the interface part. Because the implementation part of a unit hides everything it contains from the programs that use it, you can define any number of private global constants, private global objects, or even private global classes. Classes do not *have* to be defined by specifying their instance variable data and method headers in the unit interface and their method bodies in the unit implementation, you can define an entire class in the implementation portion if it is your intention to hide this class from the users of your unit. In fact, you need not make use of the unit structure at all to use the Object Pascal extensions—although most programmers do. If you want, you can define an object type and all its methods inside a single Pascal program. The only restriction in defining a class is that it must be done at the global level in a program or a unit. You cannot, for example, define a new class inside a procedure or function.

The syntactic additions to Macintosh Workshop Pascal that provide for class definition and use are shown in Figure 3-2. This figure and all the examples of this chapter assume that you are familiar with at least the syntax of standard Pascal, and preferably with the other syntactic extensions of Macintosh Workshop Pascal.

Class Definition

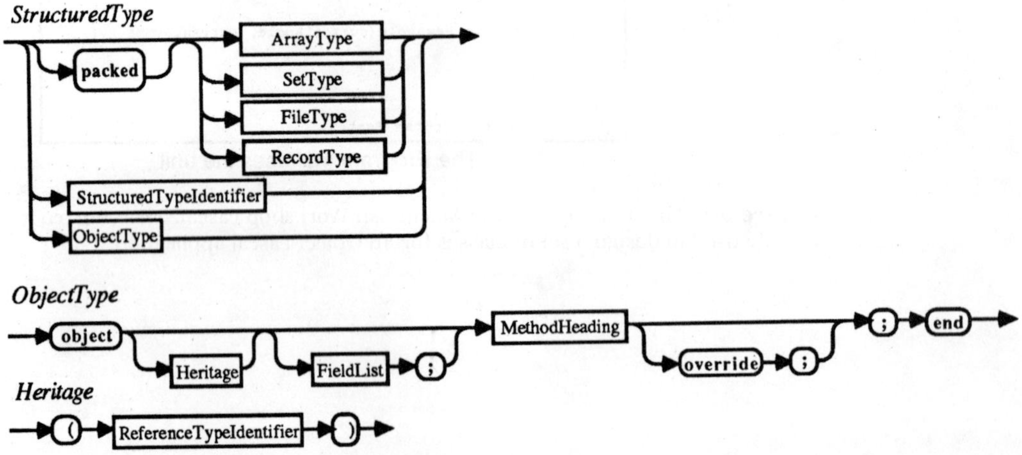

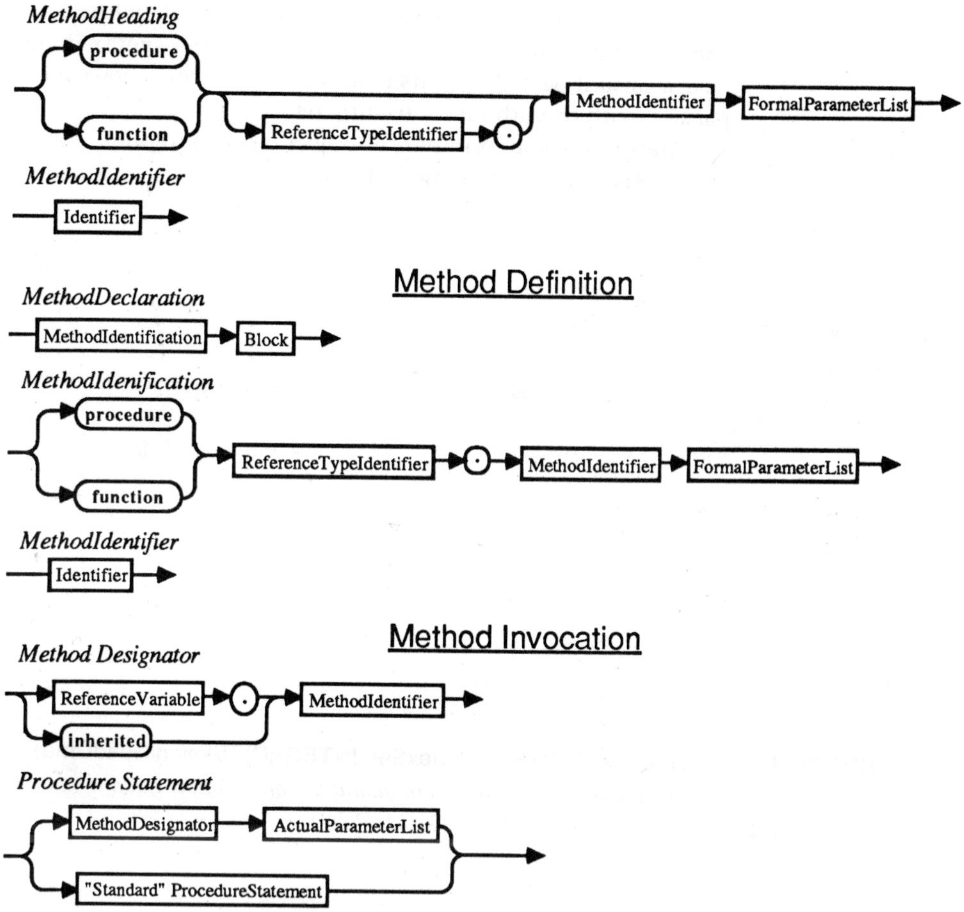

Figure 3-2 The syntax additions to Macintosh Workshop Pascal to provide the capabilities of object-oriented programming. Note that these syntax diagrams are not self-contained—they depict only the additions to the base language to provide for objects, classes, method, etc.

Notes

Note that the syntax diagrams of Figure 3-2 are not self-contained. Rather, they show only the additions and modifications to the standard Pascal syntax. Thus, for example, the FieldList metasymbol is not expanded in that figure, because it is unchanged from that of standard Pascal.

Note that the object type, unlike all other structured types, cannot be packed. Moreover, although not reflected in the syntax diagrams, it cannot have a variant part. Any of its fields can be a record, however—packed or unpacked, with or without a variant part.

Here are some examples of object-type definitions, abstracted from the Object Pascal implementation of QuadWorld:

```
TQuad = OBJECT(TObject)
  fVertex:     ARRAY[1..4] OF Point;
  fNextQuad: TQuad;
                { Successor of the linked list of quads kept in quadDocument }
  fRotated:   BOOLEAN;
                {TRUE if this quad has been rotated. Allows optimal drawing }

  {Initialization—for this class and all its subclasses: TParallelogram,
    TRhombus, etc.}
  PROCEDURE TQuad.IQuad;

{ Queries }
  FUNCTION TQuad.AsText: Str255;
  FUNCTION TQuad.EnclosingRect: Rect;

{ Modifying }
  FUNCTION TQuad.NewSketchCmd(lastVertexSet: INTEGER):TSketch QuadCmd;
                { Return an appropriate sketch command to define a new quad }
  PROCEDURE TQuad.SetPoints(pt1, pt2, pt3, pt4: Point);

END;

TParallelogram = OBJECT(TQuad)
  PROCEDURE TParallelogram.AsText: Str255; OVERRIDE;
  FUNCTION TParallelogram.NewSketchCmd(lastVertexSet:INTEGER):
    TSketchQuadCmd; OVERRIDE;

END;

TRectangle = OBJECT(TParallelogram)
  PROCEDURE TRectangle.AsText: Str255; OVERRIDE;
  FUNCTION TRectangle.NewSketchCmd(lastVertexSet: INTEGER: TSketch QuadCmd; OVERRIDE;

END;
```

Notes

This code fragment follows the naming conventions suggested by Apple for use with Object Pascal. These conventions are:

- Class names begin with "T" as in "TWindow" or "TEventHandler." "T" was chosen instead of "C" because in Object Pascal the class notion is implemented as an extension of "type" in Standard Pascal.
- Instance variable names begin with "f," which denotes that these variables are fields of the objects that are instances of this class.
- Word boundaries in variable names are indicated by capital letters rather than by underscores, which are more difficult to type.

These conventions are followed in all samples of Object Pascal code shown throughout this book and in the Object Pascal implementation of QuadWorld (Listing E).

In Object Pascal, the root class is the TObject, which corresponds to the Object class mentioned in Chapter 2. Object Pascal's TObject class is very lean: it has no instance variables and only two methods: Free and Clone. The Free method deallocates any existing object and Clone copies an object. You might wonder why an object-oriented language would have such a lean root class; most don't. Having a lean root class is an idiosyncrasy of Object Pascal. Most object-oriented languages have a dozen or so methods in the root class—methods that provide a rich functionality for all other objects in the system. Object Pascal does not take this approach in order to avoid the associated storage overhead, yet a root class is still needed for the entire hierarchy—hence the lean TObject.

The inheritance chain of the classes defined above is TObject—TQuad—TParallelogram—TRectangle. This is seen in the first line of each object type definition (TQuad=OBJECT(TObject) for the TQuad class, TParallelogram = OBJECT(TQuad) for the TParallelogram class and TRectangle = OBJECT (TParallelogram) for the TRectangle class.) Note, too, in these example classes the use of the **OVERRIDE** keyword in the two method headings for the class TParallelogram. Each method, then, overrides the corresponding method in TQuad. Object Pascal requires that overriding a method in a subclass be explicitly labeled by this keyword. Failure to do so results in a compiler error for duplicate names. The formal parameter list for such an overriding method must agree exactly with that of the overridden method. Failure to do this also will result in a compiler error.

Variables in Object Pascal can be declared to reference instances of these class types as part of a **VAR** statement, just as pointer variables can be declared to reference instances of certain **RECORD** types. Thus, to declare two variables to reference objects of the class TQuad and TParallelogram respectively, you would use the following statement:

```
VAR myQuad:                 TQuad;
    myParallelogram:        TParallellogram;
```

These variables, myQuad and myParallelogram, are examples of *reference variables* —variables of an object type. For most purposes, you can consider these object reference variables, as they are also called, to be objects. You can send an object a message, refer to one of its data fields, and so on, with no other model than this. To refer to the fRotated field of myParallelogram, for example, you would use the expression:

```
myParallelogram.fRotated
```

and to refer to the ID method of myQuad you would use a similar expression:

```
myQuad.ID
```

Definitions

Note that both expressions use the period (".") to reference the two components of an object—instance variables and methods—and thus they are syntactically similar. The difference between them is that referring to an instance variable merely accesses a field of a record (as in regular Pascal), whereas referring to a method activates it as a function or procedure. In this example, we "send the message" ID to the object referenced by myQuad. In Object Pascal, sending the message ID to the object referenced by the variable myQuad is accomplished by accessing the ID component of the object, using the same notation as field access. Of course, the actual method that gets invoked depends on the class of the object that received the message, in this case the variable myQuad. When viewed this way, the concept of "sending a message" seems a little forced. Indeed, some authors deliberately avoid the expression "sending a message" when talking about hybrid object-oriented languages like Object Pascal, considering this expression to be an unfortunate and confusing term chosen by the PARC Smalltalk group. Chief among their complaints is the fact that the expression "message sending" suggests concurrency—something not part of object-oriented programming as we have defined it here. These authors prefer to use the expression "dynamic binding of procedure calls based upon the object whose operation was invoked"—an expression that does not suggest concurrency and thus is more precise; it is, however, much more verbose and does not exactly roll off the tongue. The point of this objection is that what is important here is the additional level of indirection for a procedure invocation and this is certainly correct. However, the phrase "sending a message," while perhaps initially misleading, is certainly much easier to say and to use than "dynamic binding of procedure calls based upon the object whose operation was invoked," so it will be used throughout this book.

Like the Pascal **POINTER** type, the mere declaration of a reference variable in Object Pascal does not allocate storage for it—objects are dynamically, not statically, allocated entities. Also, like the Pascal **POINTER** type, to allocate an object of a certain class, you use the Pascal NEW procedure. The single argument to this procedure is the name of the reference variable that is to refer to the newly allocated object, as in:

```
VAR myQuad, yourQuad: TQuad;

    NEW(myQuad);
    yourQuad := myQuad;
    NEW(myQuad);
    .
    .
    .
```

(Note the strong similarity here to pointer manipulation in Pascal.)

Definitions

Strictly speaking, we have been a little free with the Object Pascal terminology. The Object Pascal Report (available from Apple) never even uses the term "class" although the notions of classes, instance variables, inheritance, method calls, and others are implemented in Object Pascal. Being very precise, Object Pascal provides an additional structured type called a *reference type.* Reference variables can be declared to refer to a dynamically allocated instance of a reference type. The reference type of such a variable is as you have declared it; the *object type* of such a variable is whatever reference type it has at any instant at run time. The reference type and object type of a reference variable can be different. An example of this would be the state of affairs after executing the following statements:

```
VAR myQuad:                  TQuad;
    myParallelogram:         TParallellogram;

NEW(myParallelogram);
    myQuad := myParallelogram;
```

At this point, the reference variable myQuad would have a reference type of TQuad (because that is how it was declared) and an object type of TParallelogram (because that is the type of its current value.) You have two choices in discussing programs written in Object Pascal: use the Object Pascal terminology very carefully and precisely, or use the standard object-oriented programming terminology and realize that it is slightly inaccurate. I prefer the latter choice.

However, some peculiarities of Object Pascal will seem mysterious unless you understand a little of how Object Pascal manages objects and uses object references. In the Macintosh implementation of Object Pascal, object reference variables are doubly indirect pointers (also called *handles*) to the Pascal storage allocation heap. When you refer to the fDocument field of an object of class TQuadView with the expression:

```
myQuadView.fDocument
```

what really happens is shown in Figure 3-3. The variable myQuadView , which you have declared to be of class type TQuadView is, in fact, a pointer to a master pointer for the object with which you are dealing. The master pointer in turn points to the space allocated on the heap for this object. This complicated structure is used so that the heap may be compacted whenever necessary without causing any change to the variables in your program. The compacting routines automatically update the master pointers for each object and guarantee that these pointers themselves do not change their location. Because it is these master pointers to which your program refers, not the objects themselves, the heap can be compacted whenever necessary. In standard Pascal you would have to refer to the myQuadView. fDocument field of such a structure with an expression like:

```
myQuadView↑↑.fDocument
```

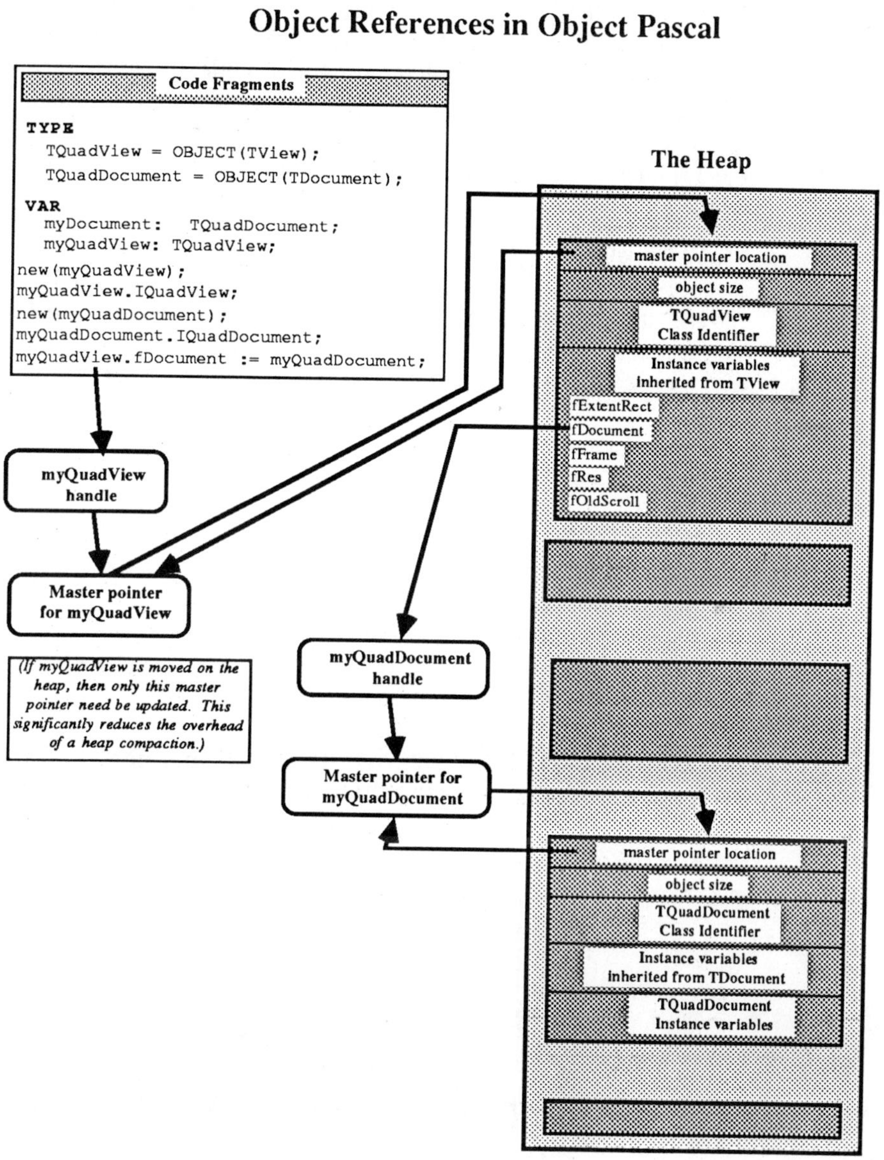

Figure 3-3 The implementation of object references in Object Pascal. The fundamentals of this implementation must be understood to avoid confusion between when automatic dereferencing is done and when it is not.

Object Pascal, however, automatically performs the double dereferencing for you and this is the point of the concern over the implementation details you need to remember when implementing your code. If you refer to a particular field (using an expression such as myQuadView.fDocument), the dereferencing is done for you. On the other hand, if you refer to the entire object by using the object reference variable alone, this dereferencing is not done. Thus, for example, the following sequence of code results in the situation shown in Figure 3-4:

```
VAR thisQuad:  TQuad;
                          { TQuad is an object-type representing quadrilaterals }
    thatQuad:  TQuad;            { in the QuadWorld application. }
                .
                .
                .
new(thisQuad);
new(thatQuad);
                .
                .
                .
thisQuad := thatQuad;
```

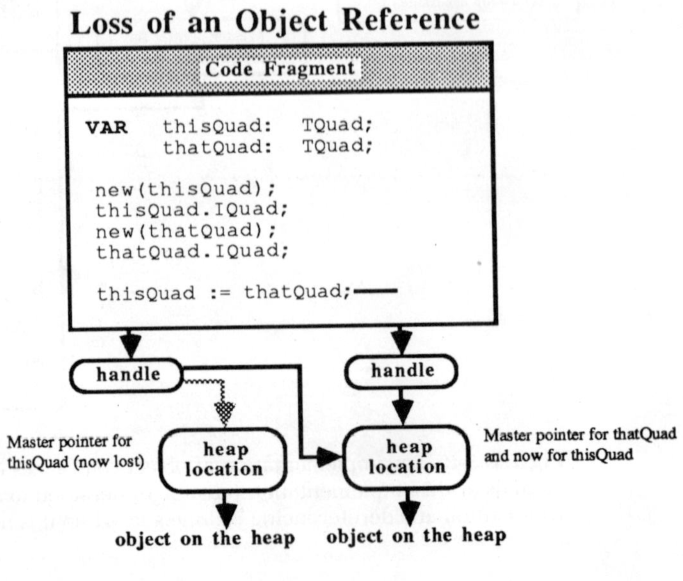

Figure 3-4 Object reference manipulation in Object Pascal.

In effect, the object once referred to by thisQuad would now be lost—it is an object without a pointer referencing it, because thisQuad and nextQuad now refer to the same master pointer and thus to the same object.

The fact that objects are referenced by doubly indirect pointers and that heap compaction takes place without your direct control also requires that you do not yourself try to construct direct pointers to objects. They would point to dead bits (or worse, bits within some other object!) should a compaction take place between the time you stored the pointer and when you used it. Thus, programmers who code constructions like the following deserve all the trouble they will bring down upon themselves:

```
VAR thisFoo:TFoo;    { Assume that class TFoo has a integer field named size. }
    x:        ↑INTEGER;
              .
              .
              .
x := @thisFoo.size;
                  { x now directly points to part of the heap. } { See note below. }
MumboJumbo;
    { a procedure which, as an uncontrollable side-effect, compacts the heap. }
x↑ := 14;
    { Will overwrite some part of the heap, though it was intended to affect
    the size field of the object referred to by thisFoo. }
```

Notes

Note that in Macintosh Workshop Pascal, the unary operator @ computes a pointer to a variable. The type of the resulting pointer is the same as that of the **NIL** pointer and, consequently, the result of the @ operator can be assigned to any pointer variable.

In addition, there are some legal-looking constructs that could cause similar problems; these are shown in Figure 3-5. The Object Pascal compiler warns you when it finds any of these in your code. The compiler warning detects all occurrences of these constructs, even the ones that are in fact safe. If you really need to use one of these constructs and if you are absolutely sure that heap compaction will not occur, you can suppress the complaint in later compilations by surrounding the offending construct with the {$H−} and {$H+} compiler commands, as shown below. The QuickDraw SetRect procedure has a **VAR** parameter as its first argument. Thus, this is an example of the second of the two constructs shown in Figure 3-5. However, SetRect merely stores some numbers and cannot possibly cause a heap compaction, so it is safe to suppress the compiler complaint. (Compiler commands are explained in more detail in the Macintosh Workshop Pascal language manual.)

```
{$H-} SetRect(myObject.outerRect, 0, 0, 100, 200); {$H+}
```

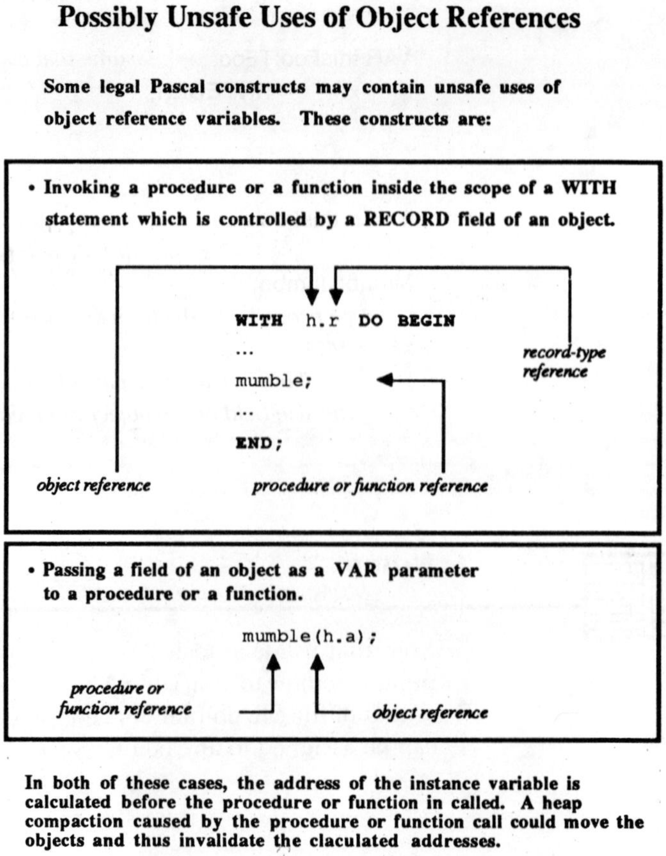

Figure 3-5 Pascal constructs that are not allowed in Object Pascal.

Part of the Object Pascal code for the methods of the TQuad, TParallelogram, and TRectangle classes is shown below. (At this point, you don't need to understand what these classes do. Just read them to get a "feel" for the language).

```
PROCEDURE TQuad.IQuad;
VAR i: INTEGER;                                          { FOR Loop index }
BEGIN
  FOR i := 1 TO 4 DO fVertex[i] := gZeroPt;
  fNextQuad := NIL;
  fRotated := FALSE;
END;

FUNCTION TQuad.AsText: Str255;
BEGIN
  AsText := 'a Quadrilateral';
END;

FUNCTION TQuad.EnclosingRect: Rect;
VAR
  minLeft, minTop, maxRight, maxBottom: INTEGER;
  thisRect:                             Rect;
  i:                                    INTEGER;         { FOR loop index }
  PROCEDURE SetMinMax(pt: Point);
  BEGIN
    minLeft := Min(minLeft, pt.h);
    minTop := Min(minTop, pt.v);
    maxRight := Max(maxRight, pt.h);
    maxBottom := Max(maxBottom, pt.v);
  END;

BEGIN                                                    { TQuad.EnclosingRect }
  minLeft := maxint; minTop := maxint;
  maxRight := 0; maxBottom := 0;

  FOR i := 1 TO 4 DO SetMinMax(SELF.fVertex[i]);

  SetRect(thisRect, minLeft, minTop, maxRight, maxBottom);
  EnclosingRect := thisRect;
END;                                                     { TQuad.EnclosingRect }

FUNCTION TQuad.NewSketchCmd(lastVertexSet: INTEGER):TSketch QuadCmd;
```

```
VAR quadSketcher: TSketchQuadCmd;
BEGIN
  NEW(quadSketcher);
  quadSketcher.ISketchQuadCmd(cAddQuadCmd, lastVertexSet);
  NewSketchCmd := quadSketcher;
END;

FUNCTION TParallelogram.AsText: Str255;
BEGIN
  AsText := 'a Parallelogram';
END;

FUNCTION TParallelogram.NewSketchCmd(lastVertexSet: INTEGER):
  TSketchQuadCmd; OVERRIDE;
VAR parallelogramSketcher: TSketchParallelogramCmd;
BEGIN
  NEW(parallelogramSketcher);
  parallelogramSketcher.ISketchQuadCmd(cAddQuadCmd,lastVertexSet);
  NewSketchCmd := parallelogramSketcher;
END;

FUNCTION TRectangle.AsText: Str255;
BEGIN
  AsText := 'a Rectangle';
END;

FUNCTION TRectangle.EnclosingRect: Rect;
VAR thisRect: Rect;
BEGIN
  IF NOT SELF.fRotated
    THEN Pt2Rect(SELF.fVertex[1], SELF.fVertex[3], thisRect)
    ELSE thisRect := INHERITED EnclosingRect;
  EnclosingRect := thisRect;
END;

FUNCTION TRectangle.NewSketchCmd(lastVertexSet: INTEGER): TSketch
  QuadCmd;
VAR rectangleSketcher: TSketchTangleCmd;
BEGIN
NEW(rectangleSketcher);
  rectangleSketcher.ISketchQuadCmd(cAddRectangleCmd, lastVertexSet);
  NewSketchCmd := rectangleSketcher;
END;
```

In this example we see that:

- Most methods are short procedures or functions that accomplish one very specific task.
- The **OVERRIDE** keyword, if used at all, need not be repeated in the implementation, but the method header must be repeated. The method TParallelogram.AsText, for example, overrides that of TQuad.AsText and in the definition of the TParallelogram class, this method is declared with the **OVERRIDE** keyword. The definition of the body of this method, as shown above, does not repeat this. On the other hand, the method TParallelogram. NewSketchCmd, which overrides the corresponding method of TQuad, has the **OVERRIDE** keyword appended to the definition of its body.
- Object Pascal is really not that different from standard Pascal. You can mix "normal" Pascal statements with Object Pascal message sends, as in the body of the method TQuad.New SketchCmd.
- The syntax for calling an overridden method is to use the **INHERITED** keyword as seen in the TRectangle.EnclosingRect method. Without going into detail about the semantics of these quadrilateral classes, the EnclosingRect function calculates the smallest upright rectangle that encloses all four of a quadrilateral's vertices. For a general quadrilateral (an instance of TQuad, for example), this is done through a test of each of the four vertices. For a quadrilateral that happens to be a rectangle (an instance of TRectangle, for example), a much simpler calculation usually is possible. This simpler calculation is possible if the rectangle has not been rotated. Thus, the Enclosing Rect method for the TRectangle class has the following form:

```
IF NOT SELF.fRotated
  THEN Simpler Calculation
  ELSE Use the standard TQuad calculation;
```

  Note that in expanding this into real Object Pascal code we could not just directly reference the EnclosingRect method like this:

```
IF NOT SELF.fRotated
  THEN Simpler Calculation
  ELSE thisRect:= SELF.EnclosingRect;                { Incorrect! }
```

  because this code would endlessly recurse invoking TRectangle.Enclosing Rect without ever invoking TQuad.EnclosingRect. Rather, we need to access the EnclosingRect method that was overridden—the one in the TQuad class. This is accomplished in Object Pascal with the **INHERITED** keyword and the following code executes correctly:

```
IF NOT SELF.fRotated
  THEN Simpler Calculation
  ELSE thisRect:= INHERITED EnclosingRect;           { Correct! }
```

This invokes the **EnclosingRect** method in the first ancestor class, going up the inheritance tree from the TRectangle class, in which it occurs. In this case, this is the TQuad class.

Notes

Usually, methods are overridden in subclasses to provide additional or alternative specialized behavior, but this example in the quadrilateral classes shows that you can also override to take advantage of special properties to reduce your computation or drawing time.

- Methods may be defined in any order in the implementation portion. There are at least three reasonable styles used to order the methods. The first style has all the methods for a given class defined in a contiguous piece of code in the implementation body. This style has the advantage of making it easy to find a particular method in the implementation part and having all the methods "in one place" should the class need to be modified. For example, changing the name or type of an instance variable may require several modifications to the methods of that class. Having those methods all together simplifies this task. The second style is to place the methods in their approximate "flow of control" order. This order makes it easier to read someone else's program because all the methods that are used in, say, setting up and opening a window, are in one place in the program code. Should there be any problem with this functional area in the application, the problem is localized to a set of methods that are in close proximity and thus can be dealt with more easily. The third style is to alphabetize all methods by their message names. This makes it easy to find a particular method, effectively grouping overridden methods together. This last style, however, suppresses the natural modularity given to an object-oriented program by its classes because the methods of any one class are scattered throughout the implementation portion.

Notes

I find the "methods-ordered-by-class" to be the only reasonable manner of organizing anything but the smallest application. This is because the class, not the method, is the basic unit of modularity in an object-oriented program. Accordingly, the Object Pascal implementation of QuadWorld, which is to be a model Object Pascal application, uses the "methods-ordered-by-class" scheme as would, in my opinion, any large application.

Semantics and Common Usage in Object Pascal

Creation and Initialization

New objects are generated in Object Pascal by using the procedure NEW, in the same manner that NEW is used to generate new dynamic data structures in standard Pascal:

Standard Pascal

```
TYPE TQuidPtr: ↑TQuid;
  TQuid = RECORD
    BEGIN
      vertex: ARRAY[1..4] OF Point;
      nextQuid:TQuidPtr
      rotated: BOOLEAN;
    END;

PROCEDURE IQuid(aQuid: TQuidPtr);
FORWARD;
PROCEDURE Draw(aQuid: TQuidPtr);
FORWARD;

VAR myQuid: TQuidPtr;

NEW(myQuid);
IQuid(myQuid);
Draw(myQuid);
myQuid↑.rotated := TRUE;
```

Object Pascal

```
TYPE TQuad = OBJECT(TObject)
  fVertex: ARRAY[1..4] OF Point;
  fNextQuad: TQuad;
  fRotated: BOOLEAN;
  PROCEDURE TQuad.IQuad;
  PROCEDURE TQuad.Draw;
END;

VAR myQuad: TQuad;

NEW(myQuad);
myQuad.IQuad;
myQuad.Draw;
myQuad.fRotated := TRUE;
```

Although not enforced in the language, it is common practice for each class to have a method to perform any necessary initialization on the instance variables of a newly created instance of that class. In addition, the name of that initialization method is usually the name of the class, with the leading capital "T" replaced by a capital "I." Thus, the initialization method for the class TView is TView.IView and for TQuadWindow, TQuadWindow.IQuadWindow. This initialization method should be invoked immediately after an object is created, as shown in the above example with the myQuad object.

STOP

Warning

Note that the argument to the NEW procedure in an Object Pascal program must not be an instance variable of some other object. This is because this argument to NEW is a **VAR** parameter and the NEW procedure might very well cause heap compaction to occur. Thus, instead of using code like this:

```
PROCEDURE TQuad.IQuad;
BEGIN
  NEW(SELF.fNextQuad);                         { Incorrect! }
  SELF.fRotated := FALSE;
END;
```

in which the object referred to by fNextQuad is allocated, you must use a temporary variable for the creation:

```
PROCEDURE TQuad.IQuad;
VAR tempQuad: TQuad;
BEGIN
  NEW(tempQuad);                               { Correct! }
  SELF.fNextQuad := tempQuad;
  SELF.fRotated := FALSE;
END;
```

Object Encapsulation

Most object-oriented languages restrict manipulation of the instance variables of an object to the methods of that object's class or one of its subclasses which ensures that an object can guarantee its own internal consistency. Object Pascal does not require this strict encapsulation, although you are encouraged to follow this restriction anyway. Thus, in Object Pascal one can write statements like the following (based on the Object Pascal code fragment shown above):

```
myQuad.fNextQuad.fVertex[1] := aNewPoint;      { bad style }
```

to change the value of the first vertex of the TQuad object following myQuad. A better way to achieve this end would be something like this:

```
myQuad.fNextQuad.SetVertices(aNewPoint, . . .);
```

An even worse violation of an object's encapsulation than the above example with a TQuad object would be something like this:

```
TYPE TWindow = OBJECT(TFrame)
            .
            .
            .
            fDocument: TDocument;
            .
            .
            .
      END;
TYPE TDocument = OBJECT(TEvtHandler)
            .
            .
            .
            fDocPrintHandler: TPrintHandler;
            .
            .
            .
      END;
TYPE TPrintHandler = OBJECT(TEvtHandler)
            .
            .
            .
            fDeviceRes: Point;
            .
            .
            .
      END;
            .
            .
            .
gFrontWindow.fDocument.fDocPrintHandler.fDeviceRes := aNewPoint;
                                                        { terrible style }
```

This is worse because there are dissimilar objects involved.

Freeing Objects

Just as you manage the creation of objects when you need them, you must manage their destruction when they are no longer needed—Object Pascal provides no automatic garbage collection. This destruction could be done using the Dispose procedure of standard Pascal, but it is better to send the message Free to the object. Using Free is better because freeing one object can sometimes require that other objects also be freed, which works best if you make each class deallocate exactly the same objects that its methods allocate. Using Free in this consistent manner simplifies the management of object storage. When you design a new class, you can either define a Free method designed specifically for this class, or you can rely on the Free method of its immediate ancestor, or superclass. Typically, you will not rely on the Free method of the superclass if your class itself creates additional objects. Because methods of your class creates these objects, methods should also be used to free them. For example:

```
TYPE TFoo = OBJECT(TSnark)
  fFirstObject: TEmployee;
  fSecondObject: TEmployee;
  fNumber: INTEGER;
  PROCEDURE TFoo.IFoo;
  PROCEDURE TFoo.Free; OVERRIDE;
  PROCEDURE TFoo.DoThis;
  PROCEDURE TFoo.DoThat;
END;

PROCEDURE TFoo.IFoo;
VAR tempObject: TEmployee;
BEGIN
  SELF.ISnark;
  NEW(tempObject);
  tempObject.IEmployee;
  SELF.fFirstObject := tempObject;
  NEW(tempObject);
  SELF.tempObject.IEmployee;
  fSecondObject := tempObject;
END;

PROCEDURE TFoo.Free;
BEGIN
  FreeObject(SELF.fFirstObject);
  FreeObject(SELF.fSecondObject);
  INHERITED Free;
END;
```

Note that in the initialization method of class TFoo two objects of class TEmployee are created. When a particular instance of TFoo is freed, these objects must be freed (assuming no other object reference variables point to them). The **TFoo.Free** method accomplishes this by first freeing these two instances of TEmployee. (This task is made somewhat easier because of the existence of a standard procedure, **FreeObject(x)**, defined in UObject, a unit supplied with Object Pascal. This procedure will send **x** the **Free** message if $x \neq$ **NIL**.) The **TFoo.Free** method then frees the TFoo object by invoking the inherited **Free** method (inherited from TSnark). Note that it would not be correct to remove the **INHERITED** in the last line of **TFoo.Free.** If you did, an invocation of **TFoo.Free** would recurse endlessly. We must invoke the **Free** method of the superclass to actually free the TFoo object. The **TFoo.Free** method frees only the objects created in TFoo's initialization method. In addition, it would not be correct to change the order of these actions in the **TFoo.Free** method like this:

```
PROCEDURE TFoo.Free;                          { Incorrectly coded! }
BEGIN
  INHERITED Free;
  FreeObject(SELF.fFirstObject);
  FreeObject(SELF.fSecondObject);
END;
```

This incorrectly designed method would first free the instance of TFoo, then try to free the two instances of TEmployee. After the instance of TFoo is freed, there are no longer any references to these instances of TEmployee — there is no way to send them messages!

Compile-Time Type Checking

Unlike many of the other object-oriented languages discussed in this book, Object Pascal can do some type checking for object reference variables at compile time. (The alternative is to defer any such checking until run time. Each alternative has its own strengths and weaknesses, explored at length in the final chapter of this book.) This compile-time checking is based upon the principle of membership of an object in a particular class. Consider the following object type declarations and associated program fragment. (Note that these classes are diagrammed in Figure 3-6.)

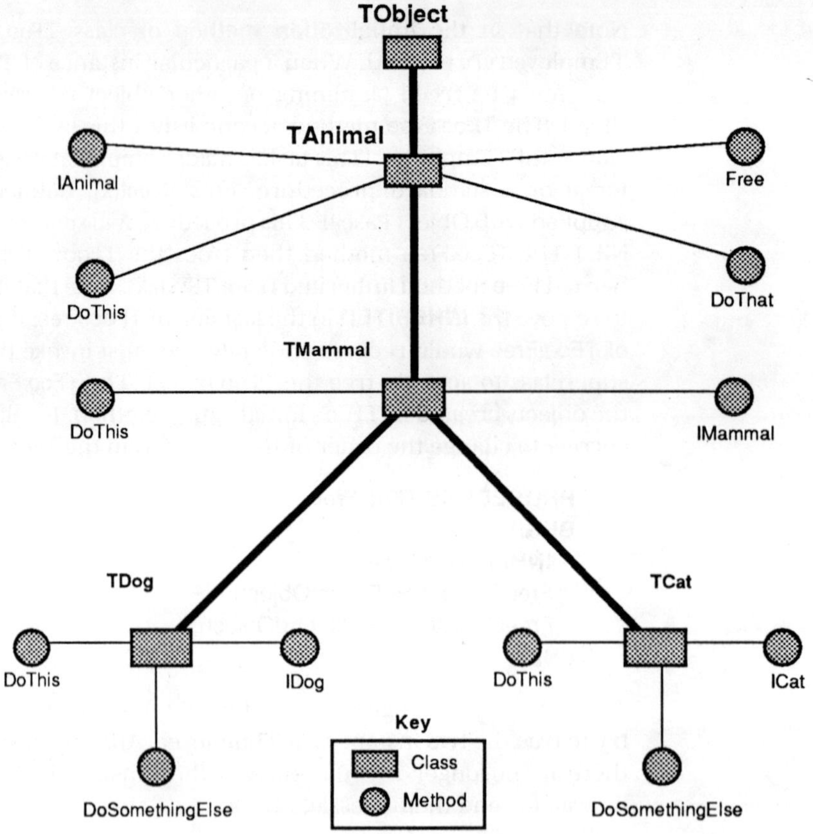

Figure 3-6 A small group of five classes used to indicate Object Pascal type checking.

```
TYPE TAnimal = OBJECT(TObject)
  fFirstObj: TOmega;
  fNumber: INTEGER;
  PROCEDURE TAnimal.IAnimal;
  PROCEDURE TAnimal.Free; OVERRIDE;
  PROCEDURE TAnimal.DoThis;
  PROCEDURE TAnimal.DoThat;
END;

TYPE TMammal = OBJECT(TAnimal)
  PROCEDURE TMammal.IMammal;
  PROCEDURE TMammal.DoThis; OVERRIDE;
END;
```

```
TYPE TDog = OBJECT(TMammal)
  PROCEDURE TDog.IDog;
  PROCEDURE TDog.DoThis; OVERRIDE;
  PROCEDURE TDog.DoSomethingElse;
END;

TYPE TCat = OBJECT(TMammal)
  PROCEDURE TCat.ICat;
  PROCEDURE TCat.DoThis; OVERRIDE;
  PROCEDURE TCat.DoSomethingElse;
END;

VAR myObject: TObject;
    anAnimal: TAnimal;
    aMammal: TMammal;
    rover: TDog;
    tabby: TCat;
    king: TDog;

NEW(anAnimal);
anAnimal.IAnimal;

NEW(aMammal);
aMammal.IMammal;

NEW(rover);
rover.IDog;

NEW(tabby);
tabby.ICat;

NEW(king);
king.IDog;
```

The object anAnimal is a member of classes TAnimal and TObject. The object aMammal is a member of classes TMammal, TAnimal, and TObject. The object **rover** is a member of classes TDog, TMammal, TAnimal, and TObject. In general, an object is a member of its class and all of its class's ancestors. Assignment statement and procedure parameters are checked for membership compatibility, in a manner analogous to type compatibility checking in standard Pascal. Thus the following are legal:

```
anAnimal := aMammal;

rover.DoThat;
```

anAnimal.DoThis;	
myObject := rover;	
aMammal.fNumber := 37;	
rover := king;	
rover.IAnimal;	(While legal, this probably doesn't "make sense" because it will not execute initialization code in the methods IDog or IMammal.)

but the following are illegal and are detected at compile-time as errors:

aMammal := anAnimal;	(Because anAnimal may reference an object other than one of class TMammal or one of TMammal 's descendant classes.)
myObject.DoThat;	(Because objects of class TObject have no DoThat method.)
anAnimal.DoSomethingElse;	(Only some objects that can be assigned to the variable anAnimal have a DoSomethingElse method because only some of TAnimal 's descendant classes have such a method. Thus, it is possible that an object referenced by the variable anAnimal would not be able to respond to the message DoSomethingElse.)
myObject.fNumber := 2;	(Because myObject does not have an fNumber field.)
anAnimal.fNumber := 'cat';	(Because the fNumber field is an integer.)
anAnimal.IGamma;	(Because objects of class TAnimal have no IGamma method.)
rover := tabby;	(Because objects of class TCat cannot be objects of class TDog.)

The example of the illegality of the statements "aMammal := anAnimal;" and "anAnimal.DoSomethingElse;" is interesting because in some circumstances it is reasonable to want to do either of these things. Those circumstances are, in the first example, when the object anAnimal, which could be an object of class TMammal, is so, and in the second example, when the object referenced by the variable anAnimal is an object of class TDog or TCat—classes that have DoSomethingElse in their message protocol. Object Pascal provides a type-casting construct to enable you to use this kind of statement. Type casts can be done using the class name, as in the following legal statement:

```
aMammal := TMammal(anAnimal);
```

This works correctly if the object anAnimal is a member of class TMammal, but otherwise it is a run-time error.

Notes

This object-type casting in Object Pascal is a special case of the general-type casting facilities in Macintosh Workshop Pascal. These facilities enable you to cast compatible types at run time with the name of the type.

To enable you to test before you try to perform a type cast coercion, the BOOLEAN function Member can be used, as in the following legal and very defensive statement:

```
IF Member(anAnimal, TMammal)
   THEN aMammal:=TMammal(anAnimal);
```

In the third of the illegal examples above, you could send the message DoSomethingElse to the object referenced by the variable anAnimal if you could be sure that the object referenced by that variable was a member of TDog or TCat:

```
IF Member(anAnimal, TCat) THEN TCat(anAnimal).DoSomethingElse;
IF Member(anAnimal, TDog) THEN TDog(anAnimal).DoSomethingElse;
```

The function Member(testObject, TSomeClass) will return **TRUE** if testObject is an instance of the class TSomeClass or any of TSomeClass's descendent classes.

Notes

The Member function can be easily misused, however. An example of such a misuse is the following:

```
IF Member(anAnimal, TMammal) THEN WeighMammal(TMammal(anAnimal))
```

```
ELSE IF Member(anAnimal, TDog) THEN
WeighDog(TDog(anAnimal))
ELSE IF Member(anAnimal, TCat) THEN
WeighCat(TCat(anAnimal));
```

All of this code could (and should) be replaced with the single line

```
aMammal.Weigh;
```

after Weigh methods are added to the classes TMammal, TDog, and TCat.

While the Object Pascal compiler can provide some assistance by performing class compatibility tests of assignment statements and message sends, there are (and must be!) things about an Object Pascal statement that cannot be known at compile time. For example, there is no way of knowing which DoThis method will be called in the statement

```
aMammal.DoThis;
```

Because each of the classes TMammal, TDog, and TCat has a DoThis method and because the variable aMammal could be of any of these classes at run-time, the determination of which method will be called cannot be made until then. Another example is that it is not possible at compile time to know the class of the object referenced by the variable anAnimal. This is because the variable anAnimal can reference objects of the class TAnimal, TMammal, TDog and TCat—all of the descendant classes of TAnimal. During the "lifetime" of the variable anAnimal it could reference objects of all of these classes, as can be seen in the following code fragment:

```
VAR anAnimal: TAnimal;
    aMammal:TMammal;
    tabby:    TCat;
    rover:    TDog;

NEW(anAnimal);
anAnimal.IAnimal;

NEW(aMammal);
aMammal.IMammal;
anAnimal := aMammal;
                    { anAnimal now references an object of class TMammal }
```

```
NEW(rover);
rover.IDog;
anAnimal := rover;          ( anAnimal now references an object of class TDog )

NEW(tabby);
tabby.ICat;
anAnimal := tabby;          (anAnimal now references an object of class TCat )
```

These examples of what Object Pascal cannot determine until run-time may give you the impression that a great deal of decisions must be delayed until then. Actually, as object-oriented languages go, Object Pascal makes very few decisions at run-time. Most object-oriented languages provide no compile-time facilities and so defer all decisions about objects until run-time. As we have shown earlier in this section, Object Pascal can check at compile time the legality of many assignment statements and can detect when there is no possibility that a message can be understood, for example, when you specify that a message be sent to an object, but there is no corresponding method in the object's class or any of its ancestor classes.

Private and Basic Methods

In designing a class there often is a need for a method that should be used only by the class designer, not by any other programmers who might use this class in application programs. Such methods are called *private methods* and some languages provide a mechanism to hide these private methods from the programs that use the class. Object Pascal, however, provides no such feature. In Object Pascal, private methods are indicated only by comments in the interface portion of a unit.

In addition to private methods, class designers may sometimes wish to ensure that a particular method is never (or at least very rarely) overridden by any of its subclasses. These methods are called *basic methods.* The manner in which these methods are distinguished is usually only in the name of the methods (that is, the message that corresponds to this method). None of the languages discussed in this book provides direct language support for basic methods, but rather suggest that basic methods be indicated by a combination of comments and carefully chosen method names, as shown in the example below:

```
INTERFACE
  TObject = OBJECT
```

```
        FUNCTION      ShallowClone: TObject;
                      { Lowest level method for copying an object; should not be
                      overridden except in very unusual cases. Simply calls
                      HandToHand to copy the object data. }
        FUNCTION      Clone: TObject;
                      { Defaults to calling ShallowClone; can be overridden to
                      clone objects referred to by fields. }
        PROCEDURE     ShallowFree;
                      { Lowest level method for freeing an object; should not be
                      overridden except in very unusual cases. Simply calls Dis-
                      posHandle to free the object data. }
        PROCEDURE     Free;
                      { Defaults to calling ShallowFree; can be overridden to free
                      objects referred to by fields. }
    END;

IMPLEMENTATION
    FUNCTION TObject.ShallowClone;
      VAR result: Handle;
    BEGIN
      result := Handle(SELF);
      IF HandToHand(result) < > noErr THEN
        BEGIN
          {$IFC qDebug}
          ProgramBreak('ShallowClone failed.');
          {$ENDC}
          result := NIL;
          END;
          ShallowClone := TObject(result);
    END;

    FUNCTION TObject.Clone;
    BEGIN
      Clone := SELF.ShallowClone;
    END;

    PROCEDURE TObject.ShallowFree;
    BEGIN
      DisposHandle(Handle(SELF));
    END;

    PROCEDURE TObject.Free;
    BEGIN
      SELF.ShallowFree;
    END;
```

The methods ShallowFree and ShallowClone are basic methods—they are never to be overridden in any class. In case the designer of a subclass needs to provide an alternative deallocation or copying method, the methods Free and/or Copy should be overridden. Note that Free and Clone in TObject do nothing beyond invoking the corresponding basic methods. These methods Free and Clone are specifically provided in the TObject class so that they can be overridden while still guaranteeing that the basic freeing and copying functionality described in the methods ShallowFree and ShallowClone is always present.

Object Pascal and MacApp

MacApp, the expandable Macintosh application previewed in Chapter 1, is a set of Object Pascal classes—a group of building blocks you can use to construct a Macintosh application easily. If you wish to implement a Macintosh application, MacApp is probably the best way for you to do so and so MacApp will be the subject of the next several chapters. For many programmers, Object Pascal and MacApp represent what they need to know to design their applications. For these individuals, the distinction between Object Pascal and MacApp is minimal because both are always used together. However, if you want to study object-oriented programming to see how this style of program design and implementation is different from traditional approaches to programming, you can use Object Pascal independent of MacApp—in the same way that you might use Pascal independent of some subroutine library that, however useful, may not be germane to the task at hand. For some programmers, the object-oriented approach is so totally new that it needs to be studied on its own for a while. For others, the ideas of object-oriented programming are so captivating that you will sometimes want to explore how these ideas can be used in areas other than application frameworks. There is no reason not to pursue these or any other paths that include Object Pascal but not, for the moment, MacApp.

Quad Classes in Object Pascal

Most of the QuadWorld application introduced in Chapter 2 is implemented using MacApp classes, but the basic classes that form the heart of this application are independent of MacApp. These classes model the pertinent properties of the geometric entities that QuadWorld enables the user to explore: the (general) quadrilateral, the parallelogram, the rhombus, the rectangle, and the square. Because these classes are independent of MacApp, we examine their design here and show that many of the benefits of object-oriented programming are independent of the use of an application framework.

The first thing you can see in the QuadWorld specification is that different quadrilaterals have behaviors. For example, each type of quadrilateral has to write a different textual representation in the QuadWorld textual view and each has a different way of being interactively drawn by the user. This suggests that each type of quadrilateral should be represented by its own class. This does not, however, tell us what data should be stored in the instances of each of these classes, nor does it indicate which inheritance structure would work best.

When considering the data that need to be stored to model a quadrilateral, you are first faced with what appears to be a dilemma. To model a general quadrilateral, all four vertices must be stored; for a parallelogram or a rhombus, only three vertices are needed; to model an upright rectangle, only two vertices are needed; and for an upright square one vertex and an edge length are sufficient. The amount of data seems to be decreasing from a general quadrilateral to a square. This does not fit well with the inheritance model of object-oriented programming. On one hand, the class-subclass relationship should go from the general to the more specific, suggesting that TQuad should be an ancestor class for all the other quadrilateral classes. On the other hand, the amount of data stored in a subclass cannot be less than that stored in its superclass. This dilemma is solved by considering two additional facts:

- If rotation of the quadrilaterals is to be allowed (as it is in QuadWorld), then two points are not enough to define a rectangle, nor will a point and an edge length suffice for a square. These are only enough if the rectangle and square remain upright, that is, parallel to the coordinate axes.
- The acts of interactively creating a particular type of object and later manipulating that same object are distinctly different. An easy way to simplify everything is to assume, for now, the existence of a separate *quadrilateral creator object* that would manage the interactive creation of these objects. The actual classes would manage only the manipulation of quadrilaterals, specifically excluding any information about creating new quadrilaterals.

These considerations suggest storing all four vertices for all types of quadrilaterals and this works extremely well. Given this design choice, the inheritance structure shown in Figure 3-7 simply "falls out."

Warning

Some simplifying omissions have been made in the class explanations given here. Chapter 8 will correct these omissions when the full QuadWorld application is developed.

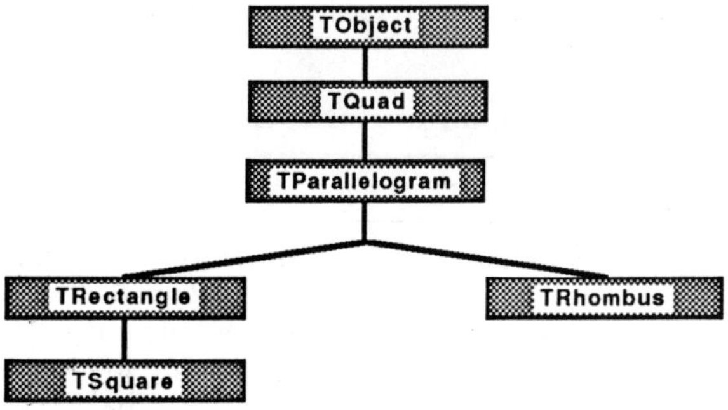

Figure 3-7 The inheritance structure of the quadrilateral classes.

The TQuad class contains all of the data and most of the functionality for all the types of quadrilaterals. Instances of TQuad have three instance variables:

TQuad Instance Variables

Variable	Type	Use
fVertex	**ARRAY** [1. .4] of Point	Records the coordinates for each of the four vertices of the quadrilateral.
fNextQuad	TQuad	Refers to a linked list of quadrilaterals, so that a variable number of quadrilateral objects can easily be managed.
fEnclosingRect	**Rect**	Records the smallest upright rectangle enclosing the quadrilateral.
fRotated	**BOOLEAN**	Records whether this quadrilateral has been rotated (fRotated = **TRUE** if the quadrilateral has been rotated). In certain cases, this enables the quadrilateral to be drawn more efficiently.

The methods of TQuad are:

TQuad Initialization and Debugging Methods

Method	Use
IQuad	Initializes a new instance of class TQuad. Also used to initialize instances of all TQuad's subclasses. Normally, each new class should have its own distinct initialization method. However, when a series of subclasses has no new instance variable data (as is the case with the quadrilateral classes), then using one initialization method is fine.
Inspect	Print out the current values of all of a quad's instance variables. This method is used only in debugging.

Definitions

Here we are using a convention common in object-oriented programming: referring to an instance of a class by using the class name (or some slight variant) without an initial capital letter. Thus, the object quad or aQuad is an instance of class TQuad. This convention rarely invites confusion and, in those cases where it might, we will use the longer but less ambiguous "an instance of class TQuad referred to by the reference variable quad" Mercifully, this will not occur often.

TQuad Query Methods

Method	Use
AsText	Returns a textual description of a quad.
Center	Calculates and return the center point of a quad.
EnclosingRect	Calculates and returns the smallest QuickDraw rectangle completely enclosing the quad. Among other things, this rectangle is used to detect whether the quad is showing in the window. TQuad's method is overridden only for efficiency in the special case that the rectangle is not rotated.

TQuad Modifying Methods

Method	Use
RotateBy	Changes a quad's vertices by rotating the quad around its center by a given number of degrees.
SetPoints	Changes a quad's vertices by replacing them by four specified points. Note that this is an example of a private method, a method needed for the full functionality of the class, but which should never be used by other classes. Unfortunately, Object Pascal provides no mechanism to hide such a method from other programs that might use this class.

TQuad Drawing Methods

Method	Use
Draw	Draws a quad in the graphical view in response to the request of the view to render itself.

TQuad Filing Methods

Method	Use
ID	Returns an integer identifying this type of quad, prior to writing a TFiledQuad record to disk. (See below.)
ReadFrom	Reads the quad from disk. (See below.)
WriteTo	Writes the quad to disk in such a way that it can be completely reconstructed later. (See below.)

Object Pascal does not provide any direct mechanism for storing objects on disk or for retrieving objects from disk. To be able to write TQuad objects to the disk as well as read them back again, the QuadWorld unit defines a standard Pascal record type, TFiledQuad:

```
TYPE
  TFiledQuad = RECORD                          { Disk version of a quad }
    theRotationState: BOOLEAN;
    theVertices: ARRAY[1..4] OF Point;
    END;
```

The TQuad method, TQuad.ID, returns an integer identifying this quad as an instance of TQuad (as opposed to an instance of TParallelogram, for example) and the method TQuad.WriteTo writes a TFiledQuad record representing a given quad to disk.

In designing the other quad classes, most of the methods of TQuad need not be overridden. The few that do are easy. TRectangle is one example:

TRectangle Query Methods

Method	Use
AsText	Returns a textual description of a rectangle object.
EnclosingRect	Calculates and returns the smallest QuickDraw rectangle completely enclosing the rectangle object. This QuickDraw rectangle is used to quickly detect if the rectangle object is showing in the window, among other things.

TRectangle Drawing Methods

Method	Use
Draw	Draws a rectangle object in the graphical view in response to the request of the view to render itself. Note that this can often be accomplished more efficiently with the QuickDraw routine FrameRect.

TRectangle Filing Methods

Method	Use
ID	Returns an integer identifying this type of rectangle object, prior to writing a TFiledQuad record to disk.

Several of these methods are like **TRectangle.AsText** in that they must be overridden to specify what it is that makes a rectangle object a rectangle. The other methods, **TRectangle.Draw** and **TRectangle.EnclosingRect**, are overridden not to provide new functionality, but to provide the same functionality in a more efficient way, as was shown earlier in the section of this chapter describing the **INHERITED** construct.

Notes

A complete listing of the implementation of the quadrilateral classes is show in Figure 3-8. This listing is a small portion of the entire Object Pascal implementation of the QuadWorld application.

```
INTERFACE

TYPE

  TQuad = OBJECT(TObject)

    fVertex:         ARRAY[1..4] OF Point;
    fNextQuad:       TQuad;               { successor in the linked list of quads kept in quadDocument  }
    fEnclosingRect: Rect;                 { the upright rectangle enclosing the quad }
    fRotated:        BOOLEAN;             { TRUE if this quad has been rotated.  Allows optimal drawing }

   { Initialization - for this class and all its subclasses, TParallelogram, TRhombus, etc. }
    PROCEDURE TQuad.IQuad;

    {$IFC qDebug}
    PROCEDURE TQuad.Inspect; OVERRIDE;              { Debugging print of the quad's instance variables }
    {$ENDC}

   { Queries }
    FUNCTION   TQuad.AsText: Str255;
    FUNCTION   TQuad.Center: Point;
    FUNCTION   TQuad.EnclosingRect: Rect;                 { Private method to calculate fExtentRect }
    FUNCTION   TQuad.NewSketchCmd: TSketchQuadCmd;        { Return an appropriate sketch command to
                                                            define a new quad }
   { Displaying }
    PROCEDURE  TQuad.Draw;

   { Modifing }
    PROCEDURE  TQuad.RotateBy(theta: INTEGER);
    PROCEDURE  TQuad.SetPoints(pt1, pt2, pt3, pt4: Point);
```

Figure 3-8 The interface and the implementation for the quadrilateral classes.

```
      { Filing }
        FUNCTION   TQuad.ID: INTEGER;
        PROCEDURE  TQuad.ReadFrom(aRefNum: INTEGER);
        PROCEDURE  TQuad.WriteTo(aRefNum: INTEGER);
    END;


    TParallelogram = OBJECT(TQuad)

        FUNCTION   TParallelogram.AsText: Str255; OVERRIDE;
        FUNCTION   TParallelogram.ID: INTEGER; OVERRIDE;
        FUNCTION   TParallelogram.NewSketchCmd: TSketchQuadCmd; OVERRIDE;
    END;

    TRhombus = OBJECT(TParallelogram)

        FUNCTION   TRhombus.AsText: Str255; OVERRIDE;
        FUNCTION   TRhombus.ID: INTEGER; OVERRIDE;
        FUNCTION   TRhombus.NewSketchCmd: TSketchQuadCmd; OVERRIDE;
    END;

    TRectangle = OBJECT(TParallelogram)

        FUNCTION   TRectangle.AsText: Str255; OVERRIDE;
        PROCEDURE  TRectangle.Draw; OVERRIDE;
        FUNCTION   TRectangle.EnclosingRect: Rect; OVERRIDE;
        FUNCTION   TRectangle.ID: INTEGER; OVERRIDE;
        FUNCTION   TRectangle.NewSketchCmd: TSketchQuadCmd; OVERRIDE;
    END;


    TSquare = OBJECT(TRectangle)

        FUNCTION   TSquare.AsText: Str255; OVERRIDE;
        FUNCTION   TSquare.ID: INTEGER; OVERRIDE;
        FUNCTION   TSquare.NewSketchCmd: TSketchQuadCmd; OVERRIDE;
    END;

IMPLEMENTATION

{ ******************************************* TQuad Methods ******************************************* }

    PROCEDURE TQuad.IQuad;
    VAR zeroPt:    Point;
        zeroRect: Rect;
        i:          INTEGER;    { FOR Loop index }
    BEGIN
        SetPt(zeroPt, 0, 0);
        FOR i := 1 TO 4 DO SELF.fVertex[i] := zeroPt;
        SetRect(zeroRect, 0, 0, 0, 0);
        SELF.fEnclosingRect := zeroRect;
        SELF.fNextQuad := NIL;
        SELF.fRotated := FALSE;
    END;

{$IFC qDebug}
{$S GDebug}
    PROCEDURE TQuad.Inspect;   OVERRIDE;
    VAR i:  INTEGER;     { FOR Loop index }
    BEGIN
        INHERITED Inspect;
        FOR i := 1 TO 4 DO WriteLn(' Vertex(', i,') is (', fVertex[i].h, ', ', fVertex[i].v, ')');
        IF SELF.fNextQuad = NIL
          THEN WriteLn('fNextQuad is NIL')
          ELSE WriteLn('fNextQuad is NOT NIL');
        WriteLn('fRotated is ', SELF.fRotated);
    END;
{$ENDC}
```

Figure 3-8 The interface and the implementation for the quadrilateral classes *(continued).*

```
{$S ARes}
    FUNCTION  TQuad.AsText: Str255;
    BEGIN
        AsText := 'a Quadrilateral';
    END;


    FUNCTION  TQuad.Center: Point;
    VAR
        thisPoint: Point;
    BEGIN
      thisPoint.h := (fVertex[1].h + fVertex[2].h + fVertex[3].h + fVertex[4].h) div 4;
      thisPoint.v := (fVertex[1].v + fVertex[2].v + fVertex[3].v + fVertex[4].v) div 4;
      Center := thisPoint;

    END;


    PROCEDURE TQuad.Draw;

        PROCEDURE DrawEdge(pt1, pt2: Point);
        BEGIN
            MoveTo(pt1.h, pt1.v);
            LineTo(pt2.h, pt2.v);
        END;  { DrawEdge }

    BEGIN
      IF RectIsVisible(SELF.fEnclosingRect) THEN          { only draw quads that will be seen }
          BEGIN
              DrawEdge(fVertex[1], fVertex[2]);
              DrawEdge(fVertex[2], fVertex[3]);
              DrawEdge(fVertex[3], fVertex[4]);
              DrawEdge(fVertex[4], fVertex[1]);
          END;
    END;  { TQuad.Draw }


    FUNCTION  TQuad.EnclosingRect: Rect;
    VAR                                                        { a PRIVATE method for this class }
        minLeft, minTop, maxRight, maxBottom:   INTEGER;
        thisRect:   Rect;
        i:          INTEGER;    { FOR loop index }

        PROCEDURE SetMinMax(pt: Point);
        BEGIN
            minLeft := Min(minLeft, pt.h);
            minTop := Min(minTop, pt.v);
            maxRight := Max(maxRight, pt.h);
            maxBottom := Max(maxBottom, pt.v);
        END;

    BEGIN  { TQuad.EnclosingRect }
        minLeft := 720;     minTop := 360;
        maxRight := 0;      maxBottom := 0;

        FOR i := 1 TO 4 DO SetMinMax(SELF.fVertex[i]);

        SetRect(thisRect, minLeft, minTop, maxRight, maxBottom);
        EnclosingRect := thisRect;
    END;  { TQuad.EnclosingRect }

{ This function returns a sketcher that will assist the user to interactively enter a quad }
    FUNCTION  TQuad.NewSketchCmd: TSketchQuadCmd;
    VAR quadSketcher:   TSketchQuadCmd;
    BEGIN
        NEW(quadSketcher);
        quadSketcher.ISketchQuadCmd(cAddQuadCmd);
        NewSketchCmd := quadSketcher;
    END;
```

Figure 3-8 The interface and the implementation for the quadrilateral classes *(continued).*

```
{ This procedure provides an id for quads written to disk }
   FUNCTION TQuad.ID: INTEGER;
   BEGIN
      ID := IDQuad;
   END;


{ This procedure reads a quad from disk.  The id has ALREADY been read. }
   PROCEDURE TQuad.ReadFrom(aRefNum: INTEGER);
   VAR data:       TFiledQuad;
       err:        OSErr;
       count:      LONGINT;
       i:          INTEGER;    { FOR Loop index }
   BEGIN
      count := SIZEOF(TFiledQuad);
      err := FSRead(aRefNum, count, @data);
      FOR i := 1 TO 4 DO SELF.fVertex[i] := data.theVertices[i];
      SELF.fRotated := data.theRotationState;
   END;

{ This procedure rotates a quad counterclockwise about its center by theta degrees }
   PROCEDURE TQuad.RotateBy(theta: INTEGER);
   VAR
      newVertex:       ARRAY[1..4] OF Point;
      sine, cosine:    REAL;
      centerPt:        Point;
      tempPt:          Point;
      radians:         REAL;
      i:               INTEGER;    { FOR loop index }

   BEGIN
      centerPt := SELF.Center;

      { Convert from degrees to radians, as required by the sine and cosine functions }
      radians := (theta * 3.14159) / 180.0;
      sine := sin(radians);
      cosine := cos(radians);
      FOR i := 1 TO 4 DO
         BEGIN
            SetPt(tempPt, SELF.fVertex[i].h - centerPt.h,      { Subtract centerPt from vertex[i]. }
                          SELF.fVertex[i].v - centerPt.v);     { Store the result in tempPt.       }
            newVertex[i].h := Num2Integer(centerPt.h + tempPt.h*cosine - tempPt.v*sine);
            newVertex[i].v := Num2Integer(centerPt.v + tempPt.v*cosine + tempPt.h*sine);
         END;

      SELF.SetPoints(newVertex[1], newVertex[2], newVertex[3], newVertex[4]);
      SELF.fRotated := TRUE;
   END;


   PROCEDURE TQuad.SetPoints(pt1, pt2, pt3, pt4: Point);
   BEGIN
      SELF.fVertex[1] := pt1;
      SELF.fVertex[2] := pt2;
      SELF.fVertex[3] := pt3;
      SELF.fVertex[4] := pt4;
      SELF.fEnclosingRect := SELF.EnclosingRect;
   END;


   PROCEDURE TQuad.WriteTo(aRefNum: INTEGER);
   VAR data:      TFiledQuad;
       count:     LONGINT;
       quadID:    INTEGER;
       err:       OSErr;
       i:         INTEGER;    { FOR Loop index }
   BEGIN
      quadID := SELF.ID;
      count := SIZEOF(INTEGER);
      err := FSWrite(aRefNum, count, @quadID);
      FOR i := 1 TO 4 DO data.theVertices[i] := SELF.fVertex[i];
      data.theRotationState := SELF.fRotated;
      count := SIZEOF(TFiledQuad);
      err := FSWrite(aRefNum, count, @data);
   END;
```

Figure 3-8 The interface and the implementation for the quadrilateral classes *(continued)*.

```
{ *************************************** TParallelogram Methods *****************************************}

   FUNCTION   TParallelogram.AsText: Str255;   OVERRIDE;
   BEGIN
        AsText := 'a Parallelogram';
   END;


   FUNCTION TParallelogram.ID: INTEGER;   OVERRIDE;
   BEGIN
       ID := IDParallelogram;
   END;


{ This function returns a sketcher that will assist the user to interactively enter a parallelogram }
   FUNCTION   TParallelogram.NewSketchCmd: TSketchQuadCmd;   OVERRIDE;
   VAR parallelogramSketcher:   TSketchParallelogramCmd;
   BEGIN
        NEW(parallelogramSketcher);
        parallelogramSketcher.ISketchQuadCmd(cAddParallelogramCmd);
        NewSketchCmd := parallelogramSketcher;
   END;


{ ****************************************** TRhombus Methods ******************************************}

   FUNCTION   TRhombus.AsText: Str255;   OVERRIDE;
   BEGIN
        AsText := 'a Rhombus';
   END;


   FUNCTION TRhombus.ID: INTEGER;   OVERRIDE;
   BEGIN
       ID := IDRhombus;
   END;


{ This function returns a sketcher that will assist the user to interactively enter a rhombus }
   FUNCTION   TRhombus.NewSketchCmd: TSketchQuadCmd;   OVERRIDE;
   VAR rhombusSketcher:   TSketchRhombusCmd;

   BEGIN
        NEW(rhombusSketcher);
        rhombusSketcher.ISketchQuadCmd(cAddRhombusCmd);
        NewSketchCmd := rhombusSketcher;
   END;


{ **************************************** TRectangle Methods ******************************************}

   FUNCTION   TRectangle.AsText: Str255;   OVERRIDE;
   BEGIN
        AsText := 'a Rectangle';
   END;


   PROCEDURE TRectangle.Draw;   OVERRIDE;
   VAR aRect: Rect;
   BEGIN
       IF NOT SELF.fRotated
         THEN
              BEGIN
                 Pt2Rect(SELF.fVertex[1], SELF.fVertex[3], aRect);
                 FrameRect(aRect);
              END

         ELSE INHERITED Draw;
   END;
```

Figure 3-8 The interface and the implementation for the quadrilateral classes *(continued)*.

```
FUNCTION  TRectangle.EnclosingRect: Rect;  OVERRIDE;
VAR thisRect:   Rect;
BEGIN
     IF NOT SELF.fRotated
       THEN Pt2Rect(SELF.fVertex[1], SELF.fVertex[3], thisRect)
       ELSE thisRect := INHERITED EnclosingRect;
     EnclosingRect := thisRect;
END;

FUNCTION TRectangle.ID: INTEGER;  OVERRIDE;
BEGIN
     ID := IDRectangle;
END;

{ This function returns a sketcher that will assist the user to interactively enter a rectangle }
FUNCTION  TRectangle.NewSketchCmd: TSketchQuadCmd;  OVERRIDE;
VAR rectangleSketcher:   TSketchTangleCmd;
BEGIN
     NEW(rectangleSketcher);
     rectangleSketcher.ISketchQuadCmd(cAddRectangleCmd);
     NewSketchCmd := rectangleSketcher;
END;

{ ******************************************** TSquare Methods ********************************************}

FUNCTION  TSquare.AsText: Str255;  OVERRIDE;
BEGIN
     AsText := 'a Square';
END;

FUNCTION TSquare.ID: INTEGER;  OVERRIDE;
BEGIN
     ID := IDSquare;
END;
```

Figure 3-8 The interface and the implementation for the quadrilateral classes *(continued)*.

Even with this minimal set of classes we can demonstrate much of the power of object-oriented programming. Recall that quadrilateral objects are dynamically allocated in response to user input (in a manner that, admittedly, has not yet been defined) and that these quadrilateral objects are linked together in a singly linked list. The algorithms for drawing the graphical and textual representations of the quadrilaterals can now be defined completely independent of these classes. To draw all the quadrilaterals, you need only traverse the list and send the **Draw** message to each quad object:

```
quad := headQuad;
WHILE quad <> NIL DO
  BEGIN
    quad.Draw;
    quad := quad.fNextQuad;
  END;
```

and similarly for the textual representation of their names:

```
quad := headQuad;
WHILE quad <> NIL DO
  BEGIN
    Calculate the correctPosition
    MoveTo(correctPosition);              { a QuickDraw graphics call }
    DrawString(quad.AsText);              { another QuickDraw graphics call }
    quad := quad.fNextQuad;
  END;
```

Notes

This is not exactly the way the drawing code for the graphic and textual views appears in the listing, but it is conceptually identical. The code in the listing is slightly more general and the details of its structure will be discussed in a later chapter.

What is important about these algorithms is that they are independent of the quadrilateral classes. If a new quadrilateral class, say, TTrapezoid, were to be added to QuadWorld, neither algorithm would have to be modified in any way. By letting each quadrilateral object decide exactly how to draw itself and represent itself as text, we have been able to express in a pristine form the drawing algorithms for the two views. We have thus insulated the view-rendering code from the objects being rendered and, to some extent, insulated the objects from the manner in which they are rendered. We will have more to say about the advantages of these types of insulation later, after we have explored the MacApp framework.

CHAPTER

4

Introduction to MacApp

One of the many benefits of object-oriented programming is the possibility of creating application frameworks—blank applications that can be easily expanded into a wide variety of specific, real applications. MacApp is one such framework. In this chapter we will:

- more precisely define application frameworks and examine how object-oriented programming can provide them,
- show how MacApp is used with Object Pascal to develop an application program, and
- construct, as a learning exercise, the smallest possible MacApp application.

In later chapters, we examine the use of MacApp with other programming languages, use the features of MacApp to build some advanced application features, including iconic menus and palettes, and use the clipboard to transfer data between different applications, whether they were written with MacApp or not. In addition, we also measure the costs and benefits of using MacApp as a base for a new application.

Application Frameworks

Prior to MacApp, most Macintosh software was developed program by program, with each program having its own code for managing all of the various interactive events that could occur while the application was running. Although these programs took advantage of the Toolbox to help develop applications that conform to the Macintosh User Interface Standard, they still had a significant amount of development inefficiency because most of the code required by the Macintosh User Interface Standard had to be re-engineered by each developer. An application framework eliminates much of this inefficiency by providing a reusable, blank application that implements much of a given user interface standard. As we will see in later chapters, Smalltalk-80 provides one such framework for the Smalltalk user interface, the Lisa Toolkit for the Lisa user interface, and MacApp for the Macintosh User Interface Standard. Applications developed by customizing this framework have as their basic skeleton the MacApp application framework shown in Figure 4-1.

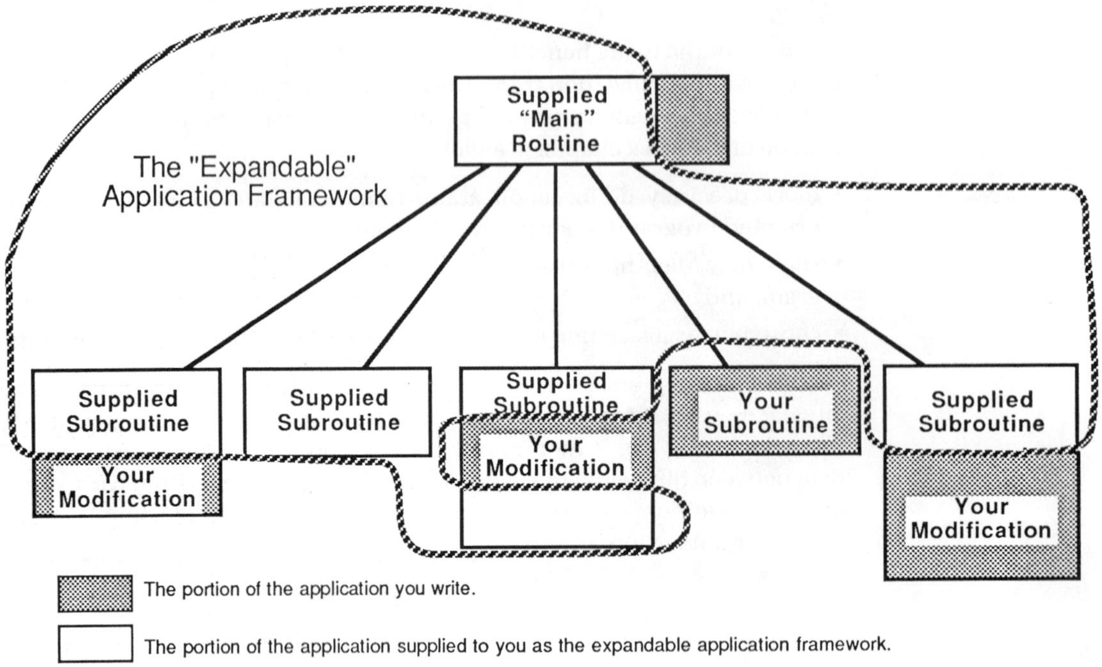

Figure 4-1 The overall design of an application built on top of the MacApp expandable application.

Notes

Don't let the term "basic" delude you into thinking that these skeleton programs are by any means trivial or simple. As we will see later in this chapter, nothing could be further from the truth.

An application framework depends heavily on many of the features of object-oriented programming. For example, the ability of the "main" routine that forms the heart of the expandable application to invoke a new application-specific "subroutine," one that was never even imagined when the main routine was written, depends on the dynamic binding feature present in object-oriented languages. (Note that the term "method" here is really more precise, but "subroutine" can be a reasonable substitute for purposes of this conceptual discussion.) The ability of the application programmer to add new functionality to a portion of the main routine depends on the ability to override a method in one class by another method in one of its descendant classes. An application framework itself, thus, must be implemented as a sequence of classes so that the user of the framework has methods to override, which implies that application frameworks must be written in an object-oriented language.

Notes

More precisely, an application framework must be written using the techniques of object-oriented programming. The easiest manner of doing this is to use an object-oriented language, but this is by no means the only way. MacExpress, an application framework not discussed in this book, is written in a standard procedural language but presents the façade of object-oriented programming to the application programmer who is using it as the core of a new application through the manipulation of pointers to the overriding procedures. As we see in Chapter 13, there are both advantages and disadvantages to this type of approach to the construction of an application framework.

MacApp is written in Object Pascal and consists of a set of six basic classes that implement many of the features of the Macintosh User Interface Standard. Because it is written in Object Pascal, it is easy for you to expand MacApp into a specific application—you do this by designing descendant classes for one or more of MacApp's classes and overriding some of the methods of each of these new classes. Before we examine how MacApp can be expanded into a particular new application, we need to outline the most important classes in MacApp: TApplication, TDocument, TWindow, TFrame, TView, and TCommand.

An Overview of the Basic Classes of MacApp

One of the principles used in designing object-oriented application programs is to have the structure of your program emulate the natural structure of the entity or entities that your program models. If you are designing a Star Trek game, for example, you will probably want to have a class that models starships like the Enterprise, another class that models Klingon warships, and still other classes for starbases, phasers, photon torpedoes, Star Fleet Headquarters, etc. If you are designing a compiler or an interpreter, you will probably want to have separate classes that model terms, factors, expressions, statements, and all the other metasymbols of your language's grammar. This design principle was followed by Apple in the design of MacApp. They were modeling a Macintosh application, so in MacApp there are classes like TApplication, TDocument, TCommand, and TWindow. These classes model the behavior that those entities have in a standard application. A window object, for example, "knows" how to open itself, how to respond to resize requests, how to move about the screen when the user clicks in the title bar, and how to expand itself to fill the screen when the user double-clicks on the zoom-window icon in the window's title bar. Figure 4-2 presents an overview of what functions each of the six main MacApp classes has responsibility for in a MacApp application and how each relates to the other five classes.

Notes

The zoom-window icon is a relatively new feature of the Macintosh User Interface Standard. It is not present yet on all applications, especially older ones.

MacApp Class	Basic Responsibilites	Relationship to the other MacApp classes
The Class TApplication 	• Manage all interactions between the application and the Finder • Manage the event queue • Display the menu bar • Handle all the menu commands	• Creates TDocument objects • Informs document objects when to perform certain actions
The Class TDocument 	• Manages everything to do with documents (files) that are owned by the application, including: - opening documents - closing documents - saving documents to disk - reverting to the previous version of a document	• Creates TView objects • Creates TWindow objects • Creates TFrame objects • Informs view objects and window objects when to perform certain actions
The Class TWindow 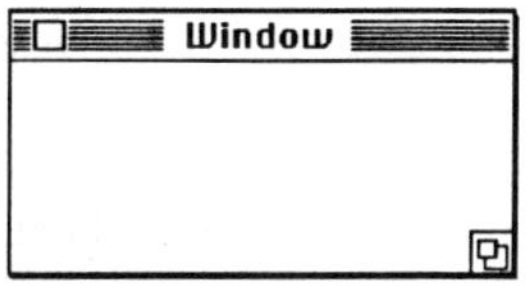	• Manages everything to do with windows including: - opening windows - closing windows - moving windows - resizing windows - activating windows - deactivating windows	• Informs the frame objects that comprise the window when to perform certain actions like scrolling
The Class TFrame 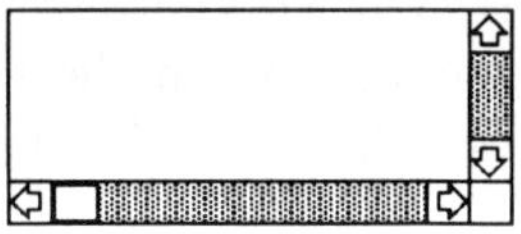	• Manages everything to do with portions of windows including: - scrolling - resizing - coordinate transformations (Note that frame objects correspond closely to QuickDraw grafPorts in that each has its own coordinate system, pen state, shading pattern, font, etc.)	• Informs the view object that it displays when to perform certain actions
The Class TView 	• Manages everything to do with rendering the images seen in a window or frame, especially drawing the image. • Highlights the current selection • Tracks the mouse • Prints the image • Assists in pagination of the image	• Creates TCommand objects
The Class TCommand 	• Manages everything to do with user interactions that affect the data in the document, including - mouse interactions and feedback - mouse commands - menu commands - keyboard input • Implements the undo and redo functions • Interacts with the clipboard, as required	• Informs a TDocument object when to perform certain actions.

Figure 4-2 The roles of the basic MacApp classes in the MacApp framework.

Following the organization of Figure 4-2, each of the basic MacApp classes has the multiple functions and relationships in the total MacApp framework:

The Class TApplication

An application object is responsible for:

- launching the application when it receives the **Open** command from the Finder (the result either of double-clicking on the application's icon or one of its documents, or of activating the **Open** command in the Finder's File menu).
- launching the application in a minimal way when it receives the **Print** command from the Finder, then causing the selected documents to be printed. (The Macintosh User Interface Standard specifies that the user need not open a document to print it, but merely needs select the document and activate the **Print** command in the Finder's File menu.) Note that the application object does not perform the actual printing operation. As we will see, printing is done by the object that renders the document's image, the view object.
- deciding which documents are displayed in the Open Which Document? dialog box. (Recall that this dialog box is displayed in response to choosing the **Open** command on the application's File menu.) Note that your application only decides which of the documents on the disk it can open—the behavior of the Open Which Document? dialog box (also known as the Standard File dialog box and shown in Figure A-14) is handled for you by MacApp.
- handling the event queue. The application object examines the event at the top of the queue and either dispatches that event to the appropriate object for further processing or processes the event itself.
- setting up the application's menus.
- responding to certain application-wide menu commands, like the **About** command on the menu or a **Help** command, which is always available to the user.
- deciding what actions need to occur when the user selects the **Close** or **Quit** commands from the application's File menu.

An application object's relationship with the other MacApp classes includes:

- creating new documents with an appropriate internal structure for this application (i.e., instances of this application's subclass of TDocument).
- informing document objects that certain actions, such as the opening and closing of documents, should be performed.

The Class TDocument

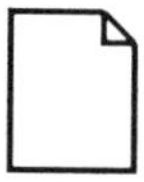

A document object is responsible for everything to do with the files (i.e., the documents) owned by the application, including:

- opening itself.
- closing itself. (Note that this is not an overlap of responsibilities with the application object—the application keeps track of which documents are open and which one it should pass the close request to. The document itself will decide exactly what to do to close properly. For example, you might want certain documents to encrypt themselves before closing and to decrypt upon opening. In an object-oriented design, the responsibility for handling this type of feature is borne by the document itself. The application merely sends the open or close message to the document.)
- processing certain menu commands such as **Save**, **Save As...**, and **Revert**.
- specifying the format for reading and writing documents to disk.

A document object's relationship with the other MacApp classes includes:

- creating the views that will render the image of the contents of the document.
- creating the windows that will display the views on the Macintosh screen. (See the discussion of class TWindow that follows.)
- creating the frames that comprise the windows. (See the discussion of class TWindow and TFrame that follows.)
- "gluing together" the views, windows, and frames that belong together. (See the discussion of class TView, TWindow and TFrame that follows.)
- informing view and window objects when to perform certain actions such as rendering a document's image or closing windows that occur in groups (e.g., a set of four windows, all of which must close if any of them closes.)

The Class TWindow

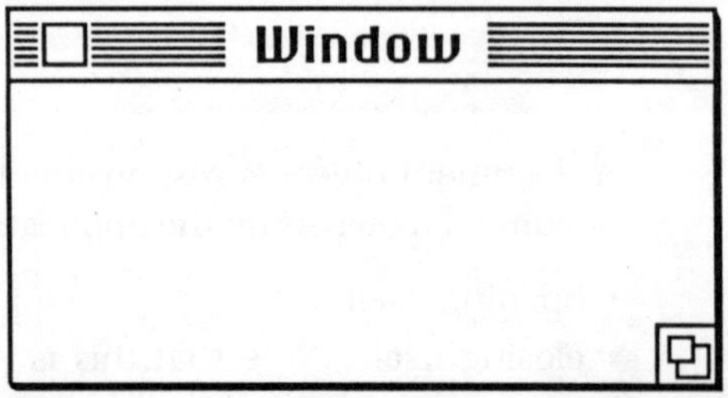

A window object partitions off portions of the screen for the display of information. As we see in the next basic MacApp class (frames), windows do not have responsibility for scrolling. This is because in the general case of a window with many panels and panes, different parts of a window may need to scroll independently. These parts are frames. The window object does, however, act as a container for a number of frame objects. A window object is responsible for:

- opening and closing itself on the screen, including drawing its boundaries.
- responding to moving and resizing requests by the user.
- activating itself when needed—for example, when the user clicks the mouse inside its borders or when the only window in front of it closes.
- deactivating itself when needed, for example, when the user clicks the mouse outside its border or when another window opens in front of it.

A window object's relationship with the other MacApp classes includes:

- determining, when the user presses or releases the mouse button, in which frame mouse events have occurred, then notifying that frame to process the event.
- sending resize messages to its frames when the window is resized.

The Class TFrame

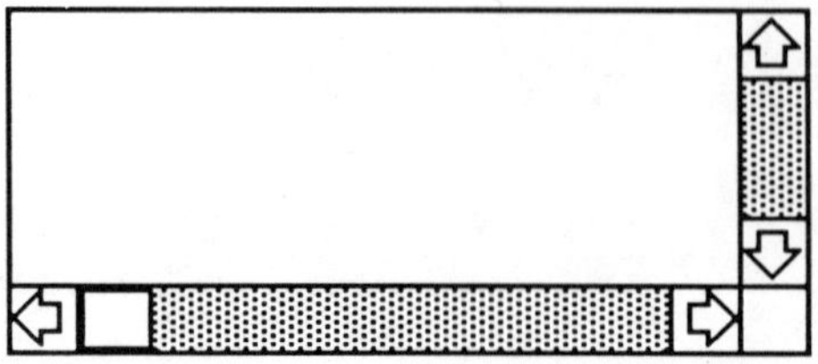

Frame objects present a portion of a view on the screen for the user to see and with which to interact. Frames are responsible for both scrolling and drawing.

Here, too, the MacApp architecture allows for the general case in which different portions of the window may have different types of drawing algorithms and may have to scroll independently.

Frames typically tile the window that contains them—the interior of the window is completely covered by nonoverlapping frames. While tiling is easy to define for a fixed-sized area, tiling becomes a little more difficult when the area can expand (such as a Macintosh window) . To maintain the tiling when a window is resized, for example, each of the frames could grow in size proportional to the resize request. This would lead, however, to the undesirable side effect that there can be no fixed-sized frames—exactly the types of frames needed for the MacDraw palette, for example. The solution to this is that when a window is constructed and frames are installed in the window, the treatment each frame will receive upon a window resize is specified.

In the whole of the application, frame objects are responsible for

- scrolling the view in response to the user actions on the scroll bars, to requests by other objects in the system (for example, the scrolling that occurs in some applications when an object partially off the screen is selected), or to auto-scrolling (the automatic scrolling that occurs when, for example, you select past the end of the currently viewed portion of the document in MacWrite, or the scrolling that should occur, but doesn't when you draw a line in MacDraw (Version 1.7) past the edge of the frame).
- drawing the scroll bars and frame boundary.
- transforming screen coordinates to and from view coordinates.
- zooming and reducing the scale of the image on the screen.
- tracking mouse movements and dispatching mouse events.

A frame object's relationship with the other MacApp classes includes:

- communicating to the view object to draw the interior of the frame, taking into account the current position of the frame with respect to the view.

The Class TView

A view object is responsible for:

- drawing an image of the data in the document. (One view object for each different visual representation of the data.)

- highlighting the current selection.
- tracking the mouse and changing the cursor shape depending upon the mouse position, if required.
- printing, which (potentially) includes properly dealing with multiple pages for large documents and views.

A view object's relationship with the other MacApp classes includes:

- creating the appropriate types of command object (the next basic MacApp class, described below) for handling menu events and mouse events (mouse button pressed, mouse button released, mouse moved) when requested to do so by the frame that displays them.

The Class TCommand

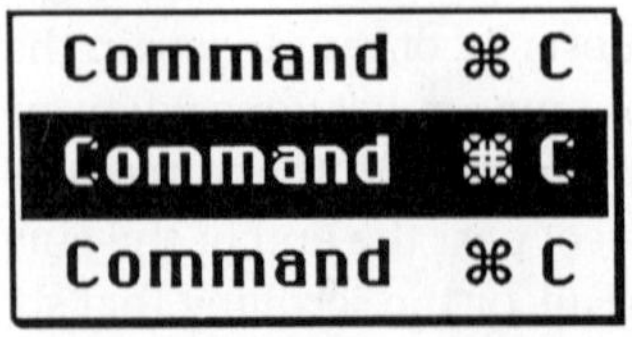

Command objects act on the application's documents or views to bring about the changes needed to reflect menu, mouse, and keyboard commands. These objects know how to both do and undo their effects. Consequently, when a command is to be performed, MacApp can simply send the command object the message DoIt and, later, if that command is to be undone, the message UndoIt. Commands isolate MacApp from the particular operations your application needs, yet enable MacApp to initiate or reverse those operations. A command object is responsible for:

- processing mouse events for a particular view.
- processing menu events.
- processing keyboard input events.
- being able to undo any document or view modification when the user selects the **Undo** command.
- being able to redo those modifications when the user selects the **Undo** command for the second time in a row.
- moving data to and from the clipboard.

A command object's relationship with the other MacApp classes includes:

- modifying the document appropriately. For example, the **Bold** command in MacWrite must know how to change the document's data structure to reflect the fact that the current selection is to appear in boldface. This should be accomplished by sending the document object a message, rather than directly affecting the document's internal structure.

There are several other classes in the main portion of the MacApp class library, but because these classes are of secondary importance in the overall structure of a MacApp application, they will be omitted in this overview. These classes will be discussed in the later description of the library.

The framework in which these objects exist at run-time in a MacApp application is shown in Figure 4-3. As can be seen in this figure, the single application object "owns" all of the document objects, each of which corresponds to an open document. (The exact manner in which this ownership is implemented will be explained shortly.) The document objects own both their windows and their views. Windows own all of their frames. Each frame object owns the view it displays. Note that there is not necessarily a single owner of any given object, because, for example, both frames and documents own the same views. (This framework is the minimal one built-in to MacApp. Should your application need additional or more complex ownership relationships, these can be added very easily.)

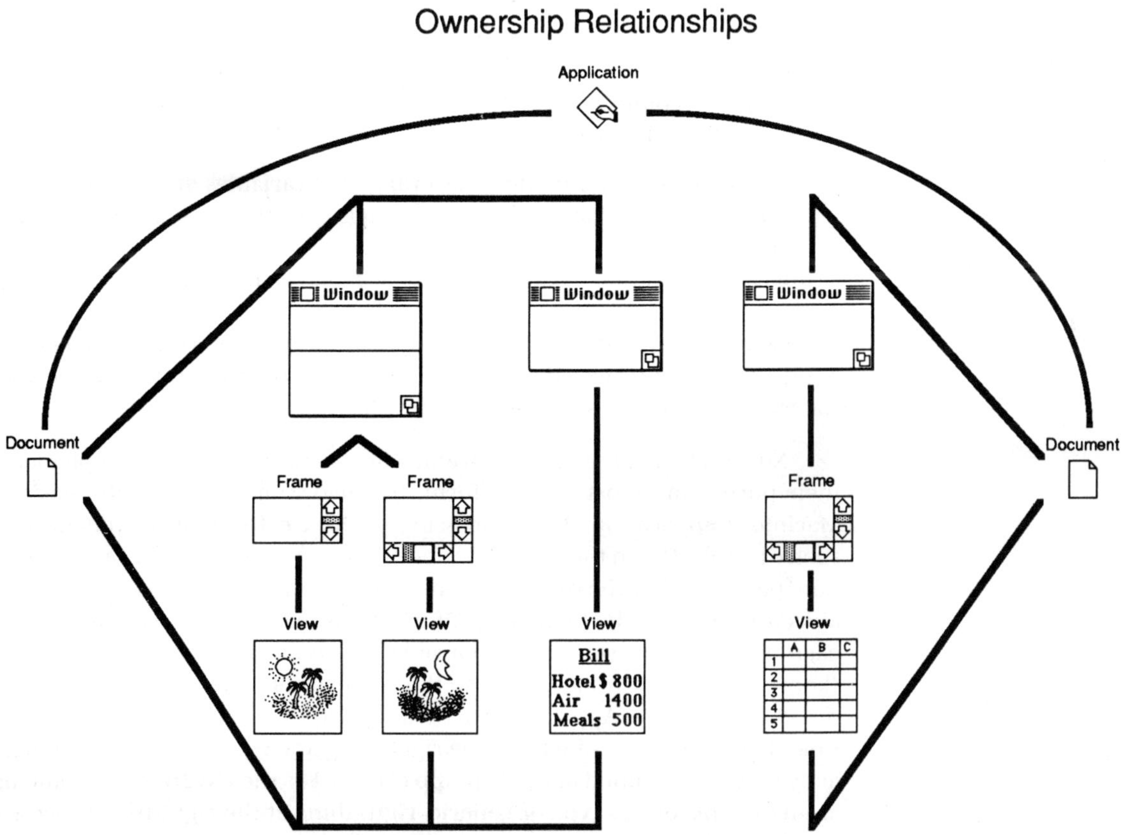

Figure 4-3 The ownership hierarchy between the various objects of the MacApp framework.

The manner of establishing ownership between these objects is through a combination of both global variables and the internal instance variables of certain objects. For example, there is a global variable, gDocList, of type TList. (Objects of the TList class manage lists of other objects. New objects can be added to the list with messages like AddLast, and objects can be retrieved with messages like First.) This global variable gDocList references all of the document objects the application owns. Because the number of open documents an application supports is not easily bounded, using a list object to maintain these references is preferable to having fields like fFirstDocument and fSecondDocument in the class TApplication. Figures 4-4 and 4-5 show many of the instance variables used for these ownership relationships. Note that in many cases both forward and backward links (or upward and downward links, depending on your point of view) are used to simplify the design of methods. Because of the presence of these links, you can easily send messages while in one of the methods of one object to other objects with which that object interacts. For example, while in a method of a TWindow object you can easily send the ForceRedraw message to that window object's first frame with a statement like this:

```
TFrame(SELF.fFrameList.First).ForceRedraw;
```

If windows didn't store references to their frames it would be significantly more complicated to accomplish such a simple task.

To further simplify matters, several global variables are maintained that refer to objects of which there is only a single occurrence at any one time. For example, because each MacApp application has only one instance of class TApplication, a global variable, gApplication, is maintained by MacApp. Methods in any class can refer to this global object. Another example of such a global object is gLastCommand. This global variable references the last command object performed. If the user chooses the **Undo** command, the gLastCommand is sent the message UndoIt by MacApp.

Note that what the MacApp framework does, in reality, is to implement, in their purest and most generic form, the algorithms that are the basis of a Macintosh application. The processing of the **Undo** menu command is one such example. When the user activates this menu command, the last "major action" performed by the user is undone. The MacApp framework has command objects for storing the knowledge of what this major action was and, thus, for each major action, you are responsible for creating a command object that "knows how" to do, undo, and redo the action it represents. You give this command object to MacApp, then trust MacApp to do the right thing at the right time. This knowledge of what is the right thing and when is the right time is exactly what is contained in the MacApp classes. For the **Undo** menu command, as an example of this type of generic, right-thing-at-the-right-time processing, MacApp will send the message UndoIt to the command object referenced by

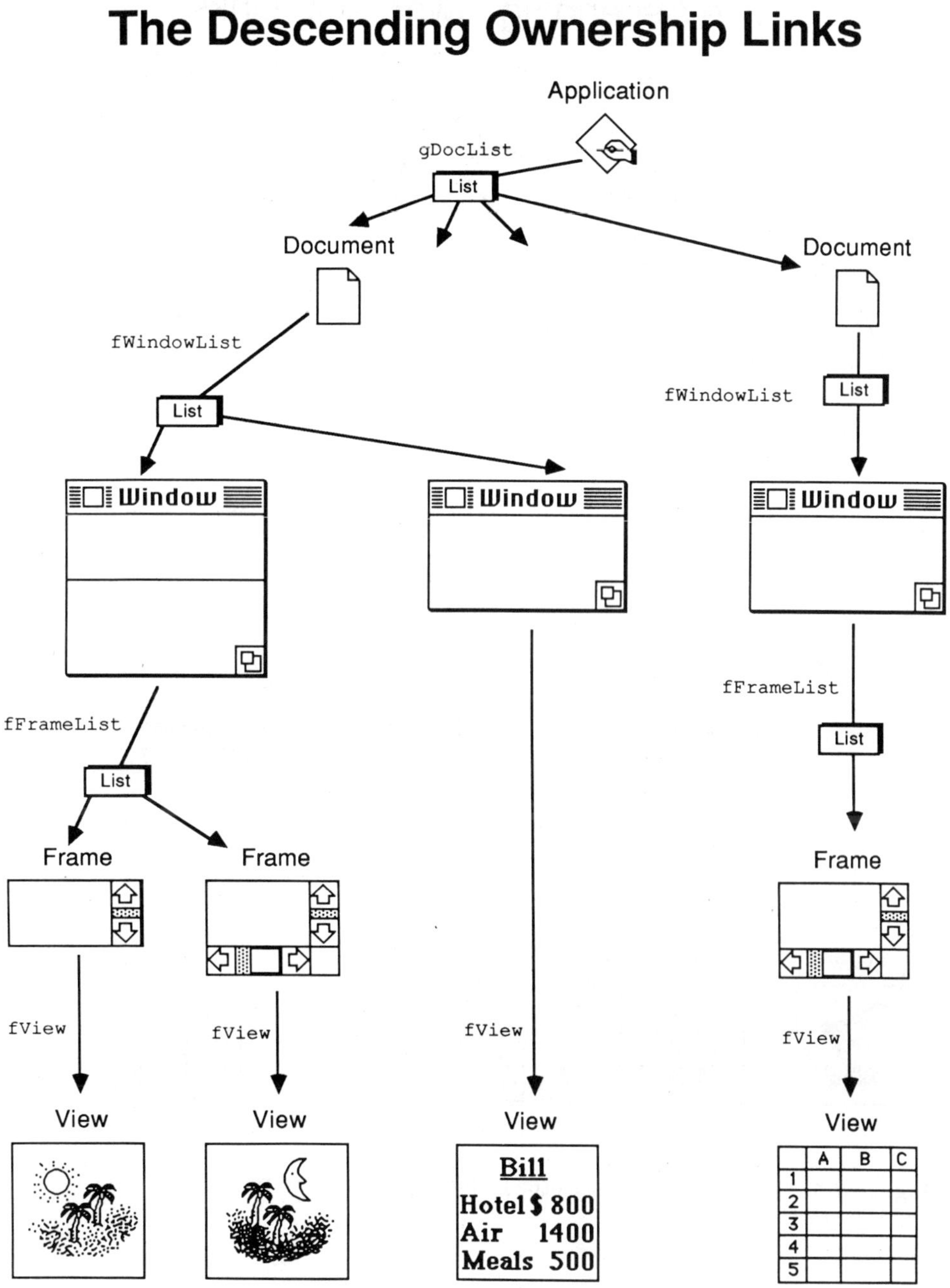

Figure 4-4 The instance variables used to implement the downward links in the ownership hierarchy.

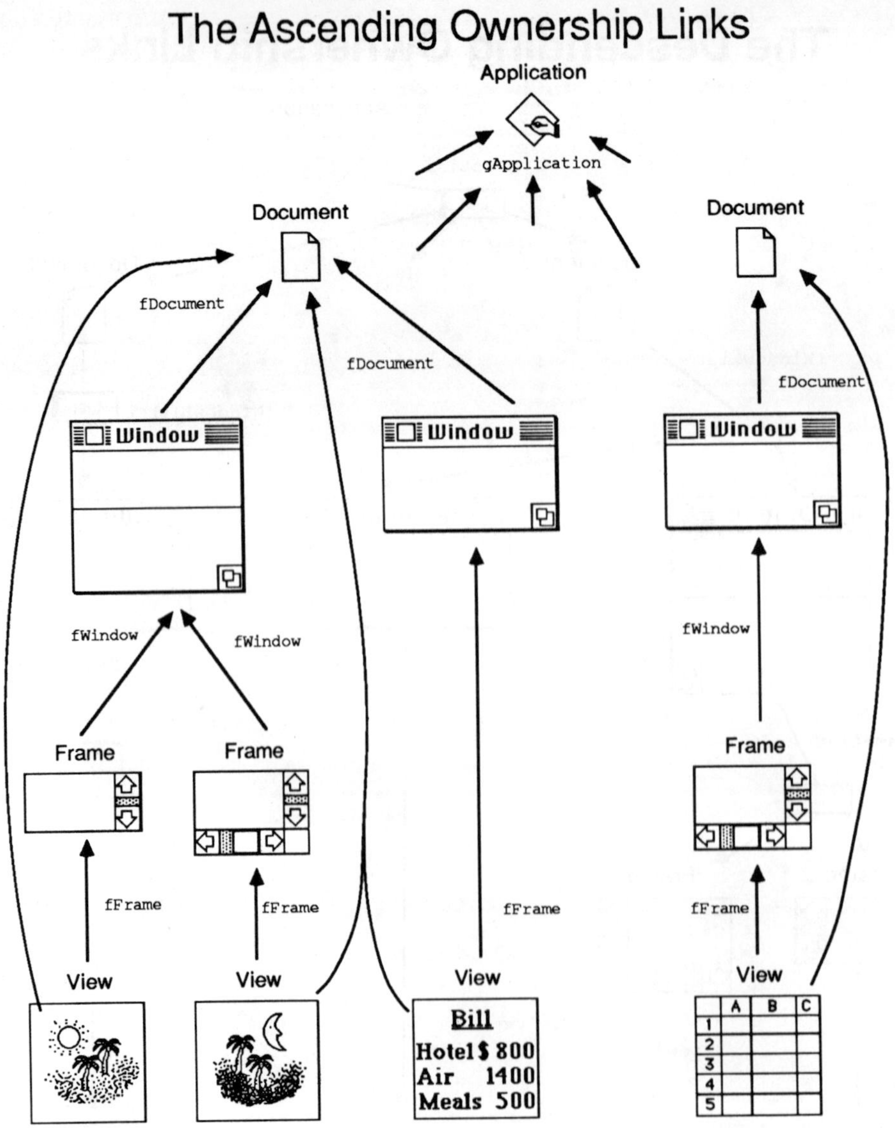

Figure 4-5 The instance variables used to implement the upward links in the ownership hierarchy.

gLastCommand, a global variable maintained by MacApp exactly for this purpose. Sending this message will accomplish the right thing and MacApp will send it at the right time. MacApp was able to process this **Undo** command correctly without ever knowing the actual operation being undone. That is, MacApp was able to purely encode the algorithm for processing the **Undo** menu command once and for all, for all commands, and in a way that could be reused by all future Macintosh applications. This is but one example of the power of object-oriented programming and of the benefits of using an application framework as the base upon which to build a new application.

Notes

Note that the reason such a framework could be written was that the actual procedure invoked by sending the message UndoIt to the object gLastCommand is not determined until run-time. At one point during the execution of the application, sending this message might invoke the method TCopyCommand.UndoIt; at another point the same message sent to gLastCommand might invoke TBoldCommand.UndoIt; and TJustifyText-Command.UndoIt might be invoked at a third point—all methods that perform completely different tasks in the application. Because of the way in which message passing works, the framework can be constructed independently of the details of the actual command.

Expanding MacApp into a Real Application

How do you begin to design an application with MacApp? Assuming you have a fairly good idea of what you want the screen to look like and how the user interactions are to appear, you can begin to match the needs of your application to the capabilities of MacApp.

Let's consider the most straightforward type of user interface. Suppose you only need a single type of window with only one type of view. You'll need to define three new classes with a total of seven methods:

1. a subclass of TDocument to define a document that will hold the information needed by your application,
2. a subclass of TView to define a view that will draw whatever your application wants to show on the screen to represent the data in your document, and
3. a subclass of TApplication to build an application that will invoke this view and use this document.

Creating these three subclasses will enable you to put up something on the Macintosh screen. You won't be able to interact with it yet in application-specific ways, but at least it will be there. You will be able to interact with this small application in application-independent ways: scrolling in both directions, using the menus, activating desk accessories, opening multiple windows, moving any of these windows, and printing the view. The interface for the code for these three tasks would look like this:

```
TYPE TSmallApplication =OBJECT(TApplication)
    PROCEDURETSmallApplication.ISmallApplication;
    FUNCTION TSmallApplication.DoMakeDocument(itsDocKind:
      INTEGER): TDocument;OVERRIDE;
  END;
  TSmallestDocument =OBJECT(TDocument)
    fView: TSmallestView;
    PROCEDURE TSmallDocument.ISmallDocument;
    PROCEDURE TSmallDocument.DoMakeViews(forPrinting:
      BOOLEAN);OVERRIDE;
    PROCEDURE TSmallDocument.DoMakeWindows;OVERRIDE;
  END;
    TSmallestView=OBJECT(TView)
    PROCEDURE TSmallView.ISmallView;
    PROCEDURE TSmallView.Draw(area: Rect);OVERRIDE;
  END;
```

This is the approach you would take, for example, to produce a screen like that of MacTerminal shown in Figure 4-6. In this application there is a single window that scrolls in both directions and a single view. (Note that we have not yet talked about interacting with that screen image or about the application-specific algorithms executing behind the scenes—in the case of MacTerminal, the communications algorithms used to connect to remote computers of various types.)

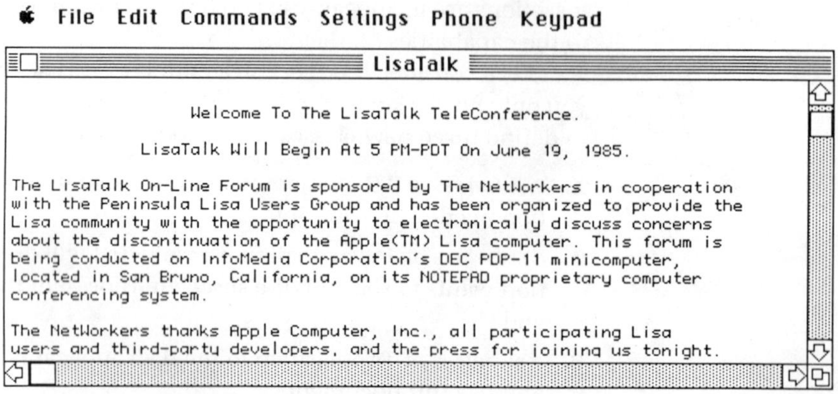

Figure 4-6 An application, MacTerminal, that follows the simplest MacApp model—a single window with a single frame and a single view.

Most novice object-oriented programmers find it difficult to measure the amount of work that has just been indicated. Their most frequent questions at this point are: "What is involved designing these three new subclasses of TApplication, TDocument, and TView? How hard is it to do?" Rather than talk about how much or how little work needs to be done to accomplish these tasks, let's just do them for the smallest possible MacApp application. This small application will draw a picture of Mickey Mouse in the middle of a scrollable window. Figure 4-7 lists all of the source code you need to build this application.

Major Unit for SmallApp (Files SmallApp.U.TEXT and SmallApp.U2.TEXT)

```
                              { The Smallest Possible MacApp Application }
                     { Copyright 1986 by Productivity Products International, Inc. }

UNIT USmallApp;

{$M+}                      { Compiler commands to generate Macintosh code }
{$X-}                      {  and turn off stack expansion }
{$E+}                      {  and automatically invoke the Editor if errors are found }
{$E Error.text}            {  and put the errors in file 'Error.text' }

INTERFACE

USES
    {$U-}                            Macintosh Software supplement }
    {$U Obj/MemTypes}          MemTypes,
    {$U Obj/QuickDraw}         QuickDraw,
    {$U Obj/OSIntf}            OSIntf,
    {$U Obj/ToolIntf}          ToolIntf,
    {$U Obj/PackIntf}          PackIntf,

    {$U Object.U}              UObject,  { This set of units are portions of MacApp }
    {$U List.U}                UList,
    {$U MacApp.U}              UMacApp,
    {$U Printing.U}            UPrinting;

CONST
    myFileType = 'MAMO';       { The file type ("MacApp MOuse') for documents of this
                                                                        application }
TYPE

    TSmallApplication = OBJECT(TApplication)

            { ----- INITIALIZE THE APPLICATION ----- }
        PROCEDURE TSmallApplication.ISmallApplication;

            { ----- MAKE A DOCUMENT ----- }
    FUNCTION  TSmallApplication.DoMakeDocument(itsCmdNumber: CmdNumber):TDocument;
                                                                          OVERRIDE;
    END;



    TSmallDocument = OBJECT(TDocument)

            { ----- FIELDS ----- }
        fSmallView:  TSmallView;

            { ----- INITIALIZE A DOCUMENT ----- }
        PROCEDURE TSmallDocument.ISmallDocument;
```

```
             { ----- MAKE A VIEW ----- }
         PROCEDURE  TSmallDocument.DoMakeViews(forPrinting: BOOLEAN); OVERRIDE;

             { ----- MAKE A WINDOW ----- }
         PROCEDURE  TSmallDocument.DoMakeWindows; OVERRIDE;

     END;



     TSmallView = OBJECT(TView)

             { ----- INITIALIZE A VIEW ----- }
         PROCEDURE TSmallView.ISmallView(itsSmallDocument: TSmallDocument);

             { ----- RENDER THE IMAGE ----- }
         PROCEDURE TSmallView.Draw(area: Rect); OVERRIDE;

     END;


IMPLEMENTATION


{$I SmallApp.U2}
                        { Copyright 1985 by Productivity Products International, Inc.}

{ USmallApp Implementation }


{ ************************************************************************************* }
{ ************************************************************************************* }
{                              METHODS FOR ALL THE SMALLAPP CLASSES                     }
{                                                                                       }
{    Note that methods are grouped by class and that the order of methods in any        }
{    class is the following(by convention only, since Object Pascal forces no order):   }
{                                                                                       }
{               (1) the initialization method, if any,                                  }
{               (2) the Inspect method - a private debugging method, if needed          }
{               (3) the Free method, if overridden, and                                 }
{               (4) the remaining methods in alphabetical order.                        }
{                                                                                       }
{ ************************************************************************************* }
{ ************************************************************************************* }



{ **************************** TSmallApplication Methods ************************** }

PROCEDURE TSmallApplication.ISmallApplication;
BEGIN
      SELF.IApplication('SMAP', myFileType);
END;

     { ----- MAKE AND INITIALIZE A DOCUMENT ----- }

FUNCTION TSmallApplication.DoMakeDocument(itsCmdNumber: CmdNumber): TDocument; OVERRIDE;
VAR aSmallDocument:TSmallDocument;
BEGIN
      NEW(aSmallDocument);
      aSmallDocument.ISmallDocument;
      DoMakeDocument := aSmallDocument;
```

```
2  -0 A END;
2  --
2  --
2  --    { ***************************** TSmallDocument Methods **************************** }
2  --
2  -- A PROCEDURE TSmallDocument.ISmallDocument;
2  0- A BEGIN
2  --         SELF.IDocument(myFileType);
2  -0 A END;
2  --
2  --
2  --         { ----- MAKE AND INITIALIZE ALL THE NECESSARY VIEWS ----- }
2  --
2  -- A PROCEDURE  TSmallDocument.DoMakeViews(forPrinting: BOOLEAN); OVERRIDE;
2  --    VAR smallView:   TSmallView;
2  0- A BEGIN
2  --         NEW(smallView);
2  --         smallView.ISmallView(SELF);
2  --         SELF.fSmallView := smallView;
2  -0 A END;
2  --
2  --
2  --         { ----- MAKE ALL THE NECESSARY WINDOWS ----- }
2  --
2  -- A PROCEDURE  TSmallDocument.DoMakeWindows; OVERRIDE;
2  --    VAR aWindow:    TWindow;
2  0- A BEGIN
2  --         aWindow := NewSimpleWindow(kIDStdWindow, NOT kDialogWindow,
2  --                                  kWantHScrollBar, kWantVScrollBar, SELF.fSmallView);
2  -0 A END;
2  --
2  --
2  --
2  --    { ****************************** TSmallView Methods ****************************** }
2  --
2  -- A PROCEDURE TSmallView.ISmallView(itsSmallDocument: TSmallDocument);
2  --    VAR viewRect:       Rect;
2  --        aStdHandler:    TStdPrintHandler;
2  0- A BEGIN
2  --         SetRect(viewRect, 0, 0, 500, 500);
2  --         IView(NIL,                      { This view has no parent view,  }
2  --               itsSmallDocument,         {  and shows a smallDocument,     }
2  --               viewRect,                 {  in a 500 x 500 rectangle,      }
2  --               sizeFixed,                {  that does not change if the frame is changed horizontally, }
2  --               sizeFixed,                {  or vertically,                 }
2  --               FALSE,                    {  and can't make selections      }
2  --               hlOff);                   {  and doesn't highlight when the window is inactive. }
2  --
2  --
2  --         New(aStdHandler);
2  --    aStdHandler.IStdPrintHandler(SELF, FALSE); { The second parameter, itsSquareDots, is FALSE since
2  --                                                 this application does not mix text and graphics.
2  --                                                 Slightly higher resolution is available with this
2  --                                                 setting. }
2  -0 A END;
2  --
2  --
2  --
2  --
2  --         { ----- RENDER THE IMAGE ----- }
2  --
2  -- A PROCEDURE TSmallView.Draw(area: Rect); OVERRIDE;
```

```
176  2  100 --
177  2  101 -- B     FUNCTION  MakeRect(top, left, bottom, right: INTEGER): Rect;
178  2  102 --       VAR r: Rect;
179  2  103 0- B     BEGIN
180  2  104 --           SetRect(r, left, top, right, bottom);
181  2  105 --           MakeRect := r;
182  2  106 -0 B     END;
183  2  107 --
184  2  108 0- A BEGIN
185  2  109 --       PenNormal;
186  2  110 --       PaintOval(MakeRect(74, 72, 139, 127));         { Outline of the mouse head }
187  2  111 --       EraseOval(MakeRect(84, 74, 138, 125));         { Outline of the mouse face }
188  2  112 --       FrameOval(MakeRect(109, 84, 129, 115));        { Mouse mouth (part 1 of 2) }
189  2  113 --       EraseRect(MakeRect(109, 84, 123, 115));        { Mouse mouth (part 2 of 2) }
190  2  114 --       FrameOval(MakeRect(98, 87, 107, 96));          { Left eye }
191  2  115 --       FrameOval(MakeRect(98, 104, 107, 113));        { Right eye }
192  2  116 --       PaintOval(MakeRect(101, 90, 104, 93));         { Left pupil }
193  2  117 --       PaintOval(MakeRect(101, 107, 104, 110));       { Right pupil }
194  2  118 --       PaintOval(MakeRect(111, 97, 117, 103));        { Nose }
195  2  119 --       PaintOval(MakeRect(53, 52, 91, 90));           { Left ear }
196  2  120 --       PaintOval(MakeRect(53, 110, 91, 148));         { Right ear }
197  2  121 --
198  2  122 --       FrameRect(MakeRect(20, 20, 170, 180));         { A bounding rectangle }
199  2  123 --
200  2  124 -0 A END;
201  2  125 --
202  2  126 --
203  1   77 --
204  1   78 --   END.
205  1   79 --
206  1   80 --
207  1   81 --
208  3    1 --                                    { The Smallest MacApp Application }
209  3    2 --                         { Copyright 1986 by Productivity Products International, Inc.}
210  3    3 --
211  3    4 --
212  3    5 --   PROGRAM SmallApp;
213  3    6 --
214  3    7 --   {$M+}                                    { Compiler commands to generate Macintosh code }
215  3    8 --   {$X-}                                    {  and turn off stack expansion }
216  3    9 --
217  3   10 --   USES
218  3   11 --       {$U-}                                { This set of units are portions of the
219  3   12 --                                              Macintosh Software supplement }
220  3   13 --       {$U Obj/MemTypes}      MemTypes,
221  3   14 --       {$U Obj/QuickDraw}     QuickDraw,
222  3   15 --       {$U Obj/OSIntf}        OSIntf,
223  3   16 --       {$U Obj/ToolIntf}      ToolIntf,
224  3   17 --
225  3   18 --       {$U Object.U}          UObject,     { This set of units are portions of MacApp }
226  3   19 --       {$U List.U}            UList,
227  3   20 --       {$U MacApp.U}          UMacApp,
228  3   21 --       {$U Printing.U}        UPrinting,
229  3   22 --
230  3   23 --       {$U SmallApp.U}        USmallApp;   { This unit has the SmallApp-specific classes }
231  3   24 --
232  3   25 --       VAR aSmallApplication:  TSmallApplication;
233  3   26 --
234  3   27 --
235  3   28 0-   BEGIN
236  3   29 --  {$S         }        { Insert this code into the blank segment }
237  3   30 --  InitToolbox(2, 10); { start with 2 extra blocks of 64 master pointers; allow up to 10 windows}
238  3   31 --  InitPrinting;       { initialize the print shop }
```

```
239  3   32 --
240  3   33 --          New(aSmallApplication);
241  3   34 --          aSmallApplication.ISmallApplication;
242  3   35 --          aSmallApplication.Run;
243  3   36 -0     END.
```

Cross Reference Listing for Major Unit and Main Program for SmallApp

```
 1. SmallApp.U.TEXT
 2. SmallApp.U2.TEXT
 3. SmallApp.M.TEXT

-A-
  area                  68*( 1)    99*( 2)
  aSmallApplicatio      25*( 3)    33 ( 3)    34 ( 3)    35 ( 3)
  aSmallDocument        33*( 2)    35 ( 2)    36 ( 2)    37 ( 2)
  aStdHandler           75*( 2)    87 ( 2)    88 ( 2)
  aWindow               63*( 2)    65=( 2)

-B-
  BOOLEAN               53 ( 1)    51 ( 2)
  bottom               101*( 2)   104 ( 2)

-C-
  CmdNumber             38 ( 1)    32 ( 2)

-D-
  DoMakeDocument        38*( 1)    32*( 2)    37=( 2)
  DoMakeViews           53*( 1)    51*( 2)
  DoMakeWindows         56*( 1)    62*( 2)
  Draw                  68*( 1)    99*( 2)

-E-
  EraseOval            111 ( 2)
  EraseRect            113 ( 2)

-F-
  FALSE                 83 ( 2)    88 ( 2)
  forPrinting           53*( 1)    51*( 2)
  FrameOval            112 ( 2)   114 ( 2)   115 ( 2)
  FrameRect            122 ( 2)
  fSmallView            47*( 1)    56=( 2)    66 ( 2)

-H-
  hlOff                 84 ( 2)

-I-
  IApplication          27 ( 2)
  IDocument             45 ( 2)
  InitPrinting          31 ( 3)
  InitToolbox           30 ( 3)
  INTEGER              101 ( 2)
  ISmallApplicatio      35*( 1)    25*( 2)    34 ( 3)
  ISmallDocument        50*( 1)    36 ( 2)    43*( 2)
  ISmallView            65*( 1)    55 ( 2)    73*( 2)
  IStdPrintHandler      88 ( 2)
  itsCmdNumber          38*( 1)    32*( 2)
  itsSmallDocument      65*( 1)    73*( 2)    79 ( 2)
  IView                 78 ( 2)
```

```
-U-
  UList              23*( 1)   19*( 3)
  UMacApp            24*( 1)   20*( 3)
  UObject            22*( 1)   18*( 3)
  UPrinting          25*( 1)   21*( 3)
  USmallApp           4*( 1)   23*( 3)

-V-
  viewRect           74*( 2)   77 ( 2)   80 ( 2)

*** End Xref: 75 id's   191 references      [1486360 bytes/4924 id's/175947 refs]
```

Figure 4-7 The complete listing of the smallest MacApp program. Note that the real heart of this listing is the USmall unit—the rest of the listing is boilerplate material required (to a great extent) in every Macintosh application

Notes

At the time this book was written, the only way to write a MacApp application was to prepare the programs for the application in the Lisa Workshop and to cross-compile those programs for the Macintosh with the Software Supplement library. In addition, the resource file for the application was built with a program called RMaker that ran in the Lisa Workshop. To use RMaker, the application programmer specified, in a cumbersome and often incomprehensible format, the characteristics of the application's menus, windows, icons, cursors, etc., and RMaker built the resource file. Plans are underway at Apple to produce a Macintosh Workshop that would enable the Macintosh developer, among other things, to write MacApp programs on the Macintosh for the Macintosh. Programming in Object Pascal will differ little whether you are using the Lisa Workshop or the Macintosh Workshop; the specification of resources may be radically different, however. The RMaker input for the smallest application is shown in Listing C for completeness, though you may be able to accomplish the same function in an easier fashion in the future.

The listings of Figure 4-7 occurs in several files:

- Small.u.Text contains the interface of the three classes that comprise this application and Small.u2.Text contains the implementation of these classes. Note that these two files, Small.u and Small.u2, contain the real heart of the application. The other files are not much more than required boilerplate material.

- Small.m.Text contains the main program that is the application. Note that there is not much to this main program other than allocating a TSmallApplication object, initializing that object, and then sending it the message Run. All of the rest of the application's functionality is contained in the units—either the USmall unit or the MacApp units. All MacApp applications have a main program that looks almost exactly like this—the only difference is a couple of the units and the class of the application object allocated.

Notes

When using the Lisa Workshop to implement a MacApp application there are two other files you must prepare:

- Small.x.Text contains the information for building the application. (This is called the "exec" file in the Workshop, hence the "x.") This information includes a list of which files to assemble or compile, how to link the object files, how to invoke RMaker, and how to transfer the resulting application to a Macintosh formatted disk so it can be run on the Macintosh.
- Small.r.Text contains the input to RMaker. Only the first three pages contain material unique to this small application; the remainder of this file contains all the application independent dialog and alert boxes.

These two additional files, SmallApp.x and SmallApp.r, plus the main files of SmallApp.u, SmallApp.u2, and SmallApp.m, are all included in the SmallApp listing in Listing C.

Typically, the only real work in designing an application is the design of the unit or units that contain the application-unique classes. For this small application, this is simply the 83 lines comprising the USmall unit (contained in the files Small.u.Text and Small.u2.Text). This small amount of code, when combined with MacApp, produced the application shown in the screen dumps of Figure 4-8. Note that scrolling, window movement, menu display, etc. are all possible. In addition, Figure 4-9 shows the output of this application on the ImageWriter and the LaserWriter. Not bad for three hours work! (For those who do not recognize it, the Mickey Mouse design was "borrowed" from the Macintosh Pascal manual.)

Continuing in our explanation of how the MacApp framework can be expanded to fit the needs of real applications, a user interface slightly more complex than TSmallApplication would consist of one type of window but several different views shown in that window at different times. This user interface is like that of the Finder, which has two types of views for a folder or a disk—an iconic view and a list view, or MacProject, which has a total of seven views that alternate in the window depending upon the user's requests, some of which are shown in Figure 4-10.

Figure 4-8 Screen dumps from the smallest MacApp application. Note that even though this application is only 83 lines of code, it can correctly manipulate multiple windows, multiple desk accessories, and correctly enable and disable entire menus and individual menu items, among other things. In short, it is a fully functional Macintosh application.

Figure 4-9 Output from the smallest MacApp application on the ImageWriter and the LaserWriter. Note that there is nothing in the listing of this application (with the exception of the call to InitPrinting in the Small main program) having to do with printing. Printing, one of the most difficult features for most application programmers, is a generic function automatically provided by MacApp.

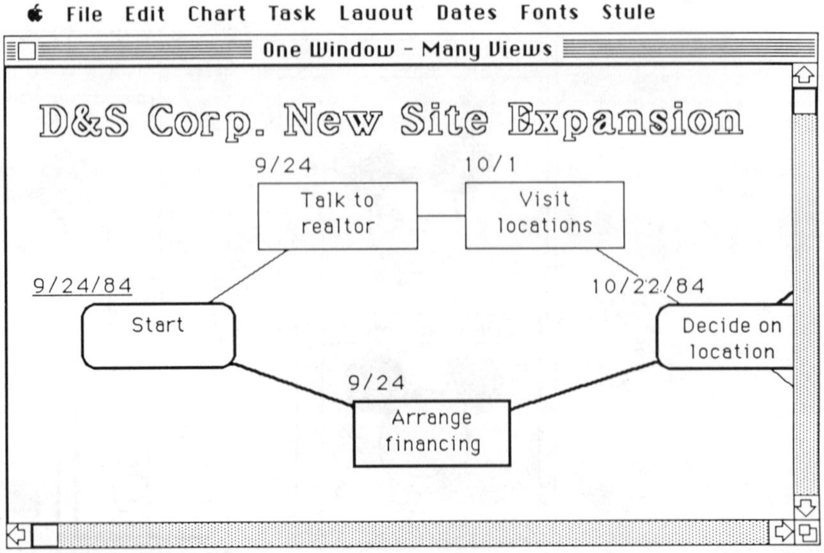

Figure 4-10 Four of the views possible in MacProject. These are shown sequentially in MacProject's single window. The application, BiggerApplication, developed in this chapter, demonstrates how to achieve this effect in a MacApp program.

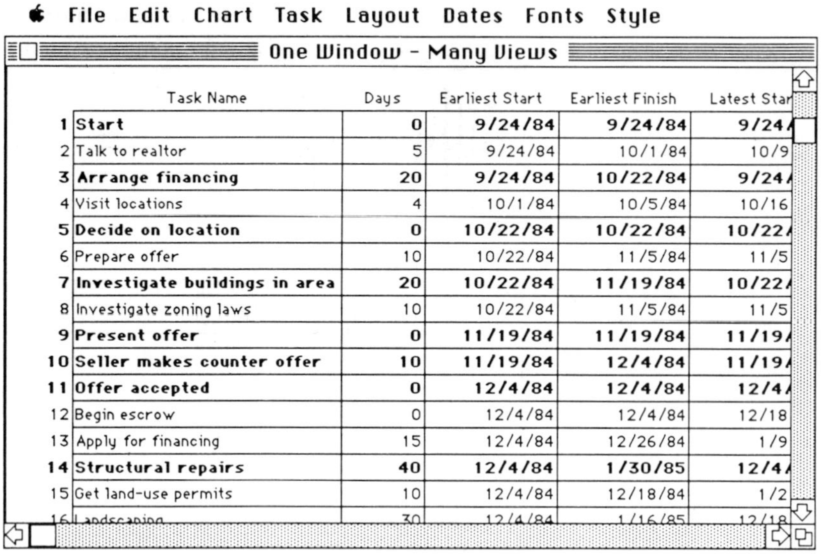

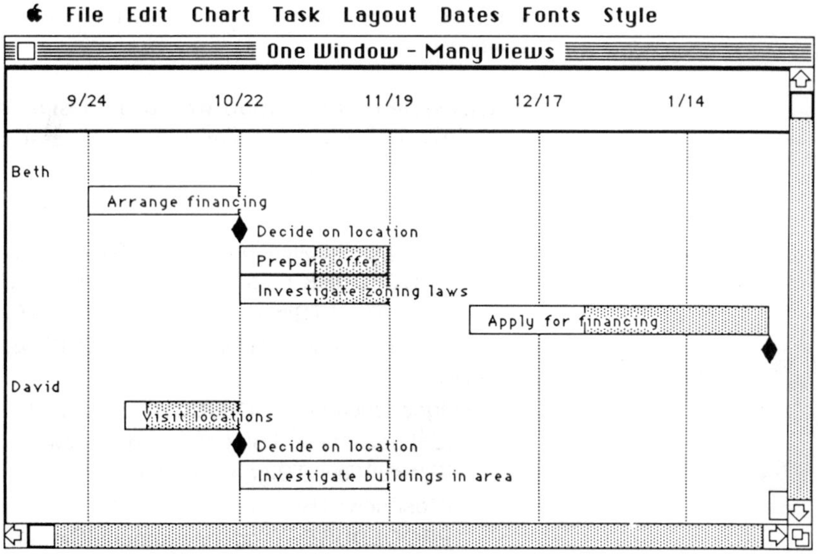

Figure 4-10 Four of the views possible in MacProject. These are shown sequentially in MacProject's single window. The application, BiggerApplication, developed in this chapter, demonstrates how to achieve this effect in a MacApp program *(continued).*

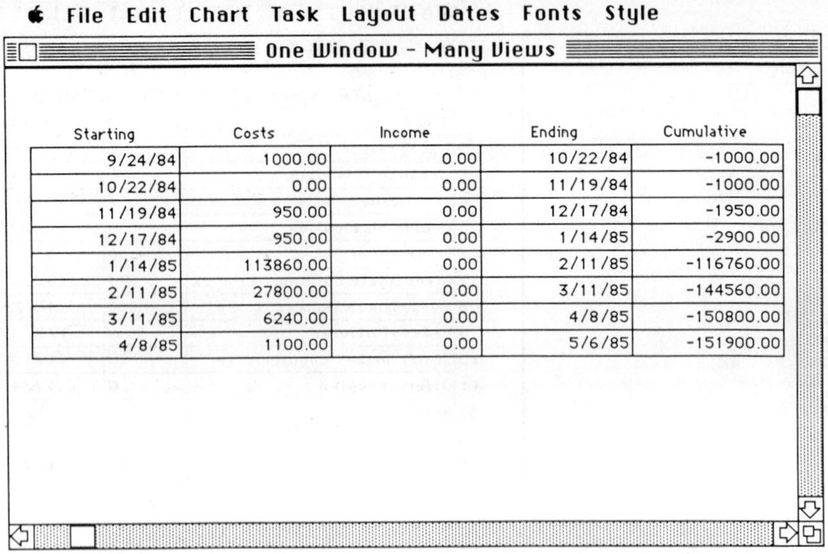

Starting	Costs	Income	Ending	Cumulative
9/24/84	1000.00	0.00	10/22/84	-1000.00
10/22/84	0.00	0.00	11/19/84	-1000.00
11/19/84	950.00	0.00	12/17/84	-1950.00
12/17/84	950.00	0.00	1/14/85	-2900.00
1/14/85	113860.00	0.00	2/11/85	-116760.00
2/11/85	27800.00	0.00	3/11/85	-144560.00
3/11/85	6240.00	0.00	4/8/85	-150800.00
4/8/85	1100.00	0.00	5/6/85	-151900.00

Figure 4-10 Four of the views possible in MacProject. These are shown sequentially in MacProject's single window. The application, BiggerApplication, developed in this chapter, demonstrates how to achieve this effect in a MacApp program *(continued).*

This style of application would be designed just like the small example above with the addition of several new subclasses of TView—one new subclass for each view. The type declarations for this application would then look something like this:

```
TYPE TBiggerApplication =OBJECT(TApplication)
    PROCEDURE TBiggerApplication.IBiggerApplication;
    FUNCTION TBiggerApplication.DoMakeDocument(itsCmdNumber:
      CmdNumber): TDocument; OVERRIDE;
  END;
  TBiggerDocument =OBJECT(TDocument)
    fScheduleView: TBiggerScheduleView;
    fProjectView: TBiggerProjectView;
    fCostView: TBiggerCostView;
    PROCEDURE TBiggerDocument.IBiggerDocument;
    PROCEDURE TBiggerDocument.DoMakeViews(forPrinting:
      BOOLEAN);OVERRIDE;
    PROCEDURE TBiggerDocument.DoMakeWindows;OVERRIDE;
  END;
  TBiggerScheduleView =OBJECT(TView)
    PROCEDURE TBiggerScheduleView.IBiggerScheduleView;
    FUNCTION TBiggerScheduleView.DoMenuCommand(aCmdNumber:
      CmdNumber): TCommand;OVERRIDE;
```

```
    PROCEDURE TBiggerScheduleView.Draw(area: Rect); OVERRIDE;
  END;
  TBiggerProjectView =OBJECT(TView)
    PROCEDURE TBiggerProjectView.IBiggerProjectView;
    FUNCTION TBiggerProjectView.DoMenuCommand(aCmdNumber:
      CmdNumber): TCommand;OVERRIDE;
    PROCEDURE TBiggerProjectView.Draw(area: Rect); OVERRIDE;
  END;
  TBiggerCostView =OBJECT(TView)
    PROCEDURE TBiggerCostView.IBiggerCostView;
    FUNCTION TBiggerCostView.DoMenuCommand(aCmdNumber:
      CmdNumber): TCommand;OVERRIDE;
    PROCEDURE TBiggerCostView.Draw(area: Rect);OVERRIDE;
  END;
```

One of the TDocument methods that must be overridden is DoMakeWindows. This procedure creates all the windows necessary to display the document. In this small example, the view shown when the application is opened (the schedule view) would be "installed" in the window during the execution of this method. To show the other views you merely install those views in the window in a similar manner whenever this is called for by the user's actions. Because this manipulation of multiple view objects is something quite common, and because it is a good example of how to use MacApp, let's go into considerably more detail as to exactly what happens in several of the methods we have just outlined for this application, which we will call BiggerApplication.

In BiggerApplication, all the view objects are usually stored with the document in the three additional instance variables of the class TSmallDocument: fScheduleView, fProjectView, and fCostView. These are called additional because TSmallDocument already has all the instance variables of TDocument and all its other ancestor classes, so the three instance variables declared with TSmallDocument are new ones added just for this new class.

These three view objects are allocated and installed in the document's instance variables in the document's DoMakeViews method. The code for that method would be something like this:

```
PROCEDURE TBiggerDocument.DoMakeViews(forPrinting: BOOLEAN);
OVERRIDE;

VAR aScheduleView: TBiggerScheduleView;
  aProjectView: TBiggerProjectView;
  aCostView: TBiggerCostView;

BEGIN
  NEW(aScheduleView);
  aScheduleView.IBiggerScheduleView;
  fScheduleView := aScheduleView; {Install schedule view in the document}
```

```
    NEW(aProjectView);
    aProjectView.IBiggerProjectView;
    fProjectView := aProjectView; {Install project view in the document}
    NEW(aCostView);
    aCostView.IBiggerCostView;
    fCostView := aCostView; { Install cost view in the document}
END;
```

Warning

In several of these code fragments I have deliberately omitted certain tests or handling for certain special cases that, I believe, are just confusing at this stage. These pedagogical simplifications are not made to the QuadWorld application (Chapters 5 and 8, and Listings D and E) and after the basic points being discussed here are mastered, you should examine the QuadWorld application to see how these details are dealt with.

To switch from one view to another, the user would probably activate a menu command. This could be processed in the DoMenuCommand method of whichever view was currently being shown in the window, because, as explained earlier, typically, it is views that create comand objects. The DoMenuCommand method of the project view would be something like this:

```
FUNCTION TBiggerProjectView.DoMenuCommand(aCmdNumber:
    CmdNumber): TCommand; OVERRIDE;
BEGIN
    DoMenuCommand := gNoChanges; { See discussion below}
    CASE aCmdNumber OF
        cProject: BEGIN END;
        cSchedule: fFrame.HaveView(TBiggerDocument(fDocument).
            fScheduleView);
        cCost: fFrame.HaveView(TBiggerDocument(fDocument).fCostView);
        .
        .
        .
        OTHERWISE DoMenuCommand := INHERITED
            DoMenuCommand(aCmdNumber);
END;
```

The DoMenuCommand for the cost view would be similar:

```
FUNCTION TBiggerCostView.DoMenuCommand(aCmdNumber:
  CmdNumber): TCommand; OVERRIDE;
BEGIN
  DoMenuCommand := gNoChanges; { See discussion below}
  CASE aCmdNumber OF
    cProject: fFrame.HaveView(TBiggerDocument(fDocument).fProjectView);
    cSchedule: fFrame.HaveView(TBiggerDocument(fDocument).
      fScheduleView);
    cCost: BEGIN END;
    .
    .
    .
    OTHERWISE DoMenuCommand := INHERITED
       DoMenuCommand(aCmdNumber);
END;
```

There are several points to note about both methods:

- The DoMenuCommand method is a function that returns a command object. MacApp will retrieve this command object and use it to correctly modify the document and/or the view by sending the command object messages like DoIt, UndoIt, and RedoIt. As we have noted earlier, this scheme is the best way to handle commands in an application framework like MacApp. However, for those commands that do not modify the document and for which **Undo** is not supported, there is no need to go to such lengths. Changing the view in a window, the operation we are discussing here, is about as simple a command as there is and it meets these two conditions. Thus, these two DoMenuCommand methods directly perform the operations necessary to change the views. These methods must still return a command object, however. MacApp maintains a special null command object in a global variable, gNoChanges, which is used when there is no need to go to the trouble of creating a command object but when you must return one. Both DoMenuCommand methods return gNoChanges.
- The new view is actually installed in the frame of the window through use of the HaveView method. The single argument to this method is the new view to be installed.
- It would not be possible for us to have written simply

```
fFrame.HaveView(fDocument.fScheduleView);
```

as the statement associated with the cSchedule switch because the fDocument field of the class TView is of type TDocument and objects of type TDocument do not have a fScheduleView instance variable. This problem would be caught at compile time and flagged as a compilation error. Because we know that fDocument really refers to an instance of TSmallDocument, we can coerce the fDocument reference so that the compiler won't complain:

```
fFrame.HaveView(TSmallDocument(fDocument).fScheduleView);
```

- TheDoMenuCommand method we have implemented processes only the menu commands unique to this application. All other commands are handled by MacApp. However, we must give MacApp a chance to do this and this is the function of the statement associated with the **OTHERWISE** clause. This statement:

  ```
  DoMenuCommand :=INHERITED DoMenuCommand(aCmdNumber);
  ```

  invokes the overridden DoMenuCommand so that standard menu commands like **Open** and **Print** can be processed properly. Note that because these menu commands may require creating a command object, our DoMenuCommands must return this command object to MacApp so the command can be handled properly.
- The basic design for view switching in BiggerApplication is to have a DoMenuCommand method in each of BiggerApplication's subclasses of TView. This DoMenuCommand would "catch" menu commands (in a manner to be explained later in Chapter 7) and process requests for a view change. While this design is straightforward, it is not necessarily the best because each view subclass must know about all the other ones (i.e., the **CASE** statement in each of the DoMenuCommand methods effectively lists all the views that are currently part of the application), and each view subclass must have its own, only slightly different DoMenuCommand. A perhaps better design would be to have the view switching processed in a DoMenuCommand method in the TBiggerlDocument class. This single method would know about all the possible views and correctly process the menu commands. The code for this method is shown below.

```
TYPE TBiggerDocument =OBJECT(TDocument)
    fScheduleView: TBiggerScheduleView;
    fProjectView: TBiggerProjectView;
    fCostView: TBiggerCostView;
    PROCEDURE TBiggerDocument.IBiggerDocument;
    PROCEDURE TBiggerDocument.DoMakeViews(forPrinting:BOOLEAN)
      ;OVERRIDE;
    PROCEDURE TBiggerDocument.DoMakeWindows; OVERRIDE;
    FUNCTION TBiggerDocument.DoMenuCommand(aCmdNumber:
      CmdNumber): TCommand;OVERRIDE;
  END;

  .

  .

  .
```

```
FUNCTION TBiggerDocument.DoMenuCommand(aCmdNumber:
  CmdNumber): TCommand;OVERRIDE;

VAR aView: TView;

BEGIN
  DoMenuCommand := gNoChanges;
  CASE aCmdNumberOF
    cProject ,cSchedule, cCost:
      BEGIN
        CASE aCmdNumberOF
          cProject: aView := fProjectView;
          cSchedule: aView := fScheduleView;
          cCostView: aView := fScheduleView;
        END;
        SELF.fHeadWindow.fHeadFrame.HaveView(aView);
      END;
    .
    .
    .
    OTHERWISE DoMenuCommand :=INHERITED DoMenuCommand
      (aCmdNumber);
  END;
```

Notes

We have not yet discussed in detail the notions mentioned above of a document object creating a command object or catching a menu command activation. The MacApp framework is more general and more robust than the discussion here indicates, which is why this chapter is entitled "Introduction to MacApp". Later chapters will explore these advanced topics in greater detail.

There are many other small ways in which we could continue to modify this application to show how it would then fit into the MacApp framework:

Desired Effect	MacApp Solution
• Several types of documents Examples: Microsoft Word has both text documents and glossaries. The Font/DA Mover has both font and desk accessory documents. MacDraw has MacDraw and PICT format documents. (Note that each type of document usually has its own distinct icon.)	Solution: Define a subclass of TDocument for each type of document needed. The initialization and Open methods in each of these subclasses will enable each kind of document to have a totally different internal format, if needed.
• Multiple views in window, all shown simultaneously Examples: Microsoft Multiplan offers multiple views of a single spreadsheet cell. Diehl Graphsoft's MiniCAD offers 11 views in the main window, all shown simultaneously (see Figure 4-11). Transylvania has the picture, the transcript, and the compass, all in different views in the main window (shown in Figure A-8).	Solution: Define a subclass of TView for each view desired and create an instance of each of these subclasses in T(Your) Document.DoMakeViews. Build a window object in the method T (Your) Document.DoMakeWindows so that this window will contain the necessary number of frames correctly positioned within its borders. Install the appropriate view in each frame in the method T (Your) Document.DoMakeWindows
• Multiple windows, each with its own view Examples: Microsoft Chart shows the series view and the chart view of the data in different windows. The game Dalek shows the main playing view, the current score, and the vanity table all in different windows. Macintosh Pascal uses several windows, especially during program debugging (shown in Figure A-10).	Solution: Define a new subclass of TView for each view needed and create an instance of each of these subclasses in T (Your) Document. DoMakeViews method. In the method T (Your) Document.DoMakeWindows create new instances of TWindow for each view, initializing each window in an appropriate manner depending on whether or not the windows need to have different numbers of frames or different scrolling capabilities.
• Splittable views Examples: Microsoft Word provides a splittable view of the textual document so the user can view disconnected portions of the document simultaneously. Microsoft Multiplan provides a splittable view of the spreadsheet for the same reason.	Solution: Use an instance of TSplitFrame which provides, as a part of its basic functionality, the ability to have several panes "looking on" noncontiguous portions of a single view.

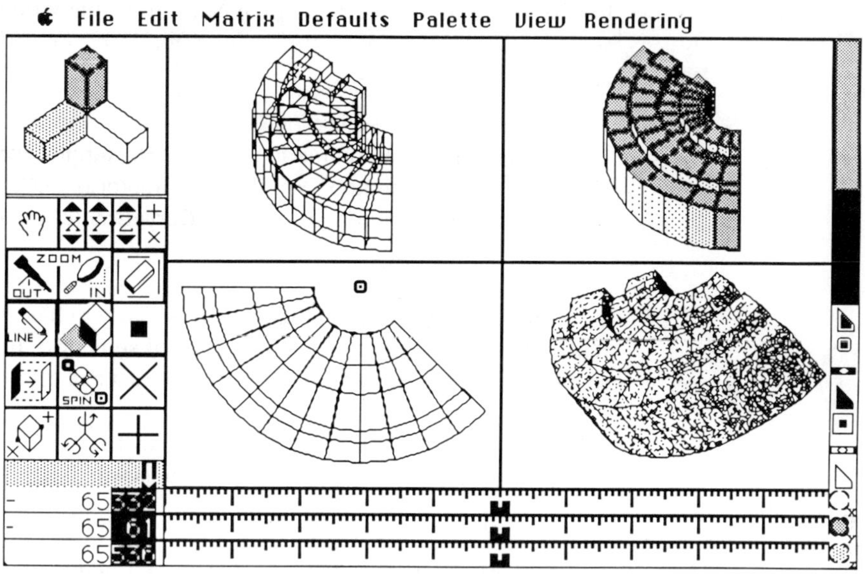

Figure 4-11 A complex window from the Mini-CAD application. This window has 11 views, all shown simultaneously.

We have not yet discussed command objects, which enable the user to interact with the image on the screen and modify a document's data. For example, in a MacDraw-like application, an instance of the class TRotateTextCmd would be created to process the user's activation of the **Rotate** command. As you might imagine, the exact procedures that need to be applied to rotate text differ from those needed to rotate a rectangle, which again differ from those needed to rotate curves. This problem is handled in an object-oriented program by having the object itself create the appropriate command object. Sound paradoxical? It works like this: suppose we have designed a MacDraw-like application in which there are text objects representing text, rectangle objects representing rectangles, and curve objects representing curves. The **Rotate** menu command, when issued, sends the message DoMenuCommand to the current selection. The single parameter of this message is the menu item number of the **Rotate** item. (Note that the menu item number is a constant for each menu item.) Thus, a line equivalent to the following is executed to create the correct kind of command object for the current selection:

```
newCommand := currentSelection.DoMenuCommand(cRotateCmd);
```

What exactly happens when the DoMenuCommand message is sent to the current selection? It depends on the current selection. Recall that one of the major tenets of object-oriented programming is that we should separate the "what" from the "how" whenever possible. In this instance, we want to create a command object that can rotate whatever type of entity is currently selected.

In a traditional approach to programming, this would have to be done with something like the following case statement, contained in the main control loop of the application:

```
CASE currentSelection.tag OF
  rectangle: newCommand := CreateRectangleCmd(cRotateCmd);
  text: newCommand := CreateTextCmd(cRotateCmd);
  curve: newCommand := CreateCurveCmd(cRotateCmd);

END;
```

The problem with this approach is that you have to modify this main control loop if you want to add a new type of selection. In addition, the main control loop is not reusable because it specifies exactly the data types that it can process.

The object-oriented solution is to let the current selection itself decide how to create a rotation command. The single line:

```
newCommand := currentSelection.DoMenuCommand(cRotateCmd);
```

takes the place of the **CASE** statement, removing all the selection type dependencies from the main control loop (enabling you to add a new selection type without modifying the main control loop), and making the main control loop more reusable.

The DoMenuCommand method is defined for all the object types the user can select and each of these methods creates and returns the correct type of command—one that will know how to properly process the current selection. When a piece of text is selected, for example, the current selection is a text object. The text object's DoMenuCommand method looks something like this:

```
FUNCTION TTextObject.DoMenuCommand(cmdNumber: CmdNumber):
  TCommand;

VAR aShadeTextCmd: TShadeTextCmd;
    aRotateTextCmd: TRotateTextCmd;

.

.

.

CASE cmdNumberOF
  cShadeCmd:BEGIN
      NEW (aShadeTextCmd);
      aShadeTextCmd.IShadeTextCmd;
      DoMenuCommand := aShadeTextCmd
    END;
```

```
cRotateCmd:BEGIN
    NEW(aRotateTextCmd);
    aRotateTextCmd.IRotateTextCmd;
    DoMenuCommand := aRotateTextCmd;
  END;

.
.
.
```

Notes

For those of you who might be interested, my mental model of the implementation of this MacDraw-like application would have an abstract superclass, TUserObject, which would be the superclass of all the graphical entities that the user could manipulate. Hence, TTextObject would be descended from this abstract superclass. TUserObject probably could be descended from either TEvtHandler (an abstract superclass that provides the funtionality for processing menu commands) or TObject.

The command that is returned from currentSelection.DoMenuCommand (in this example from TTextObject.DoMenuCommand) is sent the message DoIt, which causes it to modify the current document in whatever way it was designed to do. (See how this mechanism insulates the expandable application from the details of what the application is doing.) The current selection itself created the appropriate command to modify the document in the appropriate manner, given only the menu activation request by the user.

How do you decide the number and types of command classes in your application? The number of command classes is the number of distinctly different commands your users can perform, plus any variations needed to handle the different types of objects with which the end-user may have to deal. "Distinctly different" means that some commands, although different, can sometimes be handled by the same command class.

Notes

This is, of course, the worst case. It is not always true that you need a different command class for each type of entity that the end-use can manipulate. Even in those cases in which some methods need to change for different entities, you often can significantly reduce the amount of work you must do by making these command classes inherit from one another.

Examples of distinctly different commands in our MacDraw-like system might be the command to shade a rectangle black, the command to shade it gray, or the command to shade it white. These are really the same command with a pattern as a parameter and thus can be handled by using one command object, in which case, the command object might look like this:

```
TShadeRectCmd  = OBJECT (TCommand)
  fShadedShape: TRectObj;
  fNewShade: Color;
  fOldShade: Color;
  fDrawingDocument: TShapeDocument;
  PROCEDURE TShadeRectCmd.IShadeRectCmd(itsCommandNumber:
    INTEGER);
  PROCEDURE TShadeRectCmd.Commit;OVERRIDE;
  PROCEDURE TShadeRectCmd.DoIt;OVERRIDE;
  PROCEDURE TShadeRectCmd.RedoIt;OVERRIDE;
  PROCEDURE TShadeRectCmd.UndoIt;OVERRIDE;
END;
```

Note that instances of this command class store a sufficient amount of data to both do and undo the command. The instance variable fShadedShape references the rectangle object that this command will affect. The new shade for this rectangle is stored in fNewShade and its old shade in fOldShade. Storing its old shade ensures that the effect of this command can be undone. How this is done can be seen by examing the code for these methods:

```
PROCEDURE TShadeRectCmd.DoIt;
BEGIN
  SELF.fShadedShape.color := fNewShade; {Change the color of the rect in
    the document}
  SELF.fDrawingDocument.InvalShape(SELF.fShaded);
    {Inform the document that the area occupied by the shape needs to be
    redrawn in any views that render the document. Remember that changing
              the color in the document does not by itself affect the screen.}
```

```
END;

PROCEDURE TShadeRectCmd.RedoIt;

BEGIN
  SELF.DoIt;

END;

PROCEDURE TShadeRectCmd.UndoIt;

BEGIN
  SELF.fShadedRect.color := fOldShade;
  SELF.fDrawingDocument.InvalShape(SELF.fShaded);

END;
```

where

```
PROCEDURE TShapeDocument.InvalShape(s: TUserObject);
  PROCEDURE InvalInView(aView: TView);
  BEGIN
    aView.InvalRect(s.fExtentRect);
  END;

BEGIN
  SELF.ForAllViewsDo(InvalInView);

END;
```

Definitions

Note that these three methods qualify references to both fields and methods of SELF with "SELF." Strictly speaking, none of these is necessary and if all were removed the resulting program would be functionally identical. Whether to use "SELF." is a manner of style and there are two schools of thought on its use. The first states that because "SELF." is superfluous, it should not be used—after all, there is already enough code. For instance variables the prepended "f" is usually sufficient to indicate what is going on and for most methods the names are easily recognizable. The other school of thought believes that leaving "SELF." in place emphasizes which procedure invocations are really method calls and which referenced variables are really instance variables of the object that received the message. In a method like TShadeRectCmd.RedoIt (shown above), writing "SELF.DoIt," as opposed to just "DoIt," emphasizes that DoIt is not a global procedure. Similarly, references to SELF.fShadedRect or

SELF.fView emphasize that instance variables are being referenced. In a small method like those shown above, "SELF." may not be as helpful for instance variable references as for method calls, but in a larger method "SELF." can be quite useful for both situations. Just as using a **WITH** statement with a large enough scope in standard Pascal can make a program hard to follow, so, too, removing all of the explicit references to SELF in Object Pascal can be similarly confusing. In teaching, it is always better to be explicit about things like this, so I have made extensive use of the "SELF." qualification.

You as the application programmer need not worry about calling the DoIt, RedoIt,b and UndoIt methods yourself. These will be called by the MacApp application framework when needed. You need only make sure that when called, these methods perform the appropriate actions.

Event Sequencing in MacApp

The Macintosh User Interface Standard is an example of an event-driven user interface. Instead of a rigid, hierarchically structured set of commands that the user must traverse to reach a desired operation, most commands in a Macintosh application are available all the time. Such systems are typically designed with a central main event loop, which cycles endlessly waiting for an event to occur. When one does, it determines which of the many commands the user has indicated, and then causes the appropriate subroutine to be executed (see Figure 4-12). On the Macintosh, the lower-level system software manages an *event queue* into which events are posted for later processing. Events of various types are placed in the event queue, packaged with all their appropriate information (the current location of the mouse, the time, and the state of the keys on the keyboard, for example). The main event loop processes and dispatches these events in the order of their occurrence. The kinds of events placed in the queue include:

- mouse events—the press of the mouse button (a mouse-down event) or the release of that button (a mouse-up event).
- keyboard events—typing on the keyboard.
- window events—the activation or deactivation of a window.

MacApp preprocesses many events for you and presents your application with a higher-level event. For example, a Macintosh application must ordinarily determine if a mouse-down event has occurred in the menu bar to cause the appropriate menu to be displayed. MacApp does this for you and presents your application with a menu event if the user chooses a menu command. Your

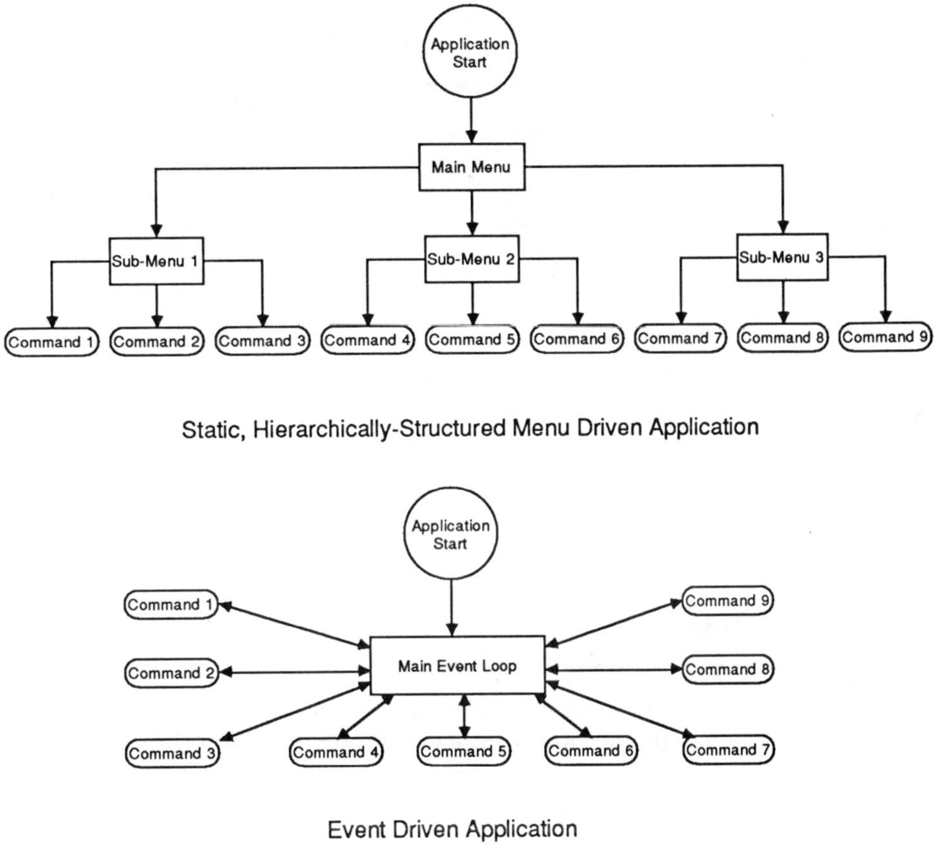

Figure 4-12 The high-level structure of an event-driven application compared to that of an application with hierarchically structured menus.

application need only handle the higher-order event—the actual choice of a menu command—and need not be concerned about menu display and interaction. Some of the higher-level events that MacApp constructs for you include:

- menu events—the user has chosen a command on a particular menu.
- mouse-down-in-content events—a mouse press inside of one of the views of one of your windows.
- Switcher events—the user has switched into or switched out of your application.
- serial events—incoming data on one of the serial communication lines.
- AppleTalk events—incoming packets on the AppleTalk network.
- alien events—a miscellaneous high-level event category.

Notes

None of these high-level events are individually differentiated by Macintosh system software at this time; they are purely the creation of MacApp. For this reason, you will find no discussion of Switcher events or even menu events in *Inside Macintosh or Macintosh Revealed.*

In addition, MacApp frees you from the design of the main event loop itself because the design of an application-independent main event loop is at the very heart of MacApp. The code of your application is invoked by MacApp so as to respond to application-unique events, but ordinary events such as mouse-downs in a window's resize control (when the user wants to resize a window) or mouse-downs in a window's title bar (when the user wants to move a window) is handled for you. (The details of MacApp's event processing will be discussed in Chapter 7.)

Coordinate Systems in MacApp

There are many coordinate systems used for drawing and for the processing of the various types of events on the Macintosh. The MacApp programmer must be aware of the most important of these and of how they interrelate, but is freed from the details of the coordinate transformations used to convert between them. The most important coordinate systems are the global or screen coordinate system, the view coordinate system, and the window or local coordinate system.

Global coordinates are the absolute Macintosh screen coordinates. The range for such coordinates on the original Macintosh is between 0 and 512 in the x direction (left to right) and between 0 and 342 in the y direction (top to bottom); on the Macintosh XL, the coordinate ranges are 0 to 720 in the x direction and 0 to 364 in the y direction. (Note that the y-coordinates are ordered in the opposite direction from their normal use in mathematics. In mathematics, the y-coordinate increases as you go up; on the Macintosh, the y-coordinate increases as you go down. This is a concession to efficiency due to current practice in hardware design.) View coordinates are used in rendering the image of the document. The range for this coordinate system is 0 to 32767 in both directions, although the view you typically create will be restricted to a small portion of this space. Window coordinates are relative to the upper left corner of the window in which the point lies. The range for these coordinates is essentially the same as for screen coordinates. Figure 4-13 shows the coordinates of a single point in each of these three systems.

For the MacApp programmer, the most important of these coordinate systems is the view coordinate system and MacApp always communicates with your application in this coordinate system. Because this is also where you define your view, your application need not be concerned with transformations between systems or with remembering that this routine deals with global coordinates, that routine with view coordinates, and the other routine with window coordinates.

The MacApp Class Library

The class inheritance structure for all MacApp classes is shown in Figures 4-14, 4-15, and 4-16. Note that these figures contain several new classes that not yet discussed:

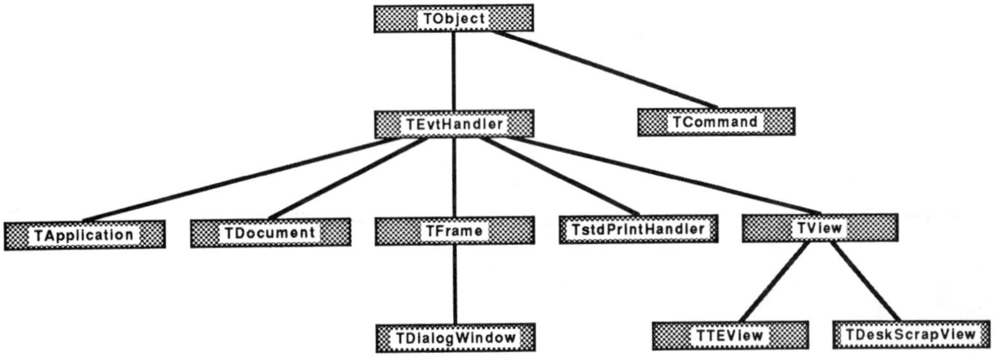

Figure 4-14 The inheritance structure of the basic MacApp classes.

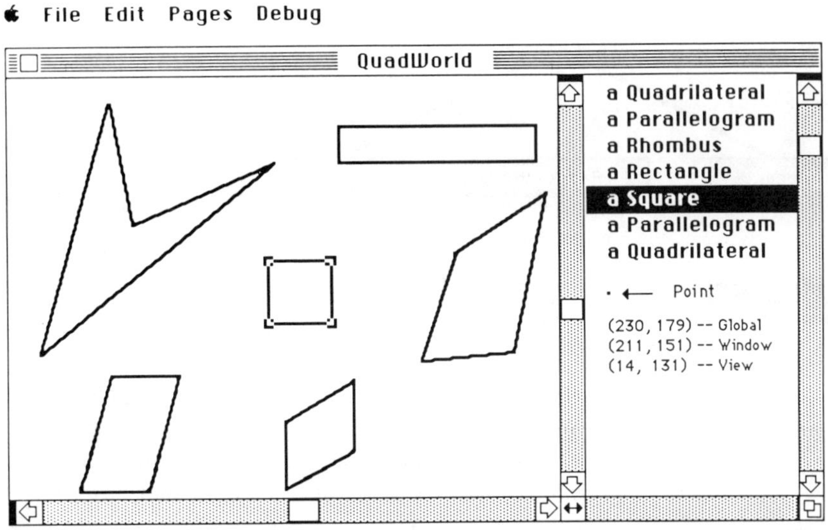

Figure 4-13 The coordinates of a single point in the three most important coordinate systems on Mac: the global coordinate system, the view coordinate system, and the local coordinate system.

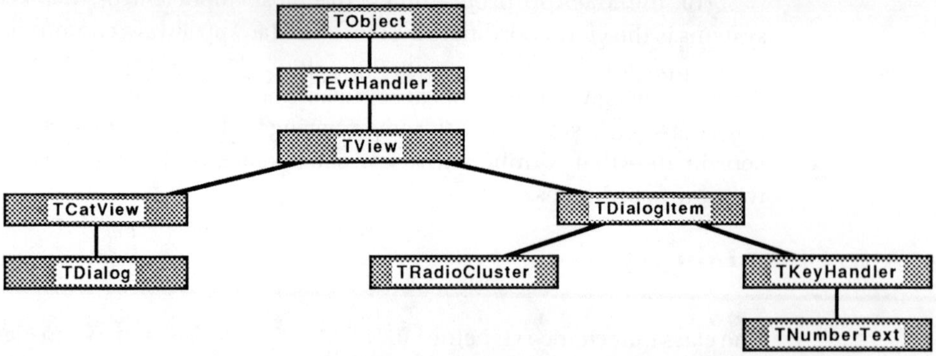

Figure 4-15 The inheritance structure of the MacApp Dialog classes.

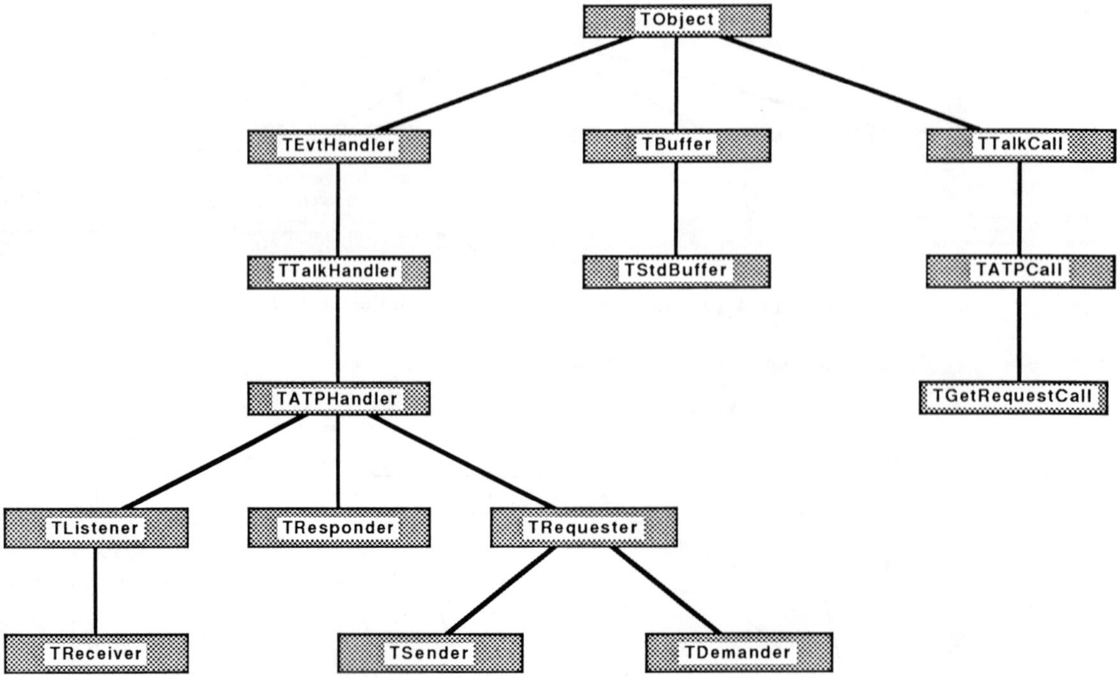

Figure 4-16 The inheritance structure of the MacApp AppleTalk classes.

Class	Basic function in the MacApp framework
TObject	An abstract superclass for all objects.
TEvtHandler	An abstract superclass that represents objects that can handle events.
TPrintHandler	A subclass of TEvtHandler that assists a view in printing. This class actually provides little printing capability but rather serves as an abstract superclass for all other classes that actually perform printing.
TStdPrintHandler	A subclass of TPrintHandler that provides a very wide range of printing capabilities on a number of output devices. This class will be used by all applications that support printing except for applications that need to provide extremely fine control of sophisticated devices like phototypesetters, and applications that provide only very simple printing support and cannot afford the overhead of a general printing class.
TTEView	A subclass of TView that supports simple editing of unformatted text, according to the Macintosh User Interface Standard.
TCatView	A subclass of TView that supports views which can contain other views
TDeskScrapView	A subclass of TView that supports the clipboard.
TDialog	A subclass of TCatView that supports the implementation of dialog boxes in accordance with the Macintosh User Interface Standard.
TDialogWindow	A subclass of TWindow specifically designed for dialog boxes.
TDialogItem	An abstract superclass for the classes that represent the various kinds of items that are part of dialog boxes.
TKeyHandler	A class that supports the use of alphanumeric text frames in dialog boxes.

TNumberText	A subclass of TKeyHandler which deals only with numeric text.
TRadioCluster	A class which supports the use of clusters of radio buttons in dialog boxes.
TTalkHandler, TTalkCall	Two abstract superclasses that deal with a single access to the AppleTalk network regardless of the protocol used.
TATPHandler, TATPCall	Subclasses of TTalkHandler and TTalkCall, respectively, that deal with the AppleTalk Transaction Protocol (ATP) used on the AppleTalk network.
TRequestor, TListener, TResponder, TSender, TDemander, TReceiver	Subclasses of TATPHandler that process various portions of the AppleTalk Transaction Protocol.
TGetRequestCall	A subclass of TATPCall that deals with a specific type of AppleTalk call.
TBuffer	A class that provides storage for and manipulation of data buffers used in processing an AppleTalk call.
TStdBuffer	A subclass of TBuffer that implements a simple, unique, relocatable buffer for use when processing AppleTalk calls.

The MacApp AppleTalk classes and MacApp Dialog classes are not discussed in this book. Consult the MacApp Reference Manual for information about these classes.

One of the most difficult tasks for the beginning object-oriented programmer (or for an experienced object-oriented programmer using a new class library for the first time) is to become acquainted with all the classes in the class library and with the functionality provided by the methods of these classes. This task can be quite formidable: for the MacApp class library alone, this is a set of more than 450 methods! Fortunately, not all methods are equally important. Rather than enumerate all 450 methods and explain what function each performs, we shall explain just how the most important ones are used. These "important" methods are those needed to implement the various versions of QuadWorld, the application introduced at the end of Chapter 2. We introduce two versions of QuadWorld: Mini-QuadWorld and full QuadWorld. Mini-QuadWorld will be developed in the Chapter 5, full QuadWorld in Chapter 8, and in Chapter 9, we examine several advanced features that could be added to QuadWorld. As we move from one version to the next we explain and use more MacApp methods in increasingly complicated ways. No claim is made, however, that even advanced QuadWorld uses every method of MacApp or displays those methods it does use in every possible way. For an explanation of the other methods, or for more information on the important ones, see Apple's MacApp Reference Manual.

CHAPTER 5

Mini-QuadWorld—A Small MacApp Application

In this chapter we develop a partial version, Mini-QuadWorld, of the QuadWorld application introduced in Chapter 2 that has the following characteristics:

- There is a fixed set of quadrilaterals stored in the quadDocument at initialization time. The user cannot add additional quadrilaterals, but can delete existing ones.
- Only one view of the quadrilaterals is provided, the graphical view.
- Any quadrilateral can be selected using the mouse.
- The selected quadrilateral is highlighted on the screen.
- The user can delete one or all quadrilaterals. Both operations can be undone.
- The user can rotate the selected quadrilateral counterclockwise by 45° any number of times. This also is undoable.

A screen dump of the MacApp implementation of Mini-QuadWorld is shown in Figure 5-1. Note that:

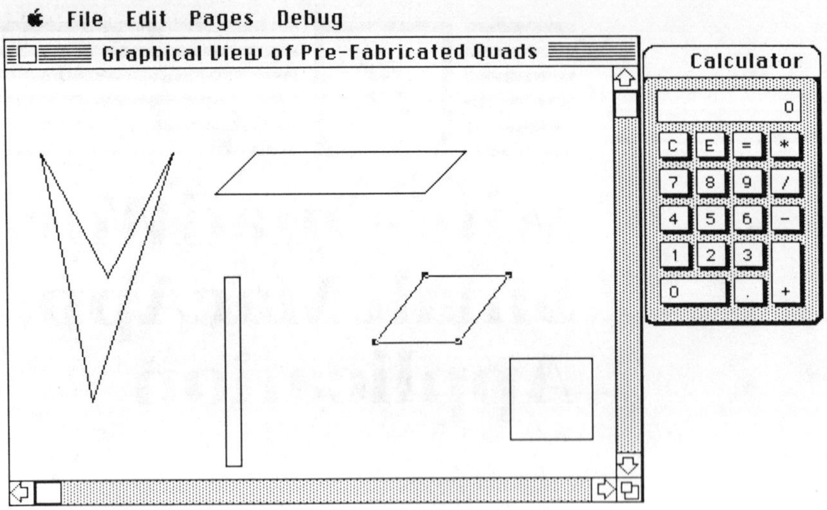

Figure 5-1 The MacApp implementation of Mini-QuadWorld.

- The window displaying the graphical view can be scrolled in both directions and can be resized.
- When a quadrilateral is selected, it is highlighted by the appearance of small, XORed squares at each vertex.
- Like all MacApp applications, Mini-QuadWorld works correctly with all desk accessories, runs under the Switcher, prints on both the ImageWriter and the LaserWriter, and works equally well on the standard Macintosh, the Macintosh Plus, and the Macintosh XL.

Warnings

The Mini-QuadWorld application was designed by removing from the full QuadWorld specification those requirements that are usually complex for the novice MacApp programmer. Accordingly, it is not truly representative of a Macintosh application or of the power and flexibility of MacApp. Rather, it is a stepping stone for the novice—first to understanding the full QuadWorld application, and then to designing totally new applications using MacApp as a base. If object-oriented programming is new to you, be sure you understand the Mini-QuadWorld application before moving on. It will be time well spent, because the problems solved here are encountered in every MacApp application.

Notes

There are several places in the design of the Mini-QuadWorld application where more generality is introduced than may be absolutely required. There are two reasons for this: to make the transition to the full QuadWorld application easy and to avoid introducing any "poor form" MacApp code that might mislead you when you start to design your own application. One example of this is the rotation of a quadrilateral. Objects of class TQuad know how to rotate themselves by any amount. To design a lobotomized TQuad class that knew only about 45° rotations would be a waste of time since it is so easy to implement general rotations. What is hard to understand about general rotations, and the reason they are deferred to the full QuadWorld, is how the user can specify the exact amount of the rotation.

There are at least two ways to describe any completed application program like Mini-QuadWorld to another programmer. The first is to describe the structure and organization of the final form of the program, explaining how each of the parts interrelate and function together. This provides an overall picture of the entire application and an understanding of how the finished application functions. However, such a description treats the program as a fait accompli—a finished structure presented as a total entity. This might help you understand how it works, but it may not be too helpful if you want to build an application yourself. For this we need another type of description. An alternate way of describing an application to another programmer is to describe how that application was constructed, giving a step-by-step, logical account of the design process—a process that can then be followed to produce new applications.

Both of these descriptive techniques are useful and to present one without the other for the first real MacApp application we discuss, Mini-QuadWorld, gives you an incomplete picture of MacApp programming. Accordingly, the next section, The Generation of Mini-QuadWorld, presents the step-by-step design description to give you one small example of how to build your own MacApp applications and the section following that, The Structure of Mini-QuadWorld, documents the overall structure of this application to give you a understanding of how an individual MacApp application fits into the MacApp framework. Both sections describe the same application and each includes portions of the Mini-QuadWorld source listing reproduced in full in Listing D. Necessarily, there is some overlap of material between these two sections—what is different, however, is the point of view.

The Generation of Mini-QuadWorld

Step 1. Data Representation

The first design step for the Mini-QuadWorld application is to decide how to represent and store the quadrilaterals. This step influences almost every other portion of the application. Much of the work of this step has already been discussed in Chapter 3 in the design and implementation of the classes TQuad, TParallelogram, TRhombus, TRectangle, and TSquare. Instances of these classes represent the quadrilaterals that you see and manipulate.

However, the design of these classes does not complete our data representation for Mini-QuadWorld. The design of Mini-Quad World will be significantly simplified if the individual quadrilateral are grouped into an object that can manage addition to or deletion from the group of an individual quadrilateral, record which quadrilateral is the selected one, and provide for the flexible enumeration of all the quadrilaterals. This object will be called the quadDocument and it will be an instance of a specially designed subclass of TDocument, TQuadDocument.

These capabilities can be easily provided by constructing a list of quadrilaterals using the **fNextQuad** links of the TQuad class together with a head quadrilateral reference in the quadDocument object (**fLastQuadAdded**) (see Figure 5-2).

Notes

Here we are using an abbreviation common to most object oriented languages: naming an instance by changing the first few characters of the class name. "quadDocument', for example, is an instance of TQuadDocument. Similarily, "quadGrView" or "aQuadGrView" means "an instance of the class TQuadGrView", and so on. This follows the style of naming object reference variables used throughout both Mini-QuadWorld and MacApp.

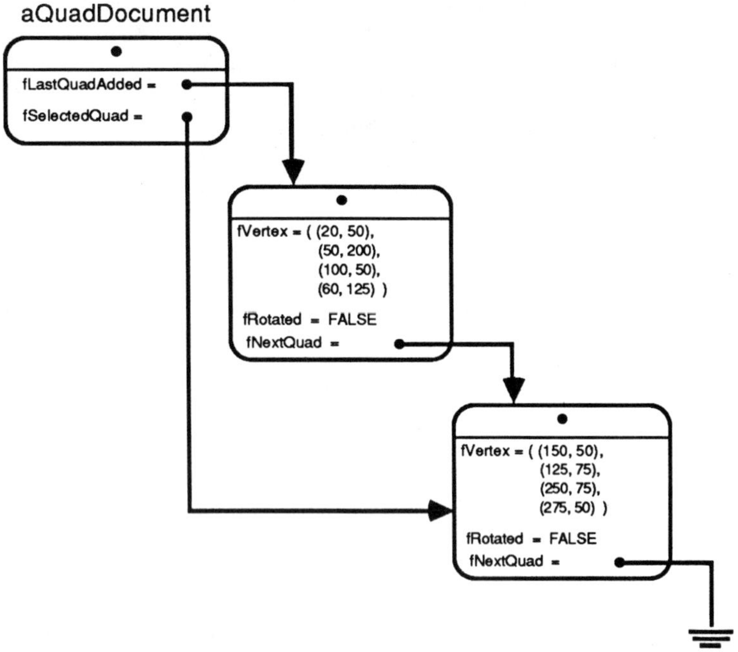

Figure 5-2 The list of quadrilaterals in a quadDocument.

Notes

It is not just convenient to store all the quadrilaterals in a quadDocument – it is required by the MacApp framework that the data of an application be stored in a document object. MacApp will send many messages to this document object, messages that will handle the opening and closing of files for storage of the document's data on disk, opening windows for the contents of the doucment to be viewed, and so on.

Adding or removing a quadrilateral object in the quadDocument then becomes merely insertion into or deletion from a singly-linked list. Executing procedures on each quadrilateral in the document is also easy: just traverse the list and invoke the desired procedure on each quad object:

```
PROCEDURE TQuadDocument.EachQuadDo(PROCEDURE DoThis(quad:
  TQuad));
VAR quad: TQuad;
```

```
BEGIN
  quad := SELF.fLastQuadAdded;
  WHILE quad <> NIL DO
    BEGIN
      DoThis(quad);
      quad := quad.fNextQuad;
    END
END;
```

To actually make a quadDocument, you must also provide an initialization routine (IQuadDocument) and make sure that this routine is called whenever a new quadDocument object is allocated:

```
PROCEDURE TQuadDocument.IQuadDocument; { ABBREVIATED
                                         —SEE NOTE BELOW }
BEGIN
  SELF.IDocument(myFileType);
  SELF.fLastQuadAdded := NIL;
  SELF.fSelectedQuad := NIL;
END;
```

The TQuadDocument.IQuadDocument method sets the initial values for the instance variables of the quadDocument: the reference to the last quadrilateral that has been added to the list of quadrilateral objects in the document (fLastQuadAdded) and the reference to the selected quadrilateral (fSelectedQuad). The value of fLastQuadAdded is maintained by the methods AddQuad and DeleteQuad to reflect the addition or deletion of a quadrilateral. The value of fSelectedQuad is maintained by a new method, TQuadDocument.SelectQuad. This method is invoked when the user changes the currently selected quadrilateral.

Notes

In this section, The Generation of Mini-QuadWorld, the code used to illustrate points is sometimes abbreviated in order to avoid a topic that hasn't been discussed yet. All such fragments have the comment { ***ABBREVIATED*** } in their first line. The next section, The Structure of Mini-QuadWorld, and the full listing of the Mini-QuadWorld application in Listing D, contain no abbreviated code.

In addition, Mini-QuadWorld, unlike many applications, has some "prefabricated" data in each document object that gets allocated automatically—the five constant quad objects. TDocument has a standard method for this, DoInitialState, and all you have to do is to override this method in the TQuadDocument class to initialize the new documents the way you want. MacApp takes care of invoking this method at the appropriate time for each new document object.

Step 2. Data Manipulation

For MacApp to be able to manipulate the data in a quadDocument, you must design command objects that perform these manipulations. MacApp won't know, for example, that to delete a quadrilateral, the quadDocument should be sent the message DeleteQuad. What MacApp will know is that when the user chooses the **Clear** command from the Edit menu, it should turn control over to a TClearQuadCommand object and let that object do to the quadDocument whatever it wants. In the data manipulation section, you design those command objects and tell MacApp when to turn over control and to whom.

STOP

Warning

In the MacApp framework, these command objects are relatively transitory. When the user chooses a menu command, a command object is created to perform that command, and then when the command can no longer be undone, the command object is freed. Deleting multiple quadrilaterals, for example, is done by separate clearQuadCmd objects, no two of which exists at the same time—each clearQuadCmd object is allocated, performs its function, and then dies. A beginning MacApp programmer may find this use of transitory objects to be a difficult programming technique to master. This is often because of a misconception about the amount of overhead associated with dynamic allocation and deallocation. In object-oriented programming, it is both common and desirable to allocate objects so that they can perform one specific task and then to deallocate them.

There are basically three things that a user of Mini-QuadWorld can do to a quadrilateral and thus there are three subclasses of TCommand you must design. Corresponding to the user action of rotating the selected quad, you need a TRotateQuadCmd class; corresponding to the clearing of a quad, a TClearQuadCmd class; and corresponding to the clearing of all quadrilaterals, a TClearAllCmd class.

The TClearQuadCmd class is representative of all three: you only have to provide new methods for several of the standard messages that TCommand objects implement: DoIt, UndoIt, RedoIt, and Commit. As the names suggest, the DoIt method of the TClearQuadCmd subclass performs any actions necessary to clear the quad, the UndoIt method does whatever is necessary to undo that action, the RedoIt method performs the action again, and the Commit method performs whatever operations are needed to commit the action and make it unable to be undone.

These methods are easy to implement. The DoIt method, for example, tells the document to deselect the currently selected quadrilateral and then delete it:

```
PROCEDURE TClearQuadCmd.DoIt; OVERRIDE;           { ABBREVIATED }
VAR quadDocument: TQuadDocument;
BEGIN
  quadDocument := TQuadDocument (SELF.fChangedDocument);
  quadDocument.SelectQuad(NIL);                     { Deselect the quad }
  quadDocument.DeleteQuad(SELF.fQuad);
END;
```

Note that the clearQuadCmd object, like all command objects, knows which document it is working on since this document is referred to by the instance variable fChangedDocument —an instance variable defined in the TCommand class and thus inherited by all its subclasses. This instance variable has TDocument class as its reference type. In order to send this document object the message SelectQuad, for example, you must tell the compiler that the document object referenced by the fChangedDocument instance variable of a clearQuadCmd has TQuadDocument as its object type—clearQuadCmds only operate on quadDocuments. Without this additional knowledge, the compiler would consider sending the SelectQuad message to the fChangedDocument to be an error—after all, most instances of TDocument would not understand the message SelectQuad. This knowledge is communicated to the compiler with the type cast in the first line of this method.

In order to be able to undo clearing a quadrilateral, the clearQuadCmd object must know which quad was deleted and so it must have an instance variable that refers to the quad involved. This variable is initialized in the IClearQuadCmd method:

```
PROCEDURE TClearQuadCmd.IClearQuadCmd(itsCmdNumber: INTEGER);
BEGIN
  SELF.ICommand(itsCmdNumber);
  SELF.fQuad := TQuadDocument(SELF.fChangedDocument).
    fSelectedQuad
END;
```

This method follows the most common format of an initialization method: first invoking the initialization method of its superclass (SELF.ICommand) and then performing any initializations that are unique to itself. Note that it would not be possible to invoke the superclass's initialization method with the **INHERITED** construct. Because initialization methods often have different argument lists and types, they are never overridden. Instead, you define a unique initialization method for each class by following the standard practice of using the name of the class with the prefixed "T" replaced by an "I".

With the deleted quad thus identified, the implementation of the UndoIt method becomes easy: just tell the document to add this quadrilateral back in and to make it the selected quadrilateral:

```
PROCEDURE TClearQuadCmd.UndoIt; OVERRIDE;        { ABBREVIATED }
VAR quadDocument: TQuadDocument;
BEGIN
  quadDocument := TQuadDocument (SELF.fChangedDocument);
  quadDocument.AddQuad(SELF.fQuad);
  quadDocument.SelectQuad(SELF.fQuad);
END;
```

These command objects are created in response to the choice of menu commands by the user. MacApp knows when a menu command is chosen and knows how to handle most of the standard commands (such as **Save, Quit**, and **Close**), but it doesn't know what do to when a menu command unique to the Mini-QuadWorld application is chosen. The method TQuadDocument.DoMenuCommand takes care of this. (Recall that in the MacApp framework there is a command number constant for each menu command. By convention, the names for these constants begin with "c".):

```
FUNCTION TQuadDocument.DoMenuCommand (aCmdNumber:
  CmdNumber): TCommand;
VAR  clearQuadCmd:      TClearQuadCmd;
     clearAllCmd:       TClearAllCmd;
     rotateQuadCmd:     TRotateQuadCmd;
BEGIN
  CASE aCmdNumber OF
    cRotateQuadCmd:   BEGIN
                        NEW(rotateQuadCmd);
                        rotateQuadCmd.IRotateQuadCmd
                          (aCmdNumber);
                        DoMenuCommand := rotateQuadCmd;
                      END;
    cClearQuadCmd:    BEGIN
                        NEW(clearQuadCmd);
                        clearQuadCmd.IClearQuadCmd
                        (aCmdNumber);
                        DoMenuCommand := clearQuadCmd;
                      END;
```

```
     cClearAllCmd:       BEGIN
                           NEW(clearAllCmd);
                           clearAllCmd.IClearAllCmd(aCmdNumber);
                           DoMenuCommand := clearAllCmd;
                         END;
       OTHERWISE         DoMenuCommand := INHERITED
                              DoMenuCommand (aCmdNumber);
   END;
 END;
```

This method is invoked by MacApp when a menu item is chosen by the user. Note that this method extends the standard DoMenuCommand of TDocument because it first tests if the chosen menu command is a command unique to Mini-QuadWorld: **Rotate by 45 degrees, Clear,** or **Clear All.** If it is, the menu command is processed by creating an appropriate command object. If it isn't, control is passed to the TDocument.DoMenuCommand with the line:

```
OTHERWISE DoMenuCommand = INHERITED DoMenuCommand
  (aCmdNumber);
```

MacApp also doesn't know about enabling the menu items unique to Mini-QuadWorld. This is taken care of by TQuadDocument.DoSetupMenus:

```
PROCEDURE TQuadDocument.DoSetupMenus; OVERRIDE;
BEGIN
  INHERITED DoSetupMenus;
  Enable(cRotateQuadCmd, SELF.fSelectedQuad <> NIL);
  Enable(cClearQuadCmd, SELF.fSelectedQuad <> NIL);
  Enable(cClearAllCmd, SELF.fLastQuadAdded <> NIL);
END;
```

This method is called by MacApp whenever a menu is to be displayed. It establishes the conditions under which the three menu commands unique to Mini-QuadWorld are enabled. The global MacApp procedure Enable is called for each menu item and the second argument of this call is a **BOOLEAN** indicating whether the command is to be enabled. If there is a selected quadrilateral (SELF.fSelectedQuad < > **NIL**), this method will enable the **Rotate** and **Clear** commands. The **Clear All** command is enabled if there are any quadrilaterals in the quadDocument (SELF.fLastQuadAdded < > **NIL**).

So, in effect, Mini-QuadWorld extends the functionality of the MacApp menu command processing routine by adding code that processes its own application specific commands. And it does so without disturbing the processing of any standard commands like **Open, Print** or **About Mini-Quad World**.

Step 3. Rendering the Data

So far, you have created a quadrilateral database and defined some operations (in the form of command objects) that can modify that data base, but you have not rendered an image of the quads in the database. This is the job of a subclass of TView, TQuadGrView, which also handles the mouse interactions that enables the user to select a quad.

You must override the view's Draw method in order to tell MacApp how your view is to be rendered. In the case of Mini-QuadWorld this is relatively simple—simply tell each quadrilateral to draw itself. The Draw method code reflects this simplicity:

```
PROCEDURE TQuadGrView.Draw(area: Rect);
    PROCEDURE DrawQuad(quad: TQuad);
    BEGIN
      quad.Draw;
    END;
  BEGIN
    TQuadDocument(SELF.fDocument).EachQuadDo(DrawQuad);
  END;
```

Since you have already written the enumeration method (TDocument. EachQuadDo), this method is particularly easy to write, with the single restriction that the procedure parameter to EachQuadDob must be a local procedure and not a method. For example, you could not have eliminated the local procedure DrawQuad and simply written:

```
TQuadDocument(SELF.fDocument).EachQuadDo(TQuad.Draw);     { illegal }
```

In addition, the quadGrView has to be able to highlight the selected quad (when told to do so by MacApp) and to erase a quad from the screen when a quad is deleted from the quadDocument. This last requirement may surprise you. Deleting a quad from the quadDocument has absolutely no effect on the view or the screen. When a quad is deleted from the quadDocument, the document has to explicitly tell the view to erase the quad. This is done in the TQuadDocument method InvalidateQuad:

```
PROCEDURE TQuadDocument.InvalidateQuad(quad: TQuad); { ABBREVIATED }
VAR invalRect: Rect;
BEGIN
  IF quad < > NIL THEN
  theQuadGrView.InvalidateQuad(quad);
END;
```

The invalidation message is passed along to the view which ensures that the quad is erased:

```
PROCEDURE TQuadGrView.InvalidateQuad(quad: TQuad);
VAR invalRect: Rect;
BEGIN
  IF quad < > NIL THEN
```

```
    BEGIN
        invalRect := quad.EnclosingRect;
        InsetRect(invalRect, -2, -2);          { Grow the rectangle to include any}
                                                { highlighting on the quad }
        SELF.fFrame.Focus;
        SELF.InvalRect(invalRect);
    END
END;
```

Like many things in a MacApp application, erasing a quad from the view is not something that you really do directly. What you really do is inform MacApp that a certain area of the view needs to be updated. MacApp remembers all such areas and, during the processing of the next update event (sent by the Window Manager to your application), it redraws these areas.

Notes

This idea of passing along a request for certain actions, as was done in TQuadGrView.Draw and TQuadDocument.InvalidateQuad, is common in object-oriented programming in general and in MacApp programming in particular. This is sometimes surprising to beginning MacApp programmers because it appears as though no method is doing any real work, but rather that all methods are merely "passing the buck" to other methods. This impression is especially strong when you examine a very general piece of code, such as the source listing for MacApp itself. But this impression is not correct. Each object contributes something along the chain of method calls, especially in a real MacApp application—unlike in Mini-QuadWorld which exists only as a teaching exercise. In the case of InvalidateQuad, for example, the quadDocument knows that when it receives the InvalidateQuad message, it should tell every view that renders the quadDocument to invalidate that quad. There is only one view, in the special case of Mini-QuadWorld, but in the full implementation of QuadWorld there are two, and in some other applications there are many more. Having a focal point of invalidation, the quadDocument, makes the application more modular and easier to extend.

Another interesting method in the TQuadGrView class is DoMouseCommand, the method that processes any mouse presses in quadGrView. In Mini-QuadWorld, a mouse press in quadGrView can mean only that the user wants to select a quadrilateral already present in the view. (In the implementation of the full QuadWorld application, where the user can sketch new quadrilaterals, the interpretation of a mouse press is considerably more involved. In fact, DoMouseCommand is the most complex method in that entire application.)

When the user presses the mouse button, the TQuadGrView.DoMouseCommand determines which quadrilateral is at the point where the cursor was when the mouse button was pressed. It asks each quadrilateral to compute the smallest rectangle that encloses itself (TQuad.EnclosingRect), and then the QuickDraw routine PtInRect is used to test if this mouse down point is inside that rectangle. As with TQuadGrView.Draw, this process is easier to write because you already have TQuadDocument.EachQuadDo.

```
FUNCTION TQuadGrView.DoMouseCommand (VAR downLocalPoint: Point;
                                     VAR info: EventInfo;
                                     VAR hysteresis: Point):
                                         TCommand; OVERRIDE;
  VAR tempQuad:     TQuad; { a temporary variable used to find the quad
                             under the cursor }
      selectedQuad: TQuad; { the currently selected quad }
    PROCEDURE CheckQuad(thisQuad: TQuad);
    BEGIN
      IF PtInRect(downLocalPoint, thisQuad.EnclosingRect) THEN
        tempQuad := thisQuad;
    END;
  BEGIN
    DoMouseCommand := gNoChanges;
    tempQuad := NIL;
    selectedQuad := TQuadDocument(SELF.fDocument).fSelectedQuad;
    TQuadDocument(SELF.fDocument).EachQuadDo(CheckQuad);
                               { tempQuad now refers to the quad,
                                 if any, beneath the cursor position }
    IF ((tempQuad <> NIL) AND (selectedQuad = tempQuad))
      THEN
      TQuadDocument(SELF.fDocument).SelectQuad(tempQuad);
                                           { Tell the document }
  END;
```

Now that the document is represented in the view, you have to make sure that the view gets properly updated when the document changes. You do this by making sure that all the command objects that modify the document tell it to do the appropriate invalidation. In TClearQuadCmd, for example, the DoIt method must tell the document to invalidate the area occupied by the deleted quad:

```
PROCEDURE TClearQuadCmd.DoIt; OVERRIDE;
VAR quadDocument: TQuadDocument;
BEGIN
  quadDocument := TQuadDocument (SELF.fChangedDocument);
  quadDocument.SelectQuad(NIL);
  quadDocument.DeleteQuad(SELF.fQuad);
  quadDocument.InvalidateQuad(SELF.fQuad);
END;
```

In addition, the quadDocument has to cause the appropriate changes in the view when the selected quadrilateral changes. This in accomplished by adding an instance variable (fQuadGrView) to TQuadDocument so that the quadDocument can easily refer to the view and by adding a SelectQuad method to TQuadDocument:

```
PROCEDURE TQuadDocument.SelectQuad(quad: TQuad);
BEGIN
  IF (quad < > SELF.fSelectedQuad) THEN
                                      { old selection < > new selection }
    BEGIN
      SELF.fQuadGrView.HighlightSelection(FALSE);
                                      { Turn off for the old selection }
      SELF.fSelectedQuad := quad;
      SELF.fQuadGrView.HighlightSelection(TRUE);
                                      { Turn on for the new selection }
    END
END;
```

This SelectQuad method invokes the HighlightSelection method of TQuadGrView:

```
PROCEDURE TQuadGrView.HighlightSelection(turnOn: BOOLEAN);
  OVERRIDE;

VAR selectedQuad: TQuad;
    cornerRect:   Rect;
    i:            INTEGER;                    { FOR loop index }

BEGIN
  selectedQuad := TQuadDocument(SELF.fDocument). fSelectedQuad;
  IF (selectedQuad < > NIL) THEN
    BEGIN
      IF RectIsVisible(selectedQuad.EnclosingRect)
        THEN                  { only do highlight if quad is visible }
```

```
            BEGIN
              PenMode(patXOr);
              SetRect(cornerRect, -2, -2, 2, 2);        { Highlighting rectangle }
              FOR i := 1 TO 4 DO
                BEGIN
                  OffsetRect(cornerRect, selectedQuad.
                    fVertex[i].h, selectedQuad.fVertex[i].v);
                  PaintRect(cornerRect);
                  OffsetRect(cornerRect,-selectedQuad.
                    fVertex[i].h, -selectedQuad.fVertex[i].v);
                END
            END
        END
    END;
```

Note that this HighlightSelection method does not use the invalidation/update mechanism that is used when a quad is deleted. Rather, it invokes QuickDraw routines directly. The reason for this is that highlighting often involves merely the XORing of small areas in the view and there is no need to completely redraw any area of the view to ensure that it is properly rendered.

Step 4. Hooking into the MacApp Framework

The last step in the design of Mini-QuadWorld is to make it possible for MacApp to invoke the code prepared in the first three steps. You do this by designing a TQuadApplication class and by adding a few pro forma methods to the TQuad-Document class. These steps are covered more fully in the following discussion on the structure of the sample MacApp application, Mini-QuadWorld.

The Structure of Mini-QuadWorld

Mini-QuadWorld is typically of MacApp applications in that it makes use of all the basic MacApp classes, either directly, by using instances of these classes (such as TWindow and TFrame) or indirectly by designing specialized subclasses that exhibit application-specific behavior (such as TQuadDocument and TQuadGrView). Figure 5-3 shows the inheritance structure for all the classes used in Mini-QuadWorld.

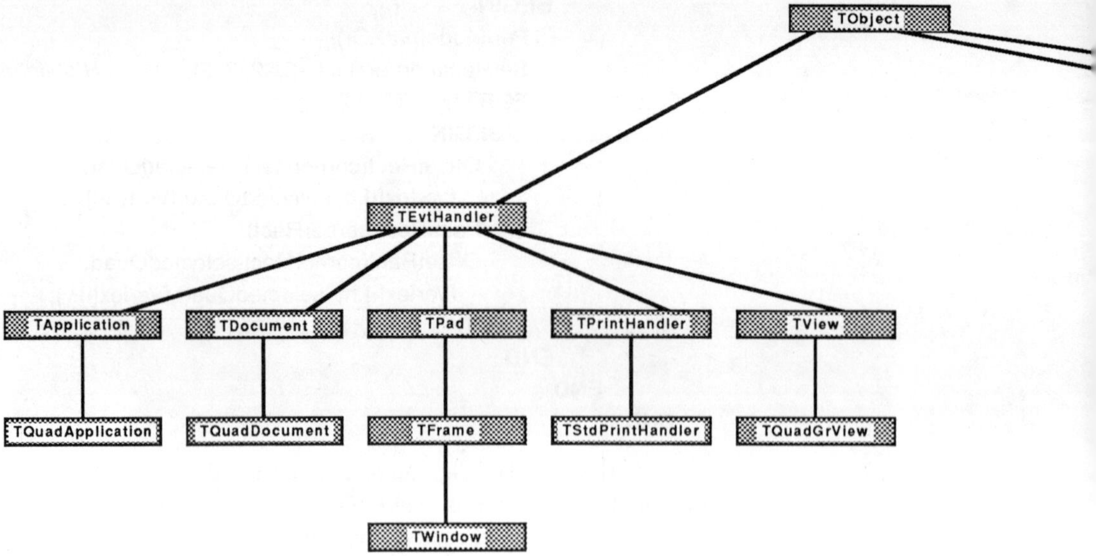

Figure 5-3 The inheritance structure of the Mini-QuadWorld classes.

The Class TQuadApplication

The highest level step in implementing Mini-QuadWorld is designing a TQuadApplication class, which is a subclass of TApplication. First you must know how an instance of TQuadApplication differs from an instance of its superclass both in terms of its instance variables and in terms of its methods.

At first glance, there isn't much difference between a TQuadApplication object and the most generic Macintosh application objects of the TApplication class. TApplication objects open when you double-click on their icons or documents, they set up menus in the menu bar, and they ask the user if changes are to be saved when the menu commands **Close** or **Quit** are chosen. Instances of TQuadApplication inherit all this behavior from TApplication. A closer inspection reveals that there doesn't seem to be any additional data that a TQuadApplication must store, so there are no new instance variables to declare for a TQuadApplication object. The only differences between a TQuadApplication and a TApplication are how they are initialized and which types of documents they use.

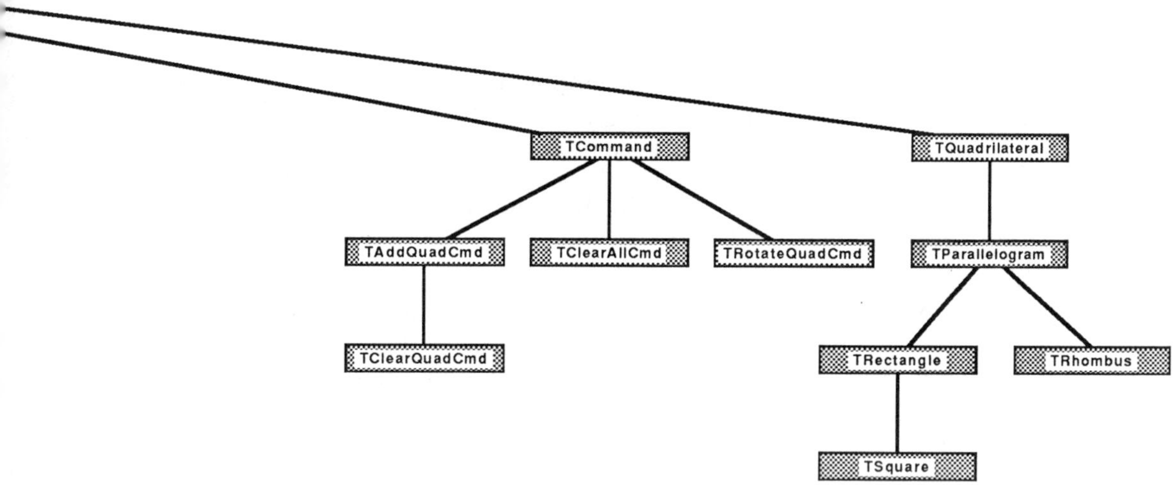

To provide for different initializations, you must add a method to TQuadApplication for initialization of TQuadApplication objects. In accordance with the conventions that Apple started, the name of this method is IQuadApplication.

To provide for a different type of document, you must override the TApplication.DoMakeDocument method to generate a document object that can store quadrilaterals. In general, an application may need many types of documents. Accordingly, the TApplication.DoMakeDocument method takes an argument that differentiates between the various types of documents that may be used in the application. Because Mini-QuadWorld has only one document type, this parameter doesn't apply yet. (See Chapter 9 for a discussion of multi-document MacApp applications.)

TQuadApplication Instance Variables

No new variables needed.

TQuadApplication Methods

Method	Use
IQuadApplication	Initializes new instances of TQuadApplication.
DoMakeDocument	Overridden method. Creates an instance of an appropriate type of document for Mini-QuadWorld—an instance of TQuadDocument.

Note that you must always override the method DoMakeDocument in designing a new application because it is through this method that MacApp is able to access the specific type of document needed for your application. This is done through one of the MacApp classes that has statements like the following:

```
theNewDocument := gApplication.DoMakeDocument;
theNewDocument.DoMakeViews(kForDisplay);
theNewDocument.DoMakeWindows;
theNewDocument.ShowWindows;
```

Notes

The actual method in which this takes place, for those who are curious, is TApplication.OpenNew. The code listed above is a simplification of the code found in that method.

When this method is invoked, gApplication refers to the application object of your TApplication subclass, TQuadApplication, and the first of these four lines invokes the DoMakeDocument method that you designed, thus returning to the MacApp code a document object specifically designed for your application—an instance of one of your subclasses of TDocument. When this document object is sent a message (like DoMakeViews, DoMakeWindows, and ShowWindows shown above) your code will be invoked if the message sent was a TDocument message you had overridden. So, MacApp can send the message DoMakeWindows to an object of your special subclass of TDocument invoking one of your methods, even though MacApp was designed and implemented long before your subclass. It is through methods like DoMakeDocument that MacApp can access the code that defines how your application differs from the generic Macintosh application.

Fortunately, since they are required, the code for DoMakeDocument is usually short and simple. Here is the full text of its code in the Mini-QuadWorld application:

```
FUNCTION TQuadApplication.DoMakeDocument(itsCmdNumber:
  CmdNumber): TDocument;
VAR quadDocument: TQuadDocument;
BEGIN
  NEW(quadDocument);
  quadDocument.IQuadDocument;
  DoMakeDocument := quadDocument;
END;
```

Note that all this method does is create a document object of the appropriate class and return it.

This technique by which MacApp accesses your code works as long as your application object is there to get everything started. But how does it get there? Your application object is created in the main program that is your application, as explained in Chapter 4 when discussing the SmallApplication. That main program is:

```
        { MacApp implementation of the Mini-QuadWorld application }
         {Copyright 1986 by Productivity Products International, Inc.}

PROGRAM MiniQW;
{$M+}
{$X-}

USES
  {$U-}
     {These units are part of the Software Supplement that enable cross-
     development of Macintosh applications from the Lisa Pascal Workshop.}
  {$U Obj/MemTypes}   MemTypes,
  {$U Obj/QuickDraw}  QuickDraw,
  {$U Obj/OSIntf}     OSIntf,
  {$U Obj/ToolIntf}   ToolIntf,
  {$U obj/SaneLib}    SANE,
                         {Floating point needed for the rotation of quads}

  { These units are part of MacApp. }
  {$U Object.U}       UObject,
  {$U MacApp.U}       UMacApp,
  {$U Printing.U}     UPrinting,

  { This unit contains the classes unique to Mini-QuadWorld. }
  {$U MiniQW.U}       UMiniQW;
```

```
VAR quadApplication: TQuadApplication;

BEGIN
{$S }                              { Put this code into the blank segment }
  InitToolbox(2, 10);
     { start with 2 extra blocks of 64 master pointers; allow up to 10 windows }

  InitPrinting;                    {initialize the print shop routines }
  NEW(quadApplication);
  quadApplication.IQuadApplication('QUAD');
  quadApplication.Run;
END.
```

Note that the main program for Mini-QuadWorld is essentially the same as that of SmallApplication. This is the case for almost all MacApp applications. Now that you have seen two such main programs and seen how similar they are, there is no need to examine yet another one.

The Class TQuadDocument

After your TApplication subclass, the next level in the structure of a MacApp application is your TDocument subclass. That subclass specifies the objects that store the information you need to represent one document. If you were designing a word processing application, your document would have to store all the text, associated font and face information, headers and footers, and paragraph styles, among other things. For the Mini-QuadWorld application you need to store the following information:

- all the quadrilaterals prefabricated in Mini-QuadWorld.
- which quadrilateral is the currently selected one.

In addition, every document class you design must contain an instance variable for each view that renders the document. A document that is rendered by several views has several such variables. Even if your application has only one type of view, your document class must still contain such an instance variable because, when several documents are open at once, each must know their individual view object.

Having outlined the instance variables, next you need to know about the methods. There are two categories of methods for the class TQuadDocument:

- methods dealing with the manipulation of the data stored in the document.
- methods providing "hooks" into the MacApp framework, i.e., methods like DoMakeDocument in TQuadApplication that are used by MacApp to install your kind of document, your type of view, and so on, to provide access to the special types of objects you have designed or to the special methods you have overridden.

The methods dealing with data manipulation enable us to execute a procedure on each quadrilateral in the document, add or delete any, change which one is selected, and redraw it in the view. Note that all of these methods are unique to the class TQuadDocument—none of them overrides any method from an ancestor class.

The four MacApp hook methods are probably the most interesting. These are also methods that you will probably override in designing your own MacApp application. The method TQuadDocument.DoMakeViews is just like the method TQuadApplication.DoMakeDocument in that it is a method you must override. In the case of TQuadDocument.DoMakeViews, you provide the overridden method to create and install the correct kind of views for your document. Its code is as simple as that of TQuadApplication.DoMakeDocument. TQuadDocument.DoMakeWindows is a method you must override to create the correct window for your application. Mini-QuadWorld has only one window which is allocated in DoLaunchWindows. DoSetupMenus enables or disables additional menu items unique to Mini-QuadWorld (that is, DoSetupMenus ensures that these menu items are displayed in black or in gray as appropriate when the menu is constructed) and DoMenuCommand processes these commands when the user chooses them.

TQuadDocument Instance Variables

Variable	Use
fLastQuad	Refers to the last quadrilateral to be added in a linked list of quadrilaterals. Note in the descriptions of quadrilateral objects in Chapter 3 that they themselves store a link to the "next" quadrilateral. Thus, fLastQuad really refers to the head quadrilateral in the list of quadrilaterals currently in the quadDocument.
fQuadGrView	Refers to the quadGraphicalView of this quadDocument.
fSelectedQuad	Refers to the currently selected quadrilateral, if any.

TQuadDocument Methods

Initialization and Freeing Methods

Method	Use
IQuadDocument	Initializes new instances of TQuadDocument.
DoInitialState	Overridden method. Stores the five prefabricated quadrilaterals in the quadDocument.
Free	Overridden method. Deallocates the quadDocument. Failure to override this method would leave TQuad objects on the heap, thereby using up heap space that the next document might need.
FreeData	Overridden method. Deallocates the quadrilaterals in the quadDocument when the document is freed. Failure to override this method would leave TQuad objects on the heap, thereby using up heap space that the next document might need.

Data Manipulation Methods

Method	Use
AddQuad	Adds a quadrilateral to the list of quadrilaterals in the quadDocument.
DeleteQuad	Deletes a quadrilateral from the list of quadrilaterals in the quadDocument.
EachQuadDo (DoThis(quad))	Executes the procedure DoThis for each of the quadrilaterals in the quadDocument.

Data Display Methods

Method	Use
InvalidateQuad	Redraws a quadrilateral.
SelectQuad	Makes a particular quadrilateral the selected quadrilateral.

MacApp "Hook" Methods

Method	Use
DoMakeViews	Overridden method. Allocates and installs the quadGraphicalView in the quadDocument.
DoMakeWindows	Overridden method. Allocates and opens the window that will display the representation of the quadDocument. Makes sure this window fills the screen regardless of screen size.
DoSetUpMenus	Overridden method. Enables the three menu commands unique to Mini-QuadWorld: **Rotate by 45 degrees, Clear,** and **Clear All.**
DoMenuCommand	Overridden method. Processes the three menu commands unique to Mini-QuadWorld: **Rotate by 45 degrees, Clear,** and **Clear All.**

Figure 5-4 shows the structure of the quadDocument (and several related objects) after the execution of TQuadDocument.DoInitialState and after the user has selected the rhombus in the quadDocument. This figure is a "snapshot" of a portion of the heap at an early point in the use of the Mini-QuadWorld application.

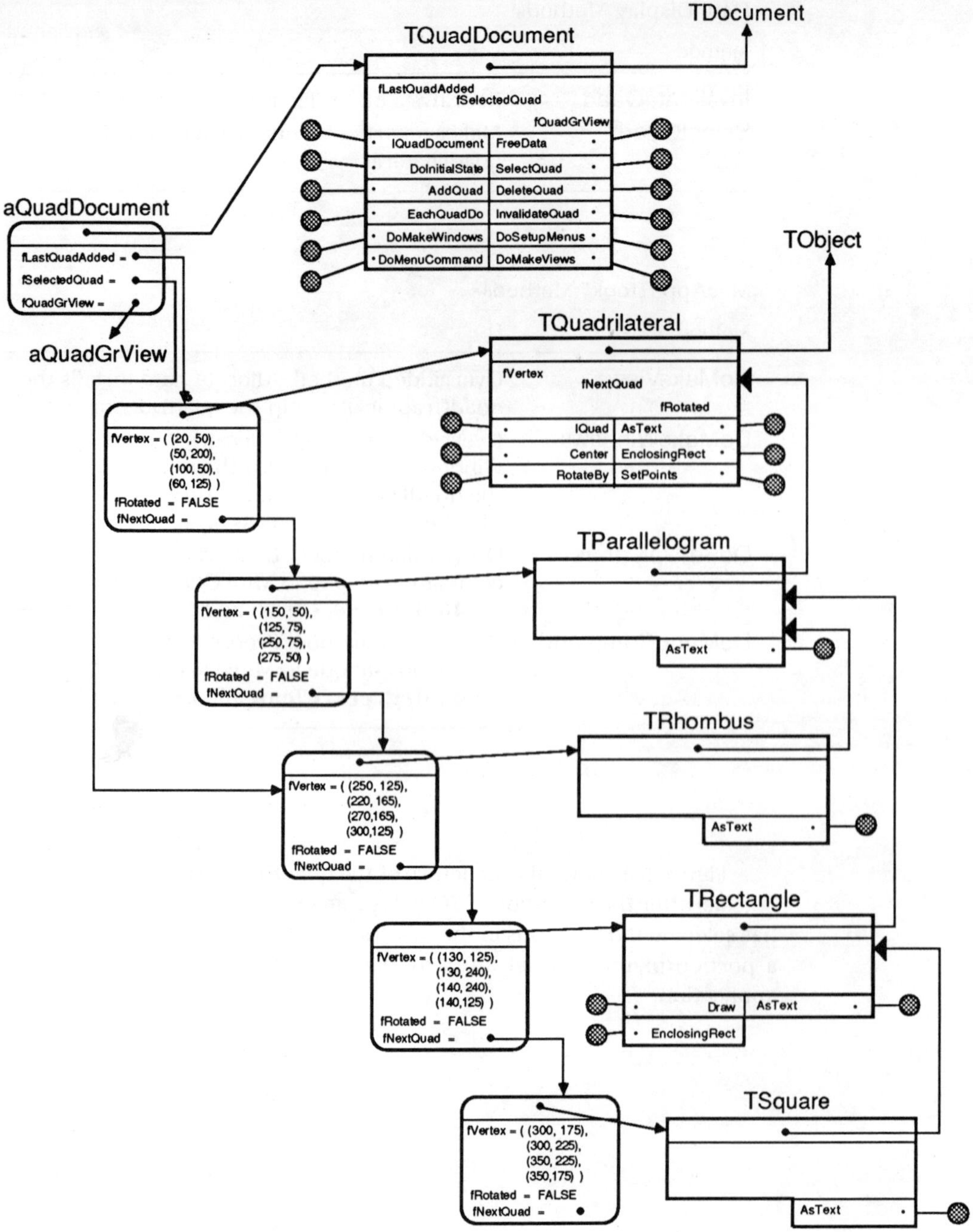

Figure 5-4 The quadDocument and other related objects depicted in the style of Figure 2-8.

Note that the Mini-QuadWorld application-specific menu commands can be both done and undone, creating command objects of the appropriate class and passing these back to MacApp to actually perform the command. We discuss the operation of each of these command objects later in this chapter.

The Class TQuadGrView

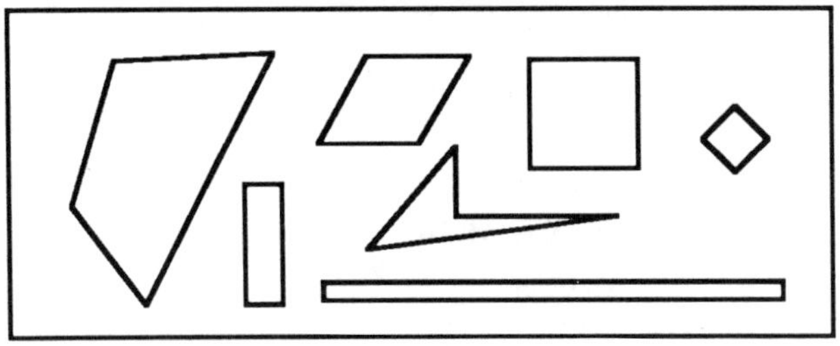

After the application subclass, TQuadApplication, and the document subclass, TQuadDocument, the next level in the structure of a MacApp application is the view subclass. The design of this class is usually relatively straightforward since TView does so many things for you and TQuadGrView is no exception.

There is no new data to be held by a quadGrView—that is, all its data is already defined in the superclass of TQuadGrView, TView.

There are a total of five methods defined in the class TQuadGrView. There are no methods to discuss in detail because all the major issues have been already covered in this chapter.

TQuadGrView Instance Variables

No new variables needed

TQuadGrView Methods

Data Manipulation Methods

Method	Use
IQuadGrView	Initializes new instances of TQuadGrView.

MacApp "Hook" Methods

Method	Use
Draw	Overridden method. Draws the graphical representation of the quadDocument.
HighlightSelection	Overridden method. Highlights the selected quadrilateral.
DoMouseCommand	Overridden method. Processes mouse presses in the quadGrView.

Display Methods

Method	Use
InvalidateQuad	Invalidates the graphical representation of a particular quadrilateral.

The Class TRotateQuadCmd

Of the various actions the user can perform with a quadrilateral, only rotating the quadrilateral has a reduced functionality compared to that of full Quad-World. In the full implementation the user can rotate a quadrilateral by any amount, whereas in Mini-QuadWorld the amount of the rotation is a fixed 45° counterclockwise. This makes TRotateQuadCmd follow the simplest model for a TCommand subclass, which requires you to override three methods, DoIt, UndoIt, and RedoIt, and then to trust MacApp to invoke these methods at the appropriate times. In designing these methods you can focus your attention on causing a quadrilateral to rotate by 45°, without worrying about such related activities as when to redraw the view, which command would be affected if the user chooses **Undo** command, and unhighlighting a menu title when its command is completed.

To perform the rotation, the rotateQuadCmd need only know which quadrilateral is to be rotated. In the interests of generality and for an easy transition to the full QuadWorld application, the angle by which to rotate the quadrilateral is stored in the rotateQuadCmd object.

TRotateQuadCmd Instance Variables

Variable	Use
fQuad	Refers to the quadrilateral that will be rotated.
fAngle	An **INTEGER** that records the angle for the rotation in degrees. In Mini-QuadWorld, this is always a constant 45°.

TRotateQuadCmd Methods

Data Manipulation Methods

Method	Use
IRotateQuadCmd	Initializes new instances of TRotateQuadCmd.

MacApp "Hook" Methods

Method	Use
DoIt	Overridden method. Performs the rotation of the quadrilateral and (indirectly) causes the newly rotated quadrilateral to be drawn in the view.
UndoIt	Overridden method. Undoes the rotation of the quadrilateral and (indirectly) causes the old quadrilateral to be drawn in the view.
RedoIt	Overridden method. Redoes the rotation of the quadrilateral and (indirectly) causes the newly re-rotated quadrilateral to be drawn in the view.

The method TRotateQuadCmd.DoIt is representative of these three methods:

```
PROCEDURE TRotateQuadCmd.DoIt; OVERRIDE;
VAR quadDocument: TQuadDocument;
BEGIN
  quadDocument := TQuadDocument(SELF.fChangedDocument);
  quadDocument.InvalidateQuad(SELF.fQuad);          { BEFORE Rotation }
  fQuad.RotateBy(SELF.fAngle);
  quadDocument.InvalidateQuad(SELF.fQuad);          { AFTER Rotation }
END;
```

This method must do more than just send the message RotateBy(45) to the quadrilateral to be rotated. It must also ensure that the appropriate portion of the view is redrawn the next time MacApp performs this drawing. This is done by:

- telling the document to invalidate the area occupied by the quad before it is rotated.
- rotating the quad.
- telling the document to invalidate the area now occupied by the quad.

These invalidation requests have the effect of adding to the update region the area occupied by the quad both before and after it is rotated. This is necessary because the rotation of the quadrilateral may result in a different invalidation area before and after the rotation. (See Figure 5-5.)

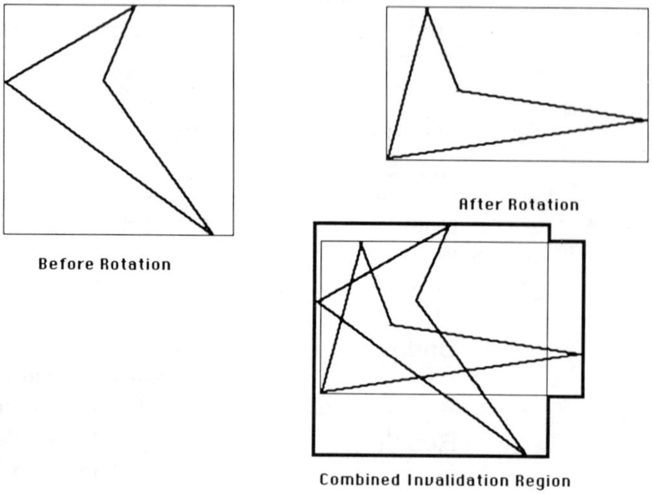

Figure 5-5 The total invalidation region following the rotation of a quadrilateral can be bigger than either the enclosing rectangle before the rotation or the enclosing rectangle after the rotation.

The Class TClearQuadCmd

The command object that deletes a single quadrilateral from the quadDocument is more complex than the command object that rotates a quadrilateral. This is because when the user can no longer undo or redo the deletion of a quadrilateral object, it must be deallocated. In MacApp terms, this action should be taken when the command is committed – that is, when it can no longer be undone. TCommand has a null method, Commit, does this—all you have to do is override Commit so that the correct actions can be taken when this method is invoked.

TClearQuadCmd Instance Variables

Variable	Use
fQuad	Refers to the quadrilateral to be deleted from the quadDocument.

TClearQuadCmd Methods

Data Manipulation Methods

Method	Use
IClearQuadCmd	Initializes new instances of TClearQuadCmd.

MacApp "Hook" Methods

Method	Use
DoIt	Overridden method. Performs the deletion of the quadrilateral and (indirectly) causes the image of the quadrilateral to be removed from the view.
UndoIt	Overridden method. Undoes the deletion of the quadrilateral—re-installs the quadrilateral in the quadDocument—and (indirectly) causes the quadrilateral to reappear in the view.
RedoIt	Overridden method. Redoes the deletion of the quadrilateral and (indirectly) causes the image of the quadrilateral to be removed from the view.
Commit	Overridden method. Frees the quadrilateral that has been removed from the document. Note that MacApp will call this method only if the command was done or redone, and only at a time when the command can no longer be undone.

The methods TClearQuadCmd.DoIt and TClearQuadCmd. Commit present most of the interesting issues in the design of this class:

```
PROCEDURE TClearQuadCmd.DoIt;OVERRIDE;
VAR quadDocument: TQuadDocument;
BEGIN
  quadDocument := TQuadDocument(SELF.fChangedDocument);
  quadDocument.SelectQuad(NIL)
  quadDocument.DeleteQuad(SELF.fQuad);
  quadDocument.InvalidateQuad(SELF.fQuad);
END;

PROCEDURE TClearQuadCmd.Commit; OVERRIDE;
BEGIN
  FreeObject(SELF.fQuad);
END;
```

Note how cleanly the DoIt method expresses in three steps what should be done to clear a quadrilateral:

1. tell the document to deselect it,
2. tell the document to delete it, and then
3. tell the document to have it redrawn. This is an example of being able to express algorithms succinctly in an object-oriented language.

The Commit method need not do anything but free the quadrilateral. This is because if this method is invoked, either TClearQuadCmd.DoIt or TClearQuadCmd.RedoIt will have already taken care of removing the quad from the quadDocument and the quadGrView.

The Class TClearAllCmd

The command object that deletes all quadrilaterals from the quadDocument must store more information than TClearQuadCmd in order to make this operation undoable. A TClearAllCmd object must remember all of the quadrilaterals in the quadDocument and must know which, if any, is selected. The selected quadrilateral must be recorded in the command object so that the state of the application is left unchanged if the **Clear All** command is executed and then undone.

TClearAllCmd Instance Variables

Variable	Use
fLastQuadAdded	Refers to root quadrilateral in the list stored in the quadDocument. By remembering this head object and by not disturbing the links between the quadrilaterals themselves, the entire list can be restored if the command is to be undone.
fSelectedQuad	Refers to the currently selected quadrilateral.

TClearAllCmd Methods

Data Manipulation Methods

Method	Use
IClearAllCmd	Initializes new instances of TClearAllCmd.

MacApp "Hook" Methods

Method	Use
DoIt	Overridden method. Performs the deletion of all the quadrilaterals and (indirectly) causes the entire view to be erased.
UndoIt	Overridden method. Undoes the deletion of the quadrilaterals—reinstalling all the quadrilaterals in the quadDocument—and (indirectly) causes the entire view to be redrawn.
RedoIt	Overridden method. Redoes the deletion of all the quadrilaterals and (indirectly) causes the entire view to be erased.
Commit	Overridden method. Frees all the quadrilaterals. Note that MacApp will call this method only if the command was done or redone, and only at a time when the command can no longer be undone.

Now that you have an idea of how the Mini-QuadWorld application is structured, you must understand more of the flow of control in MacApp before learning how a full MacApp application, QuadWorld, is developed. These topics are discussed in Chapters 7 and 8, respectively.

Notes

An interesting exercise is to modify Mini-QuadWorld so that a mouse press can have two interpretations: a mouse press on a non-selected quadrilateral deselects the current selection and selects the new quadrilateral and a mouse press on the currently selected quadrilateral lets the user to move it. One method that must be changed to provide this new functionality is TQuadGrView.DoMouseCommand—this must enable the DoMouseCommand method to distinguish between these two types of mouse presses. In addition, a new TCommand subclass, TMove-QuadCmd, must be designed to actually move the quadrilateral and MacApp must be told when to turn over control to one of these command objects.

To start you in doing this exercise, here is an indication of where a change should be made in the TQuadGrView. DoMouseCommand method:

```
FUNCTION TQuadGrView.DoMouseCommand
    (VAR downLocalPoint: Point;
    VAR info: EventInfo;
    VAR hysteresis: Point): TCommand; OVERRIDE;

VAR tempQuad:       TQuad;
        { a temporary variable used to find the quad under the cursor }
    selectedQuad:  TQuad;              { the currently selected quad }
  PROCEDURE CheckQuad(thisQuad: TQuad);
  BEGIN
    IF PtInRect(downLocalPoint, thisQuad.EnclosingRect)
      THEN
      tempQuad := thisQuad;
    END;

BEGIN
  DoMouseCommand := gNoChanges;
  tempQuad := NIL;
  selectedQuad := TQuadDocument(SELF.fDocument).
    fSelectedQuad;
  TQuadDocument(SELF.fDocument).EachQuadDo (CheckQuad);
{ tempQuad now refers to the quad, if any, beneath the cursor position }
  IF ((tempQuad < > NIL) AND (selectedQuad = tempQuad))
    THEN
      BEGIN
{Move the quad—This is left as an exercise for the reader. (See text) }
      END
    ELSE
      TQuadDocument(SELF.fDocument).SelectQuad(tempQuad);
                                                  { Tell the document }
END;
```

CHAPTER 6

The Most Frequently Asked Questions about MacApp

At this point you may want to step back and get a more complete picture of MacApp: when to use it, how to obtain it and learn it, how it handles debugging, and how it is evolving as a product. In this chapter we present the most frequently asked questions about MacApp to provide answers for you.

Learning MacApp

Must you learn Object Pascal to use MacApp?

No. While MacApp is written in Object Pascal, you can use the MacApp class library with a variety of languages, most of which are discussed in this book. Some object-oriented languages have radical differences that preclude the possibility of linking libraries in one language with libraries written in another. For these, language-specific MacApp class libraries have been designed so that they have the same class structure, protocols, and class names as the Object Pascal MacApp class library. Usually, the only difference is that the names for method and instance variables may vary slightly because of the naming conventions either required or encouraged in the particular base language.

Must you learn to program with an object-oriented language to use MacApp?

Basically, yes. Even when programming in assembly language, you must use a language that supports the notions of classes, objects, inheritance, messaging, and so on. (In assembly language this is done with macros; in other languages it is done either by modifying the compiler or interpreter or by using a preprocessor.) Typically, the amount of time you spend learning object-oriented programming and one or more object-oriented languages is paid back many times over in increased development speed, application reliability, and improved adherence to the Macintosh User Interface Standard.

How long does it take to learn to use MacApp?

Because most potential users of MacApp do not currently know an object-oriented language, two estimates are necessary: one to learn Object Pascal (or some other object-oriented language) and a second to learn the MacApp class library. These calculate the time required to "feel comfortable with" Object Pascal and MacApp and to be able to use them adequately to accomplish some given task, not necessarily the amount of time needed for an in-depth understanding, and they assume you spend at least half your time on your MacApp project. Typically, experienced Pascal programmers need about two to three weeks to learn to use Object Pascal and another one or two months to learn the MacApp class library. (These are all estimates taken before the existence of this book. This book should lower the learning curve somewhat, or at least make this time less painful.) Of course, there is widespread individual variation in these estimates, but there seem to be two contributing factors. If you have a strong background in programming languages, data structures, and data abstraction (the background gained, for example, in an undergraduate degree in computer science), these estimates will be pretty close and you may learn even quicker than they predict. If you are a dyed-in-the-wool assembly language programmer who never believed in the FORTRAN project, let alone Pascal or C, you can expect the estimates to be relatively crude and probably low. If this seems like a long time to you, just consider how much time you will save in development. The few documented controlled studies indicate that development time using the object-oriented approach is about one-quarter to one-third the time needed when using traditional development paths. In other words, what once would have taken you a year can now be done in a summer. Even if you spent two solid months learning, you would still be ahead (assuming the project would take at least three months in a traditional development path).

What is the best way to learn MacApp?

First, acquire an understanding of the vocabulary and basic concepts of object-oriented programming (Chapter 2) and MacApp (Chapter 3). Then study the two sample MacApp application programs discussed in this book. The Mini-QuadWorld application is explained in Chapter 5 with a full source text in Listing D and the full-QuadWorld application is explained in Chapter 8 with a full source code in Listing E. Although QuadWorld was specifically designed to exhibit most features necessary to begin developing your own application, it does not exhibit every MacApp feature. For example, QuadWorld uses no dialog boxes nor does it access the AppleTalk network. For examples of this sort of MacApp programming, you should look at the MacApp Cookbook and the MacApp sample programs. The MacApp Cookbook contains code fragments that exhibit programming techniques necessary for many other application effects. For example, there is a recipe in the Cookbook for building an application with several different documents and one for designing the TDialog subclass for your application's **About** box. In addition, MacApp is shipped with four or five sample programs that both demonstrate its use and ensure that you have properly installed the libraries. Study these programs to see further examples of complete MacApp applications, especially ones exhibiting different programming techniques than QuadWorld. The next step in learning MacApp is to actually write some small applications. For many people this will be sufficient to start using MacApp. In fact, even if you suspect that there are additional things about MacApp you need to know to implement your application, try to write parts of your application; writing MacApp programs is the best way to learn.

If you need to learn more, consult both the MacApp Reference Manual and the remainder of this book. Each contains a wealth of additional information. The reference manual is best if you have a very specific question about one of the MacApp classes—for example, what are its instance variables and how are they used? Or, what does the Do This method really do? This book is better if you want to learn how to use MacApp with other languages or if you want to learn about other class libraries not compatible with MacApp.

Notes

It seems somewhat counter-intuitive, but often learning about something that is similar but different can increase your understanding of both things. Consider how many American high school students really begin to understand English grammar and structure when they learn a foreign language. Such learning seems to focus your attention on aspects that you previously overlooked. When learning MacApp, also learning the LisaToolkit and the Smalltalk MVC can improve your understanding of all three. (Of course, on the other hand, learning all three could confuse you—each person is different. For me, learning about the others really did increase my understanding all of three considerably.)

Using MacApp

What are the benefits of using MacApp?

The principal benefits of using MacApp are:

- decreased development time.
- consistency and completeness with respect to the Macintosh User Interface Standard.
- improved modularity in the overall design of your application.
- decreased source code bulk.
- use of a symbolic debugger.

Let's discuss these one at a time.

Use of MacApp significantly decreases the development time for an application that adheres to the Macintosh User Interface Standard. The actual reductions vary from project to project but reductions by factors of 3 or 4 are not uncommon. There are two reasons for this: the first is that a significant portion of the application is already provided for you—the features common to all Macintosh applications. What you must program are the features that make your application unique. Second, object-oriented programming encourages you to reuse much of your own code, reducing the code you need to do this.

Almost by definition, applications built on top of the MacApp framework implement the basic features of the Macintosh User Interface Standard in exactly the same way. You are guaranteed, for example, that your windows scroll correctly, that hardcopy output faithfully mirrors the screen image, and that desk accessories are handled correctly. Even if there is some small feature of the Macintosh User Interface Standard previously unknown to you (for example, the new full-screen toggle), it is implemented in your application because it is a part of MacApp.

Using MacApp as a base enables you to modularize the design of your application along fairly natural lines. Once you have analyzed your application in terms of the basic Macintosh features of documents, views, windows, and commands, you can design each necessary subclass of the basic MacApp classes that implement these features. Each subclass can be designed independently of the details of the other subclasses. In addition, the functionality of these basic classes assists you in the organization of your whole application. For example, the code for rendering your application's images is placed in the Draw method of your subclass(es) of TView, your initial processing of a mouse press is in your view's DoMouseCommand method, and menu commands are processed in DoMenuCommand. Each of these pieces of your implementation can be dealt with and designed independently. The interactive features of your application are especially easy to organize in this approach. Adding a new feature (a new menu command, for example) to an application designed in this way is mostly a matter of adding a new subclass of TCommand that can do, undo, and redo that feature, plus adding the code to initiate that feature. (If a feature is initiated by a menu command, then add another element to the **CASE** statement of your DoMenuCommand method; if it is initiated by a mouse action, then in DoMouseCommand, etc.)

The actual amount of source code in a MacApp application is much less than in a corresponding standard procedural implementation of the same function. For example, compare the two functionally similar applications, Chernicoff's Mini-Edit program (2230 lines of Pascal) (Stephen Chernicoff, *Macintosh Revealed, Volume II—Programming with the Toolbox* (Hayden, 1985).) and the much shorter MacApp's TinyEdit sample program (212 lines of Object Pascal). While admittedly you would probably not always achieve a reduction in source code as great as this, you can reasonably expect that implementing in an object-oriented language with the MacApp class library will result in source code reductions in the neighborhood of 10,000 lines. Reductions of this magnitude are typically accompanied by corresponding reductions in maintenance costs across the board (bug correction time, the time needed to add a new feature, and time for a new staff member to understand the implementation, and so on.)

The debugging of most Macintosh applications is done with low-level hexadecimal debuggers like MacsBug and MacDB. MacApp is shipped with a higher-level symbolic debugger described later in this chapter.

In what programming environments can MacApp be used?

Currently, MacApp can be used with two different program development environments: the Lisa Workshop and the Macintosh Programmer's Workshop. The Lisa Workshop was the first development environment for Macintosh and is still used by a large percentage of Macintosh developers. Using MacApp from the Lisa Workshop requires the Macintosh Software Supplement, a set of libraries that allows cross-development for the Macintosh. MacApp is fully compatible with these libraries and with the Lisa Workshop—in fact, that is where MacApp was developed and where most of the early MacApp testers (including the author) used it. Loading the various MacApp libraries only adds about 570K to the other libraries needed for Macintosh development.

MacApp can also be used from the Macintosh Programmer's Workshop (MPW)—this is where the final development and test of MacApp took place. Apple intends for this development environment to become the mainstay of all Macintosh development—both MacApp and non-MacApp.

All of the sample programs in this book and all of the code fragments listed here have been tested in both these development environments.

Warning

Note that as Apple continues to wind down its support for Lisa and thus for the Lisa Workshop, the number of MacApp developers using Lisa will decrease. At some point, Apple will probably begin discouraging the continued use of the Lisa Workshop and eventually actually withdraw its support of it.

Can I convert my application, about half finished in standard Pascal, to the MacApp framework? Is there a way to automatically convert it to MacApp?

Unfortunately, no. The high-level structure of your application must be redesigned to fit into the MacApp framework. How difficult this will be depends on how modular you have made your design up to this point. The more modular, the easier. While the high-level design must often be redone, much of the detailed code you have developed can be reused without change. If, for example, you have been designing a new application to assist a biochemist view the three-dimensional shapes of certain chemical compounds, most of the application-specific code that handles this (drawing the molecules, interacting with that drawing, analyzing the stability of the compound, and so on) can be reused in your MacApp application.

For what types of applications is MacApp most suitable as a foundation?

Almost all, but especially vertical applications, those for yourself, for internal use in your organization, or where being the first application to market in your area of specialization is important.

For what types of applications is MacApp unsuitable?

Desk accessories and those rare applications with extremely tight performance (for example, real-time control of chemical plant) or extremely tight space requirements (say, your prototype barely fits in 512K and you have 50 new major features to add).

What application features are difficult to do in MacApp?

Without a doubt, the hardest features to put into a MacApp application are those that directly violate the Macintosh User Interface Standard. To add such a feature (using the term "feature" loosely), you would have to understand MacApp well enough to find the place where the standard behavior was implemented and override it to provide your own behavior. Clearly, the fact that this type of task is possible but difficult is not a deficiency of MacApp, but rather one of its strengths. If you adhere to the Macintosh User Interface Standard, the implementation path is cleared for you by the MacApp team; if you violate it, obstacles are strewn in your way.

The next most difficult types of features to add to a MacApp application are those that extend the Macintosh User Interface Standard in a way no other application has done before. The designers of MacApp studied the user interfaces of every piece of Macintosh software that they could find to make sure their framework was general enough to provide support for that way of doing things or at least not get in the way of an implementer who wanted to do things that way. In addition, they tried to anticipate other user interfaces and provide support for those, too. But they couldn't think of everything and if the way you want to structure the user interface is totally new, you may encounter some difficulties. It is hard to come up with an example that fits in this category, both because by its very nature totally new styles of user interaction not in conflict with the Macintosh User Interface Standard are hard to imagine, and because if I write one down here, the MacApp team will see it and provide some support for this new feature just to prove me wrong! Nevertheless, here is one example: you want your end users to be able to control interactively the amount by which the frame scrolls when the scroll bar controls are activated. Your user interface is that a mouse-down in the scroll bar scrolls by a fixed amount, a mouse-down in the scroll bar while the command key is depressed scrolls by twice that amount, and a mouse down while the shift key is depressed scrolls by three times that amount. This would be difficult to do in MacApp.

What are the speed/space penalties for using MacApp?

Because MacApp has to be quite general to provide a framework for all Macintosh applications, it has some code that your particular application may never need, plus numerous methods you override rather than execute. In most cases, the methods most applications override have been made deliberately small so that, typically, the space penalty is only about 10K to 15K. Note that the space penalty is a constant, so that the penalty is proportionally smaller for large applications.

For many developers, this small space penalty is more than offset by the reduction in development time.

Although it seems almost unbelievable, some MacApp programs actually run faster than their non-MacApp versions, despite the run-time overhead of messaging. This is because MacApp contains many of the best programming techniques that have been used across the board in Macintosh applications—techniques you would have to work for years to discover. Moreover, MacApp was designed by individuals who know the Macintosh inside and out—knowledge, again, it would take years to acquire. By merging their expert knowledge of Macintosh with your expert knowledge in your field, the result is better than either you or they could have accomplished alone. Also, messaging often is faster than the programming construct it most often replaces: **CASE** statements. Worst case, you can expect no more than a 10 percent performance penalty because you used MacApp as the framework upon which your application is built. In some cases, your application will actually be faster because you used MacApp.

Debugging MacApp application

How do you debug a MacApp application?

Debugging a MacApp program, like debugging any program on Macintosh—or, in fact, any program—is an art best learned through experience. However, debugging a MacApp program is aided by the existence of a high-level, symbolic debugger that has the following features:

- It is interactive. You can interrupt your application manually, enter the debugger, issue any number of debugging commands, see the results of those commands, and then continue your application from the interrupt point.

- It is automatically invoked when a Motorola 68000 exception such as division by zero has occurred or when the SysError routine that would normally display the bomb alert is called.
- It can trace the flow of control among the procedures and methods of your application, listing those procedures and methods by name.
- It can be used to "single step" through your application one procedure or one method at a time.
- It has its own special debugging window so the debugger output does not disturb the normal windows of your application.
- It can redirect all debugger output to a file for later examination.
- It can display the class and instance variables of any object, though the instance variables are only displayed in hexadecimal.

Figure 6-1 shows the debugger in use while the full implementation of QuadWorld (see Chapter 8) was being developed. For further information on the MacApp debugger and for detailed instruction on its use, consult the MacApp Reference Manual.

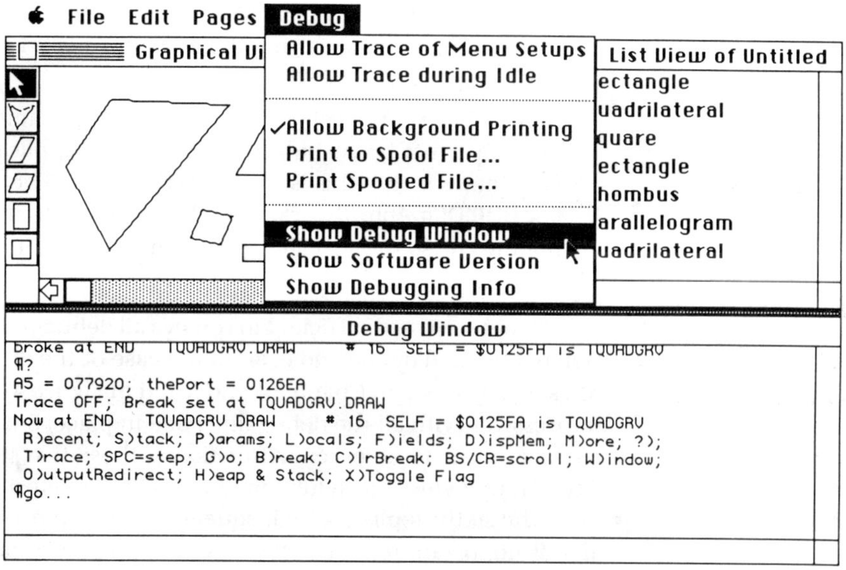

Figure 6-1 The MacApp Interactive Debugger in use. Note that the debugger output is directed to its own special window and that there is a special Debug menu for use with this window. The debugger window shows the method at which the debugger was invoked (TQuadGrView.Draw), which object received the Draw message that resulted in the invocation of this method (an instance of TQuadGrView, whose handle is stored at location $0125FA), and the verbose-mode debugger prompt.

How do I prepare a MacApp application developed with debugging code for shipment as a finished application?

When using the Lisa Workshop, there are five things you must do and a sixth that is optional. Fortunately, all but the sixth are easy to do. The first five are:

1. Change the five compile-time debugging flags in the UObject unit to FALSE. These flags are qNames (which controls whether procedure names are recorded for use in the MacApp debugger), qRangeCheck (which controls whether range checking of array subscripts is activated), qWriteLnWin (which controls the generation of the debugger window), qDebug (which controls the inclusion of miscellaneous debugging statements), and qTrace (which controls whether information is recorded so that tracing can take place.)
2. Change the debugging flag DEBUGF in Patch.A.Text to 0. This flag is a control similar to qNames.
3. Change the debugging flag DEBUGF in Object.A.Text to 0. This flag is a control similar to qNames.
4. Remove the debugging menu from your application's RMaker input file (or equivalent, if you are using the Macintosh Workshop).
5. Recompile your application. Note that because you have just changed the files that are at the very root of the MacApp framework, everything about MacApp must be recompiled before your application is recompiled. The good news is that this is transparent to you. The same one-line command ("<BUILD(myApp)") works. The bad news is that it will take a while—20 minutes or so for a small application. However, this is not something done every day.

These steps are sufficient to remove all debugging code and most information not needed by the end user. In the case of the Small Application (MacApp Mickey developed in Chapter 4 and listed in Figure 4-7), the results were most impressive. With all the debugging code in place, Small Application was 104K (103936 bytes, to be exact). After taking these five steps, the application was 51K (51200 bytes)—a reduction of 53K (52736 bytes).

The sixth step is useful if squeezing a few more bytes from your application is important to you. When a MacApp application is linked, methods that will never be called are put into a segment whose name is gNever. (An example of such a method is TApplication.DoMakeDocument. Every MacApp application must override this method, so this base method will never be called. The compiler would complain, however, if it were not present when the MacApp class library was compiled.) If you have any other methods that will never be called—for example, in one of your abstract superclasses—you should use the compiler segmentation command, {$S gNever }, to place them in this segment, too. There is no reason for this segment to be shipped with the final version of the application. To remove it you need to use the Resource Editor on the result of step 5 above. This would have saved only 500 bytes to 800 bytes in Small Application, for example, so you may not want to bother in your applications.

The details of converting to a finished application if you are using the Macintosh Programmer's Workshop were not definite at the time of this writing. They will be, however, conceptually similar and probably easier to perform.

Obtaining MacApp

Do you have to license MacApp from Apple if you use it to develop a Macintosh application that you wish to market?

Yes. Applications that use MacApp, certain portions of the Software Supplement, or certain portions of the MPW libraries must be licensed from Apple for a nominal annual fee. For additional information, contact Apple's Software Licensing Department. (The address for this department, as well as for all the other vendors whose object-oriented languages are discussed in this book, can be found in Appendix B.)

Evolution of MacApp

Why didn't MacApp exist before?

Two reasons: timing and technology. MacApp represents the embodiment of much of the knowledge gained by the designers of applications that shipped during the first 18 months of the Macintosh's life (January 1984 – July 1985). Before this knowledge could be packaged in a reusable form that was both general enough to be the basis for other applications and fast enough not to penalize the developers who used it, that knowledge had to be refined. Second, the technology of hybrid object-oriented languages is still relatively new. Smalltalk, the ancestor of all the modern object-oriented languages, was only completed in 1980. Objective-C (discussed in Chapter 13) was first shipped in 1983, and Clascal (Chapter 12) in 1984. The technology upon which MacApp is based has only recently become available.

What are the future directions for MacApp?

Apple, of course, does not publicly reveal its plans for any of its software and MacApp is no exception. My personal suggestions to Apple for future development include the following:

- Increase the functionality by adding more new units that optionally can be linked to your application. Some possible units are URuler (used to construct rulers like those used in MacWrite, Microsoft Word, and MacDraw), UPalette (used to construct palettes, keyboards, and lists), UDraw (a 32-bit coordinate version of QuickDraw and TView, for those applications that need a larger virtual drawing space), and UCollection (used to construct and manage lists, queues, sets, etc).
- Improve the speed of MacApp by recoding some parts of MacApp in hand-crafted assembly language.
- Lower the space penalty for using MacApp by recoding some parts of MacApp in hand-crafted assembly language, changing the way in which linking is done so that methods that will never be called may be stripped out, and moving parts of MacApp to system files or ROM so that they can be shared between MacApp applications running from the same disk (in the case of system files).
- Encourage other language products (both new languages and other compilers for existing languages) to provide access to MacApp, especially Macintosh Pascal, the Pascal interpreter. (Note that this implies adding all the features of Object Pascal to Macintosh Pascal.)
- Provide a means by which MacApp developers can exchange or market their new MacApp units.
- Provide a framework for a multi-level undo in MacApp in order to encourage this in future Macintosh applications. (Currently most Macintosh applications support only a single level undo—only the most recent operation can be undone. In an application with multi-level undo, the user can keep undoing operations, up to some reasonable limit, say five or ten operations.)
- Provide development tools to assist the MacApp programmer specifically, such as an intelligent window editor that would allow you to design interactively many window features for the application being coded and store those windows in a resource file that could be read by MacApp.
- Continue to update and revise MacApp so that it takes advantage of features of new members of the Macintosh family, thus insulating the application programmer from hardware changes.
- Use MacApp internally in Apple for new Macintosh software products. (This will have the effect of increasing the likelihood that the earlier suggestions will be followed.)

CHAPTER

7

The Flow of Events in MacApp

One of the most unusual aspects of designing a MacApp application is giving up the top-level control you usually have over an application's flow of control. For example, in a MacApp application, when you design a TCommand subclass, you usually override the methods TCommand.DoIt, TCommand.UndoIt, and TCommand.RedoIt. The methods you supply your subclass will provide the appropriate behavior for that command. After this is done, you pretty much forget about when these methods will be called. MacApp will invoke the correct method depending upon whether the user chooses the associated menu item for this command object, chooses **Undo** after choosing this menu command, or chooses **Redo** after having chosen **Undo.** All you, the application programmer, do is design the methods to implement the appropriate things whenever they are called. While this lack of control is really a simplification for the application programmer, it does take some getting used to. Many programmers over react by studying the internal details of MacApp in depth before beginning to design their first MacApp program. While a general understanding of MacApp is necessary for the programmer designing a first MacApp application, poring over the MacApp source listings is usually not necessary. When designing an application with the MacApp framework, the main thing is to bear in mind that it is especially important to design your methods defensively—you never know who will call them!

There are three different diagramming notations you can use to study MacApp's flow of control and in this chapter we introduce them and give a detailed examination of selected portions of the MacApp code to illustrate specifc instances of control flow within MacApp. Each diagramming notation has its particular strengths and weaknesses and each is best used in different situations. The first notation graphs the flow of control by depicting each method in the control flow as a rectangle and different types of flow constructs between these methods as different types of lines. In this notation, called *flow arrow notation*, a row of method rectangles with horizontal arrows between them (Figure 7-1) indicates straight sequential control flow—after method A comes method B, followed by C, and so on. In this situation the flow of control is from left to right.

Figure 7-1 The most elementary construct in the flow arrow notation: sequential execution.

When two methods are connected by an arrow pointing back toward the lower left (Figure 7-2), then while executing, method A "calls" method B, so that the flow of control goes from method A to method B, but then the flow of control returns to A when B has finished executing.

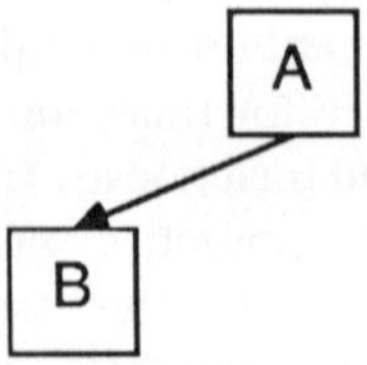

Figure 7-2 The flow arrow notation for the invocation of one method by another. In this example, method A invokes method B.

You can also indicate conditional control flow with flow arrow notation. This is done with a schematic (Figure 7-3) showing that during the execution of method A, methods B, C, D, E, and F may be invoked, depending upon the conditions represented by ovals, that apply. The flow of control may pass from method A to method B and, if so, it then returns to A; it then may pass from method A to method C and, if so, it then returns to A, and so on.

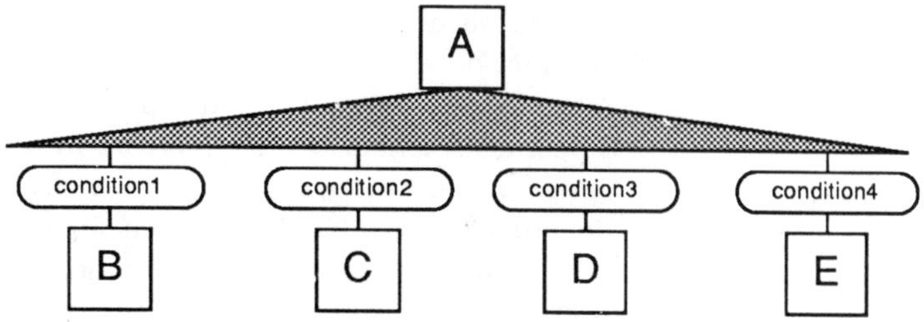

Figure 7-3 The flow arrow notation for conditional flow of control.

Notes

Clearly, this flow arrow notation is useful only for conceptually understanding the flow of control of programs, but not for writing them. The notation is nowhere near precise enough for writing programs.

You can combine these three constructs to show the overall flow of control as in the small hypothetical example shown in Figure 7-4. In this example, the sequence of method calls is A - B - C - D - E - F - G; then perhaps one or more of G1, G2, and G3; then back to G; followed by H - I - J - K. You can see that in this notation, downward arrows have precedence over horizontal ones—which is exactly what you would expect for the control flow of "subroutine" invocation and sequential execution.

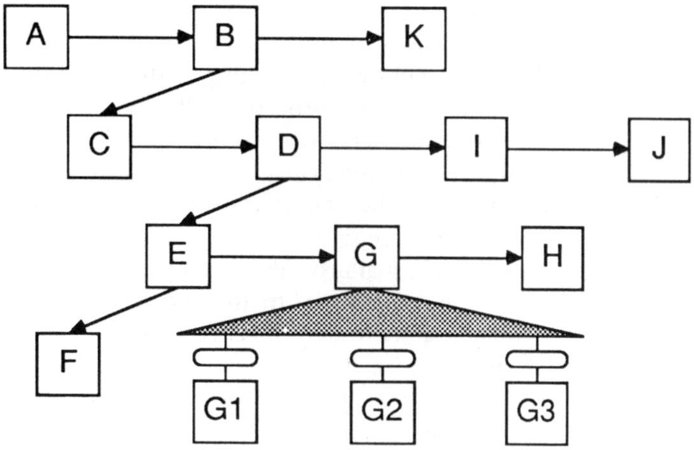

Figure 7-4 An example of flow arrow notation exhibiting all of the basic flow arrow constructs.

When flow arrow notation is actually used, the method rectangles each contain more detail than shown in these templates. When actually used, each method rectangle has the structure shown in Figure 7-5. This flow arrow notation is best used when the "big picture" of how some entire process, such as launching an application, is being discussed. Flow arrow diagrams help you see how the entire system hangs together. They are less useful when you wish to turn your attention on any specific situation, such as the appearance of a single menu when a mouse event occurs. For this you need another diagramming technique.

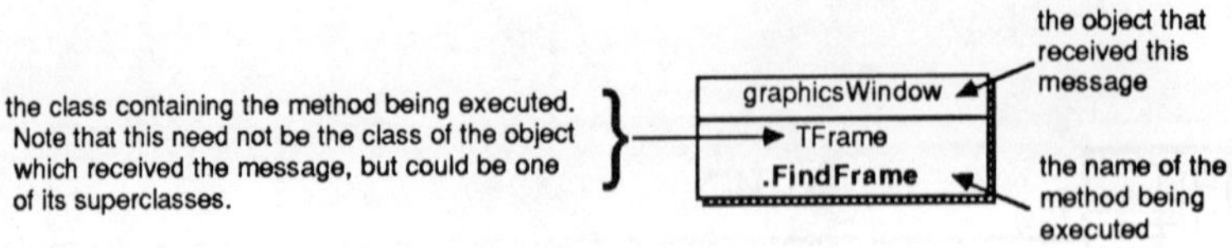

Figure 7-5 The detailed structure of a single mode in flow arrow notation.

The second diagramming technique, called *flow nest diagrams*, represents flow of control by a set of nested rounded-corner boxes and rectangles. Each box or rectangle represents a MacApp method, a MacApp global procedure, a Toolbox routine, one of your own methods, or an Object Pascal statement that is important to the overall flow of control. Like flow arrow diagramming notation, flow nest diagrams let you see the important elements of the MacApp flow of control. They are not as precise as the code itself since they remove details not necessary for the conceptual understanding of how a particular user input, such as resizing a window, is processed. In flow diagrams, placing boxes within other boxes, denotes that the enclosed procedure is called by the enclosing procedure. In the example shown in Figure 7-6, procedure A contains a call to procedures B and D. Procedure B contains a call to procedure C. The flow of control is therefore A - B - C - D. Because they can represent more than just method calls and because they can be generated automatically from code, flow diagrams are used extensively in the MacApp Reference Manual.

The strength of the flow nest diagram is in what it omits. Figure 7-6 does not imply that procedure A invokes only procedures B and D—it merely states that it does invoke them. Details inessential detail to the task at hand are deliberately removed. While flow arrow notation also shares this property of selectively omitting details, flow nest notation is best when you wish to examine only those procedures involved in a specific task.

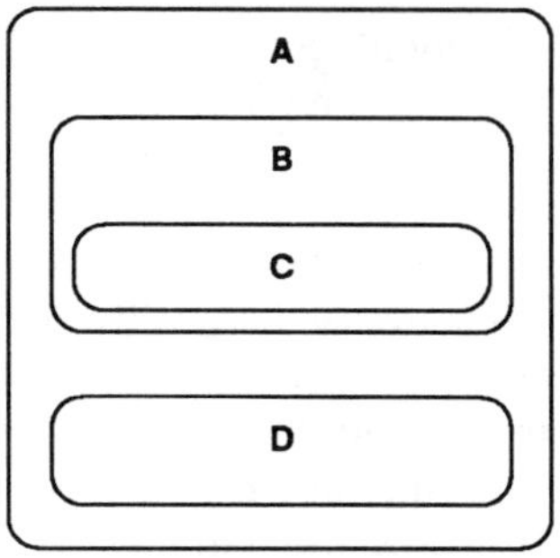

Figure 7-6 An example of the flow nest notation.

Both flow arrow diagrams and flow nest diagrams are relatively precise and detailed diagramming techniques. This is both an advantage and a disadvantage. At those times when a wealth of detail is needed, these techniques are appropriate. When large amounts of detail may confuse rather than clarify, a third diagramming technique called *conceptual diagrams* can be used. These diagrams are nowhere near as precise as the other types of diagrams. This technique merely represents artistically the portion of the flow of control under study in a way that provides a more global understanding.

We will use one or more of these techniques to represent the MacApp flow of control in several areas:

- the activation of a MacApp application, called the application's launching.
- the main MacApp event loop, where the interactive events initiated by the end user (mouse clicks, key presses, menu command activations) are first handled.
- command processing.
- application-dependent processing of mouse clicks.

While these don't exhaustively cover all of MacApp, they are the areas in which the beginning MacApp programmer most often needs to override MacApp in order to customize the application being developed.

Application Launching

When a MacApp application is launched, the basic actions that take place are:

- your application object is created in your main program.
- your application object creates one or more of your document objects depending on which icons the user opens from the Finder. If multiple document objects are created, they maybe all of the same class or instances of separate TDocument subclasses.

- your document object creates its view(s) and its window(s) and installs the view(s) in the window(s).
- the window(s) is opened and the application awaits the first user event.

These steps are shown in more detail, using flow arrow notation, in Figure 7-7. This figure depicts the simplest flow of control for application launching. Sometimes a complex MacApp application will add some new methods or otherwise modify this basic flow of control. However, even for an application like the full implementation of QuadWorld (Chapter 8), which has more than one window and many views, there is no need to modify the launching flow to provide for the additional windows. Mini-QuadWorld (Chapter 5) is another example of fitting an application to the MacApp launching sequence. In that application the document object is prefabricated, with five quad objects installed in the document when it is first allocated. The null method TDocument. DoInitialState is designed for just this purpose. The basic DoInitialState method in the TDocument class, like all null methods, does nothing; the overridden TQuadDocument.DoInitialState in the Mini-QuadWorld application is invoked during application launching (right after DoMakeDocument and right before DoMakeView), and it creates and installs the five fixed quadrilaterals in the document.

MacApp Main Event Loop

Macintosh applications are event-driven—that is, their execution is structured around the asychronous occurrence of a wide variety of user interactions. A MacApp application processes these events in its main event loop. Basically, the main event loop cycles endlessly through the following steps:

- get the next event, if one exists, from the event queue.
- if an event is found, process the event, perhaps allocating a new command object to take responsibility for doing and undoing the indicated action.
- if no event is found, execute an Idle method that provides for "background" processes.

Figure 7-8 presents this flow of control in more detail. Note the large number of different event types (mouseUp, mouseDown, updateEvent, key Event, activateEvent, switcherEvent, and even an alienEvent) for which Mac App provides. Most MacApp applications make little or no modification to this framework.

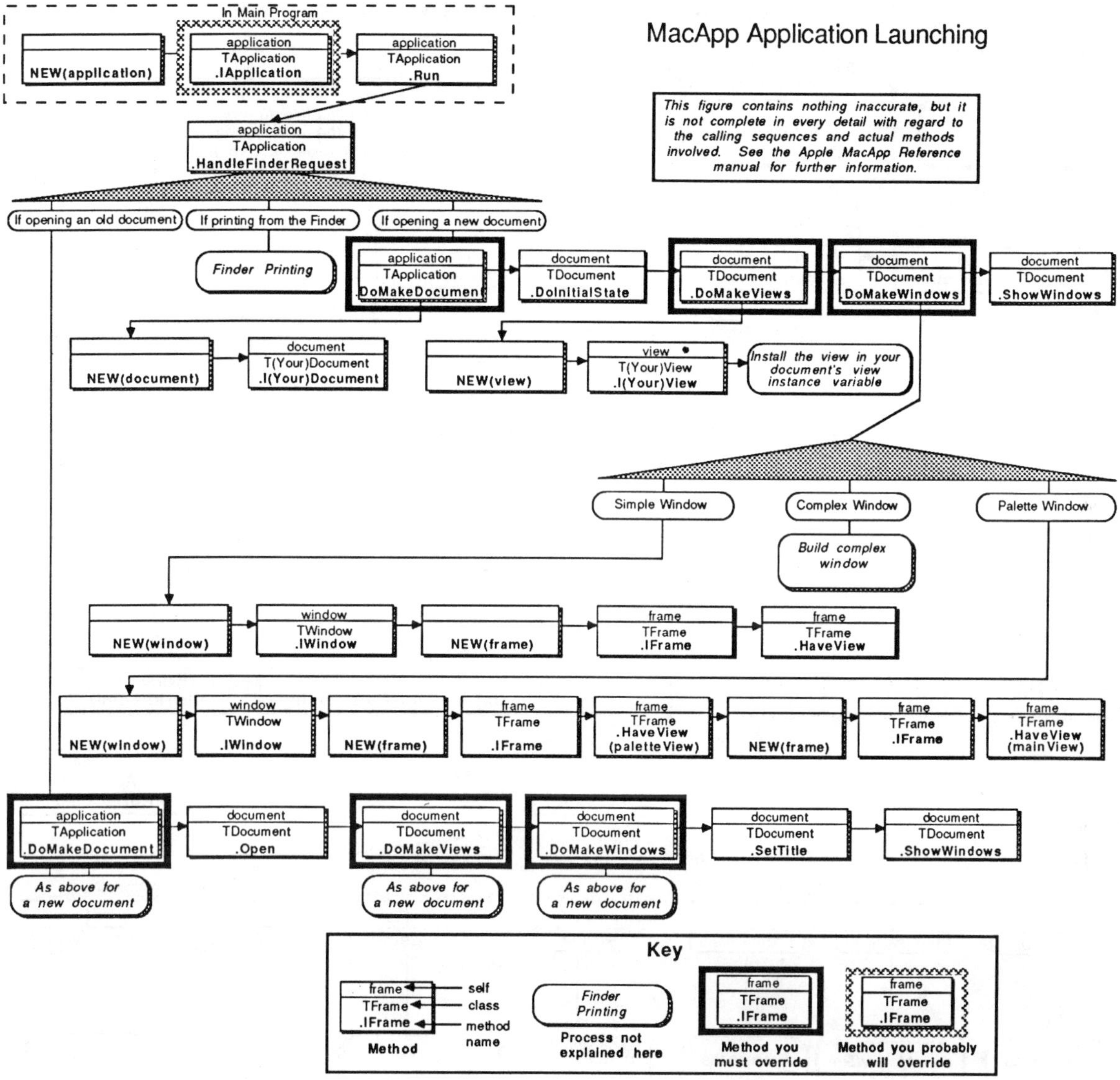

Figure 7-7 The basic flow of control in MacApp for launching an application.

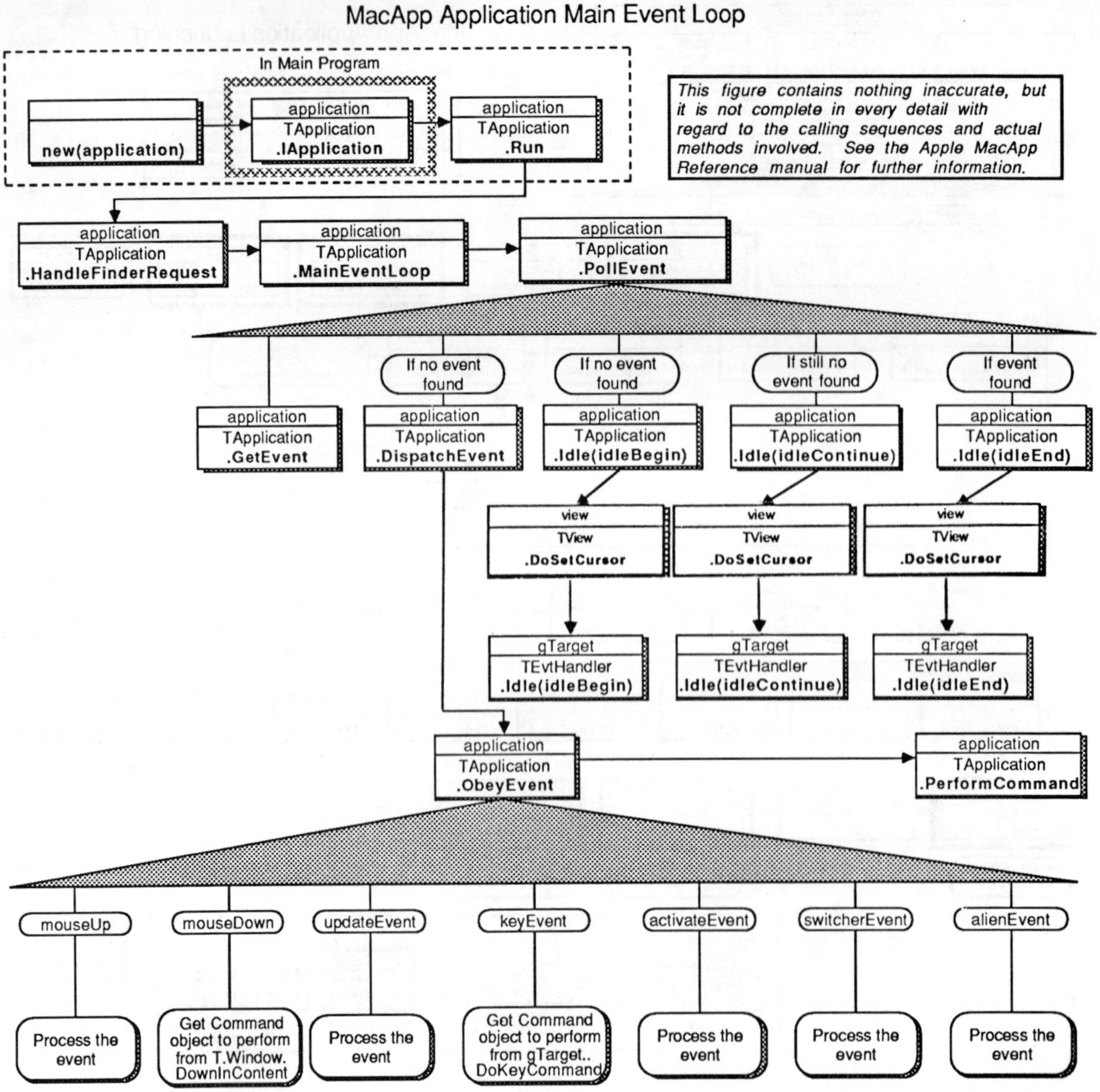

Figure 7-8 The flow of control in the MacApp main event loop.

When an interactive event initiated by the end user does occur, the series of methods actually executed depends on two things:

- which methods you have overridden and how you have overridden them.
- which instance of class TEvtHandler is given the first chance to process the event. (Note that all basic MacApp classes except TCommand are subclasses of TEvtHandler, and thus all can potentially process events.)

You have control over both of these. You decide which methods to reimplement in your descendent classes (thus overriding the standard methods) and determine the initial event handler by setting a global variable named gTarget.

gTarget references the event handler that will have the first chance to process the event. It is set to reference the most specific object (the lowest one in the ownership hierarchy from TApplication to TDocument to TView—usually a TView object) that contains the current selection. If there is no current selection, then gTarget is the active window. If there is no active window, then gTarget is the application object itself.

While your application is responsible for properly maintaining the value of gTarget, there is usually little to do in this regard after gTarget is set initially because MacApp changes the value of gTarget using standard, and usually adequate, conventions. For example, MacApp sets gTarget to the view shown in the active window whenever the user changes windows. Moreover, you do not even need to set the initial value of gTarget if you use the MacApp functions NewSimpleWindow or NewPaletteWindow because these routines will initialize gTarget for you.

Notes

Referring back to the application launching sequence in Figure 7-7, you need only worry about properly initializing gTarget if you build your own complex window. If you do so, you should use the source code for NewPaletteWindow and NewSimpleWindow as models.

The event handling sequence for menu and keyboard events, for a variety of values of gTarget, is shown in Figure 7-9. (The event handling for mouse events is handled a little differently and is covered later in this chapter.) If gTarget is your application object (which is the case only when there are no open documents and thus no windows or views), then there are potentially two chances for the event to be processed: by the methods of your application class and by the methods of TApplication. Among the menu commands, the responsibilities between these classes are:

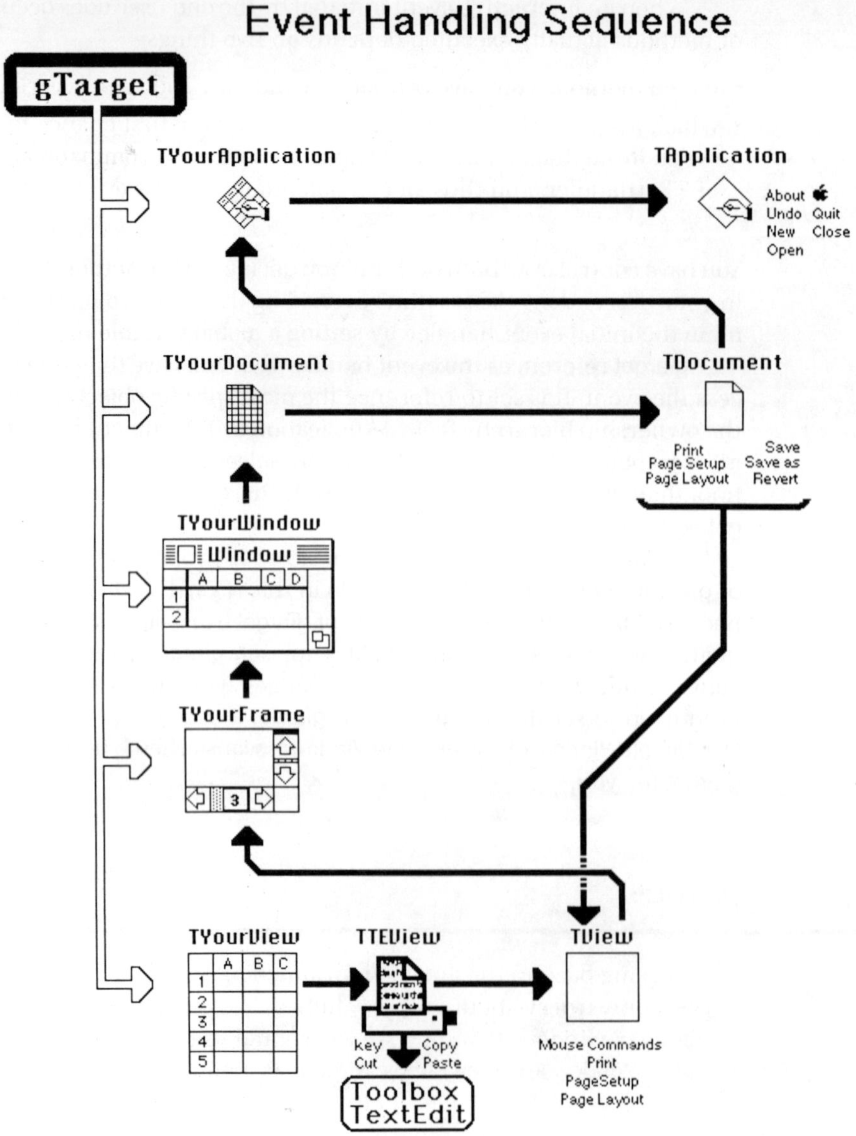

Figure 7-9 The possible event handling sequence for menu and keyboard events. The exact path a single event takes through this network depends on the value of gTarget—the first event handler that attempts to process this event.

T(Your)Application	TApplication
Anything you want, but typically commands that are "above" the level of individual documents or windows, *i.e.*, help commands, or the **About. . .** command.	All menu commands **New** **Close** **Quit** **Undo** **Open**

If gTarget is an instance of one of your TDocument subclasses, then the methods of your subclass are given the first chance to process the event, and the methods of TDocument are given the next chance. Typically, among these two classes, the division of menu command responsibilities is:

T(Your)Document	TDocument
Anything you want, but typically commands that are germane to a single document, but not just to one of its windows or views, *e.g.*, convert to (the newer) XYZ internal format.	**Save** **Save As** **Revert** **Print** **Page Setup**

If a given event cannot be processed by the methods of either document class, then the event is passed on to the application object. Thus, when a menu event like **Undo** occurs and gTarget is a document object, the DoMenuCommand methods of T(Your)Document, TDocument, T(Your)Application, and TApplication are invoked. (As you will see shortly, the DoMenuCommand of TEvtHandler also is invoked.). Let's illustrate exactly what is happening here with a hypothetical example and examine the internals of each method to follow the flow of control. Here are the methods in the order they are invoked when the user chooses **Undo** from the Edit menu. The code in each method that will be executed to invoke the next method in the event handling sequence is underlined (Some of the MacApp methods reproduced here have been slightly abbreviated, but are otherwise faithful to the actual code of MacApp).

```
FUNCTION TMyDocument.DoMenuCommand(aCmdNumber: CmdNumber):
  TCommand; OVERRIDE;

BEGIN
  IF aCmdNumber = cConvert
    THEN DoMenuCommand := SELF.FormatConversion
    ELSE DoMenuCommand :=INHERITED DoMenuCommand
      (aCmdNumber);

END;

FUNCTION TDocument.DoMenuCommand(aCmdNumber: CmdNumber):
  TCommand; OVERRIDE;

BEGIN
  DoMenuCommand := gNoChanges;
  IF (cPrFileBase <= aCmdNumber) AND (aCmdNumber <= cPrFileMax)
    THEN
      BEGIN
        IF fDocPrinter <> NIL THEN
          DoMenuCommand := fDocPrinter.DoPrintingCommand
            (aCmdNumber);
      END
    ELSE
      CASE aCmdNumberOF
        cSaveAs: BEGIN . . . END;
        cSave:BEGIN . . . END;
        cRevert: BEGIN . . . END;
        OTHERWISE DoMenuCommand := INHERITED DoMenuCommand
          (aCmdNumber);
      END;
END;

FUNCTION TEvtHandler.DoMenuCommand(aCmdNumber: CmdNumber):
  TCommand;

BEGIN
  IF fNextHandler <> NIL
    THEN DoMenuCommand := fNextHandler.DoMenuCommand
      (aCmdNumber)
    ELSE
      BEGIN
        WriteLn ('No one handled the command ', aCmdNumber);
        DoMenuCommand := gNoChanges;
      END;

END;
```

```
FUNCTION TMyApplication.DoMenuCommand(aCmdNumber:
  CmdNumber): TCommand;OVERRIDE;

BEGIN
  IF aCmdNumber = cConvertAllDocuments
    THEN DoMenuCommand := SELF.FormatConversion
    ELSE DoMenuCommand :=INHERITED DoMenuCommand
      (aCmdNumber);

END;

FUNCTION TApplication.DoMenuCommand(aCmdNumber: CmdNumber):
  TCommand; OVERRIDE;

BEGIN
  DoMenuCommand := gNoChanges;
  CASE aCmdNumberOF
    cQuit:BEGIN . . . END;
    cNew..cNewLast:BEGIN . . . END;
    cOpen..cOpenLast:BEGIN . . . END;
    cClose:BEGIN . . . END;
    cShowClipboard:BEGIN . . . END;
    cExpandWindow:BEGIN . . . END;
    cAboutApp:BEGIN . . . END;
    cUndo:BEGIN . . . END;
    OTHERWISE DoMenuCommand :=INHERITED DoMenuCommand
      (aCmdNumber);

END;

FUNCTION TEvtHandler.DoMenuCommand(aCmdNumber: CmdNumber):
  TCommand;

BEGIN
  IF fNextHandler < > NIL
    THEN DoMenuCommand := fNextHandler.DoMenuCommand
      (aCmdNumber)
    ELSE
      BEGIN
        WriteLn ('No one handled the command ', aCmdNumber);
        DoMenuCommand := gNoChanges;
      END;

END;
```

If, for example, the **Undo** menu item is chosen and the current value of gTarget is an instance of TMyDocument, which is where the command number for **Undo** is processed (in TMyDocument.DoMenuCommand). This method cannot process the global constant cUndo and thus invokes its overridden method (TDocument.DoMenuCommand). TDocument.DoMenuCommand cannot process cUndo either and thus invokes its overridden method (TEvtHandler.DoMenuCommand). This is where the transition is made from the document methods to the application methods. Your document object, as an instance of class TEvtHandler, has an instance variable, fNextHandler, which references the next handler to pass the event to if it can't handle the event. In the case of an instance of TMyDocument, this instance variable references the application object and thus the TMyApplication.DoMenuCommand method is called. This method cannot process cUndo either and thus invokes its overridden method (TApplication.DoMenuCommand). This method can handle this event. It undoes the last command (by a process detailed in the next section) and this calling sequence unwinds to return to the original caller of TMyDocument.DoMenuCommand. (Note that if TApplication.DoMenuCommand could not have handled the event, then the method TEvtHandler.DoMenuCommand would have been called again, in which case the object being sent the message would be your application object. Its fNextHandler instance variable is **NIL**, and thus the WriteLn in TEvtHandler.DoMenuCommand would have been executed, indicating a program error.)

Notes

Note that in the code fragment listed above, the method TEvtHandler. DoMenuCommand is listed twice. This is because this method is potentially invoked twice during the flow of control in the processing of a menu event. In memory, of course, the method only occurs once.

Command Processing—Choosing a Menu Command

In designing some kinds of application-dependent processing in a MacApp application, it is often necessary to understand exactly what series of actions are taken by MacApp in response to specific user actions. While this book cannot cover all such possible actions, it discusses one of the most common ones—ones that you certainly need to understand when you design almost any MacApp application: the choice of a menu command. Other actions are covered in detail in the MacApp Reference Manual.

Figure 7-10 shows the MacApp flow of control for the choice of a menu command in flow nest notation. The steps of this processing are discussed below:

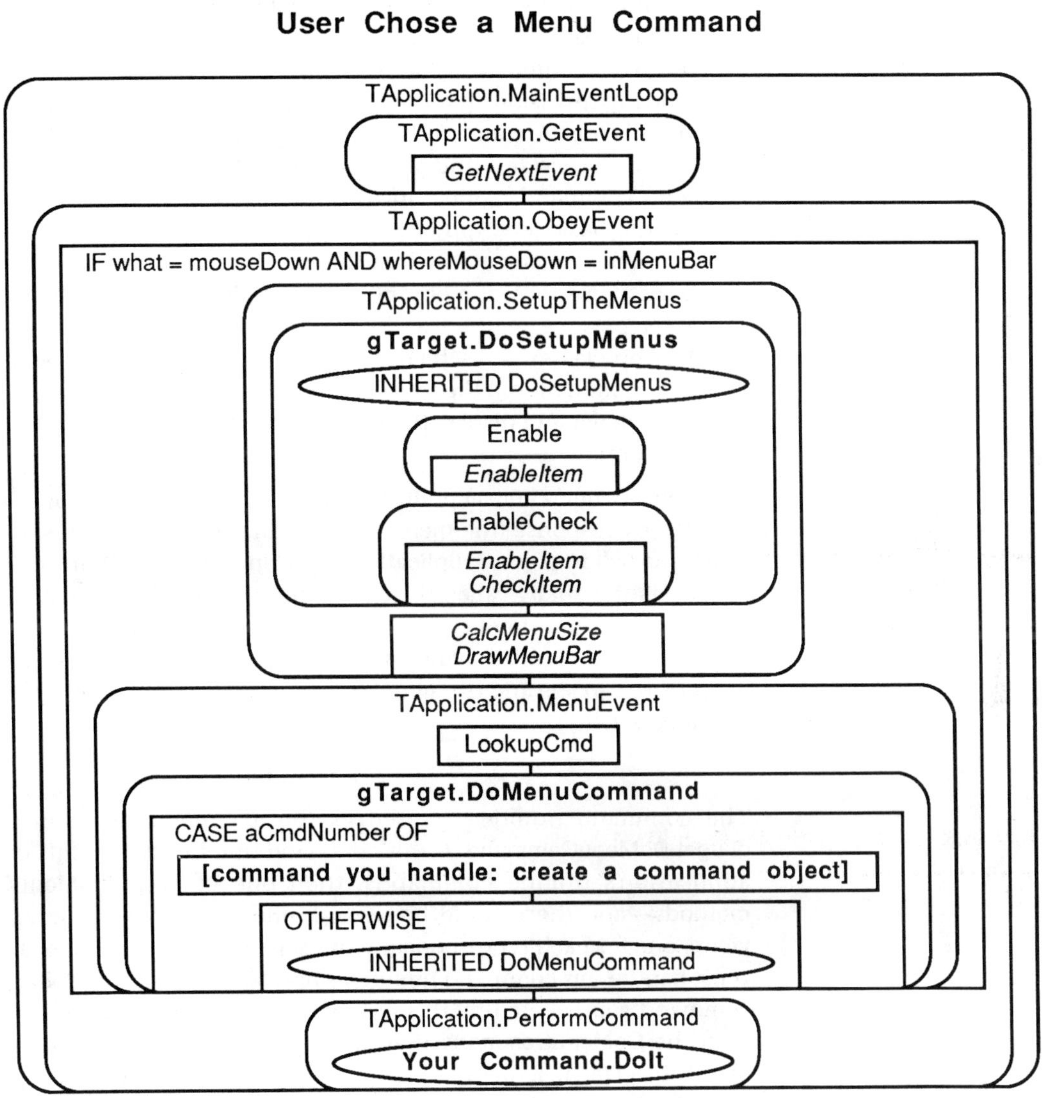

Figure 7-10 The MacApp flow of control in the processing of a menu activation in flow nest notation.

- During the execution of the MacApp main event loop, a mouse-down event in the menu bar is connected to a command number through the following steps:

  1. The appropriate menu—the one whose title is beneath the cursor position recorded in the mouseDown event—is constructed and displayed by executing the method gTarget.DoSetupMenus (among other things). This method enables (and possibly checks) each menu item that can be handled. This is done by invoking the procedure Enable (commandNumber, BooleanExpression) for each command. Note that your methods does this only for the commands unique to your application. Any DoSetMenus that you override—and you will do so if your application has unique menu commands—must invoke the inherited DoSetupMenus in order that the basic MacApp classes (TApplication, TView, TDocument, etc.) are given a chance to enable the menu items they handle (e.g., **Save, Print, Open**). Any menu items not explicitly enabled by one of your DoSetupMenus method or by one of the DoSetupMenus in the basic MacApp classes is disabled. When this information has been gathered for all commands in the menu, the appropriate Toolbox routines is called to construct and display the menu and handle the user interaction with the menu.
  2. Should a menu item actually be chosen by the user, MacApp converts the Toolbox response (the menu number and the item number packed into one word) into your application's appropriate menu item constant. This constant, usually called the *command number*, can be any integer you want, but it must not conflict with the range of integers used by MacApp for the commands it handles. The range reserved by Apple for MacApp is from 1 to 999 and the actual constants used in MacApp 1.0 are listed in Table 7-1.

- The command number is used as the argument in an invocation of gTarget.DoMenuCommand. If this command number represents one of your application's unique commands, then one of your DoMenuCommand methods—and there could be several: one for each of your application's views, one for each type of document used by your application, and so on—must handle this command number. There are two ways of doing this. If the command represented by this number is undoable or otherwise complex, then the DoMenuCommand that handles this number must create a command object (an instance of a subclass of TCommand), initialize it, and return it to MacApp. MacApp will invoke the methods of this command object as needed. (The exact mechanisms of this use of command objects by MacApp is described in the next section of this chapter.) If the command represented by this number is relatively simple, or if for some reason it is not undoable, then you may perform the appropriate computation to effect this command directly in the DoMenuCommand method that handles this number. Note that like DoSetupMenus, your DoMenuCommand method should invoke the overridden DoMenuCommand method to give MacApp the chance to handle the commands that are not application-unique.

Definitions

There is a stronger correspondence between DoSetupMenus and DoMenuCommand than the mere fact that each must override its corresponding methods in MacApp superclasses. For each DoSetupMenusDoMenuCommand pair in your subclasses, the same menu items must be handled. Thus, if your TSpecialView.DoSetupMenus enables the **Foo** menu item, your TSpecialView.DoMenuCommand must handle the command number associated with the **Foo** menu command. Conversely, if your TSpecialView.DoMenuCommand handles the command number associated with the **Foo** menu command, then your TSpecialView.DoSetupMenus must be able to enable the **Foo** menu item. This ensures that each menu command you enable is processed correctly by your application.

- If a DoMenuCommand (either one of your methods or one in the MacApp basic classes) returns a command object, then MacApp will take care of sending the DoIt messageto this object, thereby "executing" the command.

Command Processing—The Framework for Undo

MacApp provides a framework for making undoable the operations that your application provides to its end users. Without a doubt, making all of an application's operations undoable is the single most important "user-friendly" feature of the Macintosh User Interface Standard. **Undo** makes the system less threatening to beginners, encourages experts to try unusual things, and, in general, lowers the tension that would be present if an entire day's work could be wiped out with a single mistake—a situation that in itself reduces the likelihood of making a mistake in the first place. Unfortunately for implementors, **Undo** has traditionally been a feature that was difficult to build into an application. MacApp changes that.

Table 7-1 MapApp's Command Numbers

Apple has reserved the range 1–999 for MacApp's command numbers. You should not use a number in this range for any of the commands unique to your application. Here are the actual commands processed by the version 1.0 MacApp.

Command	Number	Comment
cAboutApp	1	About <appname>...
cNew	8	NEW command
cNewLast	8	
cSave	9	SAVE command
cQuit	10	command number for QUIT command
cClose	11	CLOSE command
cCloseAll	12	CLOSE ALL command
cGetInfo	13	GET INFO command
cSaveAs	14	Save as...
cSaveCopy	15	Save a copy in ...
cShowClipboard	18	Show/Hide Clipboard
cFinderNew	19	
cFinderPrint	20	
cFinderOpen	21	
cOpen	20	Open... command
cOpenLast	20	
cRevert	27	Revert To Previous Version command
cPageSetup	176	Page Setup... command
cPrintOne	177	Print One command
cPrint	178	Print... command
cStopPrinting	178	Stop Printing command, for use during Background Printing
cPrintToFile	179	Print to file... command
cPrFileBase	176	(*See cPrFileMax*)
cPrFileMax	195	command numbers between cPrFileBase and cPrFileMax are sent to a document's fDocPrintHandler even if it is not in the target chain
cPrintSpoolFile	190	Print spooled file... command
cPrViewBase	201	(*See cPrViewBase*)
cPrViewMax	250	command numbers between cPrViewBase and cPrViewMax are printing commands applied to adisplayed view which is in the Target chain
cAllowBackgroundPrinting	191	Toggle 'Allow Background Printing' switch
cCreateClipDoc	-1	Pseudo-command to TAppplication.DoMakeDocument
Zooming commands		
cReduce50	301	Reduce 50%
cReduceToFit	302	Reduce to Fit
cShowFullSize	303	Show Full Size

Editing commands

For the following command numbers, we must guarantee that <command number> - cEditBase = <appropriate number to pass to SystemEdit> . This relationship is enforced in TApplication.IApplication.

cEditBase	21	start of standard editing commands
cUndo	21	
cEditSep	22	line separating UNDO from CUT
cCut	23	
cCopy	24	
cPaste	25	
cClear	26	
cEditLast	cClear	
cTyping	36	for use in a TTypingCommand
cMouseCommand	37	generic mouse command

Debugging commands

cIdentifySoftware	100	'Identify Software' command--identification appers in debug window
cExperimenting	101	enable experimental features; controlled by menu toggle
cReportMenuChoices	102	trace menu commands; controlled by menu toggle
cShowDebugInfo	103	'Show Debug Info', for misc debugging purposes
cIntenseDebugging	104	'intense debugging', controlled by menu toggle
cTraceSetupMenus	105	Trace Enable, Disable calls etc. if gTrace is also on
cTraceIdle	106	Trace Idle if gTrace is also on
cDebugPrinting	112	temporarily used for testing gPrinting; controlled by menu toggle
cDebugWind	113	show debug window
cReportEvt	114	report events
cDoFirstClick	115	'Do First Click' toggle for a window
cVarClipPicSize	116	Pictures in Clipboard of variable Size

The framework that MacApp provides for undoable operations is built around the notion of a command object (an instance of TCommand). For each operation in your application that is to be undoable, you must design a subclass of TCommand. For purposes of this discussion, let's suppose your application has a "munge" operation that is invoked when the user chooses the **Munge** command on one of your application's menus. To make the munge operation undoable, you design the TMungeCommand class, a subclass of TCommand. In designing this class, you override the methods DoIt, UndoIt, and RedoIt and give each of these the appropriate statements to do, undo, and redo the munge operation. In addition, if the munge operation has some actions that can take place only when the munge action can no longer be undone, then you also should override the Commit method. (An example of this last case would be a clear operation like the TClearQuadCmd used in the Mini-QuadWorld application (Chapter 5)—you don't want to actually deallocate the cleared objects until you know that the user is no longer be able to undo the clear operation. Thus, in the MacApp framework, you design a TClearQuadCmd.Commit, which actually frees the cleared objects.) To respond to the choice of the **Munge** menu item, you specify in one of your DoMenuCommand methods (depending on the applicability fo the munge operation: either in your application subclass, one of your document subclasses, one of your view subclasses, depending on the applicability of the munge operation, or in very unusual cases, in a subclass of TWindow or TFrame) that a TMungeCommand object is to be created and returned to MacApp as the value of this DoMenuCommand method. MacApp will take it from there and invokes your TMungeCommand's DoIt, UndoIt, RedoIt, and Commit methods at the appropriate times.

The MacApp framework for undoable command processing is built around two variables. One is a global variable, gLastCommand, and the other is an instance variable of command objects, fCmdDone. gLastCommand refers to the last command object returned to MacApp (from one of your DoMenuCommand methods, for example) and fCmdDone is a boolean variable that records whether the command was most recently either done or redone (TRUE) or undone (FALSE). When the user chooses the **Undo** menu command, MacApp checks the gLastCommand.fCmdDone flag. If it is true, then MacApp invokes gLastCommand.UndoIt: if it is false, MacApp invokes gLastCommand RedoIt. If the last user operation was the munge operation, gLastCommand would refer to the instance of TMungeCommand that you returned to MacApp and MacApp would invoke one of your TMunge Command methods when the **Undo** command is activated. Figure 7-11 shows the flow of control for MacApp's command processing in more detail.

Application-Dependent Mouse Processing

If your application enables the end user to use the mouse to draw or select in one of your views, then you can make the best use of the MacApp framework if you design a command object to handle mouse interaction. A command object used in this way is called a *tracker* and is usually allocated in your view subclass's DoMouseCommand. Despite this name, there really isn't anything different about a tracker and a command object that is used to handle a menu command, with the exception that different methods are typically overridden. A tracker has the following methods available for overriding, in addition to the usual TCommand methods:

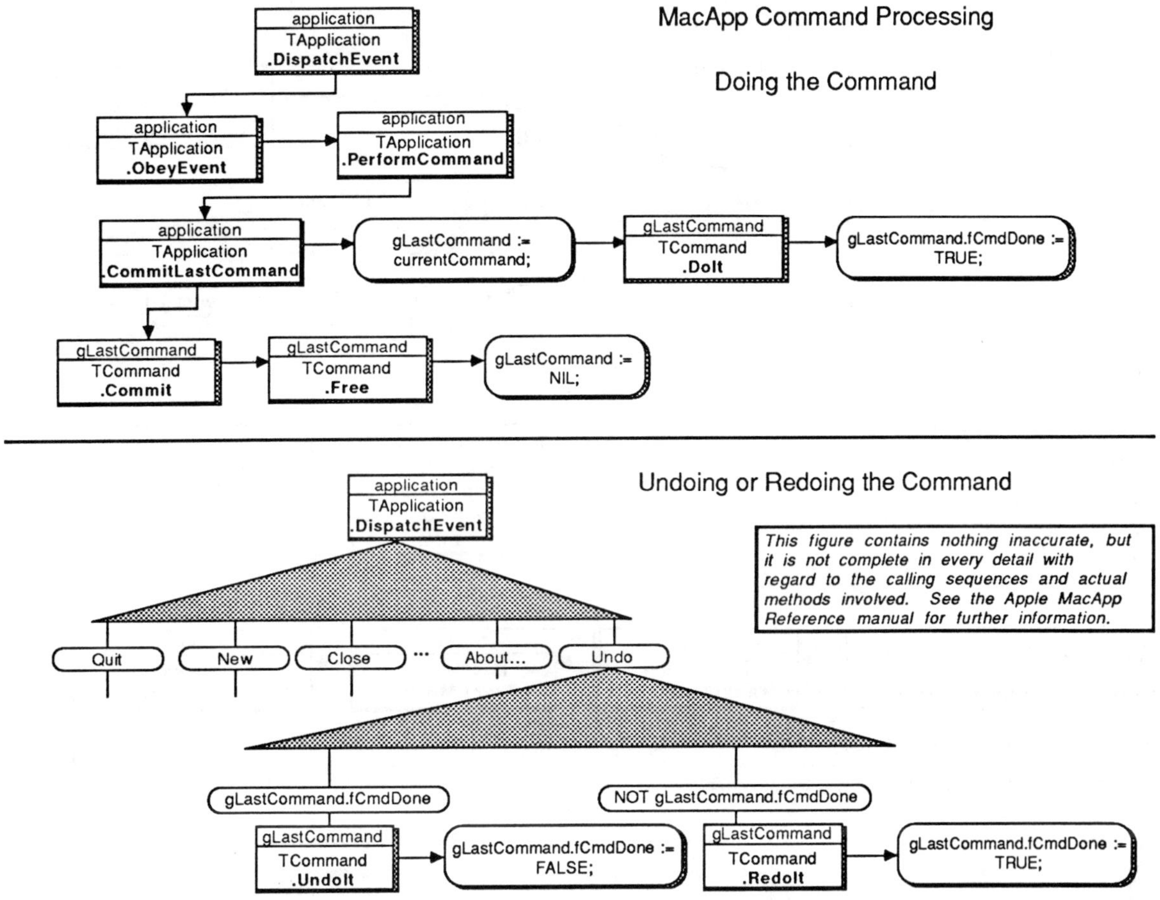

Figure 7-11 The MacApp flow of control in doing, undoing, or redoing a command.

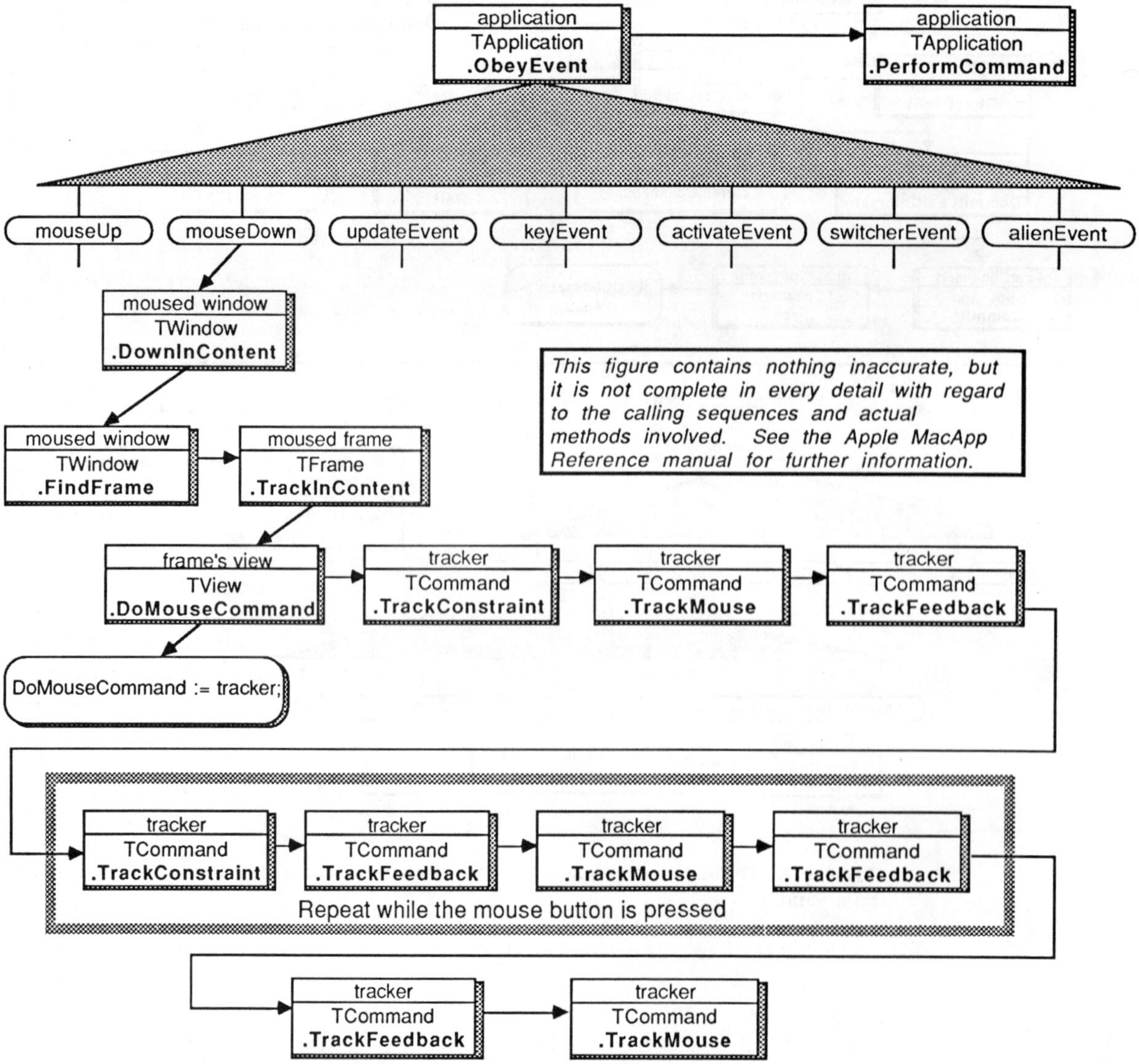

Figure 7-12 The MacApp flow of control in the application-dependent processing of mouse actions. Note that this figure ignores application-independent mouse processing (like scroll bars and window expands)

Method	Use
TrackMouse	Obtains, from MacApp, the mouse button state and the current cursor position in view coordinates. This is the method in which your application actually does something with this mouse input.
TrackFeedback	Draws any mouse movement feedback on the screen. This could be, for example, one-dimensional rubberbanding as used in MacPaint or MacDraw when lines are being entered, or two-dimensional rubberbanding as used in these same applications when rectangles are being entered.
TrackConstrain	Forces the cursor to obey certain constraints. This is can be used, for example, to "grid" the mouse (as in MacDraw) or to constrain the input to be a perfect square or circle, as in MacPaint.

Figure 7-12 shows the MacApp flow of control for mouse processing. QuadWorld, for example, uses these MacApp features for the entry of new quadrilaterals in the quadGraphicalView, using instances of the class TSketchQuadCmd (and its subclasses) as sketchers. The details involved in this are discussed in the next chapter.

Notes

There is an entire area of mouse processing that is purposely not covered in the section: application-independent mouse processing. Application-independent mouse processing is used, for example, in scrolling or in moving a window about the screen. The processing is so rarely overridden by a MacApp application (why would you want your application to do something unusual when the user was scrolling?), that it is not an appropriate topic for this text. See the MacApp Reference Manual for a full treatment of this topic as well as the mouse processing that takes place in a control unique to your application.

CHAPTER

8

QuadWorld—A Full MacApp Application

In this chapter we develop a full implementation of the QuadWorld application first introduced in Chapter 2 and partially developed (in the Mini-QuadWorld application) in Chapter 5. This full version of QuadWorld has the following functional differences from the mini-version:

- Two simultaneous views for the same quadrilaterals—the graphical view and the textual view (a menu-like list of their names).
- Interactive, undoable entry of new quadrilaterals, with all the geometric constraints associated with each type of quadrilateral automatically taken into account.
- The use of a quadrilateral palette to enable the user to easily specify the type of quadrilateral to be entered.
- Rotation of the quadrilateral by any integral angle. (Mini-QuadWorld was restricted to counterclockwise rotation by a fixed 45°.)
- There are two separate windows—one displaying the graphical view of the quadrilaterals and one displaying the textual view. Having separate windows for each of these views is more consistent with the Macintosh User Interface Standard than having one complex window with several panels. Note that each window can be separately resized and scrolled.
- The window with the graphical view has a palette of all the types of quadrilaterals. The user selects in this palette to draw a new quadrilateral.
- Quadrilaterals appear in the graphical view as they are drawn, as can be seen with the partially drawn quadrilateral in the center of the graphical window. The textual representation of a quadrilateral does not appear until the quadrilateral is completely drawn.

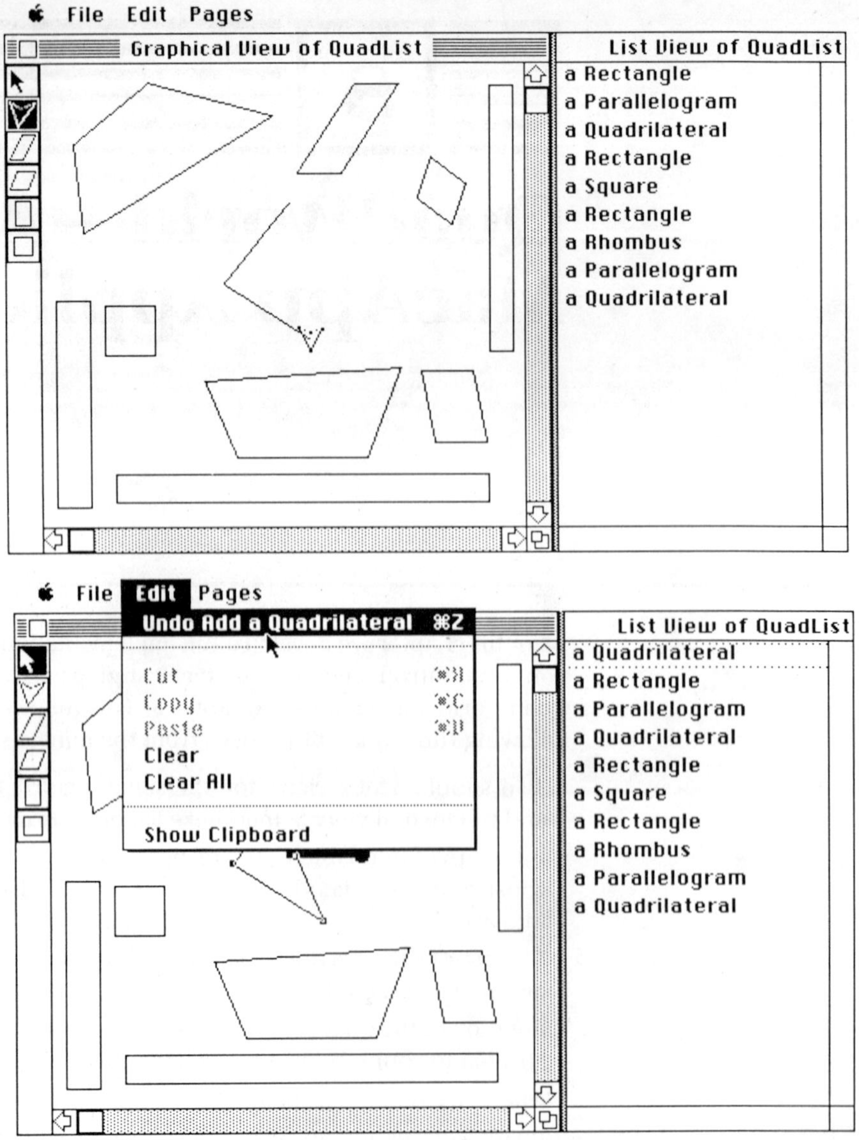

Figure 8-1 The MacApp implementation of QuadWorld.

A screen dump of the MacApp implementation of QuadWorld is shown in Figure 8-1. Note that:

- Quadrilaterals can be selected in either view. When a quadrilateral is selected, regardless of which view the selecting action took place, both of its representations, graphical and textual, are highlighted. Note that MacApp has extended the Macintosh User Interface Standard to allow for *dim highlighting*, a manner of indicating a selection in a window other than the active window. The default for dim highlighting is to highlight with gray, although it is easy to override this in a MacApp application. The quadTxView, for example, performs dim highlighting by drawing a box around the textual representation of the selected quadrilateral. This highlighting style was used instead of gray highlighting because gray highlighting of text makes the text very difficult to read. The quadGrView uses the more common gray dim highlighting.

- Various cursor shapes are used to provide user feedback of input modes that are unavoidable in most real applications. For example, quadrilateral-entry mode is indicated with the cursor shape shown in Figure 8-1.
- The user rotates a quadrilateral not through the use of a menu command, as in Mini-QuadWorld, but by a gesture with the mouse. The selected quadrilateral has a rotation handle affixed to it, also shown in Figure 8-1. Mousing down in this rotation handle enables the user to rotate that quadrilateral. The extent of the rotation is indicated by the extent to which the cursor is moved while the mouse button is pressed—in effect, the user subtends the angle by pressing the mouse button on one side of the angle and releasing it on the other.

As with Mini-QuadWorld, there are two major portions to QuadWorld: the classes that model the various types of quadrilaterals and the MacApp subclasses that present the world of quadrilaterals to the Macintosh user. QuadWorld can use the quadrilateral classes as they were developed in the Mini-QuadWorld application, but it requires major changes to the MacApp subclasses in Mini-QuadWorld. In this chapter we first describe the basic MacApp subclasses used in QuadWorld, and then describe the development of the quadrilateral sketcher classes that enable the user to interactively enter new quadrilaterals. Even within the MacApp framework there are many ways to implement QuadWorld. In the first portion of this chapter we present one implementation architecture for QuadWorld, that shown in Listing E, which has a primary guiding principle of being easy to understand. In the second portion of this chapter, we examine and compare alternative architectures.

The Structure of the QuadWorld Application Using MacApp

The QuadWorld application makes use of all the basic MacApp classes, either directly by using instances of these classes (for example, TWindow and TFrame) or indirectly by designing specialized subclasses that exhibit QuadWorld-specific behavior (for example, TQuadDocument and TQuadGr View). (Figure 8-2 shows the inheritance structure for all classes used in QuadWorld.) In this direct and indirect use of the MacApp classes, QuadWorld is typical of MacApp applications.

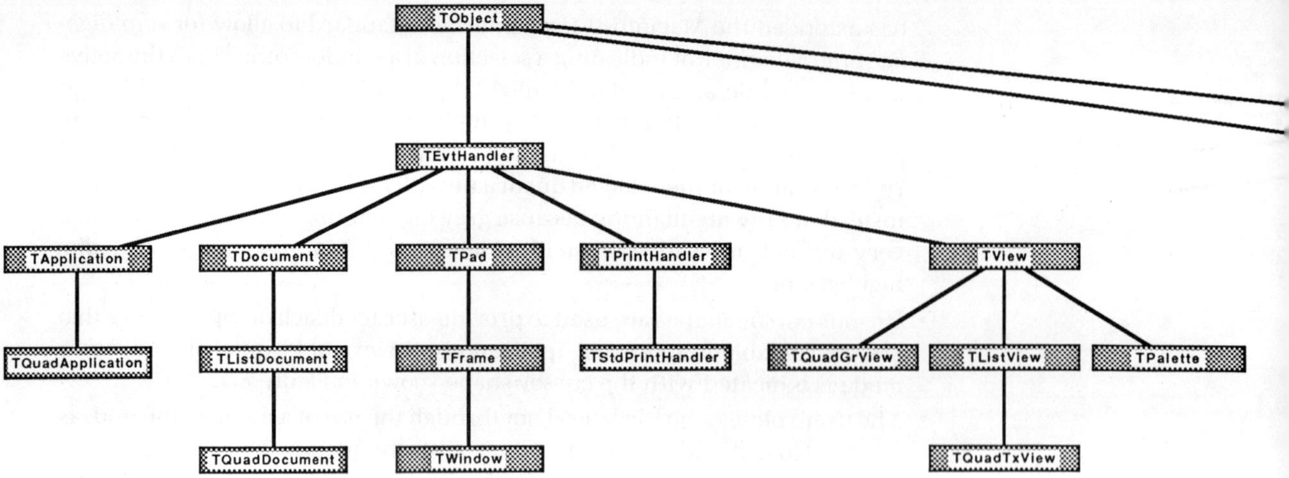

Figure 8-2 The inheritence structure of the QuadWorld classes.

To demonstrate the generation of new units and their use with the MacApp class library, a reusable portion of the QuadWorld application, the part that draws the textual view of the quadrilaterals and handles the user interaction with that view, was purposely designed as a separate, independent unit; the UListView unit. In this use of separately compiled and reusable units of classes, too, QuadWorld is typical of MacApp applications.

To keep QuadWorld (and this book) of reasonable length, QuadWorld makes no use of the secondary MacApp building blocks such as UDialog, UTEView, and UAppleTalk. In this, QuadWorld is atypical because these units are heavily used by most large applications.

The Class TQuadApplication

The first step in implementing QuadWorld is to design a TQuadApplication class, which is a subclass of TApplication. The design and implementation of this

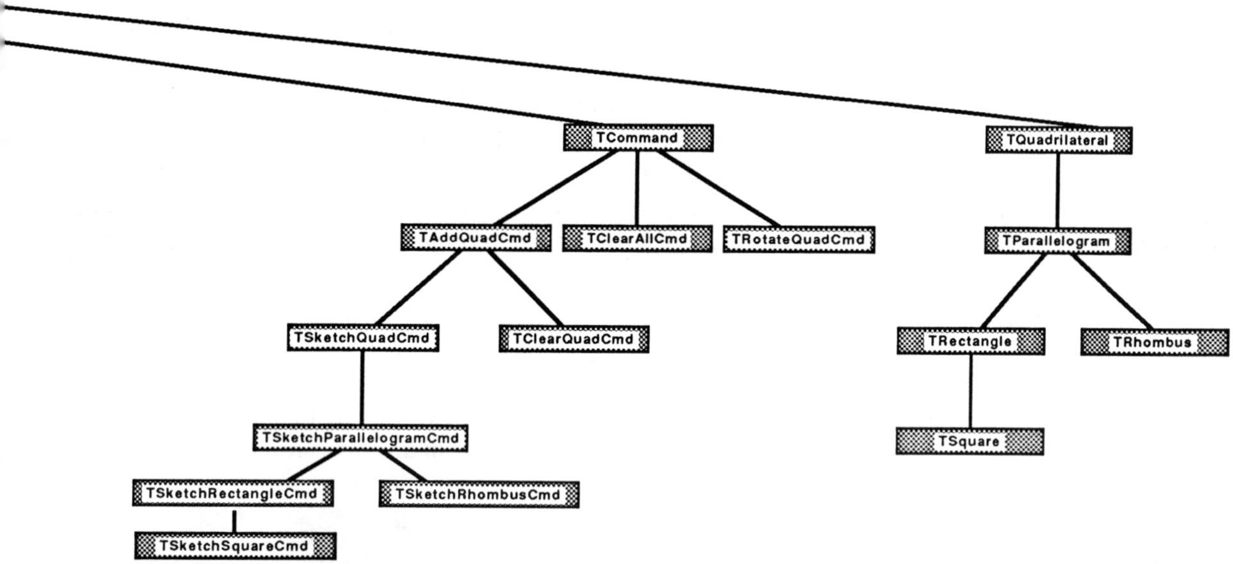

class is the same as for Mini-QuadWorld. In this, QuadWorld is typical of MacApp applications because subclasses of TApplication are relatively pro forma—each overrides DoMakeDocument, provides an initialization method, etc. As one example of an additional feature that could be done in the TApplication subclass, if QuadWorld provided a help facility (as do most Microsoft Macintosh applications, for example), this probably would be implemented in a TQuadApplication method.

The Class TQuadDocument

The TQuadDocument class for the full implementation of QuadWorld differs in several ways from that of the Mini-QuadWorld application. For the full QuadWorld application, however, you still need to store the following information:

- All the quadrilaterals the user has stored or created.
- Which quadrilateral is the currently selected one.

In addition, a quadDocument must contain references to both the graphical view and the tabular view of the quadrilaterals because every TDocument subclass must have references to the view which renders its instances.

There are four categories of methods for the class TQuadDocument:

- Methods dealing with the manipulation of the data stored in the document.
- Methods dealing with the preparation of a textual representation of the document for purposes such as generating a view.
- Methods dealing with accessing the disk.
- Methods providing hooks into the MacApp framework—methods like DoMakeViews used by MacApp to install your type of view so as to provide access to the special types of objects you have designed or to special methods you have overridden.

The methods dealing with data manipulation enable you to add a quadrilateral to or delete one from the document easily, change which one is selected, redraw one in both views, and execute a procedure on each one in the document. Note that all of these methods are unique to the class TQuad Document—none of them overrides methods in any ancestor class.

Notes

Generally, the names of these data manipulation methods are the same as in Mini-QuadWorld. The implementation of several of them, however, is slightly different because of the presence of the textual view of the quadrilaterals.

To show how a truly reusable software component could be designed using Object Pascal, I designed a special type of view that displays a series of text strings and enables the user to select any of these strings with the mouse. This reusable component is called a TListView and its code (the unit UListView) is listed along with the QuadWorld source code in Listing E. To use this component, you need to make your document class a subclass of TListDocument (also defined in UListView) and override two of its methods: SetSelection, which changes the currently selected quadrilateral in the document, and ReportListItem, which generates a textual representation for one item of the document for subsequent display in the listView. To make these methods easy to understand, I also designed two utility methods in the class TQuadDocument that convert back and forth between list indices and quadrilaterals: QuadToListIndex and ListIndexToQuad. (The TListView and TListDocument classes are documented at the end of this section.)

Definitions

The UListView unit is a general purpose software component that can be (and has been) used in other MacApp applications. It is an example of what Apple calls a *building block.* (Productivity Products International, another company doing extensive development in object-oriented programming, uses the term *software-IC* to describe this same notion.) The ability to implement such reusable and overridable software components is as significant an advantage of object-oriented programming as the ability to implement generic applications like MacApp.

The disk access methods override certain TDocument methods to deal with the special internal structure of the quadDocument. These methods provide an interesting example of how to deal with accessing and extending MacApp code without knowing the internal details of how that code works. Consider the method for writing a quadDocument to disk:

```
PROCEDURE TQuadDocument.DoWrite(aRefNum: INTEGER);
OVERRIDE;
VAR err:             OSErr;
    count:           LONGINT;
    lastQuadMarker: INTEGER;
  PROCEDURE WriteQuad(quad: TQuad);
  BEGIN
    quad.WriteTo(aRefNum);
  END;
BEGIN
  lastQuadMarker := IDLastQuad;
  count := SIZEOF(INTEGER);
  INHERITED DoWrite(aRefNum);
                              {Allow MacApp to write whatever it wants to }
  SELF.EachQuadDo(WriteQuad);
                        { Allow each quad to write itself however it wants to}
  err := FSWrite(aRefNum, count, @lastQuadMarker);
                                                   { Mark the end of the file}
END;
```

Note that this method first lets the TDocument.DoWrite write anything it wants to disk. Although currently, it only has information about the print handler, it could include window positions on the screen, view positions in the window, or many other things. After this you write each quad object to disk using a standard Pascal **RECORD** structure, TFiledQuad, not an object type (objects exist in memory only, not on disk) using the TQuad.WriteTo method:

```
PROCEDURE TQuad.WriteTo(aRefNum: INTEGER);

VAR data:    TFiledQuad;
    count:   LONGINT;
    quadID:  INTEGER;
    err:     OSErr;
    i:       INTEGER;                                {FOR Loop index}
BEGIN
  quadID := SELF.ID;
  count := SIZEOF(INTEGER);
  err := FSWrite(aRefNum, count, @quadID);
  FOR i := 1 TO 4 DO data.theVertices[i] := SELF.fVertex[i];
  data.theRotationState := SELF.fRotated;
  count := SIZEOF(TFiledQuad);
  err := FSWrite(aRefNum, count, @data);

END;
```

When all quads have been written to disk, TQuadDocument.DoWrite then writes a special "last quad" value to mark the end of the file. The format of a quadDocument on disk is shown in Figure 8-3.

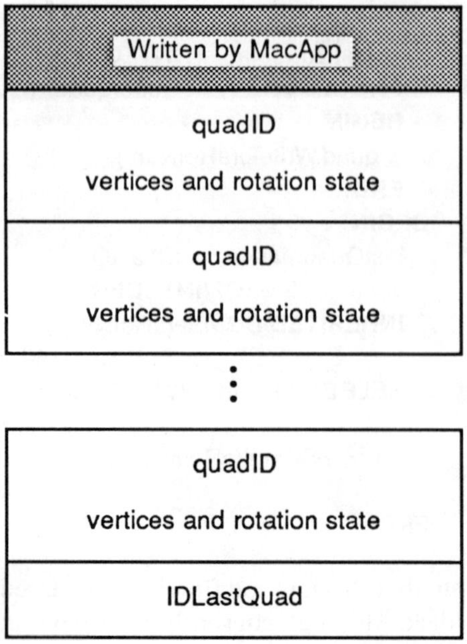

Figure 8-3 The format of a quadDocument when written to disk.

Later, when you want to read this document, you must take into account that TDocument.DoWrite has written an unknown amount of material. In fact, as MacApp programmers, you don't even have to know exactly what is written there, merely that TDocument.DoRead will read whatever TDocument.DoWrite wrote and MacApp will deal with this information appropriately. This is done by invoking TDocument.DoRead (**INHERITED** DoRead). By not assuming what or how much TDocument.DoWrite wrote into the file, you have lessened the task of converting this application to future releases of MacApp. The quads themselves are reconstituted by reading a quad ID, cloning an appropriate quad (see discussion below), and then having that new quad read its vertices and other data from the file. TQuadDocument.DoRead then reads the next quad ID and continues in this manner until the special quad ID, IDLastQuad, is found.

```
PROCEDURE TQuadDocument.DoRead(aRefNum: INTEGER; forPrinting:
  BOOLEAN); OVERRIDE;
VAR id:           INTEGER;
    count:        LONGINT;
    newQuad:      TQuad;
    err:          OSErr;
BEGIN
  INHERITED DoRead(aRefNum, forPrinting);
  count := SIZEOF(INTEGER);
  WHILE TRUE DO
    BEGIN
    err := FSRead(aRefNum, count, @id);                 { Get the next id }
    IF ((id > 0) AND (id ×= IDSquare))
       THEN newQuad := TQuad(gPrototypeQuadsArray[id].Clone)
                                                  { Clone an appropriate quad}
       ELSE IF id = IDLastQuad
         THEN LEAVE                          { Exit the loop if no more quads }
 {$IFC qDebug} ELSE ProgramBreak('Illegal quad on disk') {$ENDC};
     newQuad.ReadFrom(aRefNum);             { Tell the new quad to read itself }
     SELF.AddQuad(newQuad);                 { Add new quad to the document }
   END
 END;
```

There are several interesting points about this method:

- You have lessened the task of converting this application to future releases of MacApp by not assuming how much information MacApp will read from the file, just as you did not assume how much material MacApp would write to the file in TDocument.DoWrite.
- The algorithm used in this method allows for the possibility that each of the quads might write different types and amounts of data to disk. A upright TRectangle object, for example, could write only its two opposite corners and reconstitute itself from that data with an overridden ReadFrom method. For quadrilaterals, this is hardly worth the trouble, but for larger and more complex objects (or for larger and more complex applications) this could be a real savings. (See a further discussion of this later in the chapter when alternatives to the current QuadWorld structure are explored.)
- Cloning is an easy technique to generate new objects. In TQuadApplication. IQuadApplication, an array of quads, gPrototypeQuadsArray, is initialized. This array contains five elements: one of each of the five types of quads in QuadWorld. These quads are used as "master quadrilaterals" in QuadWorld. The quad IDs read from disk are used as indices into gPrototypeQuadsArray and a new instance of the appropriate type of quad is allocated using the Clone method inherited from TObject.

  This use of a global array of prototypical quads becomes even more useful when you consider the only alternative: a **CASE** switch on the quad IDs:

```
VAR aNewQuad:               TQuad;                          { Bad Design }
    aNewParallelogram:      TParallelogram;
    aNewRhombus:            TRhombus;
    aNewRectangle:          TRectangle;
    aNewSquare:             TSquare;

CASE id OF
        IDQuad:             BEGIN
                              NEW(aNewQuad);
                            END;
        IDParallelogram:    BEGIN
                              NEW(aNewParallelogram);
                              aNewQuad := aNewParallelogram;
                            END;
        IDRhombus:          BEGIN
                              NEW(aNewRhombus);
                              aNewQuad := aNewRhombus;
                            END;
```

```
        IDRectangle:        BEGIN
                              NEW(aNewRectangle);
                              aNewQuad := aNewRectangle;
                            END;
        IDSquare:           BEGIN
                              NEW(aNewSquare);
                              aNewQuad := aNewSquare;
                            END;
  END; { Case }
  aNewQuad.IQuad;
  aNewQuad.ReadFrom(aRefNum);
```

As with Mini-QuadWorld, the four MacApp "hook" methods are probably the most interesting because you probably will override these methods in the design of your own MacApp application. In the full implementation of QuadWorld, TQuadDocument.DoMakeViews is overridden to create and install the correct kind of views for your document. Similarly, TQuadDocument.DoMakeWindows is a method you must override to create the correct window for your application. Because the full implementation of QuadWorld has two windows, each is allocated in DoLaunchWindows. DoSetupMenus and DoMenuCommand are essentially the same as in Mini-QuadWorld, with the exception that quadrilateral rotation is no longer a menu command, but is initiated with the mouse. (Quadrilateral rotation is a mouse command because in full QuadWorld, the user specifies the angle of rotation with the mouse.)

Definitions

To be more precise, TQuadDocument.DoSetupMenus and TQuadDocument.DoMenuCommand deal with the menu items handled by the document during the menu command flow of control, as explained in Chapter 7. For the QuadWorld application, this happens to be all the QuadWorld-specific menu commands. For other applications, the various T(Your)View.DoSetupMenus and T(Your)View.DoMenuCommand methods and the T(Your)Application.DoSetUpMenus and T(Your)Application.Do MenuCommand, for example, would probably handle some menu commands specific to one of the views or the application itself, respectively.

Definitions

The class documentation blocks in this chapter indicate, in addition to listing the instance variables and methods, where differences occur between the full QuadWorld and Mini-QuadWorld. New instance variables appear in italic in the variable list. Methods that are totally new to QuadWorld have their titles italicized, while those that have new implementations have italicized explanations.

TQuadDocument Instance Variables

Variable	Use
fLastQuad	Refers to the last quadrilateral to be added in a linked list of quadrilaterals. Note the quadrilateral objects (instances of class TQuad or its subclasses) were described in Chapter 3 and that they themselves store a link to the next quadrilateral. Thus, fLastQuad really refers to the head quadrilateral in the list of quadrilaterals currently in the quadDocument.
fQuadGrView	Refers to the quadGraphicalView of this quadDocument.
fQuadTxView	Refers to the textual view of this quadDocument.
fSelectedQuad	Refers to the currently selected quadrilateral, if any.

TQuadDocument Methods

Initialization and Freeing Methods

Method	Use
IQuadDocument	Initializes new instances of TQuadDocument.

Free	Overridden method. Deallocates the quadDocument. Failure to override this method would leave TQuad objects on the heap, thereby using up heap space that the next document might need.
FreeData	Overridden method. Deallocates the quadrilaterals in the quadDocument when the document is deallocated or when the user reverts to the saved version of a document. Failure to override this method would leave TQuad objects on the heap, thereby using up heap space that the next document might need.

Data Manipulation Methods

Method	Use
AddQuad	Adds a quadrilateral to the list of quadrilaterals in the quadDocument.
DeleteQuad	Deletes a quadrilateral from the list of quadrilaterals in the quadDocument.
EachQuadDo(DoThis(quad))	Executes the procedure DoThis for each of the quadrilaterals in the quadDocument.

Data Display Methods

Method	Use
InvalidateQuad	*Redraws a quadrilateral in both views.*
SelectQuad	*Makes a particular quadrilateral the selected quadrilateral in both views.*

List View Support Methods

Method	Use
ReportListItem	Prepares a textual representation of the ith quadrilateral in the document. This representation will be used by the listView.
SetSelection	Changes the currently selected quadrilateral, presumably because the user has selected its corresponding textual representation in the listView.
QuadToListIndex	Given a particular quadrilateral, determines its index in the list of quadrilaterals and thus, for example, determines its position in the list of text strings displayed in the listView. A utility method for interface with the listView that is not required but nice to have.
ListIndexToQuad	Given a particular index value, determines which quadrilateral is in this position in the list. A utility method for interface with the listView that is not required but nice to have.

MacApp "Hook" Methods for Disk Access

Method	Use
DoNeedDiskSpace	Overridden method. Precomputes approximately how much disk space will be required to write the current quadDocument to disk.
DoWrite	Overridden method. Writes the quadDocument to disk.
DoRead	Overridden method. Reads the format written by TQuadDocument.DoWrite and "reconstitutes" the quadDocument that was stored on disk.

Other MacApp "Hook" Methods

Method	Use
DoMakeViews	*Overridden method. Allocates and installs the quadGraphicalView, the paletteView, and the listView in the quadDocument.*
DoMakeWindows	*Overridden method. Allocates and opens each of the windows which will display the two representations of the quadDocument. Makes sure these windows fill the screen regardless of screen size.*
DoSetUpMenus	*Overridden method. Enables the two menu commands unique to QuadWorld:* ***Clear****, and* ***Clear All***
DoMenuCommand	*Overridden method. Processes the two menu commands unique to QuadWorld:* ***Clear****, and* ***Clear All***

The Class TQuadGrView

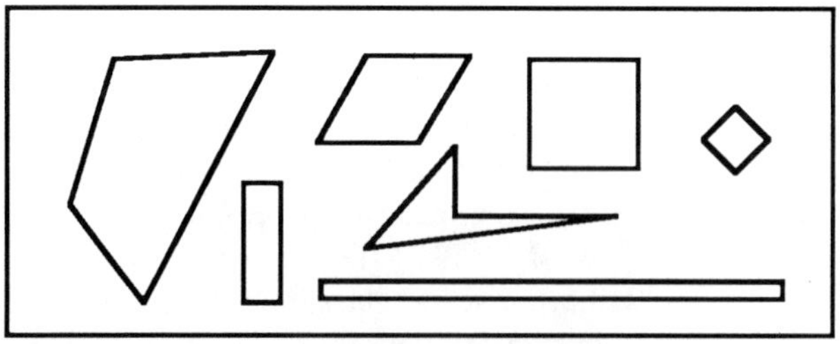

After designing the application subclass (TQuadApplication) and the document subclass (TQuadDocument), the next thing to do is design the view subclass. Even though QuadWorld has three views, you need only design two new classes, the quadrilateral graphical view class and the palette view class, because the third class, the quadrilateral textual view class, is obtained without change from the UList unit. There are a number of new tricky points in the design of TQuadGrView for the full implementation of QuadWorld, both in the specification of its instance variables and in the design of its methods.

The data that must be held by a quadGrView includes a reference to its companion palette view to make it easy to "read" the state of the palette. (Recall that the quad graphical window is divided into two portions: a fixed-sized, non-scrolling portion which displays the palette view and the rest of the window which displays the quad graphical view.) Having this piece of data stored with the quadGrView makes the TQuadGrView methods a little easier to design.

The currently selected quadrilateral is also recorded in one of the instance variables of the quadGrView. This is a change from the manner in which Mini-QuadWorld keeps track of the selection. In Mini-QuadWorld, whenever the quadGrView "needs to know" what the current selection was, it "asks" its quadDocument by directly accessing the value of the quadDocument instance variable, fSelectedQuad This subtly affects many methods in both classes. When the selection changes, for example, the quadDocument take the responsibility to tell the quadGrView to unhighlight the current selection before the selection was actually changed, to change the selection by modifying the value of fSelectedQuad, and then to tell the quadGrView to highlight the new selection. This is necessary because the quadGrView doesn't know the selection on its own. With the two views in QuadWorld and with dim highlighting in each view, this becomes a little complex for the quadDocument to manage. In QuadWorld, the view "knows" a little more about selections: they have instance variables which record the current selections and a ChangeSelection method to respond to requests by the quadDocument. Making the view smarter also makes the methods of TQuadDocument somewhat simpler.

Definitions

In the previous and other sections I often state that an object or a class "knows" some fact – for example, the class TSketchRombusCmd knows that rhombi have equal length sides. I hope no one is mislead or insulted by this common anthropomorphic slang. The only alternative is to use expressions like "the algorithms encoded in the methods of the TSketch RhombusCmd class include the calculations that enforce the equilateral constraint of rhombi." No one is served by this overly rigorous language, especially when you really know what is going on.

There is even more data that the quadGrView holds to make the user interaction during the entry of a new quadrilateral less modal and more flexible. Suppose that, while drawing a new quadrilateral, the user needed to scroll to a portion of the view that was not currently visible (to enter a really big quadrilateral, for example). This could mean that after drawing two of the lines of a quadrilateral, the user needs to suspend the drawing of this quadrilateral to use one of the scroll controls. This would result in a temporary partial quadrilateral for the duration of interruption in drawing. This partial quadrilateral must be stored somewhere; it can't be stored in the list of quadrilaterals in the quadDocument because this partial quadrilateral isn't yet a quadrilateral! This partial quadrilateral is stored in the quadGrView and, to make things even a little simpler, the state of its drawing (exactly how many vertices have been drawn so far) also is separately stored so that the drawing can be continued easily when the user returns to the quadGrView.

Notes

Note that in QuadWorld, or in any MacApp application, there is never really a need to make provisions for scrolling in the interactive entry of graphical entities since Macapp supports auto-scrolling—the automatic scrolling caused when the cursor extends outside the frame while the mouse button is pressed. There are other, more important reasons for the storage of the partial quadrilateral in the quadGrView, having to do with the interactive process by which new quadrilaterals are entered by the user. These reasons are explained later in this chapter when the use of the quadSketcher is outlined.

There are ten methods defined in the class TQuadGrView. The only ones we discuss in detail are the methods that draw the view, change the cursor, and process mouse clicks.

QuadGrView Instance Variables

Variable	Use
fSelectedQuad	Refers to the currently selected quadrilateral.
fPalette	Refers to the palette view in the same window.
fRotationRgn	The special selection "handle" used to rotate the currently selected quad around its center.

TQuadGrView Methods

Data Manipulation Methods

Method	Use
IQuadGrView	Initializes new instances of TQuadGrView.
ChangeSelection	Changes the selected quadrilateral to a particular quadrilateral.

MacApp "Hook" Methods

Method	Use
Draw	*Overridden method. Draws the graphical representation of the quadDocument.*
DoIdle	Overridden method. Makes sure that the partial quad is drawn by drawing it when nothing else is happening. (See following discussion.)
DoSetCursor	Overridden method. Changes the cursor to reflect the modes of quadrilateral entry.
HighlightSelection	Overridden method. Highlights the selected quadrilateral.
DoMouseCommand	*Overridden method. Processes mouse presses in the quadGrView. (See following discussion).*

Display Methods

Method	Use
InvalidateQuad	*Invalidates the graphical representation of a particular quadrilateral.*
DrawPartialQuad	A "subroutine" of TQuadGrView.Draw that draws the partially entered quadrilateral.
PendingSketcher	*Returns a sketching command (a tracker) that has not yet completed the interactive drawing of a new quadrilateral.*

You must always override a view's Draw method to tell MacApp how your view is to be rendered. In the case of the full implementation of QuadWorld the only aspect of the Draw method you must change (with respect to the Mini-QuadWorld implementation) is to draw the partial quadrilateral (the underlined portion of this method):

```
PROCEDURE TQuadGrView.Draw(area: Rect);
    PROCEDURE DrawQuad(quad: TQuad);
    BEGIN
      quad.Draw;
    END;
  BEGIN
    TQuadDocument(SELF.fDocument).EachQuadDo(DrawQuad);
    SELF.DrawPartialQuad;
  END;
```

The complication of the partial quadrilateral involves more than simply having to design a special drawing routine for a unique piece of data. It also involves the fact that you don't have easy control of when drawing actually takes place. MacApp schedules the actual drawing as part of its main event loop. To be sure, it will invoke your view's Draw method to determine what should be drawn, but you don't have control of exactly when this takes place. MacApp determines when to draw and what portions of the screen need to be drawn. Thus, for the partial quadrilateral not only do you have to tell MacApp how to draw it, you must make sure that MacApp draws it soon. In this QuadWorld implementation, I have chosen to do this by overriding the TView.DoIdle method so that the partial quadrilateral is drawn when there is nothing else to do.

Notes

There are actually two different places in the MacApp framework where the partial quadrilateral could be drawn: TQuadGrView.DoIdle or TQuadGrView.InvalRect. TQuadGrView.DoIdle is invoked whenever there are no other events in the event queue; TQuadGrView.InvalRect places an invalidation event in the queue so that a given rectangular area of the view is redrawn. Drawing the partial quadrilateral in the DoIdle method only requires invoking the DrawPartialQuad method in DoIdle and ensuring that this DoIdle method is itself invoked by setting the fIdlePriority instance variable of TQuadGrView to a number greater than 0. This drawing takes place when MacApp is otherwise idle, which, in practice, occurs frequently and so the resulting rubberband lines are quite responsive to mouse movements. Drawing the partial quadrilateral in the InvalRect method involves three steps:

1. adding an invocation of DrawPartialQuad in TQuadGrView.Draw
2. calculating the rectangular area around the partial quadrilateral and invoking InvalRect with this rectangle as the argument.
3. waiting for MacApp to cause the redraw of this area, and thus of the partial quadrilateral. In spite of the seemingly complex series of actions for using the InvalRect approach, it, too, is quite responsive. The difference between these two approaches to the same task lies only in the visual side effects. Because InvalRect invalidates an entire rectangular region around the partial quadrilateral, if any completed quadrilaterals happen to lie partially in that region, the portions of them that lie within the invalidation rectangle are also redrawn. The visual effect of this is a distracting blinking of nearby completed quadrilaterals. To avoid this blinking effect, I decided to use DoIdle approach for QuadWorld.

Notes

Of course, if you really want to control when drawing takes place, or anything else for that matter, you can take control from MacApp by overriding the appropriate method. In the case of fundamental operations like drawing or printing, this is very rare and unnecessary for everything but the most unusual application.

QuadWorld makes use of one visible aspect of the Macintosh User Interface Standard: the ability to change cursor shapes depending upon the position of the cursor. In the MacApp framework, this is done by overriding the TView method DoSetCursor and providing the conditions under which the cursor changes to a specified shape. In QuadWorld, for example, the cursor changes to an image of a quadrilateral with only one edge drawn during the time between the drawings of the first and second edges. This is done by checking which image in the palette is selected (fPalette.fCurrPalette) and how much of the partial quad has been drawn (Sketcher.fLastVertexSet):

```
FUNCTION TQuadGrView.DoSetCursor(localPoint: Point): BOOLEAN;
  OVERRIDE;
VAR sketcher:           TSketchQuadCmd;
    desiredCursorState: INTEGER;
BEGIN
DoSetCursor := FALSE;
IF SELF.fPalette.fCurrSelection < > 0          {the user is drawing a new quad}
  THEN
    BEGIN
      DoSetCursor := TRUE;
      sketcher := SELF.PendingSketcher;
      IF sketcher < > NIL
        THEN desiredCursorState := sketcher.fLastVertexSet
        ELSE desiredCursorState := 0;
{Set the cursor depending on the extent to which the user has entered
the new quadrilateral. Note that there is no need for a three-edged,
or a four-edged quad cursor.}
        CASE desiredCursorState OF
          0: SetCursor(GetCursor(crossCursor)↑↑);
          2: SetCursor(GetCursor(cOneEdgeQuadCursor)↑↑);
          3: SetCursor(GetCursor(cTwoEdgeQuadCursor)↑↑);
        OTHERWISE SetCursor(arrow)
      END
    END
END;
```

Cursor shapes set in this manner are changed back to the standard arrow cursor either by the DoSetCursor methods itself (for example, when the **OTHERWISE** clause of the **CASE** statement in the TQuadGrView method is executed), or when DoSetCursor returns false. MacApp invokes DoSetCursor sufficiently often so that the cursor changes as soon as the conditions you have specified occur.

The most complex method in the TQuadGrView class is DoMouse Command, which processes any mouse presses in the quadGrView. A mouse press in the quadGrView could mean any one of the following four things:

- The user wants to select a quadrilateral already present in the view.
- The user wants to begin drawing a new quadrilateral in the view.
- The user wants to continue drawing a new quadrilateral that is only partially drawn in the view.
- The user wants to rotate the selected quad.

As in MacDraw, the user distinguishes between these cases for the QuadWorld application through the use of the palette. If the selection arrow on the palette is selected, the user is selecting; if any other box of the palette is chosen, the user is drawing. This user interface thus involves modes: selection-mode, quadrilateral-drawing-mode, parallelogram-drawing-mode, among others. Though all developers strive for a modeless application, the appearance of modes is often unavoidable in real Mac applications, and QuadWorld is no exception. QuadWorld's design strives to make modes as palatable as possible by making many of them spring-loaded (for example, quadrilateral-drawing mode) or by visually indicating that the user is in a mode by changing the cursor shape, highlighting the palette, or some other means. Figure 8-4 shows the state transition diagram for the mouse modes of QuadWorld and Figure 8-5 lists the method that implements most of this modal activity, TQuadGrView. DoMouseCommand

If the user wants to draw a totally new quadrilateral, then this method clones a new quadrilateral of the appropriate type from an array of quadrilaterals (gPrototypeQuadsArray), asks the quadrilateral to create a tracker—that is, a command object with a TrackMouse method—to assist the user in drawing the quadrilateral on the screen, then installs this quadrilateral as the partial quadrilateral stored in the tracker. It is this tracker that knows about the various geometric constraints associated with the various types of quadrilaterals (rhombi, parallelograms, etc.). A tracker which also has a TrackFeedback method, and thus can draw, is called a *sketcher*. The tracker created by TQuadGrView.DoMouseCommand is also a sketcher. This sketcher is returned to MacApp; exists and is in control of the mouse until the user releases the mouse button. (The details of how these sketchers work is covered in the next section of this chapter.)

When the user wants to continue drawing a partially drawn quadrilateral, the sketcher is retrieved from to MacApp. When the user completes the drawing of the quadrilateral, the sketcher, which is also a command object, manages the addition of the newly created quadrilateral to the quadDocument. (TSketchQuadCmd contains overridden DoIt, UndoIt, and RedoIt methods to accomplish this addition.)

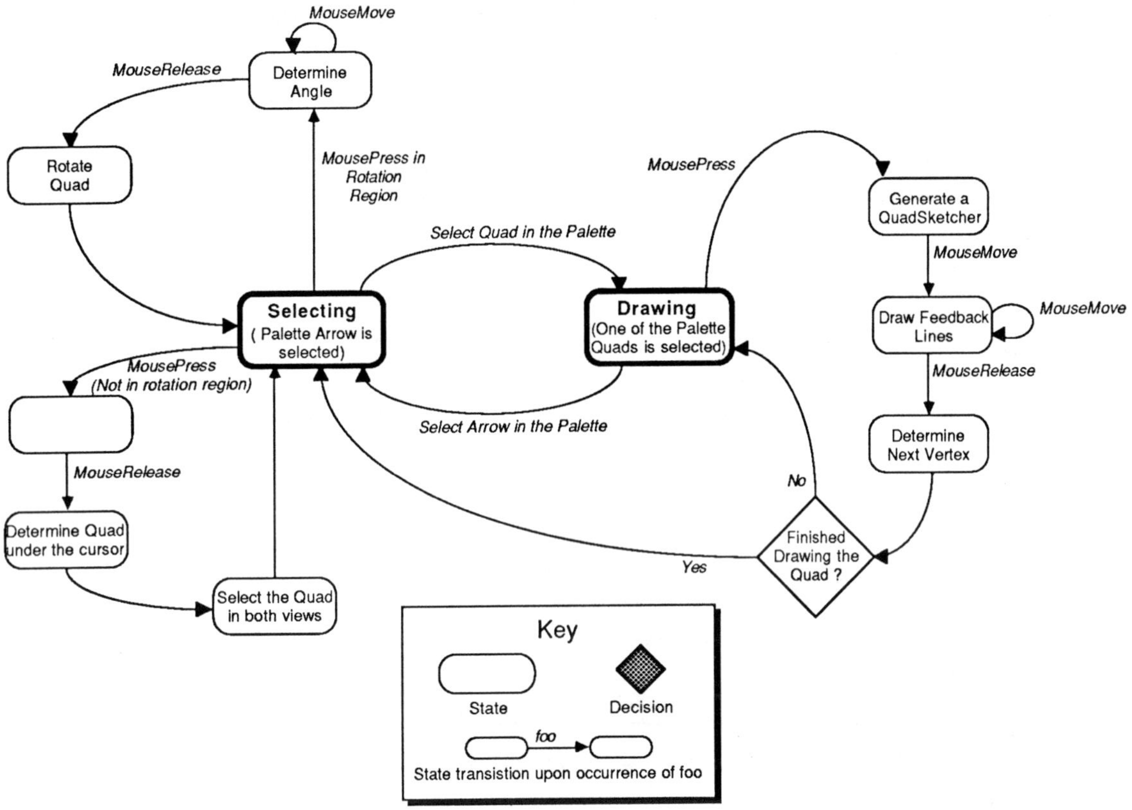

Figure 8-4 The state transitions for using the mouse in the MacApp implementation of QuadWorld.

When the user wants to select an existing quadrilateral, the TQuadGrView. DoMouseCommand method determines which quadrilateral is at the point where the cursor was when the mouse button was pressed. This is accomplished in the same way it was in Mini-QuadWorld: by asking each quadrilateral to compute the smallest rectangle that surrounds itself (TQuad. EnclosingRect) and testing if this mouse-down point is inside of that rectangle with the QuickDraw routine PtInRect. As with TQuadGrView.Draw, this process is simplified by the existence of the enumeration routine TQuadDocument. EachQuadDo

```
FUNCTION  TQuadGrView.DoMouseCommand(VAR downLocalPoint: Point; VAR info: EventInfo;
                                     VAR hysteresis: Point): TCommand;  OVERRIDE;

VAR quadSketcher:    TSketchQuadCmd;
    newQuad:         TQuad;
    quad:            TQuad;
    aRotateQuadCmd: TRotateQuadCmd;

    PROCEDURE CheckQuad(thisQuad: TQuad);
    BEGIN
       IF PtInRect(downLocalPoint, thisQuad.fEnclosingRect) THEN
           quad := thisQuad;
    END;

BEGIN
    DoMouseCommand := gNoChanges;

    IF SELF.fPalette.fCurrSelection > 0 THEN    { draw mode for some type of quad }
       BEGIN
          quadSketcher := SELF.PendingSketcher;

          IF quadSketcher = NIL  THEN        { The user wishes to start drawing a totally new quad }
             BEGIN
                TQuadDocument(SELF.fDocument).SelectQuad(NIL);  { De-select the current selection }

              { Clone appropriate quad }
                newQuad := TQuad(gPrototypeQuadsArray[SELF.fPalette.fCurrSelection].Clone);

              { Get an appropriate sketching command object }
                quadSketcher := newQuad.NewSketchCmd;
                quadSketcher.fQuad := newQuad;

                DoMouseCommand := quadSketcher;

             END { draw mode - start of new quad }

           ELSE  { Continue drawing a quad that has already been begun }
             BEGIN
                SetCursor(GetCursor(crossCursor)↑↑);
                downLocalPoint := quadSketcher.fQuad.fVertex[quadSketcher.fLastVertexSet];
                                              { Reset the mouseDownPoint to start drawing the next
                                                side.  This is done so that the rubberbanded line
                                                must be drawn from the last vertex set for the
                                                partial quad, regardless of where the mouse
                                                down occurred. }
                DoMouseCommand := quadSketcher;    { Return the stored sketcher. }
             END { draw mode - continuation of a partially drawn quad }
       END { draw mode }

    ELSE                { either a selection or a rotation.  Try for rotation first }

       IF PtInRgn(downLocalPoint, SELF.fRotationRgn)  { a rotation ? }
         THEN BEGIN
                EraseRgn(SELF.fRotationRgn);    { Feedback to the user that mouse hit detected }
                NEW(aRotateQuadCmd);
                aRotateQuadCmd.IRotateQuadCmd(cRotateQuadCmd);
                DoMouseCommand := aRotateQuadCmd;
             END

        ELSE BEGIN  { Must be a selection of a quad.  This case is tested for last since
                      it takes the longest to check }
                quad := NIL;
                TQuadDocument(SELF.fDocument).EachQuadDo(CheckQuad);

              { quad now references the quad under the cursor, if there is one }
                TQuadDocument(SELF.fDocument).SelectQuad(quad);      { Tell the document }
             END
END;
```

Figure 8-5 The TQuadGrView.DoMouseCommand method.

The Classes TSketchQuadCmd, TSketchParallelogramCmd, TSketchRhombusCmd, TSketchRectangleCmd, and TSketchSquareCmd

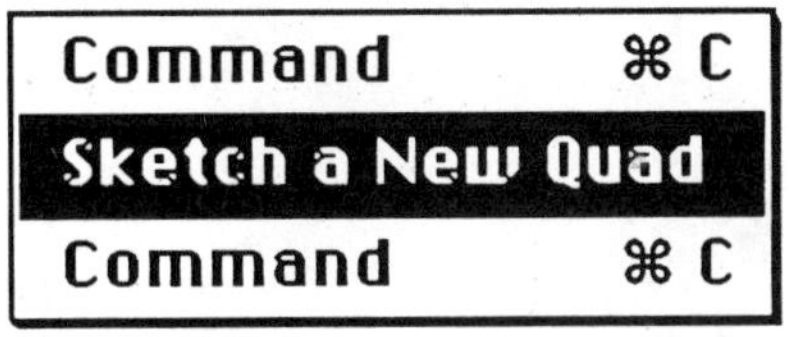

As defined in Chapter 3, instances of class TRhombus, for example, don't know that their sides are of equal length and their opposite sides are parallel nor do instances of class TRectangle know that they have 90° angles at each vertex. This knowledge belongs not in the quadrilateral object itself, but in the object that builds the quadrilateral: the TQuadSketcher objects. Corresponding to each quadrilateral class is a sketcher class to assist in the interactive building of the quadrilateral when the user enters it for the first time in the quadGrView. The inheritance structure for these quadSketcher classes is shown in Figure 8-6 and you can see that their structure parallels that of the quadrilateral classes. These sketchers are all subclasses of TCommand because the TCommand class contains the framework for processing mouse input (TCommand.TrackMouse, TCommand.TrackFeedback, and TCommand.TrackConstrain).

Notes

There is a deeper reason for this parallelism in the inheritance structures of the quadrilateral classes and the quadSketcher classes than mere coincidence. This is explained in Chapter 10 when we discuss the notions of *class methods and metaclasses.*

In the version of the QuadWorld application presented in Listing E, the user interface for entering a new quadrilateral, together with some of the underlying implementation details, is the following (in excruciating detail):

- The user selects the quadrilateral icon in the palette. When the user moves the cursor back into the quadGraphicalView, the TQuadGrView.DoSetCursor method changes it into a crosshair. This indicates that the user is in begin-draw-quadrilateral mode.

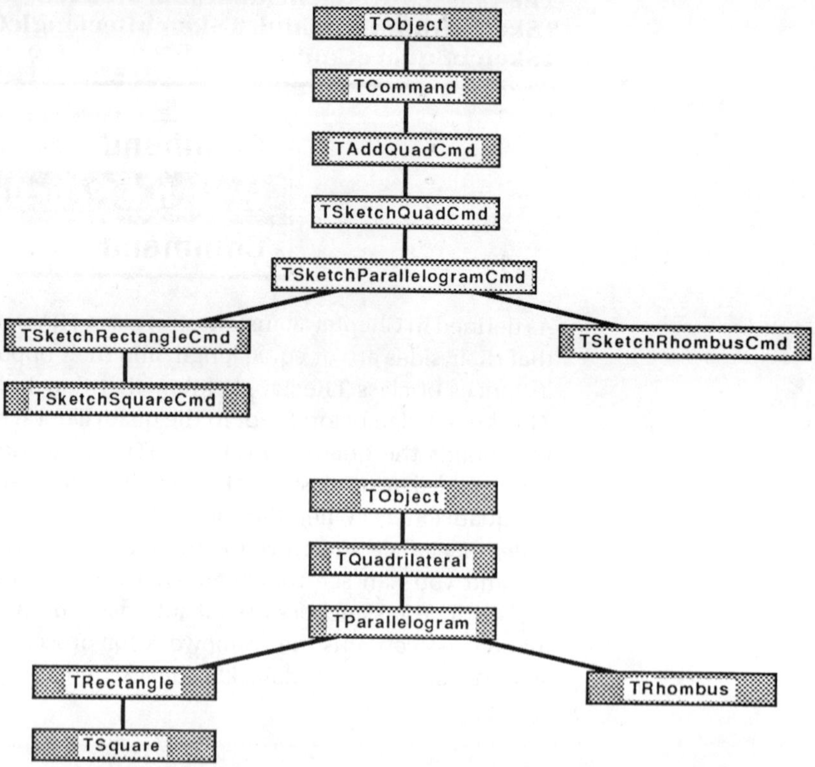

Figure 8-6 The inheritance of the TSketchQuadCmd classes.

- The user presses the mouse button while the cursor is in the quadGraphicalView to begin drawing the new quadrilateral. This eventually creates an instance of TSketchQuadCmd to handle the mouse interaction. As long as the button is pressed, this sketchQuadCmd monitors the mouse position and provides feedback to the user in the form of a rubberbanded line. During this time, the cursor remains as a crosshair.
- The user releases the mouse button. The quadSketcher (the instance of TSketchQuadCmd) is returned to MacApp and during the next idle period the method TQuadGrView.DrawPartialQuad draws the first edge of the quadrilateral being entered. This partial quadrilateral is stored in the quadSketcher as an instance variable. The user can move the cursor around the quadSketcher, use the scroll bars, pull down menus, and other components, but cannot continue drawing the quadrilateral until the mouse button is pressed inside the quadGraphicalView. At that time, the entry of this same

partial quadrilateral is continued. In effect, then, the user is in continue-draw-quadrilateral mode during this time. To let the user know that a mode has been entered, the DoSetCursor method changes the cursor into a shape that looks like a quadrilateral with only one edge drawn during this time between the end of the entry of the first edge of the quadrilateral and the beginning of the entry of the second one. As soon as the mouse button is pressed, the cursor changes back into a crosshair for drawing the second edge. The sketcher, which is retrieved from MacApp, manages this drawing.

This continues for drawing other vertices. The only difference is the shape of the cursor when drawing is not occurring: a quadrilateral with only one edge drawn or a quadrilateral with only two edges drawn.

Notes

Note that I am not claiming that this is the most ideal user interface, rather it is okay. The whole point of the later half of this chapter section and major portions of the next chapter is how to improve this and other parts of QuadWorld within the MacApp framework.

The manner in which a quadSketcher is used in QuadWorld is that TQuadGrView.DoMouseCommand gets control when the user presses the mouse button inside the graphical view, which determines, in the manner explained earlier, what interpretation to place on the use of the mouse. If the user has pressed the mouse to draw a new quad, then DoMouseCommand creates an appropriate sketcher object and returns this to MacApp. MacApp gives this sketcher object control as long as the user continues to press the mouse button and MacApp invokes the sketcher's methods for feedback to the user (TrackFeedback) and for gridding (TrackConstrain) when these are appropriate. This sketcher lives as long as this quadrilateral is being drawn, but shortly after the button is released for the last vertex, the sketcher, having served the purpose for which it was created, is deallocated. Thus, in QuadWorld, a sketcher object exists only to get from the user the quadrilateral being entered. For each new quadrilateral, different sketcher objects are created, and these are then destoyed after the specification of the quadrilateral is complete. This technique of creating an object to perform a specialized task, like obtaining a new rhombus from the user, and then destroying the object when that task is completed is very common in object-oriented programming in general and in MacApp in particular. The overhead associated with object allocation is not so large to preclude this for most tasks, especially interactive ones.

TSketchQuadCmd Instance Variables

Variable	Use
fLastVertexSet	An integer recording the last vertex that was set by the user. For example, if fLastVertexSet = 3, then the user has already specified the first three vertices of this quadrilateral, and need only specify the fourth to complete this quadrilateral object.
fQuadGrView	Refers to the quadGrView—a convenience that makes sending messages to the graphical view easier.

TSketchQuadCmd Methods

Method	Use
ISketchQuadCmd	Initializes a new instance of TQuadSketcher or of one of its subclasses.
TrackFeedback	Overridden method. Draws the feedback lines so that the user gets an impression of the quadrilateral as it is being entered.
TrackMouse	Overridden method. Decides what actions to take depending on the position of the cursor and the state of the mouse button. This is the method that causes the vertices of the partial quad to be set.
TrackConstrain	Overridden method in TRhombus and TSquare only. Corrects the cursor position to take into account the geometric constraints associated with rhombi and squares.
SetVertices	Enters one or more new vertices that have been determined.
EnclosePartialQuad	Compute the smallest upright rectangle enclosing the partial quadrilateral.

The methods of the sketcher classes work together to provide for the interactive definition of a new quadrilateral. The TrackMouse method samples the cursor position while the mouse button is pressed, TrackFeedback draws the appropriate feedback, possibly after it has been corrected by TrackConstrain, and SetVertices enters one or more vertices into the quadrilateral when the user releases the mouse button. As an example of when SetVertices sets more than one vertex, TSketchParallelogramCmd.SetVertices enters both the third and the fourth vertices of a parallelogram when the third vertex is specified as only three points are needed to define a parallelogram.

In the quadSketcher classes (the class TSketchQuadCmd and all its descendants) methods are overridden to provide exactly the additional information needed to sketch the corresponding quadrilateral. The TSketchParallelogram Cmd, for example, knows that parallelograms have opposite sides that are parallel—this knowledge is imbedded in the computation of the coordinates of the fourth vertex of the parallelogram. This computation fixes the fourth vertex in the same relative position from the third vertex as the second vertex is from the first:

```
PROCEDURE TSketchParallelogramCmd.SetVertices(newVertex: Point);
VAR diffPt: Point;
BEGIN
  INHERITED SetVertices(newVertex);
  { Set the fourth vertex of the parallelogram by compuation }
  IF SELF.fLastVertexSet = 3 THEN
    BEGIN
      diffPt.h := fQuadGrView.fPartialQuad.fVertex[1].h—
        fQuadGrView.fPartialQuad.fVertex[2].h;
      diffPt.v := fQuadGrView.fPartialQuad.fVertex[1].v—
        fQuadGrView.fPartialQuad.fVertex[2].v;
      fLastVertexSet := 4;
      fQuadGrView.fPartialQuad.fVertex[4].h := newVertex.h + diffPt.h;
      fQuadGrView.fPartialQuad.fVertex[4].v := newVertex.v + diffPt.v;
    END
END;
```

The knowledge that rhombi have equal length sides is contained in the TSketchRhombusCmd.TrackConstrain method that constrains any potential position for the third vertex of a rhombus to be the same distance from the second vertex as the second is from the first. However, there is no need to have a SetVertices method in the TSketchRhombusCmd class to enforce the constraint that rhombi have parallel opposite sides—this behavior is inherited by TSketch RhombusCmd objects from their superclass, TSketchParallelogramCmd.

The "location" of the various geometric constraints associated with quadrilaterals throughout the quadSketcher clases is shown in Figure 8-7. Note how each new sketcher class adds (or overrides) just the additional constraints needed for the corresponding type of quadrilateral. This incremental addition of knowledge is possible because of the inheritance mechanism of an object-oriented language.

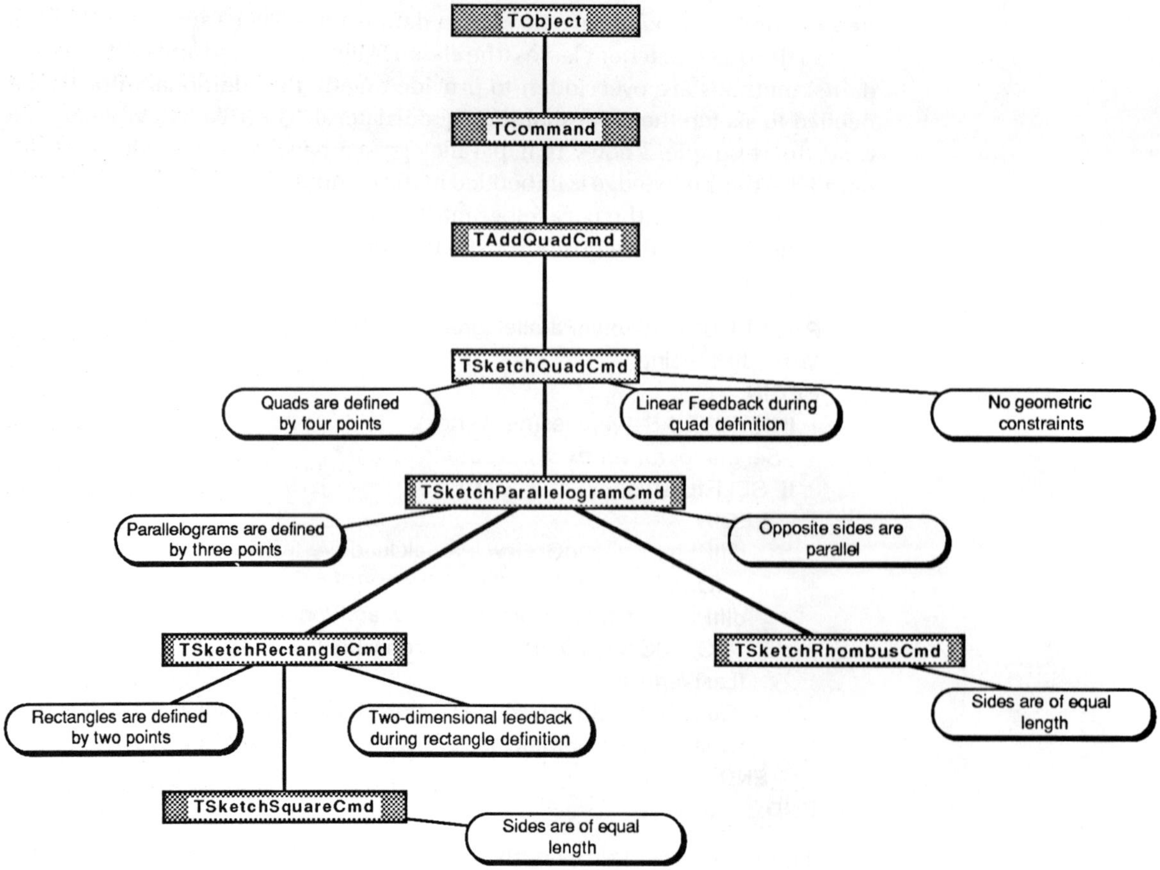

Figure 8-7 Knowledge placement in the quadSketcher classes.

The Class TRotateQuadCmd

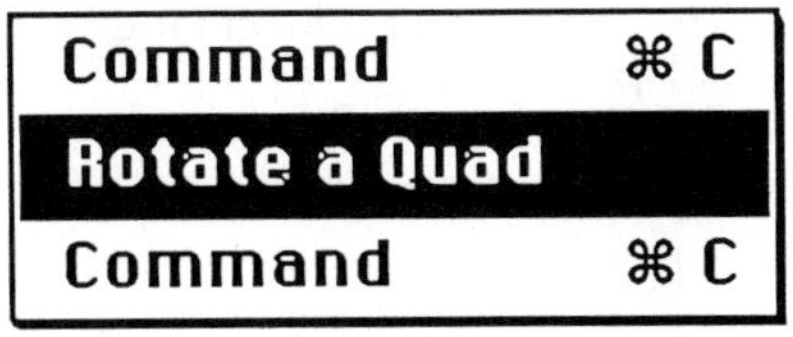

Of the various actions the user can perform with a quadrilateral, only rotating the quadrilateral has changed in this full implementation of QuadWorld, as compared to the Mini-QuadWorld application discussed in Chapter 7. In the full implementation, the user can rotate a quadrilateral by any amount. The only difficult portion about accomplishing this functionality is obtaining the desired angle from the user. Clearly, this can be done with a dialog box by having the user enter the desired angle numerically, but that is a waste of the Mac's graphics capabilities.

The way in which the user specifies the angle for rotating the currently selected quadrilateral is to draw a line through the selected quadrilateral's center, effectively subtending the angle. The user indicates the desire to do so by mousing down in a special rotation handle that appears on the selected quadrilateral. (This rotation handle can be seen in Figure 8-8.) When the user mouses down in this handle, the handle disappears, thus indicating to the user that the mouse hit was detected. From that point on, as long as the mouse button is pressed, a line rubberbands from the selected quadrilateral's center to the cursor position. When the mouse button is released, the angle of the rubberbanded line is used to rotate the quadrilateral.

Definitions

Here we are using the term "handle" to mean a lever by which the user can rotate a quadrilateral. Don't confuse this with a toolbox handle which is a double-dereferenced pointer.

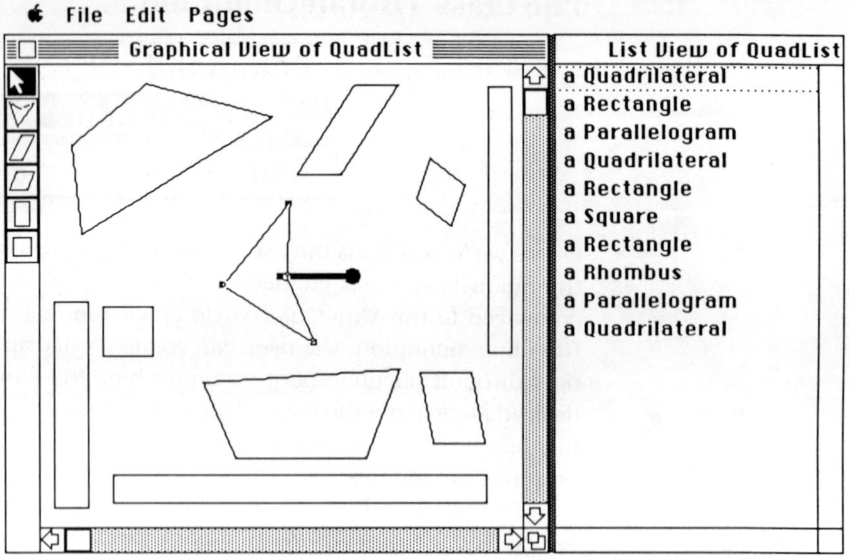

Figure 8-8 The QuadWorld rotation region.

The shape of the rotation handle is a constant QuickDraw region, regardless of the size or type of quadrilateral. The rotation handle is stored in an instance variable of the quadGrView and is moved to the center of the selected quadrilateral when the selection takes place in TQuadGrView.ChangeSelection. The region is drawn in the view by TQuadGrView.HighlightSelection. The region only appears when there is a non-nil current selection.

The Classes TListDocument and TListView

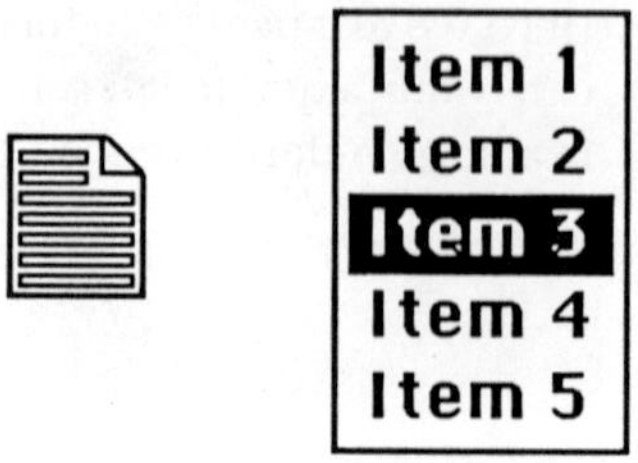

A view that displays a list of selectable text strings is useful in applications in which a large number of choices must be presented to the user. The classes TListView and TListDocument implement this notion in a way that can be reused by many MacApp applications. All programming languages provide some mechanism for reusing code. These vary in power and ease of use from physically copying and modifying code to subroutine libraries. Hybrid object-oriented languages provide these types of reusability plus another type—a type that is epitomized in *building blocks*. Together, TListView and TListDocument are an example of a reusable software component that you can design for yourself to make your application programming easier. These building blocks use the dynamic binding and inheritance features of object-oriented programming to provide components that can be reused in the most general sense: they can be reused without change if necessary or they can be customized to fit a particular need without needing access to the source code of the building block itself.

You can understand the structure and operation of the TListView class in this building block by examining two of its operations: drawing the listView and responding to mouse clicks inside the listView. The listView is drawn in the following way:

1. Setup the QuickDraw pen appropriately by sending SELF the message SetPen;
2. "Ask" the listView's document for the textual representation of the ith item by sending its the document the message ReportListItem. (Note that the document of a listView must be a listDocument. More on this later.)
3. Calculate the position of the ith item by sending SELF the message SetUpBox. This returns a rectangle that surrounds the area of the item.
4. Draw the ith item by sending SELF the message DrawOneItem.

```
PROCEDURE TListView.Draw(area: Rect);
VAR bBox: Rect;                          { the bounding box for a single item }
    itemToDraw: Str255;
    itemNumber: INTEGER;
BEGIN
    SELF.SetPen;
    itemNumber := 1;
                    { Get each item in turn from the document and draw it}
    itemToDraw := TListDocument(SELF.fDocument).ReportListItem
      (itemNumber);
    WHILE (itemToDraw < > ' ') DO
      BEGIN
                                              { Calculate the rectangle to fill}
        bBox := SELF.SetUpBox(itemNumber);
        IF RectIsVisible(bBox) THEN          { only write text that will be seen}
          BEGIN
            MoveTo(bBox.left + txMargin, bBox.top + SELF.fLineAscent);
            SELF.DrawOneItem(itemToDraw);
```

```
            END;
          itemNumber := itemNumber + 1;
          itemToDraw := TListDocument(SELF.fDocument).ReportListItem
            (itemNumber);
        END;
      SELF.fNumberOfItems := itemNumber-1;
    END;
```

The listView class (and thus the Draw method) purposely breaks down each of the logical steps in drawing the view (getting the next item, calculating its position, drawing it) into separate methods so that these methods can be overridden if necessary by application programmers who use this building block. The designer of this class has, in effect, built generality into this building block by doing this. For example, the decision as to what computation is performed to determine the position of one of the text strings can be easily changed by overriding SetUpBox in a subclass of TListView. Even if this method is overridden, the computation of the position of a text string would still take place at the appropriate place in the drawing algorithm. This is because when the message SetUpBox is sent to SELF, SELF refers to an instance of the subclass and the SetUpBox of that subclass is invoked.

When the user presses the mouse button in the listView, the TListView.DoMouseCommand determines which item is at the cursor position by sending SELF the message PtToIndex. This method determines the correct item by testing whether the cursor is inside each of the rectangles constructed by SetUpBox until it finds one that contains the cursor position:

```
FUNCTION TListView.DoMouseCommand
  (VAR downLocalPoint: Point;
   VAR info: EventInfo;
   VAR hysteresis: Point):TCommand; OVERRIDE;
VAR index: INTEGER;
BEGIN
    { If this mouse press results in a change of the current selection, let the
      document deal with it in any way it chooses. This is done because the
      document might control several views, or might deal with a changed
      selection in some other application-specific manner. }
    DoMouseCommand := gNoChanges;
    index := SELF.PtToIndex(downLocalPoint);
    IF (index > 0) THEN
      BEGIN
        IF SELF.fCurrItem = index
                        { A click on the current selection means to deselect it}
```

```
            THEN TListDocument(SELF.fDocument).SetSelection(0)
            ELSE TListDocument(SELF.fDocument).SetSelection(index);
        END
    END;
FUNCTION TListView.PtToIndex(testPoint: Point): INTEGER;
VAR i: INTEGER;                                        { FOR Loop Index }
BEGIN
    PtToIndex := 0;                          { Assume the item is NOT found}
    FOR i := 1 TO SELF.fNumberOfItems DO
      IF PtInRect(testPoint, SELF.SetUpBox(i))
        THEN BEGIN
            PtToIndex := i;
            LEAVE                   { Don't check the rest of the rectangles}
          END
    END;
```

TListView.DoMouseCommand then informs the document that the selection should be changed by sending it the message SetSelection.

If you tried to use this approach to the design of a TListView class in a separate unit, you would get (at least) two compilation errors. The compiler would warn you that instances of TDocument can't receive the messages ReportListItem and SetSelection—messages sent by the listView to its document. This warning would appear even if you had added these methods to your TDocument subclass (in your application's main unit) and implemented them. The reason for this is that the reference type of the fDocument instance variable of TListView, a variable inherited from TView, is TDocument, not your TDocument subclass, even though its object type is your document subclass and thus it can receive the messages ReportListItem and SetSelection. For this approach to the design of a TListView to work, the reference type of the fDocument instance variable must be a class that includes these two messages in its protocol and the compiler must know about this class's protocol when TListView is compiled. However, the document class of every application is different. How can a reusable TListView ever be compiled? To solve this problem, an abstract superclass, TListDocument, is designed. This class exists only to be subclassed and thus to solve this compile-time difficulty. Applications that use the TListView must design their document classes as subclasses of TListDocument, This is done in QuadWorld.

Since there will never be an instance of the abstract superclass TListDocument, there is no initialization method defined for it.

TListDocument Instance Variables

(No new variables needed)

TListDocument Methods

Method	Use
SetSelection	Changes the selection to a new value. This message is usually sent to the document as part of the processing of a mouse click in the document's listView.
ReportListItem	Returns the string representation of the ith item of the document.

TListView Instance Variables

Variable	Use
fCurrItem	The **INTEGER** index of the current selection.
fNumberOfItems	The **INTEGER** number of items currently in the list.
fLineHeight	The **INTEGER** corresponding to the minimum vertical space needed for each line of text, including the blank space between lines. This value is based entirely on the font used for the listView. The font is set in the method SetPen.
fLineAscent	The **INTEGER** corresponding to the position of the baseline of the text with respect to the top of the line. This value is based on the font used for the listView. The font is set in the method SetPen.

TListView Methods

Initialization Method

Method	Use
IListView	Initializes a new instance of TListView.

Command and Selection Processing Methods

Method	Use
ChangeSelection	Responds to a request (usually from the list-Document) to change the current selection.
DoMouseCommand	Overridden method. Processes a mouse click in the listView.
PtToIndex	Converts a point in the coordinate system of the view to the index of the list item that occurs at that point.

Display Methods

Method	Use
Draw	Overridden method. Draws the listView.
DrawOneItem	Draws one element of the list view. This method assumes that the pen has already been properly positioned. This a method in this class so that it can be easily overridden.
HighlightSelection	Overridden method. Highlights the current selection.
InvalidateItem	Invalidates one of the items so that it is redrawn the next time MacApp draws the view. However, because of the nature of a listView, this method actually invalidates the entire view whenever any item is invalidated. To do otherwise would leave "holes" in the listView.
SetUpBox	Calculates the rectangular area of the view occupied by a given list item.
SetPen	Setup the pen width, font, and pen mode before drawing the view
CalcMinExtent	Overridden method. This TView method calcualtes the extent of the view. It must be overridden in TListView since the vertical extent is variable.

Do More

Design a subclass of TListView that could be used in QuadWorld to produce two-line entires for each quad in the listView. (See Figure 8-9) These two-line entries should highlight as a single entity when a mouse click occurs anywhere on either line.

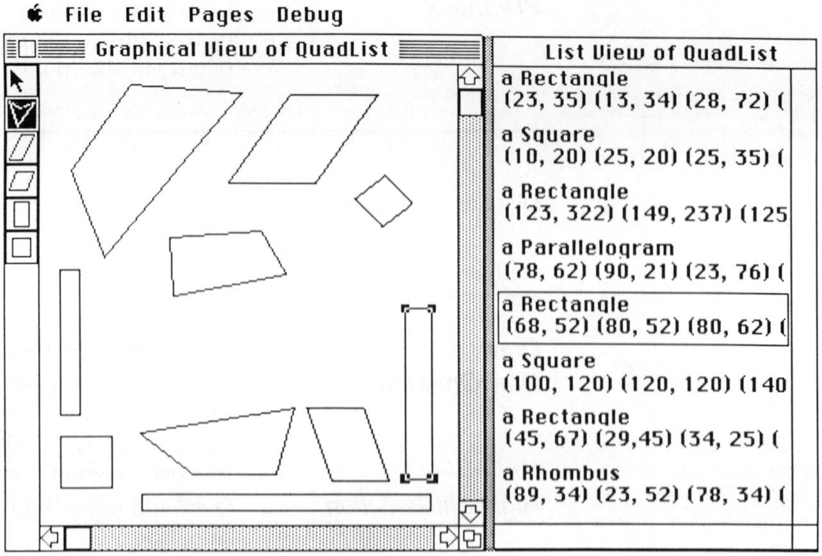

Figure 8-9 A new type of listView for QaudWorld.

This completes our discussion of the MacApp subclasses in QuadWorld, though we will use some major examples from QuadWorld in our discussion of the various advanced topics in MacApp in the next chapter.

Alternate QuadWorld Architectures

In developing the QuadWorld application, a number of design decisions were made as how to structure the classes, what instance variable data to include in each one, and how to best expand the MacApp framework into the whole of QuadWorld, among other things. In this section, several of these design decisions are reviewed and the pros and cons of alternatives presented.

Notes

Note that I certainly don't claim that the QuadWorld application source code presented in Listing E is the world's greatest MacApp application, or even that it is the best possible implementation of QuadWorld given the MacApp framework as a base. Rather, I do believe that it is a fine introductory example of the use of MacApp—an example not so small to be trivial nor so big as to be incomprehensible with a moderate effort. I encourage those who would like to learn more about MacApp by extending QuadWorld to do so in any way: by providing new features, for example, or by reimplementing portions of it in ways that you think are cleaner, more efficient, or better example of object-oriented programming. If you do so, I would like very much to hear about your efforts. I can be reached courtesy of Hayden Book Company.

The Amount of Coupling between Documents and Their View

In a MacApp application, your subclass (or subclasses) of TDocument represents the data your application manipulates and your subclass (or subclasses) of TView renders that data in a certain way for the end user. Some object-oriented programmers believe that to the maximum extent possible, the document should not know how it is rendered or even what views are available for rendering. It is hard to argue with such a position since what it really says is that there is a natural modularity in object-oriented programming—what is displayed (the data) is separate from how it is displayed (the view)—and that this modularity should be preserved. However, in practice this is often violated and in this regard QuadWorld models practice more than theory. (Note that in this discussion we are using an extended definition of the document, a definition that includes the TDocument object and the various TQuad objects that it owns because this is really the data that the view displays. Where there is a chance for confusion, we call this wider notion the *extended document*.)

This modularity is violated by the standard MacApp practice of specifically adding instance variables referring to the view in the document subclass—fQuadGrView and fQuadTxView instance variables to TQuadDocument, in the case of QuadWorld. Hence a quadDocument knows that there is a graphical representation and a textual representation of it. More precisely, a quadDocument has hardcoded information like the following:

> When one of your quadrilaterals is selected, send the ChangeSelection message to the TQuadGrView object referenced by your fQuadGrView

variable, then send the ChangeSelection message to the TListView object referenced by your fQuadTxView variable.

This is done in the TQuadDocument.SelectQuad method:

```
{ make the selection in both panels; quad = NIL means de-select;
  this routine does nothing if the old and new selections are the same }
  PROCEDURE TQuadDocument.SelectQuad(quad: TQuad);
  BEGIN
    IF (quad < > SELF.fSelectedQuad) THEN
                                        { old selection < > new selection }
      BEGIN
        SELF.fSelectedQuad := quad;
        { Select first in the graphics view }
        SELF.fQuadGrView.ChangeSelection(quad);
        { ... then in the text view }
        SELF.fQuadTxView.ChangeSelection(SELF.QuadToListIndex(quad));
      END;
  END;
```

(Note that several other TDocument methods have similar types of structural information about the QuadWorld application built into them, including InvalidateQuad, DoMakeWindows, and DoMakeViews.) The reasons for this standard practice of violating the modularity of the separation between the document and the view in a MacApp application like QuadWorld are:

- The modularity of this separation will be violated anyway because DoMakeViews and DoMakeWindows must know about the two views.
- In MacApp, documents create the views, so they should be able to send them messages.
- All document objects in MacApp can refer to their views with something like the following reference: TWindow(SELF.fWindowList.First). This inclusion of an explicit instance variable merely makes this reference a little easier to type.
- The knowledge that, for example, a quadrilateral has two representations and that when a quadrilateral is selected, both its representations must highlight, must be placed somewhere. If this information is not stored in the method of the quadDocument, the only other alternatives are the methods of:

1. the TQuad class itself.
2. a new TSelectQuadCmd class.
3. each view subclass individually.

Figure 8-10 lists the consequences of each choice, along with the choice of the document subclass. The document subclass is clearly the best choice.

Where to store the "knowledge" that a quadrilateral object has two simultaneously viewed representations each of which must be highlighted when the quadrilateral object is selected?

Class	How	Results and Implications
TQuad	Design a `TQuad.Highlight` method which would affect all views. Such a method would perform the following steps: a) Focus on quadGrView b) Paint quad's selection handles c) Focus on quadTxView d) Invert rectangle around text	1) Views cannot highlight their current selections independently, violating a MacApp application design goal that only views and commands should do any actual drawing. 2) A quadrilateral object knows its highlighting mechanism. 3) Focusing is relatively expensive and this scheme maximizes it.
TSelectQuadCmd	Design a new command class to handle the operation of selection. This command class would do the highlighting in both views.	1) Still have to have a `Highlight` method in each view to actually do the highlighting. 2) Selecting is not usually considered to be an undoable command, thus a subclass of TCommand is inappropriate. 3) To be consistent, many other command classes would have to
Each individual view class	Each view's `Highlight` method, in addition to performing the actual highlighting, would have to invoke the other views highlight method.	1) Unmodular to the extreme since every view would have to know about every other view. Adding a new view would be very troublesome. 2) Cannot make the ListView a re-usable unit for other applications to use.
TQuadDocument	Each view tells the document when a quadrilateral object has been selected in it. The document then tells all views to highlight this quadrilateral.	1) Two view instance variables needed in the document. 2) Each view must remember what the current selection is, or ask the document each time it needs thisdata. 3)To add a new view, must modify several methods of TQuadDocument * Chosen Alternative *

Figure 8-10 The possibilities for placing of the knowledge that quadrilaterals have two representations in the QuadWorld application.

In reality, the real issue on the amount of view-document coupling is not whether the document should know that two views exist because this is almost inevitable, but rather should it know about how those views render the document in detail. In QuadWorld there is only one example in the extended document in which the document knows anything about how a view is rendered and that is in the drawing of an individual quadrilateral in the quadGrView. TQuad objects know how to draw themselves. Moving this knowledge to the view would mean losing the ability to draw rectangles and squares in a more efficient manner (as discussed in Chapter 3), or worse, cluttering up the view's drawing code with tests to determine exactly what type of quadrilateral object is being drawn and then treating the unrotated rectangles and squares differently.

The Amount of Coupling between Commands and Views

It is best if adding a new command class does not require you to replicate the knowledge already stored in other classes. For example, an application with multiple views could require that each command class tell each view what was modified by the command. In QuadWorld, this design choice would have required that the TClearQuadCmd class, for example, directly cause portions of the quadGraphicalView and the quadTextualView to be redrawn by directly invoking methods of these classes. This results in a very unmodular structure and one in which knowledge about the protocol and perhaps the internal structure of the views is repeated in many separate places.

In QuadWorld, each command class invokes methods of extended TQuadDocument to modify the list of quadrilaterals and the document object then sends messages to the views that eventually cause their partial invalidation and redrawing. All such requests go to a single place (the document object), which is responsible for broadcasting the intent of these requests to the views. The commands "talk" to the document and the document "talks" to the views. This decoupling of commands and views makes it easier to add both new commands and new views, or to change a new view subclass provided in a new MacApp building block.

The Amount of Coupling between Different Views

In both theory and practice, it is best if separate views of the same document have no knowledge of the other views. To violate this makes it difficult to add a new view, use a new view subclass, use a new view unit, or change the implementation of one of your view subclasses. The MacApp implementation of QuadWorld follows this advice—neither the graphical view nor the textual view have an easy way to reference each other, nor do they do so. Note that these two views are even defined in separate Object Pascal units so that they can't even reference each others' names, let alone their internal structures or methods.

The Use of a Single Palette and List View Unit

The notion of a palette and a list view are remarkably similar. It may well be possible to design an abstract superclass, say TPalListView, that could serve as a building block for all applications that need a palette or list view. The user of such a building block would subclass TPalListView to override the DrawOne-Item method, or perhaps the Draw method. This new subclass would be initialized with data such as th number of rows, the number of columns, whether to draw lines between the entries, or whether the view was fixed in size or grew when the window was resized. Such a unit could be used by large numbers of applications without any change. This could be an improvement of the QuadWorld architecture, one that would make a fine student project.

Multiple Simple Windows versus a Single Complex Window

The user interface I originally wanted for QuadWorld was to put the two quadrilateral views in panels of a single window so that the user would be allowed to move the boundary between the panels to allow more space for one view or the other. MacApp does not yet provide adequate support for interactive resizing of paneled windows. My next choices for the QuadWorld implementation were:

1. To enhance MacApp to add interactive resizing of panels.
2. To give up resizing.
3. To use separate resizable windows.

I decided upon the last alternative of multiple, simply structured windows.

For many Macintosh applications, the choice of multiple, simple windows results in a user interface more in keeping with the Macintosh User Interface Standard. For the QuadWorld application, however, I believe that it is a less-than-optimal choice forced by the current state of the MacApp framework.

Filter and Sieves for Undo

There are two basic ways in which the DoIt, UndoIt, and RedoIt methods of a command class can work. The first way is for the DoIt method to actually modify the document's data in whatever way is appropriate for the operation associated with this command object, then for the UndoIt method to perform the inverse modification of the document, if requested by the user. For many operations, this approach is easy and efficient. For others, however, it is not so easy because the operation, by its very nature, makes many modifications throughout the document's data. To implement the inverse modification in the UndoIt method in such cases can be extremely costly in terms of both space and time. For these operations, the techniques of filters and sieves can be used.

Filters and *sieves* refer to programming techniques for modifying the view of the document without modifying the document. Consider the following simple example. Suppose that quadrilaterals in QuadWorld has shades, that the user has the ability to change the shade, and that actually changing the shade of a quadrilateral is difficult to undo (it is in fact trivial, but for the sake of the example, let us suppose it is difficult). The way to make the shade command undoable would be to make the shade of the quadrilateral seem to change on the screen without really changing it in the document. This can be done with the following code:

```
PROCEDURE TQuadGrView.Draw(area: Rect);
    PROCEDURE FilterAndDrawQuad(quad: TQuad);
    VAR tempQuad: TQuad;
    BEGIN
      IF quad < > newlyShadedQuad
        THEN quad.Draw { this quad is not the special one }
        ELSE BEGIN
            tempQuad := quad.Clone;
            tempQuad.fShade := newShade;
            tempQuad.Draw;
            tempQuad.Free;
          END
    END;
  BEGIN
    TQuadDocument(SELF.fDocument).EachQuadDo(FilterAndDrawQuad);
    SELF.DrawPartialQuad;
  END;
```

This code determines, for each quadrilateral in the quadDocument, whether the quadrilateral is the special one that should not be drawn in the normal manner, but rather in a special way—with a new shade in this example. Thus the quadrilaterals in the quadDocument are filtered through a sieve that allows most quadrilaterals to pass through to be drawn unchanged, but that affects the drawing of one special quadrilateral, the one referenced by newlyShadedQuad. This is conceptually represented in Figure 8-11.

Clearly, this small example is not representative of the way in which you would design filters and sieves in a general way for use throughout a large application. This is because this approach leads to the situation where the quirks of each commands undo requirements would be reflected in the structure of the view's Draw method—the depths of unmodularity! A more uniform and modular mechanism is needed. One way to do so is with the command object.

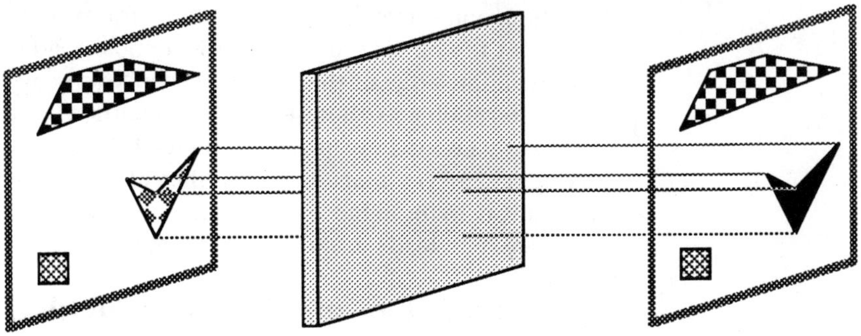

Figure 8-11 The use of filters and sieves for rendering a virtual image.

Each command object could have a FilterAndDo method and the application would access this mechanism by sending the FilterAndDo message to the gLast-Command object. This is basically the way in which the Lisa Toolkit application framework (Chapter 12) provides for undo of commands when the undo operation was difficult or costly to perform. While MacApp does not have a filtering mechanism built into the basic framework, the effect is relatively easy to achieve.

To build filtering into a MacApp application, the most reasonable course is to design two abstract superclasses, TFilterCommand and TFilteredView, that provide many of the methods needed for filtering, albeit with many as null methods. All the views and all the commands of the application are then descended from these two classes.

In the MacApp implementation of QuadWorld, because the operations on the quadDocument are easy to undo, the straightforward technique of directly modifying the list of quadrilaterals was used for all undoable commands. The Lisa Clascal implementation of QuadWorld (Listing G) uses both filters and sieves in order to demonstrate how these techniques can be employed.

Constrained Stretching of Quadrilaterals

In the current implementation of QuadWorld, the quadSketcher classes contain the knowledge of the geometric constraints associated with various types of quadrilaterals. While this makes the interactive entry of new quadrilaterals easy, it may not be the best architectural choice to support the interactive editing of quadrilaterals—a task that must preserve the geometric constraints.

Stretching one vertex of a parallelogram, for example, should be done in such a way that the object still has parallel opposite sides. For that operation, perhaps the knowledge of the geometric constraints would best be placed in the quadrilateral objects themselves. On the other hand, every quadrilateral object already knows how to allocate a sketcher of the appropriate class. Perhaps making sketchers "smarter" so that they also can edit existing quadrilaterals is the best way to for achieve this. An interesting student project would be to determine which leads to the cleanest architecture.

Handling Selections in QuadWorld

Currently, QuadWorld stores the current selection in three places: in the quadDocument, in the quadGrView, and in the quadTxView. Selection changes are initiated in the DoMouseCommands of either view. These methods inform the quadDocument that the selection has changed and the quadDocument invokes the ChangeSelection method of each view. (This process is shown in Figure 8-12.) This architecture has two problems, which may or may not be unavoidable:

- Redundant storage of the current selection information with the resulting problem of maintaining consistency between the copies.
- An inherent inefficiency—when a mouse click in the quadGrView, for example, is interpreted to require a change of selection, the quadGrView tells the quadDocument that the selection has changed and the quadDocument tells the quadTxView and the quadGrView that the selection has changed.

The only way that I could think of to solve this problem was to have the quadrilateral views interrogate the quadDocument each time they wanted to know the value of the current selection (either by sending it a message, or by directly accessing one of the quadDocument's instance variables). This was how selections were managed in Mini-QuadWorld, but the additional complexity of the two views and dim highlighting made this solution less attractive in QuadWorld.

Finding the Selected Quadrilateral

The technique used in QuadWorld for determining which of the set of quadrilaterals currently in the quadDocument has been selected when a mouse click occurs—testing the cursor point for inclusion in the enclosing rectangles of each quadrilateral—is easy and efficient, but can lead to selections which will surprise some users. Consider a quadrilateral like that in Figure 8-13 A mouse press that seems to be far away from this quad can still be within its enclosing rectangle and thus would cause the quad's selection. This would probably surprise a QuadWorld user. One way in which this surprise can be avoided is to build in a secondary test for selection of a quad. This secondary test would

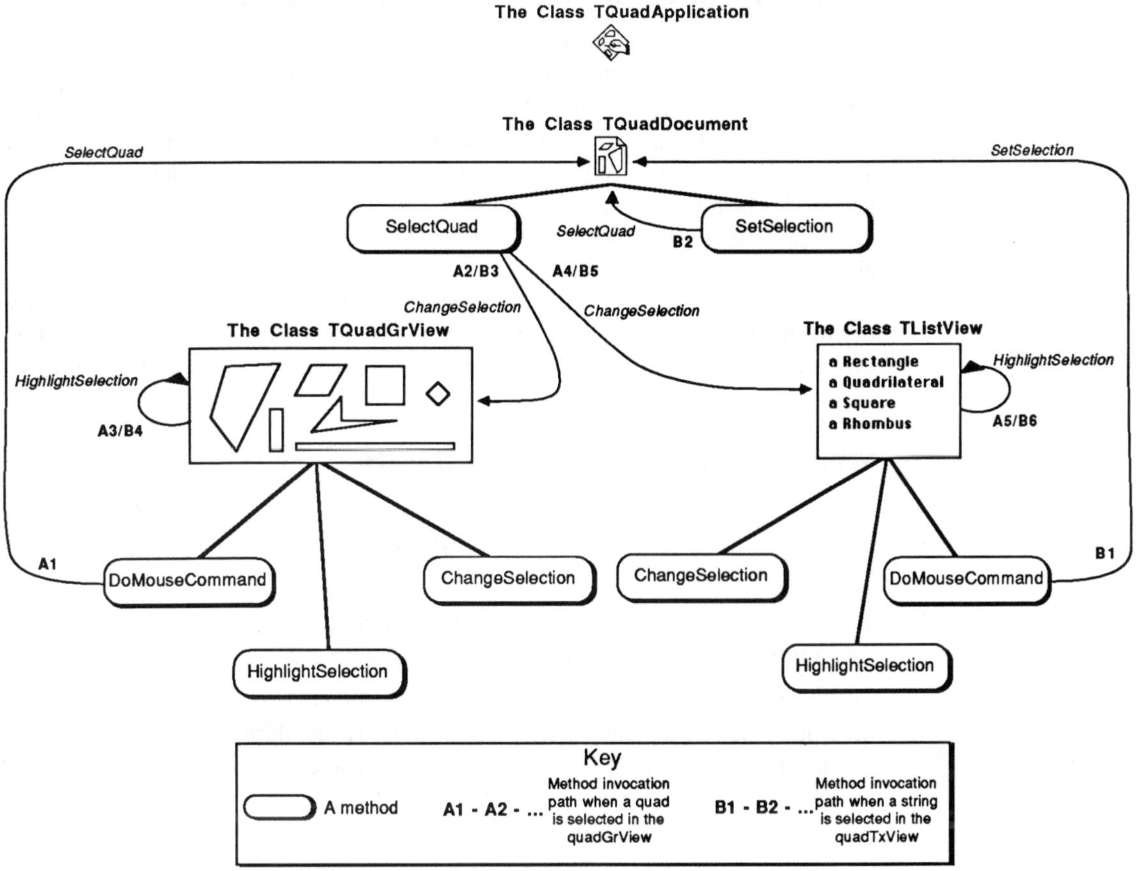

Figure 8-12 How information about the current selection is transmitted around QuadWorld.

be conducted only when the primary test—the enclosing rectangle test—succeeds, and only if the secondary test also succeeds will the selection take place. The secondary test, then, double checks the easily computed, but sometimes wrong, results of the primary test.

One possible secondary test is to construct a QuickDraw region with the same shape as the quadrilateral that passed the primary test. The QuickDraw routine PtInRgn can then be used to test if this quadrilateral really should be selected.

Store or Compute the Enclosing Rectangle

There are many occasions when you have the choice to either store a value or to compute it "on the fly" whenever it is needed. Values that are computed when needed are often called *dynamic instance variables.* QuadWorld has one such dynamic instance variable: the enclosing rectangle of a quadrilateral. This could just as easily have been an ordinary instance variable of TQuad. When this is done, it is usually called the extentRect of the object. Since quads are relatively static objects in QuadWorld, this would be a very reasonable choice.

When you have a choice between ordinary instance variables and dynamic instance variables, you should probably use ordinary instance variables for relatively stable values and dynamic instance variables when the values can change very often.

Writing Objects More Compactly

It would be easy to write the quadDocument a little more compactly by recording only the opposite corners of upright rectangles and squares. One way to do this woulld be to:

1. Define a special quadID to represent upright rectangles and squares, for example IDUpRectangle = 7, and IDUpSquare = 8.
2. Modify the use of the cloning array , gPrototypeQuadsArray, accordingly.
3. Add TRectangle.WriteTo. In this method, you must determine if the rectangle or square is upright by looking at the fRotated, then invoke the inherited WriteTo for rotated rectangles. If the quad to be written is not rotated, then just write out two opposite corners—thus saving the space occupied by two vertices.
4. Add TRectangle.ReadFrom to perform the inverse operation of WriteTo.

Using TList To Organize the QuadDocument

Ordinarily, an application like QuadWorld should use an instance of TList to organize the objects referred to in the document, rather than explictly maintaining a linkedt list. QuadWorld uses a linked list because it is a little easier for MacApp novices to understand what is going on with the various document manipulation methods if the implemenation is just a linked list and to demonstrate that the standard algorithms used in procedural programming can be used in a hybrid language like Object Pascal. If I were to do a QuadWorld-like as a real application for the marketplace, I would use a TList object in the document to organize the objects created by the user.

CHAPTER

9

Advanced MacApp Features

There are a tremendous number of "advanced topics" in any application development facility like Object Pascal or MacApp and no treatment of such topics in one chapter can hope to be comprehensive. Here we examine three areas: using MacApp for an application that must maintain several different types of documents, providing clipboard support in a MacApp application, and handling run-time errors, such as lack of additional memory, in a MacApp application. These are important topics that most MacApp developers will have to deal with eventually. In addition, there are some common stumbling blocks for the intermediate object-oriented programmer in expanding MacApp into a real application and in this chapter we examine several of these and, if appropriate, see how they could effect the further development of the QuadWorld application.

Notes

The topics explored in this chapter make excellent, small hands-on projects in object-oriented programming and the use of MacApp. Such projects could be used in a course or seminar in object-oriented programming in such a way that the relevant concepts could be thoroughly explored with a minimum of unproductive (and unappealing) drudge work. For example, given a disk with the QuadWorld source (as shown in Listing E), you could modify it so that mouse-up drawing was possible, redesign the coupling between TQuadDocument and the two TView subclasses, or add another undoable menu command to the application. The source code for all the Listings is available on Macintosh diskettes from the Hayden Book Company. (See the order form at the end of the book.)

Advanced Features

Multiple Documents

Both Mini-QuadWorld and QuadWorld need only one type of document: a document to hold and manipulate a number of quads. Accordingly, only one TDocument subclass, TQuadDocument, is defined. Most applications resemble QuadWorld in this respect and need only one type of document subclass. However, some applications need several types of documents—applications like the Font/DA mover, with font documents and desk accessory documents, and Jazz, with worksheet documents, graphics documents, database documents, form documents, word processing documents, and telecommunications documents. MacApp directly supports this type of application in the method TApplication.DoMakeDocuments. To see how this works, the first part of this section shows how you can build a multi-document application with one particular user interface on the MacApp framework and later we show how you can do this with other user interfaces.

Suppose you wish to design a multi-purpose application similar to Jazz that has four types of documents: text documents, spreadsheet document, picture documents, and business graphics documents. Further suppose that instead of a single **New** command on the File menu, there are to be four commands: **New Text, New Spreadsheet, New Picture,** and **New Business Graphic,** from which the user can choose to generate a new document of a particular type. As with all MacApp applications, these menu items are associated with the symbolic constants called command numbers – in this small example these constants are cNewText, cNewSpreadsheet, cNewPicture, and cNewBusinessGraphic.

The flow of control that begins when the user chooses one of these menu items illustrates how MacApp supports multi-document applications (Later we enumerate the steps you must take to achieve this flow of control.):

- MacApp determines the command number associated the menu item choosen. Call it thisCommandNumber.
- MacApp calls gTarget.DoMenuCommand(thisCommandNumber). Several other DoMenuCommands are invoked in the inheritance and event handler chains until TApplication.DoMenuCommand eventually handles thisCommandNumber by calling gApplication.DoMakeDocument(thisCommandNumber).

Definitions

TApplication.DoMenuCommand properly "catches" these commands requesting the allocation of new document objects if the application uses fewer than ten document types and if the command numbers of the associated commands (cNewText, cNewSpreadsheet, and so on) are appropriately chosen (more on this later). Only the most unusual application will be unable to meet these conditions.

- Your application's DoMakeDocument allocates the appropriate type of document object with code approximately like this:

```
FUNCTION TMultiApplication.DoMakeDocument(itsCmdNumber:
   CmdNumber): TDocument;
VAR textDocument: TTextDocument;
     spreadsheetDocument: TSpreadsheetDocument;
     pictureDocument: TPictureDocument;
     businessGraphicsDocument: TBusinessGraphicsDocument;
BEGIN
  CASE itsCmdNumber OF
    cNewText: BEGIN
           NEW(textDocument);
           textDocument.ITextDocument;
           DoMakeDocument := textDocument;
         END;
```

```
        cNewSpreadsheet: BEGIN
                NEW(spreadsheetDocument);
                spreadsheetDocument.ISpreadsheetDocument;
                DoMakeDocument := spreadsheetDocument;
            END;
        cNewPicture: BEGIN
                NEW(pictureDocument);
                pictureDocument.IPictureDocument;
                DoMakeDocument := pictureDocument;
            END;
        cNewBusinessGraphic: BEGIN
                NEW(businessGraphicsDocument);
                businessGraphicsDocument.IBusinessGraphicsDocument;
                DoMakeDocument := businessGraphicsDocument;
            END
        END { of CASE }
    END;
```

Note that DoMakeDocument uses command numbers to distinguish among the various type of documents. While this might seem surprising at first, it is really a great way to do so. This is because your application has declared the constants for these command numbers anyway, and because they are integers the overhead is low. All you must do in your DoMakeDocument is to test the command number passed to it, usually with a **CASE** statement, and then create the right kind of document. Applications that have only a single type of document can ignore the command number and simply create a new document—this is what QuadWorld does.

- MacApp invokes the new document's DoMakeViews and DoMakeWindows methods and then opens all the document's windows by calling TDocument.ShowWindows.

To code this multi-function application so that it works like this in the MacApp framework (with respect to new document generation), you only need to:

- Implement the classes TTextDocument, TSpreadsheetDocument, TPicture Document, and TBusinessGraphicsDocument so that they have the functionality needed by your application. (Note that this task may be significantly easier if you design some abstract superclasses, if appropriate.)
- Choose command numbers so the command numbers associated with the generation of the new documents are in the range between cNew and cNewLast, two MacApp-defined constants. (Table 7-1 shows these and all other MacApp constants.)
- Implement TMultiApplication.DoMakeDocument as shown above, using the command numbers you have defined to distinguish which type of document should be allocated.

MacApp handles the rest.

Of course, you may not want to have a menu item associated with each type of document. If you had ten document types, for example, this would result in a rather long File menu. There are many other user interfaces that can be used for this task within the MacApp framework. The Jazz user interface, for example, has a single **New** command and then presents the user with a dialog box to pick the document type that should be generated. You could easily do this in your application by adding to the steps above the modification of one of your DoMenuCommand methods, probably the one in your TApplication subclass, to take the following steps when this **New** command is "caught":

- Display a dialog box, using the classes and methods in the UDialog unit.
- Determine the type of document desired from the results of this dialog.
- Determine the command number associated with this type of document.
- Invoke **INHERITED** DoMenuCommand (with the newly computed command number) to make use of the MacApp code already in place for the generation of new documents.

Notes

Note that this is not the way in which you should usually design a DoMenuCommand. Normally, if your DoMenuCommand handles the command number, you should not invoke the inherited DoMenuCommand. However, the use above is a special case.

Clipboard Support

The model of the clipboard used by MacApp application programmers is only slightly more complex than that usually presented to the Macintosh user. To the user, the clipboard is a window that can hold any type of data and that, unlike other windows, exists across application launchings. The user moves data between documents of the same application (for example, moving a formatted paragraph between two Word documents), between documents of different applications (for example, moving a small bitmap from MacPaint to MacDraw), or between any document and the scrapbook, by first moving the data to the clipboard and then moving the data from the clipboard to its final destination. At any time during this process, the user can display the clipboard window and see the data currently on the clipboard, displayed in its proper form.

The MacApp model of the clipboard is slightly more complex. In the MacApp model, there is more than one "clipboard" and it can hold many different versions of the same information simultaneously.

Definitions

Recall that the "clipboard," like many components of the Macintosh User Interface Standard, is an end-user illusion maintained by a complex set of software. What we are discussing here is the programming effort required by the MacApp application programmer to maintain this particular illusion.

The system internal data structure that implements much of the clipboard functionality is the *public Desk Scrap*. Basically, the public Desk Scrap is a handle to a piece of data that is maintained across application launchings. The data type of the information referred to by the Desk Scrap is recorded separately and is always easily available. For reasons of efficiency, most applications also maintain a *private scrap* and move information to and from the public Desk Scrap only when absolutely required by a user request. The MacApp clipboard model uses such a private scrap.

Both the public and private scraps can hold multiple representations of the same information simultaneously. This enables applications that deal with vastly different data types to support some amount of information exchange. For example, moving a column from one Excel spreadsheet to the clipboard and then pasting it into another Excel spreadsheet retains all information about the formulas, formatting, and so on of all the cells in the column. Pasting the information on that same clipboard into MacWrite results in a set of paragraphs, each with a textual representation of a single cell; all of the formulas and much of the formatting information are lost. This happens because when an Excel column is moved to the clipboard, two different representations of that column are placed in the Excel private scrap: one is a data type private to Excel (let us, for example, call it the data type COLM); the other is a text representation that MacWrite and other text applications can process. In general, when an application pastes information from the scrap, it can pick any of the representations it finds there, although usually it picks the most specific one that it can process. Thus, in the Excel example, when there is an Excel column on the scrap at the time the Excel user chooses the **Paste** command, the COLM representation is chosen; when there is an Excel column on the scrap at the time the MacWrite user chooses the **Paste** command, the text representation is chosen because MacWrite can't use COLM data. Similiarily, when there is a MacPaint bitmap on the scrap at the time the Excel user chooses the **Paste** command, Excel behaves as if the clipboard is empty since Excel doesn't know what to do with PICT data (the kind of data that MacPaint pastes).

Definitions

As specified in *Inside Macintosh*, clipboard data types are distinguished by four-letter ASCII identifiers. Two of the most common are TEXT for textual data and PICT for graphics data. Applications that support the clipboard are expected to accept at least one of these. In addition, an application can define as many private data types, like the hypothetical COLM example above, as needed.

MacApp clipboard support is similar to MacApp filing support. In both, MacApp provides the basic framework and orchestrates much of the run-time flow of control, but it relies on methods that you must override in your application to perform such basic tasks as writing a simple piece of information to disk or determining what clipboard data types your application can process. The major methods for clipboard support, including these basic methods, are shown in Figure 9-1. This figure assumes that the object storing the data held by the private scrap is member of the TDocument class—perhaps just another instance of one of your application's TDocument classes or perhaps an instance of another TDocument class designed especially for the private scrap of your application. It also assumes that the rendering of the data on the private scrap, in the event that the user opens the clipboard window, is done by a TView object—probably just another instance of one of your application's views. Basically, there is nothing different about a document object used to store the scrap data or a view object used to render the clipboard window. TDocument objects store data and TView objects render images—you can use them for many purposes including the clipboard. However, there are some TDocument and TView methods that are invoked by MacApp only for document and view objects used with the clipboard. These also are shown in Figure 9-1.

However, to add clipboard support to a MacApp application it is not merely sufficient to override the basic methods shown in Figure 9-1. You must:

- Define a TCommand subclass to perform the cutting and copying—usually one command object can accomplish both of these similar functions—for each type of information that your application can put on the clipboard. Thus, if your application can cut and copy TEXT data, PICT data, and QUAD data (a private data type), you would have to design the three classes TCutCopyTEXTCmd, TCutCopyPICTCmd, and TCutCopyQUADCmd. The DoIt method of each of these classes installs the appropriate class of view object on the clipboard by invoking the method TApplication.ClaimClipboard.

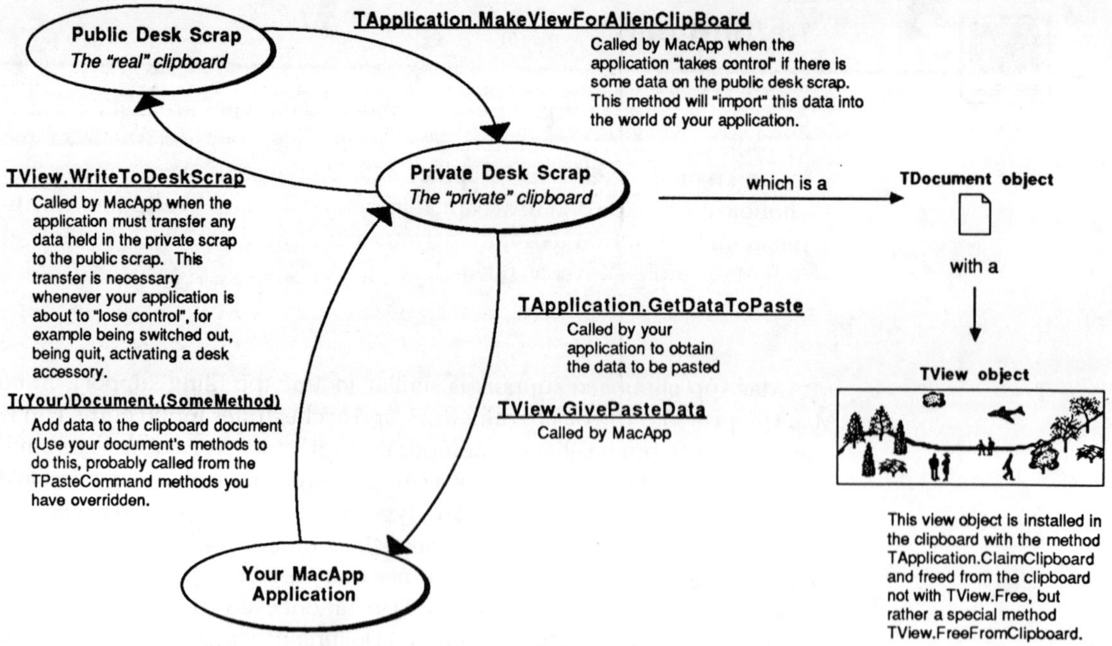

Figure 9-1 MacApp Clipboard Support.

- Implement a TCommand subclass to perform pasting. The DoIt method of this command obtains the data from the clipboard by calling TApplication.-GiveDataToPaste and then (eventually, perhaps in the Commit method) adds this data to the document.
- Implement the TView methods needed by any view that will be installed on the clipboard:
  - TView.WriteToDeskScrap—this method is called by MacApp to transfer information from the private scrap to the public scrap should that be necessary. This would be the case, for example, when the application is being terminated or switched out with the Switcher.
  - TView.FreeFromClipboard—a special view-freeing method that is called by MacApp only when a view object installed on the clipboard needs to be freed.
  - TView.ContainsClipType(dataType)—this method is called by MacApp to inquire if the view can supply a particular type of information. MacApp uses this method to decide if **Paste** should be enabled—a decision that depends in part on what type of information is on the clipboard.
  - TView.GivePasteData—this method is called by MacApp to actually retrieve a copy of the data stored on the clipboard.

Notes

You only implement these four TView methods—you never call them. MacApp calls them when it is appropriate to do so.

- Give MacApp the information about what types of data you can paste by calling the CanPaste procedure, which is defined in the MacApp units. You do not directly enable the **Paste** command yourself; rather you tell MacApp what kinds of data you can paste and let MacApp determine what is actually on the clipboard (which it does by sending the message ContainsClipType to the view object installed on the clipboard), and it decides if **Paste** should be enabled.

  CanPaste should be called in any of your DoSetupMenus methods where the **Paste** operation is supported. In each of these methods, you should call it once for each type of clipboard data that you can accept. For example, if QuadWorld allowed pasting of both quadrilaterals (a private type identified as QUAD) and text (a data type defined in *Inside Macintosh* identified as TEXT), then the TQuadDocument.DoSetupMenus method in Listing E would be modified to look like this (modifications are underlined):

```
FUNCTION TQuadDocument.DoSetupMenus; OVERRIDE;
BEGIN
  INHERITED DoSetupMenus;
  Enable(cClearQuadCmd, SELF.fSelectedQaud < > NIL);
  Enable(cClearAllCmd, SELF.fLastQuadAdded < > NIL);
  Enable(cCut, SELF.fSelectedQaud < > NIL);
  Enable(cCopy, SELF.fSelectedQaud < > NIL);
  CanPaste('TEXT');                     {Can paste textual data, but}
  CanPaste('QUAD');                     {prefer quad data if it is present}
END;
```

  The data types your application can paste are listed in order of increasing preference to your application. Thus, for QuadWorld, if a clipboard had both a TEXT and a QUAD representation of the same information, QuadWorld would prefer to receive the QUAD version. This preference is recorded in the DoSetupMenus methods by the order of the CanPaste invocations.

- Implement the TApplication method needed to create a clipboard view when there is already something on the clipboard at the time your application takes control. (An application takes control when it is launched, switched in via the Switcher, or when a desk accessory is deactivated, for example.) This method has the unusual, but appropriate name MakeView ForAlienClipboard.

Adding clipboard support to a MacApp application is a somewhat lengthy task. You must implement several new classes and many new methods. Implementing **Cut, Copy,** and **Paste** in an undoable fashion without the MacApp framework would have been a much more difficult task. After all, you need only deal with the unique aspects of the clipboard: actually moving your application-dependent types of data around. Without MacApp you would have had to do everything.

Error Handling

MacApp provides a framework for handling the various types of run-time errors that can occur while your application is executing—for example, running out of memory on the heap, trying to write to a write-protected disk, or trying to read a non-existent resource. Like the other portions of MacApp—handling of commands, processing of mouse actions, and so on—the MacApp error handling takes the right action most of the time and provides you with an easy mechanism for customization if you need it. Unlike other portions, this customization is not accomplished by overriding methods of basic MacApp classes. In fact, the error-handling mechanism makes no use of the techniques of object-oriented programming.

The MacApp error-handling framework is based on a stack of procedures that can be invoked when errors occur. As an error handler is used to process an error, it is popped off the stack. MacApp installs some generic error handlers on the stack, but you can also implement your own custom handlers and install them on the stack when appropriate. Before we examine how these custom error handlers are designed and installed, let's look at the error-handling mechanism is used when an error condition is detected.

Your appliction can detect errors by observing the results of certain Toolbox calls or Object Pascal functions. For example, running out of memory on the heap for the allocation of new instances can be detected after the **NEW** function is invoked:

```
NEW(aQuad);
IF aQuad = NIL THEN the allocation failed;
```

and an file output error can be detected by examining the return value of FSWrite:

```
err := FSWrite(aRefNum, count, @data);
IF err <> noErr THEN some kind of I/O error occurred;
```

In general, every time that you allocate an object (or a handle), you should check to see that an object was in fact allocated by testing if the object is **NIL.** You should also test the return value of any Toolbox routine that returns an error code. The MacApp error-handling framework makes this very easy to do.

To test for these conditions, you use two functions defined by MacApp, FailNIL and FailOSErr. FailNIL invokes the error handler on the top of the stack if its parameter is **NIL** and FailOSErr does likewise if its parameter is not noErr. Using these functions in the two examples above would yield the following code:

```
NEW(aQuad);
FailNIL(aQuad);
```

and

```
FailOSErr(FSWrite(aRefNum, count, @data));
```

These two functions both simplify and make more robust the code that uses them. Consider the WriteTo method for the class TQuad (developed in Chapter 8):

```
PROCEDURE TQuad.WriteTo(aRefNum: INTEGER);
VAR data: TFiledQuad;
     count: LONGINT;
     quadID: INTEGER;
     i: INTEGER; { FOR Loop index}
BEGIN
  quadID := SELF.ID;
  count := SIZEOF(INTEGER);
  FailOSErr(FSWrite(aRefNum, count, @quadID));
  FOR i := 1 TO 4 DO data.theVertices[i] := SELF.fVertex[i];
  data.theRotationState := SELF.fRotated;
  count := SIZEOF(TFiledQuad);
  FailOSErr(FSWrite(aRefNum, count, @data));
END;
```

This new version is more robust because it can deal properly with a file system error; it is simpler because there is no need to declare a local variable of type OSErr to store the result of the FSWrite invocations.

These calls to FailNIL and FailOSErr invoke the top error handler on the stack and then remove that handler from the stack. This error handler either can be one of the handlers installed by MacApp or a custom error handler designed and installed by you. A custom error handler is required whenever it is necessary to handle application-specific housekeeping details unique to a certain error condition. For example, if one of your methods allocates three objects and if all three objects must be allocated for the method to complete sucessfully, then merely using the FailNil function would not be the best way of handling an allocation failure. If an allocation error occurred while trying to allocate the third object, for example, then the first two objects would have been allocated and would be taking up space uselessly on the application heap. Because these two objects are not effective without the third, they should be deallocated if the allocation of the third object fails. This can be done with a custom error handler:

```
PROCEDURE MySpecialError(error: INTEGER; message: LONGINT);
BEGIN
  FreeObject(object1);
  FreeObject(object2);
  FreeObject(object3);
  Failure(error, message); { Propagate the error to a MacApp-installed error
    handler.}
END;
```

Such an error handler can be installed in the stack when it is appropriate with the CatchFailures function and removed from the stack with the Success function when it is no longer needed—two functions defined in the MacApp units. This would look something like this in the final application:

```
PROCEDURE TSomeClass.AllocateAllThree;
VAR object1: TSomething;
    object2: TSomethingElse;
    object3: TSomethingElseAgain;
    fi: FailInfo;       { A special MacApp-defined data type which records the
                  information necessary for error recovery—register values, etc.}
  PROCEDURE MySpecialError(error: INTEGER; message: LONGINT);
  BEGIN
    FreeObject(object1);
    FreeObject(object2);
    FreeObject(object3);
    Failure(error, message);
                     { Propagate the error to a MacApp-installed error handler.}
  END;
BEGIN
  object1 := NIL;
  object2 := NIL;
  object3 := NIL;
  CatchFailures(fi, MySpecialError);        { Install the custom error handler.}
```

```
  NEW(object1);          { A failure for any of these three allocations will }
  FailNIL(object1);      { invoke MySpecialError error handling routine}
  NEW(object2);
  FailNIL(object2);
  NEW(object3);
  FailNIL(object3);
  .
  .
  .
  Success(fi); { Remove MySpecialError from the stack.}
END;
```

Figure 9-2 summarizes the MacApp error handling framework.

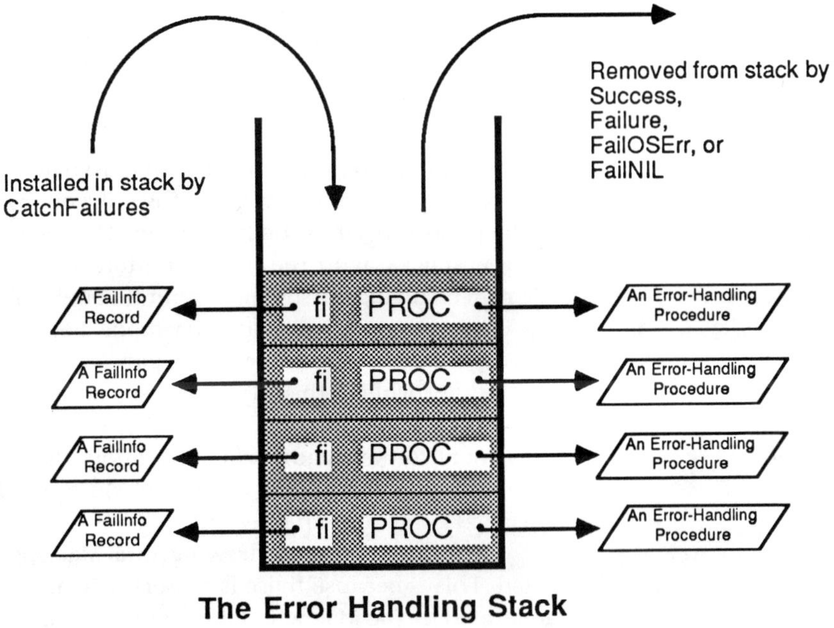

Figure 9-2 The MacApp Error-Handling mechanism.

Stumbling Blocks

Stumbling blocks involve more generic situations than the advanced features, but each MacApp developer encounters his or her own particular version of each stumbling block. Here we discuss two such situations: the first is encountered when there appears to be no clear places to override MacApp to provide the behavior your application requires and the second occurs when you wish to provide some feature in your application that MacApp does not directly support. In discussing each of these we focus on an example first and then try to generalize from this example.

Mouse-Up Drawing—Where to Override?

In the version of the QuadWorld application presented in Listing E, the user interface is highly modal. Although these modes are clearly visible to the user through palette highlighting, changing cursor shapes, and other techniques (as explained in the discussion of QuadWorld in Chapter 8), they are still undesirable.

A better user interface that would make at least some of these modes more tolerable would be similar to that used in MacDraw and MacPaint for the entry of polygons. After selecting the polygon icon in the palette, the first click of the mouse specifies the first vertex, the second the next vertex, and so on. Between clicks, with the mouse button up, the user is given feedback not through changing cursor shapes but through rubberbanded, mouse-up drawing. The user sees polygon-entry-mode because a polygon is being drawn whenever the mouse is moved, regardless of whether the mouse button is pressed. Providing this style of user interface—usually called *mouse-up drawing*—for the entry of quadrilaterals in QuadWorld would be a big improvement to the QuadWorld application. However, in doing so you run into our first stumbling block: where do you override the standard MacApp behavior to get mouse-up drawing?

Providing mouse-up drawing in a MacApp program is slightly complicated. This is because there is no series of "mouse-still-up" events continually generated by the Mac when the mouse button is not pressed that can be processed by the MacApp main event loop and thus "captured" by one of your methods. What you must do is override a method that is called very frequently in the main event loop and test, presumably by checking a flag that you have set somewhere, whether the user is in the middle of drawing a quadrilateral. If so, then you must sample the cursor position and draw the appropriate feedback lines.

Looking back at Figure 7-8, there are two possible methods that you can use for mouse-up drawing: Idle and, surprisingly, DoSetCursor. Each meets the criterion of being called regularly in the main event loop and each are methods that you previously have overridden in QuadWorld (for other reasons), so all you must do is to modify one of these existing methods in the QuadWorld application. Idle seems the better choice for psychological reasons. DoSetCursor exists to change the cursor shape, not to hide drawing code, whereas Idle exists to do exactly the sort of miscellaneous "background" task like mouse-up drawing. On the other hand, DoSetCursor seems to be the better choice for technical reasons because it performs the focusing and global-to-view coordinate transformation. Each of these operations is rather "costly", so to do them again unnecessarily in an inner loop of the application might lead to sluggish performance. This is precisely the stumbling block.

Figure 9-3 shows a new version of TQuadGrView.DoSetCursor that provides this mouse-up drawing and Figure 9-4 shows a competing version of TQuadGrView.DoIdle which would provide the same functionality. The DoIdle code, while it appears shorter, is actually much slower because of the focusing and conversion to local view coordinates. This manifests itself as a perceived difference in performance between the two versions.

Notes

These two new versions are competing ways of accomplishing the same thing. You would use either one, but not both, to add mouse-up drawing to QuadWorld.

Note that both the code in Figure 9-3 and the code in Figure 9-4 assume that:

- two new instance variables, fFeedbackOn and fLastCursorPoint, have been added to TQuadGrView. fFeedbackOn records if feedback has been drawn in the view, but not yet erased. This information is used so as not to leave "temporary" lines on the screen. fLastCursorPoint is used to record the last point to which feedback was drawn, so that erasure of the temporary lines can be done correctly. The last cursor point must be recorded in the view, rather than just being taken care of by the XORing of the lines. This covers the case in which the user is entering a new quadrilateral, moves the cursor out of the view's frame, and then returns to the view, but at a different point. Note also

```
FUNCTION  TQuadGrView.DoSetCursor(localPoint: Point): BOOLEAN;  OVERRIDE;
BEGIN
   DoSetCursor := FALSE;
   IF SELF.fPalette.fCurrPalette <> 0   { the user is drawing a new quad }
     THEN
       BEGIN
          DoSetCursor := TRUE;

       { Set the cursor depending on the extent to which the user has entered the new
         quadrilateral.  Note that there is no need for a three-edged,
         or a four-edged quad cursor. }
         CASE SELF.fStateOfPartialQuad OF
             0:              SetCursor(GetCursor(crossCursor)↑↑);
             2:              SetCursor(GetCursor(cOneEdgeQuadCursor)↑↑);
             3:              SetCursor(GetCursor(cTwoEdgeQuadCursor)↑↑);
             OTHERWISE  SetCursor(arrow);
         END
       END

   { Mouse-up drawing during the entry of a new quadrilateral }
   IF NOT EqualPt(localPoint, SELF.fLastCursorPoint)   { Did the cursor move? }
     THEN
       BEGIN
         SELF.EraseFeedback;                    { Focus on the view and erase any old feedback }
         SELF.fLastCursorPoint := localPoint;   { Record the cursor point that feedback was drawn to }
         SELF.Feedback;                         { Draw new feedback }
       END
END;


PROCEDURE TQuadGrView.EraseFeedback;
BEGIN
   SELF.fFrame.Focus;
   IF SELF.fFeedbackOn
     THEN Feedback;
    SELF.fFeedbackOn := FALSE;
END;


PROCEDURE TQuadGrView.Feedback;
VAR currentSketcher:  TSketchQuadCmd;
    lastPoint:        Point;
BEGIN
   currentSketcher := SELF.PendingSketcher;
   IF currentSketcher <> NIL
     THEN
       BEGIN
         lastPoint := currentSketcher.fQuad.fVertex[currentSketcher.fLastVertexSet];
         PenNormal;
         PenMode(patXOR);

         MoveTo(lastPoint.h, lastPoint.v);
         LineTo(SELF.fLastCursorPoint.h, SELF.fLastCursorPoint.v);

          SELF.fFeedbackOn := TRUE;
       END
     ELSE SELF.fFeedbackOn := FALSE
END;
```

Figure 9-3 A new version of TQuadGrView.DoSetCursor that provides for "mouse-up" drawing in QuadWorld.

```
PROCEDURE TQuadGrView.DoIdle(phase: IdlePhase);   OVERRIDE;
VAR localPoint:     Point;
     rawPoint:       Point;
     whatFrame:      TFrame;
     whichControl:   ControlHandle;
     partCode:        INTEGER;
     gotTheMouse:     BOOLEAN;
BEGIN
   IF phase = idleBegin   { Draw any partial quads, if necessary }
     THEN SELF.DrawPartialQuad;

  { Mouse-up drawing during the entry of a new quadrilateral }
   SELF.fFrame.Focus;   { First find the cursor }
   GetMouse(rawPoint);

 gotTheMouse := SELF.fFrame.FindFrame(rawPoint, whatFrame, localPoint, whichControl, partCode) = inContent);
 gotTheMouse := gotTheMouse AND (partCode = 0);  { Then determine if the mouse is in this view's frame }

   IF gotTheMouse
    THEN IF whatFrame.fView = SELF  { The cursor can be controlled by this view }
     THEN IF NOT EqualPt(localPoint, SELF.fLastCursorPoint)  { Did the cursor move? }
             THEN
               BEGIN
               SELF.EraseFeedback;                    { Focus on the view and erase any old feedback }
               SELF.fLastCursorPoint := localPoint;   { Record the cursor point that feedback was drawn to }
               SELF.Feedback;                         { Draw new feedback } .
               END
END;


PROCEDURE TQuadGrView.EraseFeedback;
BEGIN
    SELF.fFrame.Focus;
    IF SELF.fFeedbackOn
      THEN Feedback;
     SELF.fFeedbackOn := FALSE;
END;


PROCEDURE TQuadGrView.Feedback;
VAR currentSketcher:  TSketchQuadCmd;
    lastPoint:         Point;
BEGIN
    currentSketcher := SELF.PendingSketcher;
    IF currentSketcher <> NIL
      THEN
        BEGIN
         lastPoint := currentSketcher.fQuad.fVertex[currentSketcher.fLastVertexSet];
         PenNormal;
         PenMode(patXOR);

         MoveTo(lastPoint.h, lastPoint.v);
         LineTo(SELF.fLastCursorPoint.h, SELF.fLastCursorPoint.v);

          SELF.fFeedbackOn := TRUE;
        END
      ELSE SELF.fFeedbackOn := FALSE
END;
```

Figure 9-4 A new version of TQuadGrView.DoIdle that provides for "mouse-up" drawing in QuadWorld.

that auto-scrolling is not a feature of either of these proposed modifications nor can it be. If auto-scrolling were added, there would be no way not to finish the drawing of a new quadrilateral! This would hardly be an improvement over the modal entry of quadrilaterals developed in Chapter 8.

- two new methods, TQuadGrView.Feedback and TQuadGrView.EraseFeedback, have been added to the protocol of TQuadGrView.

Notes

For mouse-up drawing to work correctly in QuadWorld, there are several other small changes that need to be made to the methods TQuadGrView.-Draw, TSketchQuadCmd.Commit, and TSketchQuadCmd.TrackMouse. These changes are not shown here.

The difficulty in mouse-up drawing is that there was no clear-cut place in the MacApp framework for you to add the code to provide this special behavior, and mouse-up drawing is not the only example of this. The only way around a problem like this is to characterize the properties you want in a particular method (for example, by stating that the method to be overridden for mouse-up drawing would have to be invoked by MacApp very often) and then hunt for a method that has these properties. To do this effectively you must understand a considerable amount about the flow of control of MacApp under a wide variety of circumstances.

Iconic Menus—No MacApp Support

One feature that would be nice to add to QuadWorld is shades for the quadrilaterals. Given that you don't want to use valuable screen "real estate" for a shades palette, probably the best user interface for this would be an iconic shades menu like that in MacDraw, shown in the user interface appendix Figure A-24. MacApp, however, provides no menu definition facilities itself. In a simple MacApp program, all menu entries are placed into the application's resource file by the resource compiler or the Resource Editor. Neither of these utilities currently allow you to describe an iconic menu directly.

What you have here is an example of something that is completely outside the MacApp framework. It is as if you asked which method to override to change the Finder icon for an application—you are trying to do something that MacApp doesn't and isn't supposed to do. There are other tasks peripherally associated with designing an application for which MacApp provides no support, among them are designing special menus, designing the application's icon, designing and implementing any application-specific desk accesories, dealing with copy protection, and application-specific fonts. These items simply are not within the scope of MacApp. That doesn't mean, though, that MacApp stands in your way if you want to accomplish them.

Notes

To learn how to accomplish these tasks, you have to learn more about programming the Macintosh. Some of these tasks are accomplished with utilities like the Resource Editor and others are accomplished by directly calling Toolbox routines. One of the Resource Editors is documented in the *Apple Macintosh REdit manual* (Apple number 030-1212A). For more detailed information on the Toolbox, *Macintosh Revealed* (Chernicoff, Hayden, 1985) is an excellent introduction and *Inside Macintosh* (Apple Computer, Addison-Wesley, 1986) is the definitive work.

To add an iconic menu to QuadWorld, for example, you would have to directly call some of the Toolbox routines. Without getting into too much detail about menus, each menu contains a handle to a single procedure that is used to draw the menu, highlight menu items, calculate the menu's size, and report when a menu command is chosen. In most cases, the programmer never needs to worry about this procedure because the standard one used for alpha-numeric menus is installed automatically when the menu is created. For an iconic menu like the shades menu that you are trying to add to QuadWorld, you must design this procedure and install it in the menu data structure defined by the Toolbox. Basically, to add an iconic menu for shading quadrilaterals to the QuadWorld application you need to do the following:

- Design and implement this menu-definition procedure according to the specifications in *Inside Macintosh.* This procedure must track the mouse in the menu and return the "item number"—an integer between 1 and 255 to indicate which item (which shade, in the example here) was chosen, or 0 if none was chosen. This procedure must also implement the feedback to the user that a particular menu item will be chosen if the mouse button is released. The basic skeleton of this procedure is:

```
PROCEDURE ShadeMenu(message: INTEGER; theMenu: MenuHandle;
                    VAR menuRect: Rect; hitPt: Point; VAR whichItem: INTEGER);
BEGIN
  IF message < > nSizeMsg THEN (1) Save the font, text mode, and pen state, and
                               (2) Set up the menu coordinate system.
```

CASE message **OF**	
mDrawMsg:	Draw the menu;
mChooseMsg:	Figure out which item is to be highlighted (the mouse is at the point stored in hitPoint). Then do the highlighting, and return the number of the hit item in whichItem.
mSizeMsg:	Compute the menu's size (height and width) and store them in the appropriate fields of the menu record referenced by theMenu.
END; { *Case*}	
IF message < > nSizeMsg **THEN**	(1) Restore the font, text mode, and pen state, and (2) Restore the coordinate system to what it was before this procedure ws called.
END;	

Definitions

Note that: the interface of this procedure is defined by the Toolbox and that the use of the term "message" here has nothing to do with the object-oriented programming definition of a message.

- Store a handle to your menu definition procedure in the iconic menu resource. This is probably best done in the application object initialization method, TQuadApplication.IQuadApplication. It would look something like this:

```
PROCEDURE TQuadApplication.IQuadApplication;
VAR
    .
    .
    .
    PROCEDURE SetUpMenu(rsrcld: INTEGER);
    VAR menu: MenuHandle;
         r: Rect;
        item: INTEGER;
    BEGIN
      menu := GetMHandle(rsrcID);
      IF menu < > NIL
        THEN BEGIN
            menu↑↑.menuProc := gGraphicalMenu;
            ShadeMenu(mSizeMsg, menu, r, Point(0), item); { See below }
          END
```

```
    END;
    .
    .
    .
BEGIN
  .
  .
  .
  gMenuProcPointer := @ShadeMenu;
  gGraphicalMenu := @gMenuProcPointer;
  SetUpMenu(cShadeMenu);
  .
  .
  .
END;
```

- After this handle has been stored, you must cause the iconic menu to recalculate its size by invoking your menu definition procedure using as its first parameter nSizeMsg, a Toolbox constant indicating that the menu is not to be displayed, but only have its size computed. This is done at the end of the internal SetUpMenu procedure.
- Modify your DoMenuCommand to handle negative command numbers, which are returned when an iconic menu is used. The upper eight bits of the negation of the command number contain the menu ID (in case you have more than one iconic menu) and the lower eight bits contain the item number returned by your menu-definition procedure.
- Add a command class to actually perform the shading operation indicated by the menu. In the case of shading, you need only one command class, TShadeQuadCmd, because shading a quadrilateral light gray and shading it black are not very different. Note that if you want this command to be undoable, you have to store the old shade as an instance variable of the shadeQuadCmd object.

Notes

This scheme of making the shading command undoable by storing the old color in the command object works only because in QuadWorld you can only select one quadrilateral at a time, thus you need only remember one old shade (for **Undo**) and one new shade (for **Redo**). In this regard

QuadWorld is atypical because most applications that have selections have the option of an extended selection consisting of many entities. In such a case, storing all the old shades as well as all the new shades for a variable number of quadrilaterals in the command object can be troublesome. A better approach would be to have each quadrilateral store two shades and to have shadeQuadCmd manipulate this data for the list of items comprising the current selection. Because a shade can be stored easily as an integer, there isn't much storage overhead and the algorithms for the TShadeQuadCmd methods then become very simple.

The real point of this lengthy discussion of iconic menus is that you can accomplish effects for which there is no direct MacApp support because the MacApp programmer has full access to all of the Macintosh ROM routines. Iconic menus are no more complex for a MacApp developer than for any Macintosh developer. Of course, currently, they are no easier either. The stumbling block of finding no MacApp support for some unusual feature needed by your application is a problem for many developers although, ultimately the essence of this block, finding no perfect tool in a development environment, is encountered in every development path.

Notes

If you have Object Pascal and the MacApp class library, you need read no further to develop applications for the Macintosh. Refer to the Object Pascal and MacApp manuals for further information about designing and implementing MacApp applications. If you wish to learn about other object-oriented languages on the Macintosh and other class libraries, keep reading. The two object-oriented languages that most influenced Object Pascal (Smalltalk and Clascal) are discussed at length in Chapters 11 and 12. Each of these languages has its own class library used to develop new applications—class libraries which are different from MacApp. Chapter 13 surveys several other object-oriented languages on the Macintosh—some of which predate Object Pascal, some of which are its contemporaries, and some of which were designed after it. Just as knowing several standard programming languages increases your knowledge and ability to use any of them, knowing several object-oriented programming languages helps you in using any object-oriented language.

CHAPTER 10

Advanced Concepts in Object-Oriented Programming

The terminology and conceptual implementation model of object-oriented programming introduced in Chapter 2 provided only the most fundamental basis for using an object-oriented language, with only those terms and concepts necessary to write an Object Pascal MacApp program being provided. This was done so that beginning programmers could write their first MacApp program with a minimum amount of learning time. The later chapters of this book explore the use of application frameworks other than MacApp and the use of MacApp with programming languages other than Object Pascal. These other frameworks and languages use a more complex model of object-oriented programming. In this chapter several additional object-oriented programming concepts are explained so that you have a more complete conceptual implementation model. This new model suffices for the use of all the other object-oriented languages described in this book and so this model represents the union of all concepts used in these other languages. Individual differences of these languages with the common model developed here are explained when the details of those language are covered later.

A Complete Conceptual Model for the Implementation of Object-Oriented Languages

In Object Pascal, a class is simply a user-defined data type. You can think of it as describing the shared part of all the instances of a similar structure. This shared part consists of both a template for the instance variables of these objects and all the methods used by these instances. This notion of a class as the shared part of all its instances is common to all object-oriented languages, but in many object-oriented languages, there are several additional aspects to the concept of a class.

The most basic additional aspect is that classes are not merely types or shared parts but actual objects. Because classes are objects, they can respond to messages. Most of the message passing that takes place in an object-oriented program is the passing of a message to an instance of a class. However, classes themselves can respond to messages, which may be different from those to which their instances respond. For example, the instances of the Pen class (discussed in Chapter 2) respond to messages like Up and Home, that establish new values in the various data fields associated with each instance of a Pen. The Class Pen itself might respond to messages like New, that generates new instances of the class Pen, and Example1, that generates a new instance of the class Pen and uses that pen object to scribble on the screen some cute example of what a pen can do. This example of sending the message New to the Pen class to create a new instance of a pen is not merely a whimsically chosen example. In the model we are developing, the only means of allocating a new object is to send the class a message that allocates a new instance. (Remember that Objective-C called classes "factories"? This is why.) A class must have at least one message that performs this instance-creation function, if that class is to have instances. Many classes have several such messages—each allocating an object under different circumstances or with different initial conditions. In Smalltalk, for example, there is a Point class representing points in two-dimensional space. The Point class responds to the message New, which creates a new instance of a point but does not initialize it. The Point class also responds to the message x:y:, which creates a new instance of point and initializes it to a certain value.

Notes

Note that in Object Pascal it is not possible for the **NEW** procedure that generates new objects to be a method. This is because in Object Pascal all objects are created dynamically by your application program, so there would be no object to which to send the first **NEW**.

The messages to which a class responds are called its *class messages* and the methods associated with these messages to classes are called *class methods*. To differentiate methods invoked when an instance message is sent to a instance from those invoked when a class message is sent to a class, the former are called *instance methods*. Thus, in the Pen example above, the messages Up and Home are instance messages and the messages New and Example1 are class messages. In the context of this small example, you can't send the Up message to the Pen class or send the New message to an instance of Pen.

This is not as surprising as it might seem at first glance. Instances of the class Pen model the characteristics of a physical pen and have a corresponding protocol: Up, Down, Home, Draw, and so on. The Pen class, when considered as an object, models a Pen factory. One would expect a Pen factory to respond to messages like "Make me a new blue pen" (New) or "Show me a representative sample of your products" (Example1), but not to messages like Up, Down, Home, and Draw. From the system's point of view, an instance of the class Pen and the Pen class itself are merely different objects that respond to different protocols.

Definitions

In all the object-oriented languages discussed in this book, the "name spaces" for instance messages and class messages are different, so it is possible to design a class and an instance of that class that respond to the same message. However, they do not respond with the same method. This is just like the case where your TApplication object happens to respond to some of the same messages as your TView object—DoMenuCommand, for example. They have the same message in their protocols, but use different methods. In this respect, designing the set of instance messages and the set of class messages for a new class is very similar to designing the (instance) messages for two different objects—these two objects can have the same messages in their protocol but probably won't use the same methods.

One of the properties of an object is that it can store data and when classes are also considered objects, they, too, can store data. An "ordinary" object—an object as defined in the first portion of this book—stores only the instance variable data that distinguishes it from all other instances of the same class. An object that is a class can store many different types of information. Because it is an object, a class has its own instance variables called *class instance variables*. (These, however, are rarely used.) As a factory that produces other objects, a class object contains a template for the objects it may produce. This data, usually called the *instance template*, is present in any class that has or will have instances. You, as the designer of the class, must specify what is to be contained in this template, but after that, the instance template is never directly accessed by your program.

In addition to storing its own class instance variables and a template for its instances, a class object can store two other types of data. When all of the instances of a class need to have access to the same constant data, this can be stored in the class as a *class variable*. Any instance of the class can use the data as if it were stored internally in itself, but in reality there is but one copy of the data regardless of how many instances of this class exist. Class variables are a kind of global data storage although global only to the members of the same class. Class variables are used frequently in the object-oriented languages that allow them. The other type of data that a class can store is a reference to a pool of global variables. These variables, called *pool variables*, provide a mechanism for sharing data among a set of classes. You can think of a pool variable as a kind of shared class variable—shared between classes rather than between instances within a single class. Any instance of any class that contains a given pool variable can access the variables in this pool. Compared to the other types of data stored in class objects, pool variables are infrequently used. As you would expect, all of these types of data are inherited by subclasses. Thus, if in the definition of class Alpha you define a class variable named waitFlag, then all instances of subclasses of Alpha can also access waitFlag.

These various ways of storing data provide you, in effect, with different levels of data-hiding: class instance variables of a class can be accessed only by the class object itself; class variables can be accessed only by the instances of a given class; and pool variables can be accessed only by the instances of certain classes. In addition, there is usually some provision for global variables that everyone can access, but this is simply a feature of the base language, not a language extension provided to support object-oriented programming. There is a different name space for each of these levels and thus, for example, a class variable of class Alpha named foo is not confused with a class variable of Aleph named foo, as long Alpha is not a descendant of Aleph or Aleph a descendant of Alpha. There is no difference in the syntax for accessing these various levels of variables. You simply access them by name and if you make a mistake by attempting to access a class variable like waitFlag of class Alpha in the instance method of class Aleph (where Aleph is not a descendant of Alpha), then you will get a compilation error that waitFlag is undefined in the context of the class Aleph.

These new types of data require us to modify the graphical notation for classes presented in Chapter 2. The new notation is given in Figure 10-1 and an example of using this notation is shown in Figure 10-2. Note that because a class is an object it must have an is_an_instance_of link that points to its class. (More on this in a moment.)

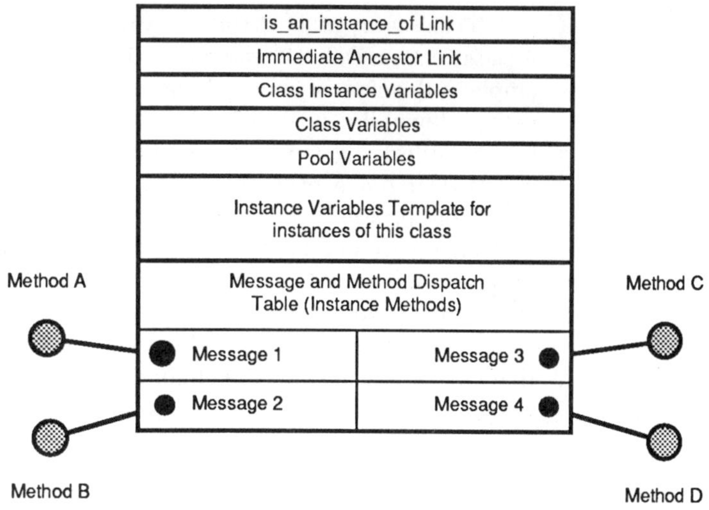

Figure 10-1 A graphical notation for a class. This notation is an extension of the one presented in Figure 2-6. The extensions provide for the additional class features available in languages like Smalltalk and Object Logo.

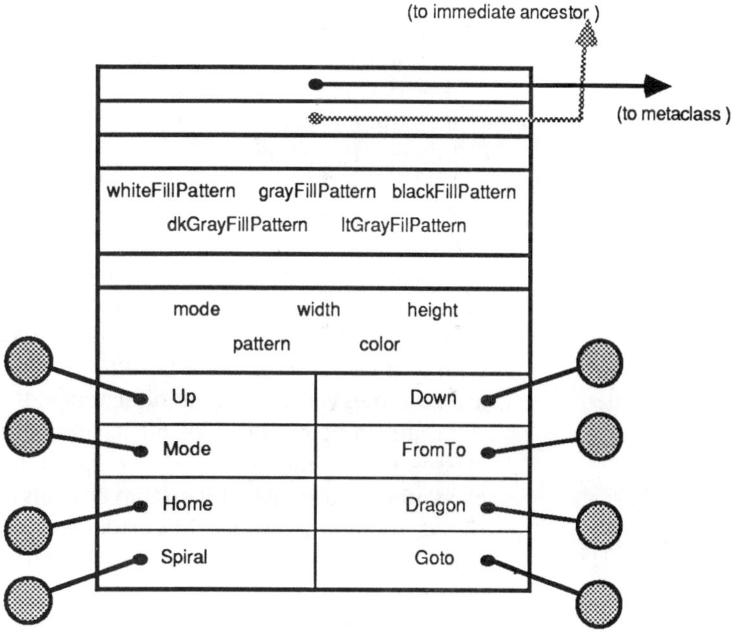

Figure 10-2 A typical class in the graphical notation of Figure 10-1. Note that this particular class does not have any class instance variables or any pool variables—these type of variables are the most rare. Also note that it is the class object that stores the shared part of all the instances of the class, in particular the instance methods like Up, Home, and so on.

If classes are objects, then they must themselves be organized into classes. A class's class is called its *metaclass*. This seemingly endless chain (what, for example, is the class of a metaclass?) is either never explored or is neatly tied together, depending on how completely the object-oriented approach is adopted by an underlying language. Smalltalk is an example of a complete object-oriented language: everything in Smalltalk is an object and everything is organized into classes, even metaclasses and the classes of metaclasses, and this chain is neatly tied back onto itself in one of the most elegant structures in programming language theory. Most other languages explored in this book stop midway along the object-class-metaclass-metaclass class chain, either for simplicity or because there is no need for this generality. Note, for example, that Object Pascal stops the chain at the class level—Object Pascal has no notion of a metaclass, and thus no notion of class messages or class methods.

Notes

A complete discussion of how this seemingly endless chain of object-class-metaclass can be resolved is beyond the scope of this book. An excellent discussion of how it is resolved in Smalltalk may be found in *Smalltalk: The Language and Its Implementation* (Adele Goldberg and David Robson, Addison-Wesley, 1983) and in Objective-C in *Object-Oriented Programming: An Evolutionary Approach* (Brad Cox, Addison-Wesley, 1986)

In addition to the simple hierarchical inheritance structure described in Chapter 2, some object-oriented languages provide for a more general type of inheritance in which a class may have two or more immediate ancestors. This type of inheritance is called *multiple inheritance* because multiple ancestors are possible. With multiple inheritance, the new class inherits all of the data, messages, and methods of all its immediate ancestors and all their superclasses. In the opinion of many researchers, multiple inheritance is a very rich class inheritance mechanism that enables class designers to easily model many things, including real-world entities like houseboats (which have characteristics of both houses and boats), mathematical entities like squares (which have characteristics of both rectangles and rhombi), and abstract concepts like circular queues (which have characteristics of both queues and linked lists). To be sure, multiple inheritance is more general, and therefore more powerful, than single inheritance. To some of these researchers, single inheritance is the exception—only a special case that is used for simplicity in analysis rather than as an accurate model of most concepts in the real world.

As a small example of the use of multiple inheritance consider the new class structure for the QuadWorld quadrilateral classes shown in Figure 10-3. In this figure, the inheritance structure for the various quadrilateral factories is shown. The Rectangle factory knows how to build quadrilaterals that have right angles and the Rhombi factory knows how to build quadrilaterals that have equal-length sides. If the Square factory inherits from both the Rectangle factory and the Rhombi factory (as is shown in this figure), there should be very little new coding necessary to implement the Square factory—all of its functionality should be inherited from one of its two immediate ancestors.

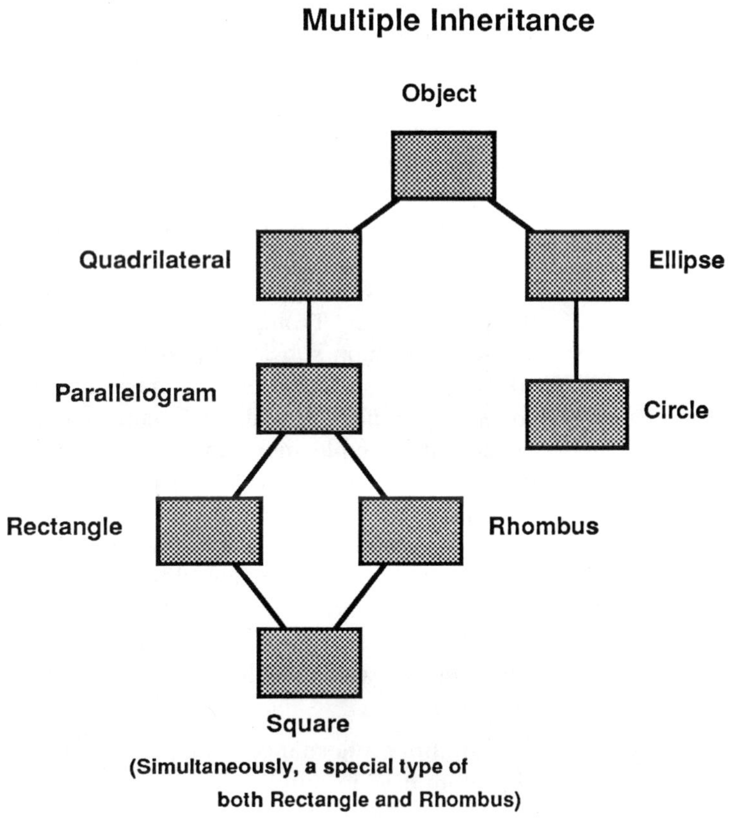

Figure 10-3 A possible use of multiple inheritance in QuadWorld.

Notes

This inheritance structure for the quadrilateral factory classes is implemented in the Smalltalk, Object Logo, and ExperCommonLISP implementations of QuadWorld. It is discussed at greater length in Chapters 11 and 13.

This additional expressive power of multiple inheritance does not come for free. The design of classes becomes more complex, new additional concepts have to be specified, and new implementation techniques must be devised. The design of classes becomes more complex because of the greater possibilities for the inheritance of both data and messages. The additional concept of a *primary immediate ancestor class* often must be distinguished from the remaining secondary ancestor classes. A primary ancestor class is the class from which more is inherited than any other superclass, or equivalently, the class from which methods are inherited if there is a inheritance conflict. Such a conflict would arise if, for example, two classes in the inheritance chain had the same message. From which of these superclasses in the inheritance chain should a common subclass inherit? (This situation is diagrammed in Figure 10-4.) The specification of a primary immediate ancestor class resolves this conflict by indicating which inheritance chain is the main one. Consider the houseboat example mentioned earlier. Two different new classes can be descended from the class House and the class Boat. One of these new classes has the class House as its primary immediate ancestor class—meaning that this new class is more like a house than a boat—and you might call this new class BoatHouse. Another new class has the class Boat as its primary immediate ancestor class, and is more like a boat than a house, so you might call this new class HouseBoat. This specification of the primary immediate ancestor is an example of an issue that did not matter when designing classes with simple inheritance.

Multiple inheritance also significantly disrupts the message-resolution algorithm used in simple inheritance. In our earlier conceptual model, a message sent to a certain object is resolved by following the object's is_an_instance_of link to its class so that the message and method dispatch table of that class is searched for the message the object received. If it is found, the corresponding method is executed. If it isn't found, the class's immediate ancestor link is followed to its superclass and the superclass's message and method dispatch table is also searched. This continues until the message is found or until the search in the message and method table of class Object fails,

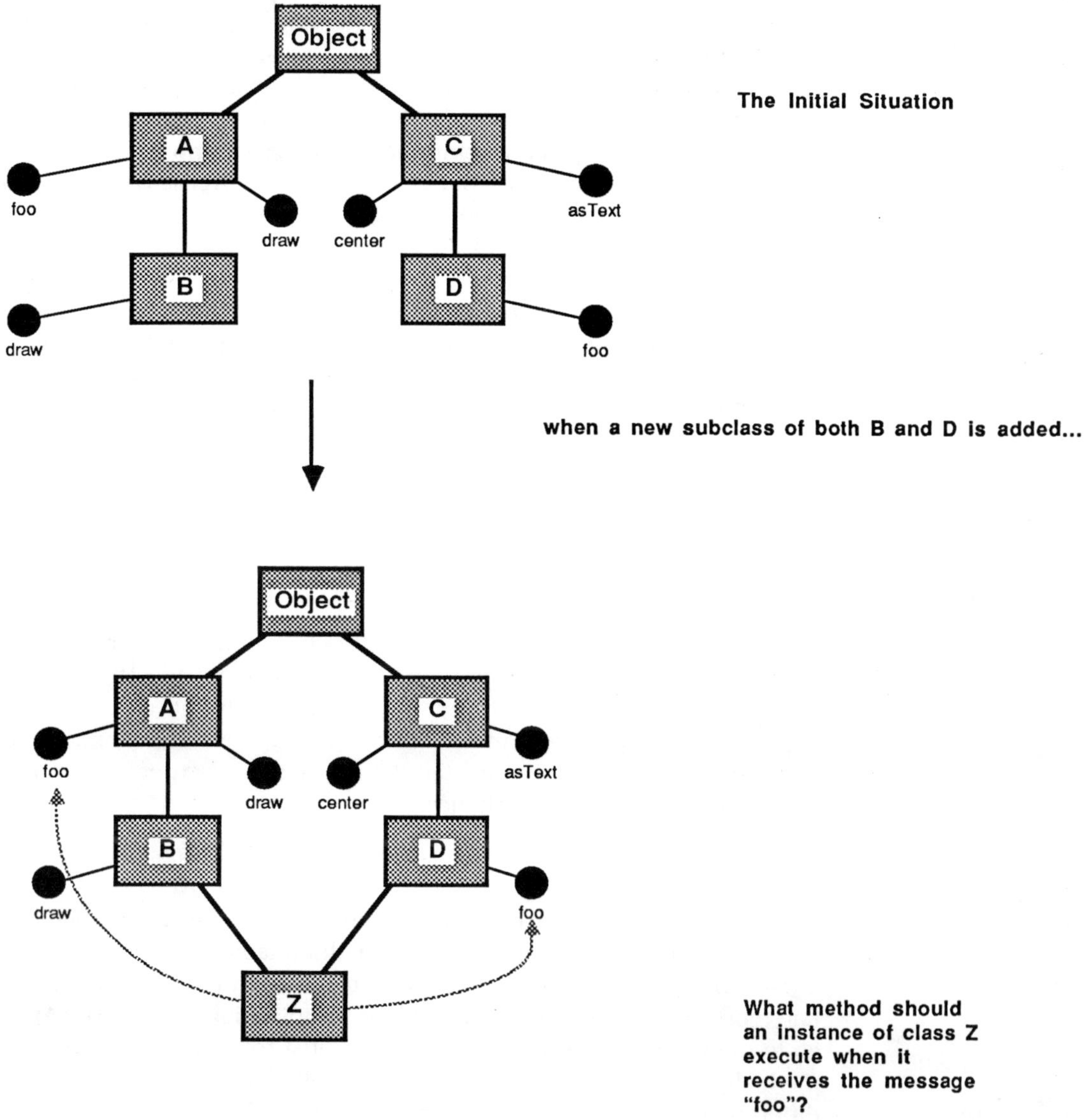

Figure 10-4 An example of an inheritance conflict possible when multiple inheritance is used.

at which time an error routine is invoked. With multiple inheritance, this algorithm cannot be followed easily because there can be more than one immediate ancestor of a given class. Basically what has happened is that the inheritance tree associated with simple inheritance has become a graph (more precisely, a directed, acyclic graph), and searching a graph is a much more difficult and time-consuming task than searching a tree. At the very least, the language implementer has to decide whether to search the graph breadth first (which, in our situation, would correspond to searching the message and method tables of all the immediate ancestor classes before searching any of the ancestor's ancestors) or depth first (search the immediate ancestor, then one of its ancestors, then one of its ancestors, until Object is reached, then begin again with the next immediate ancestor of the class you started with). However, as with simple inheritance, various implementers have devised clever ways of implementing multiple inheritance, though none have ever been able to make multiple inheritance as efficient as simple inheritance.

Definitions

Because of the many implementation difficulties with multiple inheritance ranging from conceptual entanglements to efficiency concerns, many designers of object-oriented languages have chosen not to provide multiple inheritance in their languages. Of the languages discussed in this book, only Smalltalk, Object Logo, and ExperCommon LISP provide for multiple inheritance.

Some languages have even provided for the storage of a method in an object itself, not in its class's message and method table. The motivation for this is that when you know that you are going to have only a single instance of a certain type (as with the sole instance of the TApplication class in MacApp), why go to the bother of setting up a new class just for that single object? These methods that are not stored in classes are called *unique instance methods* to differentiate them from ordinary instance methods.

Notes

Unique instance methods are a rather new concept in object-oriented languages. Of the languages discussed in this book, only Object Logo currently provides for them.

Taken all together, these new concepts are diagrammed in Figure 10-5 for the following six classes:

Object (Immediate Ancestor is NIL)
Instance Variables: (*none*)
Class Variables:
Instance Methods: WhatClass, IsNil, Copy, Release, Display
Class Methods: new, initialize, readFrom

ALPHA (Immediate Ancestor is Object)
Instance Variables: x1: **INTEGER**;
x2: **BOOLEAN**;
Class Variables: currentMin: **INTEGER**;
currentMax: **INTEGER**
Instance Methods: a, b, c
Class Methods: initialize

BETA (Immediate Ancestor is ALPHA)
Instance Variables: y1: **STRING**;
y2: **BOOLEAN**;
y3: **REAL**;
Class Variables:
Instance Methods: a, d
Class Methods: new, newWithValue

GAMMA (Immediate Ancestor is OBJECT)
Instance Variables: z1: **POINTER**;
Class Variables:
Instance Methods: a, c, e
Class Methods:

ALEPH (Immediate Ancestors are GAMMA and ALPHA)
Instance Variables: u1: **REAL**;
Class Variables:
Instance Methods: a, c, f, g
Class Methods:

OMICRON (Immediate Ancestor is ALPHA)
Instance Variables: v1: **BOOLEAN**;
v2: **STRING**;
v3: **POINTER**;
Class Variables:
Instance Methods: a, f, h, j
Class Methods:

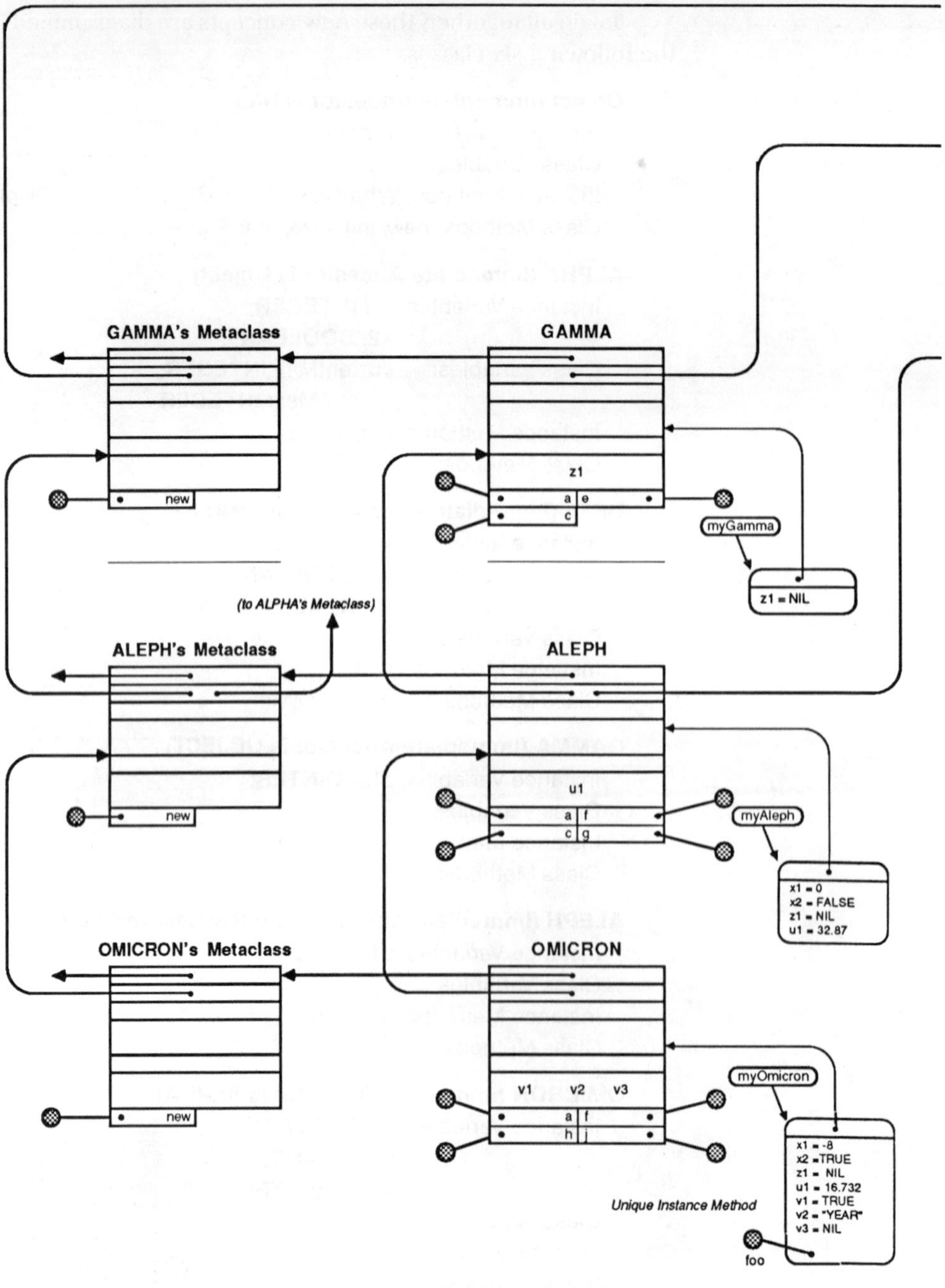

Figure 10-5 A hypothetical run-time organization of objefoo ..eir classes, and their metaclasses. This is an extension of the organization presented in Figure 2-8. New features presented in this organization are multiple inheritance, metaclasses, class methods, class variables, and unique instance methods.

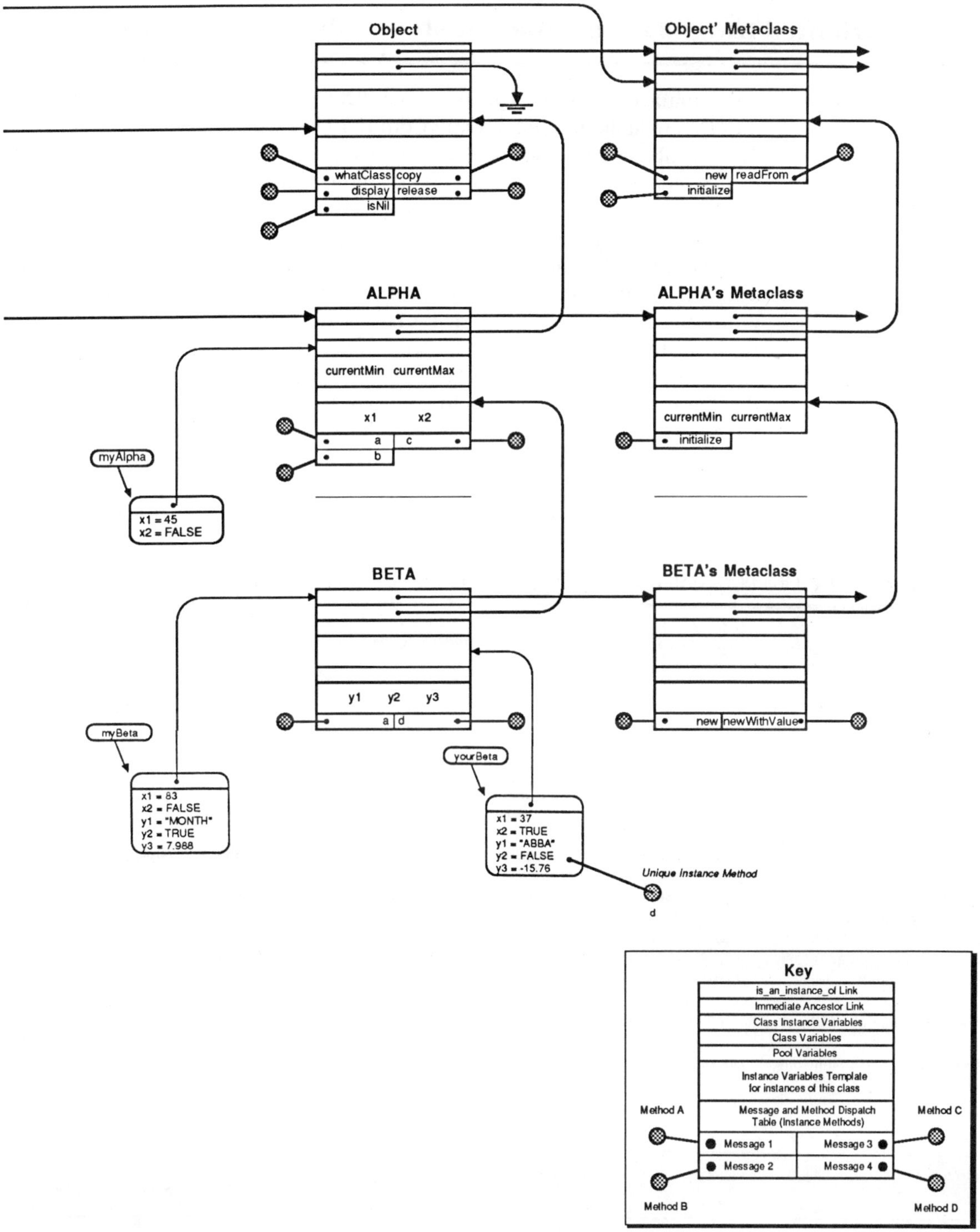

Object
whatClass
copy
display
release
isNil
Object' Metaclass
new
readFrom
initialize
ALPHA
currentMin currentMax
x1 x2
a
c
b
ALPHA's Metaclass
currentMin currentMax
initialize
myAlpha
x1 = 45
x2 = FALSE
BETA
y1 y2 y3
a
d
BETA's Metaclass
new
newWithValue
myBeta
x1 = 83
x2 = FALSE
y1 = "MONTH"
y2 = TRUE
y3 = 7.988
yourBeta
x1 = 37
x2 = TRUE
y1 = "ABBA"
y2 = FALSE
y3 = -15.76
Unique Instance Method
d
Key
is_an_instance_of Link
Immediate Ancestor Link
Class Instance Variables
Class Variables
Pool Variables
Instance Variables Template for instances of this class
Message and Method Dispatch Table (Instance Methods)
Method A
Method B
Method C
Method D
Message 1
Message 2
Message 3
Message 4

Object–Oriented Languages on Macintosh and their Terminology

The languages examined in this book (Object Pascal, Object Logo, Objective–C, Smalltalk–80, Neon, ExperCommonLisp, Object Assembler, and Lisa Clascal) all use the basic object-oriented approach to programming outlined in Chapter 2 and each implements some of the extensions to the basic concepts presented here. All of these languages have objects, classes, methods, messages, and all the rest of this new programming paradigm, however, all do not use the same terminology to describe these concepts. The introductory chapters of this book primarily uses Object pascal terminology to limit the amount of new vocabulary when discussing these notions. However, to make the various language reference manuals and other books comprehensible, each of the later chapters includes each language's standard terminology. If you wish to compare the different terms used in these languages, Table 10-1 gives the equivalent terms for each language. Note, however, that all the languages use the following terms in an identical fashion:

object method self instance ancestor descendant

Table 10-1 Object-oriented terminology as used by various languages on Macintosh

	Standard Terms								
	Root Class	***Class***	***Superclass***	***Subclass***	***Message***	***Metaclass***	***Class Methods***	***Accessing Overridden methods***	***Class Variable***
Languages									
Object Pascal	TObject	Object Type	Immediate Ancestor	Immediate Descendant	Method Call	*(none)*	*(none)*	Inherited	*(none)*
Smalltalk	Object	Class	Superclass	Subclass	Message	Metaclass	Class Methods	Super	Class Variable
Lisa Clascal	TObject	Class	Superclass	Subclass	Method Call	*(none)*	*(none)*	Super	*(none)*
Neon	Object	Class	Superclass	Subclass	Message	*(none)*	*(none)*	Super	*(none)*
ExperCommonLISP	Object	Class	Superclass	Subclass	Message	*(none)*	Metamethods	Sendsuper	Class Variable
Object Assembler	TObject	Object Type	Immediate Ancestor	Immediate Descendant	Method Call	*(none)*	*(none)*	Inherited	*(none)*
Object Logo	Something	Object	Parent	KindOf, OneOf	*(Concept not used; Standard Logo procedure call is overloaded)*	(none)	*(Concept not used; Standard Logo procedure call is overloaded)*	Usual	Variable
Objective–C	Object	Factory	Superclass	Subclass	Message	Metaclass	Factory Methods	Super	*(none)*

*Lisa Clascal allowed only one class method, *Create*, which was mandatory for each class. No special term was used to distinguish this method, however.

CHAPTER 11

Smalltalk

Smalltalk-80 is in many ways the first object-oriented language and it is certainly the most unusual one on Macintosh. The "80" in the name "Smalltalk-80" refers to the version of the Smalltalk language that was fixed by Xerox in 1980. There were earlier versions, with names like Smalltallk-76 and Small talk-72, but these are no longer in use. Smalltalk-80 is unusual because it is more than simply a programming language like Object Pascal or Clascal, it is also a comprehensive programming environment, including compilers, debuggers, change-management facilities, and a graphics editor. It is as if Object Pascal, the Mac Workshop, and the Macintosh desktop were all rolled into one. In addition, the Smalltalk-80 user interface, for both developers and users, is significantly different from that of the Macintosh. Different, but still familiar because many of the foundations upon which the Macintosh user interface rests were first explored in Smalltalk-80, including the concepts of overlapping windows, scroll bars, icons, and menus that appear on the screen when needed and then disappear after use. For these ideas and many more, Macintosh is indebted to Smalltalk-80.

Smalltalk-80 also is unusual because of its relationship to the Macintosh hardware. Part of the programming language research involved in Smalltalk-80 centered around the problem of porting a language to a new processor. Smalltalk-80 solved this problem with a virtual image—virtual machine dichotomy. A Smalltalk virtual image is a "snapshot" of all the objects in a running Smalltalk system on some workstation. For these objects to exist in a dynamic form on any type of workstation, the virtual image must be coupled with an implementation of the Smalltalk virtual machine—a precisely specified set of primitive operations that must be implemented on that new type of workstation. Usually, this task of designing and implementing the Smalltalk virtual machine is the largest portion of porting Smalltalk to a new device. What resulted when Apple performed this port to the Macintosh without making any major changes to the Smalltalk-80 class library or programming environment is The Smalltalk-80 Programming System for the Macintosh, the subject of this chapter and hereafter simply called Smalltalk.

Unlike other languages discussed in this book, Smalltalk runs in a somewhat different form on different machines, depending on how much memory is available. On a Macintosh with 512K of RAM, for example, Smalltalk runs in a somewhat "cut-down" form; with 1MB or more of RAM, a complete Smalltalk image will run; on a Macintosh with 2MB of RAM, an enhanced, experimental version of Smalltalk may be used. Everything in this chapter applies to the cut-down Smalltalk as well as to the normal Smalltalk image. Toward the end of the chapter, there is a discussion of the additional features present only in the enhanced, experimental version.

Notes

While 512K or 1MB may sound like a lot of memory by some standards, it actually is quite small for Smalltalk. Other vendors suggest system configurations with 2MB or even 3.5MB for Smalltalk applications. Prior to 1985, it was thought impossible to get Smalltalk to run on as "small" a machine as the Macintosh. It is to Apple's credit that they were able to accomplish this feat at all, and even more to their credit that they were able to do it so well.

In one other area, too, Smalltalk is unusual with respect to Macintosh. The Smalltalk-80 virtual image is designed for a workstation that has a three-button mouse, rather than the single-button mouse used by Macintosh. The optimum number of buttons for a mouse has become almost a matter of religious conviction in recent years and each vendor makes the choice it believes to be best for its customers, its workstations, and for the types of applications customers will run on that workstation. For the Xerox Smalltalk team, this choice was for a three-button mouse; for the Apple Macintosh team, a one-button mouse. Because the Xerox Smalltalk team realized that not every hardware vendor would agree with their decision or, even if they did, might not place the buttons as three vertically-aligned buttons, the three buttons of the Smalltalk system are referred to as the red button, the yellow button, and the blue button. These names have become part of the Smalltalk vocabulary and are used in the documentation of every vendor that provides a Smalltalk system. Apple has provided a very reasonable way to represent the three-button mouse that Smalltalk expects by using the one-button mouse that Macintosh has. First, the red button is the Macintosh mouse button, the yellow button is the right-hand Option button and the mouse button pressed simultaneously, and the blue button is the Enter button and the mouse button used simultaneously. Second, the Smalltalk "desktop" was modified to make single-button manipulation convenient. Certain areas, like window title frames, were "sensitized" so that pressing the mouse button in these areas would bring up one of the standard menus. (The details of the Smalltalk programmer's interface is covered in the next section.) Figure 11-1 depicts these conventions using the standard button graphic common in Smalltalk documentation.

In Smalltalk, everything is object-oriented: all the programming constructs of Smalltalk, all the elements of Smalltalk's programming environment, and all the applications written using Smalltalk. In some sense, Smalltalk is the answer to the question "Can a language be totally object-oriented, not just have objects as one portion of its functionality, as with Object Pascal?" But before you can understand the basic structure of Smalltalk, you must have an understanding of the general programming environment in which it is used. This is the topic of the next section.

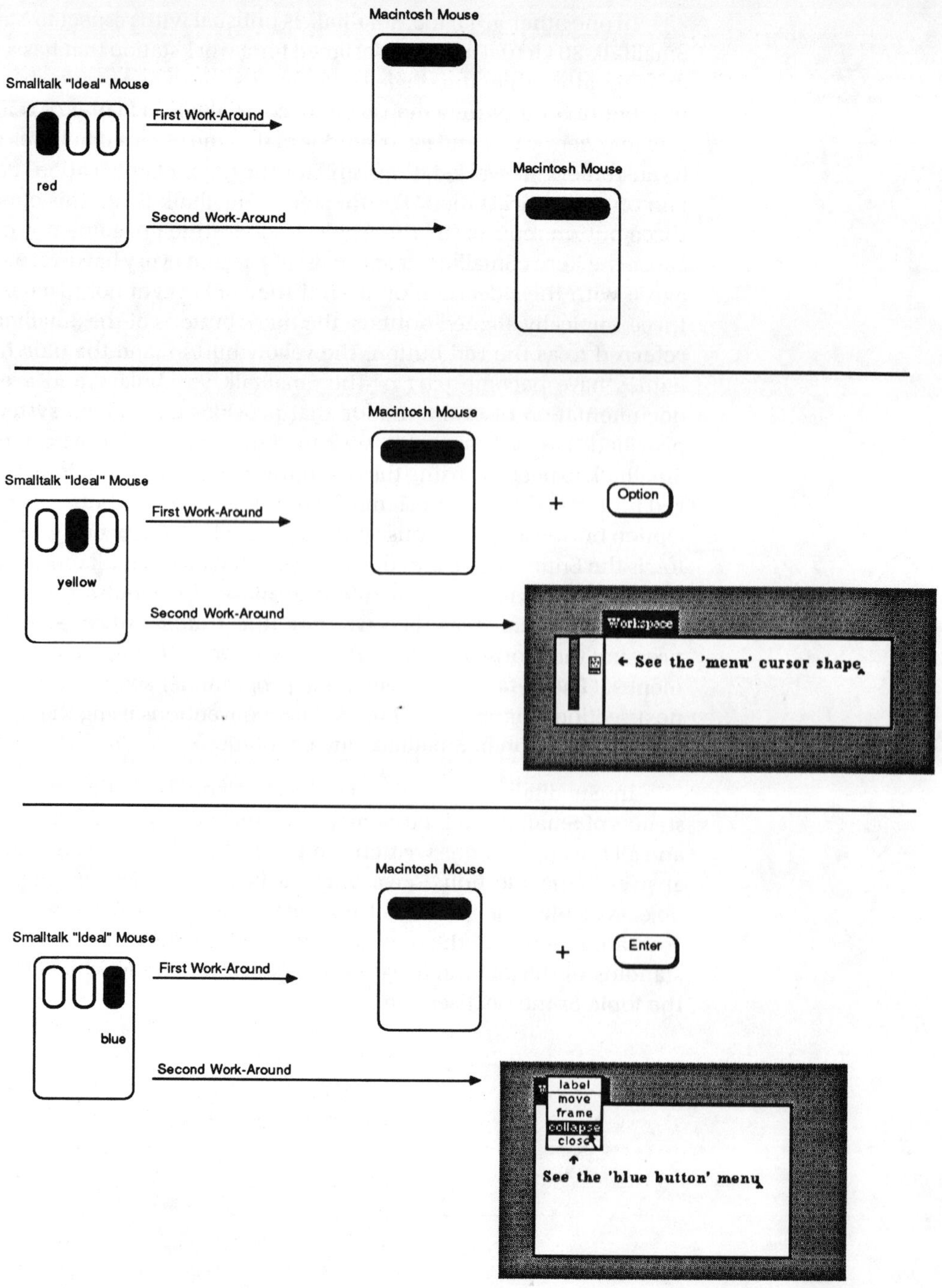

Figure 11-1 The button conventions used in The Smalltalk-80 Programming System for the Macintosh.

Smalltalk-80 Programmer Interface

It is in its programmer interface that Smalltalk differs most significantly from the other object-oriented languages discussed in this book, although it is not dramatically different from the Macintosh user interface because the latter was so heavily influenced by Smalltalk. Text is highlighted when selected, "cut" to be removed, "pasted" to be inserted, and so on. In only a couple of hours, an experienced Macintosh user can usually become comfortable with the Smalltalk conventions. It is interesting during this period of adjustment to remember that Smalltalk was the first environment to experiment with many of these notions, including overlapping windows, menus that appear when needed and then disappear, text in various fonts and styles shown in a What-You-See-Is-What-You-Get (called "WYSIWYG") manner, bitmap graphics, and extensive use of the mouse. Reflecting on this can make you truly appreciate two things: the quality of the pioneering work done by Xerox and the power it brought to the user, and the extent to which Apple improved on this basic research to provide a truly easy-to-learn system that preserved most of that power. One of the best examples of this transition can be seen in a comparison of the Smalltalk Form Editor and MacPaint. A screen image of the Form Editor is shown in Figure 11-2. The Smalltalk Form Editor provides a similar functionality to that of MacPaint but is significantly more difficult to learn. This is no criticism of the Smalltalk Form Editor. After all, the Form Editor was built to determine whether it was possible to design an application that had the same relationship to pictures as a word processing application had to text, whereas MacPaint was built already knowing this was possible and with the goal of optimizing user interactions of this type of application. Rather, this comparison between the Form Editor and MacPaint shows how much the state of the art has improved.

This small section cannot cover in detail the entire Smalltalk programmer interface, but it can highlight the areas that differ the most from the Macintosh user interface. For a detailed examination of the Smalltalk user interface as it applies to all Smalltalk systems including The Smalltalk-80 Programming System for the Macintosh, read Adele Goldberg's book, *Smalltalk-80: The Interactive Programming Environment,* (Addison-Wesley, 1984).

One of the areas where Smalltalk provides the most visibly different style of user interaction is in its use of menus. Smalltalk menus are pop-up menus that appear at the current location of the cursor whenever the yellow or blue mouse buttons are pressed. This is in contrast to Macintosh menus, which are pulled down from a fixed position at the top of the screen. The major difference in these two systems is that in the Smalltalk environment (and in most Smalltalk applications) you have only two menus available at any one moment—and you don't see menu titles to suggest what these menus contain.

This is somewhat overcome by the generally adhered-to convention in which the commands on the yellow-button menu deal with the contents of the view or window containing the cursor and the commands on the blue button menu deal with the window as a whole. Figure 11-3 shows a typical yellow-button menu and Figure 11-4 shows the standard blue-button menu.

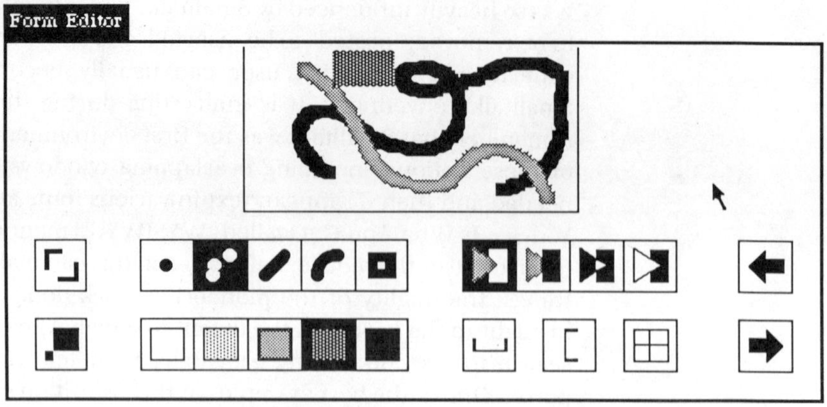

Figure 11-2 The Smalltalk Form Editor, a MacPaint predecessor.

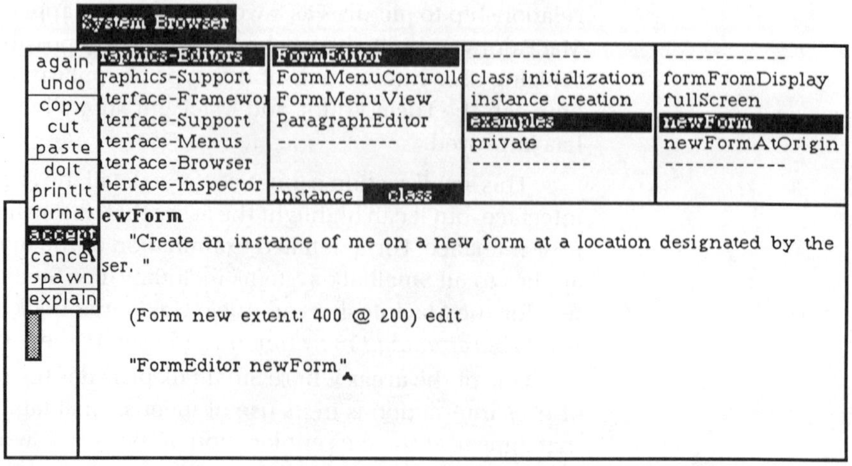

Figure 11-3 A typical yellow-button menu. This menu is the one associated with the text view in the system browser.

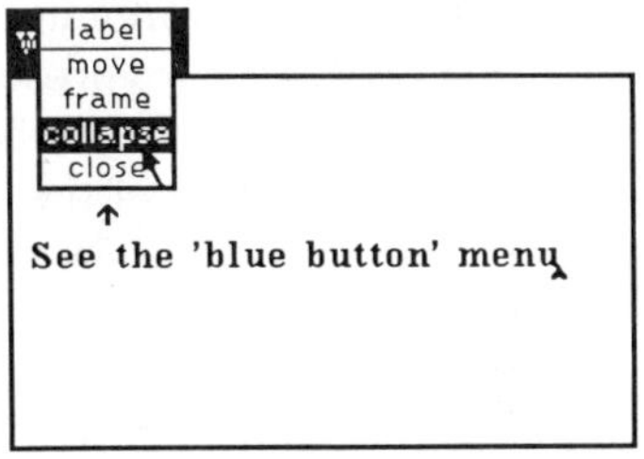

Figure 11-4 The standard Smalltalk blue button menu.

Menus are not the only portion of the Smalltalk user interface that is not visible until used. The Smalltalk-80 scroll bars have no representation on the screen until the cursor enters a scrollable view. Figure 11-5 shows a "before" and "after" screen image of a Smalltalk workspace—an area in which text may be typed and evaluated.

The cursor is outside the window...

and as soon as it moves inside, the scroll bar appears.

Figure 11-5 The appearance of the Smalltalk scroll bars in a workspace.

Extensive programming and debugging aids for the development of Smalltalk programs are present in Smalltalk. Figure 11-6 shows the format of the browser, the debugger, and the inspector. The browser is the means by which you access any of the Smalltalk classes as well as enter your own new classes. To define a new class, you edit the template of a "class defining" expression in the browser. Figure 11-6 shows the definition of the class Quad needed for the Smalltalk implementation of QuadWorld. To change an existing method of a class or to add a new method, a similar template editing takes place in the browser's largest panel. Figure 11-7 shows the definition of one of the Quad methods taking place in the browser. Should the execution of this method result in an error condition, a special debugging window can be used to determine the statement that caused the error and Figure 11-8 shows the use of the debugger to correct a method in an early version of the Quad class. Debugging also can require inspecting objects created by the execution of your statements. The inspector enables you to observe and/or modify the values of the instance variables of any object. Figure 11-9 shows an instance of the class Quad being inspected.

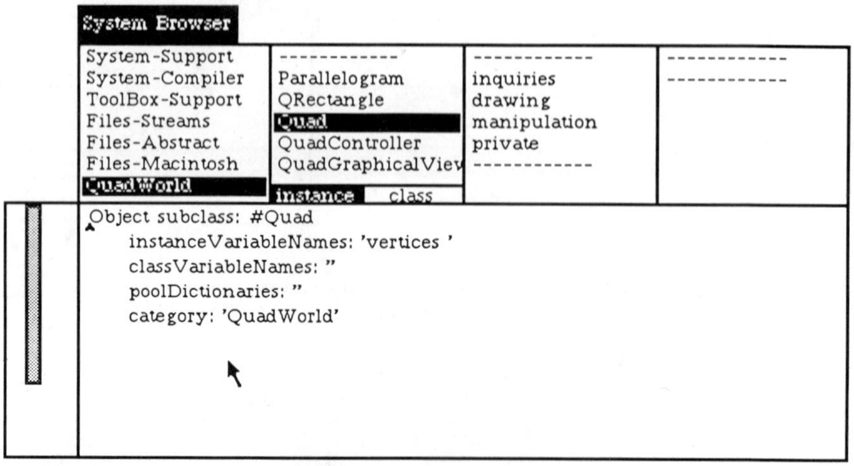

Figure 11-6 The Smalltalk system browser being used to define a new class.

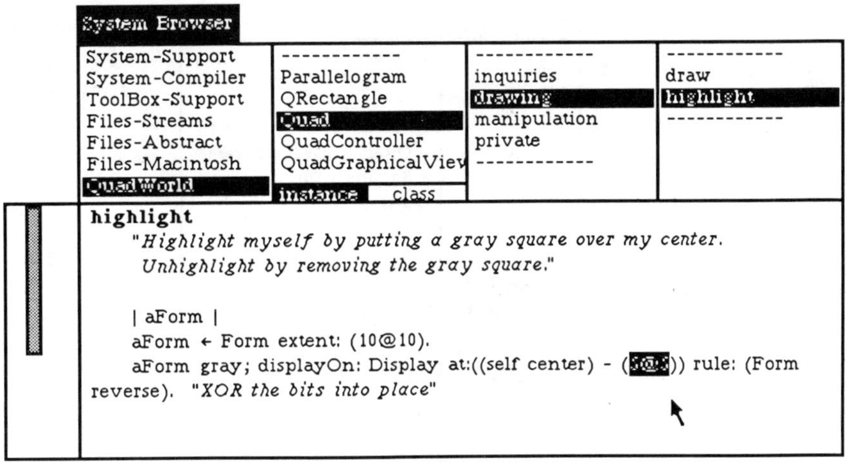

Figure 11-7 The Smalltalk system browser being used to modify an existing method.

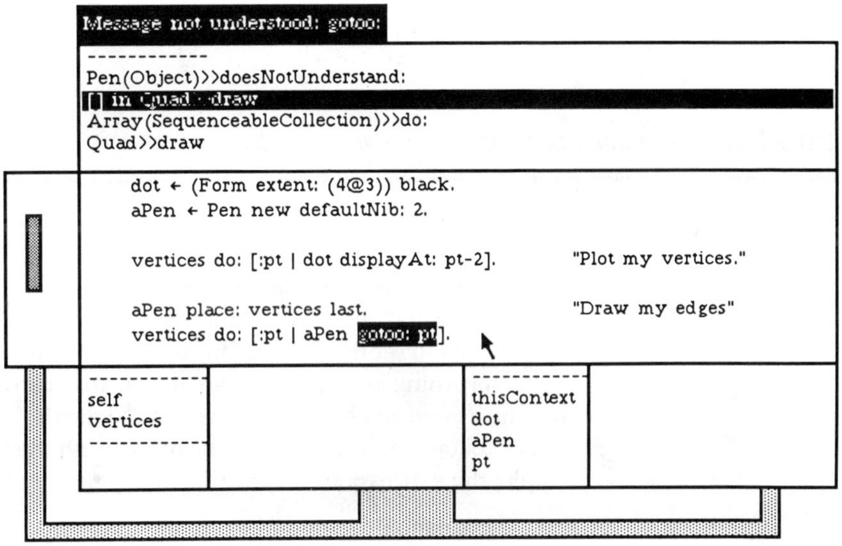

Figure 11-8 The Smalltalk debugger window.

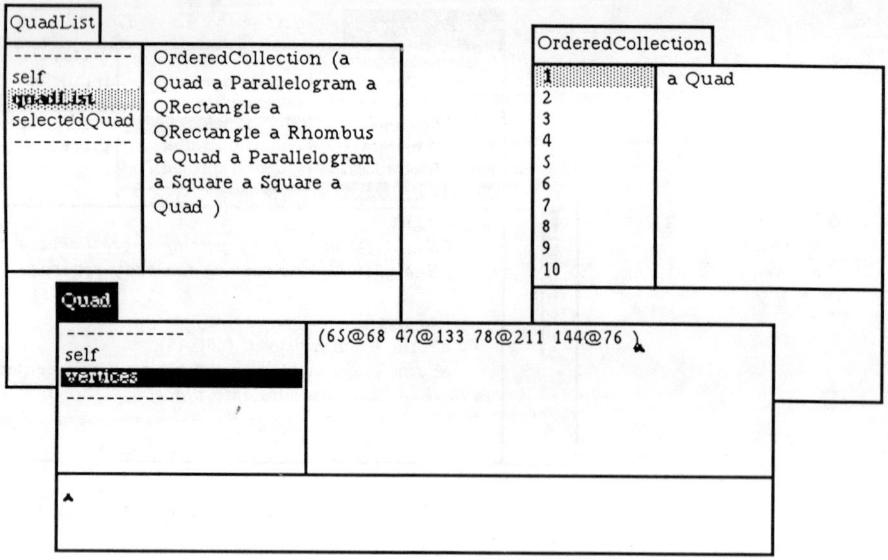

Figure 11-9 The Smalltalk inspector.

Smalltalk-80 Language

Given the background of Chapters 2 and 10, the syntax and semantics of Smalltalk are quite easy to learn. Smalltalk has all the object-oriented language features discussed in Chapter 2 and most of those discussed in Chapter 10; no version of Smalltalk has unique instance methods and Smalltalk-80 for the Macintosh currently does not have multiple inheritence.

Everything in Smalltalk is an object. To cause a computation to take place, you must send an object a message. Syntactically, you send a message to an object by following a reference to the object with the name of the message. For example, the expression

```
myRectangle center
```

sends the message center to the object myRectangle. Messages can be more complex than this, however, because there are three kinds of messages:

- *Unary messages*, the simplest type of message. Unary messages are messages without any arguments. Some examples:
  myRectangle center (Send the message center to the object myRectangle)
  aQuad asText (Send the message asText to the object aQuad)
  theWindow open (Send the message open to the object theWindow)

- *Keyword messages,* messages with (possibly) multiple arguments. In Smalltalk messages, multiple arguments are not concatenated at the end of the message as they are in Object Pascal, but rather are positioned throughout the message. Some examples (several with comparisons to Object Pascal):

```
aPoint x: 12 y: 35.                                              Smalltalk
                          (Send the message x:y: to the object aPoint)
newFrame haveView: thisView.                                     Smalltalk
newFrame.HaveView(thisView);                                Object Pascal
               (Send the message haveView: to the object newFrame)
quadApplication handleAlienEvent: nextEvent                      Smalltalk
        commandToPerform: command.
quadApplication.HandleAlienEvent(nextEvent, command);       Object Pascal
        (Send the message handleAlienEvent:commandToPerform:
        to the object newFrame)
```

- *Binary messages,* used to provide the standard infix notation for some common operators, especially arithmetic ones. Some examples:

```
a + b                        (Send the message + to the object a)
a == b                       (Send the message == to the object a)
bigString, littleString      (Send the message, to the object bigString)
```

Smalltalk also provides an easy syntax for sending a sequence of messages to the same object (cascaded messages) and for statement grouping (blocks). Some examples:

```
aPen down; go: 20; turn: 30; go: 10.
        (Send the messages down, go:, turn:, and go: to the object aPen)

sum ← 0.
1 to: 10 do: [ :i | sum ← sum + i ].
        (Sum the integers from 1 to 10 and place the result in sum)

quadList do: [ :quad | quad draw ].
        (Send each of the objects stored in the collection
        referred to by quadList the message draw)
```

The Smalltalk-80 Class Libraries

There are more than 300 classes in the standard Smalltalk library and no short overview can do more than merely give the novice Smalltalk programmer a feeling for the amount of functionality already built into the system. More extensive discussions can be found in the Goldberg and Robson text, *Smalltalk-80: The Language and Its Implementation,* Adele Goldberg and David Robson, Addison-Wesley, 1983, and in the Smalltalk-80 System Protocols manual (Evelyn Van Orden, Xerox Corporation).

There are classes in the Smalltalk library dealing with various types of numerical representations, including integers, rationals, and reals, as well as dates and time. There are geometric classes representing points, rectangles, curves, lines, fonts, cursors, and arbitrary bitmaps and bitmap manipulations. Other classes model common data structures (linked lists, ordered and unordered collections, and various types of arrays) and control structures (conditionals, repetitions, independent processes, and process scheduling). Certain classes deal with communication to external media and to the user. (The user interface classes are discussed in more detail later in this chapter.) The browsers, debuggers, compilers, and other elements previously mentioned also are implemented as classes.

Many of the examples used in Chapters 2 and 10 are taken directly from the Smalltalk library and the Smalltalk implementation of QuadWorld uses several of the classes not discussed in detail. In most instances the functionality of an object used in QuadWorld can be inferred from the name of the object and the messages it understands. Those classes that are used in the QuadWorld implementation but that might be confusing are commented on in the listing of that application (Listing F). For our purposes, the most important classes are those dealing with the construction of interactive graphical applications and the design of sophisticated user interfaces.

Smalltalk-80 Class Libraries for User Interfaces

It is somewhat ironic that the Smalltalk work, which is unusually well documented in most areas (as witnessed by the Goldberg and Robson text already mentioned as well as two other texts: *Smalltalk-80: The Interactive Programming Environment*, Adele Goldberg, Addison-Wesley, 1984 and *Smalltalk-80: Bits of History, Words of Advice*, Glenn Krasner, Addison-Wesley, 1983.), is almost not documented at all in one of the areas that is its greatest strength: the construction of highly interactive and easy-to-use user interfaces. (The sole exception is *Smalltalk-80: Creating a User Interface and Graphical Applications*, Adele Goldberg, Addison-Wesley, which is still in preparation.) Not only was this work truly pioneering, but it was adopted by many systems that followed Smalltalk, including the Lisa Toolkit (Chapter 12) and MacApp. The results of the Smalltalk research indicated many benefits to considering a user interface as consisting of three separate components: the model, the view, and the controller.

Basically, the model-view-controller design (originated by Trygve Reenskaug and usually simply called MVC) is a division of labor between the various components of an interactive graphical application. The model component stores the information to be depicted on the screen, often in a complex data structure that contains both graphical and non-graphical information. The view component renders the information contained in the model into an image that can be seen by the user. The controller, the remaining part of the MVC triad, handles the user's interactions (key presses on the keyboard, mouse interaction, menus, etc.) with the image of the model drawn by the view.

For example, in an application program used to design floor layouts, the associated data structure would perhaps be an array of record structures. In such an arrangement, the room is modeled by the entire array and each piece of furniture by a record in that array. The components of the record would include the position and orientation of the piece of furniture (data needed to draw the floor plan) as well as the weight and cost of the item (data need to evaluate the ability of the building to support the tentative arrangement and the ability of the purchasing department to buy it). This data structure would probably not include the color of the piece of furniture, for example, because such information is usually not needed to make a floor design. Thus, the model component is any data structure that you can define and interpret that captures the salient features of the same real-world situation. Smalltalk's MVC model follows this approach and any class you design can be the model for an MVC-style application. The Smalltalk model has a close analog in MacApp. In MacApp, the TDocument class is essentially analogous to the Smalltalk class Model and, as you saw in Chapter 4, your subclass of TDocument can refer to any types of data in its instance variables, just as in Smalltalk your model object can also refer to other types of objects.

Definitions

Note that there is no class in Smalltalk named "Model." The model portion of an MVC application can be any class already in the Smalltalk library or any class you design, at any position in the class hierarchy. An instance of this class would then function as the model in your application because you would "install" it as the model, much in the same way you install a view in a MacApp window by setting certain instance variables in another object to refer to it. In this sense of any object acting as the model, Smalltalk differs from MacApp, which has a specific class, TDocument, and any of its subclasses, which are the models of a MacApp application. In Smalltalk, much of the general protocol needed by a model is contained in the Object class. The designers of Smalltalk chose to design a rich Object class that could function as the abstract superclass of all MVC models. The designers of MacApp chose to design a lean TObject class and then to design another class, TDocument, to serve as the abstract superclass of all models.

The model, as vital as it is, merely stores the information that is manipulated in the application. This information is observed by the user through a view. A view of the model is some particular visible representation of the data in the model. In the room layout example, one view might be the floor plan layout in blueprint style. Another might be a three-dimensional rendering of the room from a particular vantage point with some pieces of furniture obscured by others. Another might be a purchase order specification printed by the application for the purchasing department. Still another might be a stress-loading map of the floor derived from the particular layout being examined and the weight data in the model. A model, thus, can have many views—even ones of distinctly different characteristics—associated with it. The Smalltalk implementation of QuadWorld, as you will see later in this chapter, has two views, a graphical view and a list view. Smalltalk has the following basic types of views that can be refined for the views needed in your application:

- View — The class that is a superclass of all other view classes. The instance protocol of the View class enables you to add, delete, position, and transform subviews—lower-level components of a structured picture—in addition to putting a border around a view, pointing to a model, and many other actions.
- StandardSystemView — This displays a standard Smalltalk-style window with a label in the upper-left corner and provides you with the visual component of standard window operations like framing and collapsing. (The interaction component is governed by the controller part of the MVC model. This will be discussed shortly.)
- FormView — A view for displaying and editing raster graphic images like those produced by MacPaint.
- DisplayTextView — A view for text consisting of many different fonts and styles—in a way, an elementary (by today's standards) MacWrite. This view is functionally similar to MacApp's TEView unit.
- ListView — A view for displaying and scrolling a list of items, such as the TListView class designed for the MacApp implementation of QuadWorld (Chapter 8). In fact, the Smalltalk ListView is the "mother" of the MacApp TListView class because the design of TListView was heavily influenced by the structure of the ListView.

• StringHolderView	A view for a string that is a part of a more structured object.
• BinaryChoiceView	A view for yes/no choices, as in certain types of dialog boxes.
• FillInTheBlankView	A view for a dialog box-like object into which the user types some information.
• SwitchView	A view for a dialog box-like object in which the user is presented with several mutually exclusive choices.

There are almost twenty other view classes associated with the Smalltalk programmer interface. The MacApp class TView basically corresponds to the Smalltalk View class although TView has incorporated into its functionality many features of the Smalltalk controller.

The remaining component of the MVC triad is the controller. This element prescribes the style of interaction between the user and the model. It is the controller that handles such user events as mouse clicks, selections and keyboard input. The controller portion of an MVC application then sends a message to the model (or occasionally directly to the view) to modify itself based on this input. It is here that Smalltalk differs most dramatically from MacApp or the Lisa Toolkit (Chapter 12). In essence, the MacApp Expandable Application is the controller for MacApp applications and the Lisa Toolkit Generic Application is the controller for a Lisa Toolkit application. Rather than providing one standard controller that conforms to an existing user interface standard, Smalltalk provides a number of controllers and the ability to construct new ones. In this way, Smalltalk is a useful environment for exploring alternative user interfaces. To be sure, you could override significant portions of MacApp—for example, to provide an application with a user-interface feature that is dramatically different from the Macintosh user interface standard (lift-up menus rather pull-down, for example). While such a thing could be done in MacApp, it probably is not the best starting point for such an application. The standard Smalltalk image provides more than twenty-five types of controller classes starting with the class Controller. (In general, these controller subclasses correspond directly to the View subclasses. Corresponding to the ListView, for example, there is a ListController; to the BinaryChoiceView, a BinaryChoiceController, etc.) The Smalltalk-80 implementation of QuadWorld uses two of these.

Definitions

Although a new Smalltalk controller could construct a non-standard user interface, all the Controller subclasses currently in Smalltalk actually implement a consistent user interface: the Smalltalk user interface. What has happened in the Smalltalk MVC architecture is that the same classes that are used to implement that standard user interface are also (usually) used for the application-specific behavior. In MacApp, the classes and subclasses of TApplication, TWindow, and TFrame provide most of the application-independent behavior for a new application and the classes and subclasses of TView and TCommand provide most of the application-dependent behavior.

Definitions

To be more precise, the functions of controller class are distributed in a MacApp or Toolkit application among all the basic classes. The main point is that in Smalltalk, a single object (an instance of the controller class) handles all the user interaction. In MacApp, this functionality is spread among many classes, including TView, TCommand, TApplication, TDocument, TFrame, and TWindow.

The view and controller are able to send messages to the model because each object has an instance variable that refers to the model. The model, however, has no such instance variable because the model of an MVC application can be any object. It would not be reasonable to add an instance variable to every object in the system because a few objects might be models. Rather, a capability of all objects to have dependents is used to communicate information from the model to its views and controllers. A dependent of an object A is any object that should be notified when A is modified. Objects may have any number of dependents. When an object modifies itself (recall that in Smalltalk, this is the only way an object can change because its instance variables are not directly addressable by "outsiders") it also sends itself the changed: message. The single argument to changed: is a symbol that can be used in any way by the application to record exactly how the model has changed. The standard response of an object to the changed: message is to send all of its dependents the update: message with the same symbol parameter. This has the effect of telling all dependents that the object on which they depend has changed and that it should update itself (typically through further inquiries of the model) to show the latest model information. This entire mechanism is called *change propaga-*

tion because the notified objects may themselves change and thus notify their dependents, in turn causing a flurry of messages to be sent around the system. The Smalltalk implementation of QuadWorld uses change propagation to communicate selection updates between the graphical and the textual views.

Notes

MacApp has a similar, though less general, change propagation mechanism in class TDocument. The method EachView(DoToView) announces a change in the document to each of the views that render the document.

QuadWorld in Smalltalk

A screen image from the MacWorks Smalltalk-80 implementation of QuadWorld is shown in Figure 11-10. (The source code for this implementation appears in Listing F.) This image shows two views of the quadrilaterals and one of the three available pop-up menus. The window title, border, light gray background, and the entire ListView and ListController are just some of the features in the Smalltalk QuadWorld that were inherited from the Smalltalk user inter-face classes.

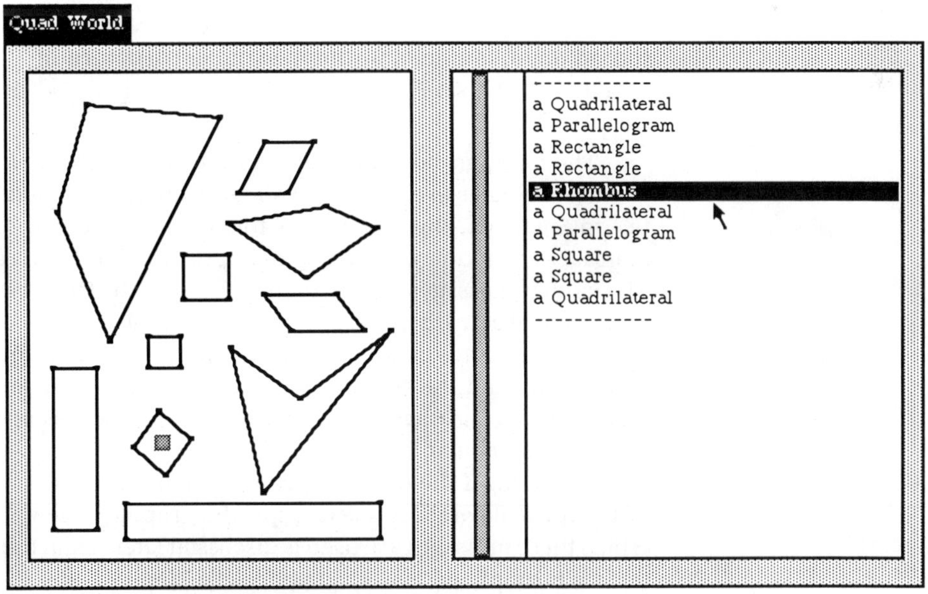

Figure 11-10 The Smalltalk implementation of QuadWorld.

In Smalltalk, the object-oriented portion of QuadWorld is implemented on two levels. On one level, the various types of quadrilaterals are implemented as a set of five classes, Quad, Parallelogram, QRectangle, Rhombus, and Square with an interrelationship between these classes that described in detail later in this section. Because Smalltalk is a pure object-oriented language, the QuadWorld user interface, too, is designed according to the object-oriented model using the Smalltalk MVC classes. The implementation of this user interface is also discussed at length in this section. The only remaining portion of the Smalltalk implementation of QuadWorld is the manner in which the instances of quadrilaterals are stored. This portion of the implementation is covered in the user interface discussion, because the Smalltalk framework for user interfaces includes such a data storage component.

In the Smalltalk QuadWorld, a quadrilateral is represented as an instance of the class Quad, itself a subclass of Object. The class Quad has four instance variables, p1, p2, p3, and p4, which all are instances of class Point, a class provided in Smalltalk's basic graphics classes. Because there are no dependencies or relationships between the vertices of a general quadrilateral, there is no way that a smaller number of vertices could be stored with each instance of a quadrilateral in the way that, for example, two opposite vertices define a square or a rectangle. The class Quad has no class variables because there is no constant data shared among all the quadrilateral instances.

The class Quad is the superclass for all other geometric classes in QuadWorld. The relationship between these classes is shown in Figure 11-11. It is interesting to note that very few of the instance methods are overridden in the subclasses. The asText method, for example, is overridden so that each type of quadrilateral can report itself correctly in the ListView. With the exception of the four methods that report the individual vertices of a quad (messages first, second, third, and fourth), the basic class structure of these quad classes in Smalltalk is the same as it is in the MacApp and Toolkit implemenations of QuadWorld.

The messages to a quad object in the Smalltalk implementation of QuadWorld are similar to those in the MacApp implementation. As is common practice in Smalltalk, the protocol of the instances of class Quad is divided into messages for inquiry, drawing, manipulation, and several private messages. The inquiry messages allow a method outside the Quad class protocol to determine each of a quadrilateral's vertices (messages first, second, third, and fourth), its center (message center), a textual representation of the quadrilateral (message asText), and the smallest upright rectangle that completely encloses the quadrilateral (message enclosingRectangle). The asText message is used in building the tabular view of QuadWorld and the enclosingRectangle message in determining if the user has pressed the mouse button in the neighborhood of the quadrilateral for selection in the graphical view. The exact manner in which these messages are used is discussed later when the QuadWorld user interface is examined.

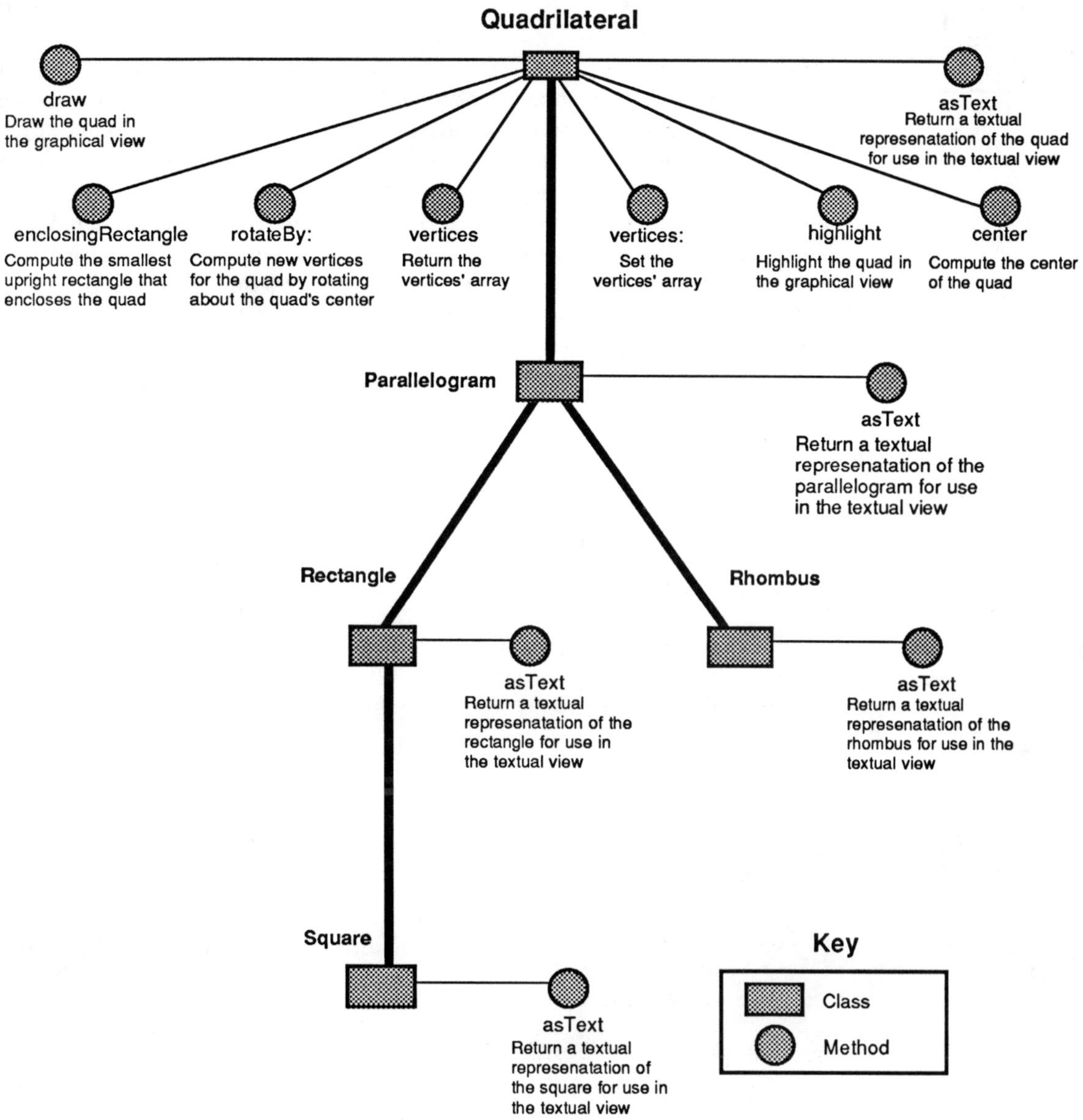

Figure 11-11 The instance methods for the class Quad and its subclasses.

Notes

The messages first, second, third, and fourth were not needed in the MacApp implementation of QuadWorld because Object Pascal allows instance variables to be accessed directly, by another object of the same class, or even by an object of another class. (Although to some, this is a major deficiency of Object Pascal since it violates one of the basic tenets of object-oriented programming; to others, it is one of Object Pascal's strengths since it provides efficient access when this is needed.) Smalltalk completely encapsulates an object and thus the only way to provide external access to its instance variables is to add messages like first, second, third, and fourth. In fact, many Smalltalk messages do nothing more than provide this type of access.

The drawing messages of class Quad provide for the drawing of a quadrilateral and for its highlighting. Special care was taken to make the highlight method the inverse of itself. That is, to unhighlight a highlighted quadrilateral, you merely send it the highlight message a second time. This was done by specifying a special combination rule, the inverse rule, for displaying a block of gray bits in the center of the quadrilateral. The first time this block of bits is displayed, it shows up; the second time, it disappears.

Notes

Note that there is no highlight message in the MacApp version of QuadWorld because in the MacApp framework highlighting is done by the TView object—by the instance of TQuadGrView, specifically in the case of QuadWorld.

The single manipulation methods, rotateBy:, while slightly complicated in its formula for the inexperienced graphics programmer, is a relatively straightforward geometric manipulation. In keeping with the standard programming practice in Smalltalk, there are private methods called by Quad class methods to initialize new instances of the class Quad.

The class methods provide a much more involved example of method organization because many of these methods must be overridden in each of the subclasses. The manner in which the methods are overridden in the subclasses shows how the principles of object-oriented programming naturally lead to the reusing of code. The relationship between these classes' methods is shown in Figure 11-12. Notice how the inheritance structure of the metaclasses exactly parallels that of the corresponding classes. This parallelism is not accidental nor is it something engineered by the application programmer. The inheritance structure of the metaclasses is automatically generated by the system to match that of their classes.

The feedbackFrom:and: method, for example, which provides visible feedback in the graphical view of the quadrilaterals while a new one is being entered, is not overridden until the QRectangle class because the type of feedback needed for quadrilaterals, parallelograms, and rhombi is essentially the same: a single rubberbanded line must be drawn. For rectangles and squares, the feedback is that of a rubberbanded rectangle, so the feedbackFrom:and: method must be overridden. It is in the fromUser methods that the number of defining points needed for each type of quadrilateral is implicitly coded. Because four points are needed for quadrilaterals, three for parallelograms and rhombi, and only two for rectangles and squares, the fromUser method is implemented in the Quadrilateral class, then overridden in the Parallelogram class and QRectangle class.

Definitions

There already is a Rectangle class in the Smalltalk class library. This class could not be used in QuadWorld as the rectangle quadrilateral because it does not have the type of protocol or instance variables we need. To avoid a naming problem, the QuadWorld rectangle class is named QRectangle in the Smalltalk implementation.

Even though parallelograms and rhombi (as one group) and rectangles and squares (as another group) have the same number of defining points, they have some different characteristics. These characteristics are encoded in the correctIt:withRespectTo:and: methods. These methods adjust the cursor position to take into account these different characteristics. For squares, this method is:

```
width ← (aPoint x)—(fixedPoint1 x).

height ← (aPoint y)—(fixedPoint1 y).

(width > height) ifTrue: [↑aPoint y: (aPoint y) + (width—height)]
                  ifFalse: [↑aPoint x: (aPoint x) + (height—width)].
```

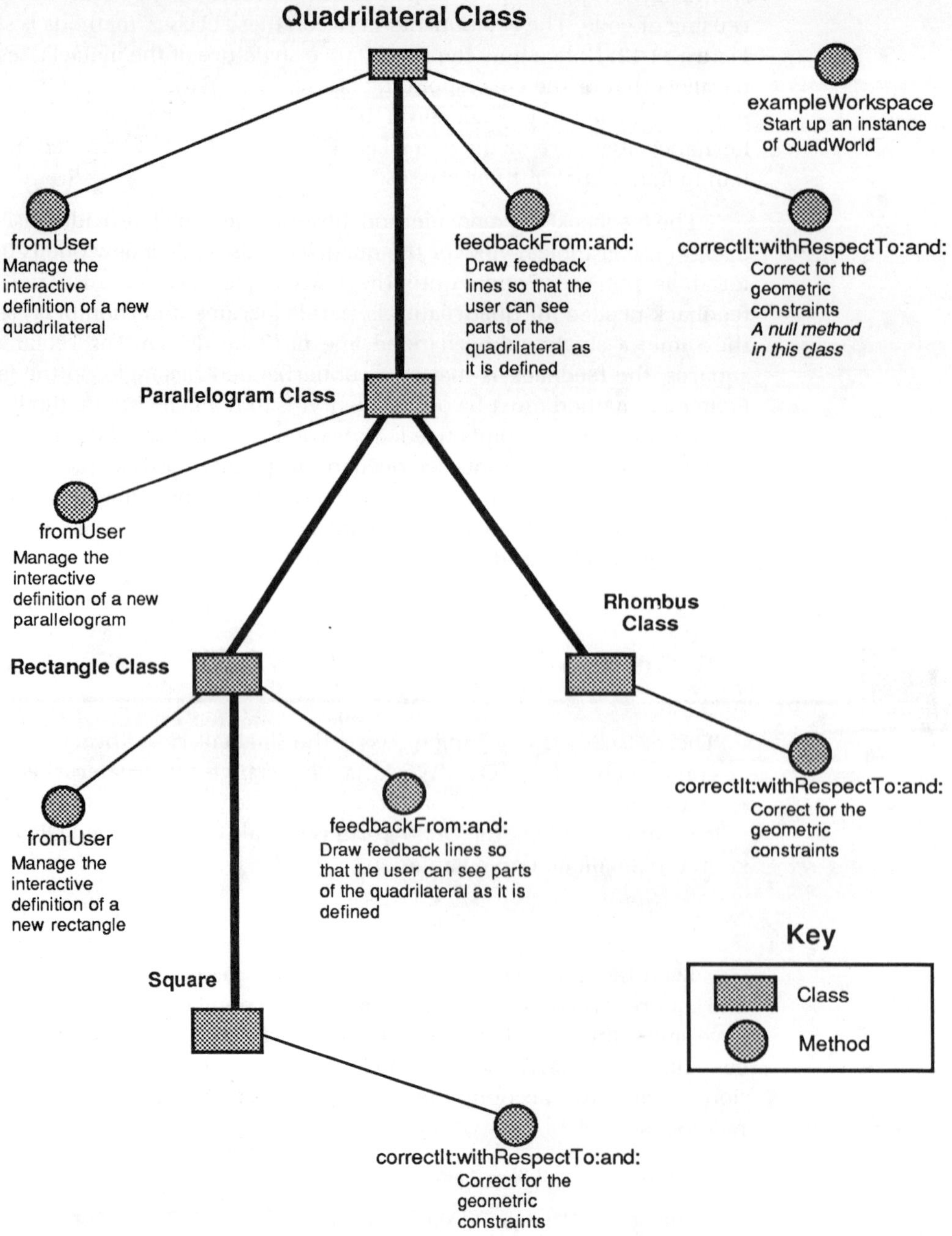

Figure 11-12 The class methods for the class Quad and its subclasses.

where aPoint is the current cursor position and fixedPoint1 is the opposite vertex of the square. This method guarantees that the rubberbanded figure is a perfect square. A similar method ensures that rhombi are constructed with equal-length sides. Including a null correctIt:withRespectTo:and: method in the Quadrilateral class allows the maximum re-use of the feedbackFrom:and: methods. The corrections take place only when constructing the appropriate type of quadrilateral.

Definitions

In Object Pascal, there are no class methods, which is also thought by some to be a deficiency in Object Pascal but by others to be one of its simplifying strenghts. In the MacApp implementation of QuadWorld, most of these responsibilities for quadrilateral creation are associated with the sketcher classes, TSketchQuadCmd and its subclasses. In fact, because Object Pascal does not have class methods, the sketcher classes had to be purposely designed to parallel the quadrilateral classes, and this parallelism has to be maintained by the programmer. (Once, during the initial development of QuadWorld, I changed the quadrilateral inheritance but forgot to make the same change in the sketcher classes. This resulted in a bug that was non-trivial to track down. No such bug is possible in Smalltalk because this metaclass parallelism is maintained automatically.) In effect, then, the sketcher classes in the MacApp implementation of QuadWorld mimic the quadrilateral metaclasses in the Smalltalk implementation.

Consistent with the original QuadWorld specification in Chapter 2, the Smalltalk QuadWorld implementation includes two distinct representations of the quadrilaterals that the user has entered, and Figure 11-10 shows a typical screen layout for the Smalltalk QuadWorld. This screen layout and the associated user interface of pop-up menus specific to the QuadWorld application are designed strictly following the model-view-controller paradigm using the interface classes included in the standard Smalltalk-80 image. In the case of QuadWorld, the model is a class called QuadList. QuadList contains an instance of OrderedCollection, a basic Smalltalk class, which stores the quadrilaterals, parallelograms, rhombi, rectangles, and squares that the user has entered. In addition, QuadList instances store the index of the currently selected quadrilateral. In any QuadWorld, there is only one instance of the QuadList model. Having a single instance of the model object is very common for a Smalltalk MVC application.

The messages of the QuadList model are specially chosen to provide the type of functionality needed for the QuadWorld application and to provide the protocol expected by a model of the system-supplied ListView class. There is an add: message to add new quadrilaterals to the ordered collection of quadrilaterals that the model is maintaining and a remove: message to delete them. Because the model communicates various types of information about itself to other objects—objects that control the pictorial renderings of the model and the user's interaction with that representation, for example—there is a rich set of reporting messages for QuadList. In QuadList, the currently selected quadrilateral can be queried with the listIndex message, set with the toggleListIndex: message and the deselectCurrentlySelectedQuad message. The ordered collection of quadrilaterals can be queried with the message listOfQuads and a textual version of this collection, used to construct the tabular view, can be obtained with the list message. The messages listIndex, toggleListIndex:, and list were chosen as messages for QuadList because they are sent by the classes ListView and ListController to their model. Thus, choosing to implement methods for these particular messages in the class QuadList means that the standard Smalltalk ListView and ListController classes can be used without subclassing. This is one of many examples in QuadWorld where a correct choice of message protocol enables the application to make great use of the existing Smalltalk class library without change.

The Smalltalk implementation of QuadWorld consists of three views: a standard system view to provide for the normal title frames, window structure, and blue-button window controls; a graphical view, which draws pictorial representations of the quadrilaterals in the QuadList model; and a list view, which presents a textual representation of the model. Smalltalk makes the design of these three views easy because they are subclasses of view classes already present in the standard Smalltalk image. Because of the rich protocol associated with each of the standard view subclasses, very little additional functionality needs to be added to the particular views used in QuadWorld. The QuadWorld list view is not even a subclass of the standard ListView, it is an instance of such a view, so no additional software is needed for this portion of QuadWorld. Even QuadGraphicalView, itself a subclass of View, needs only two additional messages and two overridden methods. The implementation of one of these overridden methods, displayView, is particularly interesting because it demonstrates vividly the power of the object-oriented approach to software design. displayView is an example of a null method, a method subclasses are expected to override but that they need not override. A null method does nothing—it performs no useful computation, but is invoked nevertheless in the other methods in the class; displayView is invoked in the display method of the View class, for example. The display method is the method that draws the borders of a view, draws the view itself, then draws its subviews.

It has the following implementation:

```
self displayBorder.

self displayView.

self displaySubViews.
```

At first glance, the self displayView statement seems like a totally useless part of this method because the message displayView in the standard View class does nothing. What it provides—and, in general, what null methods provide—is a placeholder that the application designer can override. This is not unique to Smalltalk because null methods are also used for this purpose in other frameworks including MacApp and the Lisa Toolkit. In the case of QuadGraphicalView, the new implementation of displayView is:

```
self clearInside.

(model listOfQuads) do: [ :eachQuad | eachQuad draw].

selection ← model listIndex.

self displaySelection.
```

The most important statement in this method is the second one which basically corresponds to the implementation of TQuadGrView.Draw in the MacApp version of QuadWorld. This single statement obtains the list of quadrilaterals from the model (model listOfQuads), steps through the list (do:), executing a certain block of code that draws each item in the list (eachQuad draw). Note that this block only sends the draw message to each quadrilateral—it lets each type of quadrilateral decide for itself how it should be drawn.
The displayView method does not have to be changed at all if another type of quadrilateral with its own peculiar drawing method is added to QuadWorld. It is exactly this type of isolation between the components of a system that an object-oriented architecture provides.

Note that it is not necessary to know the standard implementation of displayView or display to provide the correct override of the displayView method in QuadGraphicalView. All that is necessary to know is the general function of the displayView method in the View class. Once that is known, you can override its method in the QuadGraphicalView and design into your implementation the more specific version of that function needed in QuadWorld. If you are unsure as to whether or not the standard implementation also does something else important, you can always add super displayView at the end of your particular displayView message to get to that functionality and, in fact, this is done in the initialize method in the QuadGraphicalView class because the execution of the initialize method in the View class is crucial to the proper use of any instance of View.

In designing the controller for QuadWorld, the standard Smalltalk approach is used: find one of the existing Smalltalk classes that closely resembles the type of functionality desired in the application at hand, then subclass it to add more appropriate functionality. The particular Controller subclass that best fits the QuadWorld application is MouseMenuController. This class provides a number of standard methods for displaying custom menus when one of the three mouse buttons is pressed and also allows you to override these methods to provide for different styles of user interaction. QuadWorld does both of these to provide its user interface. Let's examine one case of each.

When the yellow button is pressed, the Smalltalk QuadWorld displays the five-item pop-up menu, "quadrilateral parallelogram rectangle rhombus square," if there is no current selection, and the three–item menu, "rotateQuad stretchQuad deleteQuad," if there is one. These menus are stored in a QuadController class variable and the yellowButtonActivity method is overridden first to decide if there is a current selection, then to set the appropriate MouseMenuController instance variables that control menu actions, and last to invoke the standard yellowButtonActivity that actually displays the menu and determines which item has been selected. Setting up custom menus involves no more work than creating an object of class PopUpMenu (a standard Smalltalk class) and linking this new menu with the instance of QuadController with the message yellowButtonMenu:yellowButtonActivity: The only tricky part is to realize that the labels: message to the PopUpMenu class requires carriage returns between each of the menu items. If you want lines between certain items on your custom menu, that, too, is easy. All you have to do is send the message labels:lines: and use as an argument to the lines: selector an array that specifies the labels that should have lines after them. This is done for the second menu, which is displayed when a quadrilateral is selected. When items on this custom menu are selected by the user, their corresponding messages (set with the yellowButtonMessages: selector) will be sent to the controller.

Confused? Here is a small example. You want the following menu to be displayed and when an item is chosen, you want the corresponding message from a list to be sent to your subclass of MouseMenuController:

To do this, generate an instance of PopUpMenu with a statement like this:

```
myMenu ← PopUpMenu labels:
'undo
grow
stretch
color
delete' lines: #(1 4).
```

Set up its corresponding messages with a statement like this:

```
myMenuMessages ← #(undo growItem stretchItem colorItem deleteItem).
```

Finally, install these in your subclass of MouseMenuController for the yellow button, for example, with the following statement (There are other analogous messages to set the menus for the two other buttons.):

```
myController yellowButtonMenu: myMenu
             yellowButtonMessages: myMenuMessages.
```

That's all there is to it.

Notes

It is interesting to compare this Smalltalk style of menu construction and handling with that of MacApp. In MacApp, the menu is stored in a resource file and is automatically handled by the TApplication object. You as the application programmer rarely get involved in menu construction and handling, other than to enter the text strings to be displayed in the menu. (The Smalltalk user interface has no notion corresponding to menu disabling or checking—the only other thing most MacApp programmers do with the actual menus.) Menus stored in resource files can be more easily translated to foreign languages or otherwise changed, compared to menus stored in the code itself— thus internationalization of MacApp applications is somewhat easier.

To design your own style of interaction, rather than using pop-up menus, you override the yellowButtonActivity method, for example, and do not invoke the standard one. In QuadWorld, this type of Smalltalk programming can be seen in the getAngle instance method in the QuadController class. The function of this method is to obtain from the user an angle after the rotation command has been entered via the pop-up menu. While this could have been done with a dialog box that required the user to type in the angle in degrees, this would be unfriendly and not visually intuitive. In QuadWorld, the user enters an angle by first drawing one line through the center of the quadrilateral to be rotated, then drawing a second one. The angle subtended by these two lines is the angle of the rotation. In this way, the user can, in effect, say "Rotate this quadrilateral so that this point is moved to here." (See Figure 11-13). The getAngle method both provides this user interaction and computes the angle.

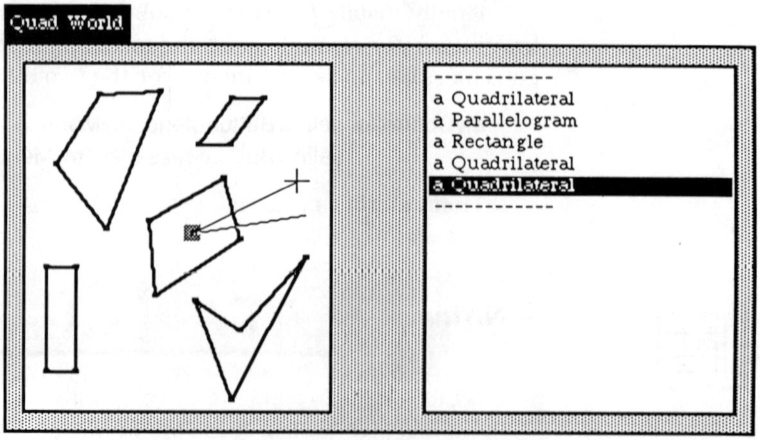

Figure 11-13 Specifying an angle for the rotation of a quadrilateral in the Smalltalk implementation of QuadWorld.

Clearly, the lines drawn by the user are just temporary construction lines. They should neither erase anything on the screen nor should they be permanent. This can be done by XOR-ing the lines on the screen and by not changing the model to record these lines. The fact that the lines are XOR-ed into place also makes their erasure easy—just redraw them. The key portion of the getAngle method in achieving this effect are the following statements:

```
aPen ← Pen new defaultNib: 1; combinationRule: (Form reverse).
.
.
.
[Sensor anyButtonPressed] whileTrue: [
  aPen drawFrom: centerPoint to: endPoint. "Erase old line "
  endPoint ← Sensor cursorPoint.
  aPen drawFrom: centerPoint to: endPoint]. "Draw new one "
```

In these statements, aPen is a thin pen that XORs its line onto the screen. When it comes time to enable the user to draw one of these lines, the line is drawn and undrawn every time the current position of the cursor is read (Sensor cursorPoint). This continues as long as the mouse button (or in fact any of the three logical mouse buttons) are pressed ([Sensor anyButtonPressed] whileTrue []:). Because the QuadGraphicalView displayView method only draws the quadrilaterals in the model, the last two lines, which are left on the screen, will be erased automatically when the view is redisplayed.

Given the three points—the center point of the currently selected quadrilateral, the end point of the first line, and the end point of the second line—it is easy to compute the cosine of the angle between the lines with the following formula:

$$\cos \varnothing = \frac{\mathbf{a} \cdot \mathbf{b}}{\| \mathbf{a} \| \ \| \mathbf{b} \|}$$

where **a** is the vector from the center point to the end point of the first line and **b** is the vector from the center point to the end point of the second line. To obtain the angle itself, you need only send the calculated cosine the message arcCos.

MacApp in Smalltalk

There is no easy way to directly access the MacApp class library from Smalltalk—the differences between Smalltalk and Object Pascal preclude that. However, it would be desirable to be able to develop applications in Smalltalk that conform to the Macintosh User Interface Standard. One way to achieve this is to replace the Smalltalk MVC classes with a set of Smalltalk classes that provide the same functionality as the MacApp classes. If there existed a Smalltalk TApplication class, a Smalltalk TDocument, and a Smalltalk TCommand for example, then a Smalltalk programmer could design an application in Smalltalk by subclassing TApplication, overriding DoMakeDocument, subclass TDocument overriding DoSetupMenus and DoMenuCommand, and so on in the normal manner that a MacApp application is developed in Object Pascal. Apple's Object-Oriented Programming group has done exactly this as an experiment in Smalltalk. (See Ken Doyle, Barry Haynes, Mark Lentczner, and Larry Rosenstein, "An Object Oriented Approach to Macintosh Application Development", *Proceedings of the 3rd Working Session on Object Oriented Languages*, Paris, France, 8-10 January 1986.)

This experimental set of Smalltalk classes provides the same functionality as the Object Pascal MacApp classes. New applications implemented in this MacApp Smalltalk are visually indistinguishable from those developed in Object Pascal, yet because of the Smalltalk programming environment, the application programmer can try out many more optional architectures in a given amount of time when working in Smalltalk, compared to what can be done while working in Object Pascal.

One of the many difficult problems in this research effort has been to guarantee that the functionality of the new Smalltalk MacApp classes are as close as possible to that of the original MacApp classes. The solution used by Apple has been to automatically generate the Smalltalk MacApp classes directly from the Object Pascal sources using an Object Pascal-to-Smalltalk conversion utility. Since the individual transformations made by this utility have been correct, the functionality of the derived classes must match that of the original classes—or, more correctly, the functionality has been very close. These derived classes have then been "hand-tuned" for performance and optimal use of Smalltalk class library.

It is still too early to say if this experimental class library will become a supported Apple product, but it has demonstrated the fact that the MacApp classes can exist in other languages—a fact that other programming language vendors will take advantage of.

CHAPTER

12

Lisa Clascal and the Lisa Toolkit

The Lisa Toolkit is the equivalent of MacApp for the Lisa 7/7 desktop environment. It provides the only fully functional development path for software that is to exist on that desktop and share data with seven standard Lisa applications (LisaWrite, LisaDraw, and others.) Specifically, the Toolkit is a set of classes that implement major portions of the Lisa user interface conventions and an application framework, called the *Generic Application,* that uses these classes. Just as with MacApp, to develop a new application, you expand the Generic Application by adding your own subclasses to the Toolkit libraries. These applications are written in the precursor of Object Pascal, Clascal. Chronologically, both the Toolkit and Clascal precede MacApp and Object Pascal and, in fact, the knowledge gained during the design and implementation of the Toolkit and Clascal had a major influence on these later two Apple projects. As is typically the case, the second time a major system is implemented it is designed cleaner and implemented better and the Toolkit-MacApp progression is no exception to this. The Toolkit is somewhat harder to use than MacApp—it requires more work and sophistication on the part of the applications programmer. There are many reasons for this, including:

- The first time any major system is implemented much new ground is broken and many new concepts are introduced. There are no precedents already established, so the resulting Toolkit contains much that was simplified and refined in the later MacApp implementation.

- The only way to program the Lisa is to use the Toolkit, so the Toolkit had to cover even the rarest cases and provide for the most unusual applications. As a result, the Toolkit is large. MacApp, on the other hand, is but one of many ways to program the Macintosh and is a way that does not exclude the others. If, while designing a MacApp application, you need to do something for which MacApp provides no support, you can call the Toolbox directly, as we did for iconic menus in Chapter 9. There is no such "safety net" on the Lisa, so the Toolkit had to do it all.
- The Lisa has a true multi-tasking operating system, so additional concepts such as background tasks had to be implemented in the Toolkit.
- In general, Lisa applications, residing on a machine with much more memory and a hard disk, can be more comprehensive than the corresponding Macintosh ones. LisaWrite, for example, provides the user with the ability to view widely separated portions of a document simultaneously as well as a spell checker and extensive page format possibilities—features missing from the 128K MacWrite. Providing an expandable application that makes it easy to implement applications of similar complexity is just a bigger task, hence the added complexity of the Toolkit compared to MacApp.

Notes

It is easy to confuse the terms "Toolkit" and "Toolbox". The Tool*kit* is the set of classes for the Lisa generic application. The Tool*box* is the set of ROM routines on the Macintosh. Lisa programmers cannot access the Toolbox and Macintosh programmers, specifically MacApp programmers, cannot access the Toolkit. One reason these terms are often confused is that the first implementation of Quickdraw is on Lisa; a later implementation is part of the Toolbox.

Notes

Shortly after the final version of the Toolkit (version 3.0) was finished, Apple decided to concentrate all its development paths on the Macintosh. Accordingly, the Toolkit is no longer supported by Apple. There is a Toolkit Users Group, however, listed in Appendix B with other suppliers and organizations associated with object-oriented programming on the Macintosh.

Just like MacApp, the Toolkit represents the combined wisdom of the Lisa software developers and provides this wisdom in the reusable manner that only an object-oriented system can provide. Because of the Toolkit, the task of designing and implementing a new desktop application for Lisa is considerably easier for you than it was for the first Lisa application designers. To use the Toolkit to design a new Lisa application, you must be familiar with the Lisa user interface guidelines. These are similar but not identical to those of the Macintosh and are documented in another book by this author, *The Complete Book of Lisa*, Harper & Row, New York, NY, 1984.

In addition to the Toolkit, or more precisely, because of it, there is one other development path possible for an application that is to be run from the Lisa desktop environment. This path is called *QuickPort*. QuickPort is itself a Toolkit application that provides standard windows in which unmodified application programs can run, much in the same way a Lisa user can use a LisaTerminal window to run an application program on a remote host. As its name implies, one of the major goals of QuickPort is to provide a means whereby existing programs can be ported quickly to the Lisa desktop. QuickPort does not, however, allow the developer to define new menu items or make extensive use of the mouse, among other things. QuickPort thus provides a relatively easy-to-use, limited means of constructing desktop software. Because the use of QuickPort by a developer does not involve the use of object-oriented languages like Object Pascal, Smalltalk, or Clascal, but rather conventional languages like Pascal and C, it is not discussed in this book. Rather, it is fully documented in the Lisa Pascal Workshop manuals.

The basic features of the Toolkit are shown in Figure 12-1. Generally, everything common to most Lisa applications is either handled automatically by the Toolkit or facilitated by the Toolkit. Opening, closing, and resizing of windows, for example, are handled completely by the Toolkit because these features are exactly the same in all Lisa applications. You need not supply any code to provide these functions in your application. One example of an area that the Toolkit cannot handle automatically is the text of the individualized menus needed by new applications. The Toolkit cannot anticipate what menu commands your application will need, but given that you write the textual representations for these commands in a text file in the Workshop, the Toolkit can construct the menus for you and handle the menu interaction. Your application is then informed if the user has activated a menu command and, if so, which command.

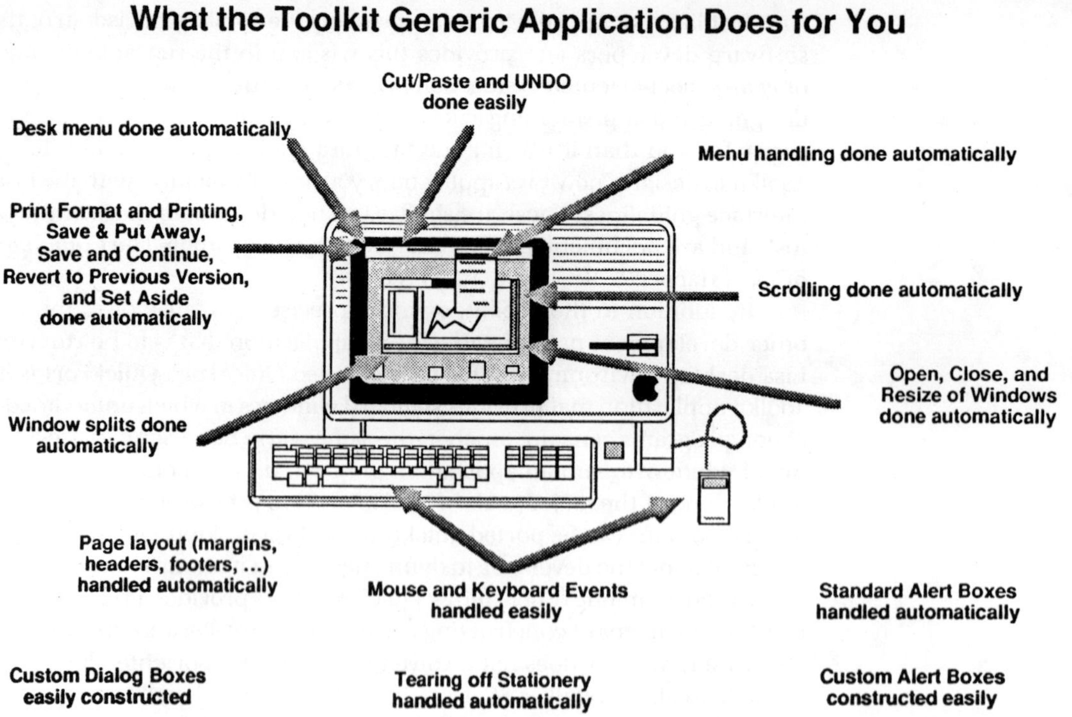

Figure 12-1 What the Toolkit does for your application. Because the Toolkit provides much of the standard behavior for applications used from the Lisa desktop, your development time and resulting source code size are significantly reduced.

Just as with MacApp, the additional expressive power and functionality of the Toolkit does not come for free. Existing applications must be extensively redesigned to take advantage of the Toolkit's features. Clascal is similar to the other hybrid object-oriented languages discussed already in that a Pascal program cannot be changed easily into a Clascal program.

Classes and Objects in Clascal

Clascal was Apple's first object—oriented extension to the Pascal language. Like Object Pascal but unlike Smalltalk, Clascal is an example of a hybrid object-oriented language. In Clascal, just as in Object Pascal, new classes are defined as additional kinds of structured types in a two-part extension to the syntax of Pascal-type statements. When defining Clascal classes, the two-part program definition facility of Lisa Pascal (*units* composed of *interface* and *implementation* parts) must be used. (Recall that in Object Pascal, the use of units is optional.) The interface part of the Clascal unit describes the structure of the new classes you define and lists their protocols. The implementation part defines the methods executed when those messages are sent to instances of the classes—in the same way Object Pascal units are usually structured.

The additions to the Lisa Pascal interface part for class definitions are shown in Figure 12-2. These diagrams and the associated examples below assume you are familiar with at least the syntax of standard Pascal and, preferably, with that of Lisa Pascal, which is almost identical to Macintosh Workshop Pascal. A sample code fragment from the interface part of the Toolkit implementation of QuadWorld is:

```
{ Common code and data of each of the two types of quadviews }
  TQuadView = SUBCLASS OF TView
    { Instance variables }
    window: TQuadWindow;  { Gives us an easy way to access the quad list,
                             since it is stored as a field in the QuadWindow. }
    { Creation method }
    FUNCTION TQuadView.CREATE(object: TObject; heap: THeap; itsExtent:
      LRect; itsPanel: TPanel): TQuadView;
  { Selection methods }
  PROCEDURE TQuadView.MousePress(mouseLPt: LPoint); OVERRIDE;
  PROCEDURE TQuadView.MouseMove(mouseLPt: LPoint); OVERRIDE;
      { Overriding the standard MouseMove method will enable the user to
                    change the selection while the mouse button is down }
  FUNCTION TQuadView.NoSelection: TSelection;OVERRIDE;
  FUNCTION TQuadView.NewSelection(quad: TQuad): TQuadSelection;
    ABSTRACT;
    { Create a new selection of the appropriate class; this is called by
      TQuadWindow.Select }
    { Utility method }
  PROCEDURE TQuadView.LPtToQuad(lPt: LPoint; VAR quad: TQuad);
    ABSTRACT;
END; { TQuadView }
```

structured–type

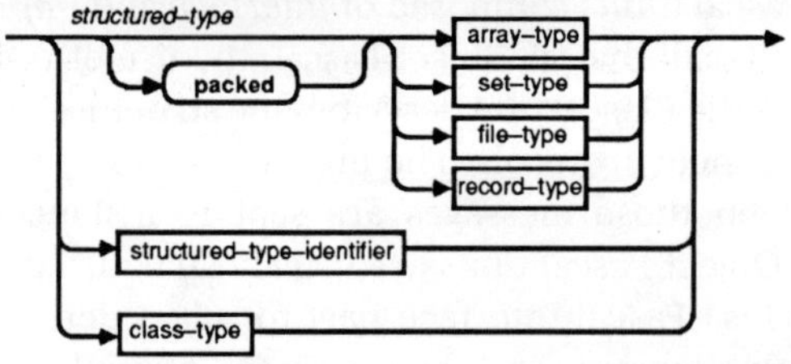

class–type

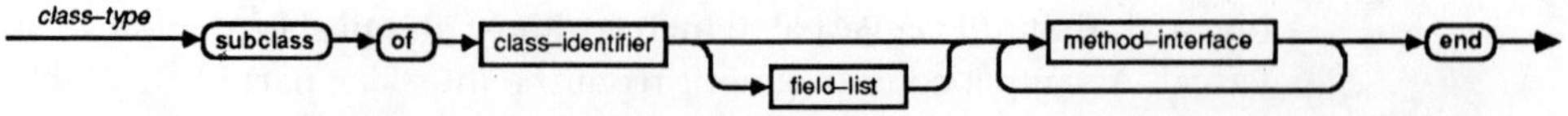

class–identifier

method–interface

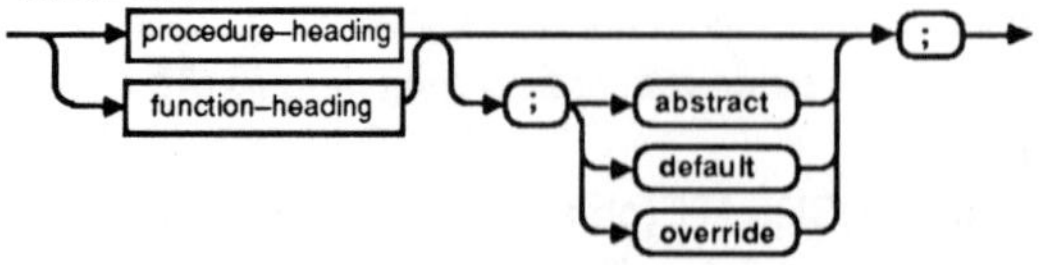

procedure–heading

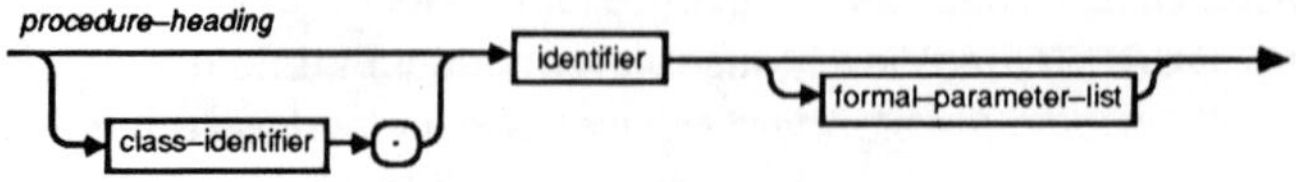

function–heading

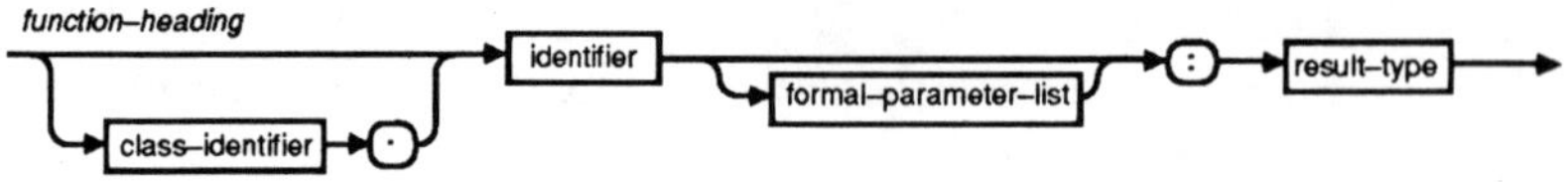

result–type

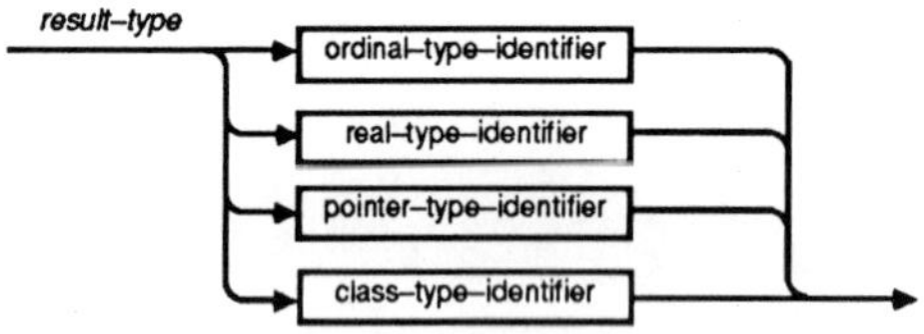

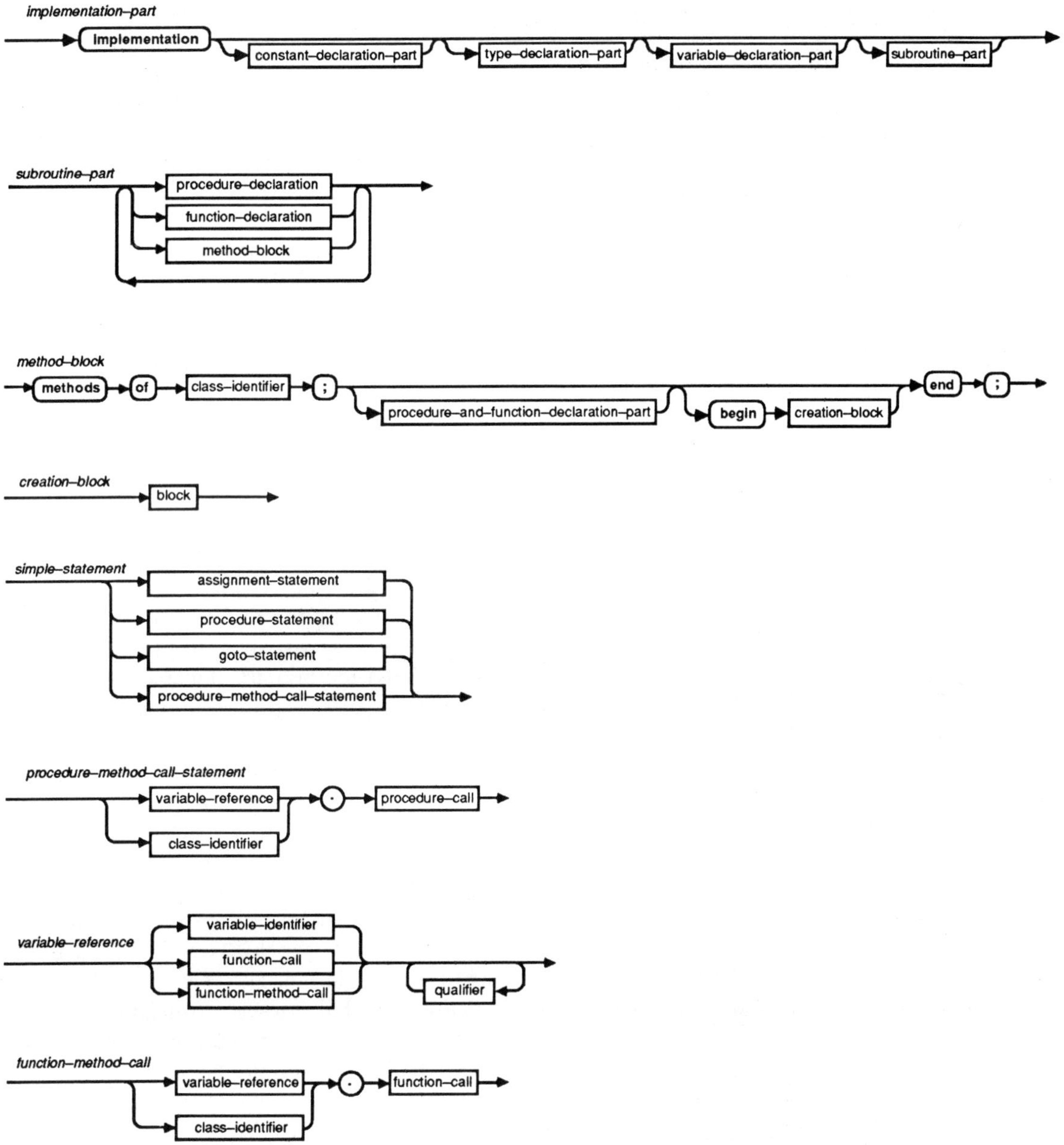

Figure 12-2 Lisa Clascal syntax diagrams

As you can see, Clascal syntax resembles that of Object Pascal in many respects, yet there are some interesting differences in both the syntax and the semantics. Two obvious syntactic differences are that the methods of a class must be grouped together in the interface and implementation parts of a unit. In the interface part they are grouped by being inside a **SUBCLASS OF ... END** block; in the implementation part they are grouped within a **METHODS OF ... END** block. Both differences are reflected in the syntax diagrams shown in Figure 12-2.

A more substantial difference is the use of additional, modifying keywords for methods. Object Pascal uses the **OVERRIDE** keyword to denote a method in a subclass. Clascal uses this keyword with the same meaning and introduces two additional ones: **ABSTRACT** and **DEFAULT**. All three keywords are used to provide the Clascal compiler with additional information for the most efficient organization of the class's method tables. An "abstract" method, one with the **ABSTRACT** keyword, is never intended to be implemented in this class. Rather, all subclasses with this type of method are expected to provide their own implementations. The **ABSTRACT** keyword is needed so that this method can be referred to in other methods of the class, even if it must be overridden in each and every concrete subclass. The compiler will not generate an error message when an **ABSTRACT** method is not, in fact, implemented in the implementation part of the unit. A **DEFAULT** method is like an **ABSTRACT** method in that it indicates that subclasses are expected to provide their own implementation, but unlike an **ABSTRACT** method, the declaring class will implement the method in a default manner. A **DEFAULT** method will probably be overridden, so the compiler "plays the odds" by storing the method pointers to **ABSTRACT** and **DEFAULT** methods in one table and all other method pointers in another table. When a subclass overrides a method, the appropriate table is copied into that subclass's data structures; if none of the methods in a table is overridden, then that table is shared with the superclass. Because only about ten percent of the Toolkit's methods are frequently overridden in any given application, this sharing of method tables can be increased by dividing the methods into those likely to be overridden (the **ABSTRACT** and **DEFAULT** methods) and the ones not likely to be overridden. The result is that about 5K bytes are saved in a typical application's global storage requirements. You can save some space in your application if you include the **DEFAULT** keyword following the methods of those classes that will sometimes be overridden in other subclasses. The QuadWorld class shown above, TQuadView, makes use of all these keywords except **DEFAULT** because only the **ABSTRACT** methods are overridden in the subclasses of TQuadView, TQuadGrView and TQuadTxView.

Definitions

The Clascal keyword **ABSTRACT** and the notion of an abstract superclass have a lot in common. Abstract superclasses typically contain several methods that their subclasses must override. These abstract methods provide subclass-specific algorithms for manipulating objects of that subclass and are present in the abstract superclass only as placeholders. The other methods of the abstract superclass implement subclass-independent algorithms using these abstract methods as building blocks. The efficiency of a Clascal application is improved if you indicate which methods of a class are abstract methods, though it is not required by the language. (For a more detailed example of the use of abstract superclasses and abstract methods, see Chapters 9 and 10 of *Smalltalk-80—The Language and Its Implementation,* Goldberg and Robson, Addison-Wesley, 1983.)

Notes

Object Pascal does not have the **ABSTRACT** and **DEFAULT** keywords because Apple found a better method of table implementation that does not require these "hints" from the applications programmer, and the syntax of the new language is not intended to reflect any implementation concerns.

Another difference between Clascal and Object Pascal is in the manner of object creation. An example of this in Clascal is:

```
VAR thisQuad: TQuad;
    thisRhombus: TRhombus;
      .
      .
      .
thisQuad := TQuad.CREATE(NIL, thisHeap);
thisRhombus := TRhombus.CREATE(NIL, thisHeap);
```

Note that, like Smalltalk, object creation in Clascal is carried out with a class message. Unlike Smalltalk, however, in which you have the freedom to construct any class message, there is only one class message in Clascal, CREATE, and it must be defined for every class.

The semantics of object creation in Clascal are somewhat unusual as can be seen in the CREATE methods for the classes TQuad and TRhombus:

```
FUNCTION TQuad.CREATE(object: TObject; itsHeap: THeap): TQuad;
VAR i: INTEGER; { FOR Loop index }
BEGIN
  IF object = NIL THEN object := NewObject(itsHeap, THISCLASS);
  SELF := TQuad(object);
  { initialize all vertices }
  FOR i := 1 TO 4 DO SELF.vertex[i] := zeroLPt;
END; { TQuad.CREATE }
FUNCTION TRhombus.CREATE(object: TObject; itsHeap: THeap):
  TRhombus;
BEGIN
  IF object = NIL THEN object := NewObject(itsHeap, THISCLASS);
  SELF := TRhombus(TParallelogram.CREATE(object, itsHeap));
END; { TRhombus.CREATE }
```

The manner in which these methods work is basically like this:

1. The CREATE method of the class of the object being created actually allocates the storage for the new object with a call to the procedure NewObject. Note that NewObject is told what class this new object is to be with the keyword **THISCLASS**.
2. This new object is then initialized by all of its superclasses (in sequential order, starting with TObject) by invoking their CREATE methods. Note that this requires a certain fixed structure to all CREATE methods—a structure that must be adhered to by the application programmer.
3. The object is finally typecast to the correct class.

A fourth difference can be seen in the following method from the Clascal implementation of QuadWorld:

```
{ Draw one quad as a text string appropriately positioned. }
PROCEDURE TQuadTxView.DrawName(quad: TQuad);
VAR tempBox: LRect;
    str: S255;
BEGIN
  { The Toolkit lets you make no assumptions about the pen. You set it when
    you want to use it. }
  SELF.SetPen;
  { Calculate the rectangle to fill }
  SELF.SetUpBox(quad, tempBox);
```

```
    IF LRectIsVisible(tempBox) THEN { only write text that will be seen }
      BEGIN
        MoveToL(tempBox.left + txMargin, tempBox.top + SELF.lineAscent);
        quad.AsText(str);
        DrawString(str);
      END;
  END;
```

Note in this method that several familiar Toolbox and MacApp types and procedures appear with slightly different names: LRect instead of Rect, LRectIsVisible instead of RectIsVisible, and MoveToL instead of MoveTo. These are examples of an extension to QuickDraw used by the Toolkit. Standard QuickDraw uses 16-bit coordinates, which means that any view constructed by QuickDraw is limited to a coordinate space extending from (0, 0) to (32767, 32767). This results in a maximum view size of about forty-one 8″ x 10″ pages in each direction (at standard resolutions). The Toolkit extension to QuickDraw uses 32-bit coordinates, resulting in a maximum view size of about four million pages in each direction. (Recall that one of the suggestions for extensions to MacApp made in Chapter 6 is to provide an optional 32-bit drawing package. This is why that suggestion was made.)

You can see several other features of Clascal by examining fragments of the Clascal implementation of the Quad World application:

```
METHODS OF TParallelogram;
  FUNCTION TParallelogram.CREATE(object: TObject; itsHeap: THeap):
    TParallelogram;
  BEGIN
    IF object = NIL THEN object := NewObject(itsHeap, THISCLASS);
    SELF := TParallelogram(TQuad.CREATE(object, itsHeap));
  END; { TParallelogram.CREATE }
{$IFC fDebugMethods}
  PROCEDURE TParallelogram.Fields(PROCEDURE Field(nameAndType:
    S255));
  BEGIN
    SUPERSELF.Fields(Field);
    Field('');
  END;
{$ENDC}
  PROCEDURE TParallelogram.AsText(VAR text: S255);
  BEGIN
    text := 'a Parallelogram';
  END; { TParallelogram.AsText }
END; { of TParallelogram methods }
METHODS OF TRhombus;
  FUNCTION TRhombus.CREATE(object: TObject; itsHeap: THeap):
    TRhombus;
```

```
    BEGIN
      IF object = NIL THEN object := NewObject(itsHeap, THISCLASS);
      SELF := TRhombus(TParallelogram.CREATE(object, itsHeap));
    END; { TRhombus.CREATE }
  {$IFC fDebugMethods}
    PROCEDURE TRhombus.Fields(PROCEDURE Field(nameAndType:
      S255));
    BEGIN
      SUPERSELF.Fields(Field);
      Field('');
    END;
  {$ENDC}
    PROCEDURE TRhombus.AsText(VAR text: S255);
    BEGIN
      text := 'a Rhombus';
    END; { TRhombus.AsText }
  END; { of TRhombus methods }
```

In this example, you see three methods from two QuadWorld classes, TParallelogram and TRhombus. There are several things to note:

- The syntactic definitions of the methods are repeated exactly as they occurred in the interface part of the QuadWorld unit, with the exception of the removal of the keywords **ABSTRACT, DEFAULT**, or **OVERRIDE**.
- Methods not declared in the interface part of the unit (the TParallelogram. Fields and TRhombus.Fields methods, for example) can be defined. These are private methods of the class.
- Conditional compilation is used to include debugging procedures. The fDebugMethods Toolkit flag is automatically set to **TRUE** when you develop your application with the debugging version of the Toolkit libraries and to **FALSE** when you use the production version. Note that this is essentially the same for MacApp.
- An ugly but important part of each method was omitted intentionally. When debugging a Toolkit application, a high-level, symbolic Toolkit debugger enables you to flag certain methods for special treatment. This is done by inserting procedure calls BP(Begin Procedure) and EP (End Procedure) to the Toolkit utilities. Simply, BP and EP call the debugger to provide an opportunity to stop at a breakpoint, trace calls, or single step through an application. Because this is necessary only when debugging, these routines are conditionally compiled, and because you never know where you will have a bug, you have to insert them into every method. Thus, the real TParallelogram.

CREATE method looks like this:

```
FUNCTION TParallelogram.CREATE(object: TObject; itsHeap: THeap):
  TParallelogram;
BEGIN
  {$IFC fTrace}BP(11);{$ENDC}
  IF object = NIL THEN object := NewObject(itsHeap, THISCLASS);
  SELF := TParallelogram(TQuad.CREATE(object, itsHeap));
  {$IFC fTrace}EP;{$ENDC}
END; { TParallelogram.CREATE }
```

Notes

Apple's Object Pascal compiler provides these features automatically and so MacApp code looks much cleaner than Toolkit code.

One of the most novel and important parts of the method block of the implementation part of a Clascal unit is the class initialization block. This compiles into a method that is invoked automatically before any first use of the class by your program. Here you can perform one-time computations that set up special values to be used in the class, or even for the entire unit. This initialization block is used in the Toolkit QuadWorld implementation in the TQuad class implementation and a portion of that code is shown below. Here, the initialization block records the unit's author and company:

```
METHODS OF TQuad;
  FUNCTION TQuad.CREATE(object: TObject; itsHeap: THeap): TQuad;
  .
  .
  .
  END; { TQuad.CREATE }
  .
  .
  .
  END; { Last method for the TQuad class }
BEGIN
  UnitAuthor('Productivity Products International, Inc./Kurt J. Schmucker');
END; { of TQuad Methods }
```

Clascal Class Libraries

There is a rich set of classes that can be used with Clascal: the Toolkit classes. In this section, the organization of these classes is outlined and their basic protocols sketched. The next section of this chapter presents in much more detail the Application Base Classes, which are the most important classes for the Generic Application. It is the ABC classes, as they are called, that implement the common features of the Lisa user interface in such a way that they can be used easily by developers to build new applications by expanding the Generic Application.

Notes

The Toolkit ABC classes are approximately the equivalent of the basic MacApp classes: TApplication, TDocument, etc.

The Clascal classes are organized into Lisa Pascal units for easy inclusion into Clascal programs. As with Object Pascal and MacApp, the standard, though not enforced, naming convention is for class type names to begin with a "T." Another standard in Clascal, similar to the one in Object Pascal, is that the interface to a unit named "UFoo" is contained in the file "UFoo.TEXT" and the implementation is in files "UFoo2.TEXT," "UFoo3.TEXT," and so on, depending on the size of the unit. The Toolkit QuadWorld application follows these conventions, as well as the Apple convention of capitalizing identifiers on word boundaries, as in "TQuadGrView." The following units are available for use with the Generic Application:

- UObject This unit is the most basic of all the class libraries. It contains the implementation of TObject, the base Clascal class from which all other classes are defined. The TObject methods provide you with the ability to allocate space on the heap, copy objects, and print out information about objects for debugging purposes. In addition, UObject contains the collection and scanning classes. The collection classes (TCollection, TList, TArray, TString, and TFile) provide the methods for dealing with various types of groups of objects. The scanning classes (TScanner, TListScanner, TStringScanner, TFileScanner) correspond to the collection classes and provide the methods for modifying and accessing these collections in various ways. For example, using the Scan method of the TScanner class you can enumerate the objects in any collection;

using the Replace method of this same class you can replace any single element of a collection with some other object. These general-purpose algorithms are coded only once and are available for every collection: the ones used by the Toolkit itself as well as any that your application might use.

- UDraw — The UDraw unit reimplements the QuickDraw library with the 32-bit drawing coordinates mentioned earlier. This has a tremendous impact on Toolkit applications. Using only QuickDraw, the maximum size of a document is about forty-one 8.5″ x 11″ pages in each direction. Using UDraw, the maximum size is about four million pages. This is not to say that documents can really get that large, but rather that there is not any real upper bound based on the drawing coordinate representation. In addition, UDraw contains the implementation of TPad, a drawing class that handles coordinate transformations, scaling, and zooming. UDraw also contains some other graphics utilities not included in QuickDraw.
- UABC — The UABC unit contains the Application Base Classes, the foundation of the Generic Application. These classes: TWindow, TClipboard, TCutCopyCommand, TPrintManager, and many others, are discussed in the next section. To design your own Toolkit application, you must become familiar with the protocols and the interaction between the ABC classes.
- UUnivText — The UUnivText unit implements the classes that enable you to cut text to and paste it from the clipboard without losing any of the font or paragraph formatting information. Typically, you do not use the classes in this unit directly but rather you use the UText classes.
- UText — UText provides classes (TParagraph, TTextSelection, TInsertionPoint, and many others) that enable you to specify a rectangular area in your application's window in which all standard Lisa text-editing operations can take place. Text can be entered from the keyboard, portions of it can be selected with the mouse, and, because UText uses UUnivText, portions of text can be cut to and pasted from the clipboard. UText also supports some rather sophisticated text applications, including chained text images (as in multicolumn documents in which text flows from one column to the next naturally) and multiple text images that are edited simultaneously. As an example of this last use of UText, consider the wide-panel view in LisaCalc. When a spreadsheet cell is selected in LisaCalc, the contents of that cell appear in the wide-panel view at the top of the LisaCalc window. This data can be edited in either position and any editing or selections that occur in one position also occur in the other.

- UDialog UDialog provides the classes (TButton, TCheckbox, TPageDesignWindow, and many others) that enable you to easily construct custom dialog boxes for your application. The dialog boxes so constructed are fully functional: the buttons highlight when selected, checkboxes invert, and the user can type into text input frames. Figure 12-3 shows one such dialog box constructed for an application in which the user provides estimates in natural language expressions. This example is from my book, *Fuzzy Sets, Natural Languages Computations, and Risk Analysis*, Computer Science Press, Rockville, MD, 1984. While it is somewhat tedious to design such a dialog box due to the exact positioning needed, it is not difficult because of the classes in the UDialog unit.

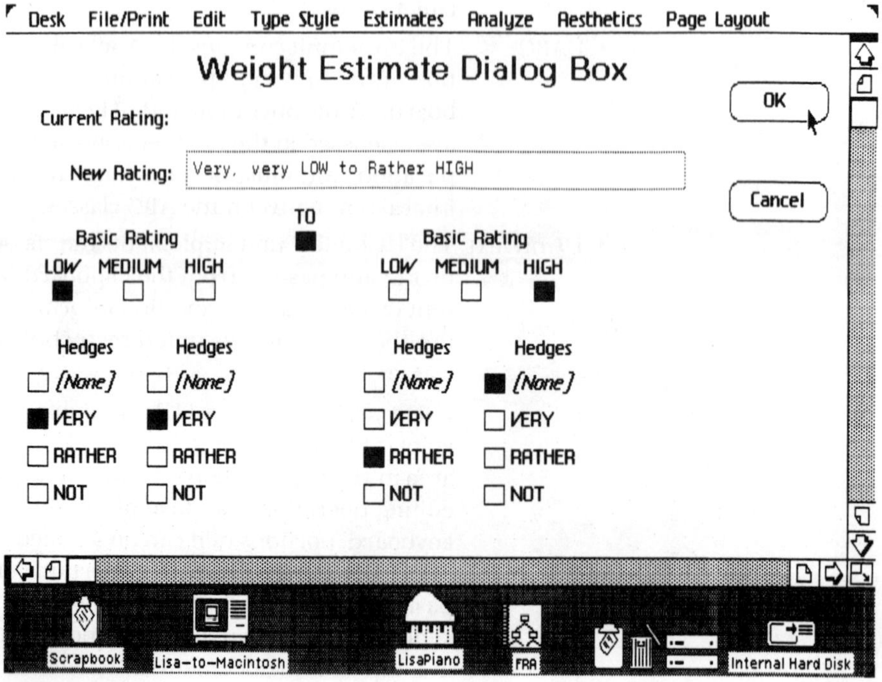

Figure 12-3 An example of a custom dialog box constructed using the classes provided in the UDialog unit.

- UPalette The UPalette unit provides classes that enable you to easily construct selection palettes like those in LisaDraw, MacDraw, and MacPaint. These palettes are fully functional in that the individual boxes in the palette highlight when selected and this information can be read by your application. What your application actually does when one of these boxes is selected is up to you. The Toolkit QuadWorld application uses the UPalette unit to provide a selection palette of the various types of quadrilaterals.
- UTimer UTimer provides easy access to the system clock for applications that need to time events.
- UIconRefs UIconRefs provides you with the classes to directly access other documents on the Lisa desktop. Unlike Macintosh, the document names that the Lisa user sees are not unique, because there can be two different LisaList document icons, for example, with exactly the same name. UIconRefs enables you to get the unique internal name for a document provided that the user has executed the **Copy Reference** command on the desktop's Edit menu. This would be necessary, for example, if you were preparing a Lisa application that would analyze the grammar and the style of the prose in LisaWrite documents.
- URuler URuler provides classes that assist in the construction and use of rulers like those used in LisaWrite for setting paragraph widths and tab stops and in LisaDraw for constructing exact size and placement drawings. Unfortunately, the URuler unit was never converted in the final version of the Toolkit. However, should your application need rulers, looking at these old version classes would still provide you with a headstart in designing such units.
- UIcon UIcon provides classes for manipulating the various nonalphabetic fonts available on Lisa. Two common example of these fonts are the tab and paragraph margin symbols used on the LisaWrite rulers and the print orientation symbols used in the **Format for Printer** Dialog Box. As with URuler, this unit was never converted to the final format of the Toolkit.

The UABC Class Library and Its Use

The classes of the UABC unit are the heart of any Toolkit application. These classes provide the control structure for the application and, to a certain extent, govern the structure of the application-unique classes you will design. In this sense, they perform the same function that the basic MacApp classes perform for the Macintosh Expandable Application. There are, however, more UABC classes than MacApp classes and the interconnections between them are different and (usually) more complex. The basic differences in the UABC classes from the MacApp classes are:

- There is exactly one window per document, so the interconnections between TDocument and TWindow classes are simpler.
- The TDocument class is only responsible for file management and it accomplishes this almost automatically with a standard file format which is little more than a heap dump.
- The Toolkit TWindow class incorporates part of the functionality of the MacApp TApplication and TDocument classes.
- Panes and filtered commands are fully supported in the Toolkit.
- Several of the building blocks (e.g., UDialog, and UText) are much more complete than their MacApp counterparts because there is no programmer's safety net beneath the Toolkit.
- The current selection was an instance of class TSelection—a class which does not even exist in MacApp.

In several areas, the Toolkit and MacApp just chose different ways of doing very similar actions. A good example of this is the idea of the current target—the object that "decides" which menu commands should be enabled and how to respond to those commands when they are chosen. In MacApp, the target can be an instance of almost any of the basic MacApp classes: TApplication, TDocument, TView, TWindow, or TFrame more precisely, the target in a MacApp application can be any instance or member of the class TEvtHandler. In the Toolkit, the target must be an instance of the class TSelection, a class, that models the notion of the current selection that is present both in the Lisa and Mac user interfaces. In the Toolkit, every panel of every window always contained an instance of TSelection, even when the user had not related anything, in which case a special null selection is the panel's selection.

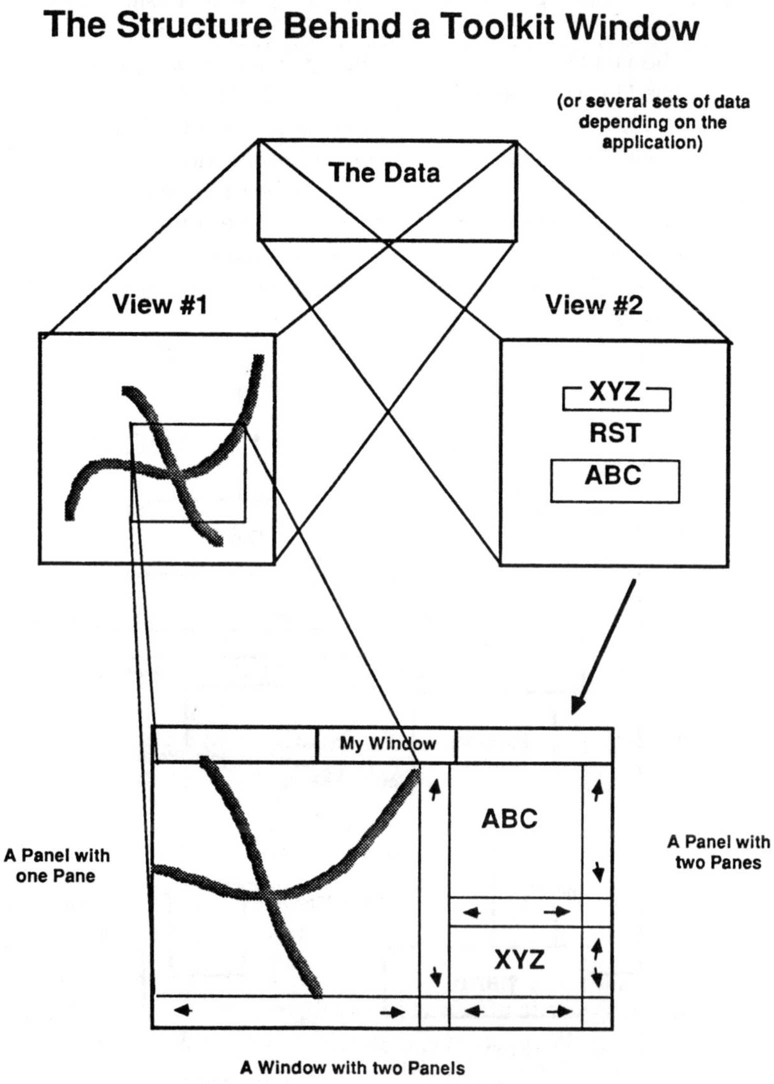

Figure 12-4 The structure behind a window of a Lisa application written using the Toolkit.

In the Toolkit, the instances of the six basic classes in UABC (TWindow, TView, TPanel, TPane, TSelection, and TCommand) are interconnected, as shown in Figure 12-5. Note that an instance of class TList, a class in UObject, is used to group objects such as panels and panes, many of which may be present in a given window, in a manner similar to the interconnections in a MacApp application. In addition to these interconnections, your application may establish additional links to simplify the application or increase its speed. The Toolkit QuadWorld implementation, for example, adds a window field to its subclasses of TView so that the view objects can access easily the QuadWorld window. The QuadWorld window, in turn, has fields pointing to each of the three panels displaying its three views.

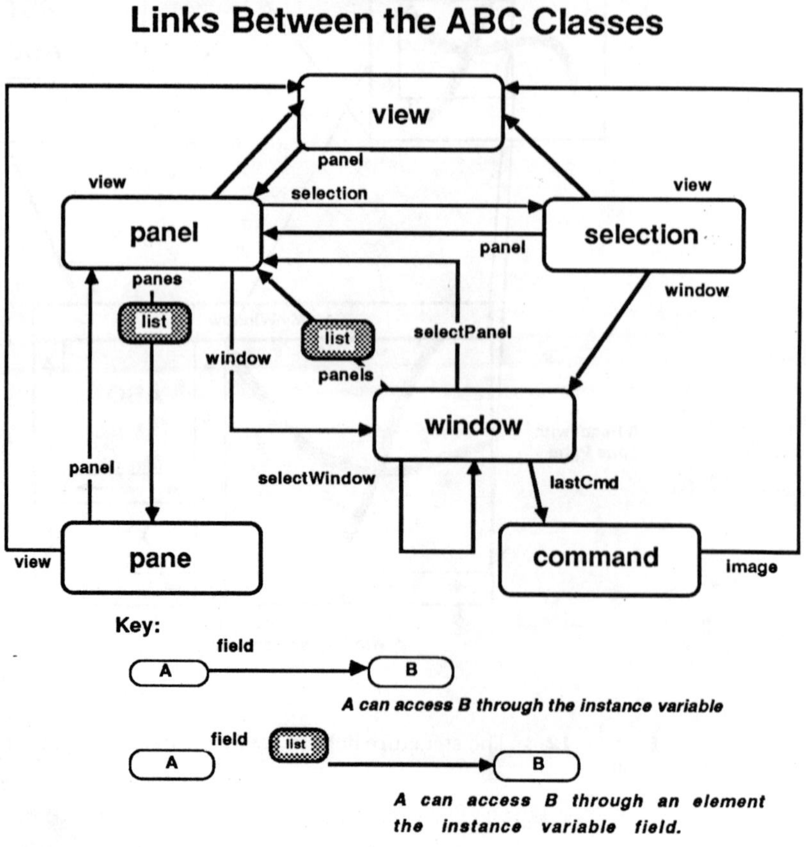

Figure 12-5 The interrelationship between the major classes in UABC. These interconnections enable the Generic Application to access the methods of the subclasses you have defined, if they are there, and to use the default methods otherwise.

Building and Installing a Toolkit Application

A Toolkit application is comprised of five files that serve the same functions and have approximately the same names as the files of a MacApp application. Like a MacApp application, the main application program for a Toolkit application is incredibly simple. For example, the QuadWorld main program is:

```
PROGRAM MQuadWorld;
  USES
    {$U UObject }     UObject,
                      QuickDraw,
    {$U UDraw }       UDraw,
    {$U UABC }        UABC,
    {$U UPalette }    UPalette,
    {$U UQuadWorld }UQuadWorld;
  CONST
    phraseVersion = 1;
  BEGIN
    process := TQuadProcess.CREATE;
    process.Commence(phraseVersion);
    process.Run;
    process.Complete(TRUE);
  END
```

Note that the Toolkit QuadWorld uses the three units required of all Toolkit applications: UObject, UDraw, and UABC (UDraw requires the use of QuickDraw). In addition, it uses the UPalette unit for the quadrilateral palette on the left side of the QuadWorld window and the UQuadWorld unit for access to the classes unique to QuadWorld. Because QuadWorld has no special dialog boxes and does no text editing, the units UDialog and UText were not needed. This main program creates a new instance of TProcess—in fact, an instance of TQuadProcess, a subclass of TProcess. This object is sent the messages Commence and Run to get everything going. After that, the Generic Application takes over and runs the application until it completes.

Just as with MacApp, there is an exec file that appropriately compiles and links a Toolkit application for you. In addition, there are two other special utilities that have direct counterparts in the Macintosh world: the Install utility and the IconEdit utility. Toolkit applications run only on the Lisa desktop, and can be compiled only in the Lisa Workshop. The Install utility properly installs a executable Toolkit application so that the desktop knows about it and its icon appears in the window of the hard disk. The Toolkit IconEdit utility enables you to design the icon for your application. On the Macintosh, RMaker or Rez, and ResEdit fulfill the same roles as Install and IconEdit, respectively.

QuadWorld in Lisa Clascal using the Toolkit

A screen image from the Toolkit implementation of QuadWorld is shown in Figure 12-6 and the source code for this implementation is in Listing G. The image shows that the Toolkit QuadWorld implementation has three views: a palette view (TActView), in which the user can select one of the five prototypical quadrilaterals and thus indicate the intention to draw one of these types of quadrilaterals; a graphical view (TQuadGrView), in which the current list of quadrilaterals is drawn; and a list view (TQuadTxView), in which the alphabetic representation of the current list of quadrilaterals is shown. These three views are displayed in three separate panels and each panel has a selection of an appropriate class. As can be seen in Figure 12-7, two of these panels can be split both horizontally and vertically. This behavior is part of the UABC classes and not a unique part of the QuadWorld implementation. Like MacApp, the Toolkit provides full support for printing on any of the output devices available to Lisa. For the Toolkit application programmer, as for the MacApp programmer, printing is "free."

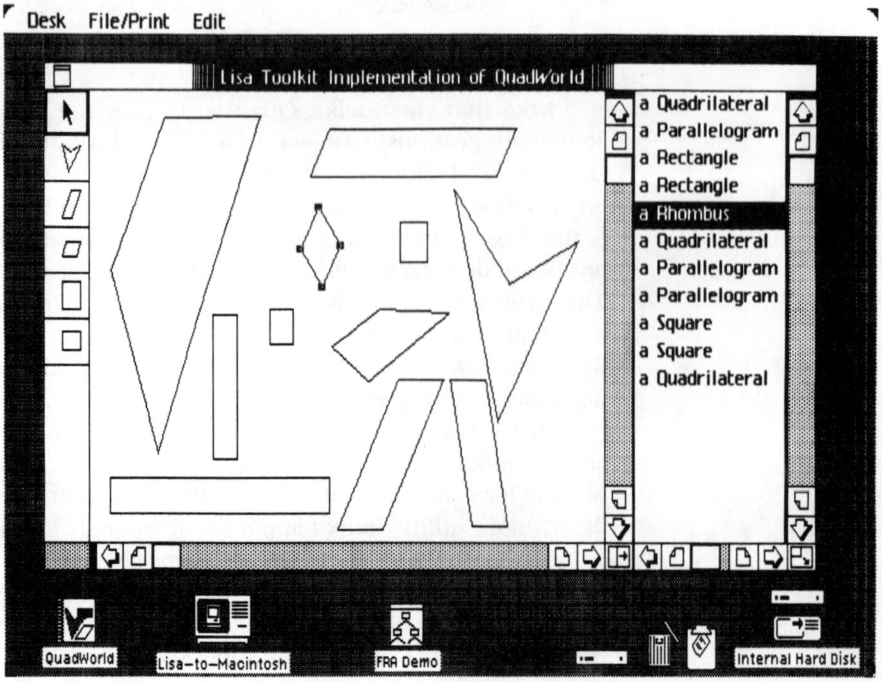

Figure 12-6 The Toolkit implementation of the QuadWorld application.

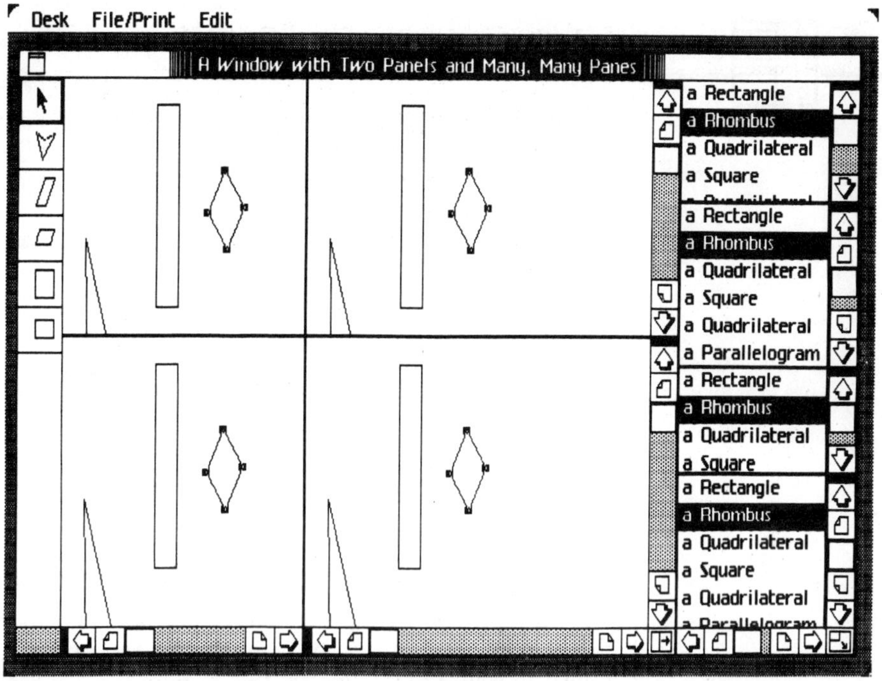

Figure 12-7 Part of the window functionality that the QuadWorld applications enjoys without having to provide any additional new programming is splitting panels, both horizontally and vertically. Note that the selection highlights correctly in each and every pane. It requires only a trivial structuring of QuadWorld to activate the Toolkit routines that accomplish this.

Because the data shown in the graphical view and the list view are the same, it is stored as a list in the window object, an instance of TQuadWindow. (Recall that in the MacApp implementation of Quad World, this data is stored in the instance of TDocument. The Toolkit has no class that fully corresponds with MacApp TDocument and thus common data must be stored in the window. Because there is a one-to-one correspondence between documents and windows on the Lisa, this use of the window to hold common data is not as inefficient as it would have been for Macintosh.) Having the data in the window means that the view methods need to refer frequently to the window and the window methods to refer often to each of the views, and because of this, appropriate instance variables are included in the design of these classes.

Notes

Note that these differences in the use of the TWindow class between the Toolkit and MacApp mean that in MacApp you rarely need to subclass TWindow and that on the Macintosh multiple windows can "belong" to the same document while on the Lisa they can't.

Notice that much of the List view (TQuadTxView) has to be implemented from scratch because it is not in any of the Clascal libraries. This is one of the reasons the Toolkit implementation of QuadWorld is so long. In retrospect, it probably would have been smarter to simply build a new unit, USpecialViews, and store the list view implementation (and maybe some others!) there. This would not have made the Toolkit implementation of QuadWorld any more (or any less) work, but it would have significantly shortened the development time and the code size of the next Lisa application that needed to use list views.

The UABC classes provide a framework for making all commands undoable that is a little different from that of MacApp. The framework for undoability in the Toolkit lies in the notions of *transparencies* and *sieves*. A transparency is used to add an object to the view without adding it to the application's data, much in the same way you can add an new image to an existing drawing by sketching the new image on a clear sheet of acetate, then placing the acetate on top of the drawing; the drawing looks modified but really isn't. The newly added image can also be easily removed. The Toolkit provides a method, TCommand.EachVirtualPart, that allows a command to add a new object to the view without actually modifying the data normally used to draw the view. Transparencies are used when adding a new quadrilateral, and the most important method used to achieve this, TAddQuadCmd.EachVirtualPart, is shown below:

```
PROCEDURE TAddQuadCmd.EachVirtualPart(PROCEDURE DoToObject
  (filteredObj: TObject));
VAR theQuadWindow: TQuadWindow;
BEGIN
  theQuadWindow := TQuadWindow(currentWindow);
  theQuadWindow.EachActualPart(DoToObject);
  DoToObject(SELF.newQuad);
END;
```

This method is called when the last command executed was the **Add Quadrilateral** command. Typically, the DoToObject procedure parameter is one that draws its argument. (It is slightly more complicated than this, but this is a reasonable simplification to use here for purposes of illustrating transparencies.) This TAddQuadCmd.EachVirtualPart method lets the window draw everything that is really part of the data (theQuadWindow.EachActualPart (DoToObject);), and then draws the new quadrilateral by executing the draw procedure itself (DoToObject(SELF.newQuad);)

A sieve is used when you want to reversibly modify an existing object in the document. Essentially what you do is look at each object before you draw it to see if it is the object you want to modify. If it isn't (the usual case), you simply draw it. If it is, you modify it, draw it, then restore it to its original state. This has the effect of making the image on the screen look as if the command has been executed without actually changing the application's data. Clearing a quadrilateral from the screen is done with the sieve shown below:

```
PROCEDURE TClearQuadCmd.FilterAndDo(actualObj: TObject;
  PROCEDURE DoToObject(filteredObj: TObject));
VAR quad: TQuad;
BEGIN
  quad := TQuad(actualObj);
  IF quad <> SELF.quad
            {Allow everything except the cleared quad to pass thru the filter}
     THEN DoToObject(quad);
END;
```

This sieve checks to see if the object it has been passed is the cleared quadrilateral (**IF** quad < > SELF.quad); if is isn't, the object is drawn (**THEN**DoToObject(quad)). If it is, it does nothing, effectively deleting the object from the screen. Note that this sieve notion could have been used to change an object's color or position by adding an **ELSE** clause that performed that action, called DoToObject with the changed object as the parameter, and then changed the object back to its original state.

All in all, transparencies and sieves only slightly complicate the application and provide undo, one of the most important features of modern, interactive software. It is a trivial price to pay for such an important addition to your application's functionality.

Definitions

As mentioned in Chapter 8, these techniques of transparencies and sieves can be used in MacApp as well as the Toolkit, but in MacApp there are no standard methods corresponding to FilterAndDo, EachVirtualPart, and EachActualPart. You must define them yourself if you find this manner of implementing undo the best one for some particular command in your application. However, MacApp does tell your command objects to Commit when they are no longer undoable, so that MacApp does provide support for making tentative changes to the view permanent in the document.

The semantics of access to the mouse are considerably different in Toolkit from those in MacApp. In the Toolkit, each subclass of TSelection and TView can override three standard mouse handling methods: MousePress, MouseMove, and MouseRelease. In the case of drawing an object such as a line or a rectangle—where the user presses the mouse button, holds it down to draw the new object, and then releases it when done (as in MacProject, MacDraw, or their Lisa equivalents)—this functionality fits perfectly with the desired user interaction. In the case of drawing an entity such as an arbitrary quadrilateral, the fit is less perfect. It seems that the most natural interaction using these primitives is like that of polygon drawing in LisaDraw and MacDraw: pressing the mouse button at the location of the first vertex, holding it down while moving to the location of the next vertex (at the same time drawing the first edge), and releasing the mouse button at the location of the second button. Pressing the mouse button again would indicate that the user now wished to indicate the location of the third vertex, which would take place when the mouse button was next released. Pressing and releasing again would indicate the fourth and final vertex. This is slightly tricky in the Toolkit because typically, a selection object is created to handle a single mouse interaction and when this interaction is completed (signaled by the release of the mouse button), the selection object creates a command object to deal with the new entity and the selection object is freed. Figure 12-8 shows which methods handle which parts of the creation of a quadrilateral.

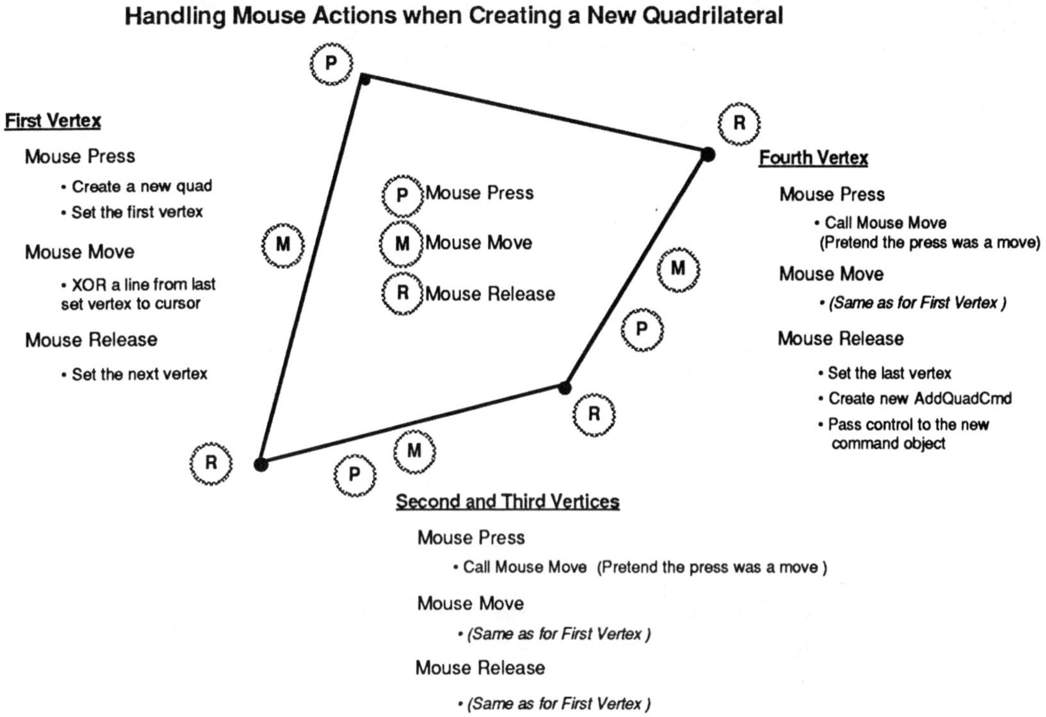

Figure 12-8 How the QuadWorld program provides for the drawing of a new quadrilateral.

Major Toolkit Products

The Lisa Toolkit is one of the few of the languages/application frameworks discussed in this book that has been available for a sufficient amount of time that major applications have been written and shipped using it. Two of these applications are the Desktop Calendar by Videx (Figure 12-9) and the Personal Composition System by Compugraphic (Figure 12-10). Figure 12-11 shows another application that I have designed—the Fuzzy Risk Analyzer/Vague Data Analyzer, from my book, *Fuzzy Sets, Natural Languages Computations, and Risk Analysis.*

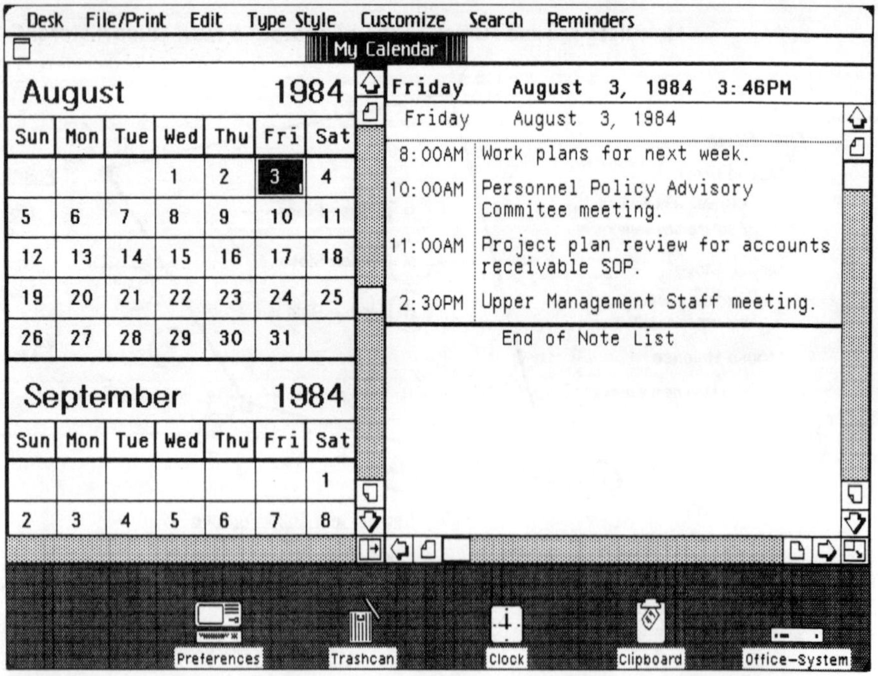

Figure 12-9 The Desktop Calendar by Videx. An application designed using the Toolkit.

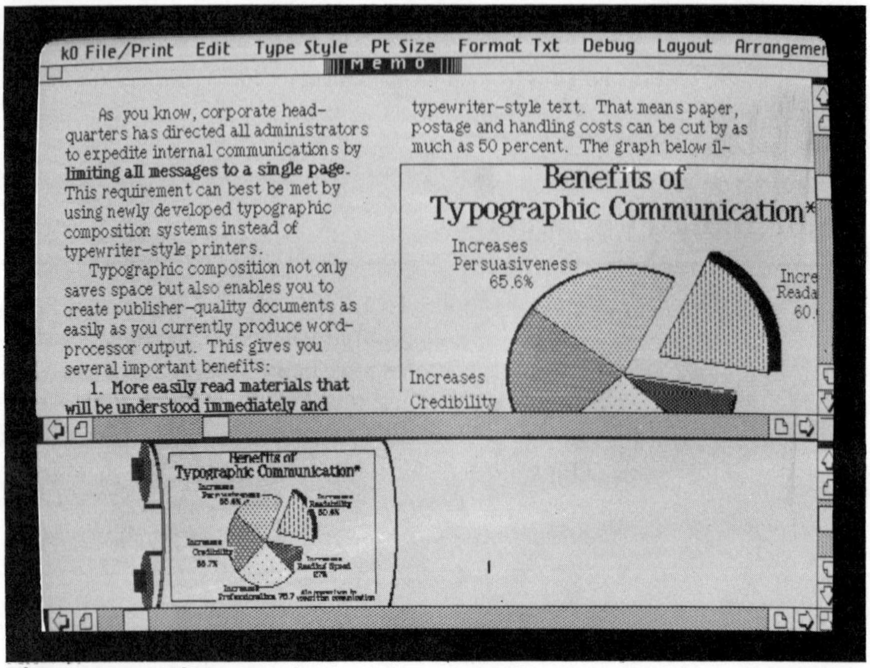

Figure 12-10 The Personal Composition System by Compugraphic, an application designed using the Toolkit.

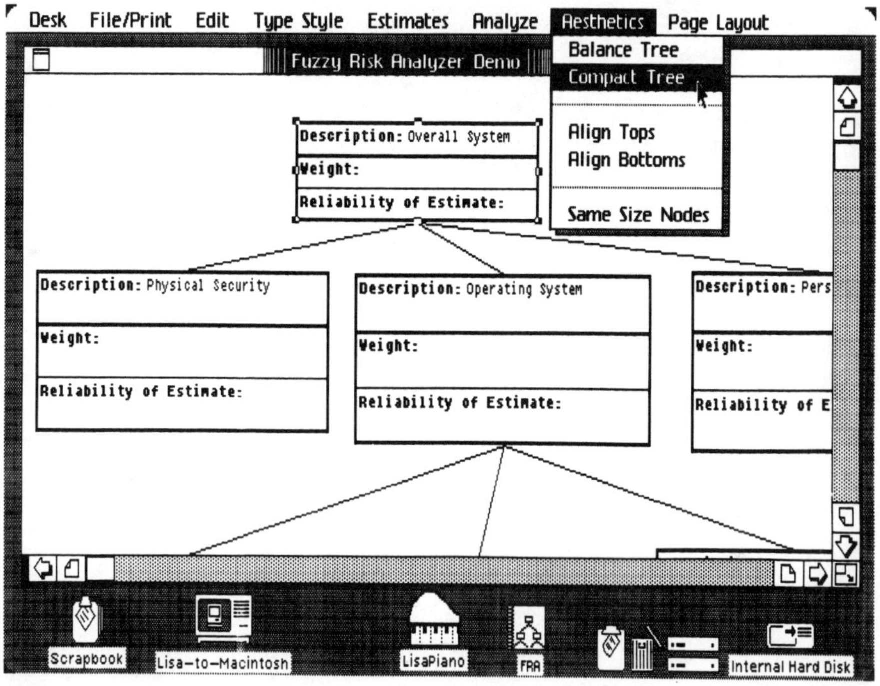

Figure 12-11 A screen image from the Toolkit implementation of the Fuzzy Risk Analyzer/Vague Data Analyzer.

CHAPTER

13

An Overview of Other Object-Oriented Languages on Macintosh

There are a large number of object-oriented languages and more being designed and implemented every year. These languages, in general, are not being designed in a vacuum, but rather are strongly influenced by previous object-oriented and procedural languages. As is true of all programming languages, the relationships among object-oriented languages can be described in terms of a family tree; this is done in Figure 13-1 for many of the object-oriented languages in use today. In addition to Object Pascal, Smalltalk, and Clascal, a number of these languages are currently available or are in development for the Macintosh. In this chapter we survey these Macintosh object-oriented languages. As we have done for Object Pascal, Smalltalk, and Clascal, we present the implementation of the quadrilateral classes in most of these languages so that you can get a feel for the syntax of each language. In addition, for each language, we present a fact sheet detailing its object-oriented characteristics, such as whether it can access the MacApp class library or whether it provides for class methods.

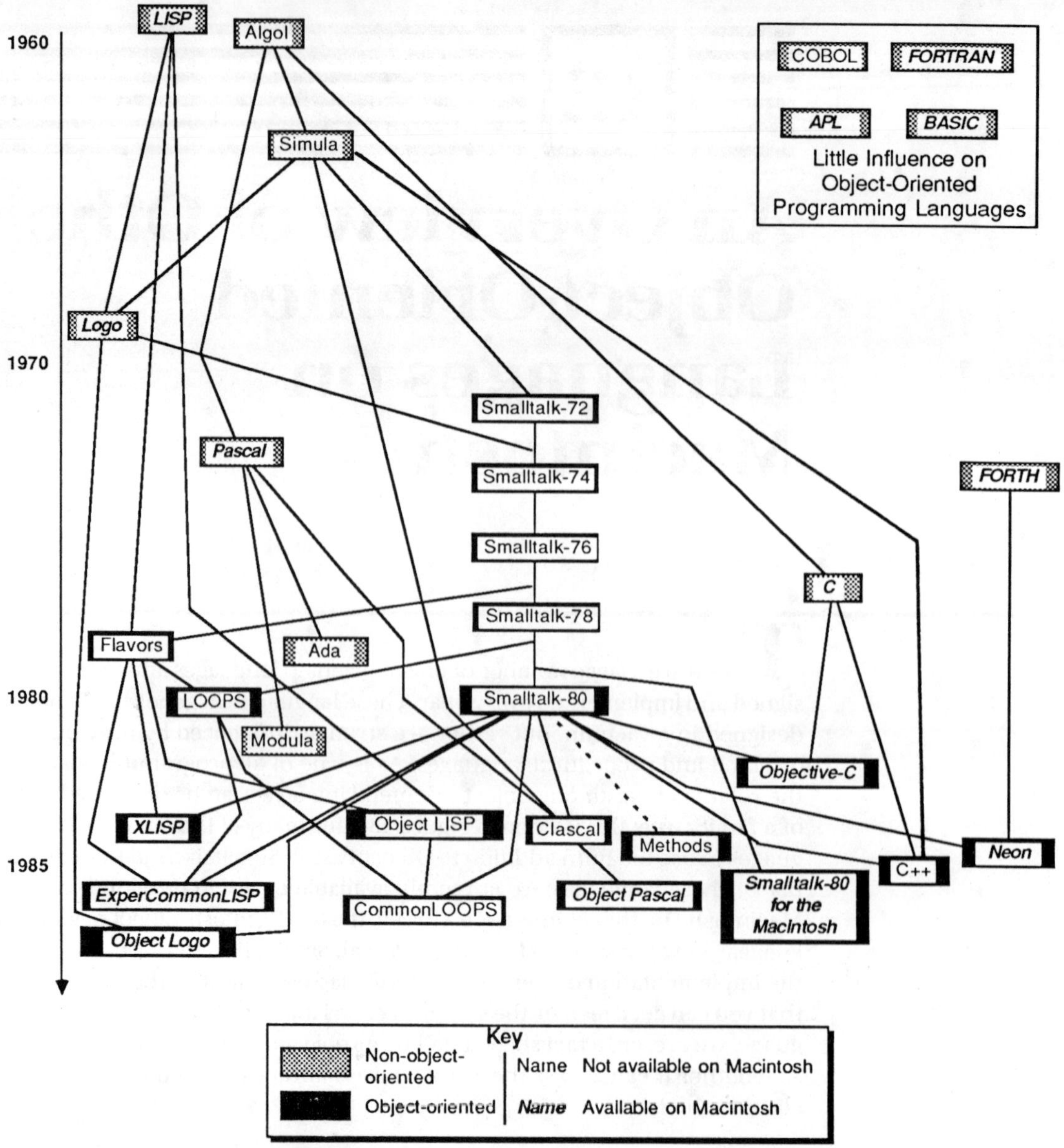

Figure 13-1 The family tree of object-oriented languages.

Summary

Object Pascal

Background Information

Base Language: Pascal

Developer: Apple

Current Version: 1.0

Programming Environment/Availability: Lisa Workshop/March 1986
Mac Programmer's Workshop/October 1986
Other: *(not applicable)*

Toolbox Access: Yes

Support for the 128K ROM: Yes

Object-Oriented Information

Instance variables and Instance Methods: Yes

Class Variables: No

Class Methods: No

Multiple Inheritance: No

Unique Instance Methods: No

Number of classes in the class library: Approximately 30

MacApp access: Yes

Sample Syntax (sending the message, msg, *with argument,* arg, *to the object referenced by* obj*):*

```
obj.msg (arg);
```

Summary Information

Greatest Strength (compared to other object-oriented languages on Mac):

Simplicity of design

Biggest Weakness (compared to other object-oriented languages on Mac):

Limited object-oriented concepts (for example, no class methods)

Other:

Apple support a big plus, even though it is a new language

Summary

Smalltalk-80 for the Macintosh

Background Information

Base Language: *(None)*

Developer: Apple

Current Version: 0.2

Programming Environment/Availability: Lisa Workshop/*(not applicable)*
Mac Programmer's Workshop/*(not applicable)*
Other: Self-contained environment
Smalltalk Programming Environment/August 1985

Toolbox Access: Yes, but difficult

Support for the 128K ROM: Not yet

Object-Oriented Information

Instance variables and Instance Methods: Yes

Class Variables: Yes

Class Methods: Yes

Multiple Inheritance: No, since this is based on the older version 1 Smalltalk from Xerox

Unique Instance Methods: No

Number of classes in the class library: Approximately 300

MacApp access: Yes, but only in an experimental version of the language

Sample Syntax (sending the message, msg, *with argument,* arg, *to the object referenced by* obj*):*

```
obj msg: arg.
```

Summary Information

Greatest Strength (compared to other object-oriented languages on Mac):
Compatability with other Smalltalk implementations

Biggest Weakness (compared to other object-oriented languages on Mac):
Speed

Other:

Not currently supported by Apple; the experimental version of the language that supports MacApp access may become a supported product.

Requires at least 1000K of RAM for serious work.

Summary

Clascal

Background Information

Base Language: Pascal

Developer: Apple

Current Version: 3.0

Programming Environment/Availability: Lisa Workshop/ September 1984
Mac Programmer's Workshop/*(not applicable)*
Other: *(not applicable)*

Toolbox Access: *(not applicable)*

Support for the 128K ROM: *(not applicable)*

Object-Oriented Information

Instance variables and Instance Methods: Yes

Class Variables: No

Class Methods: No, though there is one class method required for each class

Multiple Inheritance: No

Unique Instance Methods: No

Number of classes in the class library: Approximately 100

MacApp access: No

Sample Syntax (sending the message, msg, *with argument,* arg, *to the object referenced by* obj*):*

```
obj.msg (arg);
```

Summary Information

Greatest Strength (compared to other object-oriented languages on Mac):

Object-oriented programming for the Lisa Desktop

Biggest Weakness (compared to other object-oriented languages on Mac):
Object-oriented programming only for the Lisa Desktop

Other:
No longer supported by Apple, though a users group does exist

Notes

As this book went to press, all of the languages discussed in this chapter were just entering β-tests of new versions. I had access to all these β-versions and for this I am grateful to the respective companies. This review of β-versions is not without risk: the amount of time I had for development with these languages was limited and some details of the languages may have changed in the final releases. Consult the reference manuals of these languages for the most up-to-date information.

Neon

The language Neon is, depending on your programming language point of view, either an object-oriented extension to the Forth language or an incisive and efficient implementation of Smalltalk as a threaded, interpreted language. Regardless of which viewpoint you take, Neon is a remarkably concise language that nicely bridges the gap between the object-oriented languages (à la Smalltalk) and the threaded languages (à la Forth). Neon was developed by Kriya Systems expressly for the Macintosh and was first shipped in 1984.

Neon's Syntax and Class Library

The basic Neon syntax shows its strong Forth heritage. From the point of view of most of the other languages discussed in this book, Neon's syntax is backwards:

obj.msg(arg);	Object Pascal
obj msg: arg.	Smalltalk
arg msg: obj	Neon

(To be fair, many programmers consider the Smalltalk syntax, which has the object precede the message, to be backwards compared to the procedure call used in most languages, so perhaps Neon, with the message preceding the object, is one of the few object-oriented languages to get it right!)

New classes and methods are defined using special Neon compiler words that delimit class definitions (:CLASS and ;CLASS) and method definitions (:M and ;M). An example can be seen in the small, annotated example in Figure 13-2, which shows the Rectangle class from the basic Neon library. The basic schema are:

```
:CLASS ClassName <Super SuperClassName |n Indexed|
  |instance variable names|
  |method definitions|

;CLASS
```

and

```
:M Selector: |{ named arguments \ local variables--results}|
  |method body|

;M
```

where || denote optional portions of these schema.

One of the most useful features of Neon is the provision for both named arguments and local variables in methods. Named arguments enable you to associate a name with the arguments placed on the stack prior to the invocation of the method and then to simply refer to these arguments by name when needed in the body of the method. Local variables enable you to declare and use temporary variables in the method body. Both features greatly simplfy the use of Neon compared to the complex stack manipulations often required in Forth.

Neon allows you to choose between the efficiency of static binding and the flexibility of dynamic binding (called *early binding* and *late binding* in the Neon manual) on a message-by-message basis. At compile-time, early binding resolves a message sent to a given object into an invocation of a particular method in a particular class; while late binding leaves this resolution until run-time. The compile-time determination is made based on the declared classes for the reference variables. (Thus, Neon is like Object Pascal and Clascal, which allow a reference variable to be declared of a certain class, and unlike Smalltalk, in which all object references are equal.) The Neon line:

```
Get: myInt
```

sends the Get: message to the object referred to by myInt, with the resolution of that message determined at compile-time by the declared class of myInt. The line:

```
Get: [ myInt ]
```

sends the Get: message to the object referred to by myInt, with the resolution of that message determined at run-time by the run-time class of myInt. Late binding can be used with any construct that generates an object reference, such as:

```
Get: [ i at: myArray ]
```

Summary

Neon

Background Information

Base Language: Forth

Developer: Kriya

Current Version: 1.5

Programming Environment/Availability: Lisa Workshop/*(not applicable)*
Mac Programmer's Workshop/*(not applicable)*
Other: Self-contained environment
Neon Programming Environment/June 1985

Toolbox Access: Yes

Support for the 128K ROM: Yes

Object-Oriented Information

Instance variables and Instance Methods: Yes

Class Variables: No

Class Methods: No

Multiple Inheritance: No

Unique Instance Methods: No

Number of classes in the class library: Approximately 40

MacApp access: Not now; possibly in the near future

Sample Syntax (sending the message, msg, *with argument,* arg, *to the object referenced by* obj*):*

```
arg msg: obj
```

Summary Information

Greatest Strength (compared to other object-oriented languages on Mac):

Speed

Biggest Weakness (compared to other object-oriented languages on Mac):

The "unusual" syntax of FORTH

Other:

Large users group in existence; CompuServe conference

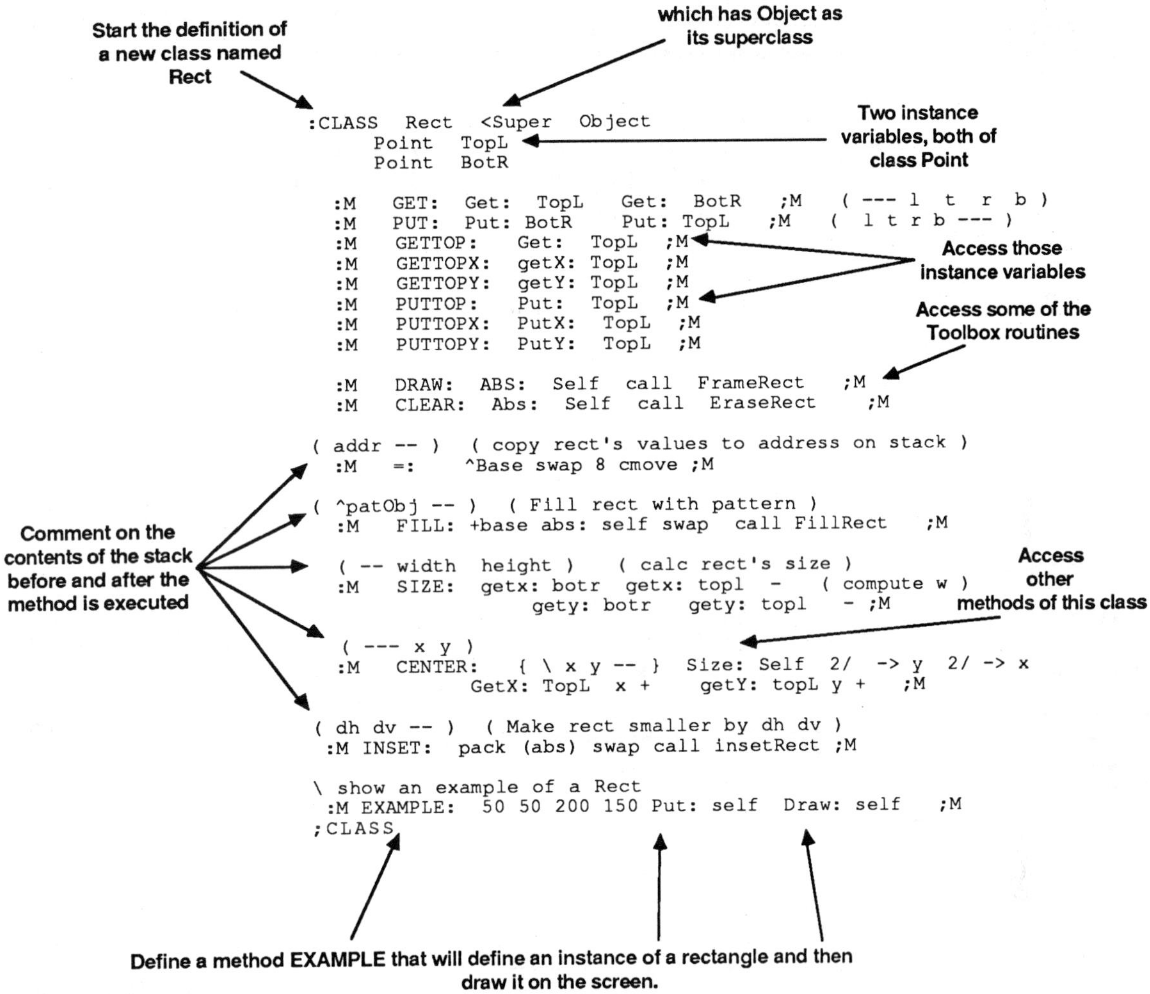

Figure 13-2 An annotated Neon class definition: a portion of the Neon Rectangle class

to send the message Get: to the object referred to by the ith element of the array object myArray, with the resolution of that message determined at run-time by the run-time class of the object stored at that element in the array.

The basic approach of the current Neon class library (Figure 13-3), unlike that of MacApp, which provides a completely functional application framework, is to "lift" the Toolbox data types to the level of classes. Accordingly, Neon provides classes like Point, Window, Dialog, and Event, that provide to the Neon programmer a more functional set of building blocks than do the basic Toolbox data type and procedures for the Pascal or C programmer, but not quite the type of building blocks that the MacApp classes provide to the Object Pascal programmer.

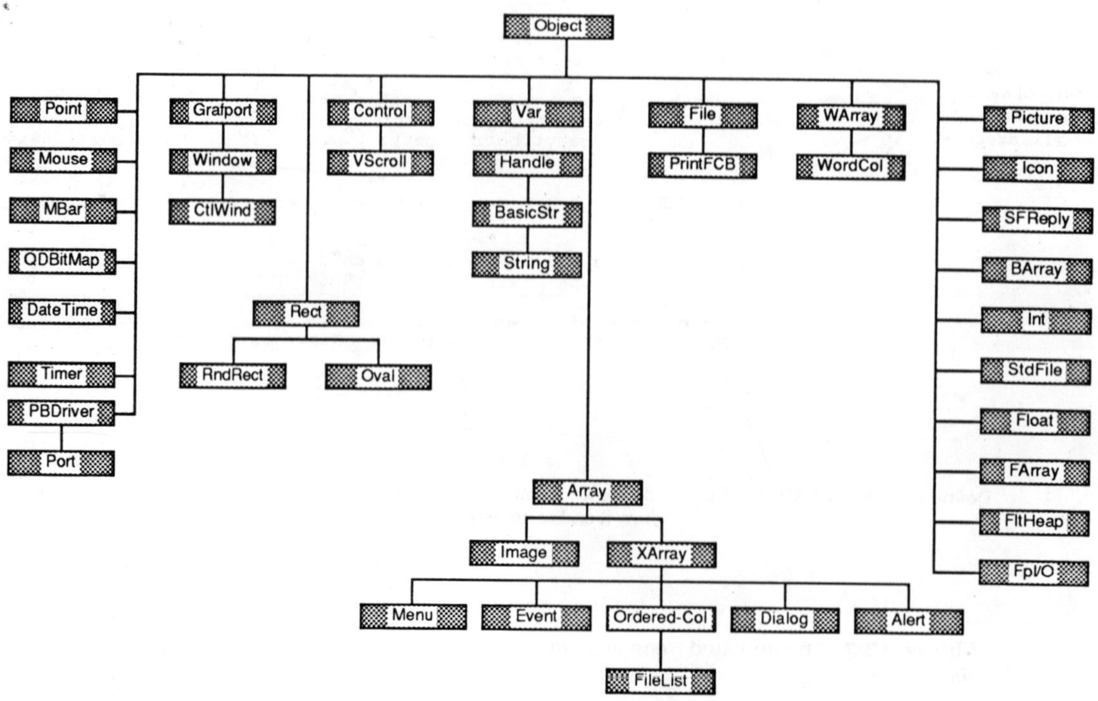

Figure 13-3 The inheritance structure of the current Neon class library.

Programming with Neon

Neon comes complete with its own self-contained development environment consisting of a text editor desk accessory, an interpreter, a compiler, and other application building tools. This development environment is generally in accordance with the Macintosh User Interface Standard. While Neon currently cannot access the MacApp class library, plans are being made to do so in the near future. This access probably will probably take the same form as that of the Smalltalk access discussed in Chapter 11—a reimplementation of the MacApp classes in Neon by Kriya so that a semantically similar set of classes is presented to the application programmer. It is currently not possible for Neon to directly access classes written in other object-oriented languages or even functions in other procedural languages like Pascal or C.

Programming in Neon is very similar to programming in Smalltalk. New classes are developed interactively with reasonably functional debugging facilities (Figure 13-4). When debugged, the new class is loaded into a working image, which then can be saved in a snapshot. Many such snapshots may be saved on disk—each representing a different development effort, a different project, and so on. Classes are used as incremental building blocks—as soon as a new class is defined, it is available for use. The results of developments in different images can be combined in a single image by recompiling the source code versions of the new classes and methods or by linking in a compiled version of a class (or set of classes) called a *module*.

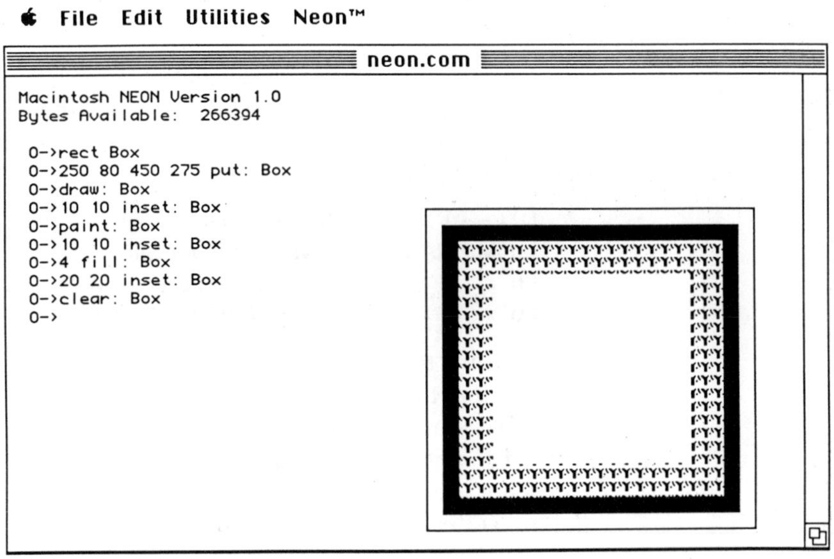

Figure 13-4 Neon in use.

Neon contains all the facilities to construct a stand-alone Macintosh application. For example, it has special routines to construct menus and to link the choice of a particular menu choice with the execution of a certain Neon word, and it has a special install utility that will "seal off" the base Neon classes so that the end-user cannnot access the Neon interpreter.

The Quadrilateral Classes in Neon

Figure 13-5 lists an implementation of the quadrilateral classes in Neon. The basic structure of these classes is identical with all other implementations in earlier chapters, although there are many small differences. Some of these differences are:

- Neon strictly supports the object encapsulation, so no access to the instance variables of an object is permitted from outside the object. This is just like Smalltalk, but unlike, for example, Object Pascal. To provide this access, additional methods were designed (PutFirst:, PutSecond:, GetFirst:, GetSecond:, and so on).
- Neon provides a special method for initializing of new instances. This method, ClassInit:, is invoked automatically whenever a new instance is allocated, so the IQuad method of the Object Pascal implementation is not present in the Neon version.
- Neon provides classes that act as "containers" of other objects so there is no need to link the quadrilateral objects in a linked list. Accordingly, the fNextQuad instance variable is not needed in Neon.
- Neon already has a rectangle class in the standard library, so the rectangle class for QuadWorld is named QRectangle, just as in Smalltalk.

Let's analyze one of these methods in detail, the Draw: method. This method is implemented in the Quad class and then overridden in the QRectangle class. Here is the Draw: implementation in the Quad class, with line numbers added to make the discussion easier:

```
(1) ( -- )        ( Draw the quad )
(2) :M DRAW:      0 at: vertex call MoveTo
(3)               4 1 DO i at: vertex call LineTo LOOP
(4)               0 at: vertex call LineTo cr          ;M
```

Line 1 is the standard comment for a Neon method. The (--) construct shows before the pair of hyphens what must be on the stack when this method is invoked (nothing) and what this method will leave on the stack when the method completes (also nothing). Having no effect on the stack is slightly unusual, but is entirely reasonable for a method like Draw: that is important for the "side-effect" of drawing on the screen.

```
\       The Quadrilateral classes in Neon
\       Copyright 1986, Productivity Products International


:CLASS Quadrilateral <Super Object

  ( INSTANCE VARIABLES )
    4 Array vertex    ( vertex will be an array of four Points )
      Int    rotated  ( rotated will be non-zero if the quad has been rotated )

  ( METHODS )
    ( -- ) ( This method will be called automatically to initialize each )
           ( instance of a quadrilateral )
  :M ClassInit: 4 0 DO heap> Point i to: vertex LOOP
                clear: rotated ;M

    ( x y -- ) ( These methods set the vertices of a quad )
  :M PutFirst:  pack 0 to: vertex   ;M
  :M PutSecond: pack 1 to: vertex   ;M
  :M PutThird:  pack 2 to: vertex   ;M
  :M PutFourth: pack 3 to: vertex   ;M

    ( -- x y ) ( These methods return the vertices of a quad )
  :M GetFirst:   0 at: vertex unpack  ;M
  :M GetSecond:  1 at: vertex unpack  ;M
  :M GetThird:   2 at: vertex unpack  ;M
  :M GetFourth:  3 at: vertex unpack  ;M

    ( -- ) ( Draw the quad )
  :M DRAW:    0 at: vertex call MoveTo
              4 1 DO  i at: vertex call LineTo LOOP
              0 at: vertex call LineTo   cr             ;M

    ( -- addr len ) ( Return the textual representation of a quad )
  :M AsText: " A Quadrilateral" ;M

;CLASS


\  THE PARALLELOGRAM CLASS
:CLASS Parallelogram <Super Quadrilateral

  ( METHODS )

    ( -- addr len ) ( Return the textual representation of a parallelogram )
  :M AsText: " A Parallelogram" ;M

;CLASS

\  THE RHOMBUS CLASS )
:CLASS Rhombus <Super Parallelogram

  ( METHODS )

    ( -- addr len ) ( Return the textual representation of a rhombus )
  :M AsText: " A Rhombus" ;M

;CLASS
```

```
\  THE RECTANGLE CLASS )
:CLASS QRectangle <Super Parallelogram

  ( METHODS )

    ( -- addr len ) ( Return the textual representation of a rectangle )
  :M AsText: " A Rectangle" ;M

    ( -- ) ( Draw a rectangle - a special type of quad )
  :M DRAW:  get: rotated IF draw: super
                         ELSE GetFirst: Self
                              GetThird: Self
                              put: tempRect
                              draw: tempRect
                         THEN                    ;M

;CLASS


\  THE SQUARE CLASS )
:CLASS Square <Super QRectangle

  ( METHODS )

    ( -- addr len ) ( Return the textual representation of a square )
  :M AsText: " A Square" ;M

;CLASS
```

Figure 13-5 The quadrilateral classes implemented in Neon

Line 2 defines Draw: as a method and begins its body. The first expression in this body sends the message at: to the object referred to by vertex. The argument to this message is 0. vertex is the array of points that form the vertices of the quadrilateral. The at: method will leave this vertex (as a point) on the stack. The Toolbox routine MoveTo is then called to position the pen at the first vertex. MoveTo expects to find a point on the stack.

Line 3 contains a Neon iteration, a DO-loop. The temporary variable i will assume in turn the values 1, 2, and 3. For each of these values the message at: will be sent to vertex, leaving the appropriate vertex on the stack. The Toolbox routine LineTo will then draw a line from the current pen position to the vertex.

Line 4 draws the last edge of the quad and then returns the Neon cursor to the left edge of the Neon interpretation window.

The override of the Draw: method in the QRectangle class is similar to its design in Object Pascal and Smalltalk:

```
(1) ( -- )          ( Draw a rectangle--a special type of quad )
(2) :M DRAW:        get: rotated IF Draw: super
(3)                          ELSE GetFirst: Self
(4)                               GetThird: Self
(5)                               put: tempRect
(6)                               draw: tempRect
(7)                          THEN                        ;M
```

In line 1, the instance variable rotated is put on the stack by sending it the message get: (a message understood by integer objects). If this integer is true (non-zero) then the Draw: method in the superclass is executed by sending the message Draw: to super. Otherwise a temporary rectangle object (an instance of the Neon class Rectangle), already allocated by the system for uses just as this, is used to efficiently draw the rectangle on the screen. This is done by pushing the opposite vertices of the QRectangle on the stack (GetFirst: self and GetThird: self—lines 3 and 4). These points are used to set the coordinates of the temporary rectangle (put: tempRect—line 5) which is then drawn by sending it the draw: message (line 6).

ExperCommonLISP

The language ExperCommonLISP is one of the most comprehensive object-oriented languages on the Macintosh in that it implements all of the features of object-oriented languages (except unique instance methods), provides a set of classes that mirror the Toolbox data types, and with the next release, will provide MacApp access. ExperCommonLISP was developed by ExperTelligence expressly for the Macintosh and was first shipped in March 1986. It was derived from the ExperLISP product available for the Macintosh since early 1985.

Notes

The exact status of the ExperCommonLISP MacApp access may have been dramatically improved by developments that were taking place at the time of this writing. This is because an automatic process has been designed for converting the original Object Pascal MacApp class library into a functionally equivalent ExperCommonLISP MacApp class library. This may significantly accelerate the completion of the ExperCommonLISP MacApp classes. See the discussion at the end of this chapter for further details.

Summary

ExperCommonLISP

Background Information

Base Language: Lisp

Developer: ExperTelligence *Current Version:* 2.0

Programming Environment/Availability: Lisp Workshop/ *(not applicable)* Mac Programmer's Workshop/*(not applicable)* Other: Self-contained environment

Toolbox Access: Yes *Support for the 128K ROM:* Yes

Object-Oriented Information

Instance variables and Instance Methods: Yes

Class Variables: Yes

Class Methods: Yes (called *metamethods*)

Multiple Inheritance: Not implemented in this version

Unique Instance Methods: No

Number of classes in the class library: Approximately 45 in the ExperCaste Class System

MacApp access: Planned, may be present in the initial release of the ExperCaste Class System

Sample Syntax (sending the message, msg, *with argument,* arg, *to the object referenced by* obj*):*

```
(obj 'msg <arg>)
```

Summary Information

Greatest Strength (compared to other object-oriented languages on Mac):

Comprehensive object-oriented features (class methods, class variables, etc.)
Size of the class library

Biggest Weakness (compared to other object-oriented languages on Mac):

For many developers, LISP is still an "unusual" language

ExperCommonLISP Syntax and Class Library

ExperCommonLISP syntax shows its strong LISP heritage. Message sending, setting object reference variables, accessing instance variables, and other object-oriented programming language features are accomplished with list functions:

(setq Triangle (send Object 'subclass))	Define a new subclass of Object, a subclass named Triangle, by sending the message subclass to the Object class.
(setq tri1 (send Triangle 'New))	Instantiate a new instance of the Triangle class and store a reference to this new instance in the variable tri1.
(send tri1 'height)	Send the message height to the object referenced by tri1.

Actually, the definition of a new class in ExperCommonLISP can be much more detailed than this simple example shows. The full class definition schema includes provisions for instance and class variables as well as instance and class methods:

General Class Definition Schema

```
(setq NewClass (CLASS (superclass1 superclass2 . . . superclassn)
  (IVS (iv1) (iv2) . . . (ivn))
  (Methods      (method1 (arg_list) (body))
                (method2 (arg_list) (body))
      .
      .
      .
                (methodn (arg_list) (body)))
  (CVS (iv1) (iv2) . . . (ivn))
  (Metamethods (method1 (arg_list) (body))
                (method2 (arg_list) (body))
      .
      .
      .
                (methodn (arg_list) (body)))))
```

where

- **IVS** is a keyword for the instance variable definition clause. Each portion of that clause names an instance variable and provides its initial value and attributes.
- **Methods** is a keyword for the method definition clause. Each portion of that clause defines a message, its argument list, and the method that is invoked when that message is received by an instance of this class.
- **CVS** is a keyword for the class variable definition clause. Like the instance variable definition clause, each portion of the CVS clause names a class variable and provides its initial value and attributes.
- **Metamethods** is a keyword for the class method definition clause. Each portion of that clause defines a class message, its argument list, and the class method that is invoked when that message is received by the class object.

Notes

Those who know LISP will observe that this schema uses terms like "arg_lists" rather than the more traditional lambda-list style common to LISP (for example, "λlist"). Here, the various lists are written out in a nonrigorous, but more informal notation. This is to make this short exposition on ExperCommonLISP more understandable to those who do not have a reading knowledge of LISP.

Even this detailed schema does not present a full picture of the facilities in ExperCommonLISP. As one example of a capability in ExperCommonLISP not exhibited by this schema and one not present in any of the other object-oriented languages discussed in this book, consider the following more detailed format of the instance variable definition clause:

(IVS (instance-variable$_1$-definition) (instance-variable$_2$-definition) . . .
  (instance-variable$_n$-definition))

where an instance variable definition has the form:

(| instance-variable-name | |default-value-form| |set| |get|)

The keywords **get** and **set** specify whether the instance variable can be accessed from outside the object. If the keyword **get** is used, the variable can be read from outside; if the keyword **set** is used, the variable can be written. Thus, the degree of encapsulation can be set on a class-by-class basis and within a class, on an instance variable-by-instance variable basis. This is a much more flexible middle ground between the unrestricted access provided by Object Pascal and the total lack of access in Smalltalk.

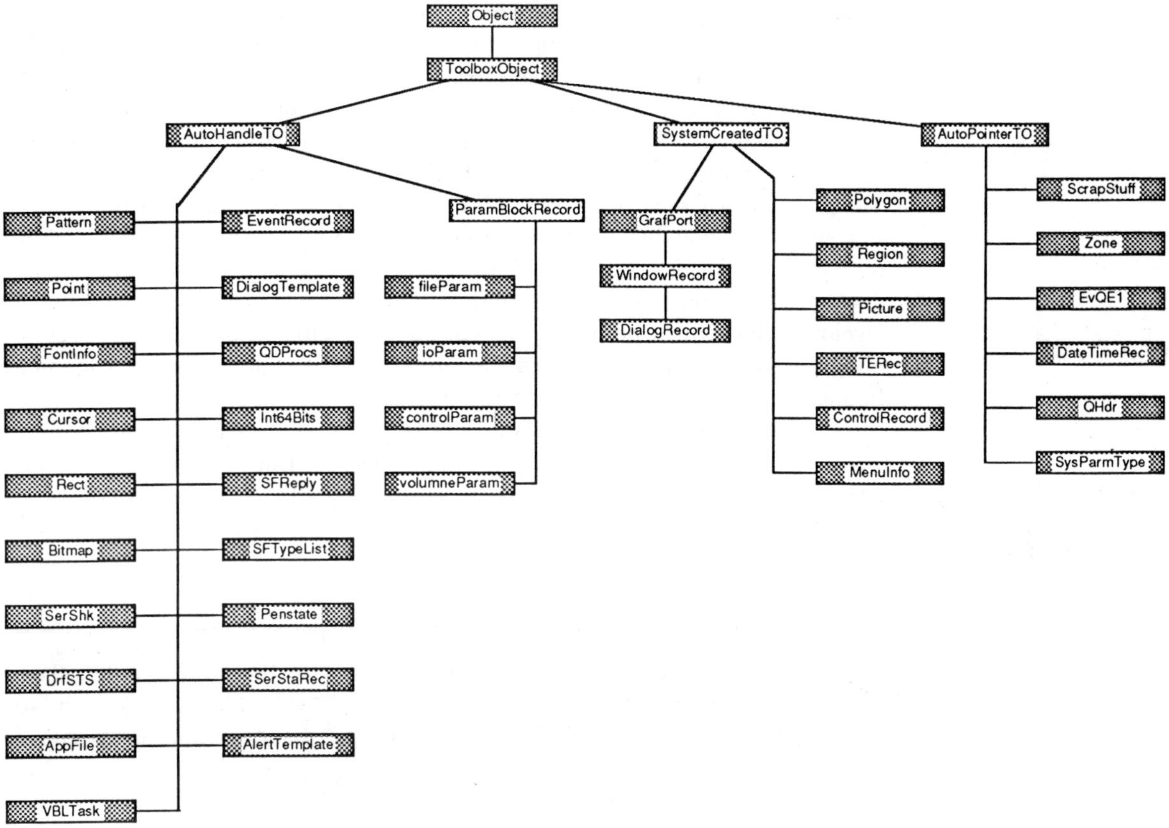

Figure 13-6 The ExperCommonLISP Class library. (Note that the MacApp classes are not repeated in this figure, though they can be accessed.)

The ExperCommonLISP class library includes a set of classes that "lift up" the Toolbox data types to the level of objects (Figure 13-6) as well as the MacApp classes. As with Smalltalk, Neon, and Object Logo, this MacApp access is achieved by a reimplementation of the MacApp class functionality by ExperTelligence.

Programming with ExperCommonLISP

ExperCommonLISP comes complete with its own self-contained development environment consisting of a text editor with a "matching parentheses" feature, an interpreter (called the Listener), a compiler, and other application-building tools. This development environment is generally in accordance with the Macintosh User Interface Standard and resembles, at a very superficial level, that of Macintosh Pascal with its Program, Text, and Graphics Windows. It is currently not possible for ExperCommonLISP to directly access classes written in other object-oriented languages, although it can access procedures and functions written in either Pascal or C.

Programming in ExperCommonLISP is very similar to programming in Neon or Smalltalk. New classes are developed interactively with reasonably functional debugging facilities (Figure 13-7). When debugged, the new class is loaded into a working image, which can then be saved in a snapshot. Many such snapshots may be saved on disk—each representing a different development effort, a different project, etc. Classes are used as incremental building blocks—as soon as a new class is defined, it is available for use. The results of developments in different images can be combined in a single image by recompiling the source code versions of the new classes and methods, or by loading the binary files produced by the file compiler.

ExperCommonLISP contains all the facilities to construct a stand-alone Macintosh application. For example, it has special routines to construct menus and to link the choice of a particular menu choice with the execution of a certain ExperCommonLISP function, and it can control all the Toolbox functions.

Object Assembler

The language Object Assembler is a set of macros for the Motorola 68000 assembly language that provides easy access to the MacApp class library and to class definition facilities. It is built on top of the macro assembly language

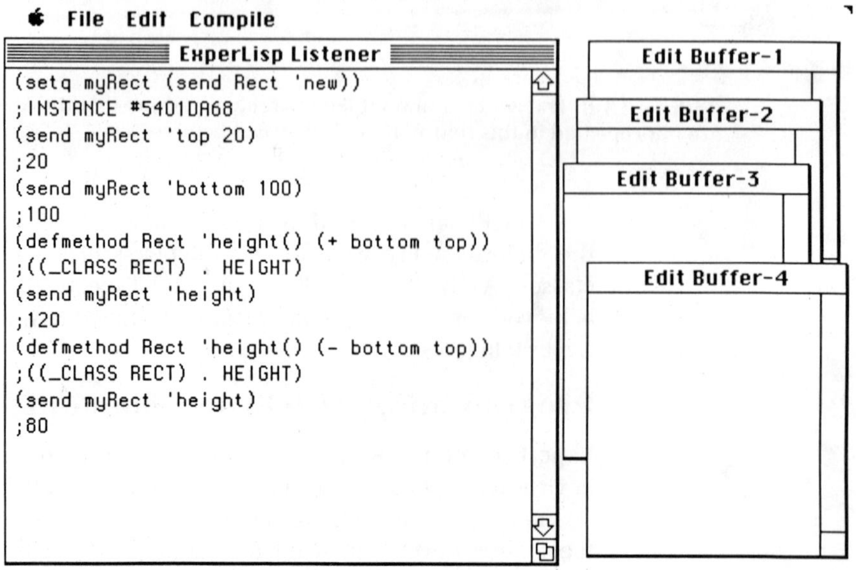

Figure 13-7 ExperCommon LISP in use.

provided by the Macintosh Programmer's Workshop assembler. Object Assembler was developed by Apple expressly for the Macintosh and will be first officially shipped late in 1986.

Summary

Object Assembler

Background Information

Base Language: Motorola 68000 Assembler

Developer: Apple — *Current Version:* 1.0

Programming Environment/Availability: Lisa Workshop/ *(not applicable)*
Mac Programmer's Workshop/October 1986
Other: *(not applicable)*

Toolbox Access: Yes — *Support for the 128K ROM:* Yes

Object-Oriented Information

Instance variables and Instance Methods: Yes

Class Variables: No

Class Methods: No

Multiple Inheritance: No

Unique Instance Methods: No

Number of classes in the class library: Approximately 30

MacApp access: Yes

Sample Syntax (sending the message, msg, *with argument,* arg, *to the object referenced by* obj*):*

```
MOVE.W    arg (A6), -(SP)
MOVE.L    obj (A6), -(SP)
MethCall  msg
```

Summary Information

Greatest Strength (compared to other object-oriented languages on Mac):

Speed

Biggest Weakness (compared to other object-oriented languages on Mac):

Limited object-oriented concepts (for example, no class methods)

The Object Assembler macros enable the assembly language programmer to define new classes, define method bodies, instantiate objects, easily reference instance variables by name, and invoke methods, including inherited ones. A few examples will suffice to demonstrate the use of these Object Assembler macros. The basic schema for defining a new class in Object Assembler, for example, is:

```
MACRO
ObjectDef &TypeName,&Heritage,&FieldList,&MethodList
```

and an example of the use of this macro is:

```
ObjectDef Shape,Object,                                    \
  ((boundRect,8),                                          \
    (borderThickness,2),                                   \
    (color,2)),                                            \
  ((Draw),                                                 \
    (MoveBy),                                              \
    (Stretch))

ObjectDef Arc,Shape,                                       \
  ((startAngle,2),                                         \
    (arcAngle,2)),                                         \
  ((Draw,OVERRIDE),                                        \
    (GetArea),                                             \
    (SetArcAngle))
```

(The "\" is required by the assembler when continuing a statement from one line to the next.)

Defining a method and referencing an instance variable by name are performed similarly:

- Defining a method
  Schema

```
MACRO
&ProcName ProcMethOf &TypeName
MACRO
EndMethod
```

  Example

```
Draw ProcMethOf Arc
  <code>
EndMethod
```

- Accessing an instance variable
  Schema

```
MACRO
ObjectWith &TypeName

MACRO
EndObjectWith
```

Example

```
ObjectWith Arc
MOVE.L startAngle(A1),-(SP)
PEA     boundRect(A1)
EndObjectWith
```

In this example of accessing an instance variable, A1 must already be loaded with an arc object reference. The ObjectWith macro simply qualifies startAngle and boundRect for you. Note that the ProcMethOf (and the corresponding FuncMethOf) macros automatically invoke the ObjectWith macro with the given class, making references to the instance variables of that class easy.

In terms of its object-oriented semantics, Object Assembler is just like Object Pascal. MacApp access is provided, as is access to any class implemented in Object Pascal. It also is possible to subclass Object Assembler classes in Object Pascal. No easy access is possible to classes implemented in other languages.

In accessing Object Pascal classes—for example, the MacApp classes—from Object Assembler you must include the interfaces of the MacApp classes in your assembler source, just as you must use the MacApp interfaces in an Object Pascal program. In the case of MacApp, an appropriate file containing all the MacApp interfaces in the form required by Object Assembler is provided with the Object Assembler macros. If you want to use any Object Pascal classes you have defined from Object Assembler, you must prepare such an interface file yourself. The same thing is true if you want to access a class defined in Object Assembler in an Object Pascal application.

Like Object Pascal, Object Assembler is used from the Macintosh Programmer's Workshop. It does not have its own development environment.

Object Logo

Object Logo is the most unusual object-oriented language on the Macintosh. This is because Object Logo is implemented as a class-less object-oriented language—an object-oriented language in which there is no firm distinction between an instance object and a factory object (a class) that makes those instances. Object Logo was developed by Coral Software Corporation expressly for the Macintosh and is scheduled to be first shipped in the summer of 1986.

Summary

Object Logo

Background Information

Base Language: Logo and CommonLisp

Developer: Coral Software Corp. *Current Version:* 1.0

Programming Environment/Availability: Lisa Workshop/ *(not applicable)* Mac Programmer's Workshop/ *(not applicable)* Other: Self-contained environment/June 1986 *(est.)*

Toolbox Access: Yes *Support for the 128K ROM:* Yes

Object-Oriented Information

Instance variables and Instance Methods: Yes

Class Variables: Yes

Class Methods: Yes

Multiple Inheritance: Yes

Unique Instance Methods: Yes

Number of classes in the class library: Approximately 30 (Actually, the number of *objects* in the *object* library)

MacApp access: Planned

Sample Syntax (sending the message, msg, *with argument,* arg, *to the object referenced by* obj*):*

```
tell :obj [msg "arg]
```

Summary Information

Greatest Strength (compared to other object-oriented languages on Mac):

Uniform treatment of objects, in the style first *proposed* for Smalltalk, but never implemented by Xerox PARC.

Easier to learn for programmers not familiar with other object-oriented languages.

Biggest Weakness (compared to other object-oriented languages on Mac):

Longer learning time for experienced object-oriented programmers because the traditional distinction between object and class is not part of Object Logo.

In designing a language that has no distinction between classes and instances, Coral Software's programmers did not leave out a concept that is at the very heart of object-oriented programming. Rather, they left out a concept that is commonly used in the implementation of object-oriented languages. Classes, after all, are really an implementation convenience—basically a way of economizing on the amount of memory required to write object-oriented programs. From Coral's point of view, the conceptual issues in using an object-oriented language are more important than implementation efficiency concerns. By removing the class "artifact", Coral has designed a language in which all objects are treated uniformly—a language they believe is much easier to learn and more flexible than traditional object-oriented languages.

There are a number of technical consequences of this philosophical decision to remove distinctions between classes and objects. In Object Logo, objects can be given instance variables and methods "on the fly" during an interactive session. You could, for example, create an object, give it two instance variables, then define a couple of methods, use those methods, clone the object, add some instance variables, remove some methods, and then clone the object. In terms of the vocabulary developed up to this point, you have created an instance (from no template), redefined the structure of an instance while it existed, added new methods while it existed, and then used it as a factory to produce a new instance just like itself—all notions that don't make sense with the traditional object-oriented vocabulary. The problem isn't with the vocabulary. The problem is that many of the notions of object-oriented programming that you have spent so long acquiring just don't apply to Object Logo as well as they did to other languages. Consequently, Object Logo is somewhat harder to learn than the other object-oriented languages described in this book if you are already familar with other object-oriented languages, just as Logo is sometimes difficult for already experienced programmers to learn. The reason for this difficulty is that learning Object Logo requires that you "unlearn" some concepts about object-oriented programming and learn some new ones that don't fit in with your conceptual model of how objects, classes, messages, and methods interrelate. Object Logo, for example, is the only language described in this book that provides for unique instance methods—methods not associated with a data structure shared among objects with a similar format, but rather methods directly "attached" to objects. In Object Logo, such a concept is very natural; in the other languages discussed here, it is most unusual.

Object Logo Syntax and Class Library

Because conceptual simplicity was one of the major goals in the design of Object Logo, Object Logo adds only a few new primitives to the Logo language:

Primitive	Semantics
KINDOF object(s)	Create a new object that inherits from object(s).
TALKTO anObject	Make anObject the "current object". (At any time during the execution of an Object Logo interactive session, there is exactly one current object. All references to variables and procedures are resolved in the context of this current object.)
HAVE name	Add the instance variable name (or the list of instance variables in name) to the current object.
HOWTO procedureName args	Add the method procedureName to the current object.
USUAL.procedureName	Invoke the inherited method. (This is essentially equivalent to the Object Pascal **INHERITED** and to sending messages to super in Smalltalk.)
TELL anObject InstructionList	Execute a list of instructions in the context of anObject without making anObject the current object. (anObject becomes the current object only for the duration of the instructions in InstructionList.)
ONEOF objects	Creates an "instance" by creating a new object that inherits from object(s), then telling the new object to EXIST. The EXIST procedure creates the object's instance variables and initializes them.
EXIST	The procedure conventionally used to initialize the state of an "instance." It is called automatically by ONEOF. New EXIST procedures should include a call to USUAL.EXIST to make sure all "superclasses" contribute to the initialization.

Figure 13-8 shows a small, annotated example of some Object Logo code that exhibits many of these operations. Note that the syntax of Object Logo is heavily influenced by Logo in which new procedures are defined with the TO

Design the "class" of visible objects

Create a collection of all visible object that is initialized to the empy list

Spiral.shape defined elsewhere

Define the instance variables of visible objects

```
; Visobs
; visible objects know how to: exist, die, setxy, draw.self, and erase.self

make "visob something
make "all.visobs []

tell :visob [howto exist]
  have [xpos ypos shape]
  make "xpos 0
  make "ypos 0
  make "shape :spiral.shape
  draw.self
  make "all.visobs fput self :all.visobs
end

tell :visob [howto die]
  make "all.visobs remove self :all.visobs
  erase.self
end

tell :visob [howto setxy :x :y]
  erase.self
  make "xpos :x
  make "ypos :y
  draw.self
end

tell :visob [howto draw.self]
  moveto :xpos :ypos
  penmode "srcXor
  stamp :shape
end

tell :visob [howto erase.self]
  draw.self
end
```

Design the "subclass" of physical objects

Create a collection of all physical objects

Access the Inherited method for EXIST

Physical objects can't occupy the same space; If moved to where other physobs are, the others will move

```
;Physobs
;Physical objects cannot appear at the same place

make "physob kindof :visob
make "all.physobs []

tell :physob [howto exist]
  usual.exist
  make "all.physobs fput self :all.physobs
end

tell :physob [howto die]
  make "all.physobs remove self :all.physobs
  usual.die
end

tell :physob [howto setxy :x :y]
  usual.setxy :x :y
  displace.if.necessary :all.physobs
end

tell :physob [howto displace.if.necessary :objs]
  if emptyp :objs [stop]
  local [x y]
  make "x :xpos
  make "y :ypos
  tell first :objs [if near :x :y :xpos :ypos [move.away.from :x :y]]
  displace.if.necessary butfirst :objs
end

tell :physob [howto move.away.from :x :y]
  setxy :xpos + 20 * sign (:xpos - :x) :ypos + 20 * (:ypos - :y)
end
```

Figure 13-8 An annotated transcript of a short Object Logo session.

primitive. For example, in (ordinary) Logo, a new command SQUARE can be defined by the following expression:

```
TO SQUARE :SIZE
  REPEAT 4 [FORWARD :SIZE RIGHT 90]
END
```

This new command draws a square with any size edge. The variable SIZE is a parameter to this command that specifies how big the square should be. Note that :SIZE means the value of SIZE and 'SIZE means the symbol 'SIZE.

Similarly, in Object Logo, a new method is defined by TELLing an object HOW TO do some operation:

```
TELL :VISOB [HOWTO ERASE.SELF]
   DRAW.SELF
 END
```

(When the object referenced by the variable VISOB (a VISibleOBject) receives the message ERASE.SELF, it is to send itself the message DRAW.SELF.)

Object Logo is one of the few languages in this book that implements multiple inheritance and Figure 13-9 shows a small example of it in use. In Object Logo, a subclass can invoke all methods for a message common to its ancestors. This style of multiple inheritance differs considerably from that of Smalltalk.

At the time of this writing, no comprehensive listing of the Object Logo class library was available. However, the plans for Object Logo class library include a complete reimplementation of the MacApp classes using their Logo primitives for accessing the Toolbox. Like Neon and ExperCommonLISP, this reimplementation will produce a semantically similar set of classes so that the MacApp programmer could move from Object Pascal or Neon to Object Logo with very little additional training about the MacApp class library.

Programming with Object Logo

Object Logo comes complete with its own self-contained development environment consisting of a text-based program editor and several debugging tools. This development environment is generally in accordance with the Macintosh User Interface Standard. It is not currently possible for Object Logo to directly access classes written in other object-oriented languages, or even procedures in other procedural languages like Pascal or C, although some kind of indirect access is likely in the future.

Programming in Object Logo is similar to programming in Smalltalk, Neon, or ExperCommonLISP. New objects are developed interactively with reasonably functional debugging facilities (Figure 13-10). When debugged, objects definitions can be saved as either text files or compiled files. These can later be loaded into any Object Logo environment. Objects are used as incremental building blocks—as soon as an object is defined, it is available for use.

```
? make "speaker something
? tell :speaker [howto say :text]
> type "###
> type :text
> print "###
> end
SAY DEFINED

? tell :speaker [say [The sky is blue]]
###The sky is blue###

? make "pessimist kindof :speaker
? tell :pessimist [say [The soup is hot]]
###The soup is hot###

? tell :pessimist [howto say :text]
> print [It's a shame.]
> usual.say :text
> end
SAY DEFINED

? tell :pessimist [say [The sun is shining]]
It's a shame.
###The sun is shining###

? make "optimist kindof :speaker
? tell :optimist [howto say :text]
> print [Wow!]
> usual.say :text
> print [It's great!]
> end
SAY DEFINED

? tell :optimist [say [Learning can be fun]]
Wow!
###Learning can be fun###
It's great!

? make "schizo (kindof :optimist :pessimist)
? tell :schizo [say [The grass is green]]
Wow!
It's a shame.
###The grass is green###
It's great!

? make "schizo2 (kindof :pessimist :optimist)
? tell :schizo2 [say [Roses are red]]
It's a shame.
Wow!
###Roses are red###
It's great!
```

Create a new object

Define the method "SAY" for that object

Test the method

Make an object that inherits from the first

Redefine the "SAY" method for that object

Test the redefinition

Make another object

And give it another definition for the "SAY" methods

Test it

Create an object the Inherits from both OPTIMIST and PESSIMIST

Send this new object the "SAY" message

The result is an intermixing of the two SAY methods

Create a new object from the same two objects, but in a different order

The result is a different intermixing of the SAY methods

Figure 13-9 An annotated transcript of an Object Logo session demonstrating the Object Logo style of multiple inheritence.

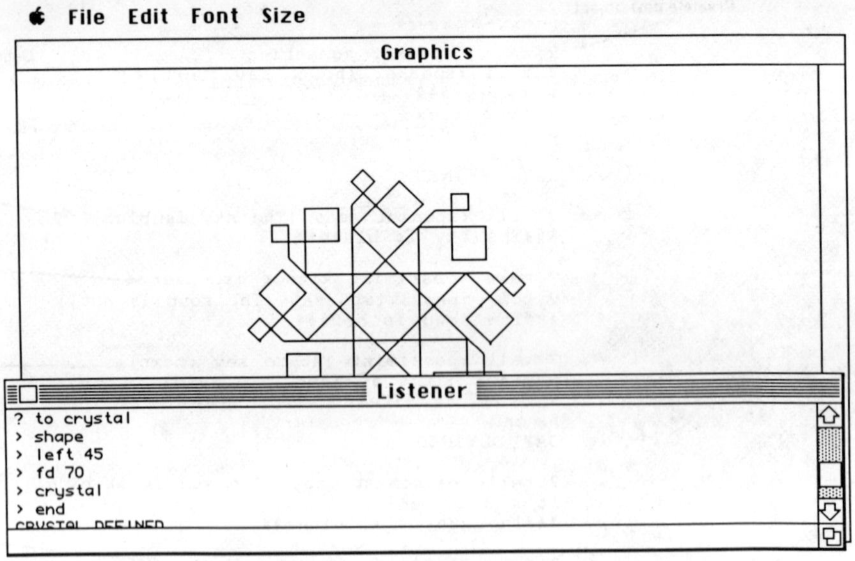

Figure 13-10 Object Logo in use.

Objective-C

The language Objective-C brings the basic notions of object-oriented programming to the C language in a manner that is machine-independent. This is accomplished by a compiler that accepts Objective-C source code and outputs an equivalent C source code. The resulting C source code can then be compiled for execution on the target machine. This basic architecture is shown in Figure 13-11. This architecture has resulted in a language that can (and does) exist on both the IBM PC and the VAX 780, and on many machines in between. Objective-C was developed by Productivity Products International (PPI) and was first shipped in 1983.

Objective-C Syntax and Class Library

The Objective-C language is a strict superset of the C language. The object-oriented extensions are achieved by adding a new expression type to the C language: the message expresion. Syntactically, this message expression is delimited by brackets. The message expression brackets are disambiguated from the standard array subscripting brackets used in ordinary C by context:

```
[obj msg: arg];
```

with an internal message syntax that is very similar to that of Smalltalk, even

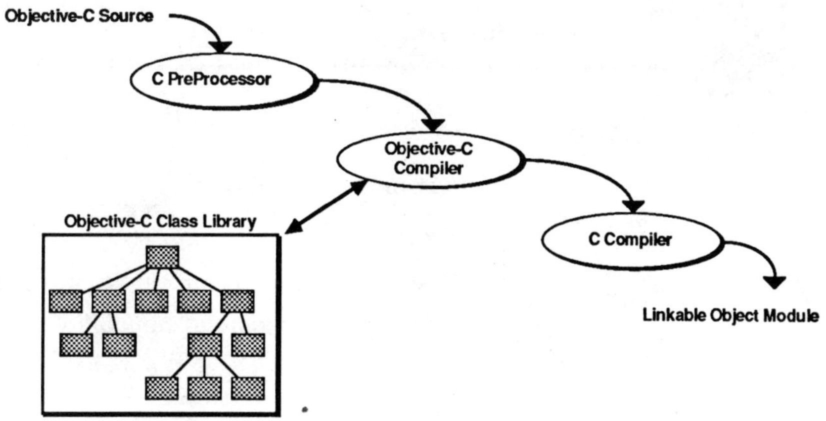

Figure 13-11 The basic architecture of Objective-C.

to the point of following Smalltalk's syntax for keyword messages. This new expression type exists on an equal level with all C expressions. The result is that a message expression can be used anywhere in an Objective-C statement that an expresion can be used in C. A sample statement that shows the resulting flexibility is:

```
[Point x: foo()+7 y: [box top]];
```

In this statement, the keyword message x:y: is being sent to the Point class. The first argument (of the x: portion) is the result of a function call and an addition (foo()+7). The second argument (of the y: portion) is the result of sending the message top to the object referred to by box.

New classes are defined in a special class description file of the following form:

```
=   ClassName: SuperClassName (PhylaList)
      { Instance Variable Declarations}
+   ClassMethodName  {Method Implementation}
–   InstanceMethodName  {Method Implementation}
=:
```

Only one class may be defined in any such file, though the number of class method definitions and instance method definitions may vary. Figure 13-12 shows an annotated example from the Objective-C class library, the Point class.

Summary

Objective-C

Background Information

Base Language: C

Developer: Productivity products — *Current Version:* 3.1

Programming Environment/Availability: Lisa Workshop/Late 1986
Mac Programmer's Workshop/Late 1986
Other: Integrated with the development environments of various C compilers on the Mac.

Toolbox Access: Yes — *Support for the 128K ROM:* Yes

Object-Oriented Information

Instance variables and Instance Methods: Yes

Class Variables: Yes, though they cannot be inherited

Class Methods: Yes

Multiple Inheritance: No

Unique Instance Methods: No

Number of classes in the class library: Approximately 25

MacApp access: Not now; possibly in the future

Sample Syntax (sending the message, msg, *with argument,* arg, *to the object referenced by* obj*):*

```
[ obj msg: arg ];
```

Summary Information

Greatest Strength (compared to other object-oriented languages on Mac):

Portability to many other workstations and hosts

Biggest Weakness (compared to other object-oriented languages on Mac):

Not a native compiler yet

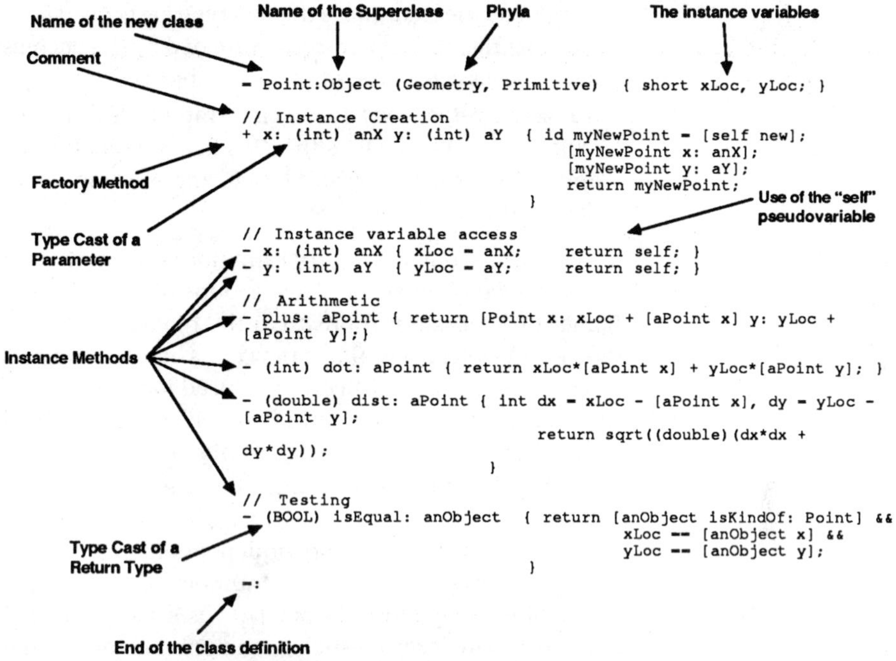

Figure 13-12 An annotated Objective-C class definition: a portion of the Point class from the Objective-C class library.

This class has two instance variables (xLoc, yLoc), one class method (x:y:) (class methods are distinguished by the leading "+"), and six instance methods (distinguished by the leading "−"). The algorithm for the plus: method, for example, is:

1. Allocate a new Point object ([Point x: y:]).
2. The value of the x-coordinate of this new Point is the sum of the value of the receiver's x-coordinate (xLoc) and the value of the argument's x-coordinate. ([aPoint x]). The y-coordinate is similarly constructed.
3. This new point object is returned to the caller of this method (return).

Note that in Objective-C:

- Message expressions can occur anywhere that an expression can occur in the standard C language. This means that messages can be used uniformly throughout the language.

- Type casts are used to provide data typing information to the Objective-C compiler. One example is the (int) type casts used for the dot product method (dot) to indicate that the value returned by the dot message is an integer—the default message return type is an object.
- All object references are declared to be of the same data type, called id in Objective-C. Thus, Objective-C is like Smalltalk in its declaration of objects and unlike Object Pascal, Clascal, and Neon in which object references are declared of a certain class.

One object-oriented programming concept that is unique to Objective-C is *phyla*. Phyla in Objective-C are groups of classes, just as phyla in biology are higher-order organizations than the biological notion of a "class". When you indicate in Objective-C that a new class belongs to a particular phylum, you are stating that this class will often be used together with the other classes in that phylum. When the Objective-C source code is compiled, this information is used to generate a more efficient method table structure.

The Objective-C class library (Figure 13-13) consists of some 25 classes that implement collection classes, basic geometric notions, and standard data structures—all in a machine-independent way. The fact that the Objective-C language is available on a large number of machines and that its class library is machine-independent is perhaps its greatest strength. PPI coined the term *software-IC* to describe such a machine-independent class, although the term is now used to describe any well-designed class.

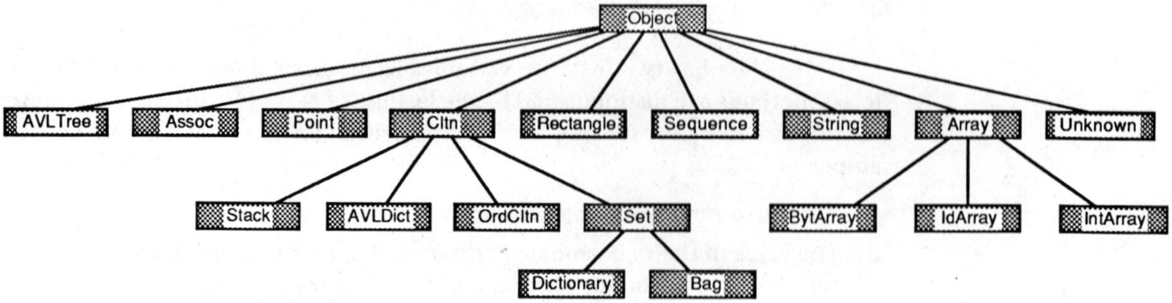

Figure 13-13 The Objective-C class library.

Programming with Objective-C

Programming in Objective-C is similar to programming in Object Pascal or Object Assembler. Classes are developed first (using a standard text editor) and compiled with the Objective-C and C compilers. Then a main program using these classes is written, compiled, and linked with the classes. It currently is not possible for Objective-C to directly access classes written in other object-oriented languages, although it can access procedures and functions written in either Pascal, C, or assembler.

Although not currently available on the Macintosh, an Objective-C interpreter (called Vici) is available. Programming in Objective-C with Vici is similar to using the interpreters of Neon, Object Logo, and ExperCommonLISP. One novel feature of Vici is the ability to work with both interpreted and compiled classes simultaneously. This means that when a large application consisting of many classes is being developed, only the classes being debugged need be run at interpreted speeds, with the remaining classes run at compiled speeds.

Like Object Pascal and Object Assembler, Objective-C itself does not contain all the facilities to construct a stand-alone Macintosh application—it relies on the facilities of the development environment in which it is used.

The Macintosh version of Objective-C provides complete access to the Macintosh Toolbox. Access like this to machine-specific libraries is not unusual for Objective-C because it is achieved transparently to the Objective-C compiler. This is because the C source produced by the Objective-C compiler is later compiled by a standard C compiler on the machine in question. In the case of the Macintosh, that C compiler is currently the Aztec C compiler produced by Manx Software, although in the future several other C compilers may be used.

It remains to be seen how Objective-C on the Macintosh will provide access to the MacApp class library. At the time of this writing, both a reimplementation of the MacApp functionality (like that done for Neon, Smalltalk, and ExperCommonLISP) and direct access to the same MacApp class library files and run-time support routines as used by Object Pascal are being considered. Objective-C probably will use the Macintosh Programmer's Workshop or the development environment of any other C compiler for which it produces C code. Objective-C currently does not have a development environment of its own on the Macintosh.

The Quadrilateral Classes in Objective-C

Figure 13-14 lists one implementation of the quadrilateral classes in Objective-C. The basic structure of these classes is identical with all of the other implementations in earlier chapters, and in particular the Quadrilateral instance variables in the Objective-C implementation are exactly the same as in the Neon implementation: an IdArray object holds the vertices, each of which is an instance of class Point, and an integer holds the boolean recording the rotation status. (In Objective-C, the class IdArray is an Array subclass that is optimized for holding references to other objects. There are many other types of such "Collection" classes, as they are usually called.)

```
#include "objc.h"              // This will define BOOL and STR

extern id IdArray, Point       // These classes are referenced

=Quadrilateral:Object(QuadWorld, Geometry, Collection, Primitive)
   // Instance variables
        { id vertices;        // An instance of IdArray four long
                              // each object in this IdArray is a Point
          BOOL rotated;       // Has the quad been rotated?
        }

//Class methods
// Instance creation
+ new { id myQuad = [super new];
        return [myQuad initialize];
      }

//Instance methods
- (STR)asText { return "a Quadrilateral"; }

- initialize { vertices = [IdArray with: 4,
                           [Point new], [Point new], [Point new], [Point new]];
               rotated = NO;
               return self;
             }

- draw { int i;
         MoveTo(PtToQDPt([vertices at: 0]));
         for (i = 1; i<4; i++) DrawTo(PTToQDPt([vertices at: i]));
         DrawTo(PTToQDPt([vertices at: 0]));
       }

- center { id points = [vertices eachElement];
           id thisPoint;
           int newX = 0;
           int newY = 0;
           while ( thisPoint = [points next] )
              { newX += [thisPoint x];   newY += [thisPoint y]; }
           [points free];
           return [Point x: newX/4  y: newY/4];
         }

=:
```

```
=Parallelogram:Quadrilateral(Geometry, Primitive)

//Instance methods
- (STR)asText { return "a Parallelogram"; }

=:
```

```
=Rhombus:Parallelogram(Geometry, Primitive)

//Instance methods
- (STR)asText { return "a Rhombus"; }

=:
```

```
=QRectangle:Paralellogram(Geometry, Primitive)

//Instance methods
- (STR)asText { return "a Rectangle"; }

- draw { id outlineRect;
         if (rotated)
                return [super draw];
         outlineRect = [Rectangle origin: [vertices at: 0]
                                  corner: [vertices at: 2]];
         FrameRect(RectToQDRect(outlineRect));
         [outlineRect free];
       }

=:
```

```
=Square:QRectangle(Geometry, Primitive)

//Instance methods
- (STR)asText { return "a Square"; }

=:
```

Figure 13-14 An implementation of the quadrilateral classes in Object-C.

However, this implementation of the quadrilateral classes contains several new and interesting variations in the design of the individual methods. The most unusual of this is the center method in the Quadrilateral class, the method which computes the center of a quadrilateral. Let's examine this method in detail. This method is listed below with line numbers to facilitate our discussion:

```
(1) - center { id points = [vertices eachElement];
(2)            id thisPoint;
(3)            int newX = 0;
(4)            int newY = 0;
(5)            while (thisPoint = [points next])
(6)                  { newX += [thisPoint x]; newY += [thisPoint y];}
(7)            [points free];
(8)            return [Point x: newX/4 y: newY/4];
(9)          }
```

Line (1) sends the message eachElement to the IdArray referred to by the vertices instance variable. Instances of class IdArray respond to the eachElement message by generating a sequence object—an object that exists to efficiently sequence through any type of collection. The points temporary variable refers to a sequence object that enumerates the objects held in the vertices IdArray. Each time the points sequence receives the next message, it returns the next element of the vertices IdArray. When the end of the IdArray is reached, a **NIL** (zero) pointer is returned. The sequence object keeps track of the position in the object it is sequencing over.

Lines (2), (3), and (4) declare other temporary variables used in the method.

Lines (5) and (6) are a C language while loop that iterates over each vertex in the quadrilateral (by way of the points sequence) and obtains the sum of all the x-coordinates and the sum of all the y-coordinates.

Line (7) frees the sequence object created in line (1). This sequence object is no longer needed and since Objective-C does not have automatic garbage collection, or its associated overhead, this unneeded object must be explicitly freed.

Line (8) sends the message x:y: to the Point class creating a new point that is located at the center of the quadrilateral. This new point is returned as the result of the center method.

In this method we have made use of IdArray, Sequence, and Point, all portions of the machine-independent Objective-C class libraries—software-ICs in PPI's terminology.

The MacApp Class Library in Other Languages

Most languages discussed in this chapter provide MacApp access by reimplementing the MacApp classes. While the goal of such a reimplementation is to maintain identical functionality between the original MacApp classes and the new ones, this is both difficult and temporary. It is difficult because MacApp is a significant amount of reasonably complex software; it is temporary because MacApp, like all software, evolves. When corrections, improvements, or changes are made to one language's MacApp class library, they are not reflected in the supposedly semantically equivalent MacApp libraries in the other object-oriented languages on Macintosh.

While there is no perfect solution to this problem, there is hope. Both Apple and PPI have succeeded in demonstrating the possibility of automatic conversion of classes written in one object-oriented language into another. Apple has a research prototype of class conversion utilities for both Object Pascal-to-Smalltalk and Smalltalk-to-ExperCommonLISP. PPI has such a prototype utility for conversion of Smalltalk classes to Objective-C. These utilities, if they can be turned into "industrial strength" applications, offer a path for automatic generation of new versions of MacApp classes from a single "master" version, presumably one maintained by Apple in Object Pascal.

There is another manner of providing MacApp access for the languages discussed in this chapter, one that is preferable but much harder to achieve. This other possibility is to directly link to the compiled Object Pascal MacApp classes. This requires, among other things, that the languages agree on a common link file format (See Snively, Paul F., "Standards Needed in Development

Systems," *MacTutor*, February 1986, pp. 5-6) and message resolution mechanism. This is how Object Assembler accesses MacApp. While in theory this is possible for other languages, it is usually considered impractical for the more "unusual" languages like Neon, Object Logo, and ExperCommonLISP. It would be technically possible for Objective-C. Whether the benefits of such an approach outweigh the considerable costs remains to be seen.

APPENDIX A

An Overview of the Macintosh User Interface Standard

The user interface is the soul of the Macintosh. Without the pull-down menus, alert boxes, cursor shapes, overlapping windows, and all the other conventions used on the Macintosh to communicate with the user, the Macintosh would be merely another personal computer. With such conventions, however, the Macintosh instantly becomes the "computer you already know how to use," in the words of Apple marketing mavens. In this chapter, we provide a conceptual framework for this user interface from the application programmer's point of view and explore many of the technical details of the Macintosh User Interface Standard. In addition, we examine why the existence of such a standard makes ever greater productivity gains possible with object-oriented programming. Since most developers are familiar with the Macintosh user interface from the user's point of view (because they themselves use the Macintosh), this chapter concentrates on providing a high-level framework describing the interface from the point of view of a developer of new Macintosh software and, accordingly, many small details are omitted from this discussion. A thorough understanding of the basic principles upon which the Macintosh user interface is built and of the framework that holds these principles together enables you to more easily extend the Macintosh user interface to the unique parts of your application—a task more important to the object-oriented programmer because MacApp, the Macintosh Expandable application, implements most of the shared common features of the Macintosh user interface for you, leaving only the unique portions of your application's user interface for you to design. For an even more thorough coverage of the details of the standard Macintosh user interface, see *Inside Macintosh*, the comprehensive programmer's reference manual produced by Apple and published by Addison-Wesley.

In general, a user interface is the sum total of everything the end user must do or know about an application program in order to accomplish the task at hand. This includes the commands the user needs to know to get things done; the actual keys the user must press and in what order to enter, manipulate, and retrieve data; the error messages the user gets when something isn't quite right; and many other things. For any given application, there are many ways to approach user interface designs. While well-designed user interfaces are received much better by the user community, they also are more difficult and more expensive to build—that is, they were until the advent of object-oriented programming techniques and the MacApp framework discussed in Chapter 4. Let us look at the characteristics of good user interfaces in general and at the details of the Macintosh user interface in particular.

On most personal computers, the user interface for each separate application program is designed to be the best possible compromise between the needs of the application at hand, the capabilities of the machine on which it is to run, and the time schedule imposed on its developers. Each developer's background, sophistication, and personal tastes influence these decisions, which, of necessity, are usually limited to the application currently under development and thus tend to be rather parochial in scope. When viewed as the result of such a three-way tug-of-war, the majority of these user interfaces are adequate and some are even excellent, but unfortunately for users, this manner of individually designing and implementing new user interfaces has two major failings:

- When push comes to shove in major decisions about a new user interface for an application, the target machine and the product schedule usually overrule the type of interface that would be most natural for the application.

- Individually crafted user interfaces tend to be, well, individual. The interaction style and interface conventions of a word processing application designed in this way usually has nothing to do with (or even conflicts with) those of a spreadsheet or a data base management system running on the same machine and used by the same user in the accomplishment of a given job. The user is thus forced into a never-ending situation in which each new application is just as hard to learn as the last. It is as if the computer were schizophrenic: a different personality with each application program.

The Macintosh changed all that.

For Macintosh developers, Apple provides (in order of increasing specialization):

- A complete specification of a user interface standard that provides guidelines for the developer covering the most basic portions of an application's user interface. Years of research, experimentation with hundreds of Macintosh users, and experience in the most easy-to-learn and easy-to-use interaction styles form the basis for these user interface guidelines—guidelines that are now a de facto standard for the Macintosh user community. These guidelines are the subject of this chapter.

- A set of routines that implement many of the small pieces of these guidelines. These routines form a portion of the Macintosh Toolbox, which is a set of routines stored in ROM that are available to every Macintosh application program. *Inside Macintosh* is, in fact, the comprehensive documentation for the Toolbox. A more elementary introduction to the Toolbox is Stephen Chernicoff's *Macintosh Revealed*.
- An expandable Macintosh Application, MacApp, which can be customized through the use of object-oriented programming. MacApp is the subject of Chapter 4 and of most of the chapters after that.

These three aids are not independent, rather they are hierarchically structured. The Toolbox routines implement the basic notions of the Macintosh user interface and MacApp "glues together" many of these Toolbox building blocks to form a framework for new Macintosh applications. As a developer you will probably use all of these aids to varying degrees depending upon the needs of your application.

There is nothing forcing you as a program developer to use MacApp as a base for your application, to call upon the Toolbox routines, or even to follow the Macintosh user interface guidelines. But it makes sense for most applications to do so. Following the Macintosh user interface standards makes the use of your application familiar to existing Macintosh users while at the same time making it consistent with the wide base of other Macintosh software. Using the Toolbox routines makes your application faster in its development and, probably, in its execution as well as making the program smaller. The benefits of using MacApp is explained at length in other chapters, but it is important to point out here that its use also provides a conceptual framework that has been shown to significantly shorten the design stage of an application. (See, Lamar Ledbetter and Brad Cox, "Software-ICs," *BYTE*, Volume 10, Number 6 (June 1985), pp. 307-316.)

The Macintosh User Interface Standard is not worthy of use simply because it is a standard—it is worthy of use because it is a well-designed user interface that conforms to most of the established principles in the design of man-machine dialogs. While a detailed examination of all such principles is outside the scope of this book, a short discussion of several of these principles and the manner in which they are implemented on the Macintosh provides an excellent introduction to the Macintosh user interface.

Three key principles to a good user interface are naturalness, consistency inside and outside the application, and the avoidance of modes. "Naturalness" is a broad and somewhat nebulous term when used to describe user interfaces—what is natural to one person may seem contrived to another. We shall, for the purposes of discussion, employ the definition of naturalness used to describe the user interface of the Lisa 7/7 software, the predecessor of the Macintosh User Interface Standard, given in my book, *The Complete Book of Lisa*, New York: Harper & Row, 1984. In general, a natural user interface is one that:

- Does not force you to remember the name of every command.
- Does not allow disastrous actions (like destruction of valuable data) to occur accidentally.
- Does not require you to understand the entire system in order to accomplish tasks.
- Allows you to switch back and forth between several different tasks without forcing you to finish one before beginning the next.
- Provides a variety of ways to input, manipulate, and retrieve data.
- Has a version for beginners and another for experts.
- Is forgiving about mistakes.
- Allows you to change your mind and undo an action.

In each of these areas, the Macintosh's user interface is exemplary. Pull-down menus provide access to the commands of an application yet don't take up much space on the screen when "rolled-up." You are not required to remember the command names of the application. Most applications alert you before a disastrous action, especially one that is irreversible, is executed. With Switcher, you almost have simultaneity of multiple tasks and with the command-key command sequences there are short-cuts for experts. The Macintosh User Interface Standard certainly meets all of the above criteria for naturalness.

Internal consistency in a user interface requires that all concepts, functions, and procedures apply across the parts of an application. Text-editing in a spreadsheet application, for example, should be the same for editing the contents of a cell or a formula. Exterior consistency requires that all concepts, functions, and procedures common across applications must be the same. Editing text in a spreadsheet application, a word-processing application, and the Pascal programming application should be essentially identical. External consistency in the user interfaces of a set of application programs shortens dramatically the time it takes to learn a new program. The "sameness" between packages maximizes the value of intuition. ("I bet this will work in Excel the same as it did in MacWrite. Let's try it.") Once you know how to edit text in one application, for example, you should know how to edit text in all applications. New programs become easier to learn, because with each program, the core concepts behind all applications can be practiced further.

The Macintosh user interface is strongest in the area of consistency—that was the very reason it was designed. Text-editing is exactly the same, for example, in all Macintosh applications even down to the I-beam cursor shape when text is being edited. Most applications have an "**About**" command as the first selection in the menu, which is itself the first menu in all applications, not because it must be the first from a technical point of view, but rather because of a conscious adherence to the user interface standard. There are many other examples of both internal and external consistency in the Macintosh's user interface standard including the clipboard, cursor shapes, and the use of command key alternatives to menu commands.

Most personal computer applications have modes to differentiate when the keyboard is being used to enter text and when it is being used to enter commands. In WordStar (a popular word processing program on non-Macintosh personal computers), for example, a 'y' entered in "main menu" mode means to delete a file, whereas a 'y' entered while in "text entry" mode appends a 'y' to the text of the document. (Moreover, WordStar uses different command modes to further differentiate command entry. A 'y' entered while in "printing" mode is a request to select the alternate ribbon color; a 'y' entered in "quick menu" mode deletes a carriage return.) Many errors and much confusion results when the user is typing in one mode while the machine is in another. Simply put, then, "a mode of an interactive computer system is a state of the user interface that lasts for a period of time, is not associated with any particular object, and has no role other than to place an interpretation on operator input. "(Larry Tesler, as quoted in "Designing the Star User Interface," David C. Smith, Charles Irby, Ralph Kimball, Bill Verplank, and Eric Harslem, *BYTE* (April 1982), pp. 242-282; see also Tesler's article, "The Smalltalk Environment," *BYTE*, (August 1981), pp.90-147.)

Modes are generally contrary to Macintosh's user interface because they limit the user to performing a certain action at a certain time or placing a special, and possibly unintended, interpretation on the user's action. As much as possible, Macintosh applications are modeless, although no application is completely modeless.

Having said that, some kinds of modes are generally tolerated when used sparingly and in good taste. The following types of modes generally conform with the Macintosh User Interface Standard:

- Modes that are long-term and procedural in nature, such as starting up Microsoft Chart and thus being in "business graphics" mode until quitting Chart.
- Modes that are "spring-loaded," that is, modes in which the user must constantly be doing something to perpetuate the mode. Selecting a command in a menu is an example of this: as long as the mouse button is pressed, the user is in "pull-down menu" mode.
- Modes that alert the user to some unusual situation that must be attended to before any other action can continue. "Please switch disks" mode is an example of this. Such modes typically block other operations to both emphasize their modularity and to draw attention to their importance.
- Modes that emulate a familiar real-life model that is itself modal, such as "picking up" different-sized paintbrushes in a graphics editor.
- Modes that change only the attributes of something, but not its nature or behavior, such as setting the font or text size for text, the shading pattern of a rectangle, or the thickness of a line.

A consistent user interface lets you learn one set of commands that may be used with many different programs. A natural user interface enables real human beings (individuals who make errors, don't like to read manuals, forget things, and use the application only occasionally) to feel comfortable and to be productive in a small amount of time. A modeless program doesn't restrict the user to certain actions at certain times, but rather presents a more flexible user interface. Note that these attributes of consistency, naturalness, and modelessness are orthogonal—a set of applications could each have a natural interface, yet each could be different from the others, or a poorly designed user interface could be used consistently across a set of applications, or could be consistently moded. However, when a user interface is natural, consistent, and modeless, both users and application developers benefit. Users gets a product that they already know how to use to some extent and application developers have a ready market trained to use their products.

These Macintosh User Interface Standard conventions are just that—conventions. They are almost universally adhered to by the many applications that now run on Macintosh, despite the fact that there is no technical reason why a new application could not change the way scroll arrows or window resizing work, for example. No reason except the tremendously important ones of market pressure and user acceptance of the resulting product. Applications that violate these conventions are generally criticized by reviewers and meet with a great deal of user resistance. Moreover, with the advent of MacApp, designing an application that violates these conventions is actually more work than following them! To violate these conventions in MacApp requires you to specifically add new code to program your own non-standard scroll bars, menus, or whatever. This just doesn't make economic or technical sense for anything but the most unusual application.

Even though much of the Macintosh User Interface Standard is embodied in MacApp and thus need not be redone, there is still a good reason for you to become familiar with the details of the Macintosh user interface conventions. No matter how much MacApp does for you, it cannot provide the features that make your application unique. If your application were an interactive musical composition system like MusicWorks or Concertware, you would have to design and implement the portions of the system that draw the lines and symbols of musical notation. MacApp cannot do that for you. In addition, you have to design and implement the routines that enable the user to interact with these symbols. To do so in a manner consistent with the conventions of the Macintosh User Interface Standard requires that you be familiar with these conventions. As a developer you need a much deeper understanding of this standard than does a Macintosh user. A Macintosh user often has an unconscious appreciation of this standard: when an application adheres to this set of guidelines, it simply feels right; when it violates one of the guidelines, something seems wrong. While this feeling may be strong, it may not be possible for a user to explicitly express what exactly is causing it. The developer's knowledge, on the other hand, must be more conscious. You must be able to express and implement all these small "things," the sum total of which is the Macintosh User Interface Standard.

In addition to the conscious application of these principles that define the Macintosh User Interface Standard, you must also test your final design on a set of real users to ensure that the sum total of the many decisions you have made still has the right feel in users' hands. This final step in fine-tuning an application often reveals small problems that, when corrected, can change a good user interface into an excellent one.

The Basic Concepts of the Macintosh User Interface Standard

The overall concept for the Macintosh user interface is succinctly expressed by stating that the Macintosh is a consistent metaphor for real life—Macintosh folders and documents, for example, act much like real file folders and documents. While this is both accurate and useful, it does not provide a sufficiently detailed conceptual model for most application programmers to work from. Macintosh's User Interface Standard exists to "flesh out" this expression.

The Macintosh User Interface Standard has nine basic concepts that, taken together, comprise everything a developer must understand about Macintosh's user interface. These concepts are:

- Applications, which enable the user to manipulate information.
- Documents, which contain information.
- Views, which present information.
- Commands, which alter the information in specific ways.
- The Finder's desktop metaphor, including icons and desk accessories, which provides a image of what is in Macintosh's memory and is a working environment for the information manipulation carried out on the Macintosh.
- Windows, which divide a portion of the Macintosh screen for the display of a portion of a view.
- Selections, which identify those portions of the information that can be affected by certain subsequent commands.
- Editing conventions, which govern the manner of specifying selections.
- Fonts, which provide a basis for manipulating text appearance.

Notes

In this section, we present an overall introduction to these nine basic concepts. In the rest of this chapter, we present detailed explanations of windows, selections, commands, and the Mac editing conventions.

As is usually the case in such a cohesive unit as the Macintosh User Interface Standard, none of these concepts is independent of each other and, thus, many explanations of these concepts refer to the other ones. For example, on the Macintosh, an application displays a view of the data in a document in a window on the Macintosh screen.

Let's step back now and define these and the other basic concepts starting with the ones that require the shortest explanations. *Applications* are pieces of software written by developers to be executed by users as turnkey programs. On most computers, pieces of software have no visible representation to the user (other than perhaps the name of the software). On the Macintosh, most things have some sort of a concrete representation and applications are no exception. Applications on Macintosh are represented in the Finder by *icons*, which are small, 32 pixel-by-32 pixel graphic objects. Icons are a method of user communication especially well-suited to Macintosh's high-resolution screen and its mouse-pointing device. (This use of icons by Apple for both the Macintosh and the Lisa was strongly influenced by the pioneering work at the Xerox Palo Alto Research Center where the workstation hardware also had a high-resolution screen and a mouse. For an excellent account of this work, see "Designing the Star User Interface," David C. Smith, Charles Irvy, Ralph Kimball, Bill Verplank, and Eric Harslem, *BYTE* (April 1982), pp. 242-282.) Sample application icons are shown in Figure A-1. Most applications have one or more types of *documents* associated with them. Documents contain the information that the application manipulates—either information entered by the user or information that is constant, such as help information or other unchanging information used by the application. Documents are also represented by icons, which are usually similar to the icon of the application that created or uses them. Thus, on the Macintosh, the user never has to worry about mixing up word-processing data with spreadsheets or dictionaries. Each has a distinctive iconic representation, in addition to the fact that opening a document automatically invokes its application. Icons have additional advantages over other methods of communication in that they are language-independent and are used on the Macintosh itself to mark the various ports as well as throughout the system documentation. Figure A-1 also shows some of the document icons associated with each application.

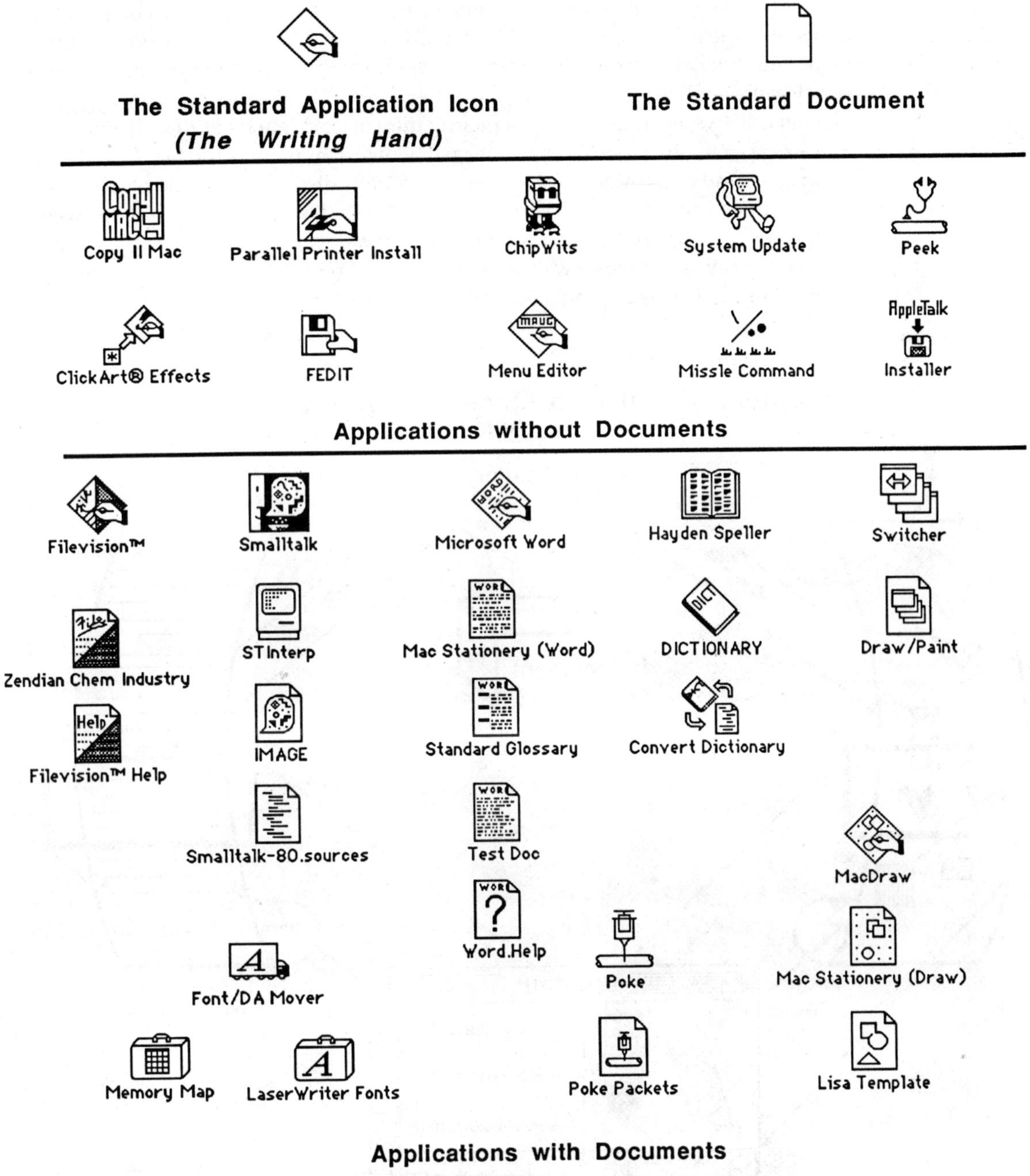

Figure A-1 A potpourri of application and document icons available on Macintosh.

When an application opens one of its documents, it usually constructs a *view* of the information stored in that document. If that information is a table of numbers, for example, then one view of that information might be a spreadsheet-like tabular display. Another view of that same data might be a bar chart. Views are manners of depicting information; each set of data can have several views. In general, a view of a particular document is too big to be shown in its entirety on a Macintosh screen. A *window* displays a portion of a view on a portion of the Macintosh screen. Figure A-2 shows the relationships between the concepts of applications, documents, views, and windows. (We have much more to say about windows later.) Figure A-3 shows these concepts as they are used in the Filevision application.

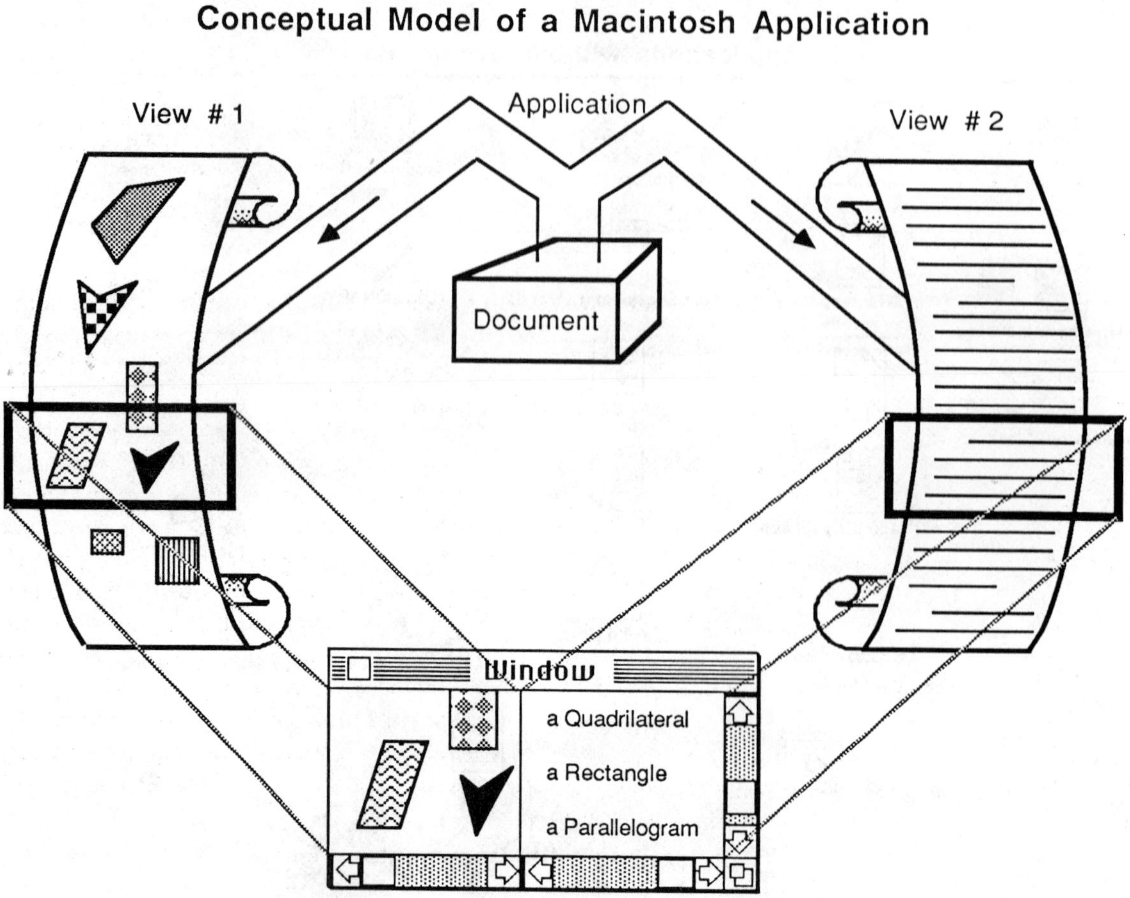

Figure A-2 The interrelationships between the basic concepts that are the foundation of the Macintosh user interface: file, application, view, window, and document.

The relationships between windows and views can be many and varied. A single window can have several different views displayed simultaneously. As you can see in Figure A-4, these views may look at the same data (i.e., the same document) or at different sets of data (different documents). A window may contain only a single view, but it may display different single views at different times depending on what the user is doing. These different views, too, may look at the same data or at different sets of data (Figure A-5). The object-oriented approach to the development of Macintosh software makes each of these potentially complex situations both easy to design and implement.

Notes

If a single window has several views, these views generally look at the same data. If your application requires that the user be presented with several sets of data simultaneously, for example, this is usually done with separate windows. Just about any relationship between windows, views, and documents is possible although some are generally preferred to others in the Macintosh User Interface Standard.

The user sees the concrete representations of applications, documents, views, and windows on the Macintosh *desktop* of the Macintosh Finder. In real life, a physical desktop gives its owner the freedom to position the items needed for the job at hand spatially: the phone is here, the memo is under the stapler, etc. The Finder's electronic desktop provides this same freedom for such items as the applications and documents mentioned earlier as well as the folders that allow users to group other icons in an effort to organize their desktops. Other icons on the desktop include disk icons that represent either removable microdiskettes or fixed hard disks. Like the stapler and hole-punch on a real-life desktop, the Macintosh desktop contains a number of desk accessories such as a calculator, a scrapbook for storing and moving information, and a control panel that enables users to adjust such things as the Macintosh sound levels and desktop background pattern. New desk accessories can be added to the desktop or old ones removed with a special utility program, the font/desk accessory mover. Figure A-6 shows a sample Macintosh desktop. Each of the items can be moved about the desktop easily—even to the extent of being partially off the desktop.

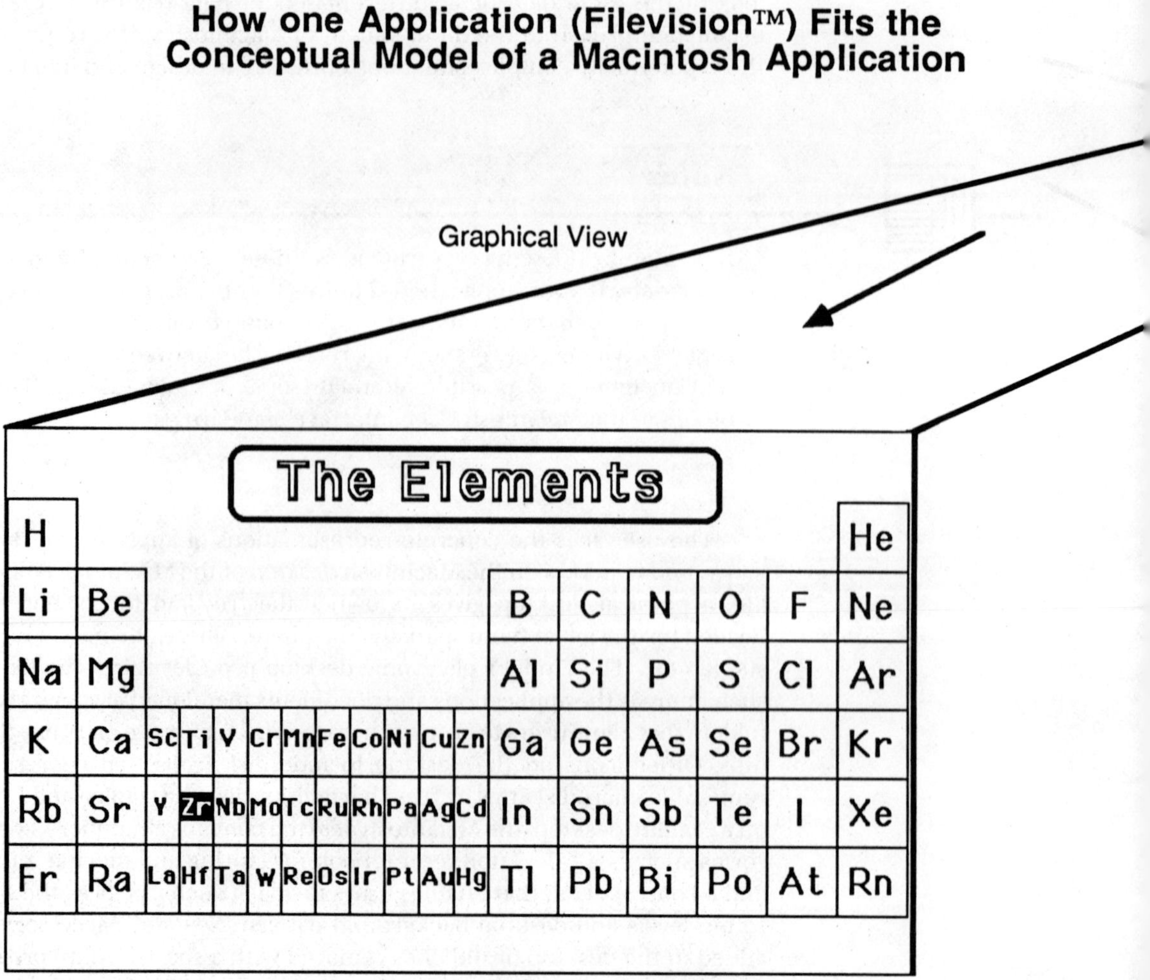

Figure A-3 The realization of the basic concepts of the Macintosh user interface in one application: Filevision. Filevision enables the user to construct a data base that is accessed graphically. In this figure we see the Filevision application icon, a Filevision document, and two Filevision windows depicting that document in two separate views: a graphical view and a tabular view. The ability to have more than one view of a given set of data is fundamental to the Macintosh user interface.

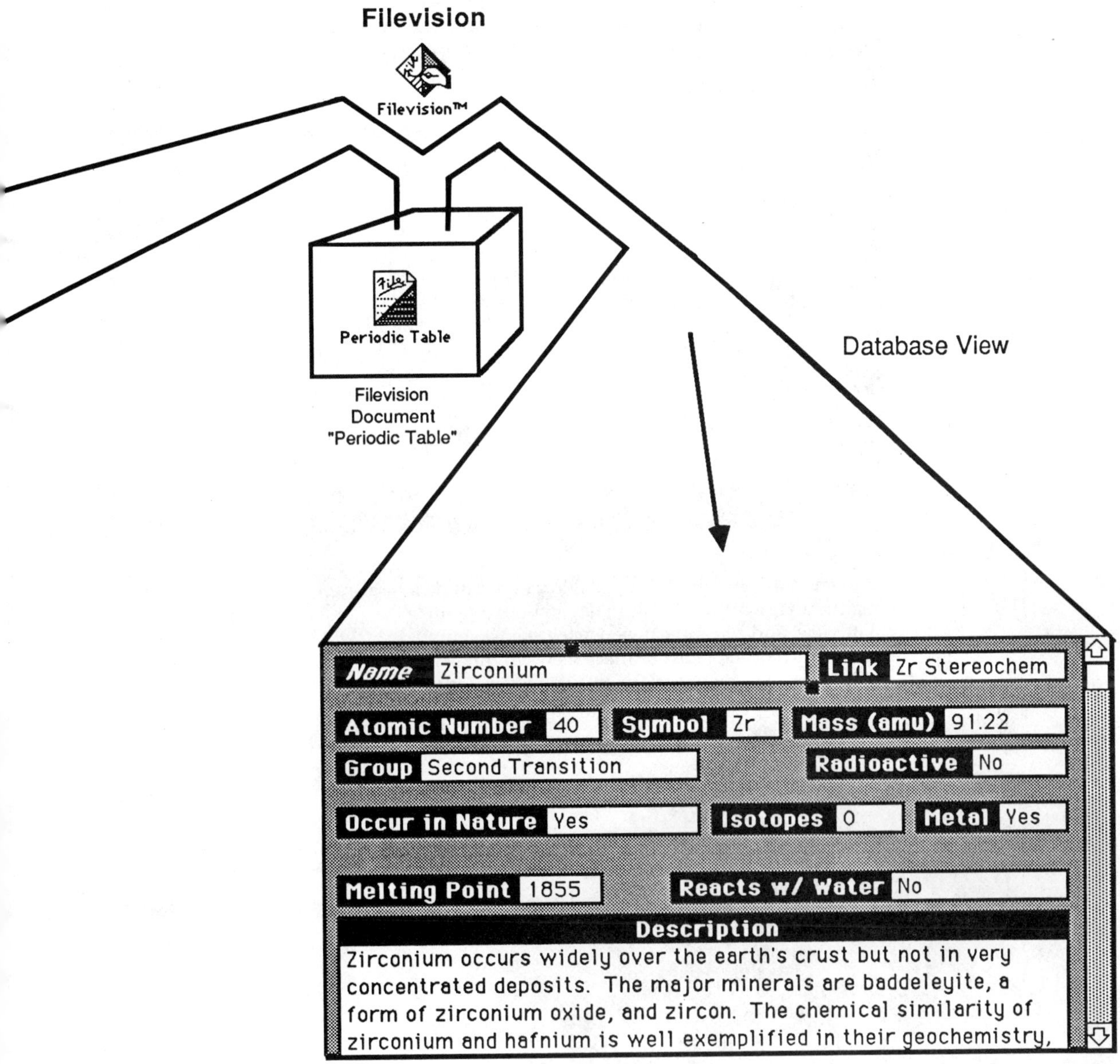
Filevision
Filevision™
Periodic Table
Filevision Document "Periodic Table"
Database View
Name Zirconium
Link Zr Stereochem
Atomic Number 40
Symbol Zr
Mass (amu) 91.22
Group Second Transition
Radioactive No
Occur in Nature Yes
Isotopes 0
Metal Yes
Melting Point 1855
Reacts w/ Water No
Description
Zirconium occurs widely over the earth's crust but not in very concentrated deposits. The major minerals are baddeleyite, a form of zirconium oxide, and zircon. The chemical similarity of zirconium and hafnium is well exemplified in their geochemistry,

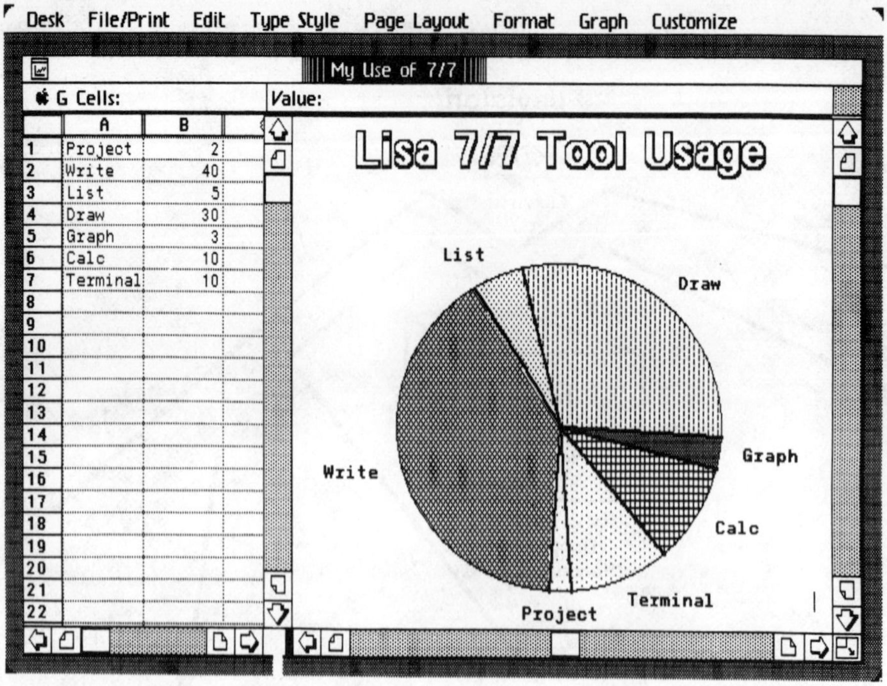

Figure A-4 Multiple simultaneous views. This is a LisaGraph window demonstrating the ability of LisaGraph to depict both a tabular view of a LisaGraph document (left view) and a graphical view (right view) simultaneously. The user can easily set the relative proportions of these views in the window, even to the extent of completely using the window for just one view. Both views are constructed from the same data, and changing that data will immediately affect both views.

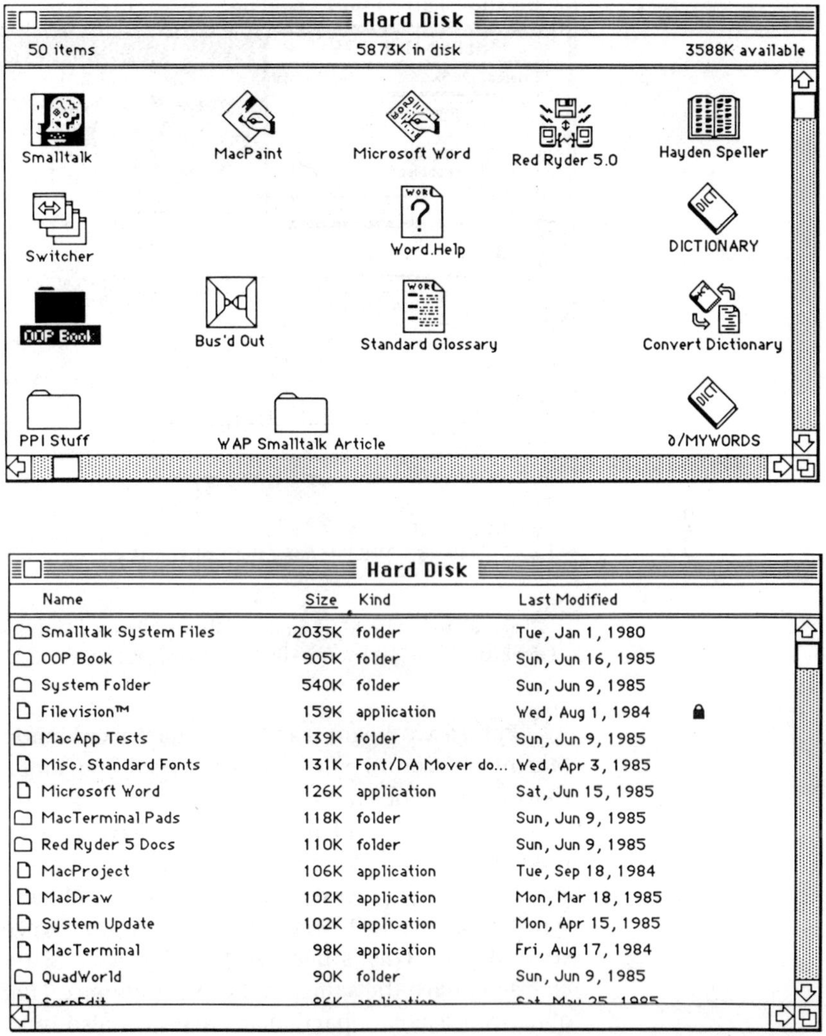

Figure A-5 Multiple sequential views. A Macintosh folder provides several different views of the entities it contains. Only one of these views may be present at a time in any given folder window, however. Here we see the icon view and the size view for the same folder.

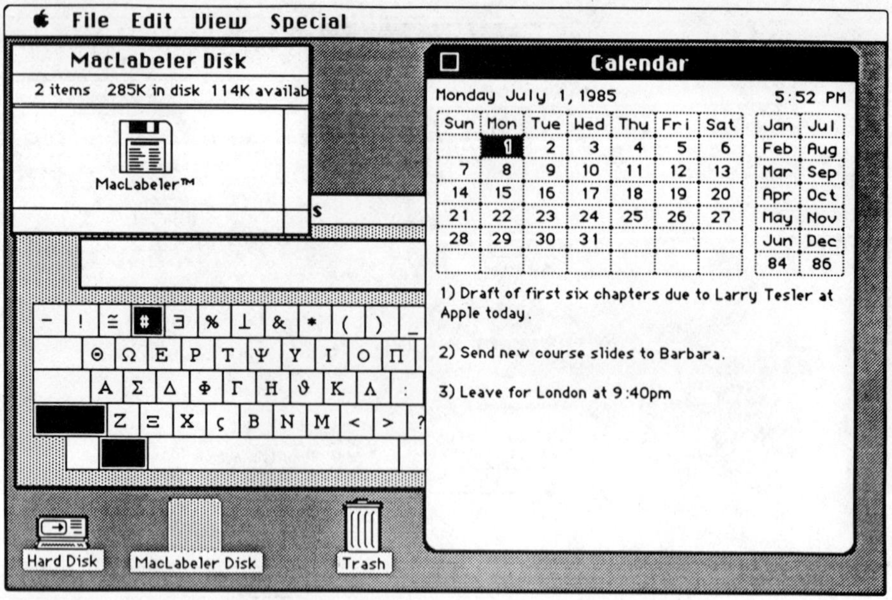

Figure A-6 The Macintosh desktop. This typical desktop shows a variety of the desktop icons and some desk accessories.

Before we begin a more detailed examination of those portions of the Macintosh user interface that are most important to the MacApp programmer, there is one more notion we must explore briefly: fonts.

In the real world, textual material is usually presented in a wide variety of type fonts, styles, and sizes that can add emphasis, enhance readability, or convey a subliminal message. On most personal computers these dimensions of typography are lost because these computers provide only a single size and style of text. This is because the identity and the appearance of individual characters are the same on these computers. That is, the byte value that uniquely represents a particular character also uniquely represents its appearance. On the Macintosh, a single character value may have many appearances. The hexadecimal value 41, for example, may appear on the Macintosh screen as any of the following, among others:

What has been done on the Macintosh is to separate the "A-ness" of the "A" from its appearance. The "A-ness" of the "A" determines its identity, i.e., its hex value; the appearance of the "A" merely shows how it is displayed on the Macintosh screen or how it will appear on Macintosh-produced hardcopy. The Macintosh thus makes available a wide range of typographic flexibility.

On Macintosh, the following typographical terms are important:

- *Font*—This is a collection of shapes for the 256 letters, numbers, punctuation marks, and other special symbols available in the Macintosh character set—a collection that has a coherent "feel" and consistent design. Its typographical attributes contain, among many other things, the presence or absence of serifs, the degree and position of curves, the thickness of the lines making up the shapes, and whether or not adjacent shapes connect. On the Macintosh many fonts are named after cities (for example, Geneva, Chicago, Athens, Cupertino, and Cairo), but this convention is beginning to break down as the number of available fonts increases. The LaserWriter fonts, for example, use such traditional typographical names as Times, Helvetica, and Courier. Remember that on the Macintosh, the font is completely independent of any particular set of text styles, and somewhat independent of its text size. (More on size and style below.)
- *Text size*—This is an indication of the font's height. The measure of text size is called "points." In typography, a point equals 1/72 of an inch and is the standard measure of text size. Points are designated by easy-to-use integral quantities (generally between 3 and 200) and the greater the point value, the larger the size of the text. On the Macintosh, you can use any font in any size, but the quality of the shapes are best when a font has been specifically designed for a particular size. When you attempt to display a text string in a given font at a certain size on the screen or on the ImageWriter printer, the Macintosh Font Manager attempts to retrieve that font in that particular size. If that size is not available, an available size is scaled up or down as appropriate to present the requested size. The results of this scaling transformation, while generally readable, are not of the high quality of a hand-designed font. On the LaserWriter, a more sophisticated technique is used and most fonts look good in most sizes.
- *Text styles*—These are the display attributes on the Macintosh, such as boldface, italics, or hollow, that are added to the appearance of a character shown in a particular font. While some typographical systems require a totally different font to be designed for, say, italic, the Macintosh applies a bitmap transformation to the shapes of any given character in any font to give that character a certain style for each particular style attribute. The fact that these transformations can be applied to any bitmap means that the style attributes are additive, e.g., the bold transformation can be applied to a character after the italic transformation to yield a bold italic style. Because of this, text styles in Pascal are modeled using the **SET** data type, giving rise to statements like the following:

```
currentStyle := oldStyle + [bold, italic];
```

  to add both bold and italic to the current text style. Figure A-7 shows a font sample for the Macintosh and Figure A-8 shows an example of how the Macintosh's font flexibility was implemented to design an easy-to-read game.

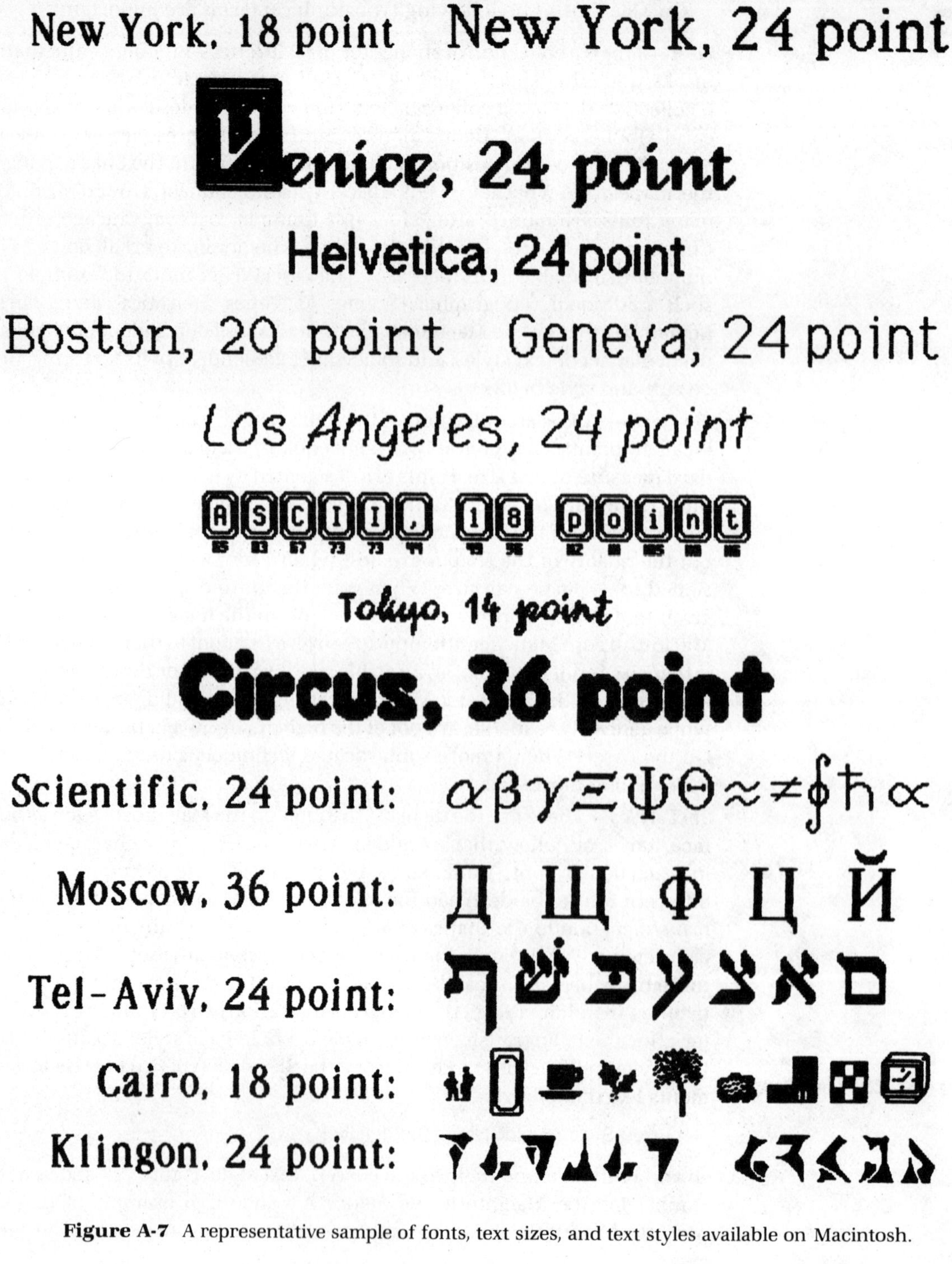

Figure A-7 A representative sample of fonts, text sizes, and text styles available on Macintosh.

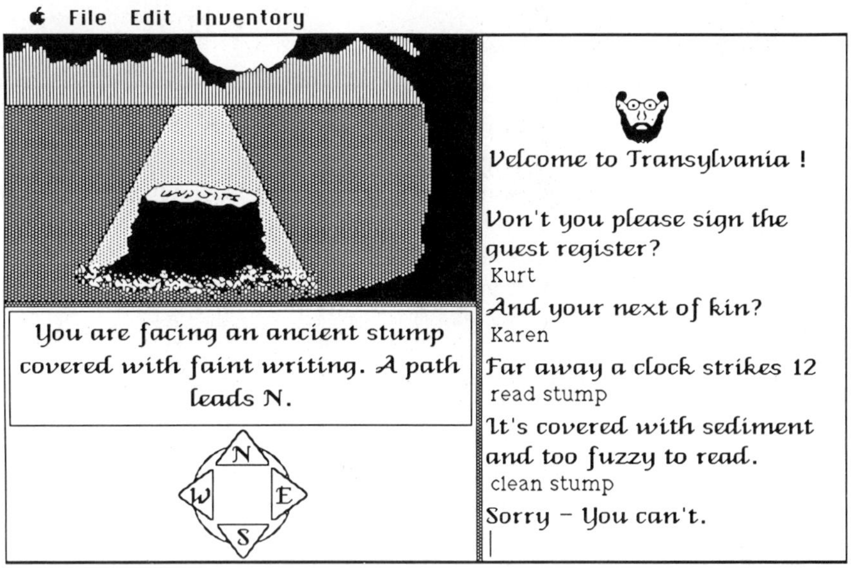

Figure A-8 The game Transylvania is an excellent example of the use of Macintosh's ability to display a wide variety of text fonts and sizes.

Definitions

Unfortunately, there doesn't seem to be universal agreement on the terms used to describe the various attributes of fonts, even within the Macintosh community. What is called a "font" here and in *Inside Macintosh* is called a "typeface" in *Macintosh Revealed.* Author Stephen Chernicoff prefers to reserve the term "font" to refer to a collection of all the character images of a given typeface in a given size. Thus, if the System File contains "New York" in five sizes and "Chicago" in two sizes, Chernicoff would say that it contains seven fonts, whereas others would say it contains only two. Each definition is useful. The slight advantage of our definition is that it deals better with applications such as Microsoft Word that do not restrict users to a small number of text sizes.

Notes

By the way, Robert Hardy, the developer of the Transylvania game shown in Figure A-8, has recorded his thoughts as one of the early Macintosh developers in a delightful article in which he explains the one instance in which he deliberately violated the Macintosh User Interface Standard: "The Adventure Writer's Adventure" by Robert Hardy, *ST. Mac*, Volume 1, Number 5, (June 1984), pp.16-20.

In the following sections, we detail the workings of windows, selections, commands, and the Macintosh editing conventions from the point of view of both the user and the application developer. In all of this discussion, the focus is the eventual use of MacApp, the Expandable Macintosh Application, as the basis for the development of new Macintosh applications.

Windows

A Macintosh window is a portal to a view. This portal is necessary because most views are considerably bigger than the Macintosh screen, and the window limits the portion of the view to be shown on a portion of the screen. An Excel spreadsheet view, for example, has a maximum 256 columns and 16,384 rows, yet the Macintosh screen can display only a very small portion of this, about 6 average-sized columns by 15 rows. It is through the window mechanism that the user chooses which 6-column-by-15-row block will actually be shown on the screen at any one time. The most common types of windows are document windows, desk accessory windows, dialog box windows, and alert box windows. Document windows are the most complex, but all types of windows are discussed in this section.

Document Windows

A Macintosh document window has a great deal of substructure to it. Figure A-9 shows a document window that contains every standard control and feature. Most applications have simpler windows because not all features and controls are appropriate in every application. Starting in the upper left corner and traversing around the window these features are:

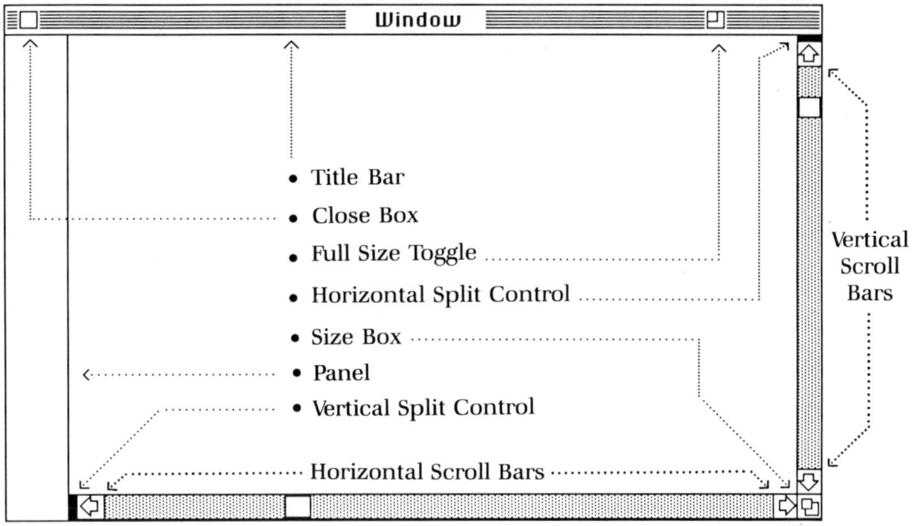

Figure A-9 A generic Macintosh document window with all components labeled. Note that this window has been "artificially" constructed to have every possible feature of a Macintosh window.

- *Close box*—A control that closes the window and removes it from the screen. (The **Close** command in the File menu generally does the same thing as this control. See the discussion of the File menu later in this chapter.) Whether or not the window is actually deallocated when it is closed is an application-dependent decision. The trade-off is the classic memory/speed trade-off: it takes storage to preserve a non-displayed window, yet it can appear on the screen again faster. If the document that this window displays has been changed, activating the close box control usually results in the display of a dialog box asking whether the user wants to save these changes. (See the discussion of dialog boxes later in this chapter.)

Definitions

More precisely, if the application does not provide a menu command or some other way to bring the closed window back (as does the Macintosh Pascal application, for example), and if the document shown in that window has changed since it was last saved, and if no other window displaying that document remains, then the application generally asks the user whether to save changes.

- *Title Bar*—The title bar displays the name of the window and provides for the movement of the window. The text string displayed in the title bar is often the name of the document shown in the view that the window looks on (MacWrite, Word, MacPaint, and MacDraw work this way), although some windows have constant titles, such as the Text, Drawing, Instant, and Observe windows of Macintosh Pascal. When a window with a varying title has no current title, it displays "Untitled" in the title position. The title bar also enables the user to reposition the window on the screen.
- *Full Size Toggle*—This control allows the user to enlarge the window to fill the screen or to reduce it back to its original size. This control was not present in early Macintosh software, so each application provided this function in its own way or not at all.
- *Horizontal Split Bar*—This is a control that enables the user to divide the window horizontally so that each portion, called a *pane*, can look at a different area of the view. Note that this control does not usually divide the window so that it looks on different views, but rather different parts of the same view, as, for example, the first and the last pages of a long textual document. Note that this control can sometimes be used several times to divide the window into many panes.
- *Vertical Scroll Bar*—This control enables the user to scroll the window over the view—either smoothly in small chunks, in full window-size chunks, or by very large amounts. The amount of scrolling is determined by which portion of the scroll bar is used. The arrows move the window a very small amount; the rest of the scroll bar moves in window-full sized components; and the scroll box itself scrolls a larger amount. The upper arrow, for example, scrolls the window up on the view (or, equivalently, scrolls the view down through the window), thus bringing a new section of the view into the upper portion of the window. Exactly how much the window scrolls depends on the individual application, but the amount is usually the smallest amount that makes sense—for example, one line of text in a text processing application, one row in a spreadsheet, or an inch or so in a graphical application. After any such use of the scroll bar (or any other action that causes scrolling), the scroll box is repositioned to show the relative position of the window on the view.
- *Size Box*—This is a control that enables the user to change the size of the window.
- *Horizontal Scroll Bar*—This is a control identical to the vertical scroll bar but for horizontal scrolling.
- *Vertical Split Control*—This is a control identical to the horizontal split control but for vertically splitting the window into left and right panes.

Note that these controls are independent of one another. Using the vertical scroll bar, for example, doesn't affect either the horizontal position of the window on the view or the horizontal scroll bar; splitting the window into two horizontal panes doesn't affect the horizontal scroll bar; moving the window around the screen (using the title bar) doesn't affect the scroll bars. Thus, with the single exception of the close box, which causes the window together with all of its controls to disappear, none of these controls has any effect on the others.

Applications may have more than one window on the Macintosh screen simultaneously. (Figure A-10 shows a sample screen from Macintosh Pascal with several windows open at once.) When this is the case, only one of these windows is actually active at a time. The active window is distinguished by its gray scroll bars, its dark title bar, and by being in front of all other windows. The active window is the only window in which the user can make a selection, edit, or perform any other activity. In the case of several activities that seem to run simultaneously, the program in control of the active window receives all commands and data entered by the user. An inactive window can become the active window (thereby deactivating the currently active window, if one exists) in one of three ways:

- Newly created windows are usually made the active window.
- When the user clicks the mouse button while the cursor is inside an inactive window, that window becomes the active window.
- The application may provide a menu command to activate an inactive (or even invisible) window.

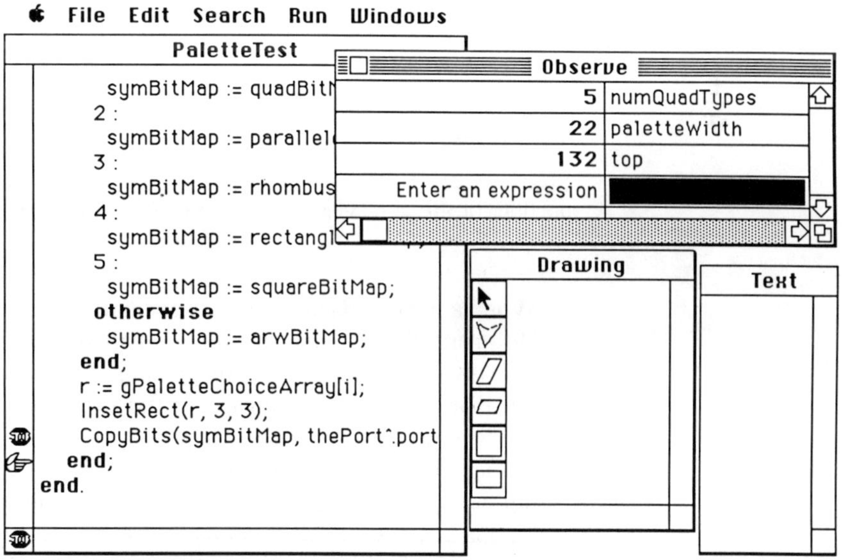

Figure A-10 Multiple windows from Macintosh Pascal.

Panels, Panes, Views, and Windows—The Interrelationships

While panes provide a way for a single window to display disjointed portions of a single view—as, for example, in a word processing program like Microsoft Word, which enables the user to view and edit both the beginning and the end of a textual document (Figure A-11) there are also other mechanisms that provide the user with the ability to see two or more things at once in a single window. Remember that the basic motivation of panes is to display disjointed portions of the same view.

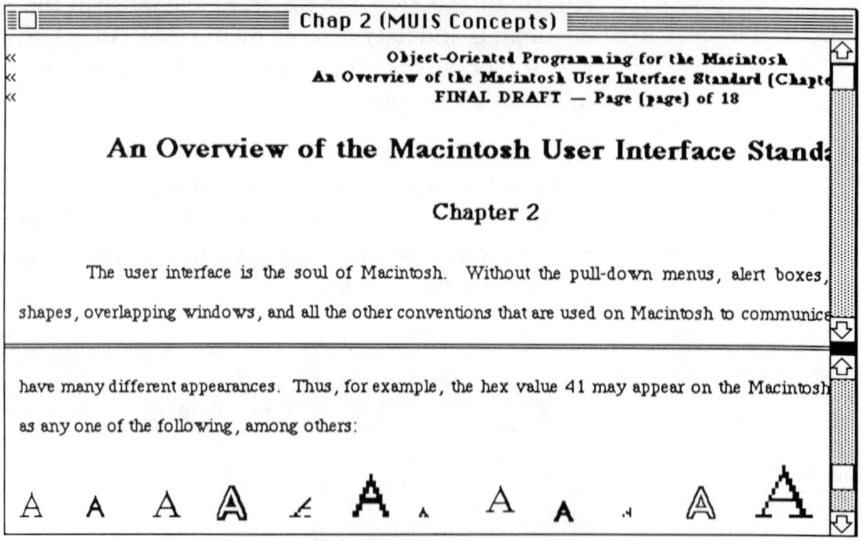

Figure A-11 Panes provide for a single window to "look on" two or more different portions of the same view, as is done here in MicroSoft Word.

When a window is more or less permanently divided into regions that display different views, these regions are called *panels*. For example, a window might be divided into one panel displaying a graphical view of a document and another displaying a tabular view of the same data (Figure A-12). Panels and panes look superficially similar. They both behave like subwindows in that they usually have both horizontal and vertical scroll bars. However, in addition to the number of views displayed, there is another difference between panes and panels: it is possible to scroll panes so that they show the same portion of the view, thus showing two images of the same piece of data on the screen at one time, something panels cannot do (Figure A-13).

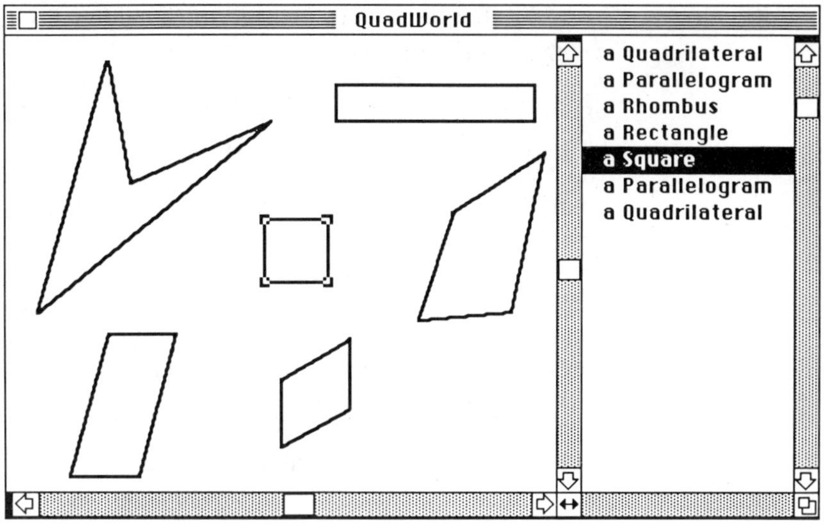

Figure A-12 A window with two panels. Panels provide for a single window to "look on" two or more different views.

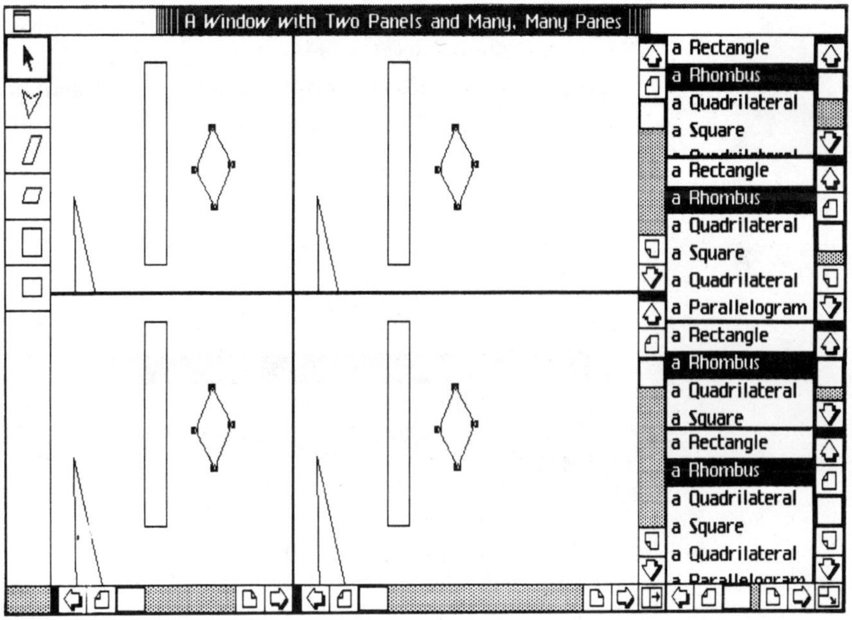

Figure A-13 A single window with two panels—one on the right and one on the left. (A scroll bar separates the two.) Each panel is split into several panes. Note that the user can scroll panes so that the same application entity has many screen images. When the user selects an entity (by clicking the mouse on any one of its images), all the entity's images must be highlighted.

Still another way to provide the functionality of being able to see two things at once is to use multiple windows. Multiple windows can display the same view (either different or the same portions of the view), different views of the same document, or different documents. Deciding whether to use multiple panels in a single window or separate windows in your application is up to you. Multiple panels in the same window are a bit more compact than separate windows, but they must be smaller because there is only a fixed amount of screen "real estate" on the Mac. Separate windows (perhaps displaying different views or different documents) can each occupy almost the entire screen, with the user toggling between them by making one or the other the active window. The biggest disadvantage of multiple panes or panels in a single window is that all the panes or panels must be moved, opened, or closed as a unit.

MacApp provides a mechanism (called frames) that enables you to easily construct whichever of these many options you believe best fits the needs of your application and its potential end users.

Dialog Windows

Dialog windows, also called dialog boxes, provide a way of obtaining from the user additional information needed to complete a command. Examples are the common Open Which Document? Dialog Box used in most Macintosh applications (Figure A-14), the Printing Dialog Box used by applications that support printing (Figure A-15), and the Search & Replace Dialog Box used by Microsoft Word (Figure A-16). These three examples represent both types of dialog boxes, modal and modeless, and also contain most of the components found on all dialog boxes.

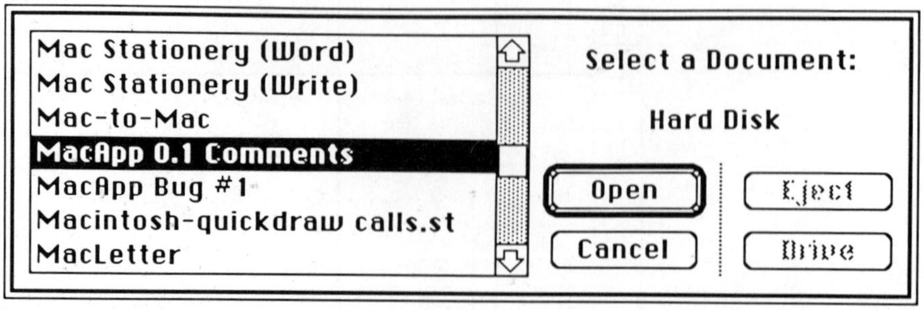

Figure A-14 The Open Which Document? Dialog Box

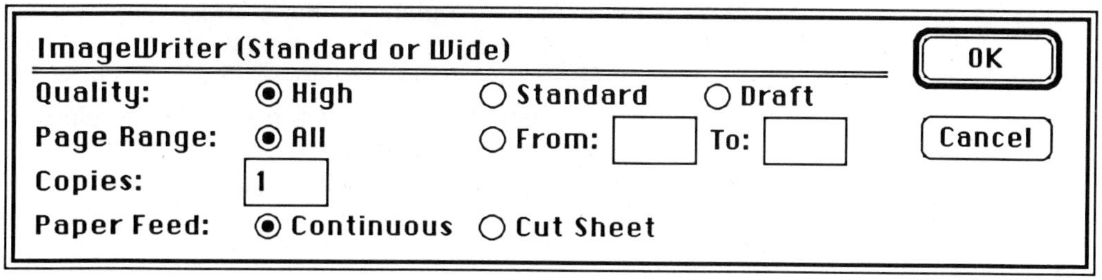

Figure A-15 The Printing Dialog Box

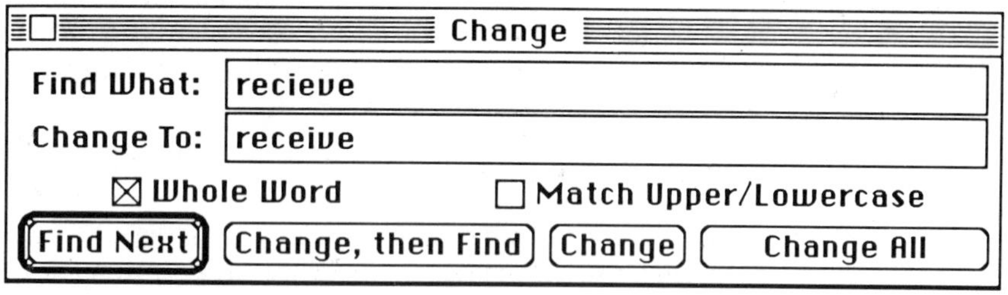

Figure A-16 The Search and Replace Dialog Box from Microsoft Word.

Fundamentally, there are two types of dialog boxes: *modal* dialog boxes, which force the user to dismiss them before taking any action outside the box, and *modeless* dialog boxes, which allow the user to perform operations outside the box while it remains on the screen. Modeless boxes are generally preferred on Macintosh because of the general trend away from modes, although there are cases where a modal box is the only reasonable choice. Modal dialog boxes are generally used for parameters to menu commands, like the Open Which Document? and the Printing Dialog Boxes. It would be impossible for these commands to continue without such information and so the mode is called for. Modeless dialog boxes, on the other hand, usually control an ongoing operation in another window. For example, the Search & Replace Dialog Box is modeless because the operation of interactively searching for a text string and deciding whether to replace it is an operation of long duration that affects the document shown in the main window. A modeless dialog window remains displayed until it is dismissed by the user and the presence of this window does not interfere with the normal operation of other commands.

In comparison with document windows, dialog windows have the following similarities and differences:

Similarities	Both have similar appearances (title bar, close box, etc.). Both "look on" a view. Both can be scrolled over their views, although this is somewhat more rare for dialog windows.
Differences	Dialog windows are generated to obtain the answer to a specific question ("How many copies should be printed?"), then are dismissed. Document windows are more permanent. Dialog windows are often modal (when present, the user has no choice but to deal with them). Many dialog windows cannot be resized, but most document windows can. Most dialog windows have internal controls (buttons, dials, etc.; see below).

Dialog boxes don't usually have the style of title bars and titles associated with Macintosh windows unless they are modeless dialog boxes. This is because the major purpose of a title bar is to enable the end user to move the window about the screen. This function is not needed for modal dialog boxes.

There are four main types of interior controls that can be present in a dialog box: buttons, check boxes, radio buttons, and dials. Examples of each are shown in Figure A-17. Each is best for acquiring certain types of data from the user:

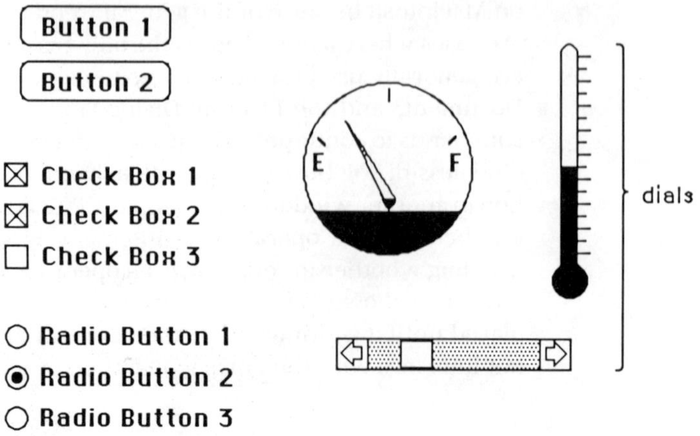

Figure A-17 The major types of controls used in dialogs and alerts on Macintosh.

- *Buttons*—The most common type of dialog box control. They provide for instantaneous execution of a certain option, usually with the resulting dismissal of the dialog box. Because the execution of a button-controlled option is immediate, the user can execute only one such option if the dialog box has a number of buttons. No other controls provide immediate execution, so buttons are often "in control" of the dialog window that is, the user operates the other controls in the window, types some text, corrects it, then changes some controls again. The other controls take no effect until the "Do It" button (often labeled "OK") is pressed and the dialog box disappears.
- *Check boxes*—These are best used to determine the values for a set of independent toggles. The user can turn the toggle on by checking the box or by removing the check. The value of any one check box does not affect the value of any other, and thus in a group of check boxes, one box might be checked, two might be checked, or all might be checked. Setting text styles is a common use of check boxes and Figure A-18 shows the use of check boxes in the character format dialog box from Microsoft Word.
- *Radio buttons*—These, on the other hand, are used to choose from a set of mutually exclusive alternatives. In any group of radio buttons, only one can be on at a time, in the same way that you can only have one button of a car radio pressed at a time. In the character format dialog box shown in Figure A-18, the position of the character with respect to the baseline is set with a group of radio buttons because the character can either be on the baseline or above it or below it, but not both above and below it.
- *Dials*—These controls are used to gather analog data from the user. With the exception of the scroll bar, which is a kind of dial used in some dialog boxes that require the user to choose between a large number of alternatives, dials are the most rarely used control.

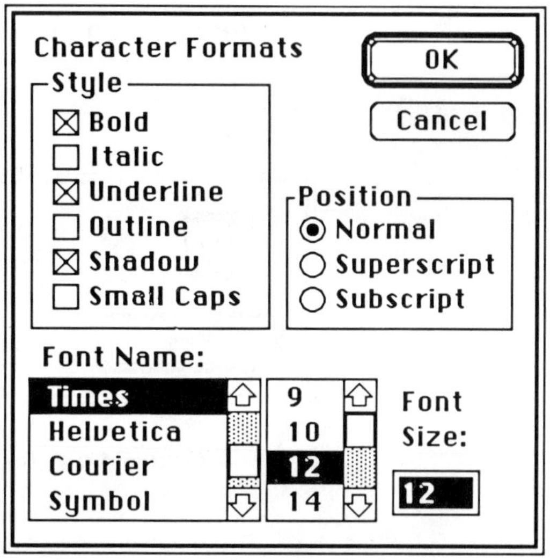

Figure A-18 The Character Formats Dialog Box from Microsoft Word. This dialog box exhibits all of the types of controls that are now used in Macintosh applications.

Notes

Two examples of dialog windows that contain scroll bar controls are the Open Which Document? Dialog Box shown in Figure A-14 and the portion of the character format Dialog Box shown in Figure A-18, in which the font is selected from a (possibly) long selection of fonts.

Alert Windows

Alert windows, also called alert boxes, provide a way to notify the user of some type of unusual situation ("The microdiskette is full.") or error ("You are trying to backspace when there is no text left in a field."). Examples of dialog windows are the common Application Missing Alert from the Finder (Figure A-19), and the Save Changes Alert used by Microsoft Word (Figure A-20). As can be seen in these examples, alert boxes are significantly less complex than dialog boxes.

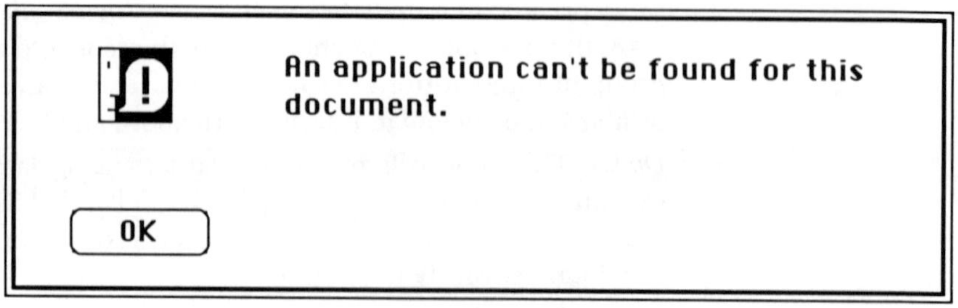

Figure A-19 The Application-Is-Missing Alert

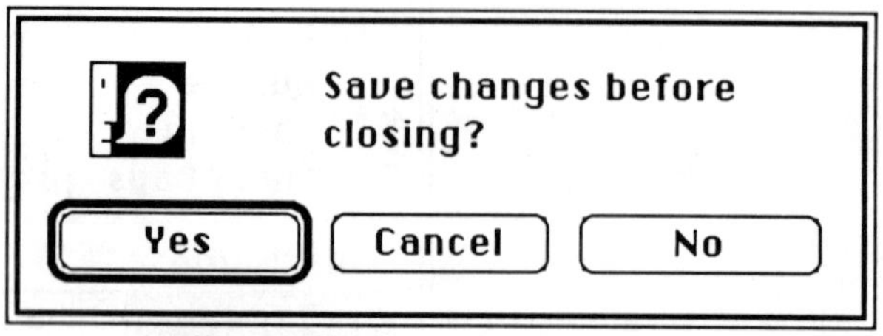

Figure A-20 The Save Changes Alert

In comparison with document windows and dialog boxes, alert windows have the following similarities and differences:

Similarities	Alert boxes are similar to simple, modal dialog boxes in structure. Both alert boxes and dialog boxes often contain icons and other pictures.
Differences	Alert boxes are generated to inform the user of some information or to confirm something; dialog windows are generated to obtain some information the application needs. Alerts are always modal. Alert boxes and dialog boxes are transitory; document windows are more permanent. Alert boxes have only buttons as internal controls. Alert boxes do not "look on" views. Alert boxes are not scrollable.

There are three types of alert boxes: notes, cautions, and stops, which differ according to the severity of the information being presented. Basically, these three different types of alerts are used in the following situations:

Situation	Alert Type	Icon
The error condition or the unusual situation that has occurred is minor and there would be no disastrous consequences if the user ignored it. Example: "That feature is not yet implemented."	NOTE	
The situation that has occurred or has been detected may have undesirable consequences if it is allowed to continue. Example: "Revert to Saved Version."	CAUTION	
Some action by the user is absolutely required because a serious, irrevocable action is about to occur or something is beyond software control. Example: "Search and Replace All," and changing microdiskettes.	STOP	

For some applications it might be appropriate to add another alert that is less serious than even a Note. This alert does not usually result in the display of an alert box, but only a beep to let the user know something mildly unusual has happened, such as trying to backspace past the left boundary of a text field.

Of the two examples above, the Application Missing Alert and the Save Changes Alert are "Stop" and a "Caution," respectively. As another, somewhat far-fetched example, if an application could read the state of a remote AppleTalk device such as the LaserWriter, then the printer being out of paper would rate a "Note" while the printer being on fire would probably rate a "Stop."

Operations on Windows

Windows can be opened, moved about the screen, resized, scrolled about the view, split over the view, and closed, although any individual window may not permit all such operations. Typically, document windows provide for most types of operations, dialog windows for some, and alert windows for none. These operations are invoked by the user in the following ways:

Operation	Invocation
Opening	Menu command or double-clicking on a desktop icon.
Moving	Mouse press anywhere in the title bar except in the close box or the full-size toggle—the outline of a window will then follow the cursor as long as the mouse button is pressed.
Resizing	Mouse press in the resize control—the outline of window's new size will then follow the cursor as long as the mouse button is pressed.
Scrolling	Mouse press in the scroll arrows or scroll box, or mouse click in the scroll elevator.
Splitting	Mouse press in one of the split controls—a full-length or full-width line will follow the cursor as long as the mouse button is pressed.
Closing	Mouse click in the close box or selecting the **Close** menu command.
Full size Enlarge	Mouse click in the full-size toggle—the first such click will enlarge the window to fill the screen, the next click will return the window to its original size.

Use of Windows

There are a multitude of ways in which windows may be used in the design of a user interface that conforms to the Macintosh User Interface Standard and thus a corresponding multitude of decisions for the application programmer. No one set of rules can work for all decisions made by all developers, but here are some of the pros and cons of some of the major issues:

- Multiple windows vs a single, complex window

  Because of the small size of the Mac screen a single, complex window consisting of several panels or panes must, of necessity, have very small pane or panel components. Therefore, multiple windows, each with their own views, are usually preferable. Because multiple windows can overlap and the component panels and panes of a single, complex window can't, each of the multiple windows can occupy all of the screen. In addition, all parts of a single window must be moved, opened, and closed as a unit and thus single windows are not as flexible as multiple windows, which can be dismissed, resized, or opened individually depending on the task at hand. Again, multiple windows are generally to be preferred.
- Splittable vs. non-splittable windows

  Splitting, is very useful for extremely large views, especially ones that have some innate structure, such as a spreadsheet or a text document. In addition, some tasks such as document preparation and spreadsheet modeling often require the user to access disjointed portions of the view simultaneously. Other applications, such as MacPaint, are severely restricted in the size of the view (a single 8" x 10" page, in the case of MacPaint) and wouldn't profit much from the ability to split a window. While splittable windows are not quite as necessary for an application like MacDraw as they are for Word or MacProject, splittable windows are preferred in general.
- Multiple documents open simultaneously?

  Providing the user with ability to open several documents at once and to switch back and forth among them is generally preferred, unless there are unusually heavy storage requirements in memory or on disk when a document is open, as is the case with MacPaint. Opening another window should be accomplished with an **Open** command (see the discussion in the command section of this chapter) and the user should be presented with a dialog box like that shown earlier in Figure A-14 to select the document to open. The documents listed in this dialog box should be all those the application can meaningfully deal with, which may be more than those that the application actually created. For example, Microsoft Word can open documents created with MacWrite as well as text documents created with other applications. The **Open** command should be disabled when the maximum number of documents is already open (see the discussion in the command section of this chapter about disabling commands).

- Allowing more than one window to look on the same document

  The ability to have multiple windows into the same document is a fine feature that can be used as an alternate to splittable windows. Sometimes it is problematical, when there are unusual mechanisms that must be used to guarantee document integrity and/or rapid execution of certain commands—those used in Filevision, for example. An application that did not provide this feature would not be looked on as in violation of the Macintosh User Interface Standard.

- Deallocating the window upon removal from screen vs. keeping it around

  Whether or not the window is deallocated upon closure depends completely upon the probability that the window will be redisplayed and upon the amount of available memory. Because this decision is invisible to the user (except for the fact that the speed of window redisplay may be slightly different) the decision cannot be made on the basis of user interface considerations alone.

Selections

One fundamental principle of the Macintosh User Interface Standard is that users first select the entity (for example, icon, text, a range of spreadsheet cells, a bar in a bar chart) to operated on and then specify the operation to be performed. Specifying of the entity first, and the action second has several advantages over working in the opposite order:

- The set of commands from which the user can pick can reflect the nature of the selection. For example, in a graphics program like MacDraw font and text style commands can be disabled when the current selection is not text. This ability to limit (or extend) the user's command choices depending on the current selection removes many possibilities for error that can occur in more traditional user interfaces.
- It is easy to apply a series of commands to a single entity in the application. For example, in a text editing application, to change a particular section of text to 24 point, bold italic New York, the user need only select the text once before activating each of the various text commands in any order.
- Mouse selection is sometimes rather tricky. For example, when selecting a single line in a complicated MacDraw drawing, or a single letter in a small font in a text editing task. By specifying the operand first, the user can retry or adjust this selection as many times as necessary without the command being executed. If, on the other hand, the command had been specified before the operand, the user would have specified the command **Cut**, then attempted to select the one line that was to be cut. An incorrect selection would have removed the wrong line. While this could be corrected via **Undo**, it just complicates things and adds unnecessary steps. With the operand specified first, the user can adjust the selection as desired, and only when the proper set of entities is choosen would the command be specified.

Selections are typically made directly with the mouse, but selection by command and selection by typing also are possible. (An example of selection by command is the common **Select All** command present on the Edit menus of many applications. An example of selection by typing is the specification of a group of spreadsheet cells by typing their names or coordinate ranges in a special part of the window.) Other manners of specifying selections also may be used, depending upon the needs of the application. When selecting with the mouse, a single click on an application entity suffices to select that entity. Applications may also provide for a special interpretation for double or triple clicking on an entity. This interpretation is application-dependent but is usually guided by the level of structure of the application's documents, as explained below.

Documents have either a user-perceived, natural ordering to the information they contain, in which case they are called *structured documents,* or they have no such ordering, in which case they are *unstructured documents.* Examples of structured documents are text documents (the ordering is the linear order of the characters), forms (the linear order of the fields), and spreadsheets (the two-dimensional order of the cells). Examples of unstructured documents include graphics documents such as those used in either MacDraw or MacPaint. Unstructured documents usually provide for the simultaneous selection of multiple entities—usually by requiring the user to individually specify the entities to be selected in some manner. Structured documents, on the other hand, usually provide only for the simultaneous selection of contiguous portions of the document, as in passages of text or ranges of cells—usually by simply specifying the first and the last items in the selection (Figure A-21). The user often indicates the extension of such a contiguous piece of a structured document by holding down the Shift key during the selection process. It is possible for an application that has structured documents to deal with noncontiguous selections, but this is very rare because of complications with the editing conventions. (See the later section in this chapter describing the editing conventions for structured and unstructured documents.)

Notes

MacDraw documents are actually structured in the sense that they are ordered by the z-value (the depth in the drawing from back to front) of the objects and this is what allows commands like **Bring To Front** and **Send to Back** to work correctly. This ordering, however, is not directly observable by the user and there is no first object in a MacDraw drawing in the same way as there is a first letter in a MacWrite document or a first cell in an Excel spreadsheet. Thus, a MacDraw document is still considered to be unstructured from the point of view of its user interface. Similar remarks about the ordering of bits in a bitmap apply to MacPaint.

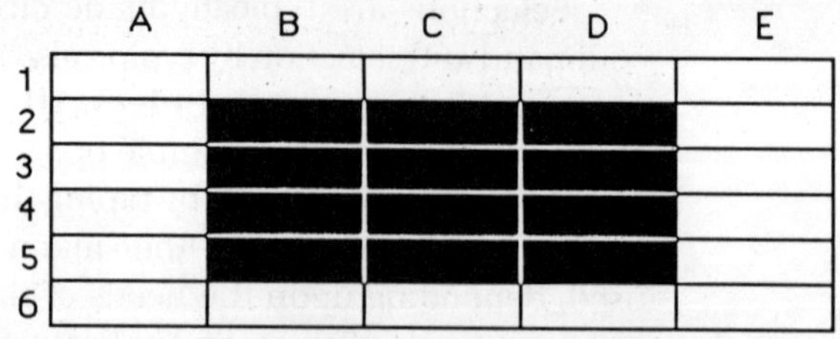

A Contiguous Selection in a tabular application. To specify this selection, the user only had to indicate the upper left cell (B2) and the lower right cell (D5). All cells "between" these two were automatically selected.

Все счастливые семьи похожи друг на друга, каждая несчастливая семья несчастлива по-своему. (Happy families are all alike; every unhappy family is unhappy in its own way.)

Anna Karenina
Leo Tolstoy

A contiguous selection in a text editing application. To select the indicated selection, the user merely had to indicate the first letter (the Russian " л ") and the last letter (the English "k") of the selection.

Figure A-21 Contiguous selections in structured documents.

The ordering of a structured document allows a natural interpretation to multiple clicking—a single click selects a individual entity; a double click selects some larger group of entities, such as a word in a text document; triple clicking selects an even larger grouping, such as a sentence or paragraph in a text document. The exact definition of the levels of grouping depends upon the application but these group definitions should be based on the ordering of the document. To be natural to the user, multiple clicks should select the same kind of entity as a single click, only more so. This naturalness is preserved, for example, when a single click in a text document selects a word, a double click a sentence, and a triple click a paragraph. To continue with the text document example, it would not be consistent with the standard to use single clicks to select text but to use double clicks to select graphics embedded in the same document.

The fact that a selection has been made—and the extent of that selection—should be made known to the user by some sort of direct, visual feedback in the window. Often, this means inverting the entity (as in highlighting text), surrounding it with a flickering outline (as in certain types of MacPaint selections), or adding one or more selection tags to the image of the selection (as in MacDraw). If a given entity can be selected in more than one way (with a correspondingly different set of possible operations), then different highlighting mechanisms should be used to differentiate between these selection styles (Figure A-22).

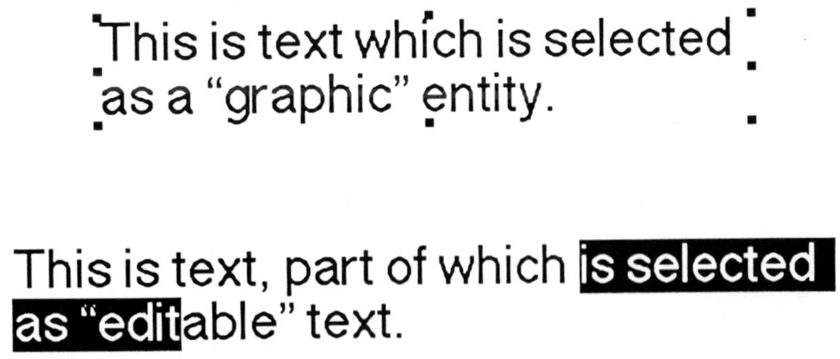

Figure A-22 An application may use different types of selection feedback to denote that the selected entity may be operated on in different ways. The two ways of selecting text in MacDraw (text as a graphic object that may be positioned, rotated, etc.; and text as a character string that may be edited) use different types of highlighting.

Commands

Once the user has selected something, a command to act upon that selection can be activated. Typically, this means choosing a command name from one of the application's pull-down menus at the top of the screen, but commands may also be entered from the keyboard and even implied by certain types of mouse actions.

The Macintosh-style pull-down menus have a number of conventions associated with their format, the order of the menu items, and the naming of the items themselves. Figure A-23 shows a menu that exhibits all of the formatting conventions. While most commands are executed immediately after they are activated, commands that terminate in an ellipsis display a dialog window for the specification of further information before the command is executed. When a command is not appropriate for the current selection, that command should be dimmed to show that it is disabled. Commands that have keyboard equivalents should be labeled with the command symbol, ⌘, followed by their keyboard equivalent. Choosing such a command via the menu or by holding down the command key and typing this character should yield the same result. Commands that are attributes (e.g., **Bold, Plain Text, 24 point**) should be preceded by a check mark if that attribute is currently in force.

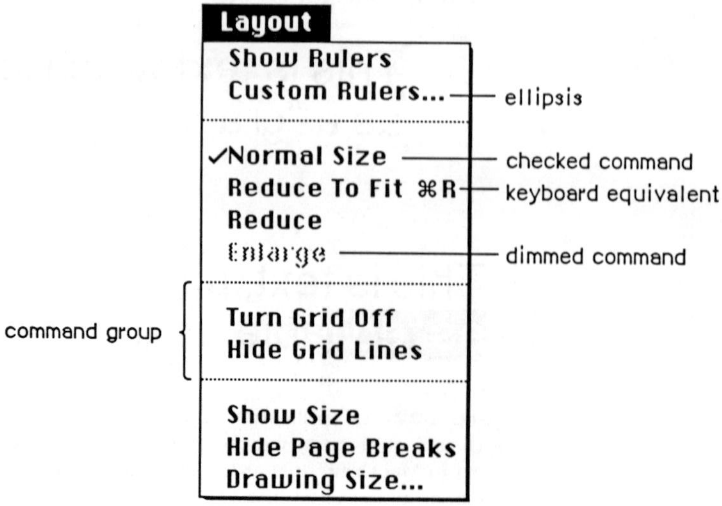

Figure A-23 An annotated Macintosh menu exhibiting all the command formatting conventions.

Commands in a menu can be divided into groups based on several criteria, including logical relationships, mutually exclusive or accumulating attribute command groups, or severity of execution. Groups assist the user to quickly recognize and activate menu items, so long as the groups are relatively small in size (fewer than 10 commands) and not overdone (no menu should have more than six groups). Commands that are logically related (such as all the text style commands) naturally form a group. Commands that are rather drastic (such as **Repaginate** in Microsoft Word, which can take over 10 minutes to execute on a long document like this appendix) are often best isolated in single-command groups, usually at the end of a menu. Commands that control the setting of accumulating attributes often belong in their own separate groups, with check marks showing the attribute or attributes currently in force. Commands that control a pair of mutually exclusive attributes (such as **Show Ruler** and **Hide Ruler**) can alternate in the same position on the menu, so that the mere availability of one of the commands shows that the other attribute is in effect.

Menus can contain text, or graphics, or both. Menus that contain anything more than just text are often called "iconic menus." Iconic menus can be fancy additions to standard menus or they can be very natural ways of presenting commands, especially when those commands are associated with graphic operations such as setting a fill pattern or setting such line style properties as line width or arrowheads. Figure A-24 shows five iconic menus. Note that when an iconic menu is used, the feedback to the user that a particular menu command will be activated if the mouse button is released may need to be changed because the standard inversion used for text menus may not be acceptable. The Fill and Pen menus in MacDraw provide two examples of menus that have custom feedback.

Definitions

Unfortunately, it is next to impossible to adequately portray the custom feedback often used in iconic menus in a static drawing because such feedback typically involves some kind of dynamic flickering of the menu item. Suffice it to say this flickering is not unlike the "marching ants" effect used in MacPaint to indicate the selection of an area of the bitmap.

Standard Menus

One of the most important ways in which the consistency of the Macintosh user interface is enforced across different applications is by the use of six standard menus: , File, Edit, and the font-related menus of Font, Style, and FontSize. It is crucial that the first three of these are also the first three menus of

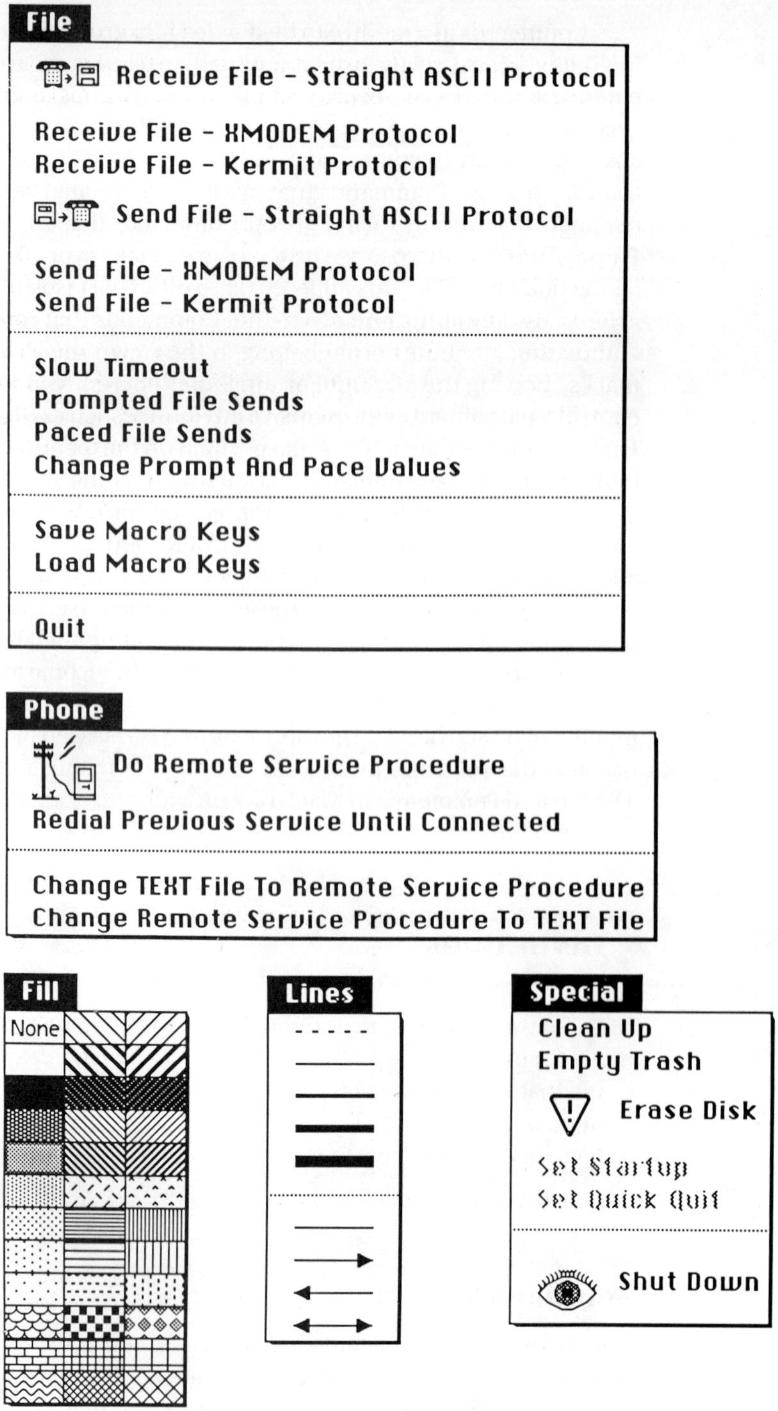

Figure A-24 A collection of iconic menus.

the application if the application is to support desk accessories. The font-related menus can be placed anywhere on the menu bar or the Style and Font-Size menus may even combined into one menu if the application needs space for other menus.

Notes

The Font menu should never be combined with other menus because users of Macintoshes with hard disks may wish to store a large number of fonts in their system folders. In this regard, the maximum length of a Macintosh menu (31 items with the "old" 64K ROMs) may be the most important limiting factor in the number of fonts that can be used at once. This is probably one of the reasons that Microsoft Word put its list of fonts not in a menu, but in the scrolling panel of a dialog box (shown earlier in Figure A-18)—thus, in theory, imposing no limit on the number of fonts that can be used with Word. This is an excellent example of extending the Macintosh User Interface Standard to overcome a current deficiency of the Macintosh: its small screen size.

The Menu The menu (Figure A-25) contains two command groups: a single command (**About**) that informs the user about the current application by displaying an alert box, and a group of commands that activate each of the desk accessories, both the accessories installed in the System Folder and those needed by the application. There seems to be a kind of contest among Macintosh developers for the production of the most spectacular alert box describing the application. Figure A-26 shows some of the better ones.

Notes

Unfortunately, there are some other About Boxes, as they are called, that are truly spectacular but which can't be reproduced here because they are dynamic. Among the best dynamic About Boxes are the ones describing the Click Arts Special Effects MacPaint accessory, the Switcher, and the Pinball Construction Set.

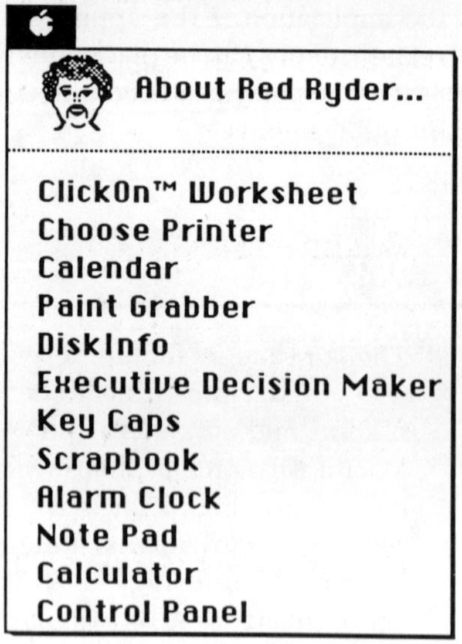

Figure A-25 An menu.

The File Menu The File menu (Figure A-27) enables the user to open documents, save documents to disk, copy documents—in short, perform some filing operations without having to leave the application and return to the Finder. In addition, it provides various commands dealing with printing. Of these two areas, printing is by far the more complex for an application developer because of the wide range of user needs and the differing capabilities of printing devices.

Some applications, such as the adventure game Transylvania, need no printing capability beyond the screen printing provided by using the Command − Shift − 4 keys and these applications may not even have any printing commands (or better yet, they may have the commands on their File menus, but they are permanently disabled). Other applications will want simple printing of just some of their views (e.g., QuadWorld), and still others will have as their primary purpose the production of exactly-as-displayed printed pages. The visual fidelity principle of the Macintosh User Interface Standard (also called *WYSIWYG* for "What You See Is What You Get") states that when a document being prepared for printing is viewed in a window on the screen, what the user sees should be as similar as possible in size and proportion to what the user wants on the printed page. The obvious way to achieve this similarity between screen and printed images is to use the same QuickDraw calls to render both images, which is exactly what is done in MacApp. There are a number of complications to this simple idea, however, including:

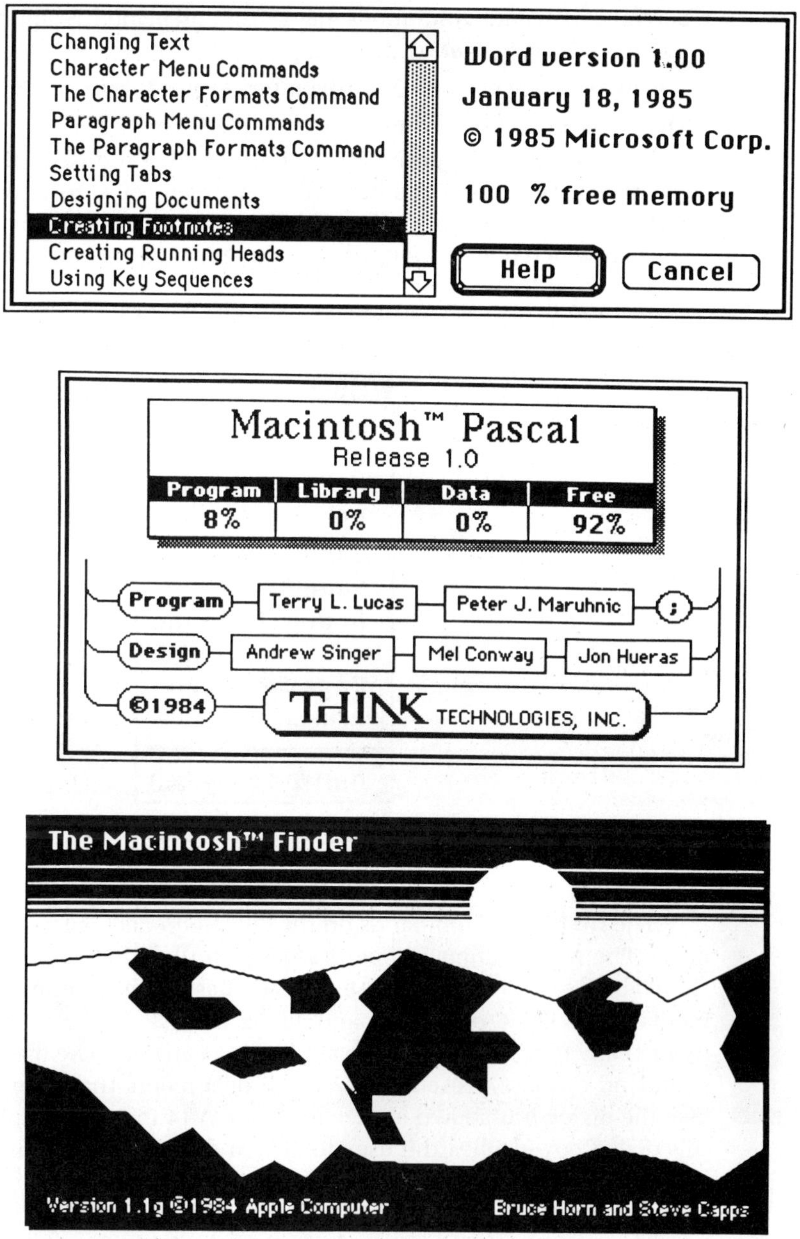

Figure A-26 Some of the better "**About**" alert boxes.

- Screen and printer resolutions may differ and printer resolutions may differ among different printing devices.
- A view typically occupies an area much larger than a single printed page.
- The large number of parameters must be directly controllable by the application or even by the user, e.g., user-specified margins, application-specific constraints (such as not splitting a spreadsheet cell across two pages, either vertically or horizontally), device-specific constraints (such as areas of the page on which one cannot print), page numbers, headers and footers, etc.

MacApp deals with all these issues in its generic support for printing.

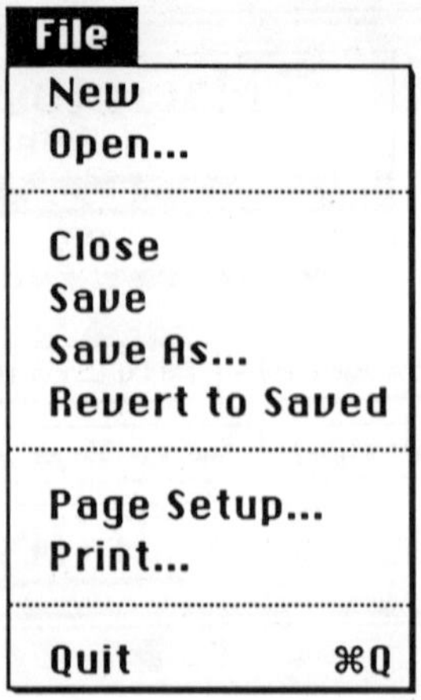

Figure A-27 The File Menu, used by most Macintosh applications.

The first set of commands on the File menu deal with opening new windows. The **New** command opens a new, untitled document. This command should be disabled when the user already has the maximum number of documents open. The **Open** command allows the user to open an existing document of any type with which the application can deal. The dialog box that this command displays presents only those documents that meet this criterion. (See the dialog box shown earlier in Figure A-14 for an example.) In addition, this dialog box enables the user to switch disks or specify an alternate disk drive for the selection of this document. The **Open** command, too, should be disabled when the user already has the maximum number of documents open.

The second set of commands deals with saving the documents shown in existing windows. **Close**, as the name suggests, closes the active window and presents an alert box asking the user if the changes to the document should be saved. **Save** saves any changes to the document in the active window and **Save As** enables the user to save a changed or unchanged document under a different name. **Revert to Saved** cancels the effect of any editing operations done since the document was opened or last saved.

The third set of commands on the File menu deals with printing. **Page Setup** enables the user to specify the printing parameters (paper orientation, paper size, etc.) that will be stored with the document. **Print Draft** prints a rough draft of a document. This command is especially useful if the application's standard printing is slow. **Print Final** (or just **Print** if there is no **Print Draft** command) enables the user to control the print quality, the number of copies to be printed, and sometimes the portion of the document to be printed, then prints the document. **Print One**, if present, prints one copy with the default print parameters.

The last set is the single command **Quit.** Execution of this command results in the display of the Save Document alert box (shown earlier in Figure A-20) if any changes have been made to the document since the last save before quitting the application.

The Edit Menu The Edit Menu (Figure A-28) enables the user to move information into or out of the document displayed in the active window, and by convention also contains the **Undo** and **Show Clipboard** commands. Even if your application does not support all commands of the Edit menu, they must be present for the use of desk accessories.

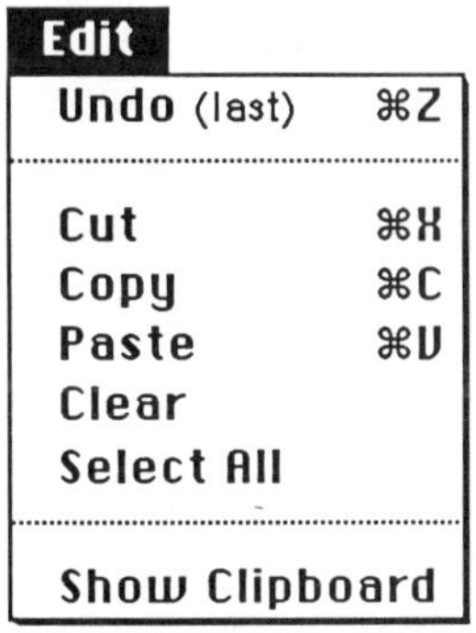

Figure A-28 The Edit Menu, used by most Macintosh applications.

Information is moved between documents via the clipboard. Information selected can be copied to the clipboard with the **Copy** command (replacing whatever was already on the clipboard), removed from the document and placed on the clipboard with the **Cut** command (also replacing whatever was on the clipboard), or copied from the clipboard to the document with the **Paste** command (without affecting whatever was on the clipboard). When the **Clear** command is chosen, the current selection is removed from the document without affecting the contents of the clipboard. The clipboard, which functions like a universal document, can hold data while one application is running or even during the launching of different applications. As such, it is the hub of all information transfers between different applications and between applications and desk accessories. The user can even display the contents of the clipboard in a clipboard window.

Notes

As is seen in detail in Chapter 9, the clipboard often holds more than one form of the same information at the same time. The application can use whatever form it can best process. This is why, for example, that textual material cut from one MacWrite document can be pasted into another MacWrite document, complete with all font and formatting information, but if that same text is pasted into MacTerminal, the font and format information is lost. MacTerminal cannot process the form of the text that has the accompanying font and format information and instead uses a form of that text without the font and format information.

The **Undo** command is usually displayed with some indication of the operation to be undone, as in "**Undo Move Rectangle**" or "**Undo Typing**." If the last operation was **Undo** itself, then the **Undo** command should appear as **Redo**. In the two examples above, this would result in the menu items: "**Redo Move Rectangle**" and "**Redo Typing**." The exact operations that can be undone are usually those that modify the active document (i.e., the user's data) in any way. Because operations such as changing the selection, scrolling the window, and moving the window do not modify the user's data, they are not usually undoable.

The Font Menus In applications that support the manipulation of text appearance, three menus are used to provide the appropriate commands (Figure A-29). The Font menu displays the names of all available fonts, the FontSize menu (also sometimes titled just Size) displays the available text sizes, and the Style menu displays the available text styles. If available at all, the commands of the Style menu are usually unchanging, but the commands of the FontSize menu are sensitive to the currently selected font, with the preferred sizes of that font are shown as outlined text. (Recall that the preferred sizes are those for which a specifically designed font is available. Any other size is mathematically generated.)

Editing Conventions

Editing conventions deal with the manner in which data are inserted into the document when one of the Edit commands is chosen or when certain editing key commands (e.g., backspace) are entered. In addition, the editing conventions deal with the types of possible selections. Because these can differ depending on whether the application deals with structured or unstructured documents, the editing conventions of the Macintosh User Interface Standard

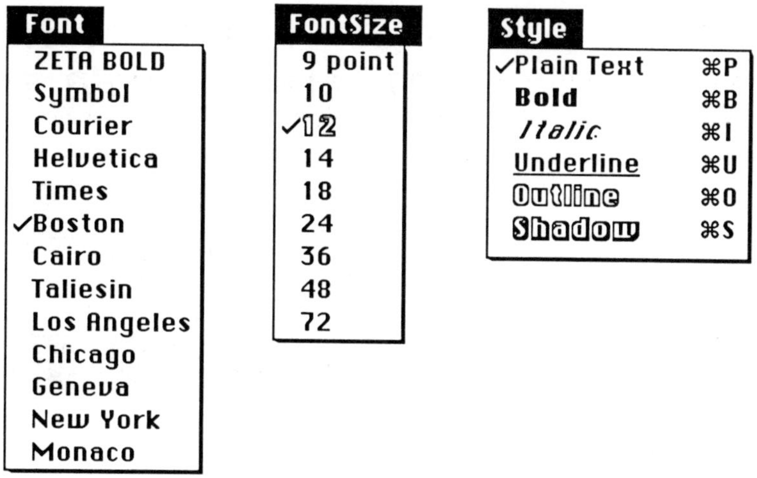

Figure A-29 The font menus, Font, FontSize, and Style, used by most Macintosh applications in some form.

can also differ. Applications with structured documents typically require that selections be contiguous, i.e., that a connected portion of the document is selected. This is because (among other reasons) when data are pasted into a structured document, they replace the current selection. If noncontiguous selections were allowed, there would be no clear cut choice for the position of the newly pasted material in the document. (Figure A-30 shows examples of contiguous and noncontiguous selections in a variety of applications.)

Unstructured documents, on the other hand, routinely allow for the selection of unrelated portions of the document. The standard conventions for the execution of a **Paste** operation in an unstructured document with a current selection is for the pasted material to be added to the document and to become the current selection, without removing the initially selected material.

Definitions

Applications with structured documents may provide the ability for the user to make noncontiguous extended selections. These applications are responsible for dealing with the resulting problems of providing reasonable meanings to the various editing operations. If so, the user indicates the desire to extend the current selection in a noncontiguous way by holding down the Command key during the selection process. (Recall that the Shift key is held down to indicate contiguous extension of the selection.

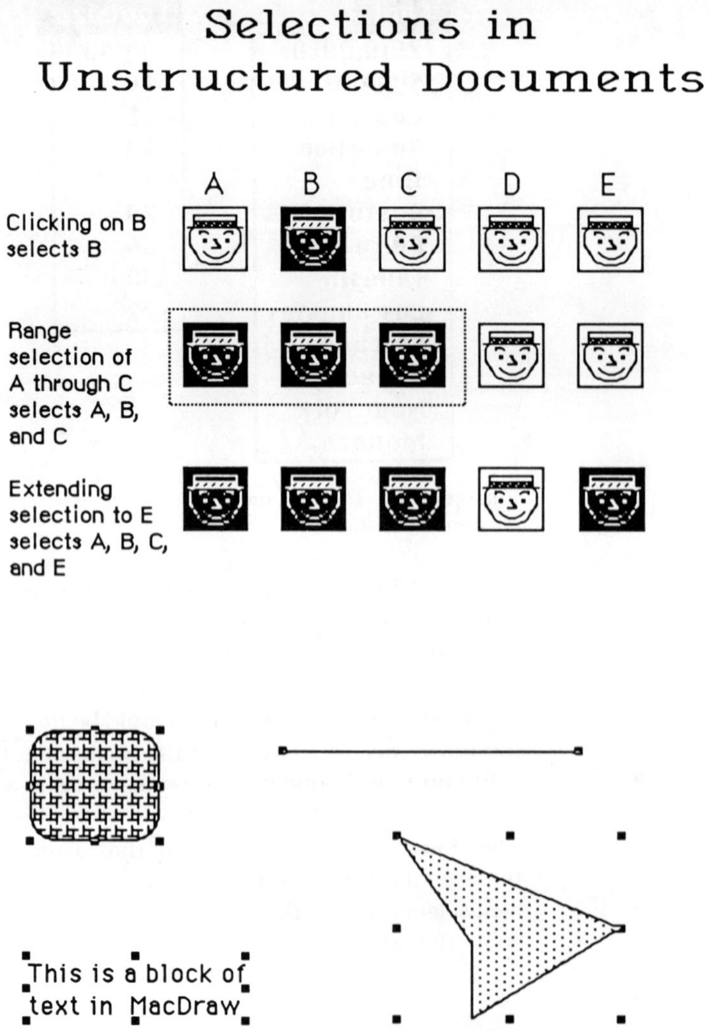

Applications that support selection by multiple clicking must also preserve the additional information available to them through such operations. For example, selecting a word in a text passage by double clicking, then cutting this selection, must also cut one of the delimiters of this word (typically spaces). Pasting this material must result in a "word paste," i.e., the delimiter must also be pasted, not merely the characters of the word. This is typically referred to as an "intelligent cut and paste."

Selections in Structured Applications

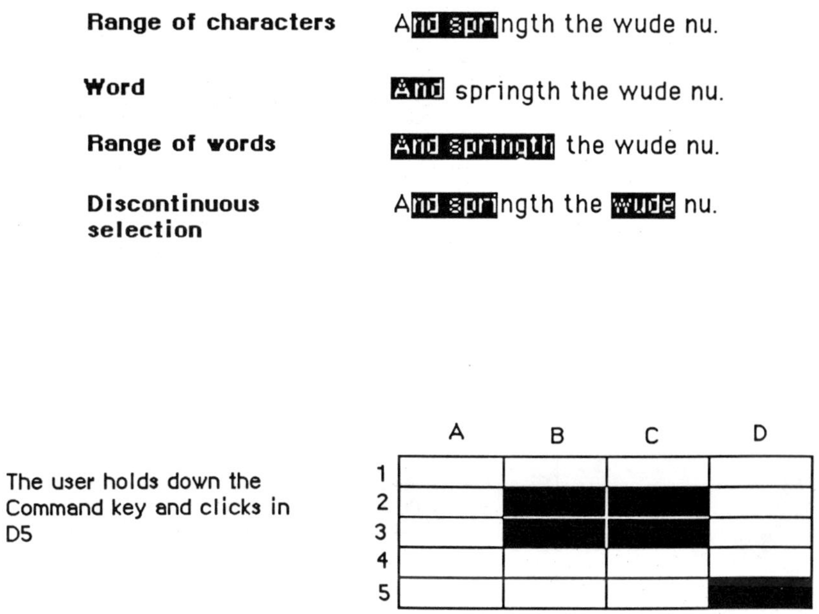

Figure A-30 Examples of contiguous and noncontiguous selections in a variety of applicatons.

Violations of the Macintosh User Interface Standard

So far, we have used many examples from the wealth of Macintosh software to illustrate the correct way to implement the principles of the Macintosh User Interface Standard. It is also possible to use examples to illustrate the wrong way. For example:

Cursor Movement

On the Macintosh, the cursor is controlled by the mouse. As the mouse is moved around a physical desktop, the cursor moves around its electronic desktop. If the mouse button is not pressed, all that happens is that the cursor moves—no other activity takes place. ThinkTank 512 (version 1.100) uses a menu to control positioning of the cursor (Figure A-31). Nothing could be further from the Macintosh User Interface Standard, as such commands are obvious carry-overs from the cursor control keys relied upon by hardware much inferior to the Macintosh. Another violation related to the cursor occurs in Smalltalk-80. Smalltalk-80 activates windows if the cursor merely moves over them, even without the mouse button being pressed.

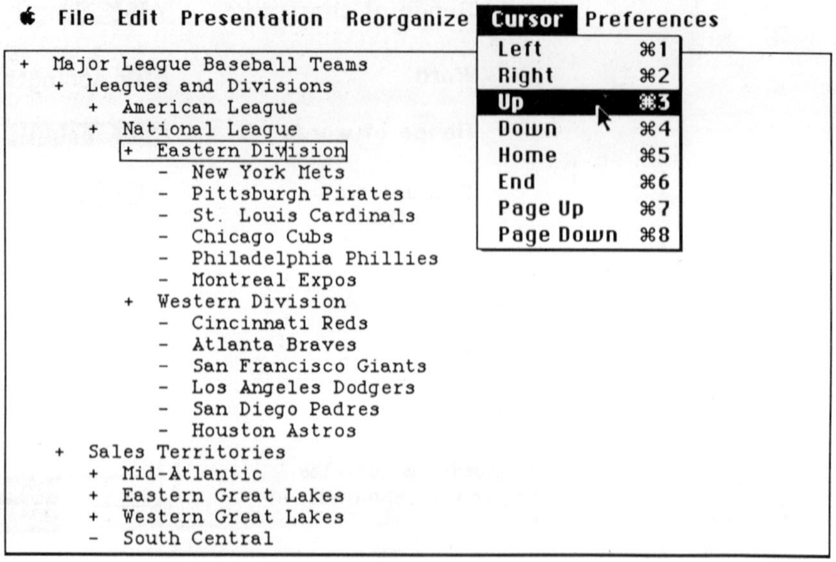

Figure A-31 The ThinkTank 512 cursor control menu—a violation of the Macintosh User Interface Standard.

Notes

Admittedly, it is grossly unfair to criticize this cursor-control model in Smalltalk-80 because Smalltalk doesn't claim to implement the Macintosh User Interface Standard and it is the original source of many of the concepts of the Macintosh User Interface Standard. Consider this Smalltalk window activation method as an example of something you should not do in a new Macintosh application. No such excuse can be made by ThinkTank's creators, however.

Scrolling

MacPaint (version 1.5) provides no window scroll bars, even though its view is considerably larger than the window. Instead, it relies on a "hand" by which the user moves the view. This method is used in several different and inconsistent mechanisms (for example, in Show Page mode) within the application. MacDraw (version 1.7) does not provide for autoscrolling and even gives the user the impression that drawing outside the window is permitted (Figure A-32). ThinkTank 512 does not provide scrolling with scroll bars, but rather with a menu command. Because ThinkTank 512 does not even use a Macintosh-style window, but rather simply blanks out a portion of the screen, the user has no indication of how much of the ThinkTank document is visible or where the portion shown is positioned with respect to the entire document.

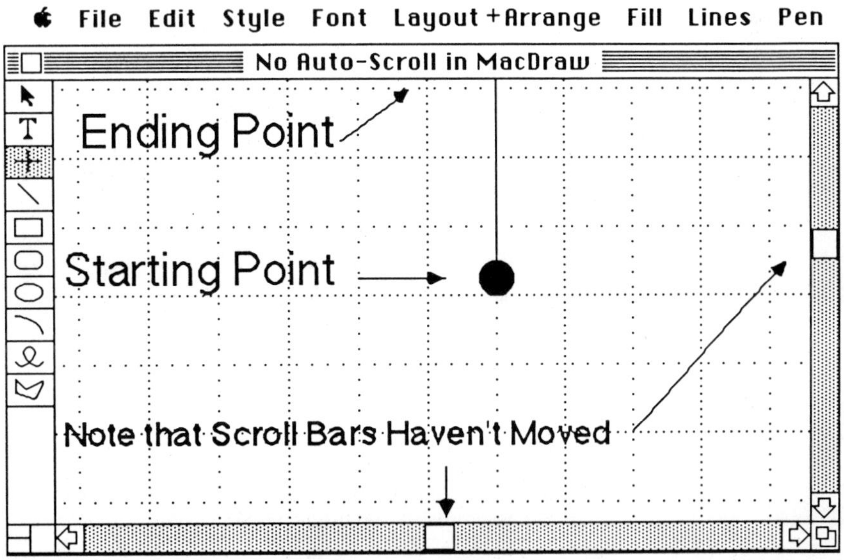

Figure A-32 The lack of auto-scrolling in MacDraw, version 1.7. Note that the user has the impression that drawing outside of the window is possible because the drawing cursor is shown in the menu bar (between the Layout and the Arrange menus). Were a new version of MacDraw to be designed on top of MacApp, this problem would be taken care of automatically.

Fonts

There are many applications that combine the Font menu with one or even two of the other font-related menus. This severely limits the number of fonts available to users of these applications. Figure A-33 shows the Font menu of version 1.7 MacDraw—notice how there is room on this menu for only 11 fonts because the rest of the menu is taken up with FontSize commands.

Figure A-33 The Font menu of version 1.7 MacDraw combines font names with font sizes. Note how this limits the MacDraw user to only 11 fonts. This is in violation of the Macintosh User Interface Standard.

APPENDIX

B

Object-Oriented Language Suppliers and User Groups

This appendix lists the suppliers of the languages discussed in this book and user groups that have a special interest in object-oriented programming.

MacApp, Object Pascal, Object Assembler, Clascal, Lisa Toolkit

Apple Computer
20525 Mariani Avenue
Cupertino, CA 95014

The Smalltalk-80 Programming System for the Macintosh

Apple Computer
20525 Mariani Avenue
Cupertino, CA 95014

Neon

Kriya Systems, Inc.
Six Export Drive
Sterling, VA 22170
(800) 345-7492; (703) 430-8800

ExperCommonLISP

ExperTelligence, Inc.
559 San Ysidro Road
Santa Barbara, CA 93108
(805) 969-7874

Object Logo

Coral Software Corporation
336 Windsor Street
Cambridge, MA 02141
(617) 547-2662

Objective-C

Productivity Products International, Inc.
27 Glen Road
Sandy Hook, CT 06482
(203) 426-1875

MacApp Users Group

Object Oriented Systems Group
Mail Stop 23AX
Apple Computer
20525 Mariana Avenue
Cupertino, CA 95014
(408) 996-1010

Toolkit Users Group

Toolkit Users Group
c/o Dave Redhed
712 35th Avenue
Seattle, WA

Object-Oriented Programming: Systems, Languages, and Applications (OOPSLA)

An Annual Conference devoted to Object-Oriented Programming

OOPSLA-86
Alan Purdy, Conference Chairman (OOPSLA '86)
Servio Logic
15025 S.W. Koll Parkway
Beaverton, OR 97006
(503) 644-4242

LISTING

A

The MacApp Interface

The MacApp class library contains over 500 methods and over two dozen classes. This section lists the interface of those portions of the MacApp class library that are used in this book—the methods most commonly used by the beginning and intermediate MacApp applications programmer. Consult Apple's *MacApp Reference Manual* for the complete listing of all classes and all methods.

This appendix has abbreviated the full MacApp interface in two ways. Certain entire classes, for example, the Apple Talk interface classes, have been completely eliminated. Other classes have had their method lists abbreviated. For example, the class TApplication has over 50 methods, some of which deal with topics like AppleTalk and which are not covered in this book. In this section, only 40 TApplication methods are listed—the ones of most commonly used. Most of the classes listed here have been similarly abbreviated.

One type of data was not abbreviated—the instance variables of the classes listed here. These are complete so that you can see the kinds of data which you may refer to in your applications.

In addition, some of the methods, constants, data types, and global variables listed here are only present in the debugging version of MacApp. These are usually clear from their names, but consult the *MacApp Reference Manual* if you are unsure.

MacApp Classes

The Class TEvtHandler

```
{The TEvtHandler type represents abstract objects that handle certain kinds of events:
        Key events: both key down and auto key events
        menu events: both enabling menus and menu items, and processing menu commands
        Read to/write from Disk
        Idle events: when there are no other events to handle
        Actual events:  EvtHandlers, through their method 'DoHandleEvent', may intercept and handle
                            actual ToolBox events
        Termination: when the application quits

 TEvtHandler are linked into a list with the most specific object (usually a selection) at the head
    of the list.  The global variable 'gTarget' contains the head of the list.  (When a window is
    deactivated, this global variable is cached in the window object, and retrieved when it is
    later activated.)

 For these kinds of events, the target (gTarget) gets the first crack at handling the event.
    The default implementation of the methods of TEvtHandler is to pass the event to the next element of
    the list.}

TEvtHandler = OBJECT (TObject)

    fNextHandler:   TEvtHandler;      {the next element of the list, or NIL}
    fIdlePriority:  INTEGER;          {unless > 0, my DoIdle will NOT be called during Idle}
    fFreeOnClosing: BOOLEAN;          {default is FALSE}

  {Init & Free}
    PROCEDURE TEvtHandler.IEvtHandler(itsNextHandler: TEvtHandler);

  {Termination}
    PROCEDURE TEvtHandler.Terminate;

  {Debugging}
    PROCEDURE TEvtHandler.IdentifySoftware;
    PROCEDURE TEvtHandler.Inspect; OVERRIDE;
    PROCEDURE TEvtHandler.ShowDebugInfo;

  {Events}
    PROCEDURE TEvtHandler.DoIdle(phase: IdlePhase);

    FUNCTION  TEvtHandler.DoHandleEvent(nextEvent: PEventRecord;
                        VAR commandToPerform: TCommand): BOOLEAN;
        {I Handle the event and return TRUE if I want it, else I don't handle it, and return FALSE}


  {Double/Triple Clicks}
    FUNCTION  TEvtHandler.DoMultiClick(lastDownPt, newDownPt: Point): BOOLEAN;
            {Called by TApplication.CountClicks.  Should return TRUE if the 2 points are
                close enough to be considered part of a double/triple click.  (Both points
                are in global coordinates.)  This is only called if the mouse down was
                within the proper time range of the previous mouse up.
             Default is to pass message to the nextEventHandler (if one exists), otherise
                to require that the sum of the x & y distances is <= 5.  }

  {Key Events}
    FUNCTION  TEvtHandler.DoKeyCommand(ch: Char; aKeyCode: INTEGER; VAR info: EventInfo): TCommand;

  {MenuEvents}
    FUNCTION  TEvtHandler.DoMenuCommand(aCmdNumber: CmdNumber): TCommand;
                    {Returns NIL if command does not change the document (also perform the
                        command), otherwise return a TCommand object.}

    PROCEDURE TEvtHandler.DoSetupMenus;

  {Miscellaneous}
    PROCEDURE TEvtHandler.DoRead(aRefNum: INTEGER; forPrinting: BOOLEAN);
    PROCEDURE TEvtHandler.DoWrite(aRefNum: INTEGER);

    END;
```

The Class TApplication

```
(*  The purpose of TApplication is to implement the main event loop that all Macintosh applications
    must have.  There is only one instance of TApplication.
    Your main program should look similar to the following:

            InitToolbox(..., ...);     {essential Toolbox initialization & other one-time initialization}
            NewObject(myApplication);
            myApplication.Run;

  One thing that TApplication does is to interpret the raw events that are posted and convert them
    into higher-level events.  For example, it converts a click in the menu bar into a 'menu event'
    that contains the menu ID/item number that was chosen by the user. *)

TApplication = OBJECT (TEvtHandler)

  {Init & Free}
    PROCEDURE TApplication.IApplication(itsSignature, itsMainFileType: OSType);
              {One-time initialization}

  {Event Loop}
    PROCEDURE TApplication.DispatchEvent(nextEvent: PEventRecord);
        {Called from MainEventLoop for every event; gives cohandlers a crack at the event, and
            if none of them takes it, dispatches the event to DoHandleEvent}

    FUNCTION  TApplication.GetEvent(eventMask: INTEGER; VAR anEvent: EventRecord): BOOLEAN;
                  {The default is to call GetNextEvent; but you can override this if
                      you have an alternate source for events.}

    PROCEDURE TApplication.HandleAlienEvent(nextEvent: PEventRecord; VAR commandToPerform: TCommand);
        {This method is called upon to deal with network events and 'application-specific' events}

    PROCEDURE TApplication.MainEventLoop;

    PROCEDURE TApplication.ObeyEvent(nextEvent: PEventRecord;  VAR commandToPerform: TCommand);
        {When this is called by MacApp, nextEvent is a pointer to
            the global variable gLastEvent.  In special circumstances, you might 'fake'
            an event record and pass a pointer to it.}

    PROCEDURE TApplication.PollEvent;

    PROCEDURE TApplication.Run;
              {HandleFinderRequest, and if not finder printing, call MainEventLoop}

  {Finder Requests}
    FUNCTION  TApplication.CanOpenDocument(itsCmdNumber: CmdNumber; VAR anAppFile: AppFile): BOOLEAN;
              {Simulates the filtering done by Std File; this is only called when
                  opening/printing documents from the finder; when using Std File, Std File
                  does the filtering.}

    PROCEDURE TApplication.HandleFinderRequest;
              {Gets the info from the finder about what files to open/print and opens/prints them.}


  {Opening / Printing Documents}
    FUNCTION  TApplication.ChooseDocument(itsCmdNumber: CmdNumber; VAR anAppFile: AppFile): BOOLEAN;
              {Call this to make a Std File Get call; returns TRUE is user selected a file.}

    FUNCTION  TApplication.DoMakeDocument(itsCmdNumber: CmdNumber): TDocument;
              {Must be overridden.  Based on itsCmdNumber create a document object of the
                  appropriate kind.}

    FUNCTION  TApplication.KindOfDocument(itsCmdNumber: CmdNumber; itsPAppFile: PAppFile): CmdNumber;
              {Given a cmd number and a specification of the file, return the cmd
                  number to pass to DoMakeDocument that indicates the type of document to make;
                  Default is to return itsCmdNumber.  If you have multiple document types,
                  a good convention is to return the cmd numbers assigned to create new
                  documents of each kind.  itsPAppFile will be NIL if we are creating a
                  brand new document, rather than opening an existing document.}

    PROCEDURE TApplication.OpenNew(itsCmdNumber: CmdNumber);
              {Called when application is opened (itsCmdNumber = cFinderNew), or when
                  NEW is chosen from menu.  If you do not want to create a new document
                  when the user opens the application, override this and do nothing if
                  itsCmdNumber = cFinderNew.}
```

```
  PROCEDURE TApplication.OpenOld(itsOpenCmd: CmdNumber; anAppFile: AppFile);
             {Called when opening an existing document from finder (itsCmdNumber = cFinderOpen) or
                 if OPEN is chosen from menu.}

  FUNCTION   TApplication.PrintDocument(anAppFile: AppFile): BOOLEAN;
             {Called to print a document from the finder.  Returns TRUE if
                 the user did not cancel printing of the rest of the documents.}

{Closing / Saving Documents}
  PROCEDURE TApplication.CloseDocument(docToClose: TDocument; VAR succeeded: BOOLEAN);
             {Close a document}


{Termination}
  PROCEDURE TApplication.Close(VAR succeeded: BOOLEAN);
             {Called when the user chooses Quit from the menu, and tries
                 to save all the open documents.  If all succeed the application terminates}

  PROCEDURE TApplication.Terminate; OVERRIDE;
             {gApplication.Terminate is called when the application terminates;
                 this is done when the ExitToShell trap is executed, even if the application
                 calls ExitToShell itself, or the user does ExitToShell from Macsbug.}

{Hierarchy}
  PROCEDURE TApplication.AddDocument(aNewDocument: TDocument);
             {Add another document to my list of documents, and make it the current one}
  PROCEDURE TApplication.DeleteDocument(docToDelete: TDocument);
             {Delete a document from my list of documents, and adjust gDocument and activeFrame if needed}

  PROCEDURE TApplication.ForAllDocumentsDo(PROCEDURE DoToDoc(aDocument: TDocument));
             {Perform the given procedure on all open documents currently owned by the application}


{Idle Events}
  PROCEDURE TApplication.Idle(phase: IdlePhase);


{Cursor}
  PROCEDURE TApplication.TrackCursor;


{Menu Events}
  FUNCTION   TApplication.MenuEvent(menuItem: LONGINT): TCommand;
             {Given a value returned by MenuKey or MenuSelect, figure out the command number
                 that was chosen, have the application create a command object,
                 and return it.}

  PROCEDURE TApplication.SetupTheMenus;
             {Initiates the process of enabling & checking menu items.}

{Opening and Closing Windows}
  PROCEDURE TApplication.CloseWindow(aWindow: TWindow; VAR succeeded: BOOLEAN);

                {Called when user closes a window either with a menu item or with
                    a GoAway box.}

  PROCEDURE TApplication.OpenWindow(aWindow: TWindow);
                {Called to open a window}


{Command Management}
  PROCEDURE TApplication.CommitLastCommand;

  PROCEDURE TApplication.PerformCommand(command: TCommand);
             {This DOES NOT check to see if command is gNoChanges.}


{Double/Triple Clicks}
  FUNCTION   TApplication.CountClicks(aPDownEvent: PEventRecord): INTEGER;
             {This is called from TApplication.ObeyEvent.  aPDownEvent is a pointer to
                 the mouse down event returns the number of clicks this mouse down represents.
             The default implementation uses some global variables declared in the implementation
                 to decide if this event is part of a double or triple click.  If you override
                 this, you will need to maintain your own state information.  You can use the
                 variable gLastUpTime to see when the last mouse up event occurred.}


{Command Handlers}
  FUNCTION   TApplication.DoMenuCommand(aCmdNumber: CmdNumber): TCommand; OVERRIDE;
  PROCEDURE TApplication.DoSetupMenus; OVERRIDE;
```

```
{Switcher Stuff}
  PROCEDURE TApplication.SwitcherEvent(switchingIn: BOOLEAN);

{Clipboard stuff}
  PROCEDURE TApplication.AboutToLoseControl;
      {Called when about to activate a Desk Accessory, switch out in Switcher, or Terminate}

  PROCEDURE TApplication.ClaimClipboard(clipView: TView);

  FUNCTION  TApplication.GetDataToPaste(aDataHandle: Handle; VAR dataType: ResType): OSErr;

  PROCEDURE TApplication.LaunchClipboard;
      {Called at Init time}

  FUNCTION  TApplication.MakeViewForAlienClipboard: TView;

{Debugging}
  PROCEDURE TApplication.IdentifySoftware; OVERRIDE;

  END;
```

The Class TDocument

```
TDocument = OBJECT (TEvtHandler)

    fWindowList:        TList;          {list of windows belonging to this document}
    fDocPrintHandler:   TPrintHandler;  {the object to be told to PRINT or DoSetUpMenus when 'Print',
                                           'Print One', or 'Page Setup...' is selected from the menu
                                           while this is the active document.}

    fChangeCount:       LONGINT;        {master count of changes since last Save}
    fSavePrintInfo:     BOOLEAN;        {if TRUE for a document saved on disk, the 'print info' record
                                            of the fDocPrintHandler will be written out to the data
                                            fork before other writing takes place}
    fSharePrintInfo:    BOOLEAN;        {if TRUE, then all printHandlers associated with views belonging
                                            to the same document will share the same 'print info' record}
    fPrintInfo:         Handle;         {if non-NIL, this is a handle to a 120-byte 'print info' record}

    fTitle:             STRING[63];     {file name}
    fFileType:          OSType;         {file type}
    fVolRefNum:         INTEGER;        {volume refNum}
    fSaveExists:        BOOLEAN;        {whether a disk file representing this document exists}

  {Init & Free}
    PROCEDURE TDocument.IDocument(itsFileType: OSType);
    PROCEDURE TDocument.Free; OVERRIDE;
    PROCEDURE TDocument.FreeData;
    PROCEDURE TDocument.FreeFromClipboard;


  {Opening / Printing Documents}
    PROCEDURE TDocument.DoInitialState;
        {Called for 'New', 'Revert' to blank, Open Tool.
         Default is to do nothing;
         You may need to do further initialization that you would not do in case of an Open...}

    PROCEDURE TDocument.DoMakeWindows;
        {Should take the views created by DoMakeViews and create windows and frames
            to display them.}

    PROCEDURE TDocument.DoMakeViews(forPrinting: BOOLEAN);
        {Create all necessary views for this document (based on forPrinting flag) and
            store into fields of your document.  The document will then be sent either
            DoMakeWindows or Print.}

    PROCEDURE TDocument.DoRead(aRefNum: INTEGER; forPrinting: BOOLEAN); OVERRIDE;
    PROCEDURE TDocument.DoWrite(aRefNum: INTEGER); OVERRIDE;
        {These just read/write the print state if necessary.}

    FUNCTION TDocument.Print(itsCmdNumber: CmdNumber): BOOLEAN;
        {Print the document, and return TRUE unless 'cancel all printing' during Finder Printing was
            requested by user; itsCmdNumber = cFinderPrint will be used if Finder Printing}
```

```
  PROCEDURE TDocument.ReadFromFile(VAR anAppFile: AppFile; forPrinting: BOOLEAN);
      {Called to read an existing file for display or printing.  IF anAppFile.fName = ''
          THEN we read from the file specified in the instance variables instead of the
          parameter, and the parameter will be updated to match the document.}

  PROCEDURE TDocument.ShowWindows;
              {Called when opening the document initially; default is to
                  call OpenWindow for all windows that have fOpenInitially TRUE}


{Closing / Saving Documents}
  PROCEDURE TDocument.Close(VAR succeeded: BOOLEAN; VAR freed: BOOLEAN);
              {Close a document.  succeeded set to TRUE if it succeeded, and freed set to TRUE if
                  as a result of the Close the document object (i.e. SELF) was freed}
          {NOTE: Must never be called for a document related to a view in the Clipboard}

  PROCEDURE TDocument.DoNeedDiskSpace(VAR dataForkBytes, rsrcForkBytes: LONGINT);
              {Bytes required to store SAVE file(s) on disk.  When called, both
                  parameters are set to 0 for you.}

  PROCEDURE TDocument.Save(itsCmdNumber: CmdNumber; onRequest, askForFilename, renameDoc: BOOLEAN);
              {Try to save the document to disk; IF necessary get file name from user; call SaveOnFile
               to actually save the data; change the document name if requested.}


{Revert}
  PROCEDURE TDocument.Revert;
  PROCEDURE TDocument.ShowReverted;
              {Called after Revert to show brand new document; default invalidates whole window}


{Miscellaneous}
  PROCEDURE TDocument.CloseWindow(aWindow: TWindow; VAR succeeded: BOOLEAN);
              {Close a window belonging to the document; set succeeded to TRUE if it succeeds}

  PROCEDURE TDocument.OpenWindow(aWindow: TWindow);

  PROCEDURE TDocument.SetTitle(aTitle: Str255);


{Command Handlers}
  FUNCTION  TDocument.DoMenuCommand(aCmdNumber: CmdNumber): TCommand; OVERRIDE;
  PROCEDURE TDocument.DoSetupMenus; OVERRIDE;


{Hierarchy}
  PROCEDURE TDocument.AddWindow(aWindow: TWindow);
  PROCEDURE TDocument.DeleteWindow(windowToDelete: TWindow);
  PROCEDURE TDocument.ForAllViewsDo(PROCEDURE DoToView(aView: TView));
        {Performs DoToView on every view in every frame of every window belonging to the document}
  PROCEDURE TDocument.ForAllWindowsDo(PROCEDURE DoToWind(aWindow: TWindow));
              {Perform the supplied proc to each window belonging to the document}
  END;
```

The Class TFrame

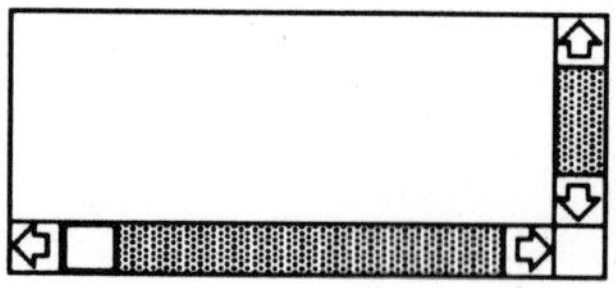

```
{The TFrame type implements the concept of a rectangular area of a window that knows how to
    scroll in each direction.  Frames also are a little like windows in that the can be resized
    and moved, they have a list of fControls that are displayed within them, and they can have
    independent coordinate systems.

 Frames are arranged in a hierarchy; each frame has a container (a TFrame) and contents (a linked
    list of Frames).  a frame's contentRect is defined in the coordinate system of its
    container.}
```

```
TFrame = OBJECT (TEvtHandler)

    fWindow:           TWindow;        {the window that contains this frame (possibly indirectly)}
    fControls:         ControlHandle;  {first of the controls displayed in this frame}
    fContainer:        TFrame;         {the window or frame that contains this frame directly}
    fContentRect:      Rect;           {boundary relative to my fContainer}
    fFrameList:        TList;          {list of frames contained in self}
    fView:             TView;
    fViewedRect:       Rect;           {The subset of the View which is currently visible within
                                           the Frame's fContentRect.  This (at the moment anyway) is
                                           not always guaranteed to be up to date; but in any case,
                                           it is set as a side effect by each call to
                                           TFrame.GetViewedRect, so that if you know that GetViewedRect
                                           has been called since the last time the viewed rect could
                                           have changed, you can confidently use fViewedRect.  The right
                                           thing would be to maintain this field correctly at all times}
    fScrollBars:       ARRAY[VHSelect] OF ControlHandle;
                                       {the scroll bars that control this frame; IMPORTANT: these are
                                           contained in the container of the frame; the refCon's of
                                           these controls is LONGINT(SELF)+1.}
    fScrollUnit:       Point;          {the standard amount to scroll by in each direction}
    fScrollLimit:      Point;          {the maximum view coordinate that can be revealed by scrolling;
                                       ??? may change later to be amount you can scroll past end
                                       of view, if there is a view ???}
    fRelOrigin:        Point;          {what to use in the SetOrigin call, relative to the fContainer's
                                       coordinate system; equals (in each direction):
                                       <scroll position> - <top(left) of fContentRect>}
    fResizeByWindow:   ARRAY[VHSelect] OF BOOLEAN;
                                       {if fResizeByWindow[vhs] if TRUE, then TWindow.ChangedSize
                                           will automatically adjust the botRight.vh[vhs]
                                           coordinate of fContentRect.}
    fShowSBars:        BOOLEAN;        {if TRUE, then the frame is supposed to show its scroll bars
                                           when its window is made active}
    fShowBorder:       BOOLEAN;        {if TRUE call SELF.DrawBorder which by default does a FrameRect
                                           of SELF.fContentRect with a (1, 1) black pen}
    fParentIsWindow:   BOOLEAN;        {TRUE iff my fContainer is a window object ??? Needed ???}
    fInOpenWindow:     BOOLEAN;        {TRUE iff my window is open on the screen}

  {Init & Free}
    PROCEDURE TFrame.IFrame(itsNextHandler: TEvtHandler;
                            itsContainer: TFrame; itsContentRect: Rect;
                            wantHScrollBar, wantVScrollBar: BOOLEAN;
                            wantHResizing, wantVResizing: BOOLEAN);
    PROCEDURE TFrame.Free; OVERRIDE;

  {Activate Events}
    PROCEDURE TFrame.Activate(entering: BOOLEAN);
              {This shows/hides the scroll bars.}
    PROCEDURE TFrame.Close(VAR succeeded: BOOLEAN; VAR freed: BOOLEAN);
              {simply tells subframes to close}
    PROCEDURE TFrame.Open;
              {simply tells subframes to open}



  {Focusing}
       {Focusing means to setup the port for drawing the contents of the frame.  This
           involves setting 'thePort', the origin and clipping of the port, and installing
           the frame's control(s) into the window.
        IMPORTANT: Before calling any control Manager routines, you must focus on the
           frame that contains those fControls, because most control Manager routines draw
           on the screen.}

    PROCEDURE TFrame.Focus;                        {focus on frame}

  {Mouse Events}
       {These are not handled by TEvtHandler because: (1) mouse events need to be handled
           relative to the image displayed in the window, and (2) the user can click anywhere
           in the window; we need to go down the frame hierarchy to figure out where the
           mouse was pressed.}

    FUNCTION  TFrame.TrackAppControl(localPt: Point; aControl: ControlHandle; partCode: INTEGER;
                            VAR info: EventInfo): TCommand;
                    {Assumes localPt is in local coordinates.
                     partCode is the initial part code as returned by FindControl.
                     This handles scrolling frames and calls SELF.DoTrackControl for
                     other fControls.}
```

```
  FUNCTION  TFrame.TrackInContent(localPoint: Point; VAR info: EventInfo): TCommand;
                {Calls SELF.fView.DoMouseCommand to get a tracker (command object), then calls
                    tracker.TrackMouse & tracker.TrackFeedback [in PatXOR mode],
                    while the button is down and returns the final command object.
                    (tracker.TrackConstrain is also called if fConstrainsMouse is TRUE)}

{Miscellaneous}
  PROCEDURE TFrame.AutoScroll(localPoint: Point; VAR deltaScroll: Point);
      {deltaScroll is set to amount to scroll by.}
  PROCEDURE TFrame.ForceRedraw;
      {invalidates entire contents of frame}
  PROCEDURE TFrame.GetViewedRect(VAR viewedRect: Rect);
      {returns, in 'viewedRect', the bounds of the area of the view which is currently projected
       into the frame}
  PROCEDURE TFrame.HaveView(aView: TView);
      {establish the link between the view and the frame}
  PROCEDURE TFrame.InvalAssumingFocused(r: Rect);
      {Same as following, but assumes already focused}
  PROCEDURE TFrame.InvalidRect(r: Rect);
      {This does SELF.Focus; INHERITED InvalRect(newRect), where newRect is
          r INTERSECT clipping region bounding box.  It also assumes that
          r is NOT a VAR parameter.}
  PROCEDURE TFrame.RevealRect(rectToReveal: Rect; minToSee: Point);
      {Undertake scrolling sufficient to reveal at least 'minToSee' worth of the rectangle
       'rectToReveal', which is given in View coordinates}
  END;
```

The Class TWindow

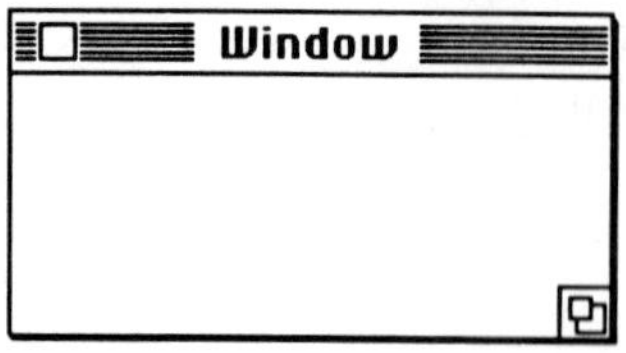


```
TWindow = OBJECT (TFrame)

    fWmgrWindow:     WindowPtr;     {The refCon of fWmgrWindow is ORD(SELF)+1}
    fIsActive:       BOOLEAN;       {is this window active; this may differ from testing if the
                                        fWmgrWindow is the FrontWindow, because of a pending activate
                                        event that hasn't been processed yet.}
    fIsDialog:       BOOLEAN;       {if TRUE, it is a DialogWindow, else it's a plain Window}
    fDocument:       TDocument;     {the document that owns it}

    fIsResizable:    BOOLEAN;       {if TRUE, resize icon will be drawn when active}
    fCanBeClosed:    BOOLEAN;       {if TRUE, menu item 'CLOSE' is enabled for it}
    fDisposeOnFree:  BOOLEAN;       {if TRUE, TWindow.Free calls DisposeWindow,
                                       otherwise it calls CloseWindow; default is FALSE}
    fCanBeActive:    BOOLEAN;       {if FALSE, window will not become the active window; default is TRUE}
    fDoFirstClick:   BOOLEAN;       {if TRUE, a click when this window is inactive will activate
                                        the window AND handle the click normally; default is FALSE}
    fNormalSize:     Rect;          {When the window is expanded to full size, this is set to the
                                        original size.}
    fTarget:         TEvtHandler;   {if this window is inactive, the gtarget to set when made active}
    fLocation:       Point;         {Where the topLeft point of the window should be, in screen
                                        coordinates, when the window is next opened.  This is set
                                        at window creation time to a point which does not conflict
                                        with the locations of existing windows; and is reset at window
                                        close time to the last location of the window's topLeft}

    fWouldCloseDoc:  BOOLEAN;       {If this is TRUE, then when the window is closed by the User, it
                                        will result in its document being closed}

    fOpenInitially:  BOOLEAN;       {If TRUE, then this window, after it has been launched for a doc,
                                        should immediately be launched}
    fPreDocname:     INTEGER;       {start of name of document in window title}
    fConstTitle:     INTEGER;       {# characters in the window title that are constant (ie., not
                                        part of document name}

    {NOTE: the fContainer's coordinate system for a window is global coordinates.}
```

```
{Init & Free}
  PROCEDURE TWindow.IWindow(itsDocument: TDocument; itsWmgrWindow: WindowPtr; isDialog: BOOLEAN;
                            canResize, canClose: BOOLEAN);
  PROCEDURE TWindow.Free; OVERRIDE;


{Hide/Show Windows}
  PROCEDURE TWindow.Close(VAR succeeded: BOOLEAN; VAR freed: BOOLEAN); OVERRIDE;
             {Calls the Toolbox HideWindow routine, and if SELF.fFreeOnClosing calls SELF.Free.}
  PROCEDURE TWindow.Open; OVERRIDE;
             {Resizes the frames as needed, and calls the Toolbox ShowWindow routine.}


{Activation/Deactivation}
  PROCEDURE TWindow.Activate(entering: BOOLEAN); OVERRIDE;
             {This calls SUPERSELF.Activate and if SELF.fIsResizable, draws the
                 grow icon.}

{Menus}
  PROCEDURE TWindow.DoSetupMenus; OVERRIDE;


{Mouse Events}
  FUNCTION  TWindow.DownInContent(globalPt: Point; VAR info: EventInfo): TCommand;
             {This is called when the mouse is pressed in a window.  It calls SELF.FindFrame
                 to find the frame that contains the mouse and calls frame.DoMousePress
                 or frame.TrackAppControl.  It returns the command object returned by those routines.}

  FUNCTION  TWindow.FindFrame(aContainerPt: Point;
                             VAR whichFrame: TFrame; VAR localPt: Point;
                             VAR whichControl: ControlHandle; VAR partCode: INTEGER): INTEGER; OVERRIDE;
             {This converts aContainerPt (which should be in global coordinates) to
                 window coordinates, and calls SUPERSELF.FindFrame.}


{Window Expanding}
  PROCEDURE TWindow.DoExpand;
  PROCEDURE TWindow.FullScreenSize(VAR r: Rect); {returns size of window when fill screen size}
  END;
```

The Class TView

```
TView = OBJECT(TEvtHandler)

    fExtentRect:          Rect;            {the bounds of the view}

    fParent:              TView;           {if non-NIL, will be same as fNextHandler}
    fSibling:             TView;           {next child of my parent, if any}

    fPrintHandler:        TPrintHandler;   {the object which handles printing for the view.  Unless you install
                                               a specific printHandler for the view (Using unit UPrinting),
                                               this field of a view will point to the global 'null'
                                               printhandler, gNullPrintHandler}

    fVisible:             BOOLEAN;         {whether the view is currently 'visible'}

    fCanSelect:           BOOLEAN;         {if true, a mouse-press here will force the deactivate of companion View}

    fHLInactive:          HLState;         {what kind of highlighting to use if window is inactive}
    fHLDesired:           HLState;         {what the highlighting should be at the current time:
                                               either hlOn if the window is active or
                                               fHLInactive if the window is inactive}
    fFrame:               TFrame;          {the frame in which I am seen, if any; will be either that frame's
                                           fView, or else a descendent of it}
    fDocument:            TDocument;       {the document I view}
    fTarget:              TEvtHandler;     {the target to install if the view is activated}
    fRes:                 Point;           {view resolution, spots per inch}
```

```
    fOldScroll:             Point;          {when not in a frame, remember fScrollOffset of last frame here}
    fMinBotRight:           Point;          {the minimum value for bottom-right point of view's extent}
    fViewPerPage:           Point;          {the default amount of view per printed page}

    fSizeDeterminer:        ARRAY[VHSelect] OF SizeDeterminer;
                                            {allows view size to fluctuate automatically according to agreed-upon
                                                rules when frame or page size changes}

    fWrittenToDeskScrap:    BOOLEAN;        {Relevant only for a view installed in the Clipboard; this flag
                                                tells whether the view has written its data to the
                                                Desk Scrap or not}

    fInformBeforeDraw:      BOOLEAN;        {If TRUE, then before the view's Draw is called, its
                                                method "AboutToDraw" is called}

    fShowExtraFeedback:     BOOLEAN;        {Whether any extra feedback will be drawn at Draw time;
                                                may be page breaks, headings, view borders, etc.}

    fShowBorders:           BOOLEAN;        {Whether to draw borders of the view on the screen;
                                                generally useful for debugging views whose sizes
                                                may change}

{Init & Free}
  PROCEDURE TView.IView(itsParent: TView; itsDocument: TDocument; itsExtent: Rect;
      itsHDeterminer, itsVDeterminer: SizeDeterminer; itsCanSelect: BOOLEAN;
      itsHLInactive: HLState);

  PROCEDURE TView.Free; OVERRIDE;

{Size}
  PROCEDURE TView.AdjustExtent;
      {See if view needs resizing, and if it does, do it}

  PROCEDURE TView.CalcMinExtent(VAR minExtent: Rect);
      {Compute the minimal bounds for the view}



{Transition}
  PROCEDURE TView.Activate(entering: BOOLEAN);
      {called when frame activates/deactivates}


{Display}
  PROCEDURE TView.AboutToDraw;
      {If a view wants to defer some action (such as reading in the data it will display from the
          Desk Scrap) until it knows that it is going to be told to Draw itself,
          it can wait for this message before doing it; the method will be called, however,
          only if the view's field fInformBeforeDraw is TRUE}

  PROCEDURE TView.DoHighlightSelection(fromHL, toHL: HLState);
      {Change the highlighting in the view from one state to the other.}

  PROCEDURE TView.Draw(area: Rect);
      {Draws self and descendents; need only actually image those pieces of the view which overlap
       with the rectangle 'area'; drawing more (or everything) takes more time, which may or may
       not matter}

  PROCEDURE TView.InvalAssumingFocused(r: Rect);
      {Same as following, but assumes already focused}

  PROCEDURE TView.InvalRect(r: Rect);
      {Mark the screen area corresponding to rectangle 'r' in the view as invalid, hence forcing
      a redraw at the next update event}



{Mouse Commands}
  FUNCTION  TView.DoMouseCommand(VAR downLocalPoint: Point; VAR info: EventInfo;
                                            VAR hysteresis: Point): TCommand;
              {Called with the coordinate of the mouseDown in local space;
                  usually, you return a TCommand object to do the tracking;
                  default is to return a generic TCommand, which will wait
                  until the mouse button is released, but will give no feedback.
               You can change downLocalPoint if you like, and the new value will be
                  passed to the command object.
               You can also change the hysteresis (which will come is as the global
                  gStdHysteresis).}
```

```
  FUNCTION  TView.WouldTakeClick(downLocalPoint: Point; VAR exclusive: BOOLEAN): BOOLEAN;
              {Returns TRUE if the view would accept a click at the the specified point;
                  Sets 'exclusive' to TRUE if any existing selection in the frame should be
                  deselected first (example:  2 different areas of editable text), and to
                  FALSE if its handling of the mouse can coexist with an existing selection
                  (example: a mouse-down in a checkbox need not deselect a blinking insertion
                  point)}


{Cursor}
  FUNCTION  TView.DoSetCursor(localPoint: Point): BOOLEAN;


{Clipboard}
  FUNCTION  TView.ContainsClipType(aType: ResType): BOOLEAN;
      {This message may be sent to a view which is installed in the Clipboard; the view
          replies by saying whether or not it 'Contains' -- i.e., can generate data for --
          the given Type of data}

  FUNCTION  TView.GivePasteData(aDataHandle: Handle; dataType: ResType): LONGINT;
      {If this view is installed as the view in the Clipboard, it may be sent this message
          which is a request for the supplied Handle to be filled with the clipboard data to be
          pasted.  Positive fn value => number of bytes successfully obtained; Negative
          fn value is an OSErr}

  PROCEDURE TView.FreeFromClipboard;
      {If this view is installed as the view in the Clipboard, it will be sent this message
          when the Undo clipboard needs to be freed; default just frees the View, but a client's
          subclass may also wish to free up other structures, such as a Document which
          perhaps holds the view's data}

  PROCEDURE TView.WriteToDeskScrap;
      {When and if necessary, a View which is installed in the Clipboard may be told to
          externalize the data it displays, by writing it to the Desk Scrap.

        The sequence is:
          The Desk Scrap will be zeroed and then this method will be called to write data to the
          actual Desk Scrap.  Your WriteToDeskScrap will then make one or more calls to
          PutDeskScrapData, to put one or more kinds of 'Scrap' data onto the Desk Scrap; it
          can alternatively call the ToolBox routine PutScrap directly}


{P r i n t i n g}

(* To be able to print a view, you need to provide a PrintHandler object to handle its printing;
   the recommended order of creation is (in your document's DoMakeView method):

        New(myView);                                      {allocate your view}
        myView.IMyView(...);                              {initialize your view}
        New(anXXPrintHandler);                            {allocate the PrintHandler}
        anXXPrintHandler.IXXPrintHandler(myView), ...);   {initialize the PrintHandler}

        Alternatively, the allocation and initialization of the printHandler can be
        done in your IMyView code.

        The PrintHandler's intialization routine will call myView.AttachPrintHandler(itself),
        which you can reimplement to do parts of your initialization which must wait until
        a PrintHandler is attached.
  *)


  FUNCTION  TView.DoMenuCommand(aCmdNumber: CmdNumber): TCommand; OVERRIDE;
      {Enables my fPrintHandler to handle commands}

  PROCEDURE TView.DoSetupMenus; OVERRIDE;
      {tells my PrintHandler to set up its menus}


  END;
```

The Class TPrintHandler

```
TPrintHandler = OBJECT (TEvtHandler)

    fView:                  TView;                       {The view whose printing is handled}
    fPageAreas:             ARRAY[ImageSpace] OF PageAreas; {metrics in view and pad space for printing}
    fDeviceRes:             Point;                       {formal printer resolution, spots per inch}
    fEffectiveDeviceRes:    Point;                       {true effective spots per inch of printer;
                                                            larger than the fDeviceRes if REDUCTION is
                                                            in effect, smaller if ENLARGEMENT is, same
                                                            as fDeviceRes is neither is in effect}

{Initialization and termination}

    PROCEDURE TPrintHandler.IPrintHandler(itsView: TView);
        {Initialize the printHandler, and associate it and 'itsView' with each other}

    END;
```

The Class TCommand

```
TCommand = OBJECT (TObject)

    fCmdNumber:          CmdNumber;      {Can be a many-to-one mapping of fCmdNumber to TCommand}
    fChangedDocument:    TDocument;      {the document changed by this command; defaults to
                                          gDocument global variable}

    fTarget:             TEvtHandler;    {The target tp set before calling UndoIt or RedoIt}
    fCanUndo:            BOOLEAN;        {Defaults to TRUE}
    fCausesChange:       BOOLEAN;        {Defaults to TRUE; Marks document changed when command is done}
    fChangesClipboard:   BOOLEAN;        {Defaults to FALSE.  Set it to true for command subclasses
                                             representing CUT and/ or COPY commands which change
                                             the Clipboard.  The generic TCommand.Commit
                                             calls a command's method WriteToClipboard if
                                             this flag is TRUE}

    fConstrainsMouse:    BOOLEAN;        {Defaults to FALSE; if you set to TRUE then TrackConstrain
                                             will be called to constrain the mouse.}

  {Init & Free}
    PROCEDURE TCommand.ICommand(itsCmdNumber: CmdNumber);

    {command processing - usually overridden}
    PROCEDURE TCommand.Commit;
    PROCEDURE TCommand.DoIt;
    PROCEDURE TCommand.RedoIt;
    PROCEDURE TCommand.UndoIt;

    {Mouse Tracking}
    PROCEDURE TCommand.TrackConstrain(anchorPoint, previousPoint: Point; VAR nextPoint: Point);
              {Override this if you want to constrain the mouse point to
                  a grid, force drawing a square, etc.  This is called only if
                  fConstrainsMouse is TRUE.}

    PROCEDURE TCommand.TrackFeedback(anchorPoint, nextPoint: Point;
                                     turnItOn, mouseDidMove: BOOLEAN);
              {Default is: IF NOT mouseDidMove THEN
                      FrameRect(<rect formed by anchorPoint and nextPoint>).
               Before TFrame.TrackInContent calls this it does a PenNormal
                  and then sets PenMode to PatXOR.}

    FUNCTION  TCommand.TrackMouse(aTrackPhase: TrackPhase;
                  VAR anchorPoint, previousPoint, nextPoint: Point;
                  mouseDidMove: BOOLEAN): TCommand;
              {This does the mouse tracking.

               The default returns SELF.
                  Override it to force gridding, to return a different type of command, or to perform
                  the command on mouse release instead of using the usual DoIt approach.
```

```
            All points are in local coordinates.

            If aTrackPhase = trackPress then all 3 points will be the same.
            If aTrackPhase = trackRelease then nextPoint will be the coordinate
               in the mouseUp event (if a mouseUp event is found), otherwise
               the same point as previousPoint.  Generally, you will ignore
               nextPoint and just look at previousPoint.

            mouseDidMove will be TRUE if aTrackPhase = trackPress or trackRelease;
            otherwise, it will indicate if nextPoint = previousPoint.

            If you change anchorPoint, the new value will be passed to you next time.
            The value of nextPoint at the time the routine exits will be passed to
               you as previousPoint the next time the routine is called.  You can
               change nextPoint if you wish.
            Usually, however, you will do gridding in the TrackConstrain method.}
      END;
```

The Class TDeskScrapView

```
TDeskScrapView = OBJECT (TView)

    fHavePicture:   BOOLEAN;
    fHaveText:      BOOLEAN;

    fDataHandle:    Handle;  {if non-NIL, will be either a PicHandle to my picture or a Handle to my Text}

    PROCEDURE TDeskScrapView.IDeskScrapView;

    PROCEDURE TDeskScrapView.AboutToDraw; OVERRIDE;
    PROCEDURE TDeskScrapView.AdjustExtent; OVERRIDE;
    PROCEDURE TDeskScrapView.Draw(area: Rect); OVERRIDE;

    END;
```

MacApp Constants

```
{M E N U S}

  {Predefined menu IDs; we will read in Menus with resource IDs starting with 1.  We append
   the desk accessories to the mApple menu.}
   mApple         =       1;
   mFile          =       2;
   mEdit          =       3;

   mLastMenu      =       63; {We manage the disabling of menu titles mFile..mLastMenu generically}

{C O M M A N D S}

   {Predefined command numbers}

    cNoCommand      =        0;     {Command number representing no command}

    cAboutApp       =        1;     {About <appname>...}

    cNew            =        8;     {NEW command }
    cNewLast        =        8;
    cSave           =        9;     {SAVE command}
    cQuit           =       10;     {command number for QUIT command}
    cClose          =       11;     {CLOSE command}
    cCloseAll       =       12;     {CLOSE ALL command }
    cGetInfo        =       13;     {GET INFO command }
    cSaveAs         =       14;     {Save as...}
    cSaveCopy       =       15;     {Save a copy in ...}
    cShowClipboard  =       18;     {Show/Hide Clipboard}

    cFinderNew      =       19;
    cFinderPrint    =       20;
    cFinderOpen     =       21;
```

```
    cOpen           =       20;     {Open... command }
    cOpenLast       =       20;
    cRevert         =       27;     {Revert To Previous Version command}

    cPageSetup      =      176;     {Page Setup... command}
    cPrintOne       =      177;     {Print One command}
    cPrint          =      178;     {Print... command}
    cStopPrinting   =      178;     {Stop Printing command, for use during Background Printing}
    cPrintToFile    =      179;     {Print to file... command}

    cPrFileBase     =      176;     {command numbers between these two bounds are sent to a document's}
    cPrFileMax      =      195;     {fDocPrintHandler even if it is not in the target chain}

    cPrintSpoolFile =      190;     {Print spooled file... command}

    cPrViewBase     =      201;     {command numbers in this range are printing commands applied to a}
    cPrViewMax      =      250;     { displayed view which is in the Target chain}

    cAllowBackgroundPrinting
                    =      191;     {Toggle 'Allow Background Printing' switch}

    cCreateClipDoc  =       -1;     {Pseudo-command to TAppplication.DoMakeDocument}

    cShowBorders    =      199;     {show view borders}


{Zooming commands}
    cReduce50       =      301;     {Reduce 50%}
    cReduceToFit    =      302;     {Reduce to Fit}
    cShowFullSize   =      303;     {Show Full Size}

  {For the following command numbers, we must guarantee that
    <command number> - cEditBase = <appropriate number to pass to SystemEdit>.
    This relationship is enforced in TApplication.IApplication.}
    cEditBase       =       21;     {start of standard editing commands}
    cUndo           =       21;
    cEditSep        =       22;     {line separating UNDO from CUT}
    cCut            =       23;
    cCopy           =       24;
    cPaste          =       25;
    cClear          =       26;
    cEditLast       =       cClear;

    cTyping         =       36;     {for use in a TTypingCommand}
    cMouseCommand   =       37;     {generic mouse command}

  {Debugging commands}
    cIdentifySoftware    =  100;    {'Identify Software' command--identification appers in debug window}
    cExperimenting       =  101;    {enable experimental features; controlled by menu toggle}
    cReportMenuChoices   =  102;    {trace menu commands; controlled by menu toggle}
    cShowDebugInfo  =       103;    {'Show Debug Info', for misc debugging purposes}
    cIntenseDebugging    =  104;    {'intense debugging', controlled by menu toggle}
    cTraceSetupMenus     =  105;    {Trace Enable, Disable calls etc. if gTrace is also on}
    cTraceIdle           =  106;    {Trace Idle if gTrace is also on}
    cDebugPrinting  =       112;    {Used to debug Printing code; controlled by menu toggle}
    cDebugWind      =       113;    {show debug window}
    cReportEvt      =       114;    {report events}
    cDoFirstClick   =       115;    {'Do First Click' toggle for a window}
    cVarClipPicSize =       116;    {Pictures in Clipboard of variable Size}
    cRefreshFrontWindow =   117;    {Refresh front window}


{A L E R T S}

    phAboutApp      =       201;    {Can hold the 'About <appName>...' message}
    phUnimplemented =       202;    {'This feature not yet implemented'}
    phMemFull       =       203;    {'Not enough memory to carry out request'}
    phNoWindows     =       204;    {'Low Memory or no more windows available'}

    phSaveChanges   =       206;    {'Save Changes Before Closing?'}
    phNoChanges     =       207;    {'There haven't been any changes since last change'}
    phRevert        =       208;    {'Revert to last version saved?'}
    phBackToBlank   =       209;    {'Revert to a blank document?'}
    phCloseOneFirst =       210;    {'Close a doc first before app can open a new one'}
    phOpenFailed    =       211;    {'Unable to open document'}
    phNoDisk        =       212;    {'No room to save document on this disk'}
    phPurgeOld      =       213;    {'OK to purge old version before saving new one?'}
    phSaveFailed    =       217;    {'The document could not be saved.'}
    phFlushPrinting =       218;    {'OK to Flush Printing', in response to Quit}
```

```
{Indices for strings in the buzz-string resource}
    bzSaveAs        =      1;       {'Save This Document As'}
    bzRescue        =      2;       {fileName to give to temporary file used during Save process}
    bzShowClip      =      3;       {'Show Clipboard'}
    bzHideClip      =      4;       {'Hide Clipboard'}
    bzUndo          =      10;      {'Undo'}
    bzRedo          =      11;      {'Redo'}

{R E S O U R C E   I D S}

    kIDMNTBbyCmdNumber  =      0;
    kIDBuzzString       =      256;     {ID of the std list of buzzwords stored as 'STR#' resources}

    kIDStdWindow        =      128;     {resource ID of std window template}
    kIDClipWindow       =      200;     {resource ID of window displaying the Clipboard}


{H I G H L I G H T I N G}
    hlOff       =   1;
    hlDim       =   2;
    hlOn        =   4;

    {these constants can be used to test for combinations of fromHL and toHL, without
        regard to which is from and which is to}
    hlOffDim    =   hlOff + hlDim;
    hlDimOff    =   hlOffDim;
    hlDimOn     =   hlDim + hlOn;
    hlOnDim     =   hlDimOn;
    hlOffOn     =   hlOff + hlOn;
    hlOnOff     =   hlOffOn;


{M I S C E L L A N E O U S}

    kWatchDelay         =      3*60;    {default # of ticks before cursor changes to a watch}

    kStdScroll          =      16;      {default value of fScrollUnit used in TFrame.IFrame}
    kStdScrLimit        =      300;     {default value of fScrollLimit used in TFrame.IFrame}
    kStdSzSBar          =      16;      {width/height of a standard vertical/horizontal scroll bar}
    kStdSzMinus1SBar    =      kStdSzSBar - 1;

    kOpenDlgKind        =      1;       {the Open... dialog}
    kSaveDlgKind        =      2;       {the standard fileName dialog}
    kPrntDlgKind        =      3;       {the gPrinting in Progress dialog}

    kClipDocumentType   =      'CLIP';  {Pass this to IDocument if the document's for the Clipboard}
    kPrintInfoSize      =      120;     {size, in bytes, of the printInfo record}

{debugging info}
    kDebugFont      =       monaco;
    kDebugSize      =       9;

    gExperimenting      =       FALSE;
    gDebugPrinting      =       FALSE;
    gReportMenuChoices  =       FALSE;
    gReportEvt          =       FALSE;
    gIntenseDebugging   =       FALSE;
    gUnloadAllSegs      =       TRUE;
    gMemMgtReport       =       FALSE;

    kNotInFrame     =       inDesk; {possible return of TFrame.FindFrame}


    kForDisplay         =   FALSE;
    kForPrinting        =   NOT kForDisplay;

        {CONSTs for use with the TFrame.IFrame method}
    kWantHScrollBar     =   TRUE;
    kWantVScrollBar     =   TRUE;
    kHFrResize          =   TRUE;
    kVFrResize          =   TRUE;


    kDialogWindow       =   TRUE;
```

```
        {For use with TDocument.Save}
    kRequestedSave      =   TRUE;
    kAskForFilename     =   TRUE;
    kRenameDocument     =   TRUE;


        {For use with NewPaletteWindow}
    kLeftPalette        =   h;
    kTopPalette         =   v;
```

MacApp Data Types

```
{E V E N T S}

  PEventRecord = ^EventRecord;

  EventInfo =     RECORD                    {stores more information about an event}
                      thePEvent:          PEventRecord;
                                                 {event used to derive the rest of the fields}
                      theBtnState:        BOOLEAN;    {bits found in the modifiers field of an EventRecord}
                      theCmdKey:          BOOLEAN;
                      theShiftKey:        BOOLEAN;
                      theAlphaLock:       BOOLEAN;
                      theOptionKey:       BOOLEAN;

                      theAutoKey:         BOOLEAN;    {TRUE iff this was an auto key event}

                      theClickCount:      INTEGER;    {0 = event was not a mouse down;
                                                 1-3 = # of multiple clicks}
                  END;

  IdlePhase = (idleBegin, idleContinue, idleEnd);
  TrackPhase = (trackPress, trackMove, trackRelease);


  CursorInfo = RECORD
      origCursor:     Cursor;         {Cursor at the time the busy cursor was put up}


      watchDelay:     INTEGER;        {time in 1/60 second before cursor changes to watch}
      inControl:      BOOLEAN;        {managed by MacApp; TRUE iff MacApp is in control; if FALSE
                                          we don't change the cursor at all}
      changeToWatch:  BOOLEAN;        {if TRUE, we automagically switch to the watch in the VBL task
                                          and switch to origCursor on a call to GetNextEvent or EventAvail;
                                          applications can changed this as necessary}
      watchOn:        BOOLEAN;        {TRUE if the busy cursor on}
      spare:          BOOLEAN;        {reserved for future use}
      watchHandle:    CursHandle;     {handle to the watch cursor}
      q:              QElem;          {vbl queue element for changing the cursor}
      END;


 {C O M M A N D S}

  CmdNumber = INTEGER;

  {the following must match the declaration in RMaker}
  MenuCmdRecord =
      RECORD
        theCmdNumber:         INTEGER;
        theMenuNumber:        INTEGER;
        theItemNumber:        INTEGER;
      END;

  CmdArray = ARRAY[1..4000] OF MenuCmdRecord;
  PCmdArray = ^CmdArray;
  CmdTable = ^PCmdArray;


  AllMenuAspects = (muEnable, muCheck, muStyle);
  MenuAspects = SET OF AllMenuAspects;
```

```
{V I E W   C O O R D I N A T E S}

  SizeDeterminer = (sizeFrame, sizePage, sizeFillPages, sizeVariable, sizeFixed);
                        {tells how a view's size is to be determined; specified separately
                         in each dimension.
                             sizeFrame:      View width or height the same as that of its frame
                             sizePage:       View to be the size of one page
                             sizeFillPages:  View to grow upward to fill an exact number of pages
                             sizeVariable:   View size fluctuates according to app-specific criteria
                             sizeFixed:      No special default handling of size issues}

  ImageSpace = (viewSpace, padSpace);
  PageAreas =
      RECORD
          thePaper:          Rect;   {physical page}
          theInk:            Rect;   {printable page}
          theMargins:        Rect;   {top, left positive; bottom, right negative}
          theInterior:       Rect;   {rect into which view-subset will be projected}
      END;

{W I N D O W   S T O R A G E}

  WindowStorage =
      RECORD
      theActualRecord:   DialogRecord; {??? make this a dialog record because it is bigger ???}
      theRecordInUse:    BOOLEAN;
      END;
  WindowArray = ARRAY[1..100] OF WindowStorage;
  WindowTable = ^WindowArray;

  WindowSlots =
      RECORD
      theCycleModulus:        INTEGER;  {default: 5}
      theBase:                Point;    {default: (8, 24)}
      theOffsetPerWindow:     Point;    {default: (20, 16)}
      END;

{S C A L I N G}

  ScaleSpecification =
      RECORD
          theNumerator:      Point; {theNumerator.h DIV theDenominator.h is the scale factor in horiz direction}
          theDenominator:    Point; {theNumerator.v DIV theDenominator.v is the scale factor in the vert. direction}
      END;

{O T H E R}

          PAppFile = ^AppFile;     {AppFile is defined in the Std File (Package Manager) section of Inside Macintosh}

          HTypeList   = ^PTypeList;
          PTypeList   = ^ArrTypeList;
          ArrTypeList = ARRAY[1..8000] OF OSType;

          Transformer = RECORD
              theViewRes:          Point;
              theDeviceRes:        Point;
              theIsScaledVH:       ARRAY[VHSelect] OF BOOLEAN;
              theScaleFactor:      ScaleSpecification;
              theScrollOffset:     Point;
              theContentRect:      Rect;
              END;

        {H I G H L I G H T I N G}
          HLState = hlOff..hlOn;
```

MacApp Global Variables

```
VAR
    gAppDone:           BOOLEAN;        {set this to TRUE when you want the application to terminate}
    gApplication:       TApplication;   {the application object}
    gBackgroundPrinting:
                        BOOLEAN;        {if true, app's main loop is running behind spooled printing}
    gClickCount:        INTEGER;        {number of 'saved up' mouse clicks; set in
                                            TApplication.ObeyEvent.
                                         If a mouseDown in content area of a window, the value is
                                            that returned by the call to TApplication.CountClicks.
                                         If a mouseUp, the value is left alone.
                                         Otherwise, set to 0.}
    gClipFrame:         TFrame;         {The frame in gClipWindow into which clipboard views are installed}
    gClipWindow:        TWindow;        {The window holding the Clipboard display}
    gClipShowing:       BOOLEAN;        {Whether the clipboard window is currently showing}

    gClipView:          TView;          {The view currently installed in the Clipboard}
    gClipUndoView:      TView;          {The view previously installed in the Clipboard}

    gCmdTable:          CmdTable;       {maps CmdNumber <-> (menu,item)}
    gCursorInfo:        CursorInfo;     {info about the state of the cursor}
    gDidLastCommand:    BOOLEAN;        {whether that last command was last done (TRUE) or undone (FALSE)}
    gDocument:          TDocument;      {the current document}
    gDocList:           TList;          {list of documents}
    gEventInfo:         EventInfo;      {refers to the last event passed to TApplication.ObeyEvent}
    gFinderPrinting:    BOOLEAN;        {TRUE iff the Finder started the App up just for printing docs}
    gFrontWindow:       TWindow;        {If non-NIL the TWindow object of the FrontWindow.}
    gLastCommand:       TCommand;       {the last command done or undone by the user}
    gLastDeskAcc:       LONGINT;        {time of the most recent possible excursion to a a Desk Accessory}

    gLastEvent:         EventRecord;    {the most recent event gotten by TApplication.MainEventLoop}
    gLastMsePt:         Point;          {coordinates of mouse in last event passed to
                                                    TApplication.CountClicks}
    gLastUpTime:        LONGINT;        {time of last mouse up event passed to TApplication.ObeyEvent}
    gMainFileType:      OSType;         {principal file type opened/printed by application;
                                            set in TApplication.IApplication; by default,
                                            TApplication.SFGetFilters returns a list of just this}
    gMenusAreSetup:     BOOLEAN;        {set FALSE after every event; set TRUE by SetupTheMenus, which
                                         is called at Idle Begin; if your DoIdle changes the target
                                         or makes other changes that would alter the appearance
                                         of menus, you must set gMenusAreSetup to FALSE there.}
    gNoChanges:         TCommand;       {special TCommand object to return if the command does not
                                            change the document.  You should carry out the command
                                            in the DoMenuCommand procedure.}
    gNullPrintHandler:  TPrintHandler;  {handles printing-relating messages for views which don't print}
    gNumDocuments:      INTEGER;        {# open documents}
    gPrintHandler:      TPrintHandler;  {a global print-handler object for use in some standard
                                            printing-related activities; this is initialized to be
                                            just a reference to gNullPrintHandler, but if you call
                                            InitPrinting, that will install a non-trivial print-handler
                                            here...}
    gPrinting:          BOOLEAN;        {true iff currently Printing}

    gRedrawMenuBar:     BOOLEAN;        {if TRUE, then DrawMenuBar will be called by
                                            TApplication.SetupTheMenus.  If you have menus that
                                            are not handled by MacApp, your implementation(s) of
                                            DoSetupMenus can set this to TRUE to force the menu
                                            bar to be redrawn.}
    gRepeatCmdKeys:     BOOLEAN;        {allow repeated cmd keys iff TRUE; default is FALSE}
    gSignature:         OSType;       {application signature}
    gTarget:            TEvtHandler;    {the TEvtHandler that gets the first chance at
                                            DoCommand, DoSetupMenu, DoKeyCommand, Idle;
                                            should never be NIL --
                                            If you do not want your own target set this to application}
    gVarClipPicSize:    BOOLEAN;      {if TRUE, Pictures in the Clipboard are treated as variable
                                            size, depending on the window size; if FALSE (default),
                                            then pictures in the Clipboard are drawn and pasted ???
                                            actual size}
    gWholeMenuAffected: BOOLEAN;        {Set by Enable/Disable(CmdFromMenuItem(aMenu, 0))}
    gZeroRect:          Rect;           {SetRect(gZeroRect, 0, 0, 0, 0);}

    gDebugPrinting:     BOOLEAN;        {simple toggle for debugging printing}
    gExperimenting:     BOOLEAN;        {simple toggle for enabling/disabling experimental features}
    gIntenseDebugging:  BOOLEAN;        {debugging toggle for intensive debugging}
    gReportEvt:         BOOLEAN;        {debugging toggle for reporting events}
    gReportMenuChoices: BOOLEAN;        {debugging toggle for tracing cmds}
    gUnloadAllSegs:     BOOLEAN;        {if TRUE, call UnloadAllSegs in main event loop}
    gDebugKeyMap:       KeyMap;         {the key state during StartVantage}
```

MacApp Global Procedures

```
PROCEDURE EntDebugger(entering: BOOLEAN);

PROCEDURE NotYetImplemented(where: Str255);
                {Put up an alert saying Not Yet Implemented and WriteLn where.}
PROCEDURE ReportEvent(ev: PEventRecord; VAR info: EventInfo);
                {WriteLn the contents of ev, and the event info}
PROCEDURE ReportMouseDown(where: INTEGER);
                {WriteLn where the mouse went down, given the result of FindWindow}

{Utility for creating simple windows that contain 1 view and may or may not scroll.
    Signals Failure if the window could not be created.}
FUNCTION  NewSimpleWindow(itsRsrcID: INTEGER; isDialogWindow: BOOLEAN;
                          wantHScrollBar, wantVScrollBar: BOOLEAN;
                          itsView: TView): TWindow;

{Utility for creating MacDraw-line windows with 1 non-scrolling palette along the left edge (whichWay = h),
        or a non-scrolling status area at the top of the window (whichWay = v),
        and a main view that may or may not scroll.
    Signals Failure if the window could not be created.}
FUNCTION  NewPaletteWindow(itsRsrcID: INTEGER; isDialogWindow: BOOLEAN;
                          wantHScrollBar, wantVScrollBar: BOOLEAN;
                          itsMainView: TView;
                          itsPaletteView: TView; sizePalette: INTEGER; whichWay: VHSelect): TWindow;


{The following routines all recognize command numbers of the form -(256 * menu + item) and -(256 * menu)}
{The former is used when there is no command number; the latter to enable/disable a whole menu (rare)}
PROCEDURE Enable(aCmd: CmdNumber; canDo: BOOLEAN);
PROCEDURE EnableCheck(aCmd: CmdNumber; canDo: BOOLEAN; checkIt: BOOLEAN);
PROCEDURE SetStyle(aCmd: CmdNumber; aStyle: Style);

{Miscellaneous}

PROCEDURE BusyDelay(newDelay: INTEGER; forceBusy: BOOLEAN);
PROCEDURE ResetBusyCursor;
    {Call BusyDelay if you want to change the busy cursor delay.
        newDelay should be in 1/60 seconds; a value <= 0 means don't change the delay.
        If forceBusy is TRUE, then the watch is put up immeidately, otherwise it doesn't
            go up until the required time has passed. (Busy delay respect the state flags
            in the cursor info record (ie., changeToWatch and inControl.)
      Call ResetBusyCursor if you want to change the cursor back to an arrow and reset the
            time before changing back to a watch.  This is called automagically if you call
            GetNextEvent or EventAvail.}

PROCEDURE CanPaste(aClipType: ResType);
    {Call this in your SetUpMenus code to register an ability to paste a particular type of Clipboard data}

PROCEDURE ClipFurtherTo(r: Rect; hDeltaOrg, vDeltaOrg: INTEGER);
    {Set clipping to:
        (r INTERSECT <current clipping>) OFFSET-BY (hDeltaOrg, vDeltaOrg)}

PROCEDURE InitToolbox(callsToMoreMasters: INTEGER; numberOfWindows: INTEGER);
    {Call this the very first thing in your main program.  Does the essential Toolbox initialization;
        If you also use the printing unit UPrinting, call InitPrinting just after you call InitToolbox}

FUNCTION PutDeskScrapData(aResType: ResType; aDataHandle: Handle): OSErr;
    {Call this from your TCommand method 'WriteToDeskScrap' (for a Command which changes the Clipboard)
        to write out data to the actual Desk Scrap.  The return code from the Scrap Manager is returned
        as the function value -- will be noErr unless something went wrong.  This procedure leaves aDataHandle
        UNLOCKED.  Rather than calling this, you can call the ToolBox routine PutScrap yourself}
        PROCEDURE ExitMacApp;
            {Call this if for some reason you want to immediately exit the application.  It calls
                gApplication.Terminate, cleans up some other internal stuff, and then calls ExitToShell.
                (Normally, you would not call this, because MacApp takes care of terminating the application.)

                You must have first called InitToolbox before calling this.}


        FUNCTION  RectIsVisible(r: Rect): BOOLEAN;              {determine if a rect is visible in a GrafPort}

        FUNCTION  RectsNest(outer, inner: Rect): BOOLEAN;       {determine if inner nests within outer}

        PROCEDURE SetHLPenState(fromHL, toHL: HLState);
                        {Set the pen state for highlighting by XOR, given the highlight transition.
                            You can use this if you use Paint<X> or Frame<X> or line drawing for your
                            highlighting.}
```

LISTING

B

Toolbox Routines Used in This Book

This appendix lists the interfaces to the Macintosh Toolbox routines mentioned in this book, or used in any of the applications we developed (SmallApp, Mini-QuadWorld, QuadWorld).

The remarkable fact is that of the more than 500 Toolbox routines which are usually the basic building block of a Macintosh application, only about 50 are needed in the MacApp applications developed here. This is not to say that a commercial strength Macintosh application will not use more of the Toolbox, but rather that with the MacApp classes as building blocks, the need for an in-depth understanding of most of the Toolbox is removed.

Notice that the vast majority of the Toolbox routines in this appendix are QuickDraw routines. This is because the only portion of your application in which MacApp can't help is the drawing of your application's views. You must develop that code yourself and it will use QuickDraw routines. It is the belief of many MacApp developers that, with the exception of the QuickDraw routines, MacApp programmers can do a lot without having to use the "low level" Toolbox directly.

QuickDraw

Rectangles

```
PROCEDURE FrameRect(r: Rect);
PROCEDURE InsetRect(VAR r: Rect; dh, dv: INTEGER);
PROCEDURE OffsetRect(VAR r: Rect; dh, dv: INTEGER);
PROCEDURE PaintRect(r: Rect);
FUNCTION  PtInRect(pt: Point; r: Rect): BOOLEAN;
PROCEDURE Pt2Rect(pt1, pt2: Point; VAR dstRect: Rect);
PROCEDURE SetRect(VAR r: Rect; left, top, right, bottom: INTEGER);
PROCEDURE UnionRect(src1, src2: Rect; VAR dstRect: Rect);
```

Pens

```
PROCEDURE GetPenState(VAR pnState: PenState);
PROCEDURE PenMode(mode: INTEGER);
PROCEDURE PenNormal;
PROCEDURE PenPat(pat: Pattern);
PROCEDURE PenSize(width, height: INTEGER);
PROCEDURE SetPenState(pnState: PenState);
```

Regions

```
PROCEDURE CloseRgn(dstRegion: RgnHandle);
PROCEDURE EraseRgn(rgn: RgnHandle);
FUNCTION  NewRgn: RgnHandle;
PROCEDURE OffsetRgn(rgn: RgnHandle; dh, dv: INTEGER);
PROCEDURE OpenRgn;
PROCEDURE PaintRgn(rgn: RgnHandle);
FUNCTION  PtInRgn(pt: Point; rgn: RgnHandle): BOOLEAN;
```

Text and Fonts

```
PROCEDURE DrawString(s: Str255);
PROCEDURE GetFontInfo(VAR info: FontInfo);
PROCEDURE TextFont(font: INTEGER);
PROCEDURE TextSize(size: INTEGER);
PROCEDURE TextFace(face: Style);
```

Other

```
PROCEDURE CopyBits(srcBits, dstBits: BitMap; srcRect, dstRect: Rect;
                   mode: INTEGER; mskRgn: RgnHandle);
PROCEDURE EraseOval(r: Rect);
FUNCTION  EqualPt(pt1, pt2: Point): BOOLEAN;
PROCEDURE FrameOval(r: Rect);
PROCEDURE LineTo(h, v: INTEGER);
PROCEDURE MoveTo(h, v: INTEGER);
PROCEDURE PaintOval(r: Rect);
PROCEDURE SetCursor(crsc: Cursor);
PROCEDURE SetPt(VAR pt: Point; h, v: INTEGER);
PROCEDURE StuffHex(thingPtr: Ptr; s: Str255);
```

File Manager

```
FUNCTION   FSRead(refNum: INTEGER; VAR count: LONGINT; buffPtr: Ptr):
                   OSErr;
FUNCTION   FSWrite(refNum: INTEGER; VAR count: LONGINT; buffPtr: Ptr):
                   OSErr;
```

Window Manager

```
PROCEDURE  SelectWindow(theWindow: WindowPtr);
```

Menu Manager

```
PROCEDURE  CustomMenuDefinitionProc(message: INTEGER;
                  theMenu: MenuHandle; VAR menuRect: Rect; hitPt: Point;
                  VAR whichItem: INTEGER);
FUNCTION   GetMHandle(menuID: INTEGER): MenuHandle;
```

Toolbox Utilities

```
FUNCTION   FixRatio(numer, denom: INTEGER): Fixed;
FUNCTION   AngleFromSlope(slope: Fixed): INTEGER;
FUNCTION   GetCursor(cursorID: INTEGER): CursHandle;
```

LISTING C

The Smallest MacApp Application

Major Unit for SmallApp (Files SmallApp.U.TEXT and SmallApp.U2.TEXT)

```
                          { The Smallest Possible MacApp Application }
                   { Copyright 1986 by Productivity Products International, Inc. }

UNIT USmallApp;

{$M+}                                   { Compiler commands to generate Macintosh code }
{$X-}                                   {  and turn off stack expansion }
{$E+}                                   {  and automatically invoke the Editor if errors are found }
{$E Error.text}                         {  and put the errors in file 'Error.text' }

INTERFACE

USES
    {$U-}                               { This set of units are portions of the
                                          Macintosh Software supplement }
    {$U Obj/MemTypes}       MemTypes,
    {$U Obj/QuickDraw}      QuickDraw,
    {$U Obj/OSIntf}         OSIntf,
    {$U Obj/ToolIntf}       ToolIntf,
    {$U Obj/PackIntf}       PackIntf,

    {$U Object.U}           UObject,    { This set of units are portions of MacApp }
    {$U List.U}             UList,
    {$U MacApp.U}           UMacApp,
    {$U Printing.U}         UPrinting;

CONST
    myFileType = 'MAMO';     { The file type ("MacApp MOuse') for documents of this application }

TYPE

    TSmallApplication = OBJECT(TApplication)

            { ----- INITIALIZE THE APPLICATION ----- }
        PROCEDURE TSmallApplication.ISmallApplication;

            { ----- MAKE A DOCUMENT ----- }
        FUNCTION  TSmallApplication.DoMakeDocument(itsCmdNumber: CmdNumber): TDocument; OVERRIDE;

    END;

```

```
      TSmallDocument = OBJECT(TDocument)

            { ----- FIELDS ----- }
         fSmallView:  TSmallView;

            { ----- INITIALIZE A DOCUMENT ----- }
         PROCEDURE TSmallDocument.ISmallDocument;

            { ----- MAKE A VIEW ----- }
         PROCEDURE  TSmallDocument.DoMakeViews(forPrinting: BOOLEAN); OVERRIDE;

            { ----- MAKE A WINDOW ----- }
         PROCEDURE  TSmallDocument.DoMakeWindows; OVERRIDE;

      END;



      TSmallView = OBJECT(TView)

            { ----- INITIALIZE A VIEW ----- }
         PROCEDURE TSmallView.ISmallView(itsSmallDocument: TSmallDocument);

            { ----- RENDER THE IMAGE ----- }
         PROCEDURE TSmallView.Draw(area: Rect); OVERRIDE;

      END;


   IMPLEMENTATION


   {$I SmallApp.U2}
                        { Copyright 1985 by Productivity Products International, Inc.}

   { USmallApp Implementation }


   { ************************************************************************************************ }
   { ************************************************************************************************ }
   {                                    METHODS FOR ALL THE SMALLAPP CLASSES                          }
   {                                                                                                  }
   {    Note that methods are grouped by class and that the order of methods in any class is the following }
   {    (by convention only, since Object Pascal forces no order):                                   }
   {                                                                                                  }
   {              (1) the initialization method, if any,                                              }
   {              (2) the Inspect method - a private debugging method, if needed                      }
   {              (3) the Free method, if overridden, and                                             }
   {              (4) the remaining methods in alphabetical order.                                    }
   {                                                                                                  }
   { ************************************************************************************************ }
   { ************************************************************************************************ }



   { *************************************** TSmallApplication Methods ******************************* }

 PROCEDURE TSmallApplication.ISmallApplication;
 BEGIN
      SELF.IApplication('SMAP', myFileType);
 END;

      { ----- MAKE AND INITIALIZE A DOCUMENT ----- }

 FUNCTION  TSmallApplication.DoMakeDocument(itsCmdNumber: CmdNumber): TDocument; OVERRIDE;
   VAR aSmallDocument:TSmallDocument;
 BEGIN
      NEW(aSmallDocument);
      aSmallDocument.ISmallDocument;
      DoMakeDocument := aSmallDocument;
 END;


   { *************************************** TSmallDocument Methods ********************************** }
```

```
2  --
2  -- A PROCEDURE TSmallDocument.ISmallDocument;
2  0- A BEGIN
2  --        SELF.IDocument(myFileType);
2  -0 A END;
2  --
2  --
2  --        { ----- MAKE AND INITIALIZE ALL THE NECESSARY VIEWS ----- }
2  --
2  -- A PROCEDURE  TSmallDocument.DoMakeViews(forPrinting: BOOLEAN); OVERRIDE;
2  --    VAR smallView:    TSmallView;
2  0- A BEGIN
2  --        NEW(smallView);
2  --        smallView.ISmallView(SELF);
2  --        SELF.fSmallView := smallView;
2  -0 A END;
2  --
2  --
2  --        { ----- MAKE ALL THE NECESSARY WINDOWS ----- }
2  --
2  -- A PROCEDURE  TSmallDocument.DoMakeWindows; OVERRIDE;
2  --    VAR aWindow:     TWindow;
2  0- A BEGIN
2  --        aWindow := NewSimpleWindow(kIDStdWindow, NOT kDialogWindow,
2  --                                  kWantHScrollBar, kWantVScrollBar, SELF.fSmallView);
2  -0 A END;
2  --
2  --
2  --
2  --    { ***************************************** TSmallView Methods ***************************************** }
2  --
2  -- A PROCEDURE TSmallView.ISmallView(itsSmallDocument: TSmallDocument);
2  --    VAR viewRect:        Rect;
2  --        aStdHandler:     TStdPrintHandler;
2  0- A BEGIN
2  --        SetRect(viewRect, 0, 0, 500, 500);
2  --        IView(NIL,                        { This view has no parent view,  }
2  --              itsSmallDocument,           {  and shows a smallDocument,     }
2  --              viewRect,                   {  in a 500 x 500 rectangle,      }
2  --              sizeFixed,                  {  that does not change if the frame is changed horizontally, }
2  --              sizeFixed,                  {  or vertically,                 }
2  --              FALSE,                      {  and can't make selections      }
2  --              hlOff);                     {  and doesn't highlight when the window is inactive. }
2  --
2  --
2  --        New(aStdHandler);
2  --        aStdHandler.IStdPrintHandler(SELF, FALSE);  { The second parameter, itsSquareDots, is FALSE since
2  --                                                      this application does not mix text and graphics.
2  --                                                      Slightly higher resolution is available with this
2  --                                                      setting. }
2  -0 A END;
2  --
2  --
2  --
2  --
2  --        { ----- RENDER THE IMAGE ----- }
2  --
2  -- A PROCEDURE TSmallView.Draw(area: Rect); OVERRIDE;
2  --
2  -- B      FUNCTION  MakeRect(top, left, bottom, right: INTEGER): Rect;
2  --         VAR r: Rect;
2  0- B      BEGIN
2  --            SetRect(r, left, top, right, bottom);
2  --            MakeRect := r;
2  -0 B      END;
2  --
2  0- A BEGIN
2  --        PenNormal;
2  --        PaintOval(MakeRect(74, 72, 139, 127));       { Outline of the mouse head }
2  --        EraseOval(MakeRect(84, 74, 138, 125));       { Outline of the mouse face }
2  --        FrameOval(MakeRect(109, 84, 129, 115));      { Mouse mouth (part 1 of 2) }
2  --        EraseRect(MakeRect(109, 84, 123, 115));      { Mouse mouth (part 2 of 2) }
2  --        FrameOval(MakeRect(98, 87, 107, 96));        { Left eye }
2  --        FrameOval(MakeRect(98, 104, 107, 113));      { Right eye }
2  --        PaintOval(MakeRect(101, 90, 104, 93));       { Left pupil }
```

```
193  2  117 --        PaintOval(MakeRect(101, 107, 104, 110));     { Right pupil }
194  2  118 --        PaintOval(MakeRect(111, 97, 117, 103));      { Nose }
195  2  119 --        PaintOval(MakeRect(53, 52, 91, 90));         { Left ear }
196  2  120 --        PaintOval(MakeRect(53, 110, 91, 148));       { Right ear }
197  2  121 --
198  2  122 --        FrameRect(MakeRect(20, 20, 170, 180));       { A bounding rectangle }
199  2  123 --
200  2  124 -0 A END;
201  2  125 --
202  2  126 --
203  1   77 --
204  1   78 --    END.
205  1   79 --
206  1   80 --
207  1   81 --
```

Main Program for SmallApp (File SmallApp.M.TEXT)

```
208  3    1 --                                   { The Smallest MacApp Application }
209  3    2 --                    { Copyright 1986 by Productivity Products International, Inc.}
210  3    3 --
211  3    4 --
212  3    5 --    PROGRAM SmallApp;
213  3    6 --
214  3    7 --    {$M+}                                { Compiler commands to generate Macintosh code }
215  3    8 --    {$X-}                                {  and turn off stack expansion }
216  3    9 --
217  3   10 --    USES
218  3   11 --        {$U-}                            { This set of units are portions of the
219  3   12 --                                           Macintosh Software supplement }
220  3   13 --        {$U Obj/MemTypes}       MemTypes,
221  3   14 --        {$U Obj/QuickDraw}      QuickDraw,
222  3   15 --        {$U Obj/OSIntf}         OSIntf,
223  3   16 --        {$U Obj/ToolIntf}       ToolIntf,
224  3   17 --
225  3   18 --        {$U Object.U}           UObject,     { This set of units are portions of MacApp }
226  3   19 --        {$U List.U}             UList,
227  3   20 --        {$U MacApp.U}           UMacApp,
228  3   21 --        {$U Printing.U}         UPrinting,
229  3   22 --
230  3   23 --        {$U SmallApp.U}         USmallApp;   { This unit has the SmallApp-specific classes }
231  3   24 --
232  3   25 --        VAR aSmallApplication:  TSmallApplication;
233  3   26 --
234  3   27 --
235  3   28 0-    BEGIN
236  3   29 --    {$S          }            { Insert this code into the blank segment }
237  3   30 --        InitToolbox(2, 10);  { start with 2 extra blocks of 64 master pointers; allow up to 10 windows}
238  3   31 --        InitPrinting;        { initialize the print shop }
239  3   32 --
240  3   33 --        New(aSmallApplication);
241  3   34 --        aSmallApplication.ISmallApplication;
242  3   35 --        aSmallApplication.Run;
243  3   36 -0    END.
```

Cross Reference Listing for Major Unit and Main Program for SmallApp

```
   1. SmallApp.U.TEXT
   2. SmallApp.U2.TEXT
   3. SmallApp.M.TEXT

-A-
  area               68*( 1)    99*( 2)
  aSmallApplicatio   25*( 3)    33 ( 3)    34 ( 3)    35 ( 3)
  aSmallDocument     33*( 2)    35 ( 2)    36 ( 2)    37 ( 2)
  aStdHandler        75*( 2)    87 ( 2)    88 ( 2)
  aWindow            63*( 2)    65=( 2)

-B-
  BOOLEAN            53 ( 1)    51 ( 2)
  bottom            101*( 2)   104 ( 2)

-C-
  CmdNumber          38 ( 1)    32 ( 2)
```

```
-D-
  DoMakeDocument      38*( 1)   32*( 2)   37=( 2)
  DoMakeViews         53*( 1)   51*( 2)
  DoMakeWindows       56*( 1)   62*( 2)
  Draw                68*( 1)   99*( 2)

-E-
  EraseOval          111 ( 2)
  EraseRect          113 ( 2)

-F-
  FALSE               83 ( 2)   88 ( 2)
  forPrinting         53*( 1)   51*( 2)
  FrameOval          112 ( 2)  114 ( 2)  115 ( 2)
  FrameRect          122 ( 2)
  fSmallView          47*( 1)   56=( 2)   66 ( 2)

-H-
  hlOff               84 ( 2)

-I-
  IApplication        27 ( 2)
  IDocument           45 ( 2)
  InitPrinting        31 ( 3)
  InitToolbox         30 ( 3)
  INTEGER            101 ( 2)
  ISmallApplicatio    35*( 1)   25*( 2)   34 ( 3)
  ISmallDocument      50*( 1)   36 ( 2)   43*( 2)
  ISmallView          65*( 1)   55 ( 2)   73*( 2)
  IStdPrintHandler    88 ( 2)
  itsCmdNumber        38*( 1)   32*( 2)
  itsSmallDocument    65*( 1)   73*( 2)   79 ( 2)
  IView               78 ( 2)

-K-
  kDialogWindow       65 ( 2)
  kIDStdWindow        65 ( 2)
  kWantHScrollBar     66 ( 2)
  kWantVScrollBar     66 ( 2)

-L-
  left               101*( 2)  104 ( 2)

-M-
  MakeRect           101*( 2)  105=( 2)  110 ( 2)  111 ( 2)  112 ( 2)  113 ( 2)  114 ( 2)  115 ( 2)  116 ( 2)
                     117 ( 2)  118 ( 2)  119 ( 2)  120 ( 2)  122 ( 2)
  MemTypes            16*( 1)   13*( 3)
  myFileType          28*( 1)   27 ( 2)   45 ( 2)

-N-
  NEW                 35 ( 2)   54 ( 2)
  New                 87 ( 2)   33 ( 3)
  NewSimpleWindow     65 ( 2)

-O-
  OBJECT              32 ( 1)   44 ( 1)   62 ( 1)
  OSIntf              18*( 1)   15*( 3)
  OVERRIDE            38*( 1)   53*( 1)   56*( 1)   68*( 1)   32*( 2)   51*( 2)   62*( 2)   99*( 2)

-P-
  PackIntf            20*( 1)
  PaintOval          110 ( 2)  116 ( 2)  117 ( 2)  118 ( 2)  119 ( 2)  120 ( 2)
  PenNormal          109 ( 2)

-Q-
  QuickDraw           17*( 1)   14*( 3)

-R-
  r                  102*( 2)  104 ( 2)  105 ( 2)
  Rect                68 ( 1)   74 ( 2)   99 ( 2)  101 ( 2)  102 ( 2)
  right              101*( 2)  104 ( 2)
  Run                 35 ( 3)

-S-
  SELF                27 ( 2)   45 ( 2)   55 ( 2)   56 ( 2)   66 ( 2)   88 ( 2)
  SetRect             77 ( 2)  104 ( 2)
```

```
  sizeFixed          81 ( 2)    82 ( 2)
  SmallApp            5*( 3)
  smallView          52*( 2)    54 ( 2)    55 ( 2)    56 ( 2)

 -T-
  TApplication       32*( 1)
  TDocument          38 ( 1)    44*( 1)    32 ( 2)
  ToolIntf           19*( 1)    16*( 3)
  top               101*( 2)   104 ( 2)
  TSmallApplicatio   32*( 1)    35*( 1)    38*( 1)    25*( 2)    32*( 2)    25 ( 3)
  TSmallDocument     44*( 1)    50*( 1)    53*( 1)    56*( 1)    65 ( 1)    33 ( 2)    43*( 2)    51*( 2)    62*( 2)
                     73 ( 2)
  TSmallView         47 ( 1)    62*( 1)    65*( 1)    68*( 1)    52 ( 2)    73*( 2)    99*( 2)
  TStdPrintHandler   75 ( 2)
  TView              62*( 1)
  TWindow            63 ( 2)

 -U-
  UList              23*( 1)    19*( 3)
  UMacApp            24*( 1)    20*( 3)
  UObject            22*( 1)    18*( 3)
  UPrinting          25*( 1)    21*( 3)
  USmallApp           4*( 1)    23*( 3)

 -V-
  viewRect           74*( 2)    77 ( 2)    80 ( 2)
```

RMaker Input File (File SmallApp.R.TEXT)

```
SmallApp.Rsrc

*  Copyright 1986 by Productivity Products International
*
*  17 February 1986
*

Type SMAP = STR
  ,0
Smallest MacApp Application Version 1.0 - 17 February 1986


Type CODE
 SmallApp,0

* Make us be Switcher-Friendly
* C000 = save screen / send suspend/resume / quit events
* 00036800 = recommended partition size (250K)
* 00023C00 = minimum partition size (175K)
*
TYPE SIZE=GNRL
  ,-1
.H
C000
00036800
00023C00


*  When user requests "About <application>" from the Apple menu, Alert # 201, by default, is displayed
*
Type ALRT
*  "About SmallApp..." message
,201 (32)
90  100  250  412
201
4444

Type DITL
*  "About SmallApp..." alert items -----------
,201 (32)
3
BtnItem Enable
130  182  150  262
OK
```

```
StatText Disable
10  80  110  270
This is the world's smallest MacApp application (only 97 lines of code!).

IconItem Disable
20  20  52  52
1



*
*  The Menu and Command-Number Table
*
Type CMNU
  ,1
  \14
    About SmallApplication…#1
    (-

  ,2
  File
    New/N#8
    Open…#20
    (-
    Close#11
    (-
    Page Setup…#176
    Print One#177
    Print …#178
    (-


    Quit/Q#10

  ,3
  Edit
    Undo/Z#21
    (-
    Cut/X#23
    Copy/C#24
    Paste/V#25
    Clear/B#26
    (-
    Show Clipboard#18


*
*  Window Definition
*
Type WIND
  ,128
  MacApp Mouse
  50 40 250 450
  Invisible GoAway
  0
  0


*
*  The Clipboard Window resource
*
Type WIND
  ,200
  Clipboard
  280 40 350 450
  Invisible GoAway
  0
  0
```

```
*
*  "Buzzwords" -- strings accessed by index  (application may wish to extend this list)
*
Type STR#
  ,256 (36)
Save this document as:
Rescue of Combo Document
Show Clipboard
Hide Clipboard
Print…
Stop Printing
Name of file to spool to:
Print Spooled File Named:
Print File
Undo
Redo
Reserved 12
Reserved 13
Reserved 14
Reserved 15


Type ICN#
*
* ICON DATA, SmallApp.Icon
  ,128
  2
00010000
00028000
00044000
00082000
00101000
00220800
00470400
00870200
013E0100
02420080
04890040
08810020
10A10010
23850008
47C23F04
833C4082
40008041
20011822
1001E414
081E3F8F
04021807
02010007
01008007
00806007
00401FE7
0020021F
00100407
00080800
00041000
00022000
00014000
00008000
00010000
00038000
0007C000
000FE000
001FF000
003FF800
007FFC00
00FFFE00
01FFFF00
03C3FF80
0781FFC0
0F81FFE0
1F81FFF0
3FC1FFF8
```

```
7FFFFFFC
FFFFFFFE
7FFFFFFF
3FFFFFFE
1FFFFFFC
0FFFFFFF
07FFFFFF
03FFFFFF
01FFFFFF
00FFFFFF
007FFFFF
003FFE1F
001FFC07
000FF800
0007F000
0003E000
0001C000
00008000


Type FREF
  ,128
  APPL 0


Type BNDL
  ,128
  SMAP 0
  2
  ICN# 1
  0   128
  FREF 1
  0   128
*
* After this point in the Resource File, all entries are Standard and can simply be copied from one
*  resource definition file to another
*
*
*********************************************************************************************
*
*  A L E R T S
*

Type ALRT

*"This feature not yet implemented" alert
,202 (32)
100  120  190  392
202
4444

Type DITL
*"This feature not yet implemented" alert items -----------
* 90x272
,202 (32)
3
BtnItem Enable
60  182  80  262
OK

StatText Disable
10  80  50  270
This feature not yet implemented

IconItem Disable
20  20  52  52
1

*
*********************************************************************************************
```

```
*
Type ALRT
*"Memory Full" alert
,203 (32)
100 120 190 392
203
4444

Type DITL
*"Memory Full" alert items
* 90x272
,203 (32)
3
BtnItem Enable
60  182  80  262
OK

StatText Disable
10  80  50  270
Not enough memory left to carry out your request!

IconItem Disable
20  20  52  52
1

*
***************************************************************************************************
*
Type ALRT
*"Memory Low or No More Windows Available" alert
,204 (32)
100  120  190  392
204
4444

Type DITL
*"This feature not yet implemented" alert items -----------
* 90x272
,204 (32)
3
BtnItem Enable
60  182  80  262
OK

StatText Disable
10  80  50  270
Memory Low or No More Windows Available

IconItem Disable
20  20  52  52
1

*
***************************************************************************************************
*
Type ALRT
*"Save changes before closing?" alert ------------------
,206 (32)
100  120  190  392
206
4444

Type DITL
*"Save changes before closing?" alert items
,206 (32)
5
BtnItem Enable
60  10  80  90
Yes

BtnItem Enable
60  100  80  172
Cancel
```

```
BtnItem Enable
60  182  80  262
No

StatText Disable
10  96  50  270
Save changes before closing?

IconItem Disable
20  20  52  52
1


*
*********************************************************************************************
*
Type ALRT
*"There haven't been any changes since the last save." alert
,207 (32)
100  120  190  392
207
4444

Type DITL
*"There haven't been any changes since the last save." alert items -----------
,207 (32)
3
BtnItem Enable
60  182  80  262
OK

StatText Disable
10  80  50  270
There haven't been any changes since the last save.

IconItem Disable
20  20  52  52
1


*
*********************************************************************************************
*
Type ALRT
*"Revert to the last version saved?" alert ------------------
,208 (32)
100  120  190  392
208
4444

Type DITL
*"Revert to the last version saved?" alert itemse
* 90x272
,208 (32)
4
BtnItem Enable
60  10  80  90
Yes

BtnItem Enable
60  182  80  262
No

StatText Disable
10  96  50  270
Revert to the last version saved?

IconItem Disable
20  20  52  52
1

*
*********************************************************************************************
```

```
*
Type ALRT
*"Revert to blank document?" alert ---------------
,209 (32)
100  120  220  392
209
4444

Type DITL
*"Revert to blank document?" alert items
,209 (32)
4
BtnItem Enable
80  10  100  90
Yes

BtnItem Enable
80  182  100  262
No

StatText Disable
10  96  70  270
Do you really want to revert to a blank document?

IconItem Disable
20  20  52  52
1

*
*******************************************************************************************
*
Type ALRT
*"Close a document first before opening a new one?" alert ---------------
,210 (32)
100  120  220  392
210
4444

Type DITL
*"Close a document first before opening a new one" alert items
* 90x272
,210 (32)
3
BtnItem Enable
60  182  80  262
OK

StatText Disable
10  80  50  270
You must close a document first before you can open another one
IconItem Disable
20  20  52  52
1

*
*******************************************************************************************
*
Type ALRT
*  "Unable to open document" alert ---------------
,211 (32)
100  120  220  392
211
4444

Type DITL
*"Unable to open document" alert items
* 90x272
,211 (32)
3
BtnItem Enable
60  182  80  262
OK
```

```
StatText Disable
10  80  50  270
Sorry, I'm unable to open the document.

IconItem Disable
20  20  52  52
1


*
*********************************************************************************************
*
Type ALRT

*"Disk Full" alert ---------------------------------
,212 (32)
100  120  190  392
212
4444

Type DITL
*"The disk is full." alert items -----------
,212 (32)
3
BtnItem Enable
60  182  80  262
OK

StatText Disable
10  80  50  270
The disk is full.

IconItem Disable
20  20  52  52
1

*
*********************************************************************************************
*
Type ALRT
* OK To purge old version before saving new? ---------------------------------
     ,213 (32)
     90  100  250  412
     213
     4444

TYPE DITL
* OK To purge old version before saving new? alert items
     ,213 (32)
     4
     BtnItem Enable
     132  20  152  100
Yes
     BtnItem Enable
     132  192  152  272
     No

     StatText Disable
     10  96  120  270
There's not enough room to save the latest version unless we first destroy the old version; are you prepared to take that risk?

     IconItem Disable
     20  20  52  52
     1

*
*********************************************************************************************
*
TYPE ALRT
*  "Printing went bad" alert
,214 (32)
100  120  190  392
214
4444
```

```
*****     "Printing went bad" alert items     ******
Type DITL

,214 (32)
3
BtnItem Enable
60  182  80  262
OK

StatText Disable
10  80  50  270
Oops... that attempt at printing didn't work (Error # ^0).  Try something else.

IconItem Disable
20  20  52  52
1

*
******************************************************************************************
*
TYPE ALRT
*  "No Pages within range" alert
,215 (32)
100  120  190  392
215
4444

*****     "No Pages within range" alert items     ******
Type DITL

,215 (32)
3
BtnItem Enable
60  182  80  262
OK

StatText Disable
10  80  50  270
This document has no pages within the requested range

IconItem Disable
20  20  52  52
1


*
******************************************************************************************
*
TYPE ALRT
*  "Run the Choose Printer Accessory" alert
,216 (32)
100  120  210  392
216
4444

*****     "Run the Choose Printer Accessory" alert items     ******

Type DITL

,216 (32)
3
BtnItem Enabled
80  182  100  262
OK

StatText Disabled
10  80  80  270
Make correct choices using "Choose Printer" Desk Accessory, then try again.

IconItem Disabled
20  20  52  52
1

*
******************************************************************************************
```

```
*
Type ALRT

*"The document could not be saved." alert ---------------------------------
,217 (32)
100  120  190  392
217
4444

Type DITL
*"The document could not be saved." alert items -----------
,217 (32)
3
BtnItem Enable
60  182  80  262
OK

StatText Disable
10  80  50  270
The document could not be saved.

IconItem Disable
20  20  52  52
1



*
*******************************************************************************************
*
Type ALRT
*  "Okay to abort background printing task?" alert
,218 (32)
100  120  190  392
218
4444

Type DITL
*****     "Okay to abort background printing task?" alert items    ******
*
,218 (32)
4
BtnItem Enable
60  10  80  90
Yes

BtnItem Enable
60  182  80  262
No

StatText Disable
10  96  50  270
Quitting now will interrupt a background printing task.  Quit anyway?

IconItem Disable
20  20  52  52
1

*
*******************************************************************************************
*


Type ALRT
*   "Value out of bounds; closest acceptable value substituted" Alert
,221 (32)
90  100  210  412
221
4444
```

```
Type DITL
,221 (32)
3
BtnItem Enabled
90  182  110  262
OK

StatText Disabled
10  80  80  270
Value out of bounds; closest acceptable value substituted.

IconItem Disabled
20  20  52  52
1




*
********************************************************************************************
*
*  D I A L O G S
*

*
Type DLOG

*"Printing In Progress..." dialog ------------------------
,256 (32)
100  120  190  392
Visible 1 NoGoAway 0
256
Print


Type DITL

*"Printing In Progress..." dialog items ----------------------------
,256 (32)
1
StatText Disabled
15  20  90  242
Printing "^0"...  To cancel printing, hold down the Command key and type period (.).


Type DLOG
* Dialog 257 -- this is the 'Proceed/Pause/Cancel' dialog running behind printing a spooled print file
  ,257 (32)
  110 30 250 476
  Visible 1 NoGoAway 0
  257

Type DITL
  ,257 (32)
  4

    BtnItem Enabled
    100 60 120 140
Proceed

    BtnItem Enabled
    100 180 120 260
Pause

    BtnItem Enabled
    100 300 120 430
Cancel Printing
    StatText Disabled
    16 50 80 410
Document '^0' is being Printed

*
********************************************************************************************
```

```
*
Type DLOG
* Dialog 258 - the 'Proceed/Pause/Cancel/Cancel-all-Printing' dialog shown during Finder Printing
  ,258 (32)
  110 30 250 476
  Visible 1 NoGoAway 0
  258

Type DITL
  ,258 (32)
  5

    BtnItem Enabled
    100 20 120 100
Proceed

    BtnItem Enabled
    100 120 120 180
Pause

    BtnItem Enabled
    100 200 120 260
Cancel

    BtnItem Enabled
    100 280 120 430
Cancel All Printing

    StatText Disabled
    16 50 80 410
Document '^0' is being Printed


*********************************************************************************************
*                                                                                           *
*    Dialog 259 -- "Starting Page Number Dialog ------------------------                   *
*                                                                                           *
*   Items are:
*
*   1   Okay button
*   2   Cancel button
*   3   "Starting Page Number" string
*   4   The editible text holding the current/desired value
*
Type DLOG

,259 (32)
50  70  150  432
Visible 1 NoGoAway 0
259
Starting Pg Num

Type DITL
  ,259 (32)
  4

    BtnItem Enabled
    70 60 90 140
Okay

    BtnItem Enabled
    70 190 90 270
Cancel

    StatText Disabled
    16 50 40 200
Starting page number:

    EditText Disabled
    16 220 30 250
vibble
```

```
*****************************************************************************************
*                                                                                       *
*  Dialog 260 --  the temporary "Margins" dialog                                        *
*                                                                                       *
Type DLOG
  ,260 (32)
  60 30 200 476
  Visible 1 NoGoAway 0
  260

Type DITL

*   temporary "Margins dialog" dialog items --------------------------------

,260 (32)
10
BtnItem Enable
100   30  120  110
OK

BtnItem Enable
100  350  120  432
Cancel

StatText Disable
16  20  36  190
Set margins to:

radioItem Enabled
44   30  64  90
0"

radioItem Enabled
44  90  64  150
1/2"

radioItem Enabled
44  150  64  200
1"

radioItem Enabled
44  200  64  270
1 1/2"

radioItem Enabled
44  270  64  330
2"

radioItem Enabled
44  330  64  400
2 1/2"

radioItem Enabled
70  120  100  400
Printable area of page
*                                                                                       *
*********
Type DLOG

,261 (32)
220  70  300  432
Visible 1 NoGoAway 0
261
Document being prepared for printing

Type DITL
  ,261 (32)
  2

    StatText Disabled
    30 50 90 310
Preparing "^0" for Printing...

    UserItem Disabled
    0 0 0 0
 *                                END of Resource Definition File
```

EXEC File for SmallApp (File SmallApp.X.TEXT)

```
;                               { The Smallest MacApp Application}
;                    { Copyright 1985 by Productivity Products International, Inc.}
;
;                    { Application "Build" File }
;Assembler Section
;
Patch.A
Object.A
MacApp.A
$
;Pascal Section
;
; The following ensures that all the sample units will be recompiled
;   if the MacApp kernel is recompiled.
WritelnWindow.U
Trace.U
Object.U
List.U
MacApp.U
Printing.U
; These are the SmallApp-specific units that must be compiled
SmallApp.U
SmallApp.M
$
;Linker Section
;
SmallApp
?
+M OBJDebug         GDebug
+M OBJFailNorm      GRes
+M OBJFailure       GRes
+M OBJInit          GInit
+M OBJRes           GRes
+M OBJTerm          GTerm
+M OBJUtil          GRes
;
+M TRCDebug         GDebug
;
+M WWInit           GInit
+M WWSeg            GDebug
;
+M GNewDoc          GDoc
+M GLowUse          GNonRes
+M GOpenDoc         GDoc
+M GClipBoard       GNonRes
+M GCloseDoc        GDoc
+M GCloseWindow     GDoc
+M Bado             GNonRes
+M GCreateD         GDoc
+M GOpenWin         GDoc
+M GWriteDo         GDoc
+M MacAppRe         GRes
+M GResize          GNonRes
+M GMove            GNonRes
+M GDefault         GNonRes
+M GResizeV         GNonRes
+M GActivat         GNonRes
+M GenAppLo         GNonRes
+M GScroll          GRes
+M MacAppLo         GNonRes
;
+M PrintInit        GInit
+M PrintActual      GPrint
+M PrintDebug       GDebug
+M PrintFromFinder  GInit
+M PrintNew         GDoc
+M PrintSetup       PrintRes
+M PrintShared      PrintRes
+M PrintSpool       GPrint
+M PrintTerm        GTerm
+M PrintMisc        GNonRes
;
```

```
+M AInit          GInit
+M ADebug         GDebug
+M ANonRes        GNonRes
obj/QuickDraw
obj/Tooltraps
obj/OStraps
obj/Prlink
obj/Packtraps
obj/RTLIB
obj/PasInit
obj/Paslib
obj/PaslibASM
$
;RMaker Section
SmallApp.R SmallApp.Rsrc
$
;MacCom Section
SmallApp.RSRC SmallestApplication
APPL
SMAP
Y
```

LISTING D

Mini-QuadWorld in Object Pascal

```
      { Object Pascal implementation of the Mini-QuadWorld application using the MacApp Class Library }
                  { Copyright 1985 by Productivity Products International, Inc. }

UNIT UMiniQW;


{$M+}                                    { Compiler commands to generate Macintosh code }
{$X-}                                    {  and turn off stack expansion }
{$E+}                                    {  and automatically invoke the Editor if errors are found }
{$E Error.text}                          {  and put the errors in file 'Error.text' }

{ ******************************************************************************************************* }
                                                    INTERFACE
{ ******************************************************************************************************* }

USES
    {$U-}                                { This set of units are portions of the
                                           Macintosh Software supplement which are used in the
                                           Lisa Pascal Workshop in order to cross develop for
                                           the Macintosh }
    {$U obj/MemTypes}         MemTypes,
    {$U obj/QuickDraw}        QuickDraw,
    {$U obj/OSIntf}           OSIntf,
    {$U obj/ToolIntf}         ToolIntf,
    {$U obj/PackIntf}         PackIntf,
    {$U obj/SaneLib}          SANE,        { Floating point library needed for the rotation of quads
                                           and for computing the distance between two points}

    {$U Object.U}             UObject,     { This set of units are portions of MacApp }
    {$U MacApp.U}             UMacApp,
    {$U Printing.U}           UPrinting;

CONST
    myFileType = 'QUAD';                           { The file type for documents of this application }

 { Command numbers used throughout QuadWorld for the operations the user can perform }
    cClearQuadCmd    =   1102;
    cClearAllCmd     =   1101;
    cRotateQuadCmd   =   1100;

TYPE

    TQuadApplication = OBJECT(TApplication)

      { Initialization }
```

```
        PROCEDURE TQuadApplication.IQuadApplication(itsSignature: OSType);

        FUNCTION  TQuadApplication.DoMakeDocument(itsCmdNumber: CmdNumber): TDocument; OVERRIDE;
    END;


    TQuadDocument = OBJECT(TDocument)
        fLastQuadAdded: TQuad;          { last quad added to the list of quads }
        fQuadGrView:    TQuadGrView;    { the graphical view of this document }
        fSelectedQuad:  TQuad;          { the selected quad, if any, else NIL }

      { Initialization/Freeing }
        PROCEDURE TQuadDocument.IQuadDocument;                               { Initialize a quadDocument }
        PROCEDURE TQuadDocument.Free; OVERRIDE;    { Free the document contents and then the doc itself }
        PROCEDURE TQuadDocument.FreeData; OVERRIDE;                          { Clear quads out of the heap }
        PROCEDURE TQuadDocument.DoInitialState; OVERRIDE;                     { Install the pre-fab quads }

      { Manipulation }
        PROCEDURE TQuadDocument.AddQuad(quad: TQuad);                   { Add to document only, not to views }
        PROCEDURE TQuadDocument.DeleteQuad(quad: TQuad);    { Delete from document only, not from views }
        PROCEDURE TQuadDocument.EachQuadDo(PROCEDURE DoThis(quad: TQuad));          { Enumerate the quads }

      { Display }
        PROCEDURE TQuadDocument.InvalidateQuad(quad: TQuad);                     { Invalidate in the view }
        PROCEDURE TQuadDocument.SelectQuad(quad: TQuad);                             { Select in the view }

      { MacApp "Hook" Methods }
        PROCEDURE TQuadDocument.DoMakeWindows; OVERRIDE;                           { Allocate the window }
        PROCEDURE TQuadDocument.DoMakeViews(forPrinting: BOOLEAN); OVERRIDE;         { Allocate the view }
        FUNCTION  TQuadDocument.DoMenuCommand(aCmdNumber: CmdNumber): TCommand; OVERRIDE; { Menu items }
        PROCEDURE TQuadDocument.DoSetupMenus; OVERRIDE;    { Enable menu items unique to mini-QuadWorld }

    END;


{ The graphical view of the quads }
    TQuadGrView = OBJECT(TView)

      { Initialization }
        PROCEDURE TQuadGrView.IQuadGrView(itsDocument: TQuadDocument);       { Initialize a quadGrView }

      { Commands and Selections }
        FUNCTION  TQuadGrView.DoMouseCommand(VAR downLocalPoint: Point;
                                             VAR info: EventInfo;
                                             VAR hysteresis: Point):
                                                 TCommand; OVERRIDE;         { Handle all mouse clicks }

      { Displaying }
        PROCEDURE TQuadGrView.Draw(area: Rect); OVERRIDE;            { Render an image of the document }
        PROCEDURE TQuadGrView.HighlightSelection(turnOn: BOOLEAN); OVERRIDE;        { Highlight a quad }
        PROCEDURE TQuadGrView.InvalidateQuad(quad: TQuad);            { Redraw the area around a quad }
    END;


    TQuad = OBJECT(TObject)

        fVertex:        ARRAY[1..4] OF Point;
        fNextQuad:      TQuad;          { successor of the linked list of quads kept in quadDocument }
        fRotated:       BOOLEAN;       { TRUE if this quad has been rotated.  Allows optimal drawing }

      { Initialization - for this class and all its subclasses, TParallelogram, TRhombus, etc.}
        PROCEDURE TQuad.IQuad;

      { Queries }
        FUNCTION  TQuad.AsText: Str255;              { Return the textual representation of the quad }
        FUNCTION  TQuad.Center: Point;                          { Return the center point of the  quad }
        FUNCTION  TQuad.EnclosingRect: Rect;     { Return the smallest rectangle enclosing the quad }

      { Displaying }
        PROCEDURE TQuad.Draw;                                 { Draw the quad in the graphical view }

      { Modifing }
        PROCEDURE TQuad.RotateBy(theta: INTEGER);                  { Rotate the quad about its center }
        PROCEDURE TQuad.SetPoints(pt1, pt2, pt3, pt4: Point);            { Set the vertices of a quad }
    END;
```

```


    TParallelogram = OBJECT(TQuad)

        FUNCTION  TParallelogram.AsText: Str255; OVERRIDE;

    END;


    TRhombus = OBJECT(TParallelogram)

        FUNCTION  TRhombus.AsText: Str255; OVERRIDE;

    END;


    TRectangle = OBJECT(TParallelogram)

        FUNCTION  TRectangle.AsText: Str255; OVERRIDE;
        PROCEDURE TRectangle.Draw; OVERRIDE;
        FUNCTION  TRectangle.EnclosingRect: Rect; OVERRIDE;

    END;


    TSquare = OBJECT(TRectangle)

        FUNCTION  TSquare.AsText: Str255; OVERRIDE;

    END;


{ This command object removes the currently selected quad from the quadDocument and is undoable}
    TClearQuadCmd = OBJECT(TCommand)
        fQuad:              TQuad;      { the quad which will be cleared }


      { Initialization }
        PROCEDURE TClearQuadCmd.IClearQuadCmd(itsCmdNumber: INTEGER);

        PROCEDURE TClearQuadCmd.Commit; OVERRIDE;          { Free the quad if the command is committed }
        PROCEDURE TClearQuadCmd.DoIt; OVERRIDE;
        PROCEDURE TClearQuadCmd.RedoIt; OVERRIDE;
        PROCEDURE TClearQuadCmd.UndoIt; OVERRIDE;
    END;


{ This command object rotates a quadrilateral by 45 degrees in the graphical view and is undoable}
    TRotateQuadCmd = OBJECT(TCommand)
        fQuad:          TQuad;       { the quad which will be rotated }
        fAngle:         INTEGER;     { In Mini-QuadWorld this is a constant }

      { Initialization }
        PROCEDURE TRotateQuadCmd.IRotateQuadCmd(itsCmdNumber: INTEGER);
        PROCEDURE TRotateQuadCmd.DoIt;    OVERRIDE;
        PROCEDURE TRotateQuadCmd.RedoIt;  OVERRIDE;
        PROCEDURE TRotateQuadCmd.UndoIt;  OVERRIDE;
    END;


{ This command object clears all the quads from the graphical view }
    TClearAllCmd = OBJECT(TCommand)
        fLastQuadAdded: TQuad;          { Save the list of quads by saving the pointer to it }
        fSelectedQuad:  TQuad;          { Save the currently selected quad }

      { Initialization }
        PROCEDURE TClearAllCmd.IClearAllCmd(itsCmdNumber: INTEGER);

        PROCEDURE TClearAllCmd.Commit; OVERRIDE;      { Free all the quads if the command is committed }
        PROCEDURE TClearAllCmd.DoIt; OVERRIDE;
        PROCEDURE TClearAllCmd.InvalidateEverything;
        PROCEDURE TClearAllCmd.RedoIt; OVERRIDE;
        PROCEDURE TClearAllCmd.UndoIt; OVERRIDE;
    END;

```

```
1 --   { ******************************************************************************************** }
1 --                                           IMPLEMENTATION
1 --   { ******************************************************************************************** }
1 --
1 --
1 --   {$I MiniQW.U2.TEXT}
2 --                       { Copyright 1985 by Productivity Products International, Inc.}
2 --
2 --   { ************************************ TQuadApplication Methods ********************************** }
2 --
2 -- A     PROCEDURE TQuadApplication.IQuadApplication(itsSignature: OSType);
2 --       VAR junk:   REAL;
2 --
2 0- A     BEGIN
2 --           SELF.IApplication('QDWD', myFileType);
2 --           junk := sin(45.0);                  { Force the loading of the transcendental function package
2 --                                                 so that there won't be a disk acces (and a corresponding
2 --                                                 delay) when the Rotate command is used.              }
2 -0 A     END;
2 --
2 --
2 -- A     FUNCTION  TQuadApplication.DoMakeDocument(itsCmdNumber: CmdNumber): TDocument; OVERRIDE;
2 --       VAR quadDocument:  TQuadDocument;
2 0- A     BEGIN
2 --           NEW(quadDocument);
2 --           quadDocument.IQuadDocument;
2 --           DoMakeDocument := quadDocument;
2 -0 A     END;
2 --
2 --
2 --   { ************************************ TQuadDocument Methods ************************************* }
2 --
2 -- A     PROCEDURE TQuadDocument.IQuadDocument;
2 0- A     BEGIN
2 --           IDocument(myFileType);
2 --           SELF.fLastQuadAdded := NIL;
2 --           SELF.fQuadGrView := NIL;
2 --           SELF.fSelectedQuad := NIL;
2 -0 A     END;
2 --
2 --
2 -- A     PROCEDURE TQuadDocument.AddQuad(quad: TQuad);
2 0- A     BEGIN
2 --           IF quad <> NIL THEN
2 1-              BEGIN
2 --              quad.fNextQuad := SELF.fLastQuadAdded;
2 --              SELF.fLastQuadAdded := quad;
2 -1              END;
2 -0 A     END;
2 --
2 --
2 -- A     PROCEDURE TQuadDocument.DeleteQuad(quad: TQuad);
2 --       VAR beforeTestQuad: TQuad;
2 --           testQuad:       TQuad;
2 0- A     BEGIN
2 --           IF (quad <> NIL) AND (SELF.fLastQuadAdded <> NIL)
2 --             THEN
2 1-                BEGIN
2 --                    IF quad = SELF.fLastQuadAdded     { Degenerate case - delete first element in list }
2 --                      THEN SELF.fLastQuadAdded := SELF.fLastQuadAdded.fNextQuad
2 --
2 --                      ELSE                          { Standard case - delete interior element }
2 2-                         BEGIN
2 --                             beforeTestQuad := SELF.fLastQuadAdded;
2 --                             testQuad := SELF.fLastQuadAdded.fNextQuad;
2 --
2 --                             WHILE (quad <> testQuad) DO
2 3-                                 BEGIN
2 --                                     beforeTestQuad := testQuad;
2 --                                     testQuad := testQuad.fNextQuad;
2 -3                                 END;
2 --                                         { Here assume that quad is in the list SOMEWHERE! }
2 --                            beforeTestQuad.fNextQuad := testQuad.fNextQuad;     { Delete the quad }
2 -2                         END;
2 -1                END;
2 -0 A     END;
2 --
```

```
2 --
2 --    { Install the pre-fab quads }
2 -- A     PROCEDURE TQuadDocument.DoInitialState; OVERRIDE;
2 --       VAR aQuad:                TQuad;
2 --           aParallelogram:       TParallelogram;
2 --           aRhombus:             TRhombus;
2 --           aRectangle:           TRectangle;
2 --           aSquare:              TSquare;
2 --           p1, p2, p3, p4:       Point;
2 --
2 0- A     BEGIN
2 --         { Install a set of pre-fabricated quads in the document - FOR MINI-QUADWORLD ONLY }
2 --
2 --           NEW(aQuad);            aQuad.IQuad;
2 --           SetPt(p1, 20, 50);  SetPt(p2, 50, 200);  SetPt(p3, 100, 50);  SetPt(p4, 60, 125);
2 --           aQuad.SetPoints(p1, p2, p3, p4);
2 --           SELF.AddQuad(aQuad);
2 --
2 --           NEW(aParallelogram);  aParallelogram.IQuad;
2 --           SetPt(p1, 150, 50);  SetPt(p2, 125, 75);  SetPt(p3, 250, 75);  SetPt(p4, 275, 50);
2 --           aParallelogram.SetPoints(p1, p2, p3, p4);
2 --           SELF.AddQuad(aParallelogram);
2 --
2 --           NEW(aRhombus);        aRhombus.IQuad;
2 --           SetPt(p1, 250, 125);  SetPt(p2, 220, 165);  SetPt(p3, 270, 165);  SetPt(p4, 300, 125);
2 --           aRhombus.SetPoints(p1, p2, p3, p4);
2 --           SELF.AddQuad(aRhombus);
2 --
2 --           NEW(aRectangle);      aRectangle.IQuad;
2 --           SetPt(p1, 130, 125);  SetPt(p2, 130, 240);  SetPt(p3, 140, 240);  SetPt(p4, 140, 125);
2 --           aRectangle.SetPoints(p1, p2, p3, p4);
2 --           SELF.AddQuad(aRectangle);
2 --
2 --           NEW(aSquare);         aSquare.IQuad;
2 --           SetPt(p1, 300, 175);  SetPt(p2, 300, 225);  SetPt(p3, 350, 225);  SetPt(p4, 350, 175);
2 --           aSquare.SetPoints(p1, p2, p3, p4);
2 --           SELF.AddQuad(aSquare);
2 -0 A     END;
2 --
2 --
2 -- A     PROCEDURE TQuadDocument.DoMakeWindows; OVERRIDE;
2 --       VAR aWindow:         TWindow;
2 --
2 0- A     BEGIN
2 --         { Graphical view window }
2 --           aWindow := NewSimpleWindow(kIDStdWindow, NOT kDialogWindow,
2 --                                      kWantHScrollBar, kWantVScrollBar, SELF.fQuadGrView);
2 --
2 --         { the following takess care of moving the window right now; probably will change later ?????}
2 --           aWindow.fLocation.h := 5;
2 --           aWindow.fLocation.v := 40;
2 -0 A     END;
2 --
2 --
2 -- A     PROCEDURE TQuadDocument.DoMakeViews(forPrinting: BOOLEAN); OVERRIDE;
2 --       VAR aQuadGrView:     TQuadGrView;
2 0- A     BEGIN
2 --           NEW(aQuadGrView);                  { Create and install the graphical view }
2 --           aQuadGrView.IQuadGrView(SELF);
2 --           SELF.fQuadGrView := aQuadGrView;
2 -0 A     END;
2 --
2 --
2 --
2 -- A     FUNCTION  TQuadDocument.DoMenuCommand(aCmdNumber: CmdNumber): TCommand; OVERRIDE;
2 --       VAR clearQuadCmd:   TClearQuadCmd;
2 --           clearAllCmd:    TClearAllCmd;
2 --           rotateQuadCmd:  TRotateQuadCmd;
2 0- A     BEGIN
2 1-           CASE aCmdNumber OF
2 2-                  cRotateQuadCmd:       BEGIN
2 --                                           NEW(rotateQuadCmd);
2 --                                           rotateQuadCmd.IRotateQuadCmd(aCmdNumber);
2 --                                           DoMenuCommand := rotateQuadCmd;
2 -2                                        END;
2 --
2 2-                  cClearQuadCmd:        BEGIN
```

```
                                            NEW(clearQuadCmd);
                                            clearQuadCmd.IClearQuadCmd(aCmdNumber);
                                            DoMenuCommand := clearQuadCmd;
                                         END;

                 cClearAllCmd:           BEGIN
                                            NEW(clearAllCmd);
                                            clearAllCmd.IClearAllCmd(aCmdNumber);
                                            DoMenuCommand := clearAllCmd;
                                         END;

                 OTHERWISE               DoMenuCommand := INHERITED DoMenuCommand(aCmdNumber);
          END;
      END;


      PROCEDURE TQuadDocument.DoSetupMenus; OVERRIDE;
      BEGIN
          INHERITED DoSetupMenus;
          Enable(cRotateQuadCmd, SELF.fSelectedQuad <> NIL);
          Enable(cClearQuadCmd, SELF.fSelectedQuad <> NIL);
          Enable(cClearAllCmd, SELF.fLastQuadAdded <> NIL);
      END;

   {$S ARes}
      PROCEDURE TQuadDocument.EachQuadDo(PROCEDURE DoThis(quad: TQuad));
          VAR quad:  TQuad;
      BEGIN
          quad := SELF.fLastQuadAdded;
          WHILE quad <> NIL DO
              BEGIN
              DoThis(quad);
              quad := quad.fNextQuad;
              END;
      END;


      PROCEDURE TQuadDocument.Free; OVERRIDE;
      BEGIN
          SELF.FreeData;                                             { Free all the quads first }
          INHERITED Free;                                            {  then free yourself      }
      END;


      PROCEDURE TQuadDocument.FreeData; OVERRIDE;
      VAR freeThisQuad:   TQuad;
          nextQuad:       TQuad;
      BEGIN
        { Free all the quads }
          IF SELF.fLastQuadAdded <> NIL                   { Are there really any quads to be freed? }
            THEN
               BEGIN
                   freeThisQuad := SELF.fLastQuadAdded;
                   nextQuad := freeThisQuad.fNextQuad;
                   FreeObject(freeThisQuad);

                   WHILE (nextQuad <> NIL) DO
                        BEGIN
                            freeThisQuad := nextQuad;
                            nextQuad := nextQuad.fNextQuad;
                            FreeObject(freeThisQuad);
                        END
               END;

          SELF.fLastQuadAdded := NIL;
          SELF.fSelectedQuad := NIL;
      END;


   { Invalidate the area occupied by the quad in the graphical view }
      PROCEDURE TQuadDocument.InvalidateQuad(quad: TQuad);
      VAR invalRect:      Rect;
      BEGIN
           IF quad <> NIL THEN
              SELF.fQuadGrView.InvalidateQuad(quad);
      END;
```

```
{ make the selection in the graphical view; quad = NIL means de-select; this routine does nothing if the
  old and new selections are the same }
  PROCEDURE TQuadDocument.SelectQuad(quad: TQuad);
  BEGIN
      IF (quad <> SELF.fSelectedQuad) THEN   { old selection <> new selection }
        BEGIN
            SELF.fQuadGrView.HighlightSelection(FALSE);          { Turn off for the old selection }
            SELF.fSelectedQuad := quad;
            SELF.fQuadGrView.HighlightSelection(TRUE);           { Turn on for the new selection }
        END
  END;


{ **************************************** TQuadGrView Methods ************************************** }

  PROCEDURE TQuadGrView.IQuadGrView(itsDocument: TQuadDocument);
  VAR r:                  Rect;
      aStdPrintHandler:   TStdPrintHandler;
      i:                  INTEGER;
  BEGIN
      SetRect(r, 0, 0, 1000, 1000);          { An arbitrary size for the drawing area of the view }
      SELF.IView(NIL, itsDocument, VRect(r), sizeFixed, sizeFixed, FALSE);
      NEW(aStdPrintHandler);
      aStdPrintHandler.IStdPrintHandler(SELF, FALSE);
  END;


  FUNCTION  TQuadGrView.DoMouseCommand(VAR downLocalPoint: Point;
                                       VAR info: EventInfo;
                                       VAR hysteresis: Point): TCommand; OVERRIDE;

  VAR tempQuad:       TQuad;      { a temporary variable used to find the quad under the cursor }
      selectedQuad:   TQuad;      { the currently selected quad }

      PROCEDURE CheckQuad(thisQuad: TQuad);
      BEGIN
         IF PtInRect(downLocalPoint, thisQuad.EnclosingRect) THEN
            tempQuad := thisQuad;
      END;

  BEGIN
      DoMouseCommand := gNoChanges;
      tempQuad := NIL;
      selectedQuad := TQuadDocument(SELF.fDocument).fSelectedQuad;

      TQuadDocument(SELF.fDocument).EachQuadDo(CheckQuad);

      { tempQuad now refers to the quad, if any, beneath the cursor position }

      IF ((tempQuad <> NIL) AND (selectedQuad = tempQuad))
        THEN
           BEGIN
               { Move the quad - This is left as an exercise for the reader.  (See text) }
           END
        ELSE
           TQuadDocument(SELF.fDocument).SelectQuad(tempQuad);              { Tell the document }

  END;



{$S ARes}
  PROCEDURE TQuadGrView.Draw(area: Rect); OVERRIDE;

      PROCEDURE DrawQuad(quad: TQuad);
      BEGIN
          quad.Draw;
      END;

  BEGIN
      TQuadDocument(SELF.fDocument).EachQuadDo(DrawQuad);
  END;


{$S ARes}
  PROCEDURE TQuadGrView.HighlightSelection(turnOn: BOOLEAN); OVERRIDE;
```

```
    VAR selectedQuad:   TQuad;
        cornerRect:     Rect;
        i:              INTEGER;    { FOR loop index }

    BEGIN
        selectedQuad := TQuadDocument(SELF.fDocument).fSelectedQuad;
        IF (selectedQuad <> NIL)  THEN
            BEGIN
              IF RectIsVisible(selectedQuad.EnclosingRect)
                THEN                                          { only do highlight if quad is visible }
                  BEGIN
                    PenMode(patXOr);
                    SetRect(cornerRect, -2, -2, 2, 2);                        { Highlighting rectangle }
                    FOR i := 1 TO 4 DO
                      BEGIN
                        OffsetRect(cornerRect, selectedQuad.fVertex[i].h, selectedQuad.fVertex[i].v);
                        PaintRect(cornerRect);
                        OffsetRect(cornerRect, -selectedQuad.fVertex[i].h, -selectedQuad.fVertex[i].v);
                      END;
                  END;
            END;
    END;


  { Invalidate the area occupied by the quad in the view }
    PROCEDURE TQuadGrView.InvalidateQuad(quad: TQuad);
    VAR invalRect:      Rect;
    BEGIN
         IF quad <> NIL THEN
             BEGIN
                 invalRect := quad.EnclosingRect;
                 InsetRect(invalRect, -2, -2);                 { Grow the rectangle to include any }
                                                                { highlighting on the quad          }
                 SELF.fFrame.Focus;
                 SELF.InvalVRect(VRect(invalRect));

             END;

    END;


  { ********************************************** TQuad Methods ******************************************** }

    PROCEDURE TQuad.IQuad;
    VAR i:       INTEGER;     {FOR Loop index}
        zeroPt: Point;
    BEGIN
        SetPt(zeroPt, 0, 0);
        FOR i := 1 TO 4 DO fVertex[i] := zeroPt;
        fNextQuad := NIL;
        fRotated := FALSE;
    END;


  {$S ARes}

    FUNCTION  TQuad.AsText: Str255;
    BEGIN
         AsText := 'a Quadrilateral';
    END;


    FUNCTION  TQuad.Center: Point;
    VAR
         thisPoint: Point;
    BEGIN
       thisPoint.h := (fVertex[1].h + fVertex[2].h + fVertex[3].h + fVertex[4].h) div 4;
       thisPoint.v := (fVertex[1].v + fVertex[2].v + fVertex[3].v + fVertex[4].v) div 4;
       Center := thisPoint;

    END;
```

```
PROCEDURE TQuad.Draw;

    PROCEDURE DrawEdge(pt1, pt2: Point);
    BEGIN
        MoveTo(pt1.h, pt1.v);
        LineTo(pt2.h, pt2.v);
    END;  {DrawEdge}

BEGIN
   IF RectIsVisible(SELF.EnclosingRect) THEN      { only draw quads that will be seen }
       BEGIN
           DrawEdge(fVertex[1], fVertex[2]);
           DrawEdge(fVertex[2], fVertex[3]);
           DrawEdge(fVertex[3], fVertex[4]);
           DrawEdge(fVertex[4], fVertex[1]);
       END;
END;  { TQuad.Draw }


FUNCTION  TQuad.EnclosingRect: Rect;
VAR
    minLeft, minTop, maxRight, maxBottom:   INTEGER;
    thisRect:   Rect;
    i:          INTEGER;     { FOR loop index }

    PROCEDURE SetMinMax(pt: Point);
    BEGIN
        minLeft := Min(minLeft, pt.h);
        minTop := Min(minTop, pt.v);
        maxRight := Max(maxRight, pt.h);
        maxBottom := Max(maxBottom, pt.v);
    END;

BEGIN  { TQuad.EnclosingRect }
    minLeft := MAXINT;     minTop := MAXINT;
    maxRight := 0;         maxBottom := 0;

    FOR i := 1 TO 4 DO SetMinMax(SELF.fVertex[i]);

    SetRect(thisRect, minLeft, minTop, maxRight, maxBottom);
    EnclosingRect := thisRect;
END;  { TQuad.EnclosingRect }


{ This method rotates a quad counterclockwise about its center by theta degrees.  Note that this
  method is considerably more general than what is needed by Mini-QuadWorld since it will rotate
  a quad by any number of degrees, whereas Mini-QuadWorld only rotates by 45 degrees.}

PROCEDURE TQuad.RotateBy(theta: INTEGER);
VAR
    newVertex:      ARRAY[1..4] of Point;
    sine, cosine:   REAL;
    centerPt:       Point;
    tempPt:         Point;
    radians:        REAL;
    i:              INTEGER;    { FOR loop index }

BEGIN
    centerPt := SELF.Center;

  { Convert from degrees to radians, as required by the sine and cosine functions }
    radians := (theta * 3.14159) / 180.0;
    sine := sin(radians);
    cosine := cos(radians);
    FOR i := 1 TO 4 DO
       BEGIN
           SetPt(tempPt, SELF.fVertex[i].h - centerPt.h,      { Subtract centerPt from vertex[i]. }
                         SELF.fVertex[i].v - centerPt.v);     { Store the result in tempPt.       }
           newVertex[i].h := Num2Integer(centerPt.h + tempPt.h*cosine - tempPt.v*sine);
           newVertex[i].v := Num2Integer(centerPt.v + tempPt.v*cosine + tempPt.h*sine);
       END;

```

```
2 --          SELF.SetPoints(newVertex[1], newVertex[2], newVertex[3], newVertex[4]);
2 --          SELF.fRotated := TRUE;
2 -0 A     END;
2 --
2 --
2 -- A     PROCEDURE TQuad.SetPoints(pt1, pt2, pt3, pt4: Point);
2 0- A     BEGIN
2 --          fVertex[1] := pt1;
2 --          fVertex[2] := pt2;
2 --          fVertex[3] := pt3;
2 --          fVertex[4] := pt4;
2 -0 A     END;
2 --
2 --
2 --     { *************************************** TParallelogram Methods ***************************************}
2 --
2 -- A     FUNCTION  TParallelogram.AsText: Str255; OVERRIDE;
2 0- A     BEGIN
2 --          AsText := 'a Parallelogram';
2 -0 A     END;
2 --
2 --
2 --     { ******************************************* TRhombus Methods ******************************************}
2 --
2 -- A     FUNCTION  TRhombus.AsText: Str255; OVERRIDE;
2 0- A     BEGIN
2 --          AsText := 'a Rhombus';
2 -0 A     END;
2 --
2 --
2 --     { **************************************** TRectangle Methods ******************************************}
2 --
2 -- A     FUNCTION  TRectangle.AsText: Str255; OVERRIDE;
2 0- A     BEGIN
2 --          AsText := 'a Rectangle';
2 -0 A     END;
2 --
2 --
2 -- A     PROCEDURE TRectangle.Draw; OVERRIDE;
2 --       VAR aRect: Rect;
2 0- A     BEGIN
2 --         IF NOT SELF.fRotated
2 --           THEN
2 1-               BEGIN
2 --                 Pt2Rect(SELF.fVertex[1], SELF.fVertex[3], aRect);
2 --                 FrameRect(aRect);
2 -1               END
2 --
2 --           ELSE INHERITED Draw;
2 -0 A     END;
2 --
2 --
2 -- A     FUNCTION  TRectangle.EnclosingRect: Rect; OVERRIDE;
2 --       VAR thisRect:   Rect;
2 0- A     BEGIN
2 --          IF NOT SELF.fRotated
2 --            THEN Pt2Rect(SELF.fVertex[1], SELF.fVertex[3], thisRect)
2 --            ELSE thisRect := INHERITED EnclosingRect;
2 --          EnclosingRect := thisRect;
2 -0 A     END;  { TRectangle.EnclosingRect }
2 --
2 --
2 --     { ******************************************* TSquare Methods *******************************************}
2 --
2 -- A     FUNCTION  TSquare.AsText: Str255; OVERRIDE;
2 0- A     BEGIN
2 --          AsText := 'a Square';
2 -0 A     END;
2 --
2 --
2 --
2 --     { ************************************** TClearQuadCmd Methods ***************************************}
2 --
```

```
2 -- A    PROCEDURE TClearQuadCmd.IClearQuadCmd(itsCmdNumber: INTEGER);
2 0- A    BEGIN
2 --          SELF.ICommand(itsCmdNumber);
2 --          SELF.fQuad := TQuadDocument(SELF.fChangedDocument).fSelectedQuad
2 -0 A    END;
2 --
2 --
2 -- A    PROCEDURE TClearQuadCmd.Commit; OVERRIDE;
2 0- A    BEGIN
2 --          FreeObject(SELF.fQuad);
2 -0 A    END;
2 --
2 --
2 -- A    PROCEDURE TClearQuadCmd.DoIt; OVERRIDE;
2 --      VAR quadDocument:   TQuadDocument;
2 0- A    BEGIN
2 --          quadDocument := TQuadDocument(SELF.fChangedDocument);
2 --          quadDocument.SelectQuad(NIL);
2 --          quadDocument.DeleteQuad(SELF.fQuad);
2 --          quadDocument.InvalidateQuad(SELF.fQuad);
2 -0 A    END;
2 --
2 --
2 -- A    PROCEDURE TClearQuadCmd.RedoIt; OVERRIDE;
2 0- A    BEGIN
2 --          SELF.DoIt;
2 -0 A    END;
2 --
2 --
2 -- A    PROCEDURE TClearQuadCmd.UndoIt; OVERRIDE;
2 --      VAR quadDocument:   TQuadDocument;
2 0- A    BEGIN
2 --          quadDocument := TQuadDocument(SELF.fChangedDocument);
2 --          quadDocument.AddQuad(SELF.fQuad);
2 --          quadDocument.InvalidateQuad(SELF.fQuad);
2 --          quadDocument.SelectQuad(SELF.fQuad);
2 -0 A    END;
2 --
2 --
2 --
2 --   { ************************************** TRotateQuadCmd Methods ****************************************}
2 --
2 --
2 -- A    PROCEDURE TRotateQuadCmd.IRotateQuadCmd(itsCmdNumber: INTEGER);
2 0- A    BEGIN
2 --          ICommand(itsCmdNumber);
2 --          SELF.fQuad := TQuadDocument(SELF.fChangedDocument).fSelectedQuad;
2 --          SELF.fAngle := 45;
2 -0 A    END;
2 --
2 --
2 -- A    PROCEDURE TRotateQuadCmd.DoIt; OVERRIDE;
2 --      VAR quadDocument:   TQuadDocument;
2 0- A    BEGIN
2 --          quadDocument := TQuadDocument(SELF.fChangedDocument);
2 --          quadDocument.InvalidateQuad(SELF.fQuad);                    { BEFORE Rotation }
2 --          fQuad.RotateBy(SELF.fAngle);
2 --          quadDocument.InvalidateQuad(SELF.fQuad);                     { AFTER Rotation }
2 -0 A    END;
2 --
2 --
2 -- A    PROCEDURE TRotateQuadCmd.RedoIt; OVERRIDE;
2 0- A    BEGIN
2 --          TQuadDocument(SELF.fChangedDocument).SelectQuad(SELF.fQuad);
2 --          SELF.DoIt;
2 -0 A    END;
2 --
2 --
2 -- A    PROCEDURE TRotateQuadCmd.UndoIt; OVERRIDE;
2 --      VAR quadDocument:   TQuadDocument;
```

```
2 0- A      BEGIN
2 --            quadDocument := TQuadDocument(SELF.fChangedDocument);
2 --            quadDocument.SelectQuad(SELF.fQuad);          { Re-establish the current selection in the view }
2 --            quadDocument.InvalidateQuad(SELF.fQuad);                                    { BEFORE Rotation }
2 --            fQuad.RotateBy(-SELF.fAngle);
2 --            quadDocument.InvalidateQuad(SELF.fQuad);                                    { AFTER Rotation }
2 -0 A      END;
2 --
2 --
2 --
2 --      { *************************************** TClearAllCmd Methods *************************************** }
2 --
2 -- A      PROCEDURE TClearAllCmd.IClearAllCmd(itsCmdNumber: INTEGER);
2 0- A      BEGIN
2 --            ICommand(itsCmdNumber);
2 --            SELF.fLastQuadAdded := TQuadDocument(SELF.fChangedDocument).fLastQuadAdded;
2 --            SELF.fSelectedQuad := TQuadDocument(SELF.fChangedDocument).fSelectedQuad;
2 -0 A      END;
2 --
2 --
2 -- A      PROCEDURE TClearAllCmd.Commit; OVERRIDE;
2 --        VAR freeThisQuad:   TQuad;
2 --            nextQuad:       TQuad;
2 0- A      BEGIN
2 --          { Free all the quads }
2 --            IF SELF.fLastQuadAdded <> NIL              { Are there really any quads to be freed? }
2 --              THEN
2 1-                 BEGIN
2 --                     freeThisQuad := SELF.fLastQuadAdded;
2 --                     nextQuad := freeThisQuad.fNextQuad;
2 --                     FreeObject(freeThisQuad);
2 --
2 --                     WHILE (nextQuad <> NIL) DO
2 2-                           BEGIN
2 --                               freeThisQuad := nextQuad;
2 --                               nextQuad := nextQuad.fNextQuad;
2 --                               FreeObject(freeThisQuad);
2 -2                           END
2 -1                 END
2 -0 A      END;
2 --
2 --
2 -- A      PROCEDURE TClearAllCmd.DoIt; OVERRIDE;
2 --        VAR quadDocument:   TQuadDocument;
2 0- A      BEGIN
2 --            quadDocument := TQuadDocument(SELF.fChangedDocument);
2 --            quadDocument.SelectQuad(NIL);
2 --            quadDocument.fLastQuadAdded := NIL;
2 --            SELF.InvalidateEverything;
2 -0 A      END;
2 --
2 --
2 -- A      PROCEDURE TClearAllCmd.InvalidateEverything;
2 --        VAR quadDocument:   TQuadDocument;
2 0- A      BEGIN
2 --            quadDocument := TQuadDocument(SELF.fChangedDocument);
2 --            quadDocument.fQuadGrView.InvalVRect(VRect(quadDocument.fQuadGrView.fExtentRect));
2 -0 A      END;
2 --
2 --
2 -- A      PROCEDURE TClearAllCmd.RedoIt; OVERRIDE;
2 0- A      BEGIN
2 --            SELF.fSelectedQuad := TQuadDocument(SELF.fChangedDocument).fSelectedQuad;
2 --                                     { In case the selection has changed between the undo and the redo }
2 --            SELF.DoIt;
2 -0 A      END;
2 --
2 --
2 -- A      PROCEDURE TClearAllCmd.UndoIt; OVERRIDE;
2 --        VAR quadDocument:   TQuadDocument;
2 0- A      BEGIN
2 --            quadDocument := TQuadDocument(SELF.fChangedDocument);
2 --            quadDocument.fSelectedQuad := SELF.fSelectedQuad;    { The selection COULDN'T have changed!!! }
```

```
870  2  667 --           quadDocument.fLastQuadAdded := SELF.fLastQuadAdded;
871  2  668 --           SELF.InvalidateEverything;
872  2  669 -0 A      END;
873  2  670 --
874  2  671 --
875  1  204 --
876  1  205 --   END.
877  1  206 --
878  1  207 --
879  1  208 --
```

```
  1. MiniQW.U.TEXT
  2. MiniQW.U2.TEXT

 -A-
   aCmdNumber           75*( 1)  136*( 2)  141 ( 2)  144 ( 2)  150 ( 2)  156 ( 2)  160 ( 2)
   AddQuad              64*( 1)   36*( 2)   88 ( 2)   93 ( 2)   98 ( 2)  103 ( 2)  108 ( 2)  557 ( 2)
   aParallelogram       76*( 2)   90 ( 2)   90 ( 2)   92 ( 2)   93 ( 2)
   aQuad                75*( 2)   85 ( 2)   85 ( 2)   87 ( 2)   88 ( 2)
   aQuadGrView         127*( 2)  129 ( 2)  130 ( 2)  131 ( 2)
   area                 94*( 1)  291*( 2)
   aRect               490*( 2)  495 ( 2)  496 ( 2)
   aRectangle           78*( 2)  100 ( 2)  100 ( 2)  102 ( 2)  103 ( 2)
   aRhombus             77*( 2)   95 ( 2)   95 ( 2)   97 ( 2)   98 ( 2)
   aSquare              79*( 2)  105 ( 2)  105 ( 2)  107 ( 2)  108 ( 2)
   aStdPrintHandler    246*( 2)  251 ( 2)  252 ( 2)
   AsText              110*( 1)  126*( 1)  133*( 1)  140*( 1)  149*( 1)  362*( 2)  364=( 2)  467*( 2)  469=( 2)
                       475*( 2)  477=( 2)  483*( 2)  485=( 2)  515*( 2)  517=( 2)
   aWindow             113*( 2)  117=( 2)  121 ( 2)  122 ( 2)

 -B-
   beforeTestQuad       47*( 2)   58=( 2)   63=( 2)   67 ( 2)

 -C-
   cClearAllCmd         38*( 1)  154 ( 2)  171 ( 2)
   cClearQuadCmd        37*( 1)  148 ( 2)  170 ( 2)
   Center              111*( 1)  368*( 2)  374=( 2)  437 ( 2)
   centerPt            431*( 2)  437=( 2)  445 ( 2)  446 ( 2)  447 ( 2)  448 ( 2)
   CheckQuad           263*( 2)  274 ( 2)
   clearAllCmd         138*( 2)  155 ( 2)  156 ( 2)  157 ( 2)
   clearQuadCmd        137*( 2)  149 ( 2)  150 ( 2)  151 ( 2)
   CmdNumber            48 ( 1)   75 ( 1)   16 ( 2)  136 ( 2)
   Commit              162*( 1)  190*( 1)  531*( 2)  614*( 2)
   cornerRect          307*( 2)  318 ( 2)  321 ( 2)  322 ( 2)  323 ( 2)
   cos                 442 ( 2)
   cosine              430*( 2)  442=( 2)  447 ( 2)  448 ( 2)
   cRotateQuadCmd       39*( 1)  142 ( 2)  169 ( 2)

 -D-
   DeleteQuad           65*( 1)   46*( 2)  542 ( 2)
   DoInitialState       61*( 1)   74*( 2)
   DoIt                163*( 1)  176*( 1)  191*( 1)  537*( 2)  549 ( 2)  575*( 2)  588 ( 2)  636*( 2)  658 ( 2)
   DoMakeDocument       48*( 1)   16*( 2)   21=( 2)
   DoMakeViews          74*( 1)  126*( 2)
   DoMakeWindows        73*( 1)  112*( 2)
   DoMenuCommand        75*( 1)  136*( 2)  145=( 2)  151=( 2)  157=( 2)  160=( 2)  160 ( 2)
   DoMouseCommand       88*( 1)  256*( 2)  270=( 2)
   DoSetupMenus         76*( 1)  166*( 2)  168 ( 2)
   DoThis               66*( 1)  176*( 2)  182 ( 2)
   downLocalPoint       88*( 1)  256*( 2)  265 ( 2)
   Draw                 94*( 1)  115*( 1)  141*( 1)  291*( 2)  295 ( 2)  379*( 2)  489*( 2)  499 ( 2)
   DrawEdge            381*( 2)  390 ( 2)  391 ( 2)  392 ( 2)  393 ( 2)
   DrawQuad            293*( 2)  299 ( 2)

 -E-
   EachQuadDo           66*( 1)  176*( 2)  274 ( 2)  299 ( 2)
   Enable              169 ( 2)  170 ( 2)  171 ( 2)
   EnclosingRect       112*( 1)  142*( 1)  265 ( 2)  314 ( 2)  336 ( 2)  388 ( 2)  398*( 2)  419=( 2)  503*( 2)
                       508 ( 2)  509=( 2)
   EventInfo            89 ( 1)  257 ( 2)
```

-F-									
FALSE	235 (2)	250 (2)	252 (2)	356 (2)					
fAngle	172*(1)	571=(2)	580 (2)	598 (2)					
fChangedDocument	527 (2)	540 (2)	556 (2)	570 (2)	578 (2)	587 (2)	595 (2)	609 (2)	610 (2)
	639 (2)	649 (2)	656 (2)	665 (2)					
fDocument	272 (2)	274 (2)	284 (2)	299 (2)	311 (2)				
fExtentRect	650 (2)								
fFrame	339 (2)								
fLastQuadAdded	53*(1)	184*(1)	30=(2)	40 (2)	41=(2)	50 (2)	53 (2)	54=(2)	54 (2)
	58 (2)	59 (2)	171 (2)	179 (2)	200 (2)	203 (2)	215=(2)	609=(2)	609 (2)
	619 (2)	622 (2)	641=(2)	667=(2)	667 (2)				
fLocation	121 (2)	122 (2)							
fNextQuad	103*(1)	40=(2)	54 (2)	59 (2)	64 (2)	67=(2)	67 (2)	183 (2)	204 (2)
	210 (2)	355=(2)	623 (2)	629 (2)					
Focus	339 (2)								
forPrinting	74*(1)	126*(2)							
fQuad	156*(1)	171*(1)	527=(2)	533 (2)	542 (2)	543 (2)	557 (2)	558 (2)	559 (2)
	570=(2)	579 (2)	580 (2)	581 (2)	587 (2)	596 (2)	597 (2)	598 (2)	599 (2)
fQuadGrView	54*(1)	31=(2)	118 (2)	131=(2)	225 (2)	235 (2)	237 (2)	650 (2)	650 (2)
FrameRect	496 (2)								
Free	59*(1)	188*(2)	191 (2)						
FreeData	60*(1)	190 (2)	195*(2)						
FreeObject	205 (2)	211 (2)	533 (2)	624 (2)	630 (2)				
freeThisQuad	196*(2)	203=(2)	204 (2)	205 (2)	209=(2)	211 (2)	615*(2)	622=(2)	623 (2)
	624 (2)	628=(2)	630 (2)						
fRotated	104*(1)	356=(2)	452=(2)	492 (2)	506 (2)				
fSelectedQuad	55*(1)	185*(1)	32=(2)	169 (2)	170 (2)	216=(2)	233 (2)	236=(2)	272 (2)
	311 (2)	527 (2)	570 (2)	610=(2)	610 (2)	656=(2)	656 (2)	666=(2)	666 (2)
fVertex	102*(1)	321 (2)	321 (2)	323 (2)	323 (2)	354=(2)	372 (2)	372 (2)	372 (2)
	372 (2)	373 (2)	373 (2)	373 (2)	373 (2)	390 (2)	390 (2)	391 (2)	391 (2)
	392 (2)	392 (2)	393 (2)	393 (2)	416 (2)	445 (2)	446 (2)	458=(2)	459=(2)
	460=(2)	461=(2)	495 (2)	495 (2)	507 (2)	507 (2)			
-G-									
gNoChanges	270 (2)								
-H-									
h	121=(2)	321 (2)	323 (2)	372=(2)	372 (2)	372 (2)	372 (2)	372 (2)	383 (2)
	384 (2)	406 (2)	408 (2)	445 (2)	445 (2)	447=(2)	447 (2)	447 (2)	448 (2)
HighlightSelecti	95*(1)	235 (2)	237 (2)	304*(2)					
hysteresis	90*(1)	258*(2)							
-I-									
i	247*(2)	308*(2)	319=(2)	321 (2)	321 (2)	323 (2)	323 (2)	350*(2)	354=(2)
	354 (2)	402*(2)	416=(2)	416 (2)	434*(2)	443=(2)	445 (2)	446 (2)	447 (2)
	448 (2)								
IApplication	9 (2)								
IClearAllCmd	188*(1)	156 (2)	606*(2)						
IClearQuadCmd	160*(1)	150 (2)	524*(2)						
ICommand	526 (2)	569 (2)	608 (2)						
IDocument	29 (2)								
info	89*(1)	257*(2)							
InsetRect	337 (2)								
INTEGER	118 (1)	160 (1)	172 (1)	175 (1)	188 (1)	247 (2)	308 (2)	350 (2)	400 (2)
	402 (2)	427 (2)	434 (2)	524 (2)	567 (2)	606 (2)			
InvalidateEveryt	192*(1)	642 (2)	646*(2)	668 (2)					
InvalidateQuad	69*(1)	96*(1)	221*(2)	225 (2)	331*(2)	543 (2)	558 (2)	579 (2)	581 (2)
	597 (2)	599 (2)							
invalRect	222*(2)	332*(2)	336=(2)	337 (2)	340 (2)				
InvalVRect	340 (2)	650 (2)							
IQuad	107*(1)	85 (2)	90 (2)	95 (2)	100 (2)	105 (2)	349*(2)		
IQuadApplication	46*(1)	5*(2)							
IQuadDocument	58*(1)	20 (2)	27*(2)						
IQuadGrView	85*(1)	130 (2)	244*(2)						
IRotateQuadCmd	175*(1)	144 (2)	567*(2)						
IStdPrintHandler	252 (2)								
itsCmdNumber	48*(1)	160*(1)	175*(1)	188*(1)	16*(2)	524*(2)	526 (2)	567*(2)	569 (2)
	606*(2)	608 (2)							
itsDocument	85*(1)	244*(2)	250 (2)						
itsSignature	46*(1)	5*(2)							
IView	250 (2)								

```
-J-
  junk             6*( 2)   10=( 2)

-K-
  kDialogWindow    117 ( 2)
  kIDStdWindow     117 ( 2)
  kWantHScrollBar  118 ( 2)
  kWantVScrollBar  118 ( 2)

-L-
  LineTo           384 ( 2)

-M-
  Max              408 ( 2)  409 ( 2)
  maxBottom        400*( 2)  409=( 2)  409 ( 2)  414=( 2)  418 ( 2)
  MAXINT           413 ( 2)  413 ( 2)
  maxRight         400*( 2)  408=( 2)  408 ( 2)  414=( 2)  418 ( 2)
  MemTypes          21*( 1)
  Min              406 ( 2)  407 ( 2)
  minLeft          400*( 2)  406=( 2)  406 ( 2)  413=( 2)  418 ( 2)
  minTop           400*( 2)  407=( 2)  407 ( 2)  413=( 2)  418 ( 2)
  MoveTo           383 ( 2)
  myFileType        34*( 1)    9 ( 2)   29 ( 2)

-N-
  NEW               19 ( 2)   85 ( 2)   90 ( 2)   95 ( 2)  100 ( 2)  105 ( 2)  129 ( 2)  143 ( 2)  149 ( 2)
                   155 ( 2)  251 ( 2)
  NewSimpleWindow  117 ( 2)
  newVertex        429*( 2)  447 ( 2)  448 ( 2)  451 ( 2)  451 ( 2)  451 ( 2)  451 ( 2)
  nextQuad         197*( 2)  204=( 2)  207 ( 2)  209 ( 2)  210=( 2)  210 ( 2)  616*( 2)  623=( 2)  626 ( 2)
                   628 ( 2)  629=( 2)  629 ( 2)
  Num2Integer      447 ( 2)  448 ( 2)

-O-
  OffsetRect       321 ( 2)  323 ( 2)
  OSIntf            23*( 1)
  OSType            46 ( 1)    5 ( 2)

-P-
  p1                80*( 2)   86 ( 2)   87 ( 2)   91 ( 2)   92 ( 2)   96 ( 2)   97 ( 2)  101 ( 2)  102 ( 2)
                   106 ( 2)  107 ( 2)
  p2                80*( 2)   86 ( 2)   87 ( 2)   91 ( 2)   92 ( 2)   96 ( 2)   97 ( 2)  101 ( 2)  102 ( 2)
                   106 ( 2)  107 ( 2)
  p3                80*( 2)   86 ( 2)   87 ( 2)   91 ( 2)   92 ( 2)   96 ( 2)   97 ( 2)  101 ( 2)  102 ( 2)
                   106 ( 2)  107 ( 2)
  p4                80*( 2)   86 ( 2)   87 ( 2)   91 ( 2)   92 ( 2)   96 ( 2)   97 ( 2)  101 ( 2)  102 ( 2)
                   106 ( 2)  107 ( 2)
  PackIntf          25*( 1)
  PaintRect        322 ( 2)
  patXOr           317 ( 2)
  PenMode          317 ( 2)
  Point             88 ( 1)   90 ( 1)  102 ( 1)  111 ( 1)  119 ( 1)   80 ( 2)  256 ( 2)  258 ( 2)  351 ( 2)
                   368 ( 2)  370 ( 2)  381 ( 2)  404 ( 2)  429 ( 2)  431 ( 2)  432 ( 2)  456 ( 2)
  pt               404*( 2)  406 ( 2)  407 ( 2)  408 ( 2)  409 ( 2)
  pt1              119*( 1)  381*( 2)  383 ( 2)  383 ( 2)  456*( 2)  458 ( 2)
  pt2              119*( 1)  381*( 2)  384 ( 2)  384 ( 2)  456*( 2)  459 ( 2)
  Pt2Rect          495 ( 2)  507 ( 2)
  pt3              119*( 1)  456*( 2)  460 ( 2)
  pt4              119*( 1)  456*( 2)  461 ( 2)
  PtInRect         265 ( 2)

-Q-
  quad              64*( 1)   65*( 1)   66*( 1)   69*( 1)   70*( 1)   96*( 1)   36*( 2)   38 ( 2)   40 ( 2)
                    41 ( 2)   46*( 2)   50 ( 2)   53 ( 2)   61 ( 2)  176*( 2)  177*( 2)  179=( 2)  180 ( 2)
                   182 ( 2)  183=( 2)  183 ( 2)  221*( 2)  224 ( 2)  225 ( 2)  231*( 2)  233 ( 2)  236 ( 2)
                   293*( 2)  295 ( 2)  331*( 2)  334 ( 2)  336 ( 2)
  quadDocument      17*( 2)   19 ( 2)   20 ( 2)   21 ( 2)  538*( 2)  540=( 2)  541 ( 2)  542 ( 2)  543 ( 2)
                   554*( 2)  556=( 2)  557 ( 2)  558 ( 2)  559 ( 2)  576*( 2)  578=( 2)  579 ( 2)  581 ( 2)
                   593*( 2)  595=( 2)  596 ( 2)  597 ( 2)  599 ( 2)  637*( 2)  639=( 2)  640 ( 2)  641 ( 2)
                   647*( 2)  649=( 2)  650 ( 2)  650 ( 2)  663*( 2)  665=( 2)  666 ( 2)  667 ( 2)
  QuickDraw         22*( 1)
```

```
-U-
  UMacApp            30*( 1)
  UMiniQW             4*( 1)
  UndoIt            165*( 1)  178*( 1)  194*( 1)  553*( 2)  592*( 2)  662*( 2)
  UObject            29*( 1)
  UPrinting          31*( 1)

-V-
  v                 122=( 2)  321 ( 2)  323 ( 2)  373=( 2)  373 ( 2)  373 ( 2)  373 ( 2)  373 ( 2)  383 ( 2)
                    384 ( 2)  407 ( 2)  409 ( 2)  446 ( 2)  446 ( 2)  447 ( 2)  448=( 2)  448 ( 2)  448 ( 2)
  VRect             250 ( 2)  340 ( 2)  650 ( 2)

-Z-
  zeroPt            351*( 2)  353 ( 2)  354 ( 2)

*** End Xref: 196 id's   1297 references   [1475976 bytes/4803 id's/174891 refs]
```

LISTING E

QuadWorld in Object Pascal

```
            { Object Pascal implementation of the QuadWorld application using the MacApp Class Library }
            { as discussed in Chapter 8 of 'Object-Oriented Programming for the Macintosh'              }
                  { Copyright 1985 by Productivity Products International, Inc. }

UNIT UQuadWorld;


{$M+}                                   { Compiler commands to generate Macintosh code }
{$X-}                                   {  and turn off stack expansion }
{$E+}                                   {  and automatically invoke the Editor if errors are found }
{$E Error.text}                         {  and put the errors in file 'Error.text' }

INTERFACE
USES
    {$U-}                               { This set of units are portions of the
                                          Macintosh Software supplement }
    {$U obj/MemTypes}       MemTypes,
    {$U obj/QuickDraw}      QuickDraw,
    {$U obj/OSIntf}         OSIntf,
    {$U obj/ToolIntf}       ToolIntf,
    {$U obj/PackIntf}       PackIntf,
    {$U obj/SaneLib}        SANE,       { Floating point library needed for the rotation of quads
                                          and for computing the distance between two points}

    {$U Object.U}           UObject,    { This set of units are portions of MacApp }
    {$U List.U}             UList,
    {$U MacApp.U}           UMacApp,
    {$U Printing.U}         UPrinting,

    {$U ListView.U}         UListView;  { List view unit for the quad textual view  }

 CONST
    myFileType = 'QUAD';                { The file type for documents written by this application }
    numQuadTypes = 5;                   { The number of types of quads, e.g., 'square' as one type,
                                          'rhombus' as another, etc., that the application can
                                          currently process }


  { Command numbers used throughout QuadWorld for the operations the user can perform }
    cClearQuadCmd    =   1102;
    cClearAllCmd     =   1101;
    cRotateQuadCmd   =   1100;

    cAddQuadCmd              =    2001;
    cAddParallelogramCmd     =    2002;
```

```
    cAddRhombusCmd          =   2003;
    cAddRectangleCmd        =   2004;
    cAddSquareCmd           =   2005;

  { The 'codes' for quads written to disk.  See the TFiledQuad Record }
    IDQuad              =       1;
    IDParallelogram     =       2;
    IDRhombus           =       3;
    IDRectangle         =       4;
    IDSquare            =       5;
    IDLastQuad          =       6;  { To mark the end of the set of quads on disk }


  { Resource ids in the QuadWorld Resource File }
    cOneEdgeQuadCursor      =  100;    { Cursor shape when only one edge of a new quad has been drawn }
    cTwoEdgeQuadCursor      =  101;    { Cursor shape when only two edges of a new quad have been drawn }


TYPE

    TFiledQuad =     RECORD                                       { Disk version of a quad }
                         theRotationState:    BOOLEAN;
                         theVertices:         ARRAY[1..4] OF Point;
                     END;


    TQuadApplication = OBJECT(TApplication)

      { Initialization }
        PROCEDURE TQuadApplication.IQuadApplication(itsSignature: OSType);

        FUNCTION  TQuadApplication.DoMakeDocument(itsCmdNumber: CmdNumber): TDocument; OVERRIDE;
    END;


    TQuadDocument = OBJECT(TListDocument)
        fLastQuadAdded: TQuad;         { last quad added to the list of quads }
        fQuadGrView:    TQuadGrView;   { the graphical view of this document }
        fQuadTxView:    TListView;     { the textual view of this document }
        fSelectedQuad:  TQuad;         { the selected quad, if any, else NIL }

      { Initialization/Freeing }
        PROCEDURE TQuadDocument.IQuadDocument;
        PROCEDURE TQuadDocument.Free; OVERRIDE;
        PROCEDURE TQuadDocument.FreeData; OVERRIDE;
        {$IFC qDebug}
        PROCEDURE TQuadDocument.Inspect; OVERRIDE;                 { Debugging print of the quadDocument }
        {$ENDC}


      { Display }
        PROCEDURE TQuadDocument.InvalidateQuad(quad: TQuad);                  { invalidate in both views }
        PROCEDURE TQuadDocument.SelectQuad(quad: TQuad);                          { select in both views }

      { Manipulation }
        PROCEDURE TQuadDocument.AddQuad(quad: TQuad);                 { add to document only, not to views }
        PROCEDURE TQuadDocument.DeleteQuad(quad: TQuad);       { delete from document only, not from views }
        PROCEDURE TQuadDocument.EachQuadDo(PROCEDURE DoThis(quad: TQuad));            { enumerate the quads }

      { List View Support (UList unit) }
        PROCEDURE TQuadDocument.SetSelection(newSelectionIndex: INTEGER); OVERRIDE;
        FUNCTION  TQuadDocument.QuadToListIndex(quad: TQuad): INTEGER;
        FUNCTION  TQuadDocument.ListIndexToQuad(index: INTEGER): TQuad;
        FUNCTION  TQuadDocument.ReportListItem(itemNumber: INTEGER): Str255;  OVERRIDE;

      { Filing }
        PROCEDURE TQuadDocument.DoNeedDiskSpace(VAR dataForkBytes, rsrcForkBytes: LONGINT); OVERRIDE;
        PROCEDURE TQuadDocument.DoRead(aRefNum: INTEGER; forPrinting: BOOLEAN); OVERRIDE;
        PROCEDURE TQuadDocument.DoWrite(aRefNum: INTEGER); OVERRIDE;

      { MacApp "Hooks" }
        PROCEDURE TQuadDocument.DoMakeWindows; OVERRIDE;
        PROCEDURE TQuadDocument.DoMakeViews(forPrinting: BOOLEAN); OVERRIDE;
        FUNCTION  TQuadDocument.DoMenuCommand(aCmdNumber: CmdNumber): TCommand; OVERRIDE;
        PROCEDURE TQuadDocument.DoSetupMenus; OVERRIDE;
    END;
```

```
{ The view used for the palette of quadrilaterals }
   TPalette = OBJECT(TView)
      fCurrSelection: INTEGER;                          { The currently selected block on the palette }
      fQuadGrView:    TQuadGrView;          { Reference to the other part of the quad graphical window }
      fChoiceRects:   ARRAY[0..numQuadTypes] of Rect;           { The individual squares of the palette }

    { Initialization }
      PROCEDURE TPalette.IPalette(itsDocument: TDocument; aQuadGrView: TQuadGrView);

      PROCEDURE TPalette.ChangeSelection(newSelection: INTEGER);
      PROCEDURE TPalette.DoHighlightSelection(fromHL, toHL: HLState); OVERRIDE;
      FUNCTION  TPalette.DoMouseCommand(VAR downLocalPoint: Point; VAR info: EventInfo;
                                   VAR hysteresis: Point): TCommand; OVERRIDE;
      PROCEDURE TPalette.Draw(area: Rect); OVERRIDE;
   END;


{ The graphical view of the quads }
   TQuadGrView = OBJECT(TView)
      fSelectedQuad:          TQuad;                 { reference to the selected quad }
      fPalette:               TPalette;              { reference to the quad palette }
      fRotationRgn:           RgnHandle;             { The small circle in which the user must
                                                       'mouse down' in order to begin specifying the
                                                       angle that the selected quad is to be rotated.  }
    { Initialization }
      PROCEDURE TQuadGrView.IQuadGrView(itsDocument: TQuadDocument);


    { Commands and Selections }
      PROCEDURE TQuadGrView.ChangeSelection(newQuad: TQuad); { Respond correctly to a selection change }
      FUNCTION  TQuadGrView.DoMouseCommand(VAR downLocalPoint: Point; VAR info: EventInfo;
                                   VAR hysteresis: Point): TCommand; OVERRIDE;

    { Displaying }
      PROCEDURE TQuadGrView.DoHighlightSelection(fromHL, toHL: HLState); OVERRIDE;
      PROCEDURE TQuadGrView.DoIdle(phase: IdlePhase); OVERRIDE;
      FUNCTION  TQuadGrView.DoSetCursor(localPoint: Point): BOOLEAN; OVERRIDE;
      PROCEDURE TQuadGrView.Draw(area: Rect); OVERRIDE;
      PROCEDURE TQuadGrView.InvalidateQuad(quad: TQuad);            { invalidate in the graphical view }

    { Interactive Entry of New Quadrilaterals }
      PROCEDURE TQuadGrView.DrawPartialQuad;    { Draw any quad yet only partially sketched by the user }
      FUNCTION  TQuadGrView.PendingSketcher: TSketchQuadCmd; { Returns the unfinished sketcher, if any }
   END;


{ The quadrilateral classes themselves }
   TQuad = OBJECT(TObject)

      fVertex:        ARRAY[1..4] OF Point;
      fNextQuad:      TQuad;               { successor of the linked list of quads kept in quadDocument  }
      fEnclosingRect: Rect;                { the upright rectangle enclosing the quad }
      fRotated:       BOOLEAN;             { TRUE if this quad has been rotated.  Allows optimal drawing }

    { Initialization - for this class and all its subclasses, TParallelogram, TRhombus, etc.}
      PROCEDURE TQuad.IQuad;

      {$IFC qDebug}
      PROCEDURE TQuad.Inspect; OVERRIDE;           { Debugging print of the quad's instance variables }
      {$ENDC}

    { Queries }
      FUNCTION  TQuad.AsText: Str255;
      FUNCTION  TQuad.Center: Point;
      FUNCTION  TQuad.EnclosingRect: Rect;                 { Private method to calculate fExtentRect }
      FUNCTION  TQuad.NewSketchCmd: TSketchQuadCmd;        { Return an appropriate sketch command to
                                                             define a new quad }
    { Displaying }
      PROCEDURE TQuad.Draw;

    { Modifing }
      PROCEDURE TQuad.RotateBy(theta: INTEGER);
      PROCEDURE TQuad.SetPoints(pt1, pt2, pt3, pt4: Point);

    { Filing }
      FUNCTION  TQuad.ID: INTEGER;
```

```
            PROCEDURE TQuad.ReadFrom(aRefNum: INTEGER);
            PROCEDURE TQuad.WriteTo(aRefNum: INTEGER);
        END;


        TParallelogram = OBJECT(TQuad)

            FUNCTION  TParallelogram.AsText: Str255; OVERRIDE;
            FUNCTION  TParallelogram.ID: INTEGER; OVERRIDE;
            FUNCTION  TParallelogram.NewSketchCmd: TSketchQuadCmd; OVERRIDE;
        END;


        TRhombus = OBJECT(TParallelogram)

            FUNCTION  TRhombus.AsText: Str255; OVERRIDE;
            FUNCTION  TRhombus.ID: INTEGER; OVERRIDE;
            FUNCTION  TRhombus.NewSketchCmd: TSketchQuadCmd; OVERRIDE;
        END;


        TRectangle = OBJECT(TParallelogram)

            FUNCTION  TRectangle.AsText: Str255; OVERRIDE;
            PROCEDURE TRectangle.Draw; OVERRIDE;
            FUNCTION  TRectangle.EnclosingRect: Rect; OVERRIDE;
            FUNCTION  TRectangle.ID: INTEGER; OVERRIDE;
            FUNCTION  TRectangle.NewSketchCmd: TSketchQuadCmd; OVERRIDE;
        END;


        TSquare = OBJECT(TRectangle)

            FUNCTION  TSquare.AsText: Str255; OVERRIDE;
            FUNCTION  TSquare.ID: INTEGER; OVERRIDE;
            FUNCTION  TSquare.NewSketchCmd: TSketchQuadCmd; OVERRIDE;
        END;


    { This abstract command object is the superclass of all commands that add quadrilaterals to or
      remove quadrilaterals from the quadDocument.  All such commands are undoable }
        TAddQuadCmd = OBJECT(TCommand)
            fQuad:              TQuad;      { the quad which will be added }
            fQuadInstalled:     BOOLEAN;    { Has the quad been added to the document?  Note that this
                                              information must be recorded here in order for the
                                              subclass (TClearQuadCmd) of this class to work correctly,
                                              since a 'done' clear command de-installs the quad yet a
                                              'done' add command installs it.}

            PROCEDURE TAddQuadCmd.IAddQuadCmd(itsCmdNumber: CmdNumber; quadToBeAdded: TQuad);
            PROCEDURE TAddQuadCmd.Free; OVERRIDE;

            PROCEDURE TAddQuadCmd.AddQuad;
            PROCEDURE TAddQuadCmd.DeleteQuad(quad: TQuad);
          { PROCEDURE TAddQuadCmd.DoIt; OVERRIDE;    Not needed, see comments in implementation }
            PROCEDURE TAddQuadCmd.RedoIt; OVERRIDE;
            PROCEDURE TAddQuadCmd.UndoIt; OVERRIDE;
        END;


    { This command object draws new quadrilaterals in the graphical view }
        TSketchQuadCmd = OBJECT(TAddQuadCmd)
            fLastVertexSet:     INTEGER;    { How far has the user gotten in constructing this quad }
            fQuadGrView:        TQuadGrView;

          { Initialization - for this class and all of its subclases}
            PROCEDURE TSketchQuadCmd.ISketchQuadCmd(aCmdNumber: CmdNumber);

            {$IFC qDebug}
            PROCEDURE TSketchQuadCmd.Inspect; OVERRIDE; { Debugging print of the sketcher's instance variables }
            {$ENDC}

            PROCEDURE TSketchQuadCmd.Commit;  OVERRIDE;
            PROCEDURE TSketchQuadCmd.EnclosePartialQuad;  { Set the enclosing rectangle for the partial quad }
            PROCEDURE TSketchQuadCmd.TrackFeedback(anchorPoint, nextPoint: Point;
                                                   turnItOn, mouseDidMove: BOOLEAN); OVERRIDE;
```

```
            FUNCTION  TSketchQuadCmd.TrackMouse(aTrackPhase: TrackPhase;
                                          VAR anchorPoint, previousPoint, nextPoint: Point;
                                          mouseDidMove: BOOLEAN): TCommand; OVERRIDE;
            PROCEDURE TSketchQuadCmd.SetVertices(newVertex: Point);  { Set one or more vertices based on the
                                                                       mouse position }
        END;


    { This command object draws new parallelograms in the graphical view }
        TSketchParallelogramCmd = OBJECT(TSketchQuadCmd)

            PROCEDURE TSketchParallelogramCmd.SetVertices(newVertex: Point);  OVERRIDE;
        END;


    { This command object draws new rhombi in the graphical view }
        TSketchRhombusCmd = OBJECT(TSketchParallelogramCmd)

            PROCEDURE TSketchRhombusCmd.TrackConstrain(anchorPoint, previousPoint: Point;
                                                       VAR nextPoint: Point); OVERRIDE;
        END;


    { This command object draws new rectangles in the graphical view }
    { NOTE: Rectangle becomes Tangle to avoid name conflict with Rhombus.  Lisa Pascal requires that
            identifiers be unique in the first eight characters. }
        TSketchTangleCmd = OBJECT(TSketchParallelogramCmd)

            PROCEDURE TSketchTangleCmd.TrackFeedback(anchorPoint, nextPoint: Point;
                                          turnItOn, mouseDidMove: BOOLEAN); OVERRIDE;
            PROCEDURE TSketchTangleCmd.SetVertices(newVertex: Point);  OVERRIDE;
        END;


    { This command object draws new squares in the graphical view }
        TSketchSquareCmd = OBJECT(TSketchTangleCmd)

            PROCEDURE TSketchSquareCmd.TrackConstrain(anchorPoint, previousPoint: Point;
                                                      VAR nextPoint: Point); OVERRIDE;
        END;


    { This command object removes the currently selected quad from the quadDocument and is undoable }
        TClearQuadCmd = OBJECT(TAddQuadCmd)

          { Initialization }
            PROCEDURE TClearQuadCmd.IClearQuadCmd(itsCmdNumber: INTEGER);

            PROCEDURE TClearQuadCmd.DoIt; OVERRIDE;
            PROCEDURE TClearQuadCmd.RedoIt; OVERRIDE;
            PROCEDURE TClearQuadCmd.UndoIt; OVERRIDE;
       END;


    { This command object rotates a quadrilateral in the graphical view and is undoable}
        TRotateQuadCmd = OBJECT(TCommand)
            fQuad:          TQuad;          { the quad which will be rotated }
            fCenterPoint:   Point;          { center point of the selected quad }
            fAngle:         INTEGER;

          { Initialization }
            PROCEDURE TRotateQuadCmd.IRotateQuadCmd(itsCmdNumber: INTEGER);

          { Command performance }
            PROCEDURE TRotateQuadCmd.DoIt;     OVERRIDE;
            PROCEDURE TRotateQuadCmd.RedoIt;   OVERRIDE;
            PROCEDURE TRotateQuadCmd.UndoIt;   OVERRIDE;

          { User feedback during the specification of the angle of rotation }
            PROCEDURE TRotateQuadCmd.TrackFeedback(anchorPoint, nextPoint: Point;
                                            turnItOn, mouseDidMove: BOOLEAN); OVERRIDE;
            FUNCTION  TRotateQuadCmd.TrackMouse(aTrackPhase: TrackPhase;
                                          VAR anchorPoint, previousPoint, nextPoint: Point;
                                          mouseDidMove: BOOLEAN): TCommand; OVERRIDE;
        END;
```

```

{ This command object clears all the quads from both views and is undoable }
   TClearAllCmd = OBJECT(TCommand)
      fLastQuadAdded: TQuad;          { Save the list of quads by saving the pointer to it }
      fSelectedQuad: TQuad;           { Save the currently selected quad }

    { Initialization }
      PROCEDURE TClearAllCmd.IClearAllCmd(itsCmdNumber: INTEGER);

      PROCEDURE TClearAllCmd.Commit; OVERRIDE;    { Free all the quads if the command is committed }
      PROCEDURE TClearAllCmd.DoIt; OVERRIDE;
      PROCEDURE TClearAllCmd.InvalidateEverything;
      PROCEDURE TClearAllCmd.RedoIt; OVERRIDE;
      PROCEDURE TClearAllCmd.UndoIt; OVERRIDE;
   END;

IMPLEMENTATION

{$I QuadWorld.U2.TEXT}
                        { Copyright 1985 by Productivity Products International, Inc.}

{ Private data }
CONST
   paletteWidth  =  20;                            { the width of the palette of quad types
                                                     on the left edge of the quad graphical
                                                     window.                                  }

VAR
   gPrototypeQuadsArray:   ARRAY [1..numQuadTypes] OF TQuad;   { An array of quads used for cloning.
                                                               See comments in IQuadApplication and
                                                               in TQuadGrView.DoMouseCommand       }


{ ******************************************************************************************* }
{ ******************************************************************************************* }
{                           METHODS FOR ALL THE QUADWORLD CLASSES                             }
{                                                                                             }
{  Note that methods are grouped by class and that the order of methods in any class is the following }
{  (by convention only, since Object Pascal forces no order):                                 }
{                                                                                             }
{             (1) the initialization method, if any,                                          }
{             (2) the Inspect method - a private debugging method, if needed                  }
{             (3) the Free method, if overridden, and                                         }
{             (4) the remaining methods in alphabetical order.                                }
{                                                                                             }
{ ******************************************************************************************* }
{ ******************************************************************************************* }


{ ************************************** TQuadApplication Methods ************************************}

   PROCEDURE TQuadApplication.IQuadApplication(itsSignature: OSType);
   VAR aQuad:             TQuad;
      aParallelogram:     TParallelogram;
      aRhombus:           TRhombus;
      aRectangle:         TRectangle;
      aSquare:            TSquare;
      junk:               REAL;

   BEGIN
      SELF.IApplication('QDWD', myFileType);

     { Set up prototype quads for all of the types of quadrilaterals.  These quads will be "cloned" as
       needed when the user adds a new quad.  Cloning is more efficient than allocating and
       initializing a new quad each time the user adds one to the document. }

      NEW(aQuad);           aQuad.IQuad;           gPrototypeQuadsArray[1] := aQuad;

      NEW(aParallelogram);  aParallelogram.IQuad;  gPrototypeQuadsArray[2] := aParallelogram;

      NEW(aRhombus);        aRhombus.IQuad;        gPrototypeQuadsArray[3] := aRhombus;

      NEW(aRectangle);      aRectangle.IQuad;      gPrototypeQuadsArray[4] := aRectangle;

      NEW(aSquare);         aSquare.IQuad;         gPrototypeQuadsArray[5] := aSquare;

      junk := sin(45.0);                  { Force the loading of the transcendental function package }
   END;
```

```
     FUNCTION  TQuadApplication.DoMakeDocument(itsCmdNumber: CmdNumber): TDocument;  OVERRIDE;
     VAR quadDocument:  TQuadDocument;
     BEGIN
         NEW(quadDocument);
         quadDocument.IQuadDocument;
         DoMakeDocument := quadDocument;

       { Notice that the cmdNumber parameter is never used in this overridden method.  This is
         because QuadWorld has only one type of document and thus just one type of 'New' menu item. }
     END;


 { *************************************** TQuadDocument Methods **************************************** }

                       { **************************************************** }
                       { **************************************************** }
                       {           THE FORMAT OF A QUADDOCUMENT ON DISK        }
                       {                                                      }
                       {     |**********************************************|  }
                       {     |                                              |  }
                       {     |           (Portion written by MacApp)        |  }
                       {     |                                              |  }
                       {     |..............................................|  }
                       {     |                   quadID                     |  }
                       {     |   vertices and rotation (TFiledQuad format)  |  }
                       {     |..............................................|  }
                       {     |                   quadID                     |  }
                       {     |   vertices and rotation (TFiledQuad format)  |  }
                       {     |..............................................|  }
                       {     |.....  (indeterminate number of quads)  ......|  }
                       {     |..............................................|  }
                       {     |                   quadID                     |  }
                       {     |   vertices and rotation (TFiledQuad format)  |  }
                       {     |..............................................|  }
                       {     |                 IDLastQuad                   |  }
                       {     |**********************************************|  }
                       {                                                      }
                       { **************************************************** }
                       { **************************************************** }

 { Initialize a new quadDocument }
     PROCEDURE TQuadDocument.IQuadDocument;
     BEGIN
         IDocument(myFileType);
         SELF.fLastQuadAdded := NIL;
         SELF.fQuadGrView := NIL;
         SELF.fQuadTxView := NIL;
         SELF.fSelectedQuad := NIL;
     END;


 {$IFC qDebug}
     PROCEDURE TQuadDocument.Inspect; OVERRIDE;                    { Debugging print of the quadDocument }

         PROCEDURE InspectOneQuad(quad: TQuad);
         BEGIN
             quad.Inspect;
             WriteLn(' The next quad: ');
         END;

     BEGIN
         INHERITED Inspect;
         SELF.EachQuadDo(InspectOneQuad);
         IF SELF.fSelectedQuad <> NIL
           THEN BEGIN
                    WriteLn(' The selected quad is: ');
                    SELF.fSelectedQuad.Inspect;
                END
           ELSE WriteLn(' There is no selected quad ');
     END;
 {$ENDC}


     PROCEDURE TQuadDocument.Free;  OVERRIDE;
     BEGIN
         SELF.FreeData;
```

```
        INHERITED Free;
    END;


{ Add a new quad to the quadDocument }
    PROCEDURE TQuadDocument.AddQuad(quad: TQuad);
    BEGIN
        IF quad <> NIL THEN
            BEGIN
            quad.fNextQuad := SELF.fLastQuadAdded;
            SELF.fLastQuadAdded := quad;
            END;
    END;


{ Delete a quad from the quadDocument }
    PROCEDURE TQuadDocument.DeleteQuad(quad: TQuad);
    VAR beforeTestQuad: TQuad;
        testQuad:       TQuad;
    BEGIN
        IF (quad <> NIL) AND (SELF.fLastQuadAdded <> NIL)
          THEN
             BEGIN
                 IF quad = SELF.fLastQuadAdded     { Degenerate case - delete first element in list }
                   THEN SELF.fLastQuadAdded := SELF.fLastQuadAdded.fNextQuad

                   ELSE                            { Standard case - delete interior element }
                      BEGIN
                          beforeTestQuad := SELF.fLastQuadAdded;
                          testQuad := SELF.fLastQuadAdded.fNextQuad;

                          WHILE (quad <> testQuad) DO
                              BEGIN
                                  beforeTestQuad := testQuad;
                                  testQuad := testQuad.fNextQuad;
                              END;
                                      { Here assume that quad is in the list SOMEWHERE! }
                         beforeTestQuad.fNextQuad := testQuad.fNextQuad;    { Delete the quad }
                      END;
             END;
    END;


{ Create all the windows necessary to represent a quadDocument to the user }
    PROCEDURE TQuadDocument.DoMakeWindows;  OVERRIDE;
    CONST   widthMacScreen = 512;
            heightMacScreen = 342;

    VAR aQuadGrView:        TQuadGrView;
        aListView:          TListView;
        grWindow:           TWindow;
        txWindow:           TWindow;
        newWindowSize:      Point;
        widthGrWindow:      INTEGER;
        extraWidth:         INTEGER;        { Additional window width/height for larger screen Macs }
        extraHeight:        INTEGER;

    BEGIN
      { Roll my own windows for both types of quad views in order to fill the screen of any size
        Mac and in order to avoid any on-screen window re-sizing }

      { Graphical view window }
        aQuadGrView := TQuadGrView(SELF.fQuadGrView);
        grWindow := NewPaletteWindow(kIDStdWindow, NOT kDialogWindow, kWantHScrollBar, kWantVScrollBar,
                                     aQuadGrView, aQuadGrView.fPalette, paletteWidth, kLeftPalette);
        extraWidth := (screenBits.bounds.right - widthMacScreen) div 2;  { Divide the extra width between
                                                                           the two windows }
        extraHeight := screenBits.bounds.bottom - heightMacScreen;
        newWindowSize.h := 325 + extraWidth;
        newWindowSize.v := 295 + extraHeight;
        widthGrWindow := newWindowSize.h;
        grWindow.ReSize(newWindowSize, FALSE);

      { Textual view window }
        aListView := SELF.fQuadTxView;    { This view object was created and installed in the method
                                            TQuadDocument.DoMakeViews }
        txWindow := NewSimpleWindow(kIDStdWindow+1, NOT kDialogWindow, kWantHScrollBar, kWantVScrollBar,
                                    aListView);
```

```
2 --
2 --           newWindowSize.h := 170 + extraWidth;          { Use the same height as the graphical view window }
2 --           txWindow.ReSize(newWindowSize, FALSE);
2 --
2 --         { move the text window to the correct horizontal position }
2 --           txWindow.fLocation.h := widthGrWindow + grWindow.fLocation.h + 5;
2 --                                    { Make it be 5 pixels from the right edge of the graphical window. }
2 --
2 --           SelectWindow(grWindow.fWmgrWindow);     { Make the grahical window the active one }
2 -0 A     END;
2 --
2 --
2 --   { Create all the views necessary to represent a quadDocument to the user }
2 -- A     PROCEDURE TQuadDocument.DoMakeViews(forPrinting: BOOLEAN);  OVERRIDE;
2 --       CONST   maxStringWidth = 400;
2 --
2 --       VAR aQuadGrView:    TQuadGrView;
2 --           aQuadTxView:    TListView;
2 --           aPalette:       TPalette;
2 --           extentRect:     Rect;
2 --
2 0- A     BEGIN
2 --           NEW(aQuadGrView);                             { Create and install the graphical view }
2 --           aQuadGrView.IQuadGrView(SELF);
2 --           SELF.fQuadGrView := aQuadGrView;
2 --
2 --           NEW(aPalette);                                { Create and install the palette view }
2 --           aPalette.IPalette(SELF, SELF.fQuadGrView);
2 --           SELF.fQuadGrView.fPalette := aPalette;
2 --
2 --           NEW(aQuadTxView);                             { Create and install the textual view }
2 --           SetRect(extentRect, 0, 0, maxStringWidth, 0);
2 --           aQuadTxView.IListView(NIL, SELF, extentRect, sizeVariable, TRUE);
2 --           SELF.fQuadTxView := aQuadTxView;
2 -0 A     END;
2 --
2 --
2 --   { Process the menu commands that are handled by the document (as opposed to those handled by the view,
2 --     the aplication, MacApp itself, etc. }
2 -- A     FUNCTION  TQuadDocument.DoMenuCommand(aCmdNumber: CmdNumber): TCommand;  OVERRIDE;
2 --       VAR clearQuadCmd:   TClearQuadCmd;
2 --           clearAllCmd:    TClearAllCmd;
2 0- A     BEGIN
2 1-           CASE aCmdNumber OF
2 2-                   cClearQuadCmd:        BEGIN
2 --                                            NEW(clearQuadCmd);
2 --                                            clearQuadCmd.IClearQuadCmd(aCmdNumber);
2 --                                            DoMenuCommand := clearQuadCmd;
2 -2                                         END;
2 --
2 2-                   cClearAllCmd:         BEGIN
2 --                                            NEW(clearAllCmd);
2 --                                            clearAllCmd.IClearAllCmd(aCmdNumber);
2 --                                            DoMenuCommand := clearAllCmd;
2 -2                                         END;
2 --
2 --                   OTHERWISE             DoMenuCommand := INHERITED DoMenuCommand(aCmdNumber);
2 -1           END;
2 -0 A     END;
2 --
2 --
2 --
2 --   { ESTIMATE how much disk space will be required to store a quadDocument }
2 -- A     PROCEDURE TQuadDocument.DoNeedDiskSpace(VAR dataForkBytes, rsrcForkBytes: LONGINT);  OVERRIDE;
2 --       VAR quad:       TQuad;
2 --           nQuads:     INTEGER;
2 0- A     BEGIN
2 --           rsrcForkBytes := 0;
2 --
2 --           quad := SELF.fLastQuadAdded;
2 --           nQuads := 0;
2 --           WHILE (quad <> NIL)  DO
2 1-               BEGIN
2 --               nQuads := nQuads + 1;
2 --               quad := quad.fNextQuad;
2 -1               END;
2 --           dataForkBytes := nQuads * (SIZEOF(TFiledQuad));
```

```
2 -0 A     END;
2 --
2 --
2 --     { Read in a quadDocument from disk, i.e., read in the special form of a quadDocument generated by
2 --       QuadWorld and "reconstitute" the quads and other information stored in the quadDocument object.
2 --       Note that this routine MAKES NO ASSUMPTIONS about the format of a quad on disk, except that
2 --       each "block" of quad data is preceeded by a quad id, or the IDLastQuad for the end of the document.
2 --       In particular, the quads could even be different sized "objects" and this method would still be
2 --       correct.  This is possible because each quad "reads itself" from disk. }
2 --     {$S ARes}
2 -- A     PROCEDURE TQuadDocument.DoRead(aRefNum: INTEGER; forPrinting: BOOLEAN);  OVERRIDE;
2 --       VAR id:           INTEGER;
2 --           count:        LONGINT;
2 --           newQuad:      TQuad;
2 --           err:          OSErr;
2 0- A     BEGIN
2 --           INHERITED DoRead(aRefNum, forPrinting);
2 --
2 --           count := SIZEOF(INTEGER);
2 --           WHILE TRUE DO
2 1-               BEGIN
2 --                   err := FSRead(aRefNum, count, @id);                              { Get the next id }
2 --                   IF ((id > 0) AND (id <= IDSquare))
2 --                     THEN newQuad := TQuad(gPrototypeQuadsArray[id].Clone)        { Clone an appropriate quad }
2 --                     ELSE IF id = IDLastQuad
2 --                          THEN LEAVE                                          { Exit the loop if no more quads }
2 --             {$IFC qDebug } ELSE ProgramBreak('Illegal quad on disk') {$ENDC } ;
2 --
2 --                   newQuad.ReadFrom(aRefNum);                                { Tell the new quad to read itself }
2 --                   SELF.AddQuad(newQuad);                                    { Add new quad to the document     }
2 -1               END
2 -0 A     END;
2 --
2 --
2 --
2 --     { Enable the menu items controlled by the document.  These are the same menu items that are
2 --       handled in TQuadDocument.DoMenuCommand.  These commands can be enabled or disabled based
2 --       on any condition that makes sense in the application.  For example, the Clear command is
2 --       only enabled when there is a selected quad. }
2 -- A     PROCEDURE TQuadDocument.DoSetupMenus;  OVERRIDE;
2 0- A     BEGIN
2 --           INHERITED DoSetupMenus;
2 --           Enable(cClearQuadCmd, SELF.fSelectedQuad <> NIL);      { Only if a quad is selected }
2 --           Enable(cClearAllCmd, SELF.fLastQuadAdded <> NIL);      { Only if there is at least one quad }
2 -0 A     END;
2 --
2 --
2 --     { Write a quadDocument to disk.  Note that this routine specifies the format that will be read
2 --       by TQuadDocument.DoRead.  This routine is independent of the way in which quads are actually
2 --       written to disk, because each quad is told to write itself. }
2 -- A    PROCEDURE TQuadDocument.DoWrite(aRefNum: INTEGER);  OVERRIDE;
2 --       VAR  err:              OSErr;
2 --            count:            LONGINT;
2 --            lastQuadMarker: INTEGER;
2 --
2 -- B          PROCEDURE WriteQuad(quad: TQuad);
2 0- B          BEGIN
2 --                quad.WriteTo(aRefNum);
2 -0 B          END;
2 --
2 0- A     BEGIN
2 --           lastQuadMarker := IDLastQuad;
2 --           count := SIZEOF(INTEGER);
2 --           INHERITED DoWrite(aRefNum);                          { Allow MacApp to write whatever it wants to }
2 --           SELF.EachQuadDo(WriteQuad);                  { Allow each quad to write itself however it wants to }
2 --           err := FSWrite(aRefNum, count, @lastQuadMarker);                        { Mark the end of the file }
2 -0 A     END;
2 --
2 --
2 --     { Enumerate all the quads, executing the procedure 'DoThis' for each one.  This method is used
2 --       from many places in QuadWorld which need to do something (like draw, or test for a mouse hit)
2 --       with each quad currently in the quadDocument. }
2 --     {$S ARes}
2 -- A     PROCEDURE TQuadDocument.EachQuadDo(PROCEDURE DoThis(quad: TQuad));
2 --           VAR quad:  TQuad;
2 0- A     BEGIN
```

```
2 --            quad := SELF.fLastQuadAdded;
2 --            WHILE quad <> NIL DO
2 1-                BEGIN
2 --                DoThis(quad);
2 --                quad := quad.fNextQuad;
2 -1                END;
2 -0 A      END;
2 --
2 --
2 --    { This routine is called when the QuadWorld application quits or when a Revert command is issued
2 --      in order to free all the quad objects that have been allocated on the heap.  }
2 -- A      PROCEDURE TQuadDocument.FreeData;  OVERRIDE;
2 --        VAR freeThisQuad:   TQuad;
2 --            nextQuad:       TQuad;
2 0- A      BEGIN
2 --            SELF.SelectQuad(NIL);
2 --
2 --          { Free all the quads }
2 --            IF SELF.fLastQuadAdded <> NIL             { Are there really any quads to be freed? }
2 --              THEN
2 1-                 BEGIN
2 --                     freeThisQuad := SELF.fLastQuadAdded;
2 --                     nextQuad := freeThisQuad.fNextQuad;
2 --                     FreeObject(freeThisQuad);
2 --
2 --                     WHILE (nextQuad <> NIL) DO
2 2-                          BEGIN
2 --                              freeThisQuad := nextQuad;
2 --                              nextQuad := nextQuad.fNextQuad;
2 --                              FreeObject(freeThisQuad);
2 -2                          END
2 -1                END;
2 --
2 --            SELF.fLastQuadAdded := NIL;
2 -0 A      END;
2 --
2 --
2 --    { Invalidate the area occupied by the quad in both views.  This will cause a redraw of this area
2 --      during the next update event }
2 -- A      PROCEDURE TQuadDocument.InvalidateQuad(quad: TQuad);
2 --        VAR invalRect:      Rect;
2 0- A      BEGIN
2 --             IF quad <> NIL THEN
2 1-                 BEGIN
2 --                      SELF.fQuadGrView.InvalidateQuad(quad);
2 --                      SELF.fQuadTxView.InvalidateItem(SELF.QuadToListIndex(quad));
2 -1                 END
2 -0 A      END;
2 --
2 --
2 --    { Determine which quad is the i-th one in the current list }
2 -- A      FUNCTION TQuadDocument.ListIndexToQuad(index: INTEGER): TQuad;
2 --        VAR quadCounter:    INTEGER;
2 --            foundQuad:      TQuad;
2 --
2 -- B          PROCEDURE FindQuad(quad: TQuad);
2 0- B          BEGIN
2 --               quadCounter := quadCounter + 1;
2 --               IF quadCounter = index
2 --                 THEN foundQuad := quad;
2 -0 B          END;
2 --
2 0- A      BEGIN
2 --           quadCounter := 0;
2 --           foundQuad := NIL;
2 --           SELF.EachQuadDo(FindQuad);
2 --           ListIndexToQuad := foundQuad;
2 -0 A      END;
2 --
2 --
2 --    { Report a textual representation of one of the quads - needed for the List View (in UList unit) }
2 -- A      FUNCTION  TQuadDocument.ReportListItem(itemNumber: INTEGER): Str255;  OVERRIDE;
2 --        VAR theQuad: TQuad;
2 0- A      BEGIN
```

```
2 --               theQuad := TQuad(SELF.ListIndexToQuad(itemNumber));
2 --               IF theQuad = NIL
2 --                 THEN ReportListItem := ' '
2 --                 ELSE ReportListItem := theQuad.AsText;
2 -0 A         END;
2 --
2 --
2 --     { make the selection in both panels; quad = NIL means de-select; this routine does nothing if the
2 --         old and new selections are the same }
2 -- A       PROCEDURE TQuadDocument.SelectQuad(quad: TQuad);
2 0- A       BEGIN
2 --             IF (quad <> SELF.fSelectedQuad) THEN    { old selection <> new selection }
2 1-                 BEGIN
2 --                      SELF.fSelectedQuad := quad;
2 --
2 --                     { Select first in the graphics view }
2 --                      SELF.fQuadGrView.ChangeSelection(quad);
2 --
2 --                     { ... then in the text view }
2 --                      SELF.fQuadTxView.ChangeSelection(SELF.QuadToListIndex(quad));
2 -1                 END;
2 -0 A       END;
2 --
2 --
2 --     { Set the current selection in response to a request from the List View (in UList unit) }
2 -- A       PROCEDURE TQuadDocument.SetSelection(newSelectionIndex: INTEGER);  OVERRIDE;
2 --         VAR quad: TQuad;
2 0- A       BEGIN
2 --             quad := SELF.ListIndexToQuad(newSelectionIndex);
2 --             SELF.SelectQuad(quad);
2 -0 A       END;
2 --
2 --     { Determine the index of a given quad in the current list }
2 -- A       FUNCTION TQuadDocument.QuadToListIndex(quad: TQuad): INTEGER;
2 --         VAR quadCounter:     INTEGER;
2 --             foundIndex:      INTEGER;
2 --
2 -- B           PROCEDURE FindIndex(currentQuad: TQuad);
2 0- B           BEGIN
2 --                quadCounter := quadCounter + 1;
2 --                IF currentQuad = quad
2 --                  THEN foundIndex := quadCounter;
2 -0 B           END;
2 --
2 0- A       BEGIN
2 --            quadCounter := 0;
2 --            foundIndex := 0;
2 --            SELF.EachQuadDo(FindIndex);
2 --            QuadToListIndex := foundIndex;
2 -0 A       END;
2 --
2 --
2 --     { ******************************************* TPalette Methods ******************************************* }
2 --
2 -- A       PROCEDURE TPalette.IPalette(itsDocument: TDocument; aQuadGrView: TQuadGrView);
2 --         VAR i:       INTEGER;
2 --             top:     INTEGER;
2 --             quad:    TQuad;
2 --             r:       Rect;
2 0- A       BEGIN
2 --             top := 0;
2 --             FOR i := 0 TO numQuadTypes DO
2 1-                 BEGIN
2 --                    SetRect(r, 0, top, paletteWidth, top + paletteWidth);
2 --                    SELF.fChoiceRect[i] := r;
2 --                    top := top + paletteWidth;
2 -1                 END;
2 --             SetRect(r, 0, 0, paletteWidth, top);
2 --             SELF.IView(NIL, itsDocument, r, sizeFixed, sizeVariable, FALSE, hlDim);
2 --             SELF.fCurrSelection := 0;
2 --             SELF.fQuadGrView := aQuadGrView;
2 -0 A       END;
2 --
2 --
```

```
2  517 -- A   PROCEDURE TPalette.ChangeSelection(newSelection: INTEGER);
2  518 0- A   BEGIN
2  519 --     {$IFC qDebug}
2  520 --        IF ((newSelection < 0) OR (newSelection > numQuadTypes))
2  521 --          THEN ProgramBreak('Illegal Palette Selection');
2  522 --     {$ENDC}
2  523 --
2  524 --        IF newSelection <> SELF.fCurrSelection THEN
2  525 1-            BEGIN
2  526 --               IF SELF.fQuadGrView.PendingSketcher <> NIL  { Are we in the middle of drawing a new quad? }
2  527 --                 THEN gApplication.CommitLastCommand;        { This will free the sketcher and its quad,
2  528 --                                                               erase the sketch lines from the view.  Thus
2  529 --                                                               the user will be able to sketch something
2  530 --                                                               else, or make selections. }
2  531 --               SELF.fFrame.Focus;
2  532 --               SELF.DoHighlightSelection(SELF.fHLDesired, hlOff);
2  533 --               SELF.fCurrSelection := newSelection;
2  534 --               SELF.DoHighlightSelection(hlOff, SELF.fHLDesired);
2  535 -1            END;
2  536 -0 A   END;
2  537 --
2  538 --
2  539 -- A   PROCEDURE TPalette.DoHighlightSelection(fromHl, toHL: HLState);  OVERRIDE;
2  540 0- A   BEGIN
2  541 --        IF fromHL <> toHL
2  542 1-          THEN BEGIN
2  543 --                    SetHLPenState(fromHL, toHL);
2  544 --                    PaintRect(SELF.fChoiceRect[SELF.fCurrSelection]);
2  545 -1               END
2  546 -0 A   END;
2  547 --
2  548 --
2  549 -- A   FUNCTION  TPalette.DoMouseCommand(VAR downLocalPoint: Point; VAR info: EventInfo;
2  550 --                                    VAR hysteresis: Point): TCommand;  OVERRIDE;
2  551 --     VAR i:  INTEGER;
2  552 0- A   BEGIN
2  553 --        DoMouseCommand := gNoChanges;
2  554 --
2  555 --        IF PtInRect(downLocalPoint, SELF.fExtentRect) THEN
2  556 1-           BEGIN
2  557 --              i := 0;
2  558 --              WHILE NOT PtInRect(downLocalPoint, SELF.fChoiceRect[i]) DO  i := i+1;
2  559 --
2  560 --              IF i > numQuadTypes
2  561 --                THEN i := numQuadTypes;    { Select the last type of quad if the mouse press is too low. }
2  562 --              SELF.ChangeSelection(i);
2  563 -1           END;
2  564 -0 A   END;
2  565 --
2  566 --
2  567 -- A   PROCEDURE TPalette.Draw(area: Rect);  OVERRIDE;
2  568 --     CONST
2  569 --        shrinkSize = (paletteWidth - 16) div 2;  { Shrink the palette rectangles by this amount in order
2  570 --                                                   not to distort the quad patterns fit into in them.   }
2  571 --
2  572 --     VAR i:           INTEGER;  { FOR Loop index }
2  573 --        symBitMap:  BitMap;
2  574 --        destRect:   Rect;
2  575 --        idealQuad, idealParallelogram, idealRhombus, idealRectangle, idealSquare: ARRAY [0..15] of INTEGER;
2  576 --
2  577 -- B         PROCEDURE FillBitMap(dataPointer: QDPtr);
2  578 0- B         BEGIN
2  579 --              WITH symBitMap DO
2  580 1-                  BEGIN
2  581 --                  rowBytes := 2;
2  582 --                  SetRect(bounds, 0, 0, 16, 16);
2  583 --                  baseAddr := dataPointer;
2  584 -1                  END;
2  585 -0 B         END;
2  586 --
2  587 0- A   BEGIN
2  588 --        { Set the images for all the ideal quadrilaterals.  Recall that all are 16-by-16 bit images
2  589 --          and thus each requires 64 hex digits for its full definition.  StuffHex is a QuickDraw routine.
```

```
             Although this looks inefficient (to compute the ideal quad images each time a palette is
             drawn), this method is invoked so infrequently that it doesn't really matter.            }
                                       {0         1         2         3         4         5         6  }
                                       {1234567890123456789012345678901234567890123456789012345678901234}
            StuffHex(@idealQuad,        '8000A003501A4C6243042008201020101020104010800880090000A0004000400');
            StuffHex(@idealParallelogram, '01FF0101020202020404040408080808101010102020202040404040808 0FF80');
            StuffHex(@idealRhombus,     '000000000FFF0801100210021002200420044008400840088010FFF000000000');
            StuffHex(@idealRectangle,   '1FF810081008100810081008100810081008100810081008100810081FF8');
            StuffHex(@idealSquare,      '000000003FFC200420042004200420042004200420042004200420043FFC00000000');

         FOR i := 0 TO numQuadTypes DO
            BEGIN
               FrameRect(SELF.fChoiceRect[i]);
               CASE i OF
                     0:                FillBitMapWith(@arrow.data);        { the arrow cursor }
                     IDQuad:           FillBitMapWith(@idealQuad);
                     IDParallelogram:  FillBitMapWith(@idealParallelogram);
                     IDRhombus:        FillBitMapWith(@idealRhombus);
                     IDRectangle:      FillBitMapWith(@idealRectangle);
                     IDSquare:         FillBitMapWith(@idealSquare);
                     OTHERWISE         FillBitMapWith(@arrow.data);
               END;
               destRect := SELF.fChoiceRect[i];
               InsetRect(destRect, shrinkSize, shrinkSize);
               CopyBits(symBitMap, thePort^.portBits, symBitMap.bounds, destRect, srcOr, NIL);
            END;
      END;


   { ****************************************** TQuadGrView Methods ****************************************** }

      PROCEDURE TQuadGrView.IQuadGrView(itsDocument: TQuadDocument);
      VAR r:                    Rect;
         aStdPrintHandler:      TStdPrintHandler;
         i:                     INTEGER;
         tempRegion:            RgnHandle;
         pnState:               PenState;
      BEGIN
         SetRect(r, 0, 0, 1000, 1000);             { Any better first guess ???}
         SELF.IView(NIL, itsDocument, r, sizeFixed, sizeFixed, FALSE, hlDim);
         SELF.fSelectedQuad := NIL;
         SELF.fPalette := NIL;

        { Generate the rotation region - it will be moved to each selected quad later }
         GetPenState(pnState);
         PenSize(1,1);
         tempRegion := NewRgn;
         OpenRgn;
               SetRect(r, 40, -5, 50, 5);
               FrameOval(r);                  { The region is a circle,   }
               SetRect(r, 0, -2, 40, +2);
               FrameRect(r);                  {   on the end of a stick.  }
         CloseRgn(tempRegion);
         SELF.fRotationRgn := tempRegion;
         SetPenState(pnState);

        { Generate and install a print handler so that the graphical view can be printed }
         NEW(aStdPrintHandler);
         aStdPrintHandler.IStdPrintHandler(SELF, FALSE);
         SELF.fIdlePriority := 1;                  { Ensure that the special DoIdle method of this class
                                                     will be invoked.  The partial quad, if it exists,
                                                     will be drawn during this idle time.}
      END;


   { Change the selected quad in the view.  Be sure to move the rotation region to the new selection. }
      PROCEDURE TQuadGrView.ChangeSelection(newQuad: TQuad);
      VAR offset: Point;
      BEGIN
         SELF.fFrame.Focus;
         SELF.DoHighlightSelection(SELF.fHLDesired, hlOff);

         IF SELF.fSelectedQuad <> NIL                  { Move rotation region back }
           THEN BEGIN
```

```
                    offset := SELF.fSelectedQuad.Center;
                    OffsetRgn(SELF.fRotationRgn, -offset.h, -offset.v);
                END;

            IF newQuad <> NIL                               { Move it to the new quad }
              THEN BEGIN
                    offset := newQuad.Center;
                    OffsetRgn(SELF.fRotationRgn, offset.h, offset.v);
                END;

            SELF.fSelectedQuad := newQuad;
            SELF.DoHighlightSelection(hlOff, SELF.fHLDesired);
        END;


    {$S ARes}
        PROCEDURE TQuadGrView.DoHighlightSelection(fromHL, toHL: HLState);  OVERRIDE;

        VAR selectedQuad:   TQuad;
            cornerRect:     Rect;
            i:              INTEGER;    { FOR loop index }

        BEGIN

            selectedQuad := SELF.fSelectedQuad;
            IF (selectedQuad <> NIL)  THEN
                 BEGIN
                   IF RectIsVisible(selectedQuad.fEnclosingRect) THEN   { only do highlight if quad is visible }
                     BEGIN
                       SetHLPenState(fromHL, toHL);           { Set the pen appropriately for the transition }
                       SetRect(cornerRect, -2, -2, 2, 2);                          { Highlighting rectangle }
                       FOR i := 1 TO 4 DO
                         BEGIN
                           OffsetRect(cornerRect, selectedQuad.fVertex[i].h, selectedQuad.fVertex[i].v);
                           PaintRect(cornerRect);
                           OffsetRect(cornerRect, -selectedQuad.fVertex[i].h, -selectedQuad.fVertex[i].v);
                         END;
                       PaintRgn(SELF.fRotationRgn);
                     END;
                 END;
        END;


        PROCEDURE TQuadGrView.DoIdle(phase: IdlePhase);  OVERRIDE;
        BEGIN
            IF phase = idleBegin
              THEN SELF.DrawPartialQuad;    { Draw any partial quad, if necessary }
            INHERITED DoIdle(phase);
        END;


    { This method will be invoked when the user presses the mouse button in the quadGrView.  Such a mouse
      press could be one of following four cases:
              CASE                                  DIFFERENTIATING CONDITION
         Select a quad                              The palette selection is the arrow
         Draw a new quad                            The palette selection is NOT the arrow
         Continue drawing a new quad                A pending sketcher exists
         Rotate a quad                              The mouse press takes place inside of the
                                                    rotation region, at its current offset

       Depending on these conditions, this method will initiate the appropriate actions. }

        FUNCTION  TQuadGrView.DoMouseCommand(VAR downLocalPoint: Point; VAR info: EventInfo;
                                             VAR hysteresis: Point): TCommand;  OVERRIDE;

        VAR quadSketcher:    TSketchQuadCmd;
            newQuad:         TQuad;
            quad:            TQuad;
            aRotateQuadCmd:  TRotateQuadCmd;

            PROCEDURE CheckQuad(thisQuad: TQuad);
            BEGIN
               IF PtInRect(downLocalPoint, thisQuad.fEnclosingRect) THEN
                   quad := thisQuad;
```

```
2 -0 B         END;
2 --
2 0- A     BEGIN
2 --           DoMouseCommand := gNoChanges;
2 --
2 --           IF SELF.fPalette.fCurrSelection > 0 THEN   { draw mode for some type of quad }
2 1-             BEGIN
2 --                 quadSketcher := SELF.PendingSketcher;
2 --
2 --                 IF quadSketcher = NIL  THEN       { The user wishes to start drawing a totally new quad }
2 2-                     BEGIN
2 --                         TQuadDocument(SELF.fDocument).SelectQuad(NIL);  { De-select the current selection }
2 --
2 --                        { Clone appropriate quad }
2 --                         newQuad := TQuad(gPrototypeQuadsArray[SELF.fPalette.fCurrSelection].Clone);
2 --
2 --                        { Get an appropriate sketching command object }
2 --                         quadSketcher := newQuad.NewSketchCmd;
2 --                         quadSketcher.fQuad := newQuad;
2 --
2 --                         DoMouseCommand := quadSketcher;
2 --
2 -2                     END { draw mode - start of new quad }
2 --
2 --                 ELSE  { Continue drawing a quad that has already been begun }
2 2-                     BEGIN
2 --                         SetCursor(GetCursor(crossCursor)^^);
2 --                         downLocalPoint := quadSketcher.fQuad.fVertex[quadSketcher.fLastVertexSet];
2 --                                                    { Reset the mouseDownPoiint to start drawing the next
2 --                                                      side.  This is done so that the rubberbanded line
2 --                                                      must be drawn from the last vertex set for the
2 --                                                      partial quad, regardless of where the mouse
2 --                                                      down occurred. }
2 --                         DoMouseCommand := quadSketcher;   { Return the stored sketcher. }
2 -2                     END { draw mode - continuation of a partially drawn quad }
2 -1             END { draw mode }
2 --
2 --
2 --         ELSE              { either a selection or a rotation.  Try for rotation first }
2 --
2 --             IF PtInRgn(downLocalPoint, SELF.fRotationRgn)  { a rotation ? }
2 1-               THEN BEGIN
2 --                         EraseRgn(SELF.fRotationRgn);    { Feedback to the user that mouse hit detected }
2 --                         NEW(aRotateQuadCmd);
2 --                         aRotateQuadCmd.IRotateQuadCmd(cRotateQuadCmd);
2 --                         DoMouseCommand := aRotateQuadCmd;
2 -1                    END
2 --
2 1-               ELSE BEGIN  { Must be a selection of a quad.  This case is tested for last since
2 --                                it takes the longest to check }
2 --                         quad := NIL;
2 --                         TQuadDocument(SELF.fDocument).EachQuadDo(CheckQuad);
2 --
2 --                       { quad now references the quad under the cursor, if there is one }
2 --                         TQuadDocument(SELF.fDocument).SelectQuad(quad);     { Tell the document }
2 -1                    END
2 -0 A     END;
2 --
2 --
2 --
2 --   { Change the cursor to a cross hair or a partial quad while the user is drawing a new quadrilateral }
2 -- A     FUNCTION  TQuadGrView.DoSetCursor(localPoint: Point): BOOLEAN;  OVERRIDE;
2 --       VAR sketcher:          TSketchQuadCmd;
2 --           desiredCursorState:     INTEGER;
2 0- A     BEGIN
2 --           DoSetCursor := FALSE;
2 --           IF SELF.fPalette.fCurrSelection <> 0    { the user is drawing a new quad }
2 --             THEN
2 1-               BEGIN
2 --                   DoSetCursor := TRUE;
2 --                   sketcher := SELF.PendingSketcher;
2 --                   IF sketcher <> NIL
2 --                     THEN desiredCursorState := sketcher.fLastVertexSet
2 --                     ELSE desiredCursorState := 0;
```

```
                  { Set the cursor depending on the extent to which the user has entered the new
                    quadrilateral.  Note that there is no need for a three-edged,
                    or a four-edged quad cursor.  }
                    CASE desiredCursorState OF
                        0:          SetCursor(GetCursor(crossCursor)^^);
                        2:          SetCursor(GetCursor(cOneEdgeQuadCursor)^^);
                        3:          SetCursor(GetCursor(cTwoEdgeQuadCursor)^^);
                        OTHERWISE   SetCursor(arrow);
                    END;
                END;
        END;


    {$S ARes}
        PROCEDURE TQuadGrView.Draw(area: Rect);  OVERRIDE;

            PROCEDURE DrawQuad(quad: TQuad);
            BEGIN
               quad.Draw;
            END;

        BEGIN
            TQuadDocument(SELF.fDocument).EachQuadDo(DrawQuad);
            SELF.DrawPartialQuad;
        END;


    { Draw the portion of the quad that is now being entered by the user }
    {$S ARes}
        PROCEDURE TQuadGrView.DrawPartialQuad;
        VAR sketcher:   TSketchQuadCmd;
            quad:       TQuad;
            i:          INTEGER;
        BEGIN
            sketcher := SELF.PendingSketcher;
            IF sketcher <> NIL THEN
              IF sketcher.fLastVertexSet > 1 THEN
                BEGIN
                   quad := sketcher.fQuad;
                   SELF.fFrame.Focus;
                   PenNormal;
                   MoveTo(quad.fVertex[1].h, quad.fVertex[1].v);
                   FOR i := 2 TO sketcher.fLastVertexSet DO LineTo(quad.fVertex[i].h, quad.fVertex[i].v);
                END;
        END;



    { Invalidate the area occupied by the quad in the graphical view.  Ensure that the rotation region,
      which is peculiar to this view, is included in the invalidation area }
        PROCEDURE TQuadGrView.InvalidateQuad(quad: TQuad);
        VAR quadRect:   Rect;
            rotRgnRect: Rect;
            quadCenter: Point;
        BEGIN
             IF quad <> NIL THEN
                 BEGIN
                     quadRect := quad.fEnclosingRect;
                     InsetRect(quadRect, -4, -4);                      { Grow the rectangle to include any }
                                                                       { highlighting on the quad.         }
                     quadCenter := quad.Center;                        { Also make sure that the rotation  }
                     SetRect(rotRgnRect, 0, -5, 50, 5);                { region is inside the invalidation }
                     OffsetRect(rotRgnRect, quadCenter.h, quadCenter.v); { rectangle.                      }
                     UnionRect(quadRect, rotRgnRect, quadRect);
                     SELF.fFrame.Focus;
                     SELF.InvalRect(quadRect);
                 END
        END;


    { Return the sketching command which is still in use }
        FUNCTION  TQuadGrView.PendingSketcher: TSketchQuadCmd;
        BEGIN
```

```
            PendingSketcher := NIL;

            IF gLastCommand <> NIL THEN                                           { there is a last command, ... }
              IF gDidLastCommand THEN                                                  { it has been done, ... }
                IF ((gLastCommand.fCmdNumber >= cAddQuadCmd) AND
                    (gLastCommand.fCmdNumber <= cAddSquareCmd)) THEN        { it was a sketching command, ... }
                  IF gLastCommand.fChangedDocument = SELF.fDocument THEN             { for this document, ... }
                    IF TSketchQuadCmd(gLastCommand).fLastVertexSet <> 4 THEN  { and its quad is not completed }
                        PendingSketcher := TSketchQuadCmd(gLastCommand);                   { THEN return it }
        END;


    { ******************************************** TQuad Methods ************************************************ }

        PROCEDURE TQuad.IQuad;
        VAR zeroPt:   Point;
            zeroRect: Rect;
            i:        INTEGER;    {FOR Loop index}
        BEGIN
            SetPt(zeroPt, 0, 0);
            FOR i := 1 TO 4 DO SELF.fVertex[i] := zeroPt;
            SetRect(zeroRect, 0, 0, 0, 0);
            SELF.fEnclosingRect := zeroRect;
            SELF.fNextQuad := NIL;
            SELF.fRotated := FALSE;
        END;

    {$IFC qDebug}
    {$S GDebug}
        PROCEDURE TQuad.Inspect;  OVERRIDE;
        VAR i:  INTEGER;    {FOR Loop index}
        BEGIN
            INHERITED Inspect;
            FOR i := 1 TO 4 DO WriteLn(' Vertex(', i,') is (', fVertex[i].h, ', ', fVertex[i].v, ')');
            IF SELF.fNextQuad = NIL
              THEN WriteLn('fNextQuad is NIL')
              ELSE WriteLn('fNextQuad is NOT NIL');
            WriteLn('fRotated is ', SELF.fRotated);
        END;
    {$ENDC}


    {$S ARes}
        FUNCTION  TQuad.AsText: Str255;
        BEGIN
             AsText := 'a Quadrilateral';
        END;


        FUNCTION  TQuad.Center: Point;
        VAR
             thisPoint: Point;
        BEGIN
           thisPoint.h := (fVertex[1].h + fVertex[2].h + fVertex[3].h + fVertex[4].h) div 4;
           thisPoint.v := (fVertex[1].v + fVertex[2].v + fVertex[3].v + fVertex[4].v) div 4;
           Center := thisPoint;

        END;


        PROCEDURE TQuad.Draw;

             PROCEDURE DrawEdge(pt1, pt2: Point);
             BEGIN
                  MoveTo(pt1.h, pt1.v);
                  LineTo(pt2.h, pt2.v);
             END;  {DrawEdge}

        BEGIN
           IF RectIsVisible(SELF.fEnclosingRect) THEN      { only draw quads that will be seen }
                BEGIN
                     DrawEdge(fVertex[1], fVertex[2]);
                     DrawEdge(fVertex[2], fVertex[3]);
                     DrawEdge(fVertex[3], fVertex[4]);
```

```
2 --                      DrawEdge(fVertex[4], fVertex[1]);
2 -1                  END;
2 -0 A      END;  { TQuad.Draw }
2 --
2 --
2 -- A      FUNCTION  TQuad.EnclosingRect: Rect;                          { a PRIVATE method for this class }
2 --        VAR
2 --             minLeft, minTop, maxRight, maxBottom:   INTEGER;
2 --             thisRect:   Rect;
2 --             i:          INTEGER;    { FOR loop index }
2 --
2 -- B           PROCEDURE SetMinMax(pt: Point);
2 0- B           BEGIN
2 --                 minLeft := Min(minLeft, pt.h);
2 --                 minTop := Min(minTop, pt.v);
2 --                 maxRight := Max(maxRight, pt.h);
2 --                 maxBottom := Max(maxBottom, pt.v);
2 -0 B           END;
2 --
2 0- A      BEGIN  { TQuad.EnclosingRect }
2 --             minLeft := 720;     minTop := 360;
2 --             maxRight := 0;      maxBottom := 0;
2 --
2 --             FOR i := 1 TO 4 DO SetMinMax(SELF.fVertex[i]);
2 --
2 --             SetRect(thisRect, minLeft, minTop, maxRight, maxBottom);
2 --             EnclosingRect := thisRect;
2 -0 A      END;  { TQuad.EnclosingRect }
2 --
2 --
2 --    { This function returns a sketcher that will assist the user to interactively enter a quad }
2 -- A      FUNCTION  TQuad.NewSketchCmd: TSketchQuadCmd;
2 --        VAR quadSketcher:   TSketchQuadCmd;
2 0- A      BEGIN
2 --             NEW(quadSketcher);
2 --             quadSketcher.ISketchQuadCmd(cAddQuadCmd);
2 --             NewSketchCmd := quadSketcher;
2 -0 A      END;
2 --
2 --
2 --    { This procedure provides an id for quads written to disk }
2 -- A      FUNCTION TQuad.ID: INTEGER;
2 0- A      BEGIN
2 --            ID := IDQuad;
2 -0 A      END;
2 --
2 --
2 --    { This procedure reads a quad from disk.  The id has ALREADY been read. }
2 -- A      PROCEDURE  TQuad.ReadFrom(aRefNum: INTEGER);
2 --        VAR data:      TFiledQuad;
2 --            err:       OSErr;
2 --            count:     LONGINT;
2 --            i:         INTEGER;    { FOR Loop index }
2 0- A      BEGIN
2 --            count := SIZEOF(TFiledQuad);
2 --            err := FSRead(aRefNum, count, @data);
2 --            FOR i := 1 TO 4 DO SELF.fVertex[i] := data.theVertices[i];
2 --            SELF.fRotated := data.theRotationState;
2 -0 A      END;
2 --
2 --
2 --
2 --    { This procedure rotates a quad counterclockwise about its center by theta degrees }
2 -- A      PROCEDURE TQuad.RotateBy(theta: INTEGER);
2 --        VAR
2 --            newVertex:       ARRAY[1..4] of Point;
2 --            sine, cosine:    REAL;
2 --            centerPt:        Point;
2 --            tempPt:          Point;
2 --            radians:         REAL;
2 --            i:               INTEGER;    { FOR loop index }
2 --
2 0- A      BEGIN
2 --             centerPt := SELF.Center;
```

```
         { Convert from degrees to radians, as required by the sine and cosine functions }
           radians := (theta * 3.14159) / 180.0;
           sine := sin(radians);
           cosine := cos(radians);
           FOR i := 1 TO 4 DO
              BEGIN
                 SetPt(tempPt, SELF.fVertex[i].h - centerPt.h,      { Subtract centerPt from vertex[i]. }
                               SELF.fVertex[i].v - centerPt.v);     { Store the result in tempPt.       }
                 newVertex[i].h := Num2Integer(centerPt.h + tempPt.h*cosine - tempPt.v*sine);
                 newVertex[i].v := Num2Integer(centerPt.v + tempPt.v*cosine + tempPt.h*sine);
              END;

           SELF.SetPoints(newVertex[1], newVertex[2], newVertex[3], newVertex[4]);
           SELF.fRotated := TRUE;
      END;


      PROCEDURE TQuad.SetPoints(pt1, pt2, pt3, pt4: Point);
      BEGIN
         SELF.fVertex[1] := pt1;
         SELF.fVertex[2] := pt2;
         SELF.fVertex[3] := pt3;
         SELF.fVertex[4] := pt4;
         SELF.fEnclosingRect := SELF.EnclosingRect;
      END;


      PROCEDURE TQuad.WriteTo(aRefNum: INTEGER);
      VAR data:   TFiledQuad;
          count:  LONGINT;
          quadID: INTEGER;
          err:    OSErr;
          i:      INTEGER;   { FOR Loop index }
      BEGIN
          quadID := SELF.ID;
          count := SIZEOF(INTEGER);
          err := FSWrite(aRefNum, count, @quadID);
          FOR i := 1 TO 4 DO data.theVertices[i] := SELF.fVertex[i];
          data.theRotationState := SELF.fRotated;
          count := SIZEOF(TFiledQuad);
          err := FSWrite(aRefNum, count, @data);
      END;


   { ****************************************** TParallelogram Methods ******************************************}
      FUNCTION  TParallelogram.AsText: Str255;  OVERRIDE;
      BEGIN
           AsText := 'a Parallelogram';
      END;


      FUNCTION TParallelogram.ID: INTEGER;  OVERRIDE;
      BEGIN
          ID := IDParallelogram;
      END;


   { This function returns a sketcher that will assist the user to interactively enter a parallelogram }
      FUNCTION  TParallelogram.NewSketchCmd: TSketchQuadCmd;  OVERRIDE;
      VAR parallelogramSketcher:   TSketchParallelogramCmd;
      BEGIN
           NEW(parallelogramSketcher);
           parallelogramSketcher.ISketchQuadCmd(cAddParallelogramCmd);
           NewSketchCmd := parallelogramSketcher;
      END;


   { ********************************************* TRhombus Methods *********************************************}
      FUNCTION  TRhombus.AsText: Str255;  OVERRIDE;
      BEGIN
           AsText := 'a Rhombus';
```

```
    END;


    FUNCTION TRhombus.ID: INTEGER;  OVERRIDE;
    BEGIN
        ID := IDRhombus;
    END;


  { This function returns a sketcher that will assist the user to interactively enter a rhombus }
    FUNCTION  TRhombus.NewSketchCmd: TSketchQuadCmd;  OVERRIDE;
    VAR rhombusSketcher:   TSketchRhombusCmd;

    BEGIN
         NEW(rhombusSketcher);
         rhombusSketcher.ISketchQuadCmd(cAddRhombusCmd);
         NewSketchCmd := rhombusSketcher;
    END;


  { **************************************** TRectangle Methods ******************************************}

    FUNCTION  TRectangle.AsText: Str255;  OVERRIDE;
    BEGIN
         AsText := 'a Rectangle';
    END;


    PROCEDURE TRectangle.Draw;  OVERRIDE;
    VAR aRect: Rect;
    BEGIN
        IF NOT SELF.fRotated
          THEN
              BEGIN
                 Pt2Rect(SELF.fVertex[1], SELF.fVertex[3], aRect);
                 FrameRect(aRect);
              END

          ELSE INHERITED Draw;
    END;


    FUNCTION  TRectangle.EnclosingRect: Rect;  OVERRIDE;
    VAR thisRect:   Rect;
    BEGIN
         IF NOT SELF.fRotated
           THEN Pt2Rect(SELF.fVertex[1], SELF.fVertex[3], thisRect)
           ELSE thisRect := INHERITED EnclosingRect;
        EnclosingRect := thisRect;
    END;  { TRectangle.EnclosingRect }


    FUNCTION TRectangle.ID: INTEGER;  OVERRIDE;
    BEGIN
        ID := IDRectangle;
    END;


  { This function returns a sketcher that will assist the user to interactively enter a rectangle }
    FUNCTION  TRectangle.NewSketchCmd: TSketchQuadCmd;  OVERRIDE;
    VAR rectangleSketcher:   TSketchTangleCmd;
    BEGIN
         NEW(rectangleSketcher);
         rectangleSketcher.ISketchQuadCmd(cAddRectangleCmd);
         NewSketchCmd := rectangleSketcher;
    END;


  { ***************************************** TSquare Methods ********************************************}

    FUNCTION  TSquare.AsText: Str255;  OVERRIDE;
    BEGIN
         AsText := 'a Square';
    END;
```

```
2 1182 --
2 1183 --
2 1184 -- A      FUNCTION TSquare.ID: INTEGER;  OVERRIDE;
2 1185 0- A      BEGIN
2 1186 --            ID := IDSquare;
2 1187 -0 A      END;
2 1188 --
2 1189 --
2 1190 --    { This function returns a sketcher that will assist the user to interactively enter a square }
2 1191 -- A      FUNCTION  TSquare.NewSketchCmd: TSketchQuadCmd;  OVERRIDE;
2 1192 --        VAR squareSketcher:   TSketchSquareCmd;
2 1193 0- A      BEGIN
2 1194 --             NEW(squareSketcher);
2 1195 --             squareSketcher.ISketchQuadCmd(cAddSquareCmd);
2 1196 --             NewSketchCmd := squareSketcher;
2 1197 -0 A      END;
2 1198 --
2 1199 --
2 1200 --    { *************************************** TAddQuadCmd Methods ****************************************}
2 1201 --
2 1202 -- A      PROCEDURE TAddQuadCmd.IAddQuadCmd(itsCmdNumber: CmdNumber; quadToBeAdded: TQuad);
2 1203 --        VAR i:      INTEGER;
2 1204 0- A      BEGIN
2 1205 --            SELF.ICommand(itsCmdNumber);
2 1206 --            SELF.fQuad := quadToBeAdded;
2 1207 --            SELF.fQuadInstalled := FALSE;
2 1208 -0 A      END;
2 1209 --
2 1210 --
2 1211 -- A      PROCEDURE TAddQuadCmd.Free;  OVERRIDE;
2 1212 0- A      BEGIN
2 1213 --    {$IFC qDebug}
2 1214 --           IF gExperimenting THEN SELF.Inspect;
2 1215 --    {$ENDC}
2 1216 --            IF NOT SELF.fQuadInstalled THEN       { the quad created for this command object isn't
2 1217 --                                                    installed in the document, so destroy it }
2 1218 --                FreeObject(SELF.fQuad);
2 1219 --            INHERITED Free;
2 1220 -0 A      END;
2 1221 --
2 1222 --
2 1223 -- A      PROCEDURE TAddQuadCmd.AddQuad;
2 1224 --        VAR quadDocument:   TQuadDocument;
2 1225 0- A      BEGIN
2 1226 --            quadDocument := TQuadDocument(SELF.fChangedDocument);
2 1227 --            quadDocument.AddQuad(SELF.fQuad);
2 1228 --            quadDocument.InvalidateQuad(SELF.fQuad);
2 1229 --            quadDocument.SelectQuad(SELF.fQuad);
2 1230 -0 A      END;
2 1231 --
2 1232 --
2 1233 -- A      PROCEDURE TAddQuadCmd.DeleteQuad(quad: TQuad);
2 1234 --        VAR quadDocument:   TQuadDocument;
2 1235 0- A      BEGIN
2 1236 --            quadDocument := TQuadDocument(SELF.fChangedDocument);
2 1237 --            quadDocument.SelectQuad(NIL);
2 1238 --            quadDocument.DeleteQuad(SELF.fQuad);
2 1239 --            quadDocument.InvalidateQuad(SELF.fQuad);
2 1240 -0 A      END;
2 1241 --
2 1242 --
2 1243 --    (*****
2 1244 --         PROCEDURE TAddQuadCmd.DoIt;  OVERRIDE;
2 1245 --         BEGIN
2 1246 --             There is nothing to do in this DoIt method.  The sketcher subclasses do the appropriate
2 1247 --             stuff in TrackMouse; the clear command has its own DoIt.
2 1248 --         END;
2 1249 --    ***)
2 1250 --
2 1251 --
2 1252 -- A      PROCEDURE TAddQuadCmd.RedoIt;  OVERRIDE;
2 1253 0- A      BEGIN
2 1254 --            TQuadDocument(SELF.fChangedDocument).SelectQuad(NIL); { Deselect current selection in both views }
2 1255 --            SELF.AddQuad;
```

```
2 1256 --            SELF.fQuadInstalled := TRUE;
2 1257 -0 A      END;
2 1258 --
2 1259 --
2 1260 -- A      PROCEDURE TAddQuadCmd.UndoIt;  OVERRIDE;
2 1261 0- A      BEGIN
2 1262 --            TQuadDocument(SELF.fChangedDocument).SelectQuad(NIL); { Deselect current selection in both views }
2 1263 --            SELF.DeleteQuad(SELF.fQuad);
2 1264 --            SELF.fQuadInstalled := FALSE;
2 1265 -0 A      END;
2 1266 --
2 1267 --
2 1268 --    { *************************************** TSketchQuadCmd Methods ****************************************}
2 1269 --
2 1270 -- A      PROCEDURE TSketchQuadCmd.ISketchQuadCmd(aCmdNumber: CmdNumber);
2 1271 --        VAR i:      INTEGER;
2 1272 0- A      BEGIN
2 1273 --            SELF.IAddQuadCommand(aCmdNumber, NIL);
2 1274 --            SELF.fQuadGrView := TQuadDocument(gDocument).fQuadGrView;
2 1275 --            SELF.fLastVertexSet := 0;
2 1276 --            SELF.fConstrainMouse := TRUE;
2 1277 -0 A      END;
2 1278 --
2 1279 --
2 1280 --    {$IFC qDebug}
2 1281 --    {$S GDebug}
2 1282 -- A      PROCEDURE TSketchQuadCmd.Inspect;  OVERRIDE;
2 1283 --        VAR i:  INTEGER;    {FOR Loop index}
2 1284 0- A      BEGIN
2 1285 --            INHERITED Inspect;
2 1286 --            IF SELF.fQuad <> NIL
2 1287 1-              THEN BEGIN
2 1288 --                      WriteLn('fQuad is NOT NIL');
2 1289 --                      SELF.fQuad.Inspect;
2 1290 -1                  END
2 1291 --              ELSE WriteLn('fQuad is  NIL');
2 1292 --
2 1293 --            WriteLn('fQuadInstalled is ', SELF.fQuadInstalled);
2 1294 --            WriteLn('fLastVertexSet is ', SELF.fLastVertexSet);
2 1295 --            {IF SELF.fNextQuad = NIL
2 1296 --              THEN WriteLn('fNextQuad is NIL')
2 1297 --              ELSE WriteLn('fNextQuad is NOT NIL')}
2 1298 -0 A      END;
2 1299 --    {$ENDC}
2 1300 --
2 1301 --
2 1302 -- A      PROCEDURE TSketchQuadCmd.Commit;  OVERRIDE;
2 1303 0- A      BEGIN
2 1304 --            IF SELF.fLastVertexSet <> 4 THEN
2 1305 --                TQuadDocument(SELF.fChangedDocument).InvalidateQuad(SELF.fQuad);
2 1306 --                                         { If the quad wasn't finished, make sure that it is erased }
2 1307 -0 A      END;
2 1308 --
2 1309 --
2 1310 --    { Set the enclosing rectangle for the partial quad }
2 1311 -- A      PROCEDURE TSketchQuadCmd.EnclosePartialQuad;
2 1312 --        VAR r1, r2, r3: Rect;
2 1313 0- A      BEGIN
2 1314 1-            CASE SELF.fLastVertexSet OF
2 1315 2-               2:   BEGIN
2 1316 --                        Pt2Rect(SELF.fQuad.fVertex[1], SELF.fQuad.fVertex[2], r1);
2 1317 --                        SELF.fQuad.fEnclosingRect := r1;
2 1318 -2                    END;
2 1319 2-               3:   BEGIN
2 1320 --                        Pt2Rect(SELF.fQuad.fVertex[1], SELF.fQuad.fVertex[2], r1);
2 1321 --                        Pt2Rect(SELF.fQuad.fVertex[2], SELF.fQuad.fVertex[3], r2);
2 1322 --                        Pt2Rect(SELF.fQuad.fVertex[1], SELF.fQuad.fVertex[3], r3);
2 1323 --                        UnionRect(r1, r2, r1);
2 1324 --                        UnionRect(r1, r3, r1);
2 1325 --                        SELF.fQuad.fEnclosingRect := r1;
2 1326 -2                    END;
2 1327 2-               4:   BEGIN
2 1328 --                        SELF.fQuad.fEnclosingRect := SELF.fQuad.EnclosingRect;
2 1329 -2                    END
```

```
        END { Case }
    END;


    PROCEDURE TSketchQuadCmd.SetVertices(newVertex: Point);
    VAR tempRect:   Rect;
    BEGIN
      { For a general quadrilateral, this method can do nothing more than just set the single new vertex
        that is passed to it.  For more specific types of quadrilaterals, additional vertices can be set.
        For example, for a rectangle all four vertices can be determined from two opposite ones.  See
        TSketch(rec)TangleCmd.SetVertices.  }

        SELF.fLastVertexSet := SELF.fLastVertexSet + 1;
        SELF.fQuad.fVertex[SELF.fLastVertexSet] := newVertex;
        SELF.EnclosePartialQuad;  { Set the enclosing rectangle for the partial quad }
    END;


    PROCEDURE TSketchQuadCmd.TrackFeedback(anchorPoint, nextPoint: Point;
                                    turnItOn, mouseDidMove: BOOLEAN);  OVERRIDE;
    BEGIN
      { For a quad, draw one new edge }
       IF mouseDidMove THEN
           BEGIN
              MoveTo(anchorPoint.h, anchorPoint.v);       { Erase old line or Draw new one }
              LineTo(nextPoint.h, nextPoint.v);
           END;
    END;


    FUNCTION  TSketchQuadCmd.TrackMouse(aTrackPhase: TrackPhase;
                                    VAR anchorPoint, previousPoint, nextPoint: Point;
                                    mouseDidMove: BOOLEAN): TCommand;  OVERRIDE;
    VAR r:              Rect;
        size:           Point;
        i:              INTEGER;
    BEGIN
        TrackMouse := SELF;   { Continue sending new events to this command object }

        IF SELF.fLastVertexSet = 0 THEN { This is true only for the first edge of a brand new quad  }
          BEGIN
            SELF.fQuad.fVertex[1] := anchorPoint;
            SELF.fLastVertexSet := 1;
          END;

        IF aTrackPhase = trackRelease THEN                          { this new point may be a new vertex }
            BEGIN
               IF NOT ( EqualPt(previousPoint, anchorPoint) AND
                        EqualPt(previousPoint, SELF.fQuad.fVertex[SELF.fLastVertexSet]) )
                 THEN                                                { No degenerate quads allowed here }
                    BEGIN
                       SELF.SetVertices(previousPoint);

                       IF SELF.fLastVertexSet = 4 THEN
                           BEGIN
                              SELF.AddQuad;
                              SELF.fQuadInstalled := TRUE;
                              SELF.fQuadGrView.fPalette.ChangeSelection(0);   { Set palette to the arrow }
                              SetCursor(arrow);                               {  and the cursor.         }
                           END
                    END
            END
    END;


{ ********************************* TSketchParallelogramCmd Methods ************************************}

    PROCEDURE TSketchParallelogramCmd.SetVertices(newVertex: Point);
    VAR diffPt: Point;
    BEGIN
        INHERITED SetVertices(newVertex);

      { Set the fourth vertex of the parallelogram by compuation  }
        IF SELF.fLastVertexSet = 3 THEN
```

```
            BEGIN
               diffPt.h := SELF.fQuad.fVertex[1].h - SELF.fQuad.fVertex[2].h;
               diffPt.v := SELF.fQuad.fVertex[1].v - SELF.fQuad.fVertex[2].v;

               SELF.fLastVertexSet := 4;
               SELF.fQuad.fVertex[4].h := newVertex.h + diffPt.h;
               SELF.fQuad.fVertex[4].v := newVertex.v + diffPt.v;
            END;
         SELF.EnclosePartialQuad;                     { Set the enclosing rectangle for the partial quad
      END;


   { ************************************ TSketchRhombusCmd Methods ***************************************

   { Adjust the value of the potential third vertices of the rhombus to ensure that the third vertex is
     the same distance from the second one as the second one is from the first.  Note that there is no need
     to enforce the parallelism constraint also associated with rhombi since this will be "inherited" from
     TSketchParallelogramCmd.}
      PROCEDURE TSketchRhombusCmd.TrackConstrain(anchorPoint, previousPoint: Point;
                                               VAR nextPoint: Point);  OVERRIDE;
      VAR tempPt:             Point;
         scale1, scale2:      INTEGER;

         FUNCTION Distance(pt1, pt2: Point): INTEGER;
         VAR temp:   INTEGER;
         BEGIN
            temp := Num2Integer( SQRT( SQR(pt1.h - pt2.h) + SQR(pt1.v - pt2.v)));
            IF temp < 2
              THEN Distance := 1
              ELSE Distance := temp;
         END;

      BEGIN
       { To perform the desired computation, start at the second vertex and add a normalized direction
         vector in the direction of the potential third vertex from the second vertex.  Multiply
         this direction vector by the distance from the first vertex to the second vertex. }

         IF SELF.fLastVertexSet = 2
           THEN
             BEGIN
               scale1 := Distance(SELF.fQuad.fVertex[1], SELF.fQuad.fVertex[2]);
               scale2 := Distance(SELF.fQuad.fVertex[2], nextPoint);
               tempPt.h := (nextPoint.h - SELF.fQuad.fVertex[2].h)*scale1;
               tempPt.v := (nextPoint.v - SELF.fQuad.fVertex[2].v)*scale1;
               tempPt.h := tempPt.h div scale2;           { Avoid underflow by these separate operations
               tempPt.v := tempPt.v div scale2;
               tempPt.h := tempPt.h + SELF.fQuad.fVertex[2].h;
               tempPt.v := tempPt.v + SELF.fQuad.fVertex[2].v;
               nextPoint := tempPt;
             END
      END;

   { ************************************ TSketchTangleCmd Methods ****************************************

      PROCEDURE TSketchTangleCmd.TrackFeedback(anchorPoint, nextPoint: Point;
                                            turnItOn, mouseDidMove: BOOLEAN);  OVERRIDE;
      VAR r:  Rect;
      BEGIN
        { For a rectangle, draw the entire rectangle }
         IF mouseDidMove THEN
            BEGIN
               Pt2Rect(anchorPoint, nextPoint, r);
               FrameRect(r);
            END;
      END;


      PROCEDURE TSketchTangleCmd.SetVertices(newVertex: Point);  OVERRIDE;
      VAR vertex1:     Point;
      BEGIN
        { Set all the remaining vertices of the rectangle by compuation  }
         SELF.fLastVertexSet := 4;
         vertex1 := SELF.fQuad.fVertex[1];
         SELF.fQuad.fVertex[3] := newVertex;
```

```
        SELF.fQuad.fVertex[2].h := newVertex.h;
        SELF.fQuad.fVertex[2].v := vertex1.v;
        SELF.fQuad.fVertex[4].h := vertex1.h;
        SELF.fQuad.fVertex[4].v := newVertex.v;
        SELF.EnclosePartialQuad;                    { Set the enclosing rectangle for the partial quad }
    END;


{ ************************************ TSketchSquareCmd Methods ****************************************}

{ Correct the nextPoint to enforce the "equal sides" constraint of the square.  Note that there is no
  need to enforce the other defining properties of a square since all of these are "inherited" from
  TSketch(Rec)TangleCmd. }
    PROCEDURE TSketchSquareCmd.TrackConstrain(anchorPoint, previousPoint: Point;
                                              VAR nextPoint: Point);  OVERRIDE;
    VAR height, width:  INTEGER;
        tempPoint:      Point;
    BEGIN
        tempPoint := nextPoint;
        width := nextPoint.h - SELF.fQuad.fVertex[1].h;
        height := nextPoint.v - SELF.fQuad.fVertex[1].v;
        IF width > height
          THEN  tempPoint.v := tempPoint.v + width - height
          ELSE  tempPoint.h := tempPoint.h - width + height;
        nextPoint := tempPoint;
    END;


{ ************************************** TClearQuadCmd Methods ****************************************}

    PROCEDURE TClearQuadCmd.IClearQuadCmd(itsCmdNumber: INTEGER);
    BEGIN
        SELF.IAddQuadCmd(itsCmdNumber, NIL);
        SELF.fQuad := TQuadDocument(SELF.fChangedDocument).fSelectedQuad
    END;


    PROCEDURE TClearQuadCmd.DoIt;  OVERRIDE;
    BEGIN
        TQuadDocument(SELF.fChangedDocument).SelectQuad(NIL); { Deselect current selection in both views }
        SELF.DeleteQuad(SELF.fQuad);
    END;


    PROCEDURE TClearQuadCmd.RedoIt;  OVERRIDE;
    BEGIN
        SELF.DoIt;
        SELF.fQuadInstalled := FALSE;   { Do free the quad when the command is committed and freed }
    END;


    PROCEDURE TClearQuadCmd.UndoIt;  OVERRIDE;
    BEGIN
        SELF.AddQuad;
        TQuadDocument(SELF.fChangedDocument).SelectQuad(SELF.fQuad);
        SELF.fQuadInstalled := TRUE;    { Don't free the quad when the command is committed and freed }
    END;


{ ************************************** TRotateQuadCmd Methods ****************************************}


    PROCEDURE TRotateQuadCmd.IRotateQuadCmd(itsCmdNumber: INTEGER);
    BEGIN
        ICommand(itsCmdNumber);
        SELF.fQuad := TQuadDocument(SELF.fChangedDocument).fSelectedQuad;
        SELF.fCenterPoint := SELF.fQuad.Center;
        SELF.fAngle := 0;
    END;


    PROCEDURE TRotateQuadCmd.DoIt; OVERRIDE;
    VAR quadDocument:   TQuadDocument;
```

```
BEGIN
    quadDocument := TQuadDocument(SELF.fChangedDocument);
    quadDocument.InvalidateQuad(SELF.fQuad);                    { BEFORE Rotation }
    fQuad.RotateBy(SELF.fAngle);
    quadDocument.InvalidateQuad(SELF.fQuad);                    { AFTER Rotation }
END;


PROCEDURE TRotateQuadCmd.RedoIt;  OVERRIDE;
BEGIN
    TQuadDocument(SELF.fChangedDocument).SelectQuad(SELF.fQuad); { Re-establish the current selection
                                                                   in both views }
    SELF.DoIt;
END;


PROCEDURE TRotateQuadCmd.UndoIt; OVERRIDE;
VAR quadDocument:   TQuadDocument;
BEGIN
    quadDocument := TQuadDocument(SELF.fChangedDocument);
    quadDocument.SelectQuad(SELF.fQuad);          { Re-establish the current selection in the view }
    quadDocument.InvalidateQuad(SELF.fQuad);                    { BEFORE Rotation }
    fQuad.RotateBy(-SELF.fAngle);
    quadDocument.InvalidateQuad(SELF.fQuad);                    { AFTER Rotation }
END;


PROCEDURE TRotateQuadCmd.TrackFeedback(anchorPoint, nextPoint: Point;
                                       turnItOn, mouseDidMove: BOOLEAN);  OVERRIDE;
BEGIN
   IF mouseDidMove THEN
       BEGIN
          MoveTo(SELF.fCenterPoint.h, SELF.fCenterPoint.v);    { Erase old line or Draw new one }
          LineTo(nextPoint.h, nextPoint.v);
       END;
END;


FUNCTION  TRotateQuadCmd.TrackMouse(aTrackPhase: TrackPhase;
                                    VAR anchorPoint, previousPoint, nextPoint: Point;
                                    mouseDidMove: BOOLEAN): TCommand;  OVERRIDE;
VAR tempPoint:      Point;
    slope:          Fixed;
    angle:          INTEGER;

BEGIN
    TrackMouse := SELF;

    IF aTrackPhase = trackRelease   { the rotation angle has been determined - calculate it }
      THEN
        BEGIN
            tempPoint.h := previousPoint.h - SELF.fCenterPoint.h;
            tempPoint.v := previousPoint.v - SELF.fCenterPoint.v;
            slope := FixRatio(tempPoint.v, tempPoint.h);
            angle := AngleFromSlope(slope);

          {$IFC qDebug}
            IF gExperimenting THEN WriteLn('QuickDraw angle is ', angle);
          {$ENDC}

          { turn the kind of angle returned by the ToolBox into the usual kind of angle }
            IF tempPoint.v >= 0
              THEN angle := angle - 180;
            angle := - angle;

          {$IFC qDebug}
            IF gExperimenting THEN WriteLn('Real angle is ', angle);
          {$ENDC}

            SELF.fAngle := angle;

            IF angle = 0
              THEN TrackMouse := gNoChanges;   { Don't bother to rotate by 0 degrees }
        END
```

```
    END;

  { **************************************** TClearAllCmd Methods ****************************************}

    PROCEDURE TClearAllCmd.IClearAllCmd(itsCmdNumber: INTEGER);
    BEGIN
        ICommand(itsCmdNumber);
        SELF.fLastQuadAdded := TQuadDocument(SELF.fChangedDocument).fLastQuadAdded;
        SELF.fSelectedQuad := TQuadDocument(SELF.fChangedDocument).fSelectedQuad;
    END;


    PROCEDURE TClearAllCmd.Commit;  OVERRIDE;
    VAR freeThisQuad:   TQuad;
        nextQuad:       TQuad;
    BEGIN
      { Free all the quads }
        IF SELF.fLastQuadAdded <> NIL             { Are there really any quads to be freed? }
          THEN
             BEGIN
                 freeThisQuad := SELF.fLastQuadAdded;
                 nextQuad := freeThisQuad.fNextQuad;
                 FreeObject(freeThisQuad);

                 WHILE (nextQuad <> NIL) DO
                      BEGIN
                          freeThisQuad := nextQuad;
                          nextQuad := nextQuad.fNextQuad;
                          FreeObject(freeThisQuad);
                      END
             END
    END;


    PROCEDURE TClearAllCmd.DoIt;  OVERRIDE;
    VAR quadDocument:   TQuadDocument;
    BEGIN
        quadDocument := TQuadDocument(SELF.fChangedDocument);
        quadDocument.SelectQuad(NIL);
        quadDocument.fLastQuadAdded := NIL;
        SELF.InvalidateEverything;
    END;


    PROCEDURE TClearAllCmd.InvalidateEverything;
    VAR quadDocument:   TQuadDocument;
    BEGIN
        quadDocument := TQuadDocument(SELF.fChangedDocument);
        quadDocument.fQuadGrView.InvalRect(quadDocument.fQuadGrView.fExtentRect);
        quadDocument.fQuadTxView.InvalRect(quadDocument.fQuadTxView.fExtentRect);
    END;


    PROCEDURE TClearAllCmd.RedoIt;  OVERRIDE;
    BEGIN
        SELF.fSelectedQuad := TQuadDocument(SELF.fChangedDocument).fSelectedQuad;  { In case the selection
                                                                                      has changed }
        SELF.DoIt;
    END;


    PROCEDURE TClearAllCmd.UndoIt;  OVERRIDE;
    VAR quadDocument:   TQuadDocument;
    BEGIN
        quadDocument := TQuadDocument(SELF.fChangedDocument);
        quadDocument.fSelectedQuad := SELF.fSelectedQuad;
        quadDocument.fLastQuadAdded := SELF.fLastQuadAdded;
        SELF.InvalidateEverything;
    END;



END.
```

```
                 { List View unit which is used in the MacApp QuadWorld Application }
                   { Copyright 1985 by Productivity Products International, Inc. }

{ This unit implements a list view like that of the Smalltalk Listview class, i.e., a vertical list
  of text items any one of which can be selected with the mouse.  Like the Smalltalk class, this
  TListView makes some assumptions about the protocol of the document it displays.  It particular,
  TListView assumes that its fDocument field refers to an instance of a subclass of TListDocument
  (defined here) and thus has the following additional document methods (at a minimum):

  T(Your)Document.SetSelection(newSelectionIndex)        This method is used to communicate to your
                                                         document that the selection has changed,
                                                         presumably because the user has selected a
                                                         text string in the TListView

  T(Your)Document.ReportListItem: Str255;                A function which returns the textual version
                                                         of a given item to be displayed by the
                                                         TListView. Note that your document can contain
                                                         primarily non-textual data - the ListView will
                                                         display a textual representation of that
                                                         data, a representation that you construct
                                                         in this method.

    To see one example of how this ListView class can be used, see the QuadWorld application.        }

UNIT UListView;

{$M+}                                      { Compiler commands to generate Macintosh code }
{$X-}                                      {  and turn off stack expansion }
{$E+}                                      {  and automatically invoke the Editor if errors are found }
{$E Error.text}                            {  and put the errors in file 'Error.text' }
INTERFACE
USES
    {$U-}                                  { This set of units are portions of the
                                             Macintosh Software supplement }
    {$U obj/MemTypes}       MemTypes,
    {$U obj/QuickDraw}      QuickDraw,
    {$U obj/OSIntf}         OSIntf,
    {$U obj/ToolIntf}       ToolIntf,
    {$U obj/PackIntf}       PackIntf,

    {$U Object.U}           UObject,       { This set of units are portions of MacApp }
    {$U List.U}             UList,
    {$U MacApp.U}           UMacApp;

TYPE
    TListDocument = OBJECT(TDocument)          { an abstract superclass that contains null methods
                                                  needed for the proper use of a list view }
        PROCEDURE TListDocument.SetSelection(newSelectionIndex: INTEGER);
        FUNCTION  TListDocument.ReportListItem(itemNumber: INTEGER): Str255;
    END;    { of TListDocument }


    TListView = OBJECT(TView)

      { Instance variables }
        fCurrItem:              INTEGER;      { index of the current selection, if any, otherwise 0 }
        fNumberOfItems:         INTEGER;      { number of items currently in the list }
        fLineHeight:            INTEGER;      { height of each line including leading }
        fLineAscent:            INTEGER;      { position of baseline relative to top of line }


      { Initialization }
        PROCEDURE TListView.IListView(itsParent: TView; itsDocument: TListDocument; itsExtent: Rect;
                                      itsVDeterminer: SizeDeterminer; itCanSelect: BOOLEAN);

      { Commands and Selections }
        PROCEDURE TListView.ChangeSelection(index: INTEGER);
        FUNCTION  TListView.DoMouseCommand(VAR downLocalPoint: Point; VAR info: EventInfo;
                                           VAR hysteresis: Point): TCommand;  OVERRIDE;
```

```
3 --         FUNCTION  TListView.PtToIndex(testPoint: Point): INTEGER;    { Convert from a point in local view
3 --                                                                        coordinates to the index of the
3 --                                                                        list of items at this point.  This
3 --                                                                        is a method so that it can easily
3 --                                                                        be overridden by clients. }
3 --
3 --       { Displaying }
3 --         PROCEDURE TListView.CalcMinExtent(VAR minExtent: Rect);  OVERRIDE;  { This method must be
3 --                                                                  overridden since a list view has a
3 --                                                                  variable vertical extent. }
3 --         PROCEDURE TListView.DoHighlightSelection(fromHL, toHL: HLState);  OVERRIDE;
3 --         PROCEDURE TListView.Draw(area: Rect);  OVERRIDE;
3 --         PROCEDURE TListView.DrawOneItem(item: Str255);      { Draw one item.  This is here so that it
3 --                                                            can easilly be overridden by a client. }
3 --         PROCEDURE TListView.InvalidateItem(itemNumber: INTEGER);
3 --         FUNCTION  TListView.SetUpBox(index: INTEGER): Rect;    { Calculate the surrounding rectangle
3 --                                                                 for an item }
3 --         PROCEDURE TListView.SetPen;      { setup the pen for drawing the text; this is a
3 --                                            method so that it can be overridden easily by clients}
3 --
3 --     END;  { TListView }
3 --
3 --
3 --
3 --   IMPLEMENTATION
3 --
3 --   {$I ListView.U2.TEXT }
4 --   { Private data }
4 --   CONST
4 --
4 --       txMargin = 4;         { horizontal space between view edge and the left edge of the text }
4 --
4 --
4 --   { ****************************  TListDocument   (an abstract superclass )   ******************************** }
4 --
4 -- A     PROCEDURE TListDocument.SetSelection(newSelectionIndex: INTEGER);
4 0- A    BEGIN
4 --          {$IFC qDebug} ProgramBreak('Call to TListDocument.SetSelection - an abstract superclass'); {$ENDC}
4 -0 A    END;
4 --
4 -- A     FUNCTION  TListDocument.ReportListItem(itemNumber: INTEGER): Str255;
4 0- A    BEGIN
4 --          {$IFC qDebug} ProgramBreak('Call to TListDocument.ReportList - an abstract superclass'); {$ENDC}
4 -0 A    END;
4 --
4 --
4 --   { ***************************************  TListView  ******************************************************* }
4 --
4 -- A     PROCEDURE TListView.IListView(itsParent: TView; itsDocument: TListDocument; itsExtent: Rect;
4 --                                     itsVDeterminer: SizeDeterminer; itCanSelect: BOOLEAN);
4 --       VAR fInfo: FontInfo;
4 0- A    BEGIN
4 --          SELF.IView(itsParent, itsDocument, itsExtent, sizeFixed, itsVDeterminer, itCanSelect, hlDim);
4 --          SELF.fCurrItem := 0;
4 --          SELF.fNumberOfItems := 0;
4 --
4 --          SELF.SetPen;
4 --          GetFontInfo(fInfo);
4 --
4 --          WITH fInfo DO
4 1-             BEGIN
4 --                SELF.fLineHeight := ascent + descent + leading + 1;
4 --                SELF.fLineAscent := ascent + (leading DIV 2) - 1;
4 -1             END
4 -0 A    END;
4 --
4 --    { This method must be overridden so that MacApp can determine the view's true extent }
4 -- A     PROCEDURE TListView.CalcMinExtent(VAR minExtent: Rect);  OVERRIDE;
4 --       VAR  itemNumber: INTEGER;
4 0- A    BEGIN
4 --        { How many items are there? }
4 --          itemNumber := 1;
4 --          WHILE (TListDocument(SELF.fDocument).ReportListItem(itemNumber) <> ' ')
4 --               DO itemNumber := itemNumber + 1;
```

```
4 --          SELF.fNumberOfItems := itemNumber - 1;
4 --
4 --       { Set the amount of room needed for that many items }
4 --          minExtent := SELF.fExtentRect;
4 --          IF SELF.fSizeDeterminer[v] <> sizeFixed      { Only need to adjust vertical extent }
4 --            THEN minExtent.botRight.v := SELF.fNumberOfItems*SELF.fLineHeight;
4 -0 A     END;
4 --
4 --
4 -- A     PROCEDURE TListView.ChangeSelection(index: INTEGER);
4 0- A     BEGIN
4 --          SELF.fFrame.Focus;
4 --          SELF.DoHighlightSelection(SELF.fHLDesired, hlOff);
4 --          SELF.fCurrItem := index;
4 --          SELF.DoHighlightSelection(hlOff, SELF.fHLDesired);
4 -0 A     END;
4 --
4 --
4 --   { Dim highlighting of text by gray XORing is not very readable, so dim highlight a text string
4 --     by framing it with a gray rectangle.  (Standard highlighting when the window displaying
4 --     the view is active is still to invert - black XORing.)  The state transition diagram is:
4 --
4 --                                                          hlTo
4 --
4 --                           |      OFF       |          DIM          |          ON
4 --               ------------|----------------|-----------------------|---------------------
4 --                   OFF     |      (NA)      |         Frame         |        Invert
4 --               ------------|----------------|-----------------------|---------------------
4 --     hlFrom        DIM     |     Frame      |         (NA)          |  Frame and Invert
4 --               ------------|----------------|-----------------------|---------------------
4 --                   ON      |     Invert     |   Invert and Frame    |         (NA)
4 --               ------------|----------------|---------------------------------------------
4 --
4 --     Since this matrix is (almost) symmetric, we can add together the hlFrom and hlTo parameters
4 --     and take one action for each of the three possible sums.  }
4 --
4 -- A     PROCEDURE TListView.DoHighlightSelection(fromHL, toHL: HLState); OVERRIDE;
4 --       VAR r:  Rect;
4 0- A     BEGIN
4 --          IF (SELF.fCurrItem > 0) THEN
4 1-            BEGIN
4 --                { Make r be the rectangle to invert }
4 --                r := SELF.SetUpBox(SELF.fCurrItem);
4 --                InsetRect(r, 1, 1);
4 --
4 --                { Set the pen pattern and mode properly }
4 --                PenPat(ltGray);
4 --                PenMode(patXor);
4 --
4 --                IF RectIsVisible(r) THEN     { only do highlighting if part of the rectangle is visible }
4 2-                  BEGIN
4 3-                      CASE (fromHl + toHL) OF
4 --                          hlOffDim:  FrameRect(r);
4 --                          hlOffOn:   InvertRect(r);
4 44                          hlDimOn:   IF fromHL = hlDim THEN BEGIN  FrameRect(r);  InvertRect(r);  END
4 44                                                   ELSE BEGIN  InvertRect(r);  FrameRect(r);  END;
4 -3                      END  { of CASE }
4 -2                  END
4 -1            END
4 -0 A     END;
4 --
4 --
4 -- A     FUNCTION  TListView.DoMouseCommand(VAR downLocalPoint: Point; VAR info: EventInfo;
4 --                                          VAR hysteresis: Point): TCommand; OVERRIDE;
4 --       VAR index: INTEGER;
4 0- A     BEGIN
4 --          { If this mouse press results in a change of the current selection, let the document
4 --            deal with it in any way it chooses.  This is done because the document might control
4 --            several views, or might deal with a changed selection in some other application-specific
4 --            manner. }
4 --
4 --          DoMouseCommand := gNoChanges;
4 --          index := SELF.PtToIndex(downLocalPoint);
4 --          IF (index > 0) THEN
```

```
4 1-            BEGIN
4 --              IF fCurrItem = index          { A click on the current selection means to deselect it }
4 --                THEN  TListDocument(SELF.fDocument).SetSelection(0)
4 --                ELSE  TListDocument(SELF.fDocument).SetSelection(index);
4 -1            END
4 -0 A      END;
4 --
4 --
4 --    { Write the textual representation of all the items, properly positioned }
4 -- A      PROCEDURE TListView.Draw(area: Rect); OVERRIDE;
4 --        VAR bBox:        Rect;           { the bounding box for a single item }
4 --            itemToDraw:  Str255;
4 --            itemNumber:  INTEGER;
4 0- A      BEGIN
4 --            SELF.SetPen;
4 --
4 --            itemNumber := 1;         { Get each item in turn from the document and draw it }
4 --            itemToDraw := TListDocument(SELF.fDocument).ReportListItem(itemNumber);
4 --            WHILE (itemToDraw <> '') DO
4 1-              BEGIN
4 --                { Calculate the rectangle to fill }
4 --                bBox := SELF.SetUpBox(itemNumber);
4 --
4 --                IF RectIsVisible(bBox) THEN      { only write text that will be seen }
4 2-                    BEGIN
4 --                      MoveTo(bBox.left + txMargin, bBox.top + SELF.fLineAscent);
4 --                      SELF.DrawOneItem(itemToDraw);
4 -2                    END;
4 --
4 --                itemNumber := itemNumber + 1;
4 --                itemToDraw := TListDocument(SELF.fDocument).ReportListItem(itemNumber);
4 -1              END;
4 --            SELF.fNumberOfItems := itemNumber - 1;
4 -0 A      END;
4 --
4 --
4 --
4 -- A      PROCEDURE TListView.DrawOneItem(item: Str255);
4 0- A      BEGIN
4 --            DrawString(item);
4 -0 A      END;
4 --
4 --
4 --    { In theory, this method invalidates the area occupied by the item, that is, the listDocument will
4 --      send this message to the view when any single item needs to be redrawn and will pass the number of
4 --      this item as the message argument.   In reality, this method invalidates the entire panel so as not
4 --      to leave "holes" in the textual representation of the document.  The argument is never used.    }
4 -- A      PROCEDURE TListView.InvalidateItem(itemNumber: INTEGER);
4 0- A      BEGIN
4 --            SELF.AdjustExtent;  { In case the size of the view has changed }
4 --            SELF.fFrame.Focus;
4 --            SELF.InvalRect(SELF.fExtentRect);
4 -0 A      END;
4 --
4 --
4 --    { Decide what item is indicated by this point; return 0 iff this point indicates no item }
4 -- A      FUNCTION  TListView.PtToIndex(testPoint: Point): INTEGER;
4 --        VAR  i: INTEGER;   { FOR Loop Index }
4 0- A      BEGIN
4 --            PtToIndex := 0;                          { Assume the item is NOT found }
4 --            FOR i := 1 TO SELF.fNumberOfItems DO
4 --              IF PtInRect(testPoint, SELF.SetUpBox(i))
4 1-                THEN BEGIN
4 --                       PtToIndex := i;
4 --                       LEAVE                 { Don't check the rest of the rectangles }
4 -1                     END
4 -0 A      END;
4 --
4 --
4 --    { Set up the pen for drawing the characters; assumes that we are focused on the correct window
4 --      (or a pad in the correct window); this is a method so it can be overridden easily }
4 -- A      PROCEDURE TListView.SetPen;
```

```
2362  4  194 0- A      BEGIN
2363  4  195 --          PenNormal;
2364  4  196 --          TextFont(SystemFont);
2365  4  197 --          TextSize(12);
2366  4  198 --          TextFace([]);
2367  4  199 -0 A      END;
2368  4  200 --
2369  4  201 --
2370  4  202 --    { Create a rectangle, for this item. }
2371  4  203 -- A      FUNCTION  TListView.SetUpBox(index: INTEGER): Rect;
2372  4  204 --        VAR  bBox: Rect;
2373  4  205 0- A      BEGIN
2374  4  206 --            { use same left and right as view, calculate the top and bottom for this item number}
2375  4  207 --            WITH bBox DO
2376  4  208 1-                BEGIN
2377  4  209 --                    left := SELF.fExtentRect.left;
2378  4  210 --                    top := (index - 1)* SELF.fLineHeight;      { Subtract 1 to get the TOP line }
2379  4  211 --                    right := SELF.fExtentRect.right;
2380  4  212 --                    bottom := top + SELF.fLineHeight;
2381  4  213 -1                END;
2382  4  214 --            SetUpBox := bBox;
2383  4  215 -0 A      END;
2384  3   98 --
2385  3   99 --    END.
```

1. QuadWorld.U.TEXT
2. QuadWorld.U2.TEXT
3. ListView.U.TEXT
4. ListView.U2.TEXT

```
-A-
  aCmdNumber        119*( 1)  266*( 1)  255*( 2)  259 ( 2)  262 ( 2)  268 ( 2)  272 ( 2) 1270*( 2) 1273 ( 2)
  AddQuad           101*( 1)  252*( 1)  143*( 2)  322 ( 2) 1223*( 2) 1227 ( 2) 1255 ( 2) 1385 ( 2) 1532 ( 2)
  AdjustExtent      171 ( 4)
  aListView         187*( 2)  212=( 2)  215 ( 2)
  anchorPoint       274*( 1)  277*( 1)  294*( 1)  304*( 1)  313*( 1)  345*( 1)  348*( 1) 1348*( 2) 1354 ( 2)
                   1354 ( 2) 1361*( 2) 1371 ( 2) 1377 ( 2) 1422*( 2) 1458*( 2) 1465 ( 2) 1492*( 2) 1579*( 2)
                   1591*( 2)
  angle            1595*( 2) 1606=( 2) 1609 ( 2) 1614=( 2) 1614 ( 2) 1615=( 2) 1615 ( 2) 1618 ( 2) 1621 ( 2)
                   1623 ( 2)
  AngleFromSlope   1606 ( 2)
  aPalette          234*( 2)  242 ( 2)  243 ( 2)  244 ( 2)
  aParallelogram     35*( 2)   50 ( 2)   50 ( 2)   50 ( 2)
  aQuad              34*( 2)   48 ( 2)   48 ( 2)   48 ( 2)
  aQuadGrView       131*( 1)  186*( 2)  200=( 2)  202 ( 2)  202 ( 2)  232*( 2)  238 ( 2)  239 ( 2)  240 ( 2)
                    497*( 2)  513 ( 2)
  aQuadTxView       233*( 2)  246 ( 2)  248 ( 2)  249 ( 2)
  area              137*( 1)  161*( 1)  567*( 2)  827*( 2)   82*( 3)  131*( 4)
  aRect            1137*( 2) 1142 ( 2) 1143 ( 2)
  aRectangle         37*( 2)   54 ( 2)   54 ( 2)   54 ( 2)
  aRefNum           113*( 1)  114*( 1)  200*( 1)  201*( 1)  303*( 2)  309 ( 2)  314 ( 2)  321 ( 2)  343*( 2)
                    350 ( 2)  356 ( 2)  358 ( 2) 1008*( 2) 1015 ( 2) 1062*( 2) 1071 ( 2) 1075 ( 2)
  aRhombus           36*( 2)   52 ( 2)   52 ( 2)   52 ( 2)
  aRotateQuadCmd    732*( 2)  781 ( 2)  782 ( 2)  783 ( 2)
  arrow             604 ( 2)  610 ( 2)  820 ( 2) 1388 ( 2)
  ascent             35 ( 4)   36 ( 4)
  aSquare            38*( 2)   56 ( 2)   56 ( 2)   56 ( 2)
  aStdPrintHandler  623*( 2)  647 ( 2)  648 ( 2)
  AsText            186*( 1)  207*( 1)  215*( 1)  223*( 1)  233*( 1)  446 ( 2)  929*( 2)  931=( 2) 1081*( 2)
                   1083=( 2) 1105*( 2) 1107=( 2) 1130*( 2) 1132=( 2) 1178*( 2) 1180=( 2)
  aTrackPhase       276*( 1)  347*( 1) 1360*( 2) 1375 ( 2) 1590*( 2) 1600 ( 2)

-B-
  baseAddr          583=( 2)
  bBox              132*( 4)  143=( 4)  145 ( 4)  147 ( 4)  147 ( 4)  204*( 4)  207 ( 4)  214 ( 4)
  beforeTestQuad    155*( 2)  166=( 2)  171=( 2)  175 ( 2)
  BitMap            573 ( 2)
  BOOLEAN            67 ( 1)  113 ( 1)  118 ( 1)  160 ( 1)  176 ( 1)  243 ( 1)  275 ( 1)  278 ( 1)  305 ( 1)
                    346 ( 1)  349 ( 1)  229 ( 2)  303 ( 2)  799 ( 2) 1349 ( 2) 1362 ( 2) 1459 ( 2) 1580 ( 2)
                   1592 ( 2)   65 ( 3)   23 ( 4)
  botRight           53 ( 4)
  bottom            205 ( 2)  212=( 4)
  bounds            203 ( 2)  205 ( 2)  582 ( 2)  614 ( 2)
```

```
  EnclosingRect      188*( 1)  225*( 1)  965*( 2)  986=( 2) 1058 ( 2) 1150*( 2) 1155 ( 2) 1156=( 2) 1328 ( 2)
  EqualPt           1377 ( 2) 1378 ( 2)
  EraseRgn           780 ( 2)
  err                307*( 2)  314=( 2)  344*( 2)  358=( 2) 1010*( 2) 1015=( 2) 1066*( 2) 1071=( 2) 1075=( 2)
  EventInfo          135 ( 1)  154 ( 1)  549 ( 2)  726 ( 2)   69 ( 3)  110 ( 4)
  extentRect         235*( 2)  247 ( 2)  248 ( 2)
  extraHeight        193*( 2)  205=( 2)  207 ( 2)
  extraWidth         192*( 2)  203=( 2)  206 ( 2)  217 ( 2)

-F-
  FALSE              209 ( 2)  218 ( 2)  511 ( 2)  629 ( 2)  648 ( 2)  803 ( 2)  910 ( 2) 1207 ( 2) 1264 ( 2)
                    1526 ( 2)
  fAngle             334*( 1) 1546=( 2) 1555 ( 2) 1574 ( 2) 1621=( 2)
  fCenterPoint       333*( 1) 1545=( 2) 1584 ( 2) 1584 ( 2) 1603 ( 2) 1604 ( 2)
  fChangedDocument   892 ( 2) 1226 ( 2) 1236 ( 2) 1254 ( 2) 1262 ( 2) 1305 ( 2) 1512 ( 2) 1518 ( 2) 1533 ( 2)
                    1544 ( 2) 1553 ( 2) 1562 ( 2) 1571 ( 2) 1633 ( 2) 1634 ( 2) 1663 ( 2) 1673 ( 2) 1681 ( 2)
                    1690 ( 2)
  fChoiceRect        507=( 2)  544 ( 2)  558 ( 2)  602 ( 2)  612 ( 2)
  fChoiceRects       128*( 1)
  fCmdNumber         890 ( 2)  891 ( 2)
  fConstrainMouse   1276=( 2)
  fCurrItem           57*( 3)   27=( 4)   61=( 4)   87 ( 4)   90 ( 4)  123 ( 4)
  fCurrSelection     126*( 1)  512=( 2)  524 ( 2)  533=( 2)  544 ( 2)  743 ( 2)  752 ( 2)  804 ( 2)
  fDocument          749 ( 2)  789 ( 2)  792 ( 2)  835 ( 2)  892 ( 2)   46 ( 4)  124 ( 4)  125 ( 4)  139 ( 4)
                     152 ( 4)
  fEnclosingRect     175*( 1)  691 ( 2)  736 ( 2)  870 ( 2)  908=( 2)  955 ( 2) 1058=( 2) 1317=( 2) 1325=( 2)
                    1328=( 2)
  fExtentRect        555 ( 2) 1674 ( 2) 1675 ( 2)   51 ( 4)  173 ( 4)  209 ( 4)  211 ( 4)
  fFrame             531 ( 2)  659 ( 2)  852 ( 2)  877 ( 2)   59 ( 4)  172 ( 4)
  fHLDesired         532 ( 2)  534 ( 2)  660 ( 2)  675 ( 2)   60 ( 4)   62 ( 4)
  fIdlePriority      649=( 2)
  FillBitMap         577*( 2)
  FillBitMapWith     604 ( 2)  605 ( 2)  606 ( 2)  607 ( 2)  608 ( 2)  609 ( 2)  610 ( 2)
  FindIndex          480*( 2)  490 ( 2)
  FindQuad           424*( 2)  434 ( 2)
  fInfo               24*( 4)   31 ( 4)   33 ( 4)
  Fixed             1594 ( 2)
  FixRatio          1605 ( 2)
  fLastQuadAdded      82*( 1)  355*( 1)  106=( 2)  147 ( 2)  148=( 2)  158 ( 2)  161 ( 2)  162=( 2)  162 ( 2)
                     166 ( 2)  167 ( 2)  285 ( 2)  336 ( 2)  369 ( 2)  387 ( 2)  390 ( 2)  402=( 2) 1633=( 2)
                    1633 ( 2) 1643 ( 2) 1646 ( 2) 1665=( 2) 1692=( 2) 1692 ( 2)
  fLastVertexSet     262*( 1)  765 ( 2)  810 ( 2)  849 ( 2)  855 ( 2)  893 ( 2) 1275=( 2) 1294 ( 2) 1304 ( 2)
                    1314 ( 2) 1342=( 2) 1342 ( 2) 1343 ( 2) 1369 ( 2) 1372=( 2) 1378 ( 2) 1383 ( 2) 1403 ( 2)
                    1408=( 2) 1441 ( 2) 1475=( 2)
  fLineAscent         60*( 3)   36=( 4)  147 ( 4)
  fLineHeight         59*( 3)   35=( 4)   53 ( 4)  210 ( 4)  212 ( 4)
  fLocation          221 ( 2)  221 ( 2)
  fNextQuad          174*( 1)  147=( 2)  162 ( 2)  167 ( 2)  172 ( 2)  175=( 2)  175 ( 2)  290 ( 2)  373 ( 2)
                     391 ( 2)  397 ( 2)  909=( 2)  920 ( 2) 1647 ( 2) 1653 ( 2)
  fNumberOfItems      58*( 3)   28=( 4)   48=( 4)   53 ( 4)  154=( 4)  182 ( 4)
  Focus              531 ( 2)  659 ( 2)  852 ( 2)  877 ( 2)   59 ( 4)  172 ( 4)
  FontInfo            24 ( 4)
  forPrinting        113*( 1)  118*( 1)  229*( 2)  303*( 2)  309 ( 2)
  foundIndex         478*( 2)  484=( 2)  489=( 2)  491 ( 2)
  foundQuad          422*( 2)  428=( 2)  433=( 2)  435 ( 2)
  fPalette           144*( 1)  202 ( 2)  244=( 2)  631=( 2)  743 ( 2)  752 ( 2)  804 ( 2) 1387 ( 2)
  fQuad              242*( 1)  332*( 1)  756=( 2)  765 ( 2)  851 ( 2) 1206=( 2) 1218 ( 2) 1227 ( 2) 1228 ( 2)
                    1229 ( 2) 1238 ( 2) 1239 ( 2) 1263 ( 2) 1286 ( 2) 1289 ( 2) 1305 ( 2) 1316 ( 2) 1316 ( 2)
                    1317 ( 2) 1320 ( 2) 1320 ( 2) 1321 ( 2) 1321 ( 2) 1322 ( 2) 1322 ( 2) 1325 ( 2) 1328 ( 2)
                    1328 ( 2) 1343 ( 2) 1371 ( 2) 1378 ( 2) 1405 ( 2) 1405 ( 2) 1406 ( 2) 1406 ( 2) 1409 ( 2)
                    1410 ( 2) 1444 ( 2) 1444 ( 2) 1445 ( 2) 1446 ( 2) 1447 ( 2) 1450 ( 2) 1451 ( 2) 1476 ( 2)
                    1477 ( 2) 1479 ( 2) 1480 ( 2) 1481 ( 2) 1482 ( 2) 1498 ( 2) 1499 ( 2) 1512=( 2) 1519 ( 2)
                    1533 ( 2) 1544=( 2) 1545 ( 2) 1554 ( 2) 1555 ( 2) 1556 ( 2) 1562 ( 2) 1572 ( 2) 1573 ( 2)
                    1574 ( 2) 1575 ( 2)
  fQuadGrView         83*( 1)  127*( 1)  263*( 1)  107=( 2)  200 ( 2)  240=( 2)  243 ( 2)  244 ( 2)  413 ( 2)
                     459 ( 2)  513=( 2)  526 ( 2) 1274=( 2) 1274 ( 2) 1387 ( 2) 1674 ( 2) 1674 ( 2)
  fQuadInstalled     243*( 1) 1207=( 2) 1216 ( 2) 1256=( 2) 1264=( 2) 1293 ( 2) 1386=( 2) 1526=( 2) 1534=( 2)
  fQuadTxView         84*( 1)  108=( 2)  212 ( 2)  249=( 2)  414 ( 2)  462 ( 2) 1675 ( 2) 1675 ( 2)
  FrameOval          639 ( 2)
  FrameRect          602 ( 2)  641 ( 2) 1143 ( 2) 1466 ( 2)  100 ( 4)  102 ( 4)  103 ( 4)
  Free                89*( 1)  250*( 1)  135*( 2)  138 ( 2) 1211*( 2) 1219 ( 2)
  FreeData            90*( 1)  137 ( 2)  380*( 2)
  FreeObject         392 ( 2)  398 ( 2) 1218 ( 2) 1648 ( 2) 1654 ( 2)
```

```
-L-
  lastQuadMarker    346*( 2)  354=( 2)  358 ( 2)
  leading            35 ( 4)   36 ( 4)
  LEAVE             318 ( 2)  186 ( 4)
  left              147 ( 4)  209=( 4)  209 ( 4)
  LineTo            855 ( 2)  951 ( 2) 1355 ( 2) 1585 ( 2)
  ListIndexToQuad   108*( 1)  420*( 2)  435=( 2)  443 ( 2)  471 ( 2)
  localPoint        160*( 1)  799*( 2)
  LONGINT           112 ( 1)  279 ( 2)  305 ( 2)  345 ( 2) 1011 ( 2) 1064 ( 2)
  ltGray             94 ( 4)

-M-
  Max               975 ( 2)  976 ( 2)
  maxBottom         967*( 2)  976=( 2)  976 ( 2)  981=( 2)  985 ( 2)
  maxRight          967*( 2)  975=( 2)  975 ( 2)  981=( 2)  985 ( 2)
  maxStringWidth    230*( 2)  247 ( 2)
  MemTypes           17*( 1)   36*( 3)
  Min               973 ( 2)  974 ( 2)
  minExtent          78*( 3)   41*( 4)   51=( 4)   53 ( 4)
  minLeft           967*( 2)  973=( 2)  973 ( 2)  980=( 2)  985 ( 2)
  minTop            967*( 2)  974=( 2)  974 ( 2)  980=( 2)  985 ( 2)
  mouseDidMove      275*( 1)  278*( 1)  305*( 1)  346*( 1)  349*( 1) 1349*( 2) 1352 ( 2) 1362*( 2) 1459*( 2)
                   1463 ( 2) 1580*( 2) 1582 ( 2) 1592*( 2)
  MoveTo            854 ( 2)  950 ( 2) 1354 ( 2) 1584 ( 2)  147 ( 4)
  myFileType         33*( 1)   42 ( 2)  105 ( 2)

-N-
  NEW                48 ( 2)   50 ( 2)   52 ( 2)   54 ( 2)   56 ( 2)   65 ( 2)  238 ( 2)  242 ( 2)  246 ( 2)
                    261 ( 2)  267 ( 2)  647 ( 2)  781 ( 2)  994 ( 2) 1097 ( 2) 1122 ( 2) 1170 ( 2) 1194 ( 2)
  NewPaletteWindow  201 ( 2)
  newQuad           153*( 1)  306*( 2)  316=( 2)  321 ( 2)  322 ( 2)  656*( 2)  668 ( 2)  670 ( 2)  674 ( 2)
                    730*( 2)  752=( 2)  755 ( 2)  756 ( 2)
  NewRgn            636 ( 2)
  newSelection      133*( 1)  517*( 2)  520 ( 2)  520 ( 2)  524 ( 2)  533 ( 2)
  newSelectionInde  106*( 1)  468*( 2)  471 ( 2)   49*( 3)    9*( 4)
  NewSimpleWindow   214 ( 2)
  NewSketchCmd      189*( 1)  209*( 1)  217*( 1)  227*( 1)  235*( 1)  755 ( 2)  991*( 2)  996=( 2) 1094*( 2)
                   1099=( 2) 1118*( 2) 1124=( 2) 1167*( 2) 1172=( 2) 1191*( 2) 1196=( 2)
  newVertex         279*( 1)  287*( 1)  306*( 1) 1025*( 2) 1043 ( 2) 1044 ( 2) 1047 ( 2) 1047 ( 2) 1047 ( 2)
                   1047 ( 2) 1334*( 2) 1343 ( 2) 1397*( 2) 1400 ( 2) 1409 ( 2) 1410 ( 2) 1471*( 2) 1477 ( 2)
                   1479 ( 2) 1482 ( 2)
  newWindowSize     190*( 2)  206 ( 2)  207 ( 2)  208 ( 2)  209 ( 2)  217 ( 2)  218 ( 2)
  nextPoint         274*( 1)  277*( 1)  295*( 1)  304*( 1)  314*( 1)  345*( 1)  348*( 1) 1348*( 2) 1355 ( 2)
                   1355 ( 2) 1361*( 2) 1423*( 2) 1445 ( 2) 1446 ( 2) 1447 ( 2) 1452=( 2) 1458*( 2) 1465 ( 2)
                   1493*( 2) 1497 ( 2) 1498 ( 2) 1499 ( 2) 1503=( 2) 1579*( 2) 1585 ( 2) 1585 ( 2) 1591*( 2)
  nextQuad          382*( 2)  391=( 2)  394 ( 2)  396 ( 2)  397=( 2)  397 ( 2) 1640*( 2) 1647=( 2) 1650 ( 2)
                   1652 ( 2) 1653=( 2) 1653 ( 2)
  nQuads            281*( 2)  286=( 2)  289=( 2)  289 ( 2)  292 ( 2)
  Num2Integer      1043 ( 2) 1044 ( 2) 1430 ( 2)
  numQuadTypes       34*( 1)  128 ( 1)   10 ( 2)  504 ( 2)  520 ( 2)  560 ( 2)  561 ( 2)  600 ( 2)

-O-
  OBJECT             72 ( 1)   81 ( 1)  125 ( 1)  142 ( 1)  171 ( 1)  205 ( 1)  213 ( 1)  221 ( 1)  231 ( 1)
                    241 ( 1)  261 ( 1)  285 ( 1)  292 ( 1)  302 ( 1)  311 ( 1)  319 ( 1)  331 ( 1)  354 ( 1)
                     47 ( 3)   54 ( 3)
  offset            657*( 2)  664=( 2)  665 ( 2)  665 ( 2)  670=( 2)  671 ( 2)  671 ( 2)
  OffsetRect        697 ( 2)  699 ( 2)  875 ( 2)
  OffsetRgn         665 ( 2)  671 ( 2)
  OpenRgn           637 ( 2)
  OSErr             307 ( 2)  344 ( 2) 1010 ( 2) 1066 ( 2)
  OSIntf             19*( 1)   38*( 3)
  OSType             75 ( 1)   33 ( 2)
  OVERRIDE           77*( 1)   89*( 1)   90*( 1)   92*( 1)  106*( 1)  109*( 1)  112*( 1)  113*( 1)  114*( 1)
                    117*( 1)  118*( 1)  119*( 1)  120*( 1)  134*( 1)  136*( 1)  137*( 1)  155*( 1)  158*( 1)
                    159*( 1)  160*( 1)  161*( 1)  182*( 1)  207*( 1)  208*( 1)  209*( 1)  215*( 1)  216*( 1)
                    217*( 1)  223*( 1)  224*( 1)  225*( 1)  226*( 1)  227*( 1)  233*( 1)  234*( 1)  235*( 1)
                    250*( 1)  255*( 1)  256*( 1)  269*( 1)  272*( 1)  275*( 1)  278*( 1)  287*( 1)  295*( 1)
                    305*( 1)  306*( 1)  314*( 1)  324*( 1)  325*( 1)  326*( 1)  340*( 1)  341*( 1)  342*( 1)
                    346*( 1)  349*( 1)  361*( 1)  362*( 1)  364*( 1)  365*( 1)   62*( 2)  114*( 2)  135*( 2)
                    182*( 2)  229*( 2)  255*( 2)  279*( 2)  303*( 2)  332*( 2)  343*( 2)  380*( 2)  440*( 2)
                    468*( 2)  539*( 2)  550*( 2)  567*( 2)  680*( 2)  707*( 2)  727*( 2)  799*( 2)  827*( 2)
                    915*( 2) 1081*( 2) 1087*( 2) 1094*( 2) 1105*( 2) 1111*( 2) 1118*( 2) 1130*( 2) 1136*( 2)
                   1150*( 2) 1160*( 2) 1167*( 2) 1178*( 2) 1184*( 2) 1191*( 2) 1211*( 2) 1252*( 2) 1260*( 2)
                   1282*( 2) 1302*( 2) 1349*( 2) 1362*( 2) 1423*( 2) 1459*( 2) 1471*( 2) 1493*( 2) 1516*( 2)
```

```
 SetSelection      106*( 1)  468*( 2)   49*( 3)    9*( 4)  124 ( 4)  125 ( 4)
 SetUpBox           86*( 3)   90 ( 4)  143 ( 4)  183 ( 4)  203*( 4)  214=( 4)
 SetVertices       279*( 1)  287*( 1)  306*( 1) 1334*( 2) 1381 ( 2) 1397*( 2) 1400 ( 2) 1471*( 2)
 shrinkSize        569*( 2)  613 ( 2)  613 ( 2)
 sin                58 ( 2) 1037 ( 2)
 sine             1026*( 2) 1037=( 2) 1043 ( 2) 1044 ( 2)
 size             1364*( 2)
 SizeDeterminer     65 ( 3)   23 ( 4)
 sizeFixed         511 ( 2)  629 ( 2)  629 ( 2)   26 ( 4)   52 ( 4)
 SIZEOF            292 ( 2)  311 ( 2)  355 ( 2) 1014 ( 2) 1070 ( 2) 1074 ( 2)
 sizeVariable      248 ( 2)  511 ( 2)
 sketcher          800*( 2)  808=( 2)  809 ( 2)  810 ( 2)  843*( 2)  847=( 2)  848 ( 2)  849 ( 2)  851 ( 2)
                   855 ( 2)
 slope            1594*( 2) 1605=( 2) 1606 ( 2)
 SQR              1430 ( 2) 1430 ( 2)
 SQRT             1430 ( 2)
 squareSketcher   1192*( 2) 1194 ( 2) 1195 ( 2) 1196 ( 2)
 srcOr             614 ( 2)
 Str255            109 ( 1)  186 ( 1)  207 ( 1)  215 ( 1)  223 ( 1)  233 ( 1)  440 ( 2)  929 ( 2) 1081 ( 2)
                  1105 ( 2) 1130 ( 2) 1178 ( 2)   50 ( 3)   83 ( 3)   14 ( 4)  133 ( 4)  159 ( 4)
 StuffHex          594 ( 2)  595 ( 2)  596 ( 2)  597 ( 2)  598 ( 2)
 symBitMap         573*( 2)  579 ( 2)  614 ( 2)  614 ( 2)
 SystemFont        196 ( 4)

-T-
 TAddQuadCmd       241*( 1)  249*( 1)  250*( 1)  252*( 1)  253*( 1)  255*( 1)  256*( 1)  261*( 1)  319*( 1)
                  1202*( 2) 1211*( 2) 1223*( 2) 1233*( 2) 1252*( 2) 1260*( 2)
 TApplication       72*( 1)
 TClearAllCmd      354*( 1)  359*( 1)  361*( 1)  362*( 1)  363*( 1)  364*( 1)  365*( 1)  257 ( 2) 1630*( 2)
                  1638*( 2) 1660*( 2) 1670*( 2) 1679*( 2) 1687*( 2)
 TClearQuadCmd     319*( 1)  322*( 1)  324*( 1)  325*( 1)  326*( 1)  256 ( 2) 1509*( 2) 1516*( 2) 1523*( 2)
                  1530*( 2)
 TCommand          119 ( 1)  136 ( 1)  155 ( 1)  241*( 1)  278 ( 1)  331*( 1)  349 ( 1)  354*( 1)  255 ( 2)
                   550 ( 2)  727 ( 2) 1362 ( 2) 1592 ( 2)   70 ( 3)  111 ( 4)
 TDocument          77 ( 1)  131 ( 1)   62 ( 2)  497 ( 2)   47*( 3)
 temp             1428*( 2) 1430=( 2) 1431 ( 2) 1433 ( 2)
 tempPoint        1495*( 2) 1497=( 2) 1501 ( 2) 1501 ( 2) 1502 ( 2) 1502 ( 2) 1503 ( 2) 1593*( 2) 1603 ( 2)
                  1604 ( 2) 1605 ( 2) 1605 ( 2) 1613 ( 2)
 tempPt           1028*( 2) 1041 ( 2) 1043 ( 2) 1043 ( 2) 1044 ( 2) 1044 ( 2) 1424*( 2) 1446 ( 2) 1447 ( 2)
                  1448 ( 2) 1448 ( 2) 1449 ( 2) 1449 ( 2) 1450 ( 2) 1450 ( 2) 1451 ( 2) 1451 ( 2) 1452 ( 2)
 tempRect         1335*( 2)
 tempRegion        625*( 2)  636=( 2)  642 ( 2)  643 ( 2)
 testPoint          71*( 3)  178*( 4)  183 ( 4)
 testQuad          156*( 2)  167=( 2)  169 ( 2)  171 ( 2)  172=( 2)  172 ( 2)  175 ( 2)
 TextFace          198 ( 4)
 TextFont          196 ( 4)
 TextSize          197 ( 4)
 TFiledQuad         66*( 1)  292 ( 2) 1009 ( 2) 1014 ( 2) 1063 ( 2) 1074 ( 2)
 thePort           614 ( 2)
 theQuad           441*( 2)  443=( 2)  444 ( 2)  446 ( 2)
 theRotationState   67*( 1) 1017 ( 2) 1073=( 2)
 theta             195*( 1) 1023*( 2) 1036 ( 2)
 theVertices        68*( 1) 1016 ( 2) 1072=( 2)
 thisPoint         937*( 2)  939 ( 2)  940 ( 2)  941 ( 2)
 thisQuad          734*( 2)  736 ( 2)  737 ( 2)
 thisRect          968*( 2)  985 ( 2)  986 ( 2) 1151*( 2) 1154 ( 2) 1155=( 2) 1156 ( 2)
 TListDocument      81*( 1)   47*( 3)   49*( 3)   50*( 3)   64 ( 3)    9*( 4)   14*( 4)   22 ( 4)   46 ( 4)
                   124 ( 4)  125 ( 4)  139 ( 4)  152 ( 4)
 TListView          84 ( 1)  187 ( 2)  233 ( 2)   54*( 3)   64*( 3)   68*( 3)   69*( 3)   71*( 3)   78*( 3)
                    81*( 3)   82*( 3)   83*( 3)   85*( 3)   86*( 3)   88*( 3)   22*( 4)   41*( 4)   57*( 4)
                    84*( 4)  110*( 4)  131*( 4)  159*( 4)  169*( 4)  178*( 4)  193*( 4)  203*( 4)
 TObject           171*( 1)
 toHL              134*( 1)  158*( 1)  539*( 2)  541 ( 2)  543 ( 2)  680*( 2)  693 ( 2)   81*( 3)   84*( 4)
                    99 ( 4)
 ToolIntf           20*( 1)   39*( 3)
 top               499*( 2)  503=( 2)  506 ( 2)  506 ( 2)  508=( 2)  508 ( 2)  510 ( 2)  147 ( 4)  210=( 4)
                   212 ( 4)
 TPalette          125*( 1)  131*( 1)  133*( 1)  134*( 1)  135*( 1)  137*( 1)  144 ( 1)  234 ( 2)  497*( 2)
                   517*( 2)  539*( 2)  549*( 2)  567*( 2)
 TParallelogram    205*( 1)  207*( 1)  208*( 1)  209*( 1)  213*( 1)  221*( 1)   35 ( 2) 1081*( 2) 1087*( 2)
                  1094*( 2)
 TQuad              82 ( 1)   85 ( 1)   97 ( 1)   98 ( 1)  101 ( 1)  102 ( 1)  103 ( 1)  107 ( 1)  108 ( 1)
                   143 ( 1)  153 ( 1)  162 ( 1)  171*( 1)  174 ( 1)  179*( 1)  182*( 1)  186*( 1)  187*( 1)
                   188*( 1)  189*( 1)  192*( 1)  195*( 1)  196*( 1)  199*( 1)  200*( 1)  201*( 1)  205*( 1)
```

LISTING F

QuadWorld in Smalltalk

Class Name — **Quad**
Superclass Name — **Object**
Instance Variable Names — **vertices**
Class Variable Names — *(none)*
Pool Dictionaries — *(none)*
Class comment:

'The Quad class represents the most general case of a quadrilateral. The instance methods of this class display the quadriateral and allow for inquiries of its internal state. The class methods allow for the interactive creation of a new instance of a quad. Note that some of the class methods ("correctIt:withRespectTo:and:" and "feedbackFrom:" in particular, are present to provide an overall simple structure to the class Quad together with its subclasses of Paralelogram, Rhombus, Rectangle, and Square.

VARIABLES: Instances of class Quad have only one instance variable: vertices. This is an Array of the four vertices - each one of which is an instance of class Point. There are no class variables.'

Instance Messages and Methods

Quad methodsFor: 'inquiries'

```
asText
      "Return my textual description for the Tabular view"
      ↑ 'a Quadrilateral'

center
      "Return my center."
      ↑ (self vertices    inject: 0@0
                          into: [:centerPoint :nextVertex | centerPoint + nextVertex])//4.

enclosingRectangle
       "Return a rectangle enclosing me."

       | partialRect1 partialRect2 |
       partialRect1 ← Rectangle  origin: ( (self vertices at: 1) min: (self vertices at: 3))
                                 corner: ( (self vertices at: 1) max: (self vertices at: 3)).
       partialRect2 ← Rectangle  origin: ( (self vertices at: 2) min: (self vertices at: 4))
                                 corner: ( (self vertices at: 2) max: (self vertices at: 4)).
       ↑ partialRect1 merge: partialRect2
```

```
vertices
        "Return an Array containing my four vertices."
        ↑ vertices

Quad methodsFor: 'drawing'

draw
        "Draw myself on the screen."

        | dot aPen |
        dot ← (Form extent: (4@3)) black.
        aPen ← Pen new defaultNib: 2.
        vertices do: [:pt | dot displayAt: pt-2].          "Plot my vertices."

        aPen place: vertices last.                         "Draw my edges"
        vertices do: [:pt | aPen goto: pt].

highlight
        "Highlight myself by putting a gray square over my center.
         Unhighlight by removing the gray square."

        | aForm |
        aForm ← Form extent: (10@10).
        aForm gray.
        aForm displayOn: Display at:((self center) - (5@5)) rule: (Form reverse).  "XOR the bits into place"


Quad methodsFor: 'manipulation'

rotateBy: anAngle
        "Rotate myself counterclockwise about my center by anAngle radians"
        | centerPoint cosine sine tempPoint |
        centerPoint ← self center.
        cosine ← anAngle cos.
        sine ← anAngle sin.
        self vertices:
              (vertices
                  collect: [ :vertex | tempPoint ← vertex - centerPoint.
                              ( ((centerPoint x) + ((tempPoint x)*cosine) - ((tempPoint y)*sine) )
                              @ ( (centerPoint y) + ((tempPoint y)*cosine) + ((tempPoint x)*sine) ))]).


Quad methodsFor: 'private'

vertices: anArrayOfVertices
        "Set the vertex values for a new quadrilateral"

        vertices ← anArrayOfVertices.
```

<u>Class Messages and Methods</u>

<u>Class instance variable names</u> *(none)*

```
Quad class methodsFor: 'instance creation'

correctIt: aPoint withRespectTo: fixedPoint1 and: fixedPoint2
        "Adjust the value of aPoint to reflect the geometric constraints of the quadrilateral
         being entered.  Note that for quadrilaterals and parallelograms, no adjusment is necessary."

        ↑ aPoint
```

```
(tempPoint ~= lastVertex)
            ifTrue: [↑ tempPoint ]
            ifFalse: [↑ self  feedbackFrom: lastVertex and: otherVertex]     "No degenerate quads"
```

feedbackFrom: lastVertex and: otherVertex

```
    "Provide the user with feedback while the next vertex is being entered.  Do this
     by drawing a line from the last vertex to the (possibly adjusted) current cursor point.
     Return the cursor point when the mouse button is pressed."

    | tempPoint aPen |
    aPen ← Pen new defaultNib: 1; combinationRule: (Form reverse).  "Thin, XOR line"
    tempPoint ← self correctIt: (lastVertex copy) withRespectTo: lastVertex and: otherVertex.
    [Sensor noButtonPressed]
         whileTrue: [ aPen drawFrom: lastVertex to: tempPoint.
                     tempPoint ← self correctIt: (Sensor cursorPoint)
                                     withRespectTo: lastVertex and: otherVertex.
                     aPen drawFrom: lastVertex to: tempPoint.].
```

fromUser

```
    "Answer an instance of me that is determined by having the user designate
    the four vertices of a quadrilateral."

    | p1 p2 p3 p4 newSelf |
    Cursor square showWhile: [ p1 ← Sensor waitClickButton.
                              p2 ← self feedbackFrom: p1 and: nil.
                              p3 ← self feedbackFrom: p2 and: nil.
                              p4 ← self feedbackFrom: p3 and: nil].
    ↑ super new vertices: (Array with: p1 with: p2 with: p3 with: p4)
```

Quad class methodsFor: 'examples'

exampleWorkspace

```
    "Execute the following expression in order to examine the behavior of the QuadWorld"

    "QuadGraphicalView open: QuadList initializeQuadList."
```

Class Name	**Parallelogram**
Superclass Name	**Quad**
Instance Variable Names	*(none)*
Class Variable Names	*(none)*
Pool Dictionaries	*(none)*

Class comment:

'The class Parallelogram represents those quadrilaterals that are parallelograms. Note that most of the behaviour of this class is inherited from its superclass, Quad.

VARIABLES: This class has no new instance or class variables.'

Instance Messages and Methods

Parallelogram methodsFor: 'inquiries'

asText

```
    "Return my textual description for the Tabular view"

     ↑ 'a Parallelogram'
```

Class Messages and Methods

Class instance variable names *(none)*

Parallelogram class methodsFor: 'instance creation'

fromUser

```
        "Answer an instance of me that is determined by having the user designate
        the three vertices necessary to define a parallelogram or a rhombus."

        | p1 p2 p3 |
        Cursor square showWhile: [ p1 ← Sensor waitClickButton.
                                   p2 ← self feedbackFrom: p1 and: nil.
                                   p3 ← self feedbackFrom: p2 and: p1].

        ↑ super new vertices: (Array with: p1
                                      with: p2
                                      with: p3
                                      with: ( (p3 x + p1 x - p2 x) @ (p3 y + p1 y - p2 y) ))
```

Class Name	**Rhombus**
Superclass Name	**Parallelogram**
Instance Variable Names	*(none)*
Class Variable Names	*(none)*
Pool Dictionaries	*(none)*

Class comment:

'The class Rhombus represents those quadrilaterals that are rhombi. Note that it inherites most of it behavior from its two superclasses, Quad and Parallelogram.

VARIABLES: This class has no new instance or class variables.'

Instance Messages and Methods

Rhombus methodsFor: 'inquiries'

asText

```
        "Return my textual description for the Tabular view"

        ↑ 'a Rhombus'
```

Class Messages and Methods

Class instance variable names *(none)*

Rhombus class methodsFor: 'instance creation'

correctIt: aPoint withRespectTo: fixedPoint1 and: fixedPoint2

```
        "Adjust the value of aPoint to reflect the geometric constraints of the quadrilateral
         being entered.  Note that for a rhombus this only involves making sure that the third vertex
         is the same distance from the second vertex as the second vertex is from the first.  The
        parallelism is 'inherited' from parallelograms."
         "To perform this compuation, start at the last vertex and add a normalized direction vector
        of the direction from the last vertex to aPoint multiplied by the distance from the first
        vertex to the second vertex."

        ((fixedPoint2 == nil) or: [aPoint = fixedPoint1])
            ifTrue: [↑ aPoint]
            ifFalse: [↑ fixedPoint1 +
              (( (aPoint - fixedPoint1) * (fixedPoint2 dist: fixedPoint1) ) // (aPoint dist: fixedPoint1) )
```

Class Name — **QRectangle**
Superclass Name — **Parallelogram**
Instance Variable Names — *(none)*
Class Variable Names — *(none)*
Pool Dictionaries — *(none)*
Class comment:

'The class QRectangle represents those quadrilaterals that are rectangles. Do NOT confuse this with Rectangle class which is a part of Smalltalk-80 - in fact, the name of this class must be "QRectangle" that the system will be able to make this differentiation. Note that QRectangle inherites most of behavior from its superclasses, Quad, and Parallelogram.

VARIABLES: This class has no new instance or class variables.'

Instance Messages and Methods

QRectangle methodsFor: 'inquiries'

```
asText
      "Return my textual description for the Tabular view"

      ↑ 'a Rectangle'
```

Class Messages and Methods

Class instance variable names *(none)*

QRectangle class methodsFor: 'instance creation'

```
feedbackFrom: firstVertex and: otherVertex
      "Provide the user with feedback while he is entering the next vertex
       by drawing a rectangle (or a corrected square) from the first vertex to
       the current cursor point. Note that for rectangles and squares,
       otherVertex is nil. Return the cursor point when the mouse button is pushed."

      | tempPoint aPen |
      aPen ← Pen new defaultNib: 1; combinationRule: (Form reverse). "Thin, XOR line"
      tempPoint ← self correctIt: (firstVertex copy) withRespectTo: firstVertex and: nil.
      [Sensor noButtonPressed] whileTrue:
                 [aPen drawFrom: firstVertex to: ((tempPoint x) @ (firstVertex y)).
                  aPen drawFrom: firstVertex to: ((firstVertex x) @ (tempPoint y)).
                  aPen drawFrom: ((tempPoint x) @ (firstVertex y)) to: tempPoint.
                  aPen drawFrom: ((firstVertex x) @ (tempPoint y)) to: tempPoint.

                  tempPoint ← self correctIt: (Sensor cursorPoint) withRespectTo: firstVertex and: nil.

                  aPen drawFrom: firstVertex to: ((tempPoint x) @ (firstVertex y)).
                  aPen drawFrom: firstVertex to: ((firstVertex x) @ (tempPoint y)).
                  aPen drawFrom: ((tempPoint x) @ (firstVertex y)) to: tempPoint.
                  aPen drawFrom: ((firstVertex x) @ (tempPoint y)) to: tempPoint.].
      ↑ tempPoint

fromUser
      "Answer an instance of me that is determined by having the user designate
      the four vertices of a quadrilateral."

      | p1 p3 |
      Cursor square showWhile:
                 [p1 ← Sensor waitClickButton.
                  p3 ← self feedbackFrom: p1 and: nil.
```

```
"Assume that p1 is less than p3 (This is following the standard
 Smalltalk-80 convention for entering rectangles.)"
(p1 < p3)
      ifFalse: [self halt: 'You entered a recangle or a square the wrong way.']].

↑ super new vertices: (Array with: p1 with: ((p3 x)@(p1 y)) with: p3 with: ((p1 x)@(p3 y)))
```

Class Name **Square**
Superclass Name **QRectangle**
Instance Variable Names *(none)*
Class Variable Names *(none)*
Pool Dictionaries *(none)*
Class comment:
'The class Square represents those quadrilaterals that are Squares. Note that it inherites most of its behavior from its superclasses, Quad, Parallelogram, and QRectangle.

Class Name **QuadList**
Superclass Name **Object**
Instance Variable Names quadList
selectedQuad
Class Variable Names *(none)*
Pool Dictionaries *(none)*
Class comment:
'This class is the model for the Smalltalk-80 implementation of Quad World. Since Quad World has a standard ListView, instances of QuadList respond to the message list and listIndex, as is required of all models which are viewed thru a ListView. These messages are also used in the graphical view, QuadGraphicalView. Note that QuadList controlls the extent to which each of the views is updated through the use of the parameter to the changed: message, again in accordance with what is expected by the ListView.

VARIABLES: No class variables. Two instance variables, the OrderedCollection of the quadrilaterals in the model (quadList) and the integer index into this ordered collection corresponding to the currently selected quadrilateral. Note that this model, the QuadGraphicalView, and the ListView all record the currently selected quad. This seeming redundancy is needed to correctly handle the various ways in which a selection may be changed.'

Instance Messages and Methods

QuadList methodsFor: 'additions-deletions'

add: aQuad

```
"Add a quadrilateral to the quadList ordered Collection and then re-draw each view."

quadList add: aQuad.
self changed: #list.
```

VARIABLES: This class has no new instance or class variables.'

Instance Messages and Methods

Square methodsFor: 'inquiries'

asText

```
"Return my textual representation for the Tabular view"

↑ 'a Square'
```

Class Messages and Methods

Class instance variable names (none)

Square class methodsFor: 'instance creation'

```
correctIt: aPoint withRespectTo: fixedPoint1 and: fixedPoint2
	"Adjust the value of aPoint to reflect the geometric constraints of the quadrilateral
	 being entered. Note that for a square this only involves making sure that the sides are
	 all of equal length. The right angles are 'inherited' from rectangles. Also note that for
	 squares, fixedPoint2 is always nil."

	| width height |
	width ← (aPoint x) - (fixedPoint1 x).
	height ← (aPoint y) - (fixedPoint1 y).
	(width > height)
			ifTrue: [↑ aPoint y: (aPoint y) + (width - height)]
			ifFalse: [↑ aPoint x: (aPoint x) + (height - width)].

remove: aQuad
	"Remove a quadrilateral to the quadList ordered Collection and then re-draw the views"

	self deselectCurrentlySelectedQuad.
	quadList remove: aQuad ifAbsent: [self error: 'No quadrilateral found.'].
	self changed: #list.

rotateBy: anAngle
	"Rotate the currently selected quadrilateral by anAngle and then re-draw just the graphical view"
	(quadList at: selectedQuad) highlight; rotateBy: anAngle.
	self changed: #draw.
```

QuadList methodsFor: 'reporting'

```
list
	"Return a textual version of my quadList for the ListView. Note that every model which uses
	 the standard ListView and standard ListController must implement this message."
	| aTextualQuadList |

	aTextualQuadList ← OrderedCollection new: (quadList size).
	quadList do: [:quad | aTextualQuadList addLast: (quad asText)].
	↑ aTextualQuadList

listIndex
	"Return index to my currently selected quad, or 0 if none is selected Note that every model
	 which uses the standard ListView and standard ListController must implement this message."

	↑ selectedQuad

listOfQuads
	"Return my current quadList"

	↑ quadList
```

QuadList methodsFor: 'selecting'

```
deselectCurrentlySelectedQuad
	"Un-highlight the currently selected quad, if any, and set the current selection to 0"

	 self toggleListIndex: 0.
```

```
toggleListIndex:  anInteger
       "Highlight and set the value of the currently selected quad"

       (selectedQuad ~= anInteger)
                   ifTrue: [ selectedQuad ← anInteger.
                             self changed: #listIndex.].  "Tell each view to update the selection"
```

QuadList methodsFor: 'private'

```
initialQuadList
       "Initialize the instance variables quadList and selectedQuad"

       quadList ← OrderedCollection new.
       selectedQuad ← 0.
```

Class Messages and Methods

Class instance variable names (*none*)

QuadList class methodsFor: 'class initialization'

```
initializeQuadList
       "Create the quadList and initialize its instance variables"

       ↑ super new initialQuadList
```

Class Name	**QuadGraphicalView**
Superclass Name	**View**
Instance Variable Names	selection
Class Variable Names	(*none*)
Pool Dictionaries	(*none*)

Class comment:

'The class QuadGraphicalView class displays the QuadWorld window. It completely implements the graphical view portion of the window and creates an instance of ListView to provide the list view portion of the window. Note that the model (an instance of QuadList), the QuadGraphicalView, and the ListView all record the currently selected quad. This seeming redundancy is needed to correctly handle the various ways in which a selection may be changed.

VARIABLES: One instance variables, selection, which holds an integer corresponding to the index of the currently selected quad in the model of this application.'

Instance Messages and Methods

QuadGraphicalView methodsFor: 'initialize-release'

```
initialize
       super initialize.
       selection ← 0.
```

QuadGraphicalView methodsFor: 'displaying'

```
displaySelection
       "Highlight the current selection in this view"
```

```
        selection ~= 0
               ifTrue: [((model listOfQuads) at: selection) highlight].

displayView
        "Redraw the entire contents of the graphical view and update selection."

        self clearInside.
        (model listOfQuads) do: [:eachQuad | eachQuad draw].
        selection ← model listIndex.
        self displaySelection.

moveSelection:  anInteger
        "The selection has changed.  Unhighlight the previous selection and highlight
         the new one.  Note that anInteger is the index of the new selection in the model."

        (anInteger ~= selection and: [selection ~= 0])
               ifTrue: [((model listOfQuads) at: selection) highlight].     "Unhighlight the old selection
        selection ← anInteger.                          "Update the record of the current selection in this vie
        self displaySelection.

update:  aSymbol
        "Re-display the entire view if the model has changed significantly.
         If just the selection has changed, then move the indication of the current selection"

        ((aSymbol == #list) or: [aSymbol == #draw])
               ifTrue:
                      [self displayView.
                      ↑self].

        (aSymbol == #listIndex)
               ifTrue:
                      [self moveSelection: model listIndex.
                      ↑self]


QuadGraphicalView methodsFor: 'controller access'

defaultControllerClass
        "Establish the type of controller used by a QuadGraphicalView"

        ↑ QuadController
```

Class Messages and Methods

Class instance variable names   *(none)*

```
QuadGraphicalView class methodsFor: 'instance creation'

open:  aQuadList
       "Set up the threeviews in the QuadWorld window.
        The top view is a standard system view.  It provides the standard blue button activity
       and the window name.
       The instance of the standard system view holds the graphical view of the list of quads (the
       model for this application) and the tabular view of the same model."

       | topView aQuadGraphicalView aQuadTabularView |
       topView ← StandardSystemView new.
       topView model: aQuadList.
       topView borderWidth: 2.
```

```
topView insideColor: Form lightGray.
topView label: 'Quad World'.
topView minimumSize: (300@200).

QuadController initialize.
aQuadGraphicalView ← QuadGraphicalView new model: aQuadList.
aQuadGraphicalView window: (10@10 extent: 35@35).
aQuadGraphicalView insideColor: Form white.
aQuadGraphicalView borderWidth: 2.
aQuadGraphicalView controller: QuadController new.
topView addSubView: aQuadGraphicalView.

aQuadTabularView ← ListView new model: aQuadList.
aQuadTabularView window: (55@10 extent: 35@35).
aQuadTabularView insideColor: Form white.
aQuadTabularView borderWidth: 2.
aQuadTabularView controller: ListController new.
topView addSubView: aQuadTabularView.

topView controller open.
```

Class Name	**QuadController**
Superclass Name	**MouseMenuController**
Instance Variable Names	*(none)*
Class Variable Names	NoQuadYellowButtonMenu QuadYellowButtonMenu NoQuadYellowButtonMessages QuadYellowButtonMessages
Pool Dictionaries	*(none)*

Class comment:

'The class QuadController contains the user interface (menus and interaction methods) for the MacWorks Smalltalk-80 implementation of QuadWorld. See the "getStretch" method for a student project related to QuadWorld.

VARIABLES: No instance variables. Four class variables holding the text of the two pop-up menus and their associated messages.'

Instance Messages and Methods

QuadController methodsFor: 'initialize-release'

initialize

```
    super initialize.
    self initializeYellowButtonMenu
```

QuadController methodsFor: 'menu messages'

deleteQuad

```
    "Delete the currently selected quad from the model"

    model remove: (model listOfQuads at: (model listIndex)).
```

getAngle

```
    "get an angle from the user and rotate the currently selected quadrilateral by this angle"

    | quadList centerPoint endPoint arcPoint aPen anAngle |
    aPen ← Pen new defaultNib: 1; combinationRule: (Form reverse). "thin, XOR line"
```

```
        quadList ← model listOfQuads.
        centerPoint ← (quadList at: (model listIndex)) center.
        Cursor crossHair showWhile:
               [Sensor waitButton.
                endPoint ← Sensor cursorPoint.
                aPen drawFrom: centerPoint to: endPoint.
                [Sensor anyButtonPressed] whileTrue:
                      [aPen drawFrom: centerPoint to: endPoint.      "Erase old line"
                       endPoint ← Sensor cursorPoint.
                       aPen drawFrom: centerPoint to: endPoint].
                Sensor waitButton.
                Sensor cursorPoint: endPoint + 2.       "Move cursor to end of first line (stable line)"
                arcPoint ← endPoint + 2.
                aPen drawFrom: centerPoint to: arcPoint.          "Draw first image of angle line"
                [Sensor anyButtonPressed] whileTrue:
                      [aPen drawFrom: centerPoint to: arcPoint.      "Erase old line"
                       arcPoint ← Sensor cursorPoint.
                       aPen drawFrom: centerPoint to: arcPoint]].

        "Compute the angle by normalizing the dot product to get the cosine, and then mapping back"
        anAngle ← (arcPoint - centerPoint) dotProduct: (endPoint - centerPoint).
        anAngle ← anAngle / ((arcPoint dist: centerPoint) * (endPoint dist: centerPoint)).
        anAngle ← anAngle arcCos.

        self model rotateBy: anAngle.

getStretch
        "Obtain from the user the manner in which to modify the currently selected quad"

        self halt: 'Stretching currently not implemented.  Sorry'.

parallelogram
        "Add a parallelogram to the model"

        | aParallelogram |
        aParallelogram ← Parallelogram fromUser.
        model add: aParallelogram.

quadrilateral
        "Add a quadrilateral to the model"

        | aQuad |
        aQuad ← Quad fromUser.
        model add: aQuad.

rectangle
        "Add a rectangle to the model"

        | aRectangle |
        aRectangle ← QRectangle fromUser.
        model add: aRectangle.

rhombus
        "Add a rhombus to the model"

        | aRhombus |
        aRhombus ← Rhombus fromUser.
        model add: aRhombus.
```

```
square
	"Add a square to the model"

	| aSquare |
	aSquare ← Square fromUser.
	model add: aSquare.


QuadController methodsFor: 'control defaults'

isControlActive
	"Determine whether QuadController or the 'higher' standard system controller should be in control'

	↑ super isControlActive & Sensor blueButtonPressed not

redButtonActivity
	"Detect selections of quads in the graphical view"

	| testPosition  listOfQuads  currentlySelectedQuadIndex foundIt |
	testPosition ← Sensor cursorPoint.
	listOfQuads ← model listOfQuads.
	currentlySelectedQuadIndex ← model listIndex.

	"If the currently selected quad is hit by the mouse, de-select it."
	(currentlySelectedQuadIndex ~= 0)
	    ifTrue:
	        [((listOfQuads at: currentlySelectedQuadIndex)
	                enclosingRectangle containsPoint: testPosition) ifTrue:
	                        [model deselectCurrentlySelectedQuad]].

	"Run thru the list of quads looking for the last one that is hit by the mouse."

	foundIt ← 0.
	listOfQuads do: [ :quad | (quad enclosingRectangle containsPoint: testPosition)
	                        ifTrue:  [foundIt ← listOfQuads indexOf: quad]].

	"Select the found quad, or if none, deselect the currently selected quad."
	(foundIt ~= 0)
	    ifTrue:  [model toggleListIndex: foundIt]
	    ifFalse: [model deselectCurrentlySelectedQuad].

yellowButtonActivity
	"Determine which yellow button menu to put up, then execute the standard behavior"

	(self model listIndex = 0)
	    ifTrue: [self  yellowButtonMenu: NoQuadYellowButtonMenu
	                   yellowButtonMessages: NoQuadYellowButtonMessages]
	    ifFalse: [self yellowButtonMenu: QuadYellowButtonMenu
	                   yellowButtonMessages: QuadYellowButtonMessages].
	super yellowButtonActivity.


QuadController methodsFor: 'private'

initializeYellowButtonMenu
	self yellowButtonMenu: QuadYellowButtonMenu yellowButtonMessages: QuadYellowButtonMessages
```

Class Messages and Methods

Class instance variable names *(none)*

QuadController class methodsFor: 'class initialization'

```
initialize
	"Specify the two types of yellow button menu items and their corresponding actions"

   "Yellow button menu when no quad is selected"
	NoQuadYellowButtonMenu ← PopUpMenu labels:
						'quadrilateral
						parallelogram
						rhombus
						rectangle
						square'.
	NoQuadYellowButtonMessages ← #(quadrilateral parallelogram rhombus rectangle square).

   "Yellow button menu when a quad is selected"
	QuadYellowButtonMenu ← PopUpMenu labels:
						'rotate Quad
						stretch Quad
						delete Quad' lines: #(2).
	QuadYellowButtonMessages ← #(getAngle getStretch deleteQuad).

	QuadController initialize
```

LISTING G

QuadWorld in Clascal Using the Lisa Toolkit Classes

```
                { Lisa Clascal and Lisa Toolkit implementation of the QuadWorld application }
                        { Copyright 1985 by Productivity Products International, Inc. }

UNIT UQuadWorld;

{ *************************************************************************************************** }
{ *************************************************************************************************** }

                                                INTERFACE

{ *************************************************************************************************** }
{ *************************************************************************************************** }

    USES
        {$U UObject}            UObject,        { TObject and all collection classes }
                                QuickDraw,
        {$U UDraw}              UDraw,          { Toolkit 32-bit coordinate graphics library }
        {$U UABC}               UABC,           { Toolkit Application Base Classes, windows, views, etc. }
        {$U UPalette}           UPalette;       { A LisaDraw-like palette class.  Note: UPalette.OBJ must
                                                  be on the prefix volume for UQuadWorld to compile}

{$IFC fSymOK}   { If using the debugging version of the Toolkit libaries, }
{$D+}           { then leave procedure names in the object file for LisaBug to use }
{$ELSEC}        { otherwise don't. }
{$D-}
{$ENDC}
{$IFC fDbgOK}   { If using the debugging version of the Toolkit libaries, }
{$R+}           { then enable range checking in arrays, enumeration types, and lists }
{$ELSEC}        { otherwise don't }
{$R-}
{$ENDC}

{$E ERRORS.TEXT}
{$E+}                   {go into the editor automagically in the rare event that an error is found}


  CONST
      maxQuad      = 25;          { maximum number of quadrilaterals currently supported      }

    { Menu commands }

      uClearQuadCmd    = 1101;
      uClearAllCmd     = 1102;
      uRotateQuadCmd   = 1100;

```

```
      uAddQuadCmd      = 2001;  { Implied commands.  These commands are not initiated by   }
      uAddParagramCmd  = 2002;  { menu events but rather by mouse actions in the palette.  }
      uAddRhombusCmd   = 2003;  { Making them commands is in accordance with the Lisa User }
      uAddRectCmd      = 2004;  { Interface standards, since they modify the document.     }
      uAddSquareCmd    = 2005;

   { Selection kinds }
      quadKind      = 1;
      paragramKind  = 2;
      rhombusKind   = 3;
      rectangleKind = 4;
      squareKind    = 5;

   { Dimensions of a box in palette }
      palWidth  = 36;
      palHeight = 24;

   { Distance between edge of palette box and the prototype quads }
      hPalMargin = 6;
      vPalMargin = 4;

   { row numbers in action palette }
      symArrow          =   1;
      symQuad           =   2;
      symParallelogram  =   3;
      symRhombus        =   4;
      symRectangle      =   5;
      symSquare         =   6;

   { phrase constants }
      phMaxQuads = 1001;    { "You have entered the max number of quads." }


   TYPE

    QuadIndex = 0..maxQuad;


    TQuad = SUBCLASS OF TObject

      { instance variables }
         vertex:   ARRAY[1..4] OF LPoint;

      { Creation method }
         FUNCTION  TQuad.CREATE(object: TObject; itsHeap: THeap): TQuad;

      { Inquiry methods }
         FUNCTION  TQuad.AddCmdNumber: INTEGER;                  { Report the command number to add a quad }
         PROCEDURE TQuad.AsText(VAR text: S255);            { Report the textual representation of a quad }
         PROCEDURE TQuad.Center(VAR centerLPt: LPoint);                         { Report the center of a quad }
         FUNCTION  TQuad.CreateSelection
                        (aQuadGrView: TQuadGrView): TCreateQuadSelection;    { Return a quad sketcher }
         PROCEDURE TQuad.EnclosingLRect(VAR encloseLRect: LRect);     { Report the rect enclosing a quad }

      { Modifing methods }
         PROCEDURE TQuad.SetPoints(pt1, pt2, pt3, pt4: LPoint);                  { Set a quad's vertices }
         PROCEDURE TQuad.RotateBy(theta: REAL);                          { Rotate a quad by theta radians }

    END;  { TQuad }


    TParallelogram = SUBCLASS OF TQuad

      { methods }
         FUNCTION  TParallelogram.CREATE(object: TObject; itsHeap: THeap): TParallelogram;
         FUNCTION  TParallelogram.AddCmdNumber: INTEGER;  OVERRIDE;
         PROCEDURE TParallelogram.AsText(VAR text: S255); OVERRIDE;
         FUNCTION  TParallelogram.CreateSelection
                                   (aQuadGrView: TQuadGrView): TCreateQuadSelection;  OVERRIDE;

    END;  { TParallelogram }


    TRhombus = SUBCLASS OF TParallelogram

      { methods }
         FUNCTION  TRhombus.CREATE(object: TObject; itsHeap: THeap): TRhombus;
```

```
          FUNCTION  TRhombus.AddCmdNumber: INTEGER;  OVERRIDE;
          PROCEDURE TRhombus.AsText(VAR text: S255); OVERRIDE;
          FUNCTION  TRhombus.CreateSelection(aQuadGrView: TQuadGrView): TCreateQuadSelection;  OVERRIDE;

     END;  { TRhombus }


     TRectangle = SUBCLASS OF TParallelogram

       { methods }
          FUNCTION  TRectangle.AddCmdNumber: INTEGER;  OVERRIDE;
          FUNCTION  TRectangle.CREATE(object: TObject; itsHeap: THeap): TRectangle;
          PROCEDURE TRectangle.AsText(VAR text: S255); OVERRIDE;
          FUNCTION  TRectangle.CreateSelection(aQuadGrView: TQuadGrView): TCreateQuadSelection;  OVERRIDE;

     END;  { TRectangle }


     TSquare = SUBCLASS OF TRectangle

       { methods }
          FUNCTION  TSquare.AddCmdNumber: INTEGER;  OVERRIDE;
          FUNCTION  TSquare.CREATE(object: TObject; itsHeap: THeap): TSquare;
          PROCEDURE TSquare.AsText(VAR text: S255); OVERRIDE;
          FUNCTION  TSquare.CreateSelection(aQuadGrView: TQuadGrView): TCreateQuadSelection;  OVERRIDE;

     END;  { TSquare }

{ ****************************************************************************************************** }

 { Common code and data of each of the two types of quadviews - an abstract superclass }
     TQuadView = SUBCLASS OF TView

       { Instance variables }
          window:      TQuadWindow; { Gives us an easy way to access the quad list, since it is stored
                                      as a field in the QuadWindow. }

       { Creation method }
          FUNCTION  TQuadView.CREATE(object: TObject; heap: THeap; itsExtent: LRect;
                                     itsPanel: TPanel): TQuadView;

       { Selection methods }
          PROCEDURE TQuadView.MouseMove(mouseLPt: LPoint); OVERRIDE;
          PROCEDURE TQuadView.MousePress(mouseLPt: LPoint); OVERRIDE;
                                     { Overriding the standard MouseMove method will enable the user to
                                       change the selection while the mouse button is down }
          FUNCTION  TQuadView.NoSelection: TSelection; OVERRIDE;

          FUNCTION  TQuadView.NewSelection(quad: TQuad): TQuadSelection; ABSTRACT;
                { Create a new selection of the appropriate class; this is called by TQuadWindow.Select }

       { Utility method }
          PROCEDURE TQuadView.LPtToQuad(lPt: LPoint; VAR quad: TQuad); ABSTRACT;

       END;  { TQuadView }


 { This view controls the graphic interpretation of the quads }
     TQuadGrView = SUBCLASS OF TQuadView

       { Creation method }
          FUNCTION  TQuadGrView.CREATE(object: TObject; heap: THeap; itsPanel: TPanel): TQuadGrView;

       { Drawing methods }
          PROCEDURE TQuadGrView.Draw; OVERRIDE;

       { Selection method }
          FUNCTION  TQuadGrView.NewSelection(quad: TQuad): TQuadSelection; OVERRIDE;

       { Utility methods }
          PROCEDURE TQuadGrView.LPtToQuad(lPt: LPoint; VAR quad: TQuad); OVERRIDE;

       END;  { TQuadGrView }


 { This view controls the textual interpretation of the quads }
     TQuadTxView = SUBCLASS OF TQuadView
```

```

    { Instance variables }
       lineHeight: INTEGER;      { height of each line including leading }
         lineAscent: INTEGER;     { position of baseline relative to top of line }

    { Creation method }
       FUNCTION  TQuadTxView.CREATE(object: TObject; heap: THeap; itsPanel: TPanel): TQuadTxView;

    { Selection method }
       FUNCTION  TQuadTxView.NewSelection(quad: TQuad): TQuadSelection; OVERRIDE;


    { Drawing methods }
       PROCEDURE TQuadTxView.Draw; OVERRIDE;
       PROCEDURE TQuadTxView.DrawName(quad: TQuad);
       PROCEDURE TQuadTxView.SetUpBox(quad: TQuad; VAR bBox: LRect);
       PROCEDURE TQuadTxView.SetPen;          { setup the pen for drawing the text; this is a method so
                                                that the pen is setup the same way throughout the program
                                                and so it can be overridden }

    { Utilities }
       PROCEDURE TQuadTxView.LPtToQuad(lPt: LPoint; VAR quad: TQuad); OVERRIDE;

    END;  { TQuadTxView }

 { ************************************************************************************************** }

  { This is the common code and info for both the panel's selections - an abstract superclass. }
    TQuadSelection = SUBCLASS OF TSelection

    { Instance variables }
       quad: TQuad;            { the quad which is selected }

    { Creation method }
       FUNCTION  TQuadSelection.CREATE(object: TObject; heap: THeap; itsView: TQuadView;
                                             itsKind: INTEGER; itsQuad: TQuad): TQuadSelection;

    { Command execution methods }
       FUNCTION  TQuadSelection.CanDoCommand(cmdNumber: TCmdNumber;
                                       VAR checkIt: BOOLEAN): BOOLEAN; OVERRIDE;
                                   { set up (gray, check, etc.) the menu items that a selection
                                     responds to before the user has a chance to see them }

       FUNCTION  TQuadSelection.NewCommand(cmdNumber: TCmdNumber): TCommand; OVERRIDE;

    END;  { TQuadSelection }


  { This selection is the graphic representation of the selection }
    TQuadGrSelection = SUBCLASS OF TQuadSelection

    { Creation method }
       FUNCTION  TQuadGrSelection.CREATE(object: TObject; heap: THeap;
                         itsView: TQuadView; itsQuad: TQuad): TQuadGrSelection;

    { Highlighting method }
       PROCEDURE  TQuadGrSelection.Highlight(highTransit: THighTransit); OVERRIDE;

    END;  { TQuadGrSelection }


  { This selection is the text representation of the selection }
    TQuadTxSelection = SUBCLASS OF TQuadSelection

    { Creation method }
       FUNCTION  TQuadTxSelection.CREATE(object: TObject; heap: THeap;
                         itsView: TQuadView; itsQuad: TQuad): TQuadTxSelection;

    { Highlighting method }
       PROCEDURE  TQuadTxSelection.Highlight(highTransit: THighTransit); OVERRIDE;

    END;  { TQuadTxSelection }

 { ************************************************************************************************** }

  { This selection is used to provide visual feedback during the creation of new quads }
    TCreateQuadSelection = SUBCLASS OF TSelection

```

```
      { Instance variables }
          quad:             TQuad;                    { the quad being created }
          vertex:           ARRAY [1..4] OF LPoint;  { the vertices of the new quad }
          lastVertexSet:    INTEGER;                  { the last vertex that has been indicated by the user }

      { Creation method }
          FUNCTION  TCreateQuadSelection.CREATE(object: TObject; itsHeap: THeap; itsView: TQuadView;
                                                     itsAnchorLPt: LPoint): TCreateQuadSelection;

      { Mouse action feedback methods }
          PROCEDURE TCreateQuadSelection.MouseConstrain(mouseLPt: LPoint; VAR correctedLPt: LPoint);
          PROCEDURE TCreateQuadSelection.MouseMove(mouseLPt: LPoint); OVERRIDE;
          PROCEDURE TCreateQuadSelection.MousePress(mouseLPt: LPoint); OVERRIDE;
          PROCEDURE TCreateQuadSelection.MouseRelease; OVERRIDE;
          PROCEDURE TCreateQuadSelection.SetVertices(newVertex: LPoint);

      END;  { TCreateQuadSelection }


  { This selection is used to provide visual feedback during the creation of new parallelograms }
     TCreateParallelogramSelection = SUBCLASS OF TCreateQuadSelection

      { Creation method }
          FUNCTION  TCreateParallelogramSelection.CREATE(object: TObject; itsHeap: THeap;
                               itsView: TQuadView; itsAnchorLPt: LPoint): TCreateParallelogramSelection;

      { Mouse action feedback methods }
          PROCEDURE TCreateParallelogramSelection.SetVertices(newVertex: LPoint);  OVERRIDE;

      END;  { TCreateParallelogramSelection }


  { This selection is used to provide visual feedback during the creation of new rhombi }
     TCreateRhombusSelection = SUBCLASS OF TCreateParallelogramSelection

      { Creation method }
          FUNCTION  TCreateRhombusSelection.CREATE(object: TObject; itsHeap: THeap; itsView: TQuadView;
                                                 itsAnchorLPt: LPoint): TCreateRhombusSelection;

      { Mouse action feedback methods }
          PROCEDURE TCreateRhombusSelection.MouseConstrain(mouseLPt: LPoint;
                                                        VAR correctedLPt: LPoint);  OVERRIDE;

      END;  { TCreateRhombusSelection }


  { This selection is used to provide visual feedback during the creation of new quads }
     TCreateTangleSelection = SUBCLASS OF TCreateParallelogramSelection

      { Creation method }
          FUNCTION  TCreateTangleSelection.CREATE(object: TObject; itsHeap: THeap; itsView: TQuadView;
                                                itsAnchorLPt: LPoint): TCreateTangleSelection;

      { Mouse action feedback methods }
          PROCEDURE TCreateTangleSelection.MouseMove(mouseLPt: LPoint); OVERRIDE;
          PROCEDURE TCreateTangleSelection.SetVertices(newVertex: LPoint);  OVERRIDE;

      END;  { TCreateTangleSelection }


  { This selection is used to provide visual feedback during the creation of new quads }
     TCreateSquareSelection = SUBCLASS OF TCreateTangleSelection

      { Creation method }
          FUNCTION  TCreateSquareSelection.CREATE(object: TObject; itsHeap: THeap; itsView: TQuadView;
                                                itsAnchorLPt: LPoint): TCreateSquareSelection;

      { Mouse action feedback methods }
          PROCEDURE TCreateSquareSelection.MouseConstrain(mouseLPt: LPoint;
                                                        VAR correctedLPt: LPoint); OVERRIDE;

      END;  { TCreateSquareSelection }

 { ************************************************************************************************ }

  { The window for this Application }
     TQuadWindow = SUBCLASS OF TWindow
```

```
    { Instance variables }
        quadList:  TList;  { putting the quad list here means that it can easily be shared by both
                             panels and that we can use a filtering approach to undo }

        grPanel:   TPanel;  { the panel for the graphic view }
        txPanel:   TPanel;  { the panel for the textual view }
        actions:   TPanel;  { the palette panel }

    { Creation method }
        FUNCTION  TQuadWindow.CREATE(object: TObject; heap: THeap;
                                     itsWmgrId: TWindowId): TQuadWindow;

    { Command execution method }
        FUNCTION  TQuadWindow.CanDoCommand(cmdNumber: TCmdNumber;
                                           VAR checkIt: BOOLEAN): BOOLEAN; OVERRIDE;
                                       { set up (gray, check, etc.) the menu items that the window
                                         responds to before the user has a chance to see them }

        FUNCTION  TQuadWindow.NewCommand(cmdNumber: TCmdNumber): TCommand; OVERRIDE;


    { Actions palette method }
        PROCEDURE TQuadWindow.SetAction(action: INTEGER; doHilite: BOOLEAN);

    { Filtering }
        PROCEDURE TQuadWindow.EachActualPart(PROCEDURE DoToObject(filteredObj: TObject)); OVERRIDE;
        PROCEDURE TQuadWindow.EachVirtualPart(PROCEDURE DoToObject(filteredObj: TObject)); OVERRIDE;
        PROCEDURE TQuadWindow.FilterAndDo(actualObj: TObject;
                                          PROCEDURE DoToObject(filteredObj: TObject)); OVERRIDE;
        PROCEDURE TQuadWindow.SpecialFilter(actualObj: TObject;
                                            PROCEDURE DoToObject(filteredObj: TObject));

    { Other Methods }
        PROCEDURE  TQuadWindow.BlankStationery; OVERRIDE;              { set up a blank document }

        PROCEDURE TQuadWindow.InvalidateQuad(quad: TQuad);       { invalidates a quad in both panels }

        PROCEDURE TQuadWindow.Select(selectPanel: TPanel; quad: TQuad);
                                    { change selection in both panels, and update highlighting;
                                      quad = NIL means change to no selection }

    END;  { TQuadWindow }

{ ************************************************************************************************ }

{ Palette subclass  -- Note: UPalette.OBJ must be on the prefix volume for UQuadWorld to compile}
{       This illustrates the small amount of work needed to use a Toolkit building block        }

    TActView = SUBCLASS OF TPalView

      { Creation method }
        FUNCTION  TActView.CREATE(object: TObject; itsHeap: THeap; itsPanel: TPanel): TActView;

      { Display methods }
        PROCEDURE  TActView.DrawSymbol(atCol, atRow: INTEGER); OVERRIDE;
        PROCEDURE  TActView.ChangedSelection(atCol, atRow: INTEGER); OVERRIDE;

      { Mouse tracking method }
        PROCEDURE  TActView.MouseRelease; OVERRIDE;

    END;  { TActView }

{ ************************************************************************************************ }

            {Command objects that act on all the subclasses of quadrilaterals}


{ This command adds new quadrilaterals to the quadList and is undoable }

    TAddQuadCmd = SUBCLASS OF TCommand

      { Instance variables}
        newQuad:    TQuad;

      { Creation method}
        FUNCTION  TAddQuadCmd.CREATE(object: TObject; itsHeap: THeap; itsCmdNumber: TCmdNumber;
                                     itsQuad: TQuad): TAddQuadCmd;
```

```
        { Command Execution methods }
          PROCEDURE TAddQuadCmd.Commit; OVERRIDE;
          PROCEDURE TAddQuadCmd.Perform(cmdPhase: TCmdPhase); OVERRIDE;
          PROCEDURE TAddQuadCmd.EachVirtualPart(PROCEDURE DoToObject(filteredObj: TObject)); OVERRIDE;

      END;  { TAddQuadCmd }


  { This command rotates quadrilaterals and is undoable }

      TRotateQuadCmd = SUBCLASS OF TCommand

        { Instance variables }
          quad:      TQuad;                { the quad being rotated }
          angle:     REAL;                 { the angle to rotate by, in radians }

        { Creation method }
          FUNCTION  TRotateQuadCmd.CREATE(object: TObject; itsHeap: THeap; itsCmdNumber: TCmdNumber;
                                          itsQuad: TQuad; itsAngle: REAL): TRotateQuadCmd;

        { Command execution methods }
          PROCEDURE TRotateQuadCmd.Perform(cmdPhase: TCmdPhase); OVERRIDE;

      END;  { TRotateQuadCmd }


  { This command clears one quad and is undoable }

      TClearQuadCmd = SUBCLASS OF TCommand

        { Instance variables }
          quad:  TQuad;                { the quad being removed }

        { Creation method }
          FUNCTION  TClearQuadCmd.CREATE(object: TObject; itsHeap: THeap; itsCmdNumber: TCmdNumber;
                                         itsQuad: TQuad): TClearQuadCmd;

        { Command execution methods }
          PROCEDURE  TClearQuadCmd.Perform(cmdPhase: TCmdPhase); OVERRIDE;
          PROCEDURE  TClearQuadCmd.FilterAndDo(actualObj: TObject;
                                          PROCEDURE DoToObject(filteredObj: TObject)); OVERRIDE;
          PROCEDURE  TClearQuadCmd.EachVirtualPart(PROCEDURE DoToObject(filteredObj: TObject)); OVERRIDE;

      END;  { TClearQuadCmd }


  { This command clears all the quads and is undoable }

      TClearAllCmd = SUBCLASS OF TCommand

        { Instance variables}
          kind:  INTEGER;   { Stores the kind of the current selection so that UNDO works correctly }

        { Creation method}
          FUNCTION  TClearAllCmd.CREATE(object: TObject; itsHeap: THeap; itsCmdNumber: TCmdNumber)
                                        : TClearAllCmd;

        { Command Execution methods }
          PROCEDURE TClearAllCmd.Commit; OVERRIDE;
          PROCEDURE TClearAllCmd.Perform(cmdPhase: TCmdPhase); OVERRIDE;
          PROCEDURE TClearAllCmd.EachVirtualPart(PROCEDURE DoToObject(filteredObj: TObject)); OVERRIDE;

      END;  { TClearAllCmd }


  { ****************************************************************************************** }

   { The "process" controlling this application }
      TQuadProcess = SUBCLASS OF TProcess

        { Creation method }
          FUNCTION  TQuadProcess.CREATE: TQuadProcess;

          FUNCTION  TQuadProcess.NewDocManager(volumePrefix: TFilePath; openAsTool: BOOLEAN)
                                  : TDocManager; OVERRIDE;
          PROCEDURE TQuadProcess.Commence(phraseVersion: INTEGER); OVERRIDE;

      END;  { TQuadProcess }
```

```
  { Manager of the application's document}
     TQuadDocManager = SUBCLASS OF TDocManager

       { Creation method }
          FUNCTION  TQuadDocManager.CREATE(object: TObject; heap: THeap;
                                         itsPathPrefix: TFilePath): TQuadDocManager;
          FUNCTION  TQuadDocManager.NewWindow(heap: THeap; WmgrId: TWindowId): TWindow; OVERRIDE;

       END;  { TQuadDocManager }

  { ************************************************************************************** }
  { ************************************************************************************** }

                                      IMPLEMENTATION

  { ************************************************************************************** }
  { ************************************************************************************** }


  {$I UQuadWorld2.TEXT }
  { Private data }
  CONST

     txMargin    = 4;          { horizontal space between text view and edge of text }

  VAR
     { The data and bitmaps for the images for the action palette.  These are initialized
       in TQuadProcess.Commence. Note that for the selection arrow, we just use the data for
       the arrow cursor which is supplied with QuickDraw. }

     idealQuad, idealParallelogram, idealRhombus, idealRectangle, idealSquare: ARRAY [0..15] of INTEGER;
     arwBitMap, quadBitMap, parallelogramBitMap, rhombusBitMap, rectBitMap, squareBitMap: BitMap;


  { ************************************************************************************** }
  { ************************************************************************************** }
  {                           METHODS FOR ALL THE QUADWORLD CLASSES                        }
  {                                                                                        }
  {    Note the order of methods in a methods block is the following (by convention):     }
  {                                                                                        }
  {              (1) the creation method - a class method,                                 }
  {              (2) the Fields method - a private debugging method, NOT listed in the interface, }
  {              (3) the Free method, if needed, and                                       }
  {              (4) the remaining methods in alphabetical order.                          }
  {                                                                                        }
  { ************************************************************************************** }
  { ************************************************************************************** }


  METHODS OF TQuad;

       FUNCTION  TQuad.CREATE(object: TObject; itsHeap: THeap): TQuad;

       VAR  i: INTEGER;  { FOR Loop index }
       BEGIN
          {$IFC fTrace}BP(11);{$ENDC}
           IF object = NIL THEN object := NewObject(itsHeap, THISCLASS);
           SELF := TQuad(object);

           { initialize all vertices }
            FOR i := 1 TO 4 DO SELF.vertex[i] := zeroLPt;

          {$IFC fTrace}EP;{$ENDC}
       END; { TQuad.CREATE }


       {$IFC fDebugMethods}
       PROCEDURE TQuad.Fields(PROCEDURE Field(nameAndType: S255));
       BEGIN
           SUPERSELF.Fields(Field);
           Field('vertex: ARRAY[1..4] OF LPoint');
           Field('');
       END;
       {$ENDC}
```

```
FUNCTION  TQuad.AddCmdNumber: INTEGER;
BEGIN
    {$IFC fTrace}BP(10);{$ENDC}
    AddCmdNumber := uAddQuadCmd;
    {$IFC fTrace}EP;{$ENDC}
END;


PROCEDURE TQuad.AsText(VAR text: S255);
BEGIN
    {$IFC fTrace}BP(11);{$ENDC}
     text := 'a Quadrilateral';
    {$IFC fTrace}EP;{$ENDC}
END;  { TQuad.AsText }


PROCEDURE TQuad.Center(VAR centerLPt: LPoint);
VAR
     thisPoint:      LPoint;
BEGIN
    {$IFC fTrace}BP(11);{$ENDC}
     WITH SELF DO
        BEGIN
              thisPoint.h := (vertex[1].h + vertex[2].h + vertex[3].h + vertex[4].h) div 4;
              thisPoint.v := (vertex[1].v + vertex[2].v + vertex[3].v + vertex[4].v) div 4;
        END;
     centerLPt := thisPoint;

    {$IFC fTrace}EP;{$ENDC}
END;  { TQuad.Center }


FUNCTION  TQuad.CreateSelection(aQuadGrView: TQuadGrView): TCreateQuadSelection;
VAR aCreateQuadSelection: TCreateQuadSelection;
BEGIN
    {$IFC fTrace}BP(10);{$ENDC}
    aCreateQuadSelection := TCreateQuadSelection.CREATE(NIL, SELF.heap, aQuadGrView, zeroLPt);
    CreateSelection := aCreateQuadSelection;
    {$IFC fTrace}EP;{$ENDC}
END;


PROCEDURE TQuad.EnclosingLRect(VAR encloseLRect: LRect);
VAR
     minLeft, minTop, maxRight, maxBottom:    LONGINT;
     thisRect:    LRect;
     i:           INTEGER;     { FOR loop index }

     PROCEDURE SetMinMax(pt: LPoint);
     BEGIN
           minLeft := Min(minLeft, pt.h);
           minTop := Min(minTop, pt.v);
           maxRight := Max(maxRight, pt.h);
           maxBottom := Max(maxBottom, pt.v);
     END;

BEGIN  { TQuad.EnclosingLRect }
    {$IFC fTrace}BP(11);{$ENDC}
     minLeft := 720;     minTop := 360;
     maxRight := 0;      maxBottom := 0;

     FOR i := 1 TO 4 DO SetMinMax(SELF.vertex[i]);

     SetLRect(thisRect, minLeft, minTop, maxRight, maxBottom);
     encloseLRect := thisRect;

    {$IFC fTrace}EP;{$ENDC}
END;  { TQuad.EnclosingRectangle }


PROCEDURE TQuad.SetPoints(pt1, pt2, pt3, pt4: LPoint);
BEGIN
    {$IFC fTrace}BP(11);{$ENDC}
     WITH SELF DO
        BEGIN
              vertex[1] := pt1;
              vertex[2] := pt2;
```

```
2 --                 vertex[3] := pt3;
2 --                 vertex[4] := pt4;
2 -1             END;
2 --         {$IFC fTrace}EP;{$ENDC}
2 -0 A   END;  { TQuad.SetPoints }
2 --
2 --
2 --     { This procedure rotates a quad counterclockwise about its center by theta radians }
2 -- A   PROCEDURE TQuad.RotateBy(theta: REAL);
2 --     VAR
2 --         newVertex:      ARRAY[1..4] of LPoint;
2 --         sine, cosine:   REAL;
2 --         centerLPt:      LPoint;
2 --         tempLPt:        LPoint;
2 --         i:              INTEGER;   { FOR loop index }
2 --
2 0- A   BEGIN
2 --         {$IFC fTrace}BP(10);{$ENDC}
2 --
2 --          SELF.Center(centerLPt);
2 --          sine := sin(theta);
2 --          cosine := cos(theta);
2 --
2 --          FOR i := 1 TO 4 DO
2 1-             BEGIN
2 --                 LPtMinusLPt(SELF.vertex[i], centerLPt, tempLPt);
2 --                 newVertex[i].h := TRUNC(centerLPt.h + tempLPt.h*cosine - tempLPt.v*sine);
2 --                 newVertex[i].v := TRUNC(centerLPt.v + tempLPt.v*cosine + tempLPt.h*sine);
2 -1             END;
2 --
2 --          SELF.SetPoints(newVertex[1], newVertex[2], newVertex[3], newVertex[4]);
2 --
2 --         {$IFC fTrace}EP;{$ENDC}
2 -0 A   END;
2 --
2 --
2 --   END;  { of TQuad Methods }
2 --
2 --   { ********************************************************************************************** }
2 --
2 --   METHODS OF TParallelogram;
2 --
2 -- A   FUNCTION  TParallelogram.CREATE(object: TObject; itsHeap: THeap): TParallelogram;
2 0- A   BEGIN
2 --        {$IFC fTrace}BP(11);{$ENDC}
2 --         IF object = NIL THEN object := NewObject(itsHeap, THISCLASS);
2 --         SELF := TParallelogram(TQuad.CREATE(object, itsHeap));
2 --        {$IFC fTrace}EP;{$ENDC}
2 -0 A   END; { TParallelogram.CREATE }
2 --
2 --
2 --     {$IFC fDebugMethods}
2 -- A   PROCEDURE TParallelogram.Fields(PROCEDURE Field(nameAndType: S255));
2 0- A   BEGIN
2 --         SUPERSELF.Fields(Field);
2 --         Field('');
2 -0 A   END;
2 --     {$ENDC}
2 --
2 --
2 -- A   FUNCTION  TParallelogram.AddCmdNumber: INTEGER;
2 0- A   BEGIN
2 --         {$IFC fTrace}BP(10);{$ENDC}
2 --         AddCmdNumber := uAddParagramCmd;
2 --         {$IFC fTrace}EP;{$ENDC}
2 -0 A   END;
2 --
2 --
2 -- A   PROCEDURE TParallelogram.AsText(VAR text: S255);
2 0- A   BEGIN
2 --         {$IFC fTrace}BP(11);{$ENDC}
2 --          text := 'a Parallelogram';
2 --         {$IFC fTrace}EP;{$ENDC}
2 -0 A   END;  { TParallelogram.AsText }
```

```
    FUNCTION  TParallelogram.CreateSelection(aQuadGrView: TQuadGrView): TCreateQuadSelection;
    VAR aCreateParallelogramSelection: TCreateParallelogramSelection;
    BEGIN
        {$IFC fTrace}BP(10);{$ENDC}
        aCreateParallelogramSelection := TCreateParallelogramSelection.CREATE(NIL, SELF.heap,
                                                                  aQuadGrView, zeroLPt);
        CreateSelection := aCreateParallelogramSelection;
        {$IFC fTrace}EP;{$ENDC}
    END;

END;  { of TParallelogram methods }

{ *********************************************************************************************** }

METHODS OF TRhombus;

    FUNCTION  TRhombus.CREATE(object: TObject; itsHeap: THeap): TRhombus;
    BEGIN
       {$IFC fTrace}BP(11);{$ENDC}
        IF object = NIL THEN object := NewObject(itsHeap, THISCLASS);
        SELF := TRhombus(TParallelogram.CREATE(object, itsHeap));
       {$IFC fTrace}EP;{$ENDC}
    END; { TRhombus.CREATE }


    {$IFC fDebugMethods}
    PROCEDURE TRhombus.Fields(PROCEDURE Field(nameAndType: S255));
    BEGIN
        SUPERSELF.Fields(Field);
        Field('');
    END;
    {$ENDC}


    FUNCTION  TRhombus.AddCmdNumber: INTEGER;
    BEGIN
        {$IFC fTrace}BP(10);{$ENDC}
        AddCmdNumber := uAddRhombusCmd;
        {$IFC fTrace}EP;{$ENDC}
    END;


    PROCEDURE TRhombus.AsText(VAR text: S255);
    BEGIN
        {$IFC fTrace}BP(11);{$ENDC}
         text := 'a Rhombus';
        {$IFC fTrace}EP;{$ENDC}
    END;  { TRhombus.AsText }


    FUNCTION  TRhombus.CreateSelection(aQuadGrView: TQuadGrView): TCreateQuadSelection;
    VAR aCreateRhombusSelection: TCreateRhombusSelection;
    BEGIN
        {$IFC fTrace}BP(10);{$ENDC}
        aCreateRhombusSelection := TCreateRhombusSelection.CREATE(NIL, SELF.heap, aQuadGrView, zeroLPt);
        CreateSelection := aCreateRhombusSelection;
        {$IFC fTrace}EP;{$ENDC}
    END;


END;  { of TRhombus methods }

{ *********************************************************************************************** }

METHODS OF TRectangle;

    FUNCTION  TRectangle.CREATE(object: TObject; itsHeap: THeap): TRectangle;
    BEGIN
       {$IFC fTrace}BP(11);{$ENDC}
        IF object = NIL THEN object := NewObject(itsHeap, THISCLASS);
        SELF := TRectangle(TParallelogram.CREATE(object, itsHeap));
       {$IFC fTrace}EP;{$ENDC}
```

```
2 -0 A     END; { TRectangle.CREATE }
2 --
2 --
2 --       {$IFC fDebugMethods}
2 -- A     PROCEDURE TRectangle.Fields(PROCEDURE Field(nameAndType: S255));
2 0- A     BEGIN
2 --           SUPERSELF.Fields(Field);
2 --           Field('');
2 -0 A     END;
2 --       {$ENDC}
2 --
2 --
2 -- A     FUNCTION  TRectangle.AddCmdNumber: INTEGER;
2 0- A     BEGIN
2 --           {$IFC fTrace}BP(10);{$ENDC}
2 --           AddCmdNumber := uAddRectCmd;
2 --           {$IFC fTrace}EP;{$ENDC}
2 -0 A     END;
2 --
2 --
2 -- A     PROCEDURE TRectangle.AsText(VAR text: S255);
2 0- A     BEGIN
2 --           {$IFC fTrace}BP(11);{$ENDC}
2 --            text := 'a Rectangle';
2 --           {$IFC fTrace}EP;{$ENDC}
2 -0 A     END;  { TRectangle.AsText }
2 --
2 --
2 -- A     FUNCTION  TRectangle.CreateSelection(aQuadGrView: TQuadGrView): TCreateQuadSelection;
2 --       VAR aCreateRectangleSelection: TCreateTangleSelection;
2 0- A     BEGIN
2 --           {$IFC fTrace}BP(10);{$ENDC}
2 --           aCreateRectangleSelection := TCreateTangleSelection.CREATE(NIL, SELF.heap, aQuadGrView, zeroLPt);
2 --           CreateSelection := aCreateRectangleSelection;
2 --           {$IFC fTrace}EP;{$ENDC}
2 -0 A     END;
2 --
2 --
2 --   END;  { of TRectangle methods }
2 --
2 --   { ************************************************************************************************ }
2 --
2 --   METHODS OF TSquare;
2 --
2 -- A     FUNCTION  TSquare.CREATE(object: TObject; itsHeap: THeap): TSquare;
2 0- A     BEGIN
2 --          {$IFC fTrace}BP(11);{$ENDC}
2 --           IF object = NIL THEN object := NewObject(itsHeap, THISCLASS);
2 --           SELF := TSquare(TRectangle.CREATE(object, itsHeap));
2 --          {$IFC fTrace}EP;{$ENDC}
2 -0 A     END; { TSquare.CREATE }
2 --
2 --
2 --       {$IFC fDebugMethods}
2 -- A     PROCEDURE TSquare.Fields(PROCEDURE Field(nameAndType: S255));
2 0- A     BEGIN
2 --           SUPERSELF.Fields(Field);
2 --           Field('');
2 -0 A     END;
2 --       {$ENDC}
2 --
2 --
2 -- A     FUNCTION  TSquare.AddCmdNumber: INTEGER;
2 0- A     BEGIN
2 --           {$IFC fTrace}BP(10);{$ENDC}
2 --           AddCmdNumber := uAddSquareCmd;
2 --           {$IFC fTrace}EP;{$ENDC}
2 -0 A     END;
2 --
2 --
2 -- A     PROCEDURE TSquare.AsText(VAR text: S255);
2 0- A     BEGIN
2 --           {$IFC fTrace}BP(11);{$ENDC}
2 --            text := 'a Square';
```

```
            {$IFC fTrace}EP;{$ENDC}
        END;  { TSquare.AsText }


        FUNCTION  TSquare.CreateSelection(aQuadGrView: TQuadGrView): TCreateQuadSelection;
        VAR aCreateSquareSelection: TCreateSquareSelection;
        BEGIN
            {$IFC fTrace}BP(10);{$ENDC}
            aCreateSquareSelection := TCreateSquareSelection.CREATE(NIL, SELF.heap, aQuadGrView, zeroLPt);
            CreateSelection := aCreateSquareSelection;
            {$IFC fTrace}EP;{$ENDC}
        END;


    END;  { of TSquare methods }

    {***************************************************************************************************}

                  {*************************************************************************}
                  {*****************     New Views for this application     *******************}
                  {*************************************************************************}

    METHODS OF TQuadView;

        FUNCTION  TQuadView.CREATE(object: TObject; heap: THeap; itsExtent: LRect;
                                  itsPanel: TPanel): TQuadView;
        BEGIN
            {$IFC fTrace}BP(11);{$ENDC}
             IF object = NIL THEN object := NewObject(heap, THISCLASS);
             SELF := TQuadView(itsPanel.NewView(object, itsExtent,
                                       TPrintManager.CREATE(NIL, heap), stdMargins, TRUE));
             SELF.window := TQuadWindow(itsPanel.window);
            {$IFC fTrace}EP;{$ENDC}
        END;

        {$IFC fDebugMethods}
        PROCEDURE TQuadView.Fields(PROCEDURE Field(nameAndType: S255));
        BEGIN
            SUPERSELF.Fields(Field);
            Field('window: TQuadWindow');
            Field('');
        END;
        {$ENDC}

    { just make believe it was a mouse press; the selection code does nothing if the same box is selected }
        PROCEDURE TQuadView.MouseMove(mouseLPt: LPoint);
        BEGIN
            {$IFC fTrace}BP(11);{$ENDC}
            SELF.MousePress(mouseLPt);
            {$IFC fTrace}EP;{$ENDC}
        END;

    { Calculate the new selected quad, and make the selection in both panels }
        PROCEDURE TQuadView.MousePress(mouseLPt: LPoint);
        VAR  thisQuad:      TQuad;
             thisPanel:     TPanel;
             theSelection:  TSelection;
        BEGIN
            {$IFC fTrace}BP(12);{$ENDC}
            thisPanel := SELF.panel;
            theSelection := thisPanel.selection;

            IF InClass(theSelection, TQuadSelection) THEN   { Not a TCreateQuadSelection, so we are not
                                                              drawing a new quad with the mouse. }
                BEGIN
                   SELF.LPtToQuad(mouseLPt, thisQuad);
                   SELF.window.Select(thisPanel, thisQuad);
                   IF thisQuad = NIL THEN
                       SELF.window.SetAction(symArrow, TRUE);  { Select the arrow in the palette }
                END
             ELSE
                SUPERSELF.MousePress(mouseLPt);  { The standard action is to pass the mouse data to the
                                                   mouse press method of the select panel's current selection
            {$IFC fTrace}EP;{$ENDC}
```

```
    END;


    FUNCTION  TQuadView.NoSelection: TSelection;
    BEGIN
        {$IFC fTrace}BP(11);{$ENDC}
        noSelection := TQuadSelection.CREATE(NIL, SELF.heap, SELF, nothingKind, NIL);
        {$IFC fTrace}EP;{$ENDC}
    END;

END;  { of TQuadView Methods }

{ *************************************************************************************************** }

METHODS OF TQuadGrView;

    FUNCTION  TQuadGrView.CREATE(object: TObject; heap: THeap; itsPanel: TPanel):
                                 TQuadGrView;
    VAR r:          LRect;
    BEGIN
        {$IFC fTrace}BP(11);{$ENDC}
        IF object = NIL THEN object := NewObject(heap, THISCLASS);

        SetLRect(r, 0, 0, 1000, 1000);
        SELF := TQuadGrView(TQuadView.CREATE(object, heap, r, itsPanel));
        {$IFC fTrace}EP;{$ENDC}
    END;

    {$IFC fDebugMethods}
    PROCEDURE TQuadGrView.Fields(PROCEDURE Field(nameAndType: S255));
    BEGIN
        SUPERSELF.Fields(Field);
        Field('');
    END;
    {$ENDC}

 { Draw all the quadrilarterals; Note that this routine does not optimize the drawing of rectangles }
    PROCEDURE TQuadGrView.Draw;

        PROCEDURE DrawQuad(object: TObject);
            VAR  quad:   TQuad;
                 thisLRect:  LRect;

                 PROCEDURE DrawEdge(pt1, pt2: LPoint);
                 BEGIN
                      MoveToL(pt1.h, pt1.v);
                      LineToL(pt2.h, pt2.v);
                 END;  { DrawEdge }

            BEGIN  { DrawQuad }
                quad := TQuad(object);
                quad.EnclosingLRect(thisLRect);

                IF LRectIsVisible(thisLRect) THEN      { only draw quads that will be seen }
                  {$H-} WITH quad DO
                          BEGIN
                               DrawEdge(vertex[1], vertex[2]);
                               DrawEdge(vertex[2], vertex[3]);
                               DrawEdge(vertex[3], vertex[4]);
                               DrawEdge(vertex[4], vertex[1]);
                          END;   {$H+}
            END;  { TQuad.Draw }

    BEGIN { TQuadGrView.Draw }
        {$IFC fTrace}BP(11);{$ENDC}
         SELF.window.EachVirtualPart(DrawQuad);             { Draw all quads, even a 'virtual' one }
        {$IFC fTrace}EP;{$ENDC}
    END;


 { Decide what quad is indicated by this point; return NIL in quad iff none }
    PROCEDURE TQuadGrView.LPtToQuad(lPt: LPoint; VAR quad: TQuad);
    VAR  thisLRect:  LRect;

```

```
            PROCEDURE TestAQuad(object: TObject);
               VAR  testQuad:   TQuad;
               BEGIN
                   testQuad := TQuad(object);
                   testQuad.EnclosingLRect(thisLRect);
                   IF LRectHasLPt(thisLRect, lPt) THEN
                       quad := testQuad;
               END;
       BEGIN
           {$IFC fTrace}BP(11);{$ENDC}
            quad := NIL;
            SELF.window.EachVirtualPart(TestAQuad);
           {$IFC fTrace}EP;{$ENDC}
       END;


   { return a new selection appropriate to this view }
       FUNCTION  TQuadGrView.NewSelection(quad: TQuad): TQuadSelection;
       BEGIN
           {$IFC fTrace}BP(11);{$ENDC}
           NewSelection := TQuadGrSelection.CREATE(NIL, SELF.heap, SELF, quad);
           {$IFC fTrace}EP;{$ENDC}
       END;


   END;  { of TQuadGrView Methods }

   { **************************************************************************************************** }

   METHODS OF TQuadTxView;

       FUNCTION  TQuadTxView.CREATE(object: TObject; heap: THeap; itsPanel: TPanel): TQuadTxView;
       VAR longStr:    S255;
           fInfo:      FontInfo;
       BEGIN
           {$IFC fTrace}BP(11);{$ENDC}
           IF object = NIL THEN object := NewObject(heap, THISCLASS);

           { use a temporary extent rect, until we can calculate the correct one }
           SELF := TQuadTxView(TQuadView.CREATE(object, heap, zeroLRect, itsPanel));

           PushFocus;
           itsPanel.window.Focus;
           SELF.SetPen;                                { set pen assumes that focus has been done }
           GetFontInfo(fInfo);
           longStr := 'A Parallelogram';

           WITH fInfo, SELF, extentLRect DO
               BEGIN
               lineHeight := ascent + descent + leading + 1;
               lineAscent := ascent + (leading DIV 2) - 1;
         {$H-} right := StringWidth(longStr) + 2*txMargin; {$H+}
               bottom := maxQuad*lineHeight;
               END;

           PopFocus;
           {$IFC fTrace}EP;{$ENDC}
       END;

       {$IFC fDebugMethods}
       PROCEDURE TQuadTxView.Fields(PROCEDURE Field(nameAndType: S255));
       BEGIN
           SUPERSELF.Fields(Field);
           Field('lineHeight:    INTEGER');
           Field('lineAscent:    INTEGER');
           Field('');
       END;
       {$ENDC}


   { Write the textual representation of all the quads }
       PROCEDURE TQuadTxView.Draw;

           PROCEDURE DrawQuadName(object: TObject);
```

```
2 --               VAR  quad:   TQuad;
2 0- B             BEGIN
2 --                   quad := TQuad(object);
2 --                   SELF.DrawName(quad);
2 -0 B             END;
2 --
2 0- A       BEGIN
2 --             {$IFC fTrace}BP(11);{$ENDC}
2 --              SELF.window.EachVirtualPart(DrawQuadName);
2 --             {$IFC fTrace}EP;{$ENDC}
2 -0 A       END;
2 --
2 --
2 --    { Draw one quad as a text string appropriately positioned. }
2 -- A       PROCEDURE TQuadTxView.DrawName(quad: TQuad);
2 --         VAR tempBox:         LRect;
2 --             str:             S255;
2 0- A       BEGIN
2 --             {$IFC fTrace}BP(11);{$ENDC}
2 --             { The tool kit makes no assumptions about the pen.  You set it when you want to use it. }
2 --             SELF.SetPen;
2 --
2 --             { Calculate the rectangle to fill }
2 --             SELF.SetUpBox(quad, tempBox);
2 --
2 --             IF LRectIsVisible(tempBox) THEN      { only write text that will be seen }
2 1-                BEGIN
2 --                MoveToL(tempBox.left + txMargin, tempBox.top + SELF.lineAscent);
2 --                quad.AsText(str);
2 --                DrawString(str);
2 -1                END;
2 --             {$IFC fTrace}EP;{$ENDC}
2 -0 A       END;
2 --
2 --
2 --    { Decide what quad is indicated by this point; return NIL in quad iff this point indicates no quad }
2 -- A       PROCEDURE TQuadTxView.LPtToQuad(lPt: LPoint; VAR quad: TQuad);
2 --
2 -- B           PROCEDURE CheckQuad(obj: TObject);
2 --             VAR   thisQuad:   TQuad;
2 --                   thisBox:    LRect;
2 0- B          BEGIN
2 --                thisQuad := TQuad(obj);
2 --                SELF.SetUpBox(thisQuad, thisBox);
2 --                IF LRectHasLPt(thisBox, lPt) THEN
2 --                    quad := thisQuad;
2 -0 B          END;
2 --
2 0- A       BEGIN
2 --             {$IFC fTrace}BP(11);{$ENDC}
2 --             quad := NIL;
2 --             SELF.window.EachVirtualPart(CheckQuad);
2 --             {$IFC fTrace}EP;{$ENDC}
2 -0 A       END;
2 --
2 --
2 -- A       FUNCTION  TQuadTxView.NewSelection(quad: TQuad): TQuadSelection;
2 0- A       BEGIN
2 --             {$IFC fTrace}BP(11);{$ENDC}
2 --             NewSelection := TQuadTxSelection.CREATE(NIL, SELF.heap, SELF, quad);
2 --             {$IFC fTrace}EP;{$ENDC}
2 -0 A       END;
2 --
2 --
2 --    { Set up the pen for drawing the characters; assumes that we are focused on the right window
2 --            (or a pad in the right window); this is a method so it can be overridden easily }
2 -- A       PROCEDURE TQuadTxView.SetPen;
2 0- A       BEGIN
2 --           {$IFC fTrace}BP(10);{$ENDC}
2 --           PenNormal;
2 --           TextFont(fIDSystem);          { system font }
2 --           TextFace([]);
2 --           {$IFC fTrace}EP;{$ENDC}
2 -0 A       END;
```

```
2   652 --
2   653 --
2   654 --     { Create a rectangle, for this quad. }
2   655 -- A      PROCEDURE TQuadTxView.SetUpBox(quad: TQuad; VAR bBox: LRect);
2   656 --        VAR  thisIndex:                QuadIndex;
2   657 --             virtualQuadListSize:      INTEGER;
2   658 --
2   659 -- B           PROCEDURE SearchVirtualQuadList(obj: TObject);
2   660 --             VAR   thisQuad:    TQuad;
2   661 0- B           BEGIN
2   662 --                thisQuad := TQuad(obj);
2   663 --                virtualQuadListSize := virtualQuadListSize + 1;
2   664 --                IF thisQuad = quad THEN
2   665 --                    thisIndex := virtualQuadListSize;      { Current postion in the virtual list }
2   666 -0 B           END;
2   667 --
2   668 0- A       BEGIN
2   669 --             {$IFC fTrace}BP(11);{$ENDC}
2   670 --              thisIndex := 0;
2   671 --              virtualQuadListSize := 0;
2   672 --              SELF.window.EachVirtualPart(SearchVirtualQuadList);
2   673 --
2   674 --              IF thisIndex = 0 THEN    { This quad has just been drawn and is not yet installed in the window }
2   675 --                  thisIndex := virtualQuadListSize + 1;
2   676 --
2   677 --             { use same left and right as view, calculate the top and bottom }
2   678 --             WITH SELF, bBox DO
2   679 1-                 BEGIN
2   680 --                 left := SELF.extentLRect.left;
2   681 --                 top := (thisIndex - 1)* lineHeight;       { Subtract 1 to get the TOP line }
2   682 --                 right := SELF.extentLRect.right;
2   683 --                 bottom := top + lineHeight;
2   684 -1                 END;
2   685 --             {$IFC fTrace}EP;{$ENDC}
2   686 -0 A       END;
2   687 --
2   688 --     END;  { of TQuadTxView Methods }
2   689 --
2   690 --     { ****************************************************************************************************** }
2   691 --
2   692 --                   {****************************************************************************}
2   693 --                   {**************      New Selections for this application      *****************}
2   694 --                   {****************************************************************************}
2   695 --
2   696 --     METHODS OF TQuadSelection;
2   697 --
2   698 -- A       FUNCTION  TQuadSelection.CREATE(object: TObject; heap: THeap; itsView: TQuadView; itsKind: INTEGER;
2   699 --                                          itsQuad: TQuad): TQuadSelection;
2   700 0- A       BEGIN
2   701 --             {$IFC fTrace}BP(12);{$ENDC}
2   702 --             IF object = NIL THEN object := NewObject(heap, THISCLASS);
2   703 --
2   704 --             SELF := TQuadSelection(TSelection.CREATE(object, heap, itsView, itsKind, zeroLPt));
2   705 --             SELF.quad := itsQuad;
2   706 --             {$IFC fTrace}EP;{$ENDC}
2   707 -0 A       END;
2   708 --
2   709 --         {$IFC fDebugMethods}
2   710 -- A       PROCEDURE TQuadSelection.Fields(PROCEDURE Field(nameAndType: S255));
2   711 0- A       BEGIN
2   712 --             SUPERSELF.Fields(Field);
2   713 --             Field('quad:    TQuad');
2   714 --             Field('');
2   715 -0 A       END;
2   716 --         {$ENDC}
2   717 --
2   718 --
2   719 --     { set up the state of all the menu items controlled by the selection before the user gets to see them }
2   720 --
2   721 -- A       FUNCTION   TQuadSelection.CanDoCommand(cmdNumber: TCmdNumber; VAR checkIt: BOOLEAN): BOOLEAN;
2   722 --         VAR enable:          BOOLEAN;
2   723 --
2   724 0- A       BEGIN
2   725 --             {$IFC fTrace}BP(10);{$ENDC}
```

```
        enable := SELF.kind <> nothingKind;
        CASE cmdNumber OF
            uClearQuadCmd, uRotateQuadCmd:   CanDoCommand := enable;
            OTHERWISE
                CanDoCommand := SUPERSELF.CanDoCommand(cmdNumber, checkIt);
            END;
        {$IFC fTrace}EP;{$ENDC}
    END;


    FUNCTION  TQuadSelection.NewCommand(cmdNumber: TCmdNumber): TCommand;
    VAR  quadView:   TQuadView;
    BEGIN
        {$IFC fTrace}BP(11);{$ENDC}
        NewCommand := NIL;
        quadView := TQuadView(SELF.view);

        CASE cmdNumber OF
            uClearQuadCmd:
                    NewCommand := TClearQuadCmd.CREATE(NIL, SELF.heap, cmdNumber, SELF.quad);

            uRotateQuadCmd:
                    NewCommand := TRotateQuadCmd.CREATE(NIL, SELF.heap, cmdNumber,
                                                        SELF.quad, 3.14159*45.0/180.0);   { 45 degrees }

            OTHERWISE     { The Toolkit ABCs do the rest! }
                NewCommand := SUPERSELF.NewCommand(cmdNumber);
            END;
        {$IFC fTrace}EP;{$ENDC}
    END;

END;  { of TQuadSelection Methods }

{ ************************************************************************************************ }


METHODS OF TQuadGrSelection;

    FUNCTION  TQuadGrSelection.CREATE(object: TObject; heap: THeap; itsView: TQuadView;
                                      itsQuad: TQuad): TQuadGrSelection;
    VAR thisKind: INTEGER;
    BEGIN
        {$IFC fTrace}BP(12);{$ENDC}
        IF object = NIL THEN object := NewObject(heap, THISCLASS);
        IF itsQuad = NIL
            THEN  thisKind := nothingKind
            ELSE  thisKind := quadKind;
        SELF := TQuadGrSelection(TQuadSelection.CREATE(object, heap, itsView, thisKind, itsQuad));
        {$IFC fTrace}EP;{$ENDC}
    END;


 { Required to highlight the indication in the already-focused pad }
    PROCEDURE TQuadGrSelection.Highlight(highTransit: THighTransit);
    VAR r:  LRect;

        PROCEDURE PaintHandles(quad: TQuad);
        VAR
            highLightLRect:    LRect;
            i:                 INTEGER;    { FOR loop index }

        BEGIN
            SetLRect(highLightLRect, -3, -2, 3, 2);    { Highlighting rectangle }

            {$H-} WITH quad DO
                    FOR i := 1 TO 4 DO
                        BEGIN
                            OffsetLRect(highLightLRect, vertex[i].h, vertex[i].v);
                            PaintLRect(highLightLRect);
                            OffsetLRect(highLightLRect, -vertex[i].h, -vertex[i].v);
                        END;  {$H+}
        END;  { PaintHandles }

    BEGIN  { TQuadGrselection.Highlight }
```

```
            {$IFC fTrace}BP(12);{$ENDC}
            IF (HighTransit <> hNone) AND (SELF.kind <> nothingKind) THEN
                BEGIN
                   SELF.quad.EnclosingLRect(r);
                   PenMode(patXOr);
                   IF LRectIsVisible(r) THEN    { only do highlight if part of the quad is visible }
                      PaintHandles(SELF.quad);
                END;
            {$IFC fTrace}EP;{$ENDC}
        END;

    END;  { of TQuadGrSelection }

    { ************************************************************************************************ }

    METHODS OF TQuadTxSelection;

        FUNCTION  TQuadTxSelection.CREATE(object: TObject; heap: THeap; itsView: TQuadView;
                                          itsQuad: TQuad): TQuadTxSelection;
        VAR thisKind:  INTEGER;
        BEGIN
            {$IFC fTrace}BP(12);{$ENDC}
            IF object = NIL THEN object := NewObject(heap, THISCLASS);
            IF itsQuad = NIL
                THEN  thisKind := nothingKind
                ELSE  thisKind := quadKind;
            SELF := TQuadTxSelection(TQuadSelection.CREATE(object, heap, itsView, thisKind, itsQuad));
            {$IFC fTrace}EP;{$ENDC}
        END;

    { Required to highlight the indication in the already-focused pad }
        PROCEDURE TQuadTxSelection.Highlight(highTransit: THighTransit);
        VAR r:           LRect;
            quadTxView:  TQuadTxView;
        BEGIN
            {$IFC fTrace}BP(12);{$ENDC}
            IF (HighTransit <> hNone) AND (SELF.kind <> nothingKind) AND (SELF.quad <> NIL) THEN
                BEGIN

                    { This application inverts the text string to indicate it is selected; when deactivated,
                      the highlighting changes to a thin black rectangle }

                    { Make r be the rectangle to invert }
                    quadTxView := TQuadTxView(SELF.view);
                    quadTxView.SetUpBox(SELF.quad, r);

                    IF LRectIsVisible(r) THEN    { only do highlighting if part of the rectangle is visible }
                        BEGIN
                            PenNormal;
                            PenSize(1, 1);

                            IF (highTransit = hOffToDim) OR (highTransit = hDimToOff) THEN
                                FrameLRect(r)
                            ELSE
                                BEGIN
                                IF (highTransit = hOnToDim) OR (highTransit = hDimToOn) THEN
                                    InsetLRect(r, 1, 1);
                                InvrtLRect(r);
                                END;
                        END;
                END;
            {$IFC fTrace}EP;{$ENDC}
        END;

    END;  { of TQuadTxSelection Methods }

    { ************************************************************************************************ }

                    {*******************************************************************}
                    {*********     New Sketching Selections for this application     ************}
                    {*******************************************************************}

    METHODS OF TCreateQuadSelection

```

```
2 -- A     FUNCTION  TCreateQuadSelection.CREATE(object: TObject; itsHeap: THeap; itsView: TQuadView;
2 --                                            itsAnchorLPt: LPoint): TCreateQuadSelection;
2 --       VAR  i:     INTEGER;     { FOR Loop index}
2 --            quad: TQuad;
2 0- A     BEGIN
2 --           {$IFC fTrace}BP(10);{$ENDC}
2 --           IF object = NIL THEN object := NewObject(itsHeap, THISCLASS);
2 --           SELF := TCreateQuadSelection(TSelection.CREATE(object, itsHeap, itsView,
2 --                                                               quadKind, itsAnchorLPt));
2 --           FOR i := 1 TO 4 DO SELF.vertex[i] := zeroLPt;
2 --           SELF.lastVertexSet := 0;
2 --           quad := TQuad.CREATE(NIL, itsHeap);
2 --           SELF.quad := quad;
2 --           {$IFC fTrace}EP;{$ENDC}
2 -0 A     END;
2 --
2 --       {$IFC fDebugMethods}
2 -- A     PROCEDURE TCreateQuadSelection.Fields(PROCEDURE Field(nameAndType: S255));
2 0- A     BEGIN
2 --           SUPERSELF.Fields(Field);
2 --           Field('quad: TQuad');
2 --           Field('vertex:  ARRAY [1..4] OF LPoint');
2 --           Field('lastVertexSet: INTEGER');
2 --           Field('');
2 -0 A     END;
2 --       {$ENDC}
2 --
2 --
2 -- A     PROCEDURE TCreateQuadSelection.Free;
2 0- A     BEGIN
2 --           {$IFC fTrace}BP(11);{$ENDC}
2 --             Free(SELF.quad);
2 --             SUPERSELF.Free;
2 --           {$IFC fTrace}EP;{$ENDC}
2 -0 A     END;
2 --
2 --
2 -- A     PROCEDURE TCreateQuadSelection.MouseConstrain(mouseLPt: LPoint; VAR correctedLPt: LPoint);
2 0- A     BEGIN
2 --           {$IFC fTrace}BP(12);{$ENDC}
2 --            correctedLPt := mouseLPt;        { No geometric constraints for a general quadrilateral }
2 --           {$IFC fTrace}EP;{$ENDC}
2 -0 A     END;
2 --
2 --
2 -- A     PROCEDURE TCreateQuadSelection.MouseMove(mouseLPt: LPoint);
2 --       VAR  diffLPt:                LPoint;
2 --            correctedMousePoint:    LPoint;
2 --            theQuadWindow:          TQuadWindow;
2 --
2 -- B          PROCEDURE DrawTheLine;
2 0- B          BEGIN
2 --               PenNormal;
2 --               PenMode(patXOr);   {Draw with reversible ink }
2 --               MoveToL(SELF.vertex[SELF.lastVertexSet].h, SELF.vertex[SELF.lastVertexSet].v);
2 --               LineToL(SELF.currLPt.h,   SELF.currLPt.v);
2 -0 B          END;
2 --
2 0- A     BEGIN
2 --           {$IFC fTrace}BP(12);{$ENDC}
2 --            theQuadWindow := TQuadWindow(SELF.window);
2 --            SELF.MouseConstrain(mouseLPt, correctedMousePoint);
2 --            LPtMinusLPt(correctedMouseLPt, SELF.currLPt, diffLPt);
2 --            IF NOT EqualLPt(diffLPt, zeroLPt) THEN
2 1-             BEGIN
2 --                 theQuadWindow.grPanel.OnAllPadsDo(DrawTheLine);   { Undraw the line }
2 --                 SELF.currLPt := correctedMouseLPt;
2 --                 theQuadWindow.grPanel.OnAllPadsDo(DrawTheLine);   { Draw the line }
2 -1             END;
2 --           {$IFC fTrace}EP;{$ENDC}
2 -0 A     END;
2 --
2 --
2 -- A     PROCEDURE TCreateQuadSelection.MousePress(mouseLPt: LPoint);
```

```
VAR  itsQuad:        TQuad;
     theQuadWindow: TQuadWindow;
     itsHeap:        THeap;
BEGIN
    {$IFC fTrace}BP(12);{$ENDC}
    IF SELF.lastVertexSet <> 0      { This will be true every time except the first time that }
       THEN                         { MousePress is called.                                  }
          BEGIN
             SELF.MouseMove(mouseLPt);
          END

       ELSE                         { This block will be executed only the first time that this }
          BEGIN                     { method is called.                                         }
             itsHeap := SELF.heap;
             theQuadWindow := TQuadWindow(currentWindow);
             IF theQuadWindow.quadList.size = maxQuad
                THEN
                   BEGIN
                      { Put up alert box and replace current selection}
                       process.Stop(phMaxQuads);
                       TQuadWindow(currentWindow).Select(SELF.panel, NIL);
                   END
                ELSE
                   BEGIN
                      SELF.anchorLPt := mouseLPt;  { These were NOT set correctly in the CREATE }
                      SELF.currLPt := mouseLPt;    { method since that method was called from   }
                                                   { TActView.MousePress.                       }
                      SELF.vertex[1] := mouseLPt;
                      SELF.lastVertexSet := 1;
                   END;
          END;
    {$IFC fTrace}EP;{$ENDC}
END;


PROCEDURE TCreateQuadSelection.MouseRelease;
VAR  newCmdNumber:  TCmdNumber;
     theQuadWindow: TQuadWindow;
     tempQuad:      TQuad;
BEGIN
    {$IFC fTrace}BP(12);{$ENDC}
     theQuadWindow := TQuadWindow(SELF.window);

     SELF.SetVertices(SELF.currLPt);

     IF SELF.lastVertexSet = 4 THEN   { Done creating this quad }
        BEGIN
 {$H-}     WITH SELF DO quad.SetPoints(vertex[1], vertex[2], vertex[3], vertex[4]);    {$H+}
           newCmdNumber := SELF.quad.AddCmdNumber;
           tempQuad := SELF.quad;
           SELF.quad := NIL;        { the quad will be installed in the list of quads.  The
                                      createQuadSelection object is no longer 'respnsible' for it. }

           theQuadWindow.PerformCommand(TAddQuadCmd.CREATE(NIL, SELF.heap, newCmdNumber, tempQuad));
                  { Note that the newly created command object will replace the current selection
                    (an instance of TCreateQuadSelection) with another selection object.        }

        END;
    {$IFC fTrace}EP;{$ENDC}
END;


PROCEDURE TCreateQuadSelection.SetVertices(newVertex: LPoint);
BEGIN
    { For a general quadrilateral, this method can do nothing more than just set the single new
      vertexthat is passed to it.  For more specific types of quadrilaterals, additional vertices
      can be set.  For example, for a rectangle all four vertices can be determined from two
      opposite corners. See TCreate(Rec)TangleSelection.SetVertices.  }

    {$IFC fTrace}BP(12);{$ENDC}
     SELF.lastVertexSet := SELF.lastVertexSet + 1;
     SELF.vertex[SELF.lastVertexSet] := newVertex;
    {$IFC fTrace}EP;{$ENDC}
END;
```

```
2 --
2 --
2 --    END;  { of TCreateQuadSelection }
2 --
2 --    { ************************************************************************************************ }
2 --
2 --    METHODS OF TCreateParallelogramSelection
2 --
2 -- A      FUNCTION  TCreateParallelogramSelection.CREATE(object: TObject; itsHeap: THeap; itsView: TQuadView;
2 --                                                   itsAnchorLPt: LPoint): TCreateParallelogramSelection;
2 --        VAR  i:              INTEGER;     { FOR Loop index}
2 --             parallelogram: TParallelogram;
2 0- A     BEGIN
2 --            {$IFC fTrace}BP(10);{$ENDC}
2 --            IF object = NIL THEN object := NewObject(itsHeap, THISCLASS);
2 --            SELF := TCreateParallelogramSelection(
2 --                        TCreateQuadSelection.CREATE(object, itsHeap, itsView, itsAnchorLPt));
2 --            Free(SELF.quad);
2 --            parallelogram := TParallelogram.CREATE(NIL, itsHeap);
2 --            SELF.quad := parallelogram;
2 --            SELF.kind := paragramKind;
2 --            {$IFC fTrace}EP;{$ENDC}
2 -0 A     END;
2 --
2 -- A      PROCEDURE TCreateParallelogramSelection.SetVertices(newVertex: LPoint);
2 --        VAR  diffLPt: LPoint;
2 0- A     BEGIN
2 --            {$IFC fTrace}BP(12);{$ENDC}
2 --             SUPERSELF.SetVertices(newVertex);
2 --
2 --            { Set the fourth vertex of the parallelogram by computation }
2 --            IF SELF.lastVertexSet = 3 THEN
2 1-             BEGIN
2 --                LPtMinusLPt(SELF.vertex[1], SELF.vertex[2], diffLPt);
2 --                LPtPlusLPt(SELF.vertex[3], diffLPt, diffLPt);
2 --                SELF.vertex[4] := diffLPt;
2 --                SELF.lastVertexSet := 4;
2 -1             END;
2 --            {$IFC fTrace}EP;{$ENDC}
2 -0 A     END;
2 --
2 --
2 --    END;  { of TCreateParallelogramSelection }
2 --
2 --    { ************************************************************************************************ }
2 --
2 --    METHODS OF TCreateRhombusSelection
2 --
2 -- A      FUNCTION  TCreateRhombusSelection.CREATE(object: TObject; itsHeap: THeap; itsView: TQuadView;
2 --                                             itsAnchorLPt: LPoint): TCreateRhombusSelection;
2 --        VAR  i:        INTEGER;     { FOR Loop index}
2 --             rhombus: TRhombus;
2 0- A     BEGIN
2 --            {$IFC fTrace}BP(10);{$ENDC}
2 --            IF object = NIL THEN object := NewObject(itsHeap, THISCLASS);
2 --            SELF := TCreateRhombusSelection(
2 --                     TCreateParallelogramSelection.CREATE(object, itsHeap, itsView, itsAnchorLPt));
2 --
2 --            Free(SELF.quad);
2 --            rhombus := TRhombus.CREATE(NIL, itsHeap);
2 --            SELF.quad := rhombus;
2 --            SELF.kind := rhombusKind;
2 --            {$IFC fTrace}EP;{$ENDC}
2 -0 A     END;
2 --
2 --      { See comments in the Object Pascal implementation of QuadWorld }
2 -- A      PROCEDURE TCreateRhombusSelection.MouseConstrain(mouseLPt: LPoint; VAR correctedLPt: LPoint);
2 --        VAR  tempLPt: LPoint;
2 --             scale1To2, scale2To3: INTEGER;
2 --
2 -- B           FUNCTION Distance(pt1, pt2: LPoint): INTEGER;
2 --             VAR   temp:  INTEGER;
2 0- B          BEGIN
2 --                temp := TRUNC(SQRT( SQR(pt1.h - pt2.h) + SQR(pt1.v - pt2.v)));
```

```
2 1096 --                IF temp < 2
2 1097 --                  THEN Distance := 1
2 1098 --                  ELSE Distance := temp;
2 1099 -0 B          END;
2 1100 --
2 1101 0- A     BEGIN
2 1102 --           {$IFC fTrace}BP(12);{$ENDC}
2 1103 --           correctedLPt := mouseLPt;          { the default is no correction }
2 1104 --
2 1105 --            IF SELF.lastVertexSet = 2 THEN     { but if the THIRD vertex is being determined, then ... }
2 1106 1-              BEGIN
2 1107 --                  scale1To2 := Distance(SELF.vertex[1], SELF.vertex[2]);
2 1108 --                  scale2To3 := Distance(SELF.vertex[2], mouseLPt);
2 1109 --                  tempLPt.h := (mouseLPt.h - SELF.vertex[2].h)*scale1To2;
2 1110 --                  tempLPt.v := (mouseLPt.v - SELF.vertex[2].v)*scale1To2;
2 1111 --                  tempLPt.h := tempLPt.h div scale2To3;
2 1112 --                  tempLPt.v := tempLPt.v div scale2To3;
2 1113 --                  LPtPlusLPt(tempLPt, SELF.vertex[2], tempLPt);
2 1114 --                  correctedLPt := tempLPt;
2 1115 -1              END;
2 1116 --           {$IFC fTrace}EP;{$ENDC}
2 1117 -0 A     END;
2 1118 --
2 1119 --
2 1120 --   END;  { of TCreateRhombusSelection }
2 1121 --
2 1122 --   { ****************************************************************************************** }
2 1123 --
2 1124 --   METHODS OF TCreateTangleSelection
2 1125 --
2 1126 -- A     FUNCTION  TCreateTangleSelection.CREATE(object: TObject; itsHeap: THeap; itsView: TQuadView;
2 1127 --                                              itsAnchorLPt: LPoint): TCreateTangleSelection;
2 1128 --       VAR  i:          INTEGER;     { FOR Loop index}
2 1129 --            rectObj : TRectangle;
2 1130 0- A     BEGIN
2 1131 --           {$IFC fTrace}BP(10);{$ENDC}
2 1132 --           IF object = NIL THEN object := NewObject(itsHeap, THISCLASS);
2 1133 --           SELF := TCreateTangleSelection(
2 1134 --                    TCreateParallelogramSelection.CREATE(object, itsHeap, itsView, itsAnchorLPt));
2 1135 --
2 1136 --           Free(SELF.quad);
2 1137 --           rectObj := TRectangle.CREATE(NIL, itsHeap);
2 1138 --           SELF.quad := rectObj;
2 1139 --           SELF.kind := rectangleKind;
2 1140 --           {$IFC fTrace}EP;{$ENDC}
2 1141 -0 A     END;
2 1142 --
2 1143 -- A     PROCEDURE TCreateTangleSelection.MouseMove(mouseLPt: LPoint);
2 1144 --       VAR  diffLPt:                LPoint;
2 1145 --            correctedMousePoint:    LPoint;
2 1146 --            theQuadWindow:          TQuadWindow;
2 1147 --
2 1148 -- B          PROCEDURE DrawTheBox;
2 1149 --            VAR   tempLRect:  LRect;
2 1150 0- B          BEGIN
2 1151 --               PenNormal;
2 1152 --               PenMode(patXOr);    {Draw with reversible ink }
2 1153 --               tempLRect.topLeft := SELF.vertex[1];
2 1154 --               tempLRect.botRight := SELF.currLPt;
2 1155 --               RectifyLRect(tempLRect);
2 1156 --               FrameLRect(tempLRect);
2 1157 -0 B          END;
2 1158 --
2 1159 0- A     BEGIN
2 1160 --           {$IFC fTrace}BP(12);{$ENDC}
2 1161 --            theQuadWindow := TQuadWindow(SELF.window);
2 1162 --            SELF.MouseConstrain(mouseLPt, correctedMousePoint);
2 1163 --            LPtMinusLPt(correctedMouseLPt, SELF.currLPt, diffLPt);
2 1164 --            IF NOT EqualLPt(diffLPt, zeroLPt) THEN
2 1165 1-               BEGIN
2 1166 --                  theQuadWindow.grPanel.OnAllPadsDo(DrawTheBox);    { Undraw the box }
2 1167 --                  SELF.currLPt := correctedMouseLPt;
2 1168 --                  theQuadWindow.grPanel.OnAllPadsDo(DrawTheBox);    { Draw the box }
2 1169 -1               END;
```

```
2 --             {$IFC fTrace}EP;{$ENDC}
2 -0 A        END;
2 --
2 --
2 -- A        PROCEDURE TCreateTangleSelection.SetVertices(newVertex: LPoint);
2 --          VAR  vertex1: LPoint;
2 0- A        BEGIN
2 --              {$IFC fTrace}BP(12);{$ENDC}
2 --              { Set both other vertices by compuation }
2 --               SELF.lastVertexSet := 4;
2 --               SELF.vertex[3] := newVertex;
2 --               vertex1 := SELF.vertex[1];
2 --
2 --               SELF.vertex[2].h := newVertex.h;
2 --               SELF.vertex[2].v := vertex1.v;
2 --               SELF.vertex[4].h := vertex1.h;
2 --               SELF.vertex[4].v := newVertex.v;
2 --              {$IFC fTrace}EP;{$ENDC}
2 -0 A        END;
2 --
2 --
2 --      END;  { of TCreateTangleSelection }
2 --
2 --      { ********************************************************************************************** }
2 --
2 --      METHODS OF TCreateSquareSelection
2 --
2 -- A        FUNCTION  TCreateSquareSelection.CREATE(object: TObject; itsHeap: THeap; itsView: TQuadView;
2 --                                                   itsAnchorLPt: LPoint): TCreateSquareSelection;
2 --          VAR  i:       INTEGER;    { FOR Loop index}
2 --               square: TSquare;
2 0- A        BEGIN
2 --              {$IFC fTrace}BP(10);{$ENDC}
2 --              IF object = NIL THEN object := NewObject(itsHeap, THISCLASS);
2 --              SELF := TCreateSquareSelection(
2 --                        TCreateTangleSelection.CREATE(object, itsHeap, itsView, itsAnchorLPt));
2 --
2 --              Free(SELF.quad);
2 --              square := TSquare.CREATE(NIL, itsHeap);
2 --              SELF.quad := square;
2 --              SELF.kind := squareKind;
2 --              {$IFC fTrace}EP;{$ENDC}
2 -0 A        END;
2 --
2 -- A        PROCEDURE TCreateSquareSelection.MouseConstrain(mouseLPt: LPoint; VAR correctedLPt: LPoint);
2 --          VAR  tempLPt: LPoint;
2 --               width, height: INTEGER;
2 0- A        BEGIN
2 --              {$IFC fTrace}BP(12);{$ENDC}
2 --               tempLPt := mouseLPt;
2 --               width := tempLPt.h - SELF.vertex[1].h;
2 --               height := tempLPt.v - SELF.vertex[1].v;
2 --               IF width > height
2 --                 THEN  tempLPt.v := tempLPt.v + width - height
2 --                 ELSE  tempLPt.h := tempLPt.h - width + height;
2 --               correctedLPt := tempLPt;
2 --              {$IFC fTrace}EP;{$ENDC}
2 -0 A        END;
2 --
2 --
2 --      END;  { of TCreateSquareSelection }
2 --
2 --
2 --      { ********************************************************************************************** }
2 --
2 --                    {****************************************************************************}
2 --                    {***************     A New Window for this application     ******************}
2 --                    {****************************************************************************}
2 --
2 --      METHODS OF TQuadWindow;
2 --
2 -- A        FUNCTION  TQuadWindow.CREATE(object: TObject; heap: THeap; itsWmgrId: TWindowId): TQuadWindow;
2 --          VAR  thisList: TList;
2 0- A        BEGIN
```

```
2 1244 --          {$IFC fTrace}BP(10);{$ENDC}
2 1245 --          IF object = NIL THEN object := NewObject(heap, THISCLASS);
2 1246 --          SELF := TQuadWindow(TWindow.CREATE(object, heap, itsWmgrId, TRUE));
2 1247 --
2 1248 --          thisList := TList.CREATE(NIL, heap, 10);
2 1249 --          WITH SELF DO
2 1250 1-              BEGIN
2 1251 --                  quadList := thisList;
2 1252 --                  grPanel := NIL;
2 1253 --                  txPanel := NIL;
2 1254 --                  actions := NIL;
2 1255 -1              END;
2 1256 --          {$IFC fTrace}EP;{$ENDC}
2 1257 -0 A    END;
2 1258 --
2 1259 --      {$IFC fDebugMethods}
2 1260 -- A    PROCEDURE TQuadWindow.Fields(PROCEDURE Field(nameAndType: S255));
2 1261 0- A    BEGIN
2 1262 --          SUPERSELF.Fields(Field);
2 1263 --          Field('quadList:   TList');
2 1264 --          Field('cbPanel:    TPanel');
2 1265 --          Field('txPanel:    TPanel');
2 1266 --          Field('actions:    TPanel');
2 1267 --          Field('');
2 1268 -0 A    END;
2 1269 --      {$ENDC}
2 1270 --
2 1271 -- A    PROCEDURE TQuadWindow.Free;
2 1272 0- A    BEGIN
2 1273 --          {$IFC fTrace}BP(11);{$ENDC}
2 1274 --            SELF.quadList.DelAll(TRUE);
2 1275 --            Free(SELF.quadList);
2 1276 --            SUPERSELF.Free;
2 1277 --          {$IFC fTrace}EP;{$ENDC}
2 1278 -0 A    END;
2 1279 --
2 1280 --
2 1281 --  { Create a blank document }
2 1282 -- A    PROCEDURE  TQuadWindow.BlankStationery;
2 1283 --      VAR  docHeap:              THeap;
2 1284 --           mainPanel:            TPanel;
2 1285 --           panel:                TPanel;
2 1286 --           aGraphicalQuadView:   TQuadGrView;
2 1287 --           aTextualQuadView:     TQuadTxView;
2 1288 --           aActView:             TActView;
2 1289 --           selection:            TSelection;
2 1290 --
2 1291 0- A    BEGIN
2 1292 --          {$IFC fTrace}BP(11);{$ENDC}
2 1293 --          docHeap := SELF.heap;
2 1294 --
2 1295 --          { Make the main panel first so that it will be the selectPanel and the clickPanel }
2 1296 --          mainPanel := TPanel.CREATE(NIL, docHeap, SELF, 2*palHeight, 2*palWidth,
2 1297 --                                      [aScroll, aSplit], [aScroll, aSplit]);
2 1298 --          SELF.grPanel := mainPanel;
2 1299 --
2 1300 --          { ... and its view and selection }
2 1301 --          aGraphicalQuadView := TQuadGrView.CREATE(NIL, docHeap, mainPanel);
2 1302 --          selection := mainPanel.selection.FreedAndReplacedBy(
2 1303 --                                    TQuadGrSelection.CREATE(NIL, docHeap, aGraphicalQuadView, NIL));
2 1304 --          selection.kind := nothingKind;
2 1305 --
2 1306 --
2 1307 --          { ... and the palette panel }
2 1308 --          panel := mainPanel.Divide(h, palWidth+1, pixelsFromEdge, [], palWidth, [aScroll], [aBar]);
2 1309 --          SELF.actions := panel;
2 1310 --
2 1311 --          { ... and its view and selection }
2 1312 --          aActView := TActView.CREATE(NIL, docHeap, panel);
2 1313 --          selection := panel.selection.FreedAndReplacedBy(TPalSelection.CREATE(NIL, docHeap, aActView));
2 1314 --
2 1315 --
2 1316 --          { ... then the Text panel (about one-quarter of the horizontal space in the main panel) ... }
2 1317 --          panel := mainPanel.Divide(h, -25, percentFromEdge, [userCanResizeIt, windowCanResizeIt],
```

```
2 --                                   0, [aScroll, aSplit], [aScroll]);
2 --              SELF.txPanel := panel;
2 --
2 --              { ... and its view ... }
2 --              aTextualQuadView := TQuadTxView.CREATE(NIL, docHeap, panel);
2 --              selection := panel.selection.FreedAndReplacedBy(
2 --                                   TQuadTxSelection.CREATE(NIL, docHeap, aTextualQuadView, NIL));
2 --              selection.kind := nothingKind;
2 --
2 --              {$IFC fTrace}EP;{$ENDC}
2 -0 A        END;
2 --
2 --
2 --      { set up the state of all the menu items before the user gets to see them }
2 -- A        FUNCTION  TQuadWindow.CanDoCommand(cmdNumber: TCmdNumber; VAR checkIt: BOOLEAN): BOOLEAN;
2 0- A        BEGIN
2 --              {$IFC fTrace}BP(10);{$ENDC}
2 1-              CASE cmdNumber OF
2 --                  uClearAll:    CanDoCommand := TRUE;
2 --                  OTHERWISE     CanDoCommand := SUPERSELF.CanDoCommand(cmdNumber, checkIt);
2 -1              END;
2 --              {$IFC fTrace}EP;{$ENDC}
2 -0 A        END;
2 --
2 --
2 --      { Enumerate all of the quads that are "really" there }
2 -- A        PROCEDURE TQuadWindow.EachActualPart(PROCEDURE DoToObject(filteredObj: TObject));
2 0- A        BEGIN
2 --              {$IFC fTrace}BP(11);{$ENDC}
2 --              SELF.quadList.Each(DoToObject);
2 --              {$IFC fTrace}EP;{$ENDC}
2 -0 A        END;
2 --
2 --
2 --      { Enumerate all of the quads, even the one that may not "really" be there yet }
2 -- A        PROCEDURE TQuadWindow.EachVirtualPart(PROCEDURE DoToObject(filteredObj: TObject));
2 0- A        BEGIN
2 --              {$IFC fTrace}BP(11);{$ENDC}
2 --              SELF.SpecialFilter(NIL, DoToObject);
2 --              {$IFC fTrace}EP;{$ENDC}
2 -0 A        END;
2 --
2 --
2 --      { Check all of the quads to see if one has been changed to prepare the virtual image shown to the user }
2 -- A        PROCEDURE TQuadWindow.FilterAndDo(actualObj: TObject; PROCEDURE DoToObject(filteredObj: TObject));
2 0- A        BEGIN
2 --              {$IFC fTrace}BP(11);{$ENDC}
2 --              SELF.SpecialFilter(actualObj, DoToObject);
2 --              {$IFC fTrace}EP;{$ENDC}
2 -0 A        END;
2 --
2 --
2 -- A        PROCEDURE TQuadWindow.InvalidateQuad(quad: TQuad);
2 --          VAR
2 --               panel:          TPanel;
2 --               invalRect:      LRect;
2 0- A        BEGIN
2 --             {$IFC fTrace}BP(12);{$ENDC}
2 --              IF quad <> NIL THEN
2 1-                  BEGIN
2 --                      { Invalidate in the graphical view }
2 --                       quad.EnclosingLRect(invalRect);
2 --                       InsetLRect(invalRect, -3, -2);              { Grow the rectangle to include any }
2 --                       SELF.grPanel.InvalLRect(invalRect);         { highlighting on the quad          }
2 --
2 --                     { Invalidate in the textual view }
2 --                      SELF.txPanel.Invalidate;                     { Invalidate the entire panel so as not }
2 --                                                                   { to leave "holes" in the list of quads }
2 -1                  END;
2 --
2 --             {$IFC fTrace}EP;{$ENDC}
2 -0 A        END;
2 --
2 --
```

```
2 -- A      FUNCTION  TQuadWindow.NewCommand(cmdNumber: TCmdNumber): TCommand;
2 --        VAR  windowHeap: THeap;
2 0- A      BEGIN
2 --            {$IFC fTrace}BP(11);{$ENDC}
2 --            windowHeap := SELF.heap;
2 1-            CASE cmdNumber OF
2 --
2 --                uClearAll:         NewCommand := TClearAllCmd.CREATE(NIL, windowHeap, cmdNumber);
2 --
2 --                OTHERWISE      { The ABCs do the rest! }
2 --                    NewCommand := SUPERSELF.NewCommand(cmdNumber);
2 -1                END;
2 --            {$IFC fTrace}EP;{$ENDC}
2 -0 A      END;
2 --
2 --
2 --    { make the selection in both panels; quad = NIL means de-select; this routine does nothing if the
2 --        old and new selections are the same }
2 -- A      PROCEDURE TQuadWindow.Select(selectPanel: TPanel; quad: TQuad);
2 --        VAR
2 --          needToSelect:      BOOLEAN;         { TRUE iff old and new selections are different }
2 --          panel:             TPanel;
2 --          aQuadView:         TQuadView;
2 --          aQuadSelection:    TQuadSelection;
2 --
2 -- B        PROCEDURE SelectItInOnePanel(thePanel: TPanel);
2 0- B        BEGIN
2 --              { un-highlight the old selection }
2 --              thePanel.Highlight(thePanel.selection, hOnToOff);
2 --
2 --              aQuadView := TQuadView(thePanel.view);
2 --              IF quad = NIL THEN
2 --                  aQuadSelection := TQuadSelection(aQuadView.NoSelection)
2 --              ELSE
2 --                  aQuadSelection := TQuadSelection(aQuadView.NewSelection(quad));
2 --
2 --              aQuadSelection := TQuadSelection(thePanel.selection.FreedAndReplacedBy(aQuadSelection));
2 --
2 --              { highlight the new selection }
2 --              thePanel.Highlight(thePanel.selection, hOffToOn);
2 --
2 --              IF panel = selectPanel THEN
2 --                  panel.BeSelectPanel(TRUE);
2 -0 B        END;
2 --
2 0- A      BEGIN { TQuadWindow.Select }
2 --            {$IFC fTrace}BP(12);{$ENDC}
2 --            IF NOT InClass(SELF.selectPanel.selection, TQuadSelection) THEN
2 --                needToSelect := TRUE
2 --            ELSE
2 1-                BEGIN
2 --                    aQuadSelection := TQuadSelection(SELF.selectPanel.selection);
2 --                    aQuadSelection.MarkChanged;
2 --                    IF aQuadSelection.kind = nothingKind THEN
2 --                        needToSelect := quad <> NIL
2 --                    ELSE
2 --                        needToSelect := (quad <> aQuadSelection.quad);
2 -1                END;
2 --
2 --            IF needToSelect THEN
2 1-                BEGIN
2 --                    { First for the graphics panel }
2 --                    SelectItInOnePanel(SELF.grPanel);
2 --
2 --                    { ... then for the text panel }
2 --                    SelectItInOnePanel(SELF.txPanel);
2 -1                END;
2 --            {$IFC fTrace}EP;{$ENDC}
2 -0 A      END;
2 --
2 --
2 --    { Communicate with the actions palette }
2 -- A      PROCEDURE TQuadWindow.SetAction(action: INTEGER; doHilite: BOOLEAN);
2 --            VAR actPanel:       TPanel;
```

```
2 0- A     BEGIN
2 --           {$IFC fTrace}BP(11);{$ENDC}
2 --           actPanel := SELF.actions;
2 --
2 --           IF (action >= symArrow) AND (action <= symSquare)
2 --            THEN
2 --               TPalSelection(actPanel.selection).SetSelection(1, action, doHilite, FALSE, TRUE);
2 --           {$IFC fTrace}EP;{$ENDC}
2 -0 A     END;
2 --
2 --
2 --   { A special filter that can be used when the window holds the data.  Note: this corrects a deficiency
2 --     in the Toolkit routine TWindow.FilterDispatch.  That routine will not work correctly with applications
2 --     that store the data in the window, since TWindow.FilterDispatch expects the view to hold the data.   }
2 --
2 -- A     PROCEDURE TQuadWindow.SpecialFilter(actualObj: TObject; PROCEDURE DoToObject(filteredObj: TObject));
2 --       VAR  filterCommand: TCommand;
2 --            filtering:     BOOLEAN;
2 0- A     BEGIN
2 --           {$IFC fTrace}BP(11);{$ENDC}
2 --           filterCommand := SELF.lastCmd;
2 --
2 --           filtering := FALSE;
2 --           IF filterCommand <> NIL THEN
2 --               IF filterCommand.doing THEN
2 --                   filtering := TRUE;
2 --
2 --           IF filtering THEN
2 --               IF actualObj <> NIL THEN                           { This call to SpecialFilter came from  }
2 --                   filterCommand.FilterAndDo(actualObj, DoToObject) { FilterAndDo, thus call the         }
2 --                                                                  { command's FilterAndDo method.        }
2 --                ELSE                                              { This call to SpecialFilter came from  }
2 --                   filterCommand.EachVirtualPart(DoToObject)      { EachVirtualPat, thus call the         }
2 --                                                                  { command's EachVirtualPart method.    }
2 --           ELSE   { No filtering }
2 --               IF actualObj <> NIL THEN                          { The null filter - Everything goes thru }
2 --                   DoToObject(actualObj)
2 --               ELSE                                              { There are no virtual objects, so just }
2 --                   SELF.EachActualPart(DoToObject);              { get the actual ones.                 }
2 --
2 --           {$IFC fTrace}EP;{$ENDC}
2 -0 A     END;
2 --
2 --
2 --   END;  { of TQuadWindow methods }
2 --
2 --   { ******************************************************************************************************* }
2 --
2 --                 {*************************************************************************}
2 --                 {************      A New Palette View for this application      ***************}
2 --                 {*************************************************************************}
2 --
2 --   METHODS OF TActView;
2 --
2 -- A     FUNCTION  TActView.CREATE(object: TObject; itsHeap: THeap; itsPanel: TPanel): TActView;
2 0- A     BEGIN
2 --           {$IFC fTrace}BP(10);{$ENDC}
2 --           IF object = NIL THEN object := NewObject(itsHeap, THISCLASS);
2 --           SELF := TActView(TPalView.CREATE(object, itsHeap, itsPanel, palWidth, palHeight, 1, 6));
2 --           SELF.extentLRect.bottom := 500;       { increase view height so rest of palette will be white }
2 --           {$IFC fTrace}EP;{$ENDC}
2 -0 A     END;
2 --
2 --       {$IFC fDebugMethods}
2 -- A     PROCEDURE TActView.Fields(PROCEDURE Field(nameAndType: S255));
2 0- A     BEGIN
2 --           SUPERSELF.Fields(Field);
2 --           Field('');
2 -0 A     END;
2 --       {$ENDC}
2 --
2 -- A     PROCEDURE TActView.DrawSymbol(atCol, atRow: INTEGER);
```

```
2 --        VAR lr:      LRect;
2 --            r:       Rect;
2 --            bounds: Rect;
2 --
2 -- B          PROCEDURE DrawOneSymbol(symBitMap: BitMap);
2 0- B          BEGIN
2 --                SELF.GetBoxLRect(atCol, atRow, lr);
2 --                thePad.lRectToRect(lr, r);
2 --                SetRect(bounds, 0, 0, 16, 16);
2 --                OffsetRect(bounds, r.left + (LengthRect(r, h)-8) DIV 2,
2 --                                   r.top  + (LengthRect(r, v)-16) DIV 2);
2 --
2 --                CopyBits(symBitMap, thePort^.portBits, symBitMap.bounds, bounds, srcOr, NIL);
2 -0 B          END;
2 --
2 0- A      BEGIN
2 --            {$IFC fTrace}BP(12);{$ENDC}
2 1-            CASE atRow OF
2 --                symArrow:         DrawOneSymbol(arwBitMap);
2 --                symQuad:          DrawOneSymbol(quadBitMap);
2 --                symParallelogram: DrawOneSymbol(parallelogramBitMap);
2 --                symRhombus:       DrawOneSymbol(rhombusBitMap);
2 --                symRectangle:     DrawOneSymbol(rectBitMap);
2 --                symSquare:        DrawOneSymbol(squareBitMap);
2 -1            END;
2 --
2 --            {$IFC fTrace}EP;{$ENDC}
2 -0 A      END;
2 --
2 --
2 -- A      PROCEDURE TActView.MouseRelease;
2 --        VAR panel:          TPanel;
2 --            palSelection:   TPalSelection;
2 --            selectedSymbol: INTEGER;
2 --            theQuadWindow:  TQuadWindow;
2 --            newSelection:   TCreateQuadSelection;
2 --            viewHeap:       THeap;
2 --            aQuadGrView:    TQuadGrView;
2 --            aSelection:     TSelection;
2 --
2 0- A      BEGIN
2 --            {$IFC fTrace}BP(12);{$ENDC}
2 --            panel := SELF.panel;
2 --            palSelection := TPalSelection(panel.selection);
2 --            palSelection.MouseRelease;
2 --            selectedSymbol := palSelection.selRow;
2 --            viewHeap := SELF.heap;
2 --            theQuadWindow := TQuadWindow(panel.window);
2 --            aQuadGrView := TQuadGrView(theQuadWindow.grPanel.view);
2 --
2 --            IF (selectedSymbol  >= symQuad) AND (selectedSymbol <= symSquare)
2 --                 THEN     { The user wants to draw another quad }
2 1-                    BEGIN
2 --                       { Deselect any currently selected quad }
2 --                        theQuadWindow.Select(theQuadWindow.grPanel, NIL);
2 --
2 --                       { Create an appropriate instance of TCreateQuadSelection or one of its subclasses }
2 2-                        CASE selectedSymbol OF
2 --                            symQuad:            newSelection := TCreateQuadSelection.CREATE(NIL,
2 --                                                                          viewHeap, aQuadGrView, zeroLPt);
2 --                            symParallelogram:   newSelection := TCreateParallelogramSelection.CREATE(NIL,
2 --                                                                          viewHeap, aQuadGrView, zeroLPt);
2 --                            symRhombus:         newSelection := TCreateRhombusSelection.CREATE(NIL,
2 --                                                                          viewHeap, aQuadGrView, zeroLPt);
2 --                            symRectangle:       newSelection := TCreateTangleSelection.CREATE(NIL,
2 --                                                                          viewHeap, aQuadGrView, zeroLPt);
2 --                            symSquare:          newSelection := TCreateSquareSelection.CREATE(NIL,
2 --                                                                          viewHeap, aQuadGrView, zeroLPt);
2 -2                        END;
2 --
2 --                        aSelection := theQuadWindow.grPanel.selection.FreedAndReplacedBy(newSelection);
2 -1                    END
2 --
```

```
                ELSE  { The selection arrow has been chosen in the palette.  Make sure the selection in
                        the graphics panel is a QuadSelection. }
                    BEGIN
                      aSelection := theQuadWindow.grPanel.selection.FreedAndReplacedBy(
                                          aQuadGrView.NoSelection);
                    END;

            {$IFC fTrace}EP;{$ENDC}
        END;

    END;  { of TActView methods }

    { ************************************************************************************************ }

                {***********************************************************************}
                {**************        New Commands for this application      ******************}
                {***********************************************************************}

    METHODS OF TAddQuadCmd;

        FUNCTION  TAddQuadCmd.CREATE(object: TObject; itsHeap: THeap; itsCmdNumber: TCmdNumber;
                                     itsQuad: TQuad): TAddQuadCmd;
        VAR  theQuadWindow: TQuadWindow;
        BEGIN
            {$IFC fTrace}BP(10);{$ENDC}
            IF object = NIL THEN object := NewObject(itsHeap, THISCLASS);
            SELF := TAddQuadCmd(TCommand.CREATE(object, itsHeap, itsCmdNumber, NIL, TRUE, revealAll));
            SELF.newQuad := itsQuad;

            theQuadWindow := TQuadWindow(currentWindow);
            theQuadWindow.Select(theQuadWindow.grPanel, itsQuad);
            theQuadWindow.SetAction(symArrow, TRUE);              { Select the arrow in the palette }
            {$IFC fTrace}EP;{$ENDC}
        END;


        {$IFC fDebugMethods}
        PROCEDURE TAddQuadCmd.Fields(PROCEDURE Field(nameAndType: S255));
        BEGIN
            TCommand.Fields(Field);
            Field('newQuad: TQuad');
            Field('');
        END;
        {$ENDC}


        PROCEDURE TAddQuadCmd.Commit;
        VAR theQuadWindow:    TQuadWindow;
        BEGIN
            {$IFC fTrace}BP(12);{$ENDC}
            theQuadWindow := TQuadWindow(currentWindow);
            theQuadWindow.quadList.InsLast(SELF.newQuad);
            SELF.newQuad := NIL;
            {$IFC fTrace}EP;{$ENDC}
        END;


        PROCEDURE TAddQuadCmd.EachVirtualPart(PROCEDURE DoToObject(filteredObj: TObject));
        VAR  theQuadWindow: TQuadWindow;
        BEGIN
            {$IFC fTrace}BP(12);{$ENDC}
            theQuadWindow := TQuadWindow(currentWindow);
            theQuadWindow.EachActualPart(DoToObject);
            DoToObject(SELF.newQuad);
            {$IFC fTrace}EP;{$ENDC}
        END;


        PROCEDURE TAddQuadCmd.Perform(cmdPhase: TCmdPhase);
        VAR theQuadWindow:         TQuadWindow;
            thisQuadSelection:     TQuadSelection;

        BEGIN
            {$IFC fTrace}BP(12);{$ENDC}
```

```
2 1687 --            theQuadWindow := TQuadWindow(currentWindow);
2 1688 --
2 1689 --            { Fix the graphics selection }
2 1690 --            thisQuadSelection := TQuadSelection(theQuadWindow.grPanel.selection);
2 1691 --            WITH thisQuadSelection DO
2 1692 1-                CASE cmdPhase OF
2 1693 --                    doPhase, redoPhase:   kind := quadKind;
2 1694 --                    undoPhase:            kind := nothingKind;
2 1695 -1                END;  {CASE}
2 1696 --
2 1697 --            { ... and the text selection }
2 1698 --            thisQuadSelection := TQuadSelection(theQuadWindow.txPanel.selection);
2 1699 --            WITH thisQuadSelection DO
2 1700 1-                CASE cmdPhase OF
2 1701 --                    doPhase, redoPhase:   kind := quadKind;
2 1702 --                    undoPhase:            kind := nothingKind;
2 1703 -1                END;  {CASE}
2 1704 --
2 1705 --            theQuadWindow.InvalidateQuad(thisQuadSelection.quad);
2 1706 --           {$IFC fTrace}EP;{$ENDC}
2 1707 -0 A      END;
2 1708 --
2 1709 --
2 1710 --    END;    { of TAddQuadCmd Methods }
2 1711 --
2 1712 --    { ************************************************************************************************** }
2 1713 --
2 1714 --    METHODS OF TClearQuadCmd;
2 1715 --
2 1716 -- A      FUNCTION  TClearQuadCmd.CREATE(object: TObject; itsHeap: THeap;
2 1717 --                                  itsCmdNumber: TCmdNumber; itsQuad: TQuad): TClearQuadCmd;
2 1718 0- A      BEGIN
2 1719 --           {$IFC fTrace}BP(10);{$ENDC}
2 1720 --           IF object = NIL THEN object := NewObject(itsHeap, THISCLASS);
2 1721 --           SELF := TClearQuadCmd(TCommand.CREATE(object, itsHeap, itsCmdNumber, NIL, TRUE, revealNone));
2 1722 --           SELF.quad := itsQuad;
2 1723 --           {$IFC fTrace}EP;{$ENDC}
2 1724 -0 A      END;
2 1725 --
2 1726 --
2 1727 --    {$IFC fDebugMethods}
2 1728 -- A      PROCEDURE TClearQuadCmd.Fields(PROCEDURE Field(nameAndType: S255));
2 1729 0- A      BEGIN
2 1730 --           TCommand.Fields(Field);
2 1731 --           Field('quad: TQuad');
2 1732 -0 A      END;
2 1733 --     {$ENDC}
2 1734 --
2 1735 --
2 1736 -- A      PROCEDURE TClearQuadCmd.Commit;
2 1737 --        VAR theQuadWindow:    TQuadWindow;
2 1738 0- A      BEGIN
2 1739 --           {$IFC fTrace}BP(12);{$ENDC}
2 1740 --           theQuadWindow := TQuadWindow(currentWindow);
2 1741 --           theQuadWindow.Select(theQuadWindow.grPanel, NIL);
2 1742 --           theQuadWindow.quadList.DelObject(SELF.quad, TRUE);
2 1743 --           {$IFC fTrace}EP;{$ENDC}
2 1744 -0 A      END;
2 1745 --
2 1746 --
2 1747 -- A      PROCEDURE TClearQuadCmd.EachVirtualPart(PROCEDURE DoToObject(filteredObj: TObject));
2 1748 --        VAR  theQuadWindow: TQuadWindow;
2 1749 --
2 1750 -- B          PROCEDURE DoToFilteredObject(actualObj: TObject);
2 1751 0- B          BEGIN
2 1752 --                SELF.FilterAndDo(actualObject, DoToObject);
2 1753 -0 B          END;
2 1754 --
2 1755 0- A      BEGIN
2 1756 --           {$IFC fTrace}BP(12);{$ENDC}
2 1757 --           theQuadWindow := TQuadWindow(currentWindow);
2 1758 --           theQuadWindow.EachActualPart(DoToFilteredObject);
2 1759 --           {$IFC fTrace}EP;{$ENDC}
2 1760 -0 A      END;
```

```
2 --
2 --
2 -- A     PROCEDURE TClearQuadCmd.FilterAndDo(actualObj: TObject; PROCEDURE DoToObject(filteredObj: TObject));
2 --           VAR quad: TQuad;
2 0- A     BEGIN
2 --           {$IFC fTrace}BP(12);{$ENDC}
2 --               quad := TQuad(actualObj);
2 --               IF quad <> SELF.quad      { Allow everything except the cleared quad to pass thru the filter }
2 --                   THEN DoToObject(quad);
2 --           {$IFC fTrace}EP;{$ENDC}
2 -0 A     END;
2 --
2 --
2 -- A     PROCEDURE TClearQuadCmd.Perform(cmdPhase: TCmdPhase);
2 --       VAR thisSelection:  TSelection;
2 --           theQuadWindow:  TQuadWindow;
2 --
2 -- B         PROCEDURE PerformInPanel(panel: TPanel);
2 0- B         BEGIN
2 --               thisSelection := panel.selection;
2 --
2 --               WITH thisSelection DO
2 1-                  CASE cmdPhase OF
2 --                       doPhase, redoPhase:    kind := nothingKind;
2 --                       undoPhase:             kind := quadKind;
2 -1                  END;
2 -0 B         END;
2 --
2 0- A     BEGIN
2 --           {$IFC fTrace}BP(12);{$ENDC}
2 --           {Recall that the quad to be deleted is also the quad stored in the current selection.  Make sure
2 --            that the selection will not show up when the quad is invalidated. }
2 --           theQuadWindow := TQuadWindow(currentWindow);
2 --           PerformInPanel(theQuadWindow.grPanel);
2 --           PerformInPanel(theQuadWindow.txPanel);
2 --           theQuadWindow.InvalidateQuad(SELF.quad);
2 --           {$IFC fTrace}EP;{$ENDC}
2 -0 A     END;
2 --
2 --   END;  { of TClearQuadCmd methods }
2 --
2 --   { ************************************************************************************************ }
2 --
2 --   METHODS OF TClearAllCmd;
2 --
2 -- A     FUNCTION  TClearAllCmd.CREATE(object: TObject; itsHeap: THeap;
2 --                                                 itsCmdNumber: TCmdNumber): TClearAllCmd;
2 --       VAR  theQuadWindow: TQuadWindow;
2 0- A     BEGIN
2 --           {$IFC fTrace}BP(10);{$ENDC}
2 --           IF object = NIL THEN object := NewObject(itsHeap, THISCLASS);
2 --           SELF := TClearAllCmd(TCommand.CREATE(object, itsHeap, itsCmdNumber, NIL, TRUE, revealNone));
2 --           theQuadWindow := TQuadWindow(currentWindow);
2 --           SELF.kind := theQuadWindow.grPanel.selection.kind;
2 --           {$IFC fTrace}EP;{$ENDC}
2 -0 A     END;
2 --
2 --
2 --    {$IFC fDebugMethods}
2 -- A     PROCEDURE TClearAllCmd.Fields(PROCEDURE Field(nameAndType: S255));
2 0- A     BEGIN
2 --           TCommand.Fields(Field);
2 --           Field('kind: INTEGER');
2 -0 A     END;
2 --     {$ENDC}
2 --
2 --
2 -- A     PROCEDURE TClearAllCmd.Commit;
2 --       VAR theQuadWindow:    TQuadWindow;
2 0- A     BEGIN
2 --           {$IFC fTrace}BP(12);{$ENDC}
2 --           theQuadWindow := TQuadWindow(currentWindow);
2 --           theQuadWindow.quadList.DelAll(TRUE);
2 --           theQuadWindow.Select(theQuadWindow.grPanel, NIL);
```

```
        {$IFC fTrace}EP;{$ENDC}
    END;


    PROCEDURE TClearAllCmd.EachVirtualPart(PROCEDURE DoToObject(filteredObj: TObject));
    BEGIN
        {$IFC fTrace}BP(12);{$ENDC}
          { There are no quads in the vitrual document after a clear all!! }
        {$IFC fTrace}EP;{$ENDC}
    END;


    PROCEDURE TClearAllCmd.Perform(cmdPhase: TCmdPhase);
    VAR thisSelection:  TSelection;
        theQuadWindow:  TQuadWindow;

        PROCEDURE PerformInPanel(panel: TPanel);
        BEGIN
            thisSelection := panel.selection;

            WITH thisSelection DO
               CASE cmdPhase OF
                   doPhase, redoPhase:     kind := nothingKind;
                   undoPhase:              kind := SELF.kind;
               END;

            { Invalidate the whole panel }
            panel.Invalidate;
        END;

    BEGIN
        {$IFC fTrace}BP(12);{$ENDC}
        theQuadWindow := TQuadWindow(currentWindow);
        PerformInPanel(theQuadWindow.grPanel);
        PerformInPanel(theQuadWindow.txPanel);
        {$IFC fTrace}EP;{$ENDC}
    END;


END;  { of TClearAllCmd methods }

{ ************************************************************************************************ }

METHODS OF TRotateQuadCmd;

    { Note that there is no need to do filtering for this command.  Undo is implemented by just
      rotating back the affected quad }

    FUNCTION  TRotateQuadCmd.CREATE(object: TObject; itsHeap: THeap;
                                    itsCmdNumber: TCmdNumber;
                                    itsQuad: TQuad;
                                    itsAngle: REAL): TRotateQuadCmd;
    BEGIN
        {$IFC fTrace}BP(10);{$ENDC}
        IF object = NIL THEN object := NewObject(itsHeap, THISCLASS);

        SELF := TRotateQuadCmd(TCommand.CREATE(object, itsHeap, itsCmdNumber, NIL, TRUE, revealAll));
        WITH SELF DO
            BEGIN
            quad := itsQuad;
            angle := itsAngle;
            END;
        {$IFC fTrace}EP;{$ENDC}
    END;


    {$IFC fDebugMethods}
    PROCEDURE TRotateQuadCmd.Fields(PROCEDURE Field(nameAndType: S255));
    BEGIN
        SUPERSELF.Fields(Field);
        Field('quad:          TQuad');
        Field('angle:        REAL');
        Field('');
    END;
```

```
      {$ENDC}


   PROCEDURE TRotateQuadCmd.Perform(cmdPhase: TCmdPhase);
   VAR theQuadWindow:     TQuadWindow;
   BEGIN
       {$IFC fTrace}BP(12);{$ENDC}
       theQuadWindow := TQuadWindow(currentWindow);
        theQuadWindow.InvalidateQuad(SELF.quad);        { Invalidate before rotating }

       CASE cmdPhase OF
            doPhase, redoPhase:  SELF.quad.RotateBy(SELF.angle);
            undoPhase:           SELF.quad.RotateBy(-SELF.angle);
         END;

        {Invalidate the quad }
        theQuadWindow.InvalidateQuad(SELF.quad);        { Invalidate after rotating }
      {$IFC fTrace}EP;{$ENDC}
   END;


END;  { of TRotateQuadCmd methods }

{ *************************************************************************************************** }

             {*********************************************************************}
             {**********     New BoilerPlate Classes for this application     ************}
             {*********************************************************************}

METHODS OF TQuadProcess;

{ Required boiler plate }
   FUNCTION  TQuadProcess.CREATE;
   BEGIN
       {$IFC fTrace}BP(11);{$ENDC}
       SELF := TQuadProcess(TProcess.CREATE(NewObject(mainHeap, THISCLASS), mainHeap));
       {$IFC fTrace}EP;{$ENDC}
   END;


{ Required boiler plate }
   FUNCTION  TQuadProcess.NewDocManager(volumePrefix: TFilePath; openAsTool: BOOLEAN): TDocManager;
   BEGIN
       {$IFC fTrace}BP(11);{$ENDC}
        IF openAsTool THEN
          NewDocManager := NIL
         ELSE
          NewDocManager := TQuadDocManager.CREATE(NIL, mainHeap, volumePrefix);
       {$IFC fTrace}EP;{$ENDC}
   END;


{ Initialize the symbols used in the palette }
   PROCEDURE TQuadProcess.Commence(phraseVersion: INTEGER);

        PROCEDURE FillBitMap(dataPointer: QDPtr; VAR thisBitMap: BitMap);
        BEGIN
            WITH thisBitMap DO
                BEGIN
                rowBytes := 2;
                SetRect(bounds, 0, 0, 16, 16);
                baseAddr := dataPointer;
                END;
        END;

   BEGIN
     {$IFC fTrace}BP(10);{$ENDC}
     SUPERSELF.Commence(phraseVersion);

     { Set the images for all the ideal quadrilaterals.  Recall that all are 16-by-16 bit rectangles
       and thus each requires 64 hex digits for its full definition.  StuffHex is a QuickDraw routine. }
                                    {0        1         2         3         4         5         6    }
                                    {1234567890123456789012345678901234567890123456789012345678901234}
       StuffHex(@idealQuad,         '8000A003501A4C6243042008201020101020104010800880090000A0004000400');
```

```
            StuffHex(@idealParallelogram, '01FF0101020202020404040408080808101010102020202040404040408080FF80');
            StuffHex(@idealRhombus,       '0000000000001FFF100120022002400440044004800 8FFF80000000000000000');
            StuffHex(@idealRectangle,     'FFFF80018001800180018001800180018001800180018001800180018001FFFF');
            StuffHex(@idealSquare,        '00000000FFFF8001800180018001800180018001800180 01FFFF000000000000');

           { Build the arrow bitmap using the arrow cursor bitmap supplied by QuickDraw }
            FillBitMap(@arrow.data, arwBitMap);

           { Build the rest from the definitions stored above }
            FillBitMap(@idealQuad, quadBitMap);
            FillBitMap(@idealParallelogram, parallelogramBitMap);
            FillBitMap(@idealRhombus, rhombusBitMap);
            FillBitMap(@idealRectangle, rectBitMap);
            FillBitMap(@idealSquare, squareBitMap);

           {$IFC fTrace}EP;{$ENDC}
        END;


    END;  { of TQuadProcess Methods }

    { *********************************************************************************************** }

    METHODS OF TQuadDocManager;

    { Required boiler plate}
        FUNCTION  TQuadDocManager.CREATE(object: TObject; heap: THeap;
                                             itsPathPrefix: TFilePath): TQuadDocManager;
        BEGIN
            {$IFC fTrace}BP(11);{$ENDC}
            IF object = NIL THEN object := NewObject(heap, THISCLASS);
            SELF := TQuadDocManager(TDocManager.CREATE(object, heap, itsPathPrefix));
            {$IFC fTrace}EP;{$ENDC}
        END;


    { Required boiler plate}
        FUNCTION  TQuadDocManager.NewWindow(heap: THeap; WmgrId: TWindowId): TWindow;
        BEGIN
            {$IFC fTrace}BP(11);{$ENDC}
            NewWindow := TQuadWindow.CREATE(NIL, heap, WmgrId);
            {$IFC fTrace}EP;{$ENDC}
        END;


    END;  { of TQuadDocManager }


    END.
```

```
 1. UQuadWorld.TEXT
 2. UQuadWorld2.TEXT

-A-
 aActView          1288*( 2) 1312=( 2) 1313 ( 2)
 aBar              1308 ( 2)
 ABSTRACT           171*( 1)  175*( 1)
 aCreateParallelo   211*( 2)  214=( 2)  216 ( 2)
 aCreateQuadSelec    90*( 2)   93=( 2)   94 ( 2)
 aCreateRectangle   311*( 2)  314=( 2)  315 ( 2)
 aCreateRhombusSe   261*( 2)  264=( 2)  265 ( 2)
 aCreateSquareSel   361*( 2)  364=( 2)  365 ( 2)
 action             378*( 1) 1464*( 2) 1470 ( 2) 1470 ( 2) 1472 ( 2)
 actions            362*( 1) 1254=( 2) 1309=( 2) 1468 ( 2)
 actPanel          1465*( 2) 1468=( 2) 1472 ( 2)
 actualObj          383*( 1)  385*( 1)  473*( 1) 1362*( 2) 1365 ( 2) 1481*( 2) 1494 ( 2) 1495 ( 2) 1503 ( 2) 1504 ( 2)
                   1750*( 2) 1763*( 2) 1767 ( 2)
 actualObject      1752 ( 2)
 AddCmdNumber        93*( 1)  111*( 1)  123*( 1)  133 ( 1)  144 ( 1)   57*( 2)   60=( 2)  194*( 2)  197=( 2)  244*( 2)
                    247=( 2)  294*( 2)  297=( 2)  344*( 2)  347=( 2)  996 ( 2)
 aGraphicalQuadVi  1286*( 2) 1301=( 2) 1303 ( 2)
 anchorLPt          972=( 2)
 angle              448*( 1) 1895=( 2) 1920 ( 2) 1921 ( 2)
```

```
  itsQuad          235*( 1)  253*( 1)  266*( 1)  432*( 1)  452*( 1)  469*( 1)  699*( 2)  705 ( 2)  765*( 2)  770 ( 2)
                   773 ( 2)  818*( 2)  823 ( 2)  826 ( 2)  948*( 2) 1634*( 2) 1640 ( 2) 1643 ( 2) 1717*( 2) 1722 ( 2)
                  1885*( 2) 1894 ( 2)
  itsView          234*( 1)  253*( 1)  266*( 1)  284*( 1)  302*( 1)  314*( 1)  328*( 1)  342*( 1)  698*( 2)  704 ( 2)
                   764*( 2)  773 ( 2)  817*( 2)  826 ( 2)  874*( 2)  881 ( 2) 1030*( 2) 1038 ( 2) 1070*( 2) 1078 ( 2)
                  1126*( 2) 1134 ( 2) 1197*( 2) 1205 ( 2)
  itsWmgrId        366*( 1) 1241*( 2) 1246 ( 2)

-K-
  kind             485 ( 1)  726 ( 2)  801 ( 2)  836 ( 2) 1042=( 2) 1083=( 2) 1139=( 2) 1210=( 2) 1304=( 2) 1325=( 2)
                  1445 ( 2) 1693=( 2) 1694=( 2) 1701=( 2) 1702=( 2) 1784=( 2) 1785=( 2) 1814=( 2) 1814 ( 2) 1857=( 2)
                  1858=( 2) 1858 ( 2)

-L-
  lastCmd         1486 ( 2)
  lastVertexSet    281*( 1)  884=( 2)  928 ( 2)  928 ( 2)  953 ( 2)  976=( 2)  993 ( 2) 1018=( 2) 1018 ( 2) 1019 ( 2)
                  1053 ( 2) 1058=( 2) 1105 ( 2) 1179=( 2)
  leading          553 ( 2)  554 ( 2)
  left             605 ( 2)  680=( 2)  680 ( 2) 1549 ( 2)
  LengthRect      1549 ( 2) 1550 ( 2)
  lineAscent       203*( 1)  554=( 2)  605 ( 2)
  lineHeight       202 ( 1)  553=( 2)  556 ( 2)  681 ( 2)  683 ( 2)
  LineToL          476 ( 2)  929 ( 2)
  LONGINT          101 ( 2)
  longStr          536*( 2)  549=( 2)  555 ( 2)
  LPoint            87 ( 1)   95 ( 1)  101 ( 1)  165 ( 1)  166 ( 1)  175 ( 1)  193 ( 1)  221 ( 1)  280 ( 1)  285 ( 1)
                   288 ( 1)  288 ( 1)  289 ( 1)  290 ( 1)  292 ( 1)  302 ( 1)  305 ( 1)  315 ( 1)  318 ( 1)  319 ( 1)
                   329 ( 1)  332 ( 1)  333 ( 1)  343 ( 1)  346 ( 1)  347 ( 1)   73 ( 2)   75 ( 2)  105 ( 2)  127 ( 2)
                   144 ( 2)  146 ( 2)  147 ( 2)  401 ( 2)  409 ( 2)  473 ( 2)  501 ( 2)  614 ( 2)  875 ( 2)  911 ( 2)
                   911 ( 2)  919 ( 2)  920 ( 2)  921 ( 2)  947 ( 2) 1010 ( 2) 1031 ( 2) 1046 ( 2) 1047 ( 2) 1071 ( 2)
                  1088 ( 2) 1088 ( 2) 1089 ( 2) 1092 ( 2) 1127 ( 2) 1143 ( 2) 1144 ( 2) 1145 ( 2) 1174 ( 2) 1175 ( 2)
                  1198 ( 2) 1214 ( 2) 1214 ( 2) 1215 ( 2)
  lPt              175*( 1)  193*( 1)  221*( 1)  501*( 2)  509 ( 2)  614*( 2)  622 ( 2)
  LPtMinusLPt      159 ( 2)  936 ( 2) 1055 ( 2) 1163 ( 2)
  LPtPlusLPt      1056 ( 2) 1113 ( 2)
  LPtToQuad        175*( 1)  193*( 1)  221*( 1)  421 ( 2)  501*( 2)  614*( 2)
  lr              1540*( 2) 1546 ( 2) 1547 ( 2)
  LRect             98 ( 1)  161 ( 1)  215 ( 1)   99 ( 2)  102 ( 2)  380 ( 2)  448 ( 2)  471 ( 2)  502 ( 2)  593 ( 2)
                   618 ( 2)  655 ( 2)  780 ( 2)  784 ( 2)  832 ( 2) 1149 ( 2) 1373 ( 2) 1540 ( 2)
  LRectHasLPt      509 ( 2)  622 ( 2)
  LRectIsVisible   483 ( 2)  603 ( 2)  805 ( 2)  846 ( 2)
  lRectToRect     1547 ( 2)

-M-
  mainHeap        1944 ( 2) 1944 ( 2) 1956 ( 2)
  mainPanel       1284*( 2) 1296=( 2) 1298 ( 2) 1301 ( 2) 1302 ( 2) 1308 ( 2) 1317 ( 2)
  MarkChanged     1444 ( 2)
  Max              109 ( 2)  110 ( 2)
  maxBottom        101*( 2)  110=( 2)  110 ( 2)  116=( 2)  120 ( 2)
  maxQuad           38*( 1)   81 ( 1)  556 ( 2)  963 ( 2)
  maxRight         101*( 2)  109=( 2)  109 ( 2)  116=( 2)  120 ( 2)
  Min              107 ( 2)  108 ( 2)
  minLeft          101*( 2)  107=( 2)  107 ( 2)  115=( 2)  120 ( 2)
  minTop           101*( 2)  108=( 2)  108 ( 2)  115=( 2)  120 ( 2)
  MouseConstrain   288*( 1)  318*( 1)  346*( 1)  911*( 2)  935 ( 2) 1088*( 2) 1162 ( 2) 1214*( 2)
  mouseLPt         165*( 1)  166*( 1)  288*( 1)  289*( 1)  290*( 1)  318*( 1)  332*( 1)  346*( 1)  401*( 2)  404 ( 2)
                   409*( 2)  421 ( 2)  427 ( 2)  911*( 2)  914 ( 2)  919*( 2)  935 ( 2)  947*( 2)  956 ( 2)  972 ( 2)
                   973 ( 2)  975 ( 2) 1088*( 2) 1103 ( 2) 1108 ( 2) 1109 ( 2) 1110 ( 2) 1143*( 2) 1162 ( 2) 1214*( 2)
                  1219 ( 2)
  MouseMove        165*( 1)  289*( 1)  332*( 1)  401*( 2)  919*( 2)  956 ( 2) 1143*( 2)
  MousePress       166*( 1)  290*( 1)  404 ( 2)  409*( 2)  427 ( 2)  947*( 2)
  MouseRelease     291*( 1)  414*( 1)  983*( 2) 1570*( 2) 1584 ( 2)
  MoveToL          475 ( 2)  605 ( 2)  928 ( 2)

-N-
  nameAndType       48*( 2)  186*( 2)  236*( 2)  286*( 2)  336*( 2)  392*( 2)  459*( 2)  564*( 2)  710*( 2)  891*( 2)
                  1260*( 2) 1532*( 2) 1650*( 2) 1728*( 2) 1820*( 2) 1902*( 2)
  needToSelect    1412*( 2) 1440=( 2) 1446=( 2) 1448=( 2) 1451 ( 2)
  newCmdNumber     984*( 2)  996=( 2) 1001 ( 2)
  NewCommand       243*( 1)  374*( 1)  736*( 2)  740=( 2)  745=( 2)  748=( 2)  752=( 2)  752 ( 2) 1392*( 2) 1399=( 2)
                  1402=( 2) 1402 ( 2)
  NewDocManager    507*( 1) 1950*( 2) 1954=( 2) 1956=( 2)
  NewObject         37 ( 2)  179 ( 2)  229 ( 2)  279 ( 2)  329 ( 2)  384 ( 2)  451 ( 2)  540 ( 2)  702 ( 2)  769 ( 2)
```

```
thePad            1547 ( 2)
thePanel          1417*( 2) 1420 ( 2) 1420 ( 2) 1422 ( 2) 1428 ( 2) 1431 ( 2) 1431 ( 2)
thePort           1552 ( 2)
theQuadWindow      922*( 2)  934=( 2)  939 ( 2)  941 ( 2)  949*( 2)  962=( 2)  963 ( 2)  985*( 2)  989=( 2) 1001 ( 2)
                  1146*( 2) 1161=( 2) 1166 ( 2) 1168 ( 2) 1574*( 2) 1587=( 2) 1588 ( 2) 1594 ( 2) 1594 ( 2) 1610 ( 2)
                  1616 ( 2) 1635*( 2) 1642=( 2) 1643 ( 2) 1643 ( 2) 1644 ( 2) 1660*( 2) 1663=( 2) 1664 ( 2) 1671*( 2)
                  1674=( 2) 1675 ( 2) 1682*( 2) 1687=( 2) 1690 ( 2) 1698 ( 2) 1705 ( 2) 1737*( 2) 1740=( 2) 1741 ( 2)
                  1741 ( 2) 1742 ( 2) 1748*( 2) 1757=( 2) 1758 ( 2) 1776*( 2) 1793=( 2) 1794 ( 2) 1795 ( 2) 1796 ( 2)
                  1808*( 2) 1813=( 2) 1814 ( 2) 1829*( 2) 1832=( 2) 1833 ( 2) 1834 ( 2) 1834 ( 2) 1849*( 2) 1867=( 2)
                  1868 ( 2) 1869 ( 2) 1913*( 2) 1916=( 2) 1917 ( 2) 1925 ( 2)
theSelection       412*( 2)  416=( 2)  418 ( 2)
theta              102*( 1)  142*( 2)  154 ( 2)  155 ( 2)
THighTransit       256 ( 1)  269 ( 1)  779 ( 2)  831 ( 2)
thisBitMap        1964*( 2) 1966 ( 2)
thisBox            618*( 2)  621 ( 2)  622 ( 2)
THISCLASS           37 ( 2)  179 ( 2)  229 ( 2)  279 ( 2)  329 ( 2)  384 ( 2)  451 ( 2)  540 ( 2)  702 ( 2)  769 ( 2)
                   822 ( 2)  880 ( 2) 1036 ( 2) 1076 ( 2) 1132 ( 2) 1203 ( 2) 1245 ( 2) 1525 ( 2) 1638 ( 2) 1720 ( 2)
                  1811 ( 2) 1889 ( 2) 1944 ( 2) 2013 ( 2)
thisIndex          656*( 2)  665=( 2)  670=( 2)  674 ( 2)  675=( 2)  681 ( 2)
thisKind           766*( 2)  771=( 2)  772=( 2)  773 ( 2)  819*( 2)  824=( 2)  825=( 2)  826 ( 2)
thisList          1242*( 2) 1248=( 2) 1251 ( 2)
thisLRect          471*( 2)  481 ( 2)  483 ( 2)  502*( 2)  508 ( 2)  509 ( 2)
thisPanel          411*( 2)  415=( 2)  416 ( 2)  422 ( 2)
thisPoint           75*( 2)   80 ( 2)   81 ( 2)   83 ( 2)
thisQuad           410*( 2)  421 ( 2)  422 ( 2)  423 ( 2)  617*( 2)  620=( 2)  621 ( 2)  623 ( 2)  660*( 2)  662=( 2)
                   664 ( 2)
thisQuadSelectio  1683*( 2) 1690=( 2) 1691 ( 2) 1698=( 2) 1699 ( 2) 1705 ( 2)
thisRect           102*( 2)  120 ( 2)  121 ( 2)
thisSelection     1775*( 2) 1780=( 2) 1782 ( 2) 1848*( 2) 1853=( 2) 1855 ( 2)
TList              357 ( 1) 1242 ( 2) 1248 ( 2)
TObject             84 ( 1)   90 ( 1)  110 ( 1)  122 ( 1)  134 ( 1)  145 ( 1)  161 ( 1)  184 ( 1)  206 ( 1)  234 ( 1)
                   252 ( 1)  265 ( 1)  284 ( 1)  301 ( 1)  314 ( 1)  328 ( 1)  342 ( 1)  365 ( 1)  381 ( 1)  382 ( 1)
                   383 ( 1)  384 ( 1)  385 ( 1)  386 ( 1)  407 ( 1)  431 ( 1)  437 ( 1)  451 ( 1)  468 ( 1)  473 ( 1)
                   474 ( 1)  475 ( 1)  488 ( 1)  494 ( 1)  518 ( 1)   32 ( 2)  176 ( 2)  226 ( 2)  276 ( 2)  326 ( 2)
                   380 ( 2)  446 ( 2)  469 ( 2)  504 ( 2)  535 ( 2)  577 ( 2)  616 ( 2)  659 ( 2)  698 ( 2)  764 ( 2)
                   817 ( 2)  874 ( 2) 1030 ( 2) 1070 ( 2) 1126 ( 2) 1197 ( 2) 1241 ( 2) 1344 ( 2) 1353 ( 2) 1362 ( 2)
                  1362 ( 2) 1481 ( 2) 1481 ( 2) 1522 ( 2) 1633 ( 2) 1670 ( 2) 1716 ( 2) 1747 ( 2) 1750 ( 2) 1763 ( 2)
                  1763 ( 2) 1806 ( 2) 1839 ( 2) 1883 ( 2) 2009 ( 2)
top                605 ( 2)  681=( 2)  683 ( 2) 1550 ( 2)
topLeft           1153=( 2)
TPalSelection     1313 ( 2) 1472 ( 2) 1572 ( 2) 1583 ( 2)
TPalView           404 ( 1) 1526 ( 2)
TPanel             162 ( 1)  184 ( 1)  206 ( 1)  360 ( 1)  361 ( 1)  362 ( 1)  393 ( 1)  407 ( 1)  381 ( 2)  411 ( 2)
                   446 ( 2)  535 ( 2) 1284 ( 2) 1285 ( 2) 1296 ( 2) 1372 ( 2) 1410 ( 2) 1413 ( 2) 1417 ( 2) 1465 ( 2)
                  1522 ( 2) 1571 ( 2) 1778 ( 2) 1851 ( 2)
TParallelogram     107*( 1)  110 ( 1)  110 ( 1)  111*( 1)  112*( 1)  113*( 1)  119 ( 1)  130 ( 1)  174*( 2)  176*( 2)
                   176 ( 2)  180 ( 2)  186*( 2)  194*( 2)  202*( 2)  210*( 2)  230 ( 2)  280 ( 2) 1033 ( 2) 1040 ( 2)
TPrintManager      386 ( 2)
TProcess           502 ( 1) 1944 ( 2)
TQuad               84*( 1)   90*( 1)   90 ( 1)   93*( 1)   94*( 1)   95*( 1)   96*( 1)   98*( 1)  101*( 1)  102*( 1)
                   107 ( 1)  171 ( 1)  175 ( 1)  190 ( 1)  193 ( 1)  209 ( 1)  214 ( 1)  215 ( 1)  221 ( 1)  231 ( 1)
                   235 ( 1)  253 ( 1)  266 ( 1)  279 ( 1)  391 ( 1)  393 ( 1)  428 ( 1)  432 ( 1)  447 ( 1)  452 ( 1)
                   465 ( 1)  469 ( 1)   30*( 2)   32*( 2)   32 ( 2)   38 ( 2)   48*( 2)   57*( 2)   65*( 2)   73*( 2)
                    89*( 2)   99*( 2)  127*( 2)  142*( 2)  180 ( 2)  410 ( 2)  470 ( 2)  480 ( 2)  501 ( 2)  505 ( 2)
                   507 ( 2)  521 ( 2)  578 ( 2)  580 ( 2)  592 ( 2)  614 ( 2)  617 ( 2)  620 ( 2)  634 ( 2)  655 ( 2)
                   660 ( 2)  662 ( 2)  699 ( 2)  765 ( 2)  782 ( 2)  818 ( 2)  877 ( 2)  885 ( 2)  948 ( 2)  986 ( 2)
                  1370 ( 2) 1410 ( 2) 1634 ( 2) 1717 ( 2) 1764 ( 2) 1767 ( 2) 1885 ( 2)
TQuadDocManager    515*( 1)  518 ( 1)  519 ( 1)  520*( 1) 1956 ( 2) 2006*( 2) 2009*( 2) 2010 ( 2) 2014 ( 2) 2020*( 2)
TQuadGrSelection   249*( 1)  252 ( 1)  253 ( 1)  256*( 1)  524 ( 2)  762*( 2)  764*( 2)  765 ( 2)  773 ( 2)  779*( 2)
                  1303 ( 2)
TQuadGrView         97 ( 1)  114 ( 1)  125 ( 1)  136 ( 1)  147 ( 1)  181*( 1)  184 ( 1)  184 ( 1)  187*( 1)  190*( 1)
                   193*( 1)   89 ( 2)  210 ( 2)  260 ( 2)  310 ( 2)  360 ( 2)  444*( 2)  446*( 2)  447 ( 2)  454 ( 2)
                   459*( 2)  467*( 2)  501*( 2)  521*( 2) 1286 ( 2) 1301 ( 2) 1577 ( 2) 1588 ( 2)
TQuadProcess       502*( 1)  505 ( 1)  505 ( 1)  507*( 1)  509*( 1) 1938*( 2) 1941*( 2) 1944 ( 2) 1950*( 2) 1962*( 2)
TQuadSelection     171 ( 1)  190 ( 1)  209 ( 1)  228*( 1)  234*( 1)  235 ( 1)  238*( 1)  243*( 1)  249 ( 1)  262 ( 1)
                   418 ( 2)  436 ( 2)  521 ( 2)  634 ( 2)  696*( 2)  698*( 2)  699 ( 2)  704 ( 2)  710*( 2)  721*( 2)
                   736*( 2)  773 ( 2)  826 ( 2) 1415 ( 2) 1424 ( 2) 1426 ( 2) 1428 ( 2) 1439 ( 2) 1443 ( 2) 1683 ( 2)
                  1690 ( 2) 1698 ( 2)
TQuadTxSelection   262*( 1)  265 ( 1)  266 ( 1)  269*( 1)  637 ( 2)  815*( 2)  817*( 2)  818 ( 2)  826 ( 2)  831*( 2)
                  1324 ( 2)
TQuadTxView        199*( 1)  206*( 1)  206 ( 1)  209*( 1)  213*( 1)  214*( 1)  215*( 1)  216*( 1)  221*( 1)  533*( 2)
                   535*( 2)  535 ( 2)  543 ( 2)  564*( 2)  575*( 2)  592*( 2)  614*( 2)  634*( 2)  644*( 2)  655*( 2)
                   833 ( 2)  843 ( 2) 1287 ( 2) 1322 ( 2)
TQuadView          154*( 1)  161*( 1)  162 ( 1)  165*( 1)  166*( 1)  169*( 1)  171*( 1)  175*( 1)  181 ( 1)  199 ( 1)
                   234 ( 1)  253 ( 1)  266 ( 1)  284 ( 1)  302 ( 1)  314 ( 1)  328 ( 1)  342 ( 1)  378*( 2)  380*( 2)
```

Index